Secret Obsession

Isabella Montague

CHAPTER ONE

CHALLENGING TIMES

Students are about to board the coach in the chaos of positioning vehicles. Donald saw a young child running in front of an oncoming coach entering the car park. He ran horrified, using his rugby skills, scooped her up in his arms, holding her to his chest to protect from injury rolling on the lawn. The child's mother screamed, standing on the pavement, suspecting the worst. The girl, unhurt, crying, Donald returned the distraught child to her mother with a brief smile. She expressed her gratitude with a hug.

Donald stepped aboard the coach to applause, sitting with his friend. Mrs Josephine Gibbs from Strawberry Estate, parking alongside the coach, waiting for her daughter Christine. Donald could see her short yellow miniskirt from his elevated position. Michael commented, "Nice legs."

Christine turned to wave to Donald and Michael climbing in her mother's black Range Rover, driven away at high speed.

"Hi, mother," Christine smiled, pleased to be heading home.

Josephine smiled, "I have a surprise for you, darling. Dr Sir Rodney Battersby has agreed to meet you. Hopefully, you will start associating with a good circle of friends instead of the riffraff you're presently socialising with. I'm annoyed with your father. He should enrol you in a private girl's school where you would become a lady. I will not have you mixing with trash and ending up like me marrying a commoner."

Christine sighed heavily, looking at her mother, "I hope you are not trying to sell me off to some rich dirty old man; father would disapprove. He's warned you before, mother. I don't mind meeting wealthy people. Surely you realise love comes into the equation somewhere. What do you expect of me this time, mother?"

Josephine smiled, "Dr Sir Rodney is 78 years old and a conservative party member. He's searching for a suitable well-bred young lady to associate with his grandson. You must remember Christine, the family are in banking, and Sir Rodney happens to own the casino where I occasionally visit. Unfortunately, I'm ten thousand pounds in debt, the casino limit for me. Whatever happens, young lady, you will be pleasant, and if he suggests you should meet his grandson, you will oblige. I placed a change of clothes on your bed. I want you to run upstairs and return immediately, make sure you apply deodorant; you won't have time to shower."

Christine sighed, dreading what was to happen next. She's been down this road before, her mother trying to find suitors for her, remembering some unpleasant experiences. She couldn't understand the rush. Although Christine was more concerned about the ten thousand pounds her mother owes the casino and what her father would say if he ever found out.

Christine and her mother arrived at Strawberry estate, a three-thousand-acre farm, observing a limousine parked. Christine grabbed her briefcase, dashed into the house, and ran upstairs, changing out of her school clothes and sighing heavily. She changed into what her mother had selected. Christine Observed in the full-length mirror, frowning. Wasn't much you couldn't see of her legs. The skirt was short, and the black lace bra could easily be viewed through the material of her blouse. Christine quickly tidied her hair, slipped on her shoes and headed downstairs into the lounge.

Josephine smiling confidently introduced Christine to what appeared to be a bold frail man clutching his walking stick in a suit. "I have the pleasure to introduce you to Sir Rodney Battersby. He has travelled some distance to meet you on behalf of his grandson."

Sir Rodney smiled, standing to his feet, embracing Christine, taking her entirely by surprise, especially when he kissed her on the cheek and neck, expressing, "Pleased to meet you, Christine. I've received favourable reports concerning your conduct." He stepped away a few feet looking at her as if she were a piece of meat on a hook. Christine felt his eyes burning into her. He grinned, almost leering at her white ankle socks, lifting his eyes slowly to the hemline of her miniskirt, continuing upward, staring at her blouse and, finally, her disapproving expression.

Josephine, rather pleased by Sir Rodney's response, stands by Christine, encouraging her to turn around on the spot for Sir Rodney to have a view of her daughter. "You are a pretty thing, Christine," he commented. "I think my grandson would be satisfied to have you on his arm in the future and certainly have the bone structure of your mother. Unfortunate, you haven't pure blonde hair, and your eyes are brown, not blue; you are certainly attractive. I presume you are a virgin?"

Christine stared at her mother, not expecting a question so personal. Josephine commented quickly, "She is and not permitted to associate with riff-raff, I can assure you; she's saving herself for the right person. I want Christine to succeed; she has excellent grades, and her father refused to send her to a private girl's school."

"I see we are on the same page; Josephine, unfortunate, her father's a commoner; however, your bloodline is excellent." Christine stood like a statue, unsure of what would happen next from the conversation. For sale, whether she approved or not.

Sir Rodney smiled at Christine, "Don't look so concerned young lady," he glanced at Josephine, pointing his ivory-handled walking stick at Christine. Sir Rodney walked around Christine; she felt his eyes burning into her. He paused in front of her using the handle of his walking stick, gently pressing against her covered breast. Christine stepped back, shocked.

Josephine placed her hands on her daughter's shoulders from behind, attempting to stop Christine from moving.

Christine frowned, "No need to touch me!"

Josephine swiftly turned Christine to face her, glaring, hoping she'd understand she must comply. Christine stood annoyed. Sir Rodney smiled, "I'm not concerned, Josephine; at least the girl won't permit anyone to touch her, a good sign." Sir Rodney removed a signed cheque for ten thousand pounds from his pocket, showing Christine. "What your mother owes at my casino. Would you like me to give it to your mother to pay her debt?"

"Yes, please, Sir Rodney, my father can't keep paying her gambling debts; the farm will go bankrupt," Christine said, nervously trembling.

"You have a business head on your shoulders; you understand the value of money. I will add you to the list for my grandson to consider marrying," he smiled, sitting on the settee.

Josephine quickly passed him a whisky. Sir Rodney patted the seat beside him, "Sit with me, Christine."

Josephine offered her daughter a small glass of whisky; she accepted, drinking slowly, trembling. She's shocked by her mother's actions and how Sir Rodney behaved. Christine remarked, "Excuse me for a moment," she left the settee and her whisky, heading for the loo. She breathed a sigh of relief to be out of the room. Christine remembered reading a newspaper about Sir Rodney being involved with a pawnshop. Christine returned moments later, pausing before she entered the room, listening to them talk. She peers through the crack in the door jamb, observing Sir Rodney and her mother kissing, which didn't surprise her. She hoped her father would discover what her mother was like one day.

Christine made a noise; her mother turned her back, walking away from Sir Rodney. He patted the seat beside him, ensuring Christine sat close to him. Christine continued drinking her whisky, observing Sir Rodney's hand on her leg and her mother watching from a chair across the room, unconcerned. Sir Rodney slid his hand along the top of Christine's leg and gently squeezed, "Thank you, Christine, you can go," Sir Rodney voiced, "I need to talk to your mother privately."

Christine never said a word, vacating the room in haste, partially closing the door. She ran into the kitchen and out the back door hiding behind a large oak tree a short distance from the lounge. Christine views Sir Rodney and her mother. As she suspected, her mother kissed him, permitting his hand to venture inside her blouse.

Christine turned her back, not wanting to see any more and returned to her bedroom, immediately settling to complete her homework. Half an hour later, she looked from her bedroom window, watching the limousine leave, hearing her mother running upstairs and coming into her bedroom. "I thought you were about to throw a tantrum, Christine, for a moment, especially when he touched your leg. Don't worry. He left me the cheque to settle my debt, leaving a happy man, and I'm sure you are in the running to marry his grandson."

"The same as the others wild promises mother looking for excitement which he certainly achieved with you. You must remember; he won't miss ten thousand. He'll simply write the debt off. I wonder how father would feel if he found out."

"You certainly won't say anything, Christine, not in your interests if you want to own half of Strawberry Estate with your wonderful brother Dixon. The way you're performing, I very much doubt you will. I suspect the chances of you finding a wealthy husband are highly unlikely; you are too scared to advance your position." Josephine left Christine's bedroom and headed downstairs, relieved she had a cheque to cover her debt.

***

Donald Selwyn stepped from the coach, walking the cobbled drive to Crabtree Farm. Winter had arrived with a vengeance. "Hi, son," Martin smiled, placing his hand on Donald's shoulder as they walked to the cottage together across the cobbled stones laid hundreds of years ago. Martin was a well-built man in his forties; his father had died the year before. Martin found the situation rather daunting, managing the farm almost solo until his son finished his education.

Mary laid the table a well-built lass used to the hard work of running a household and helping on the farm, which usually meant manual labour unless you were extremely wealthy and could afford modern equipment. Donald approaching 17, is a definite favourite with the girls at school with his blonde hair and blue eyes. He enjoyed rugby and football, which would soon drift into history; once he'd sat his exams, he'd leave school to help on the three-hundred-acre farm, which consisted of cereals, sheep, cattle, and a couple of pigs, providing bacon for the household. Any surplus the pigs produced was sold.

After tea, Donald moved from the table to his bedroom to complete his homework. Martin shone his torch, walked around the buildings, checked the yard before closing the door on the day, and sat down by the fire with Mary. "You can't go on, Martin trying to manage the sheep and cattle on your own plus the cereals. Donald has another year at school, although he helps during the holidays and evenings."

"I know Mary, my back is worse! I can't consider an operation until Donald finishes his education; we certainly can't afford to employ anyone," he remarked, kissing her cheek.

She smiled, "That idea will not improve your back," moving to make a cup of tea, grinning, understanding what her husband was after even with a bad back.

Martin smiled, wondering whether he should sell the farm and work for somebody else. Let someone else worry about the taxman and VAT, finding the money for another tractor. Mary returned, sitting beside him, placing the cups on the flagstone hearth. "Shall we sell Mary? We should be able to live quite comfortably."

"What about Donald if you're really serious, Martin? You should discuss with him his future; once the farm is gone, he'll have nothing?"

Martin frowned, "Perhaps I'm depressed, off to bed. I'm absolutely knackered," he sighed, patting Mary's backside, gently holding her covered breasts from behind, hearing her chuckle.

At 6 o'clock in the morning, Martin walked across the yard, milking the old cow, returning to the cottage with the milk placing the bucket on the table for Mary to deal with. Although quite chilly, he released Geraldine into the paddock to shelter from the wind behind the buildings. Martin walked into the old tractor shed. He started the Ferguson 20, his father's favourite tractor, which he purchased brand-new in 1955; delivered with a three-cylinder Perkins diesel engine.

He backed up to the small trailer by the barn throwing on three bales of hay, two bags of nuts and two wheelbarrow loads of swedes. The ground was still quite frosty, travelling across the fields; you could hear the ground under the tyres crunching. Sheep surrounded Martin when he reached the troughs and hay rack. Martin quickly ran along the troughs with a bag of nuts. With their impatience, the sheep determined to trip him at every opportunity, finally placing two hay bales in the sheep rack. He moved away across the field using his pitchfork; he threw swedes, leaving some for the cattle.

He moved on to the following field to the bullocks, throwing the remainder of the swedes giving him a chance while they were occupied to place a bale of hay in the feeder. Some signs of grass in the field, silently praying for the weather to improve along with the grass. He knew he would have to increase their daily rations; otherwise, they soon lose weight. Martin would keep the bullocks for a while longer before sending to market, hoping to improve carcass weight.

Martin checked to see how much fodder they had left, realising; he'd have to transport another round bale later in the day. He checked the water butt by the gate wasn't frozen, a stroke of luck; he'd wrapped the pipework in old hessian sacks filled with straw, hoping to keep the frost away to some degree; one job he wouldn't have to do today.

By the time Martin had returned to the yard, almost 8 o'clock breakfast time. He looked at the pigpen seeing the two old saddleback sows waiting for their breakfast. Martin quickly grabbed half a bucket of pig nuts casting in the sty; everything else could wait until after breakfast. Rubbing his hands, he entered the kitchen, Donald's finishing his cornflakes, ready to catch the school bus at the end of the drive. "Everything okay, dad?" he asked eagerly.

"Yes, apart from cold, son," Martin remarked, sitting at the table and tucking into his egg, bacon, and fried bread. "Dad, why don't you sell the livestock? Grow cereals would make life so much easier for you. I can always find a job elsewhere when I leave school," Donald suggested.

"That's all your eggs in one basket. If you have a crop failure, what do we do?" Martin replied, less than impressed. "Don't you want the place left to you, Donald? If you're not interested in farming, say so now," Martin snapped.

"You have the wrong end of the stick dad, of course, I'm interested in the farm. Do you know how much oilseed rape is fetching a ton? Wheat has gone through the roof. You only have to sit on your backside, driving a tractor. Far better than fighting with old ewe's trying to clip feet and shear, not forgetting, dagging. If you're fortunate, they won't drop dead on you."

"I'll give it some thought; you'd better hurry; you'll miss the bus. Don't forget your face mask coronavirus hasn't finished with society Donald," Martin advised sipping his coffee. Mary looked on, somewhat concerned with the conversation. She knew they couldn't afford to suddenly change operations. They had some equipment to handle cereals, most worn out. The old combine harvester, which only cut a hundred acres a year, usually broke down three times a day. A new one would be an enormous figure to purchase or even a good second-hand one, and you don't know what you're really buying.

Mary poured herself a coffee sitting by Martin, "I don't think Donald worked things out properly, Martin. He only looked at the prices of cereals, not the cost of the equipment, which would swallow anything we made for several years if we went down that road," she sighed, wishing they could.

Martin smiled briefly, "At least he showed an interest; I'd love nothing better than to dispose of the sheep; they are a pain in the neck, and half the time, we never make enough money on them.

Occasionally, the cattle do well. Dare I ask our financial state, Mary?"

"This month, we're not in the red yet; we won't have to pay the bank any interest," she smiled.

Donald arrived at school and sat with his friend Michael in the cafeteria, enjoying lunch. Donald sighed heavily, "I tried to convince my father to dispose of those bloody sheep; his back can't take it anymore."

Michael half smiled, "My dad, you can't stop him. He won't listen; he looks at me as if I haven't a brain." Both laughed. "Our farm is about the same size as yours, Donald. Our income is hit and miss. I've suggested he goes arable; I'd find a job at least he could make an easier living. Grain prices are only rising; now, we're out of the EU and, of course, the war abroad. Most weeks, mum and dad sit up late trying to decide what to do next," Michael suggested leaving the table to fetch drinks.

Christine Gibbs approached the table, an attractive girl always prim and proper. Donald patted the seat. She sat beside him smiling and asked, "What are you two moaning about now?"

"Okay, Miss Prim and proper," Donald joked. "You have more acres and money than you know what to do with on Strawberry Estate," he grinned, receiving a jab in the ribs from Christine.

"Perhaps you two should work harder because we own land doesn't mean we're wealthy, although the subsidies help," she grinned.

Michael laughed, "We discussed the best way forward for our parents. Probably sell up and move to the Bahamas; sitting in the sun all day would be the solution. No worries and no rich neighbours gloating on their success."

"I'm not gloating," Christine protested. "If you saw the bills coming into the office at home, you'd cry. You must remember. We have to pay staff, the equipment we have to buy is enormous and very expensive, our diesel bill, need I go on," she exhaled.

"And we thought you just rode your horse around the estate with your little whip keeping everyone under control," Donald smiled.

Christine jabbed him in the ribs again, grinning, "I must study for my exams," Christine remarked, leaving the table and grabbing her briefcase.

"There's your solution, Donald," Michael laughed, "Marry her; you won't be short of money."

"You must be joking; she's a looker, but I bet she'd be a nightmare to live with. You realise every exam passed with distinction. That one will be heading towards university probably become a solicitor, marry some rich prat," Donald commented.

Christine strolled along the school corridor, churning over in her mind what her mother had said during their conversation in her bedroom. She wanted to marry someone she loved; money would be a bonus. Her future is secure with Strawberry Estate; she's convinced her father would see to that. She would need to marry someone interested in farming, although she could run the estate herself. "Hey, daydreamer," Kevin commented, joining her in the corridor. "Where are you heading, Christine?"

"Studying that's all, and you?"

"Classroom two is empty for the rest of the day. If you sit in the back corner on the right, no one can see you," he grinned.

Christine smiled, following Kevin into the classroom; they sat at the back and placed books on the table to study. Christine commented, "My mother keeps trying to find someone for me, embarrassing. She seems to think I should marry some rich guy. What do you think, Kevin?"

"My parents are the same. My father owns several factories; he's panicking I won't find the right girl. He looks at every girl I take home to see if she's liable to divorce me, and I'd lose his little empire," Kevin moaned.

"Can I ask you a personal question, Kevin, please?" She watched him nod. "Have you had sex, and would you marry a girl you knew had been to bed with other men?"

"Never thought about Christine; I suppose it wouldn't matter if you love the person. I don't know the answer. I certainly wouldn't want an old bike." They chuckled.

"I haven't a boyfriend. Although asked several times, I don't know whether to go all the way or save myself. Unless they collected me in a Ferrari or a Rolls-Royce, mother wouldn't allow them in the house," she shrugged her shoulders.

The day's final bell rang. Donald boarded the coach for home with Michael, watching Christine jump in her mother's black Range Rover and driven home rather than travel on the bus like everyone else.

Early the following day the usual routine. Donald finished breakfast and prepared to walk down the drive. Mary's mobile rang, realising something must be wrong, "Martin, you what! You, okay?"

"No, phone for an ambulance. I can't move, a bloody old ewe trip me, I've fallen across the steel troughs; oh, my back."

"Don't move, Martin; we are coming. Donald, ring for an ambulance now! Your fathers had an accident," Mary glared, worried.

Donald didn't need asking twice; he rang the emergency services. "You stay here, wait for the ambulance, and come to your father; he's with the ewes."

Mary quickly grabbed blankets throwing in the back of the old Land Rover. Shouting the sheepdog. "Biscuit, where are you," realising he's still in his kennel, Martin hadn't released him. She'd scolded Martin time and time again for not taking Biscuit to keep the sheep away while he placed food in the troughs. She concluded that he wouldn't be in this mess if he'd listened, releasing Biscuit from his chain. He jumped in the back of the Land Rover with some eagerness. Mary drove across the field, finding Martin surrounded by sheep trying to remove food from the bag he dropped.

Biscuit went to work the old ewes scattered. Donald heard the ambulance approaching; he ran out to intercept. Thanks to the frost, they could drive across the field; otherwise, they would be stuck in the mud. Taking half an hour to prepare Martin for transport, finally easing him into the back of the ambulance.

"Don't worry, Dad, I'll take care of the animals," Donald assured. He's worried about his father, watching the ambulance leave the frozen field.

"I'll look after the animal's mum. You go with dad, don't worry, I can manage."

"What about your exams this afternoon?"

Donald shrugged his shoulders, "I can't be in two places at once; the farm has to come first and the animals," he sighed.

Mary frowned, "I'll phone the school and explain, Donald. I'm sure they will allow you to sit at a later date."

Donald watched his mother drive away. Donald placed the remainder of the sheep nuts in the troughs, took a hay bale for the hay rack, and moved the tractor across the field. Tossing swedes on the frozen grass, moving on to repeat the process with the cattle, seeing they needed another bale of silage. He drove to the buildings, parked the old tractor in the shed, walked into the house, poured a coffee, holding it with both hands feeling the warmth finally penetrate his fingers. He sat at the kitchen table, worried about his father, praying nothing too serious. Although he knew his father had suffered from his back for years. Reality returned with his mobile ringing Michael Pearce, his friend.

"Hey Donald, an announcement in assembly. What happened to your dad? How serious, Donald?"

"I don't know, Michael; he fell across the steel trough; it could be the end of everything," Donald sighed. "I'm waiting for mum to ring me; there's no more I can say. I'll text you as soon as I know; good luck with your exams."

"Thanks, mate; I'll be thinking of you. Bye for now."

Donald continued with his chores after changing out of his school uniform. He climbed aboard the JCB, speared a round bale, and slowly transported across the field for the cattle, peeling off the plastic and netting. He dropped the bale in the feeder, feeling his phone vibrate in his pocket. Donald looked at his phone. Christine Gibbs, he answered, puzzled and sighing. "I've heard Donald; Michael texts me; I'm at home today. I don't have any exams until next week. How serious is the situation," she asked with trepidation.

"Mothers at hospital with dad, I'm looking after the farm. She hasn't phoned me, so I have no news. I'll text you, Christine, when I hear. Thanks for ringing."

"Don't be silly, Donald. We're friends; I'm aware you all think I'm a little rich spoiled bitch," she ended the call, not waiting for him to respond.

Christine found her father, Gerald Gibbs, in his 50s, an intelligent gentleman farmer. Josephine's parents owned the estate relinquishing it to their daughter and new son-in-law as a wedding present when they were married. "Father, can I take the quad bike and drive to Crabtree Farm? Donald Selwyn's father had an accident; he's in hospital; they don't know his condition. I'd like to help," she asked, with an ulterior motive.

"I don't see why not, Christine; it doesn't hurt to be neighbourly," her father suggested kissing her forehead. "Besides, you attend the same school; I'm sure his parents don't have coronavirus."

Christine's mother, Josephine, entered the kitchen asking, "What's this I hear," she asked with her polished voice.

Christine explained. "You are certainly not riding a quad bike, Christine, and probably come home with coronavirus from a peasant farm," Josephine assured, looking at her cascading blonde hair and new earrings in the mirror. "You are a young lady, not a farmhand. Hopefully, you will marry someone when you finish university with some promise and not be so foolish as your mother."

"Of course, mother, you want me to be like my brother Dixon, a drug addict and the rest of his friends at university. They'll have AIDS before long. They spend more time with prostitutes than learning anything," Christine swiftly replied, annoyed.

Josephine spun around on her heels, tidying her skirt and blouse, about to slap Christine's face. Gerald grabbed her wrist. "You will not strike our daughter for speaking her mind and expressing the truth you fail to face. Dixon's a bloody mess, and you know it. How many times have we paid for that little bugger to attend rehab," he shouted.

"Be quiet, Gerald! The servant will hear you."

"Let her strike me, father; I'll show you how to become rich. I'll sue her for every penny she has for assault," Christine glared at her mother in defiance, watching her walk off muttering. "Sorry, father, I didn't mean to cause you more strife with mother," Christine exhaled.

"Make sure you wear a crash helmet, love, and don't go too fast, the quads full of fuel in the garage. Cut across the fields. You're only a mile from Crabtree Farm; for christ's sake, be bloody careful," kissing her on the forehead.

Christine ran upstairs and changed into warmer clothing using the crash helmet in the garage. She started the quad bike, roaring off down the drive cutting through the farmyard across the fields, keeping to the tracks. She sneaked down the short distance on a minor road turning into Crabtree Farm, slowly heading up the rutted drive and parked in the yard.

Donald's in the house, warming his hands by the Aga. He looked out the window, realising Christine when she removed her crash helmet and placed it on the seat.

Donald smiled, opening the door and pouring the coffee. He joked, "I didn't know you had work clothes."

"If you're going to insult me, Donald, I'll go home," she scolded. "Have you heard anything about your father?"

"He's in surgery as far as I understand," he sighed. "We won't know the extent of the damage for an hour or two, I don't think."

They sat around the kitchen table. "I thought I'd come over and help if I can; perhaps I could make your lunch or something. Have you finished feeding the animals?"

"Yes! I have fifty acres to plough; I think too hard now. Besides, dad will go loopy if he wasn't there to watch me start off."

"I don't think you have to worry about your father; he'll be out of action for a while. We'll walk down the field and see how hard the ground is, not wishing to blow my own trumpet," she says, smiling. "I don't know whether you're aware I won a ploughing competition."

Donald paused, not believing what he was hearing.

"Yes, wasn't in this County at my cousin's farm with a Ferguson 20 TVO last year. My mother went ballistic when she found out. She said young ladies are not to drive tractors and operate machinery. My father strongly disagrees with her. He permits me to drive the tractors at every opportunity and demonstrates how to operate them. He's convinced I will take over the farm; he wants me to understand how every operation is carried out correctly," she grinned.

"Not just a pretty face. I thought the most you performed is to look at the accounts to see how much you can spend on clothes."

She kicked out with her steel-capped boots catching Donald on the shin. "That hurt."

"Good! I actually do the accounts with my father saves employing someone."

"Sorry, Christine, only teasing."

They entered the fifty-acre field of old pasture the sheep had virtually destroyed.

"Our old reversible plough and Massey tractor wouldn't touch this too hard and probably spend more on spares. The mouldboards are that thin they'd break if you look at them, another job I have to do, replace at some stage," he sighed.

"What are you planting here, Donald?"

" Barley, I would have liked winter wheat. It's too late; I should have ploughed and planted before now, but we needed the grass for the lambs because so dry, we were short of pasture." Donald's phone rang, Mum. "He's broken his back, Donald. The surgeons repaired; he'll be out of action for some time," she sighed.

"Don't worry, mum, we'll manage. We always do bye. I guess you heard, Christine." She nodded, looking to the ground and removing her mobile. Donald's somewhat puzzled by her actions.

"Father, Saturday morning, can I borrow the John Deere and the 10-furrow reversible. I have fifty acres to plough; it won't take me long."

Her father laughed, "If I said no, you'd take it anyway, daughter. Don't break, brand-new, and for christ's sake, don't mention to your mother she will go mental."

"Thanks, father; by the way, Mr Selwyn has broken his back; he'll be out of action for some time; bye for now."

"Come on, Donald, you can make me another coffee freezing out here," she smiled, looking at the astonished expression on Donald's face. "That's what neighbours are for; Donald, help each other. I hope the tractor will fit through the gateways, 600 horsepower, on rubber tracks." Donald didn't say anything; he was trying to comprehend what was happening; by the time they returned to the farm, his mother was home. Donald opened the door for Christine.

"Mother, I'd like you to meet Christine Gibbs; we attend the same school." They embraced each other warmly. Mary poured them a coffee relieved her husband wouldn't be a cripple.

"I've spoken to the school because of the extenuating circumstances. The headteacher will allow you to sit your exams as soon as things are settled here," she smiled with relief.

"That's good news, Donald," Christine remarked. "May I suggest if I come early in the morning, say about 5 o'clock, you think Donald we can feed the animals before we have to catch the school bus, then you can attend school. I'm ploughing the fifty acres Saturday morning, weather permitting. What do you think?"

"We can't ask you to do that, Christine; this isn't your problem. Besides, your father and mother would not allow you to do so, I'm sure," Mary advised, firmly aware of Josephine's opinion of the locals.

"No, don't ruin your future, Christine; you need to concentrate on your exams," Donald insisted.

"What's this about ploughing fifty acres," Mary asked, "Who decided this?" Christine put her hand up. "I spoke to father, and he said I could use our tractor and plough. It will cut through the ground like butter, even if slightly frozen; I'm trying to be helpful. I told Donald I know how to operate a tractor and plough."

Donald interrupted, "She won a ploughing match last year, mum. She eats exams, Christine has passed everyone with distinction, she's a bloody genius. Michael and I were discussing her yesterday," he ended his sentence abruptly, not wishing Christine to know the topic of the conversation.

"I think I should speak to your father and mother first, Christine, before we do anything else. I appreciate your offering to help us but not without their consent. I won't allow you to sacrifice your own future because we have a few issues," Mary smiled, kissing Christine.

Christine removed her mobile, "No time like the present," she phoned her father, somewhat frustrated. "Father, will you speak with Mrs Selwyn? I've offered to rise early and assist in feeding the animals before attending school with Donald. I've also explained about ploughing the fifty acres. She needs your approval."

She passed the phone to Mrs Selwyn before he had a chance to argue. "Mr Gibbs, you have a marvellous daughter who is very strong-willed and pig-headed; you agree to what she suggests. We'd appreciate the help, don't misunderstand me, but we can't have her education suffering."

Gerald laughed, "Christine's education won't suffer; Mrs Selwyn, the girl is a walking genius. Regards operating equipment, you have nothing to worry about. I trained her myself when her mother wasn't looking."

"Oh," Mary laughed, "Slightly difficult?"

"You could say that," he answered. "Josephine has wild ideas for Christine's future, which will fail miserably; my daughter doesn't take prisoners or suffer fools. Honestly, I'm proud of her offering to help a neighbour with misfortune. Don't worry about the tractor and plough. I'll cover the cost; I'm only too pleased to help. I know Christine can't wait to climb aboard my new tractor and plough," he laughed, "Goodbye."

Christine sat drinking coffee with a smug expression. "Thanks, Christine," Mary grinned, passing back her mobile.

"When you've had enough, Christine, you must pack up and come to the house; you are far more generous than anyone I know." Mary cuddled Christine with tear-filled eyes of gratitude, not worried about the coronavirus, always forgetting to wear her mask-like everyone else in the farming community.

"Good, I'm glad that's settled," she smiled, patting Donald's cheek. "Right, I'm off home; I'll see you in the morning; Donald bright and early at 5 o'clock, kick him out of bed, Mrs Selwyn," Christine smiled.

"You can count on it," Mary grinned. Donald escorted Christine to her quad bike.

"Thanks, I owe you one."

Christine hugged him, "See you in the morning, bye," she grinned, riding her quad bike. Her plan is falling into place.

Donald returned to the house to have another coffee, wasn't much he could do in this weather. "What a lovely young girl Donald?"

"Yes, I thought stuck-up Miss prim and proper, I'm very much mistaken. Michael suggested I wouldn't be short of money if I married her. I expressed to him she'd be a bloody nightmare. I wasn't wrong; she takes control by the looks of things."

"Sounds like she has problems with her mother," Mary advised. "Her father seems a lovely man. I don't think we've ever met sociably. I remember Gerald Gibbs; he dated Josephine Spires, and she became pregnant. Quite a stink over the whole situation. Some believed that Gibbs wasn't the father; Josephine apparently liked to play around. Anyway, they were allowed to marry to cover up the mess. Christine's brother, he's a nightmare from talk around the village drug addict or something prosecuted twice."

"I thought you were just a farmer's wife, mum; how did you acquire this information?"

"Usually, when your father took me to the cattle market and chat with a few farmer's wives, Josephine wouldn't lower herself to walk into a cattle market. Butter wouldn't melt in her mouth. Anyway, leave the subject alone. None of our business."

Donald made the sound of a cat meowing. Mary turned slightly red-faced, flicking Donald with a towel realising she was sharing gossip with her son. Donald ran outside laughing; he'd never considered his mother one for gossip until now, mind you all interesting. Donald prepared the animal rations ready for feeding at night. He walked around the lambs with Biscuit, his sheepdog, deciding whether they had any lambs suitable for market.

Donald realised he couldn't transport the animals to market; he'd be prosecuted for taking the Land Rover and trailer on the road without a licence. He ran to the cottage; Mary looked at him out of breath; what could have gone wrong. "What's the matter, Donald?"

"I can't drive the Land Rover and trailer to market. We may have between ten or fifteen lambs ready to go," he smiled cautiously.

"I can drive the Land Rover and trailer not difficult; I've done it before," she grinned confidently.

Donald breathed a sigh of relief. The thought of hiring in transport would swallow any profit they make from the lambs. Mary could see his worried expression. She rubbed his hair, "Silly boy, you never saw me taking animals to market before, oh I suppose not, you are always at school," she smiled.

She slipped on her coat, "Show me what you think is ready, Donald. If you're right, we'll take them this coming Tuesday; we could do with some cash," she smiled reassuringly. They walked across the field together, Biscuit close to their heels. "Have the lamb's penned, Donald, make sure our eyes are not deceiving us? Away Biscuit," Mary commanded, not long before the lambs were penned. Mary removed an aerosol from her coat pocket, checking each lamb that looked suitable and marked with a red spot. After two hours, they'd managed to find fifteen, just enough for the stock trailer to carry. Mary patted Donald on the shoulder, "Well done, Donald, for noticing. We'll make a farmer of you yet," Mary smiled.

Mary returned to the house; Donald continued with his chores, finally coming into the house at 5 o'clock in the evening. "Another frost tonight, mum. Are we visiting dad?"

"No, I've spoken to him on the phone, tearing his hair out; he wants to come home. I explained that we have everything under control and not to worry."

9 o'clock, Donald retired to bed, worn out. "Don't forget to set your alarm unless you want to embarrass yourself and not be ready for when Christine arrives; I wouldn't want to be in your shoes, son," Mary grinned.

"No, she'd make sure everybody at school knew I couldn't get out of bed," he laughed. Donald set the alarm for 4 o'clock to give him ample time to be ready. Donald closed his eyes the next thing he heard, his alarm feeling like he'd never been to sleep. He dressed in his work clothes quickly, making coffees. His mother came down to join him in her dressing gown. 5 o'clock on the dot, they saw a Range Rover come into the yard. Christine kissed her father on the cheek, jumping out with her briefcase and a suitcase of clothes to change into after they'd fed the animals.

Mary opened the front door and waved. Mr Gibbs smiled, acknowledging, driving out of the yard. Christine ran into the house, smiling, "I thought I'd have to throw a bucket of water over you this morning Donald," she smirked, drinking her coffee swiftly. "Right, I'll milk the cow, feed the chickens and pigs, and you feed the bullocks and sheep, don't forget to take Biscuit; I don't want to have to visit you in hospital."

"Very good, your ladyship," Donald laughed.

Mary smiled, watching them both scurry out of the cottage. Christine carried the milking bucket, and Donald ran to the tractor shed. Christine returned with the milk, "I've left Geraldine in the stable with hay and nuts. I think it's too cold, and nothing out there for her to eat. I hope that's okay, Mrs Selwyn?"

" Mary, please, and yes, the correct course of action, she will only end up with sore teats; the cold, bitter wind will make them crack."

Christine fed the pigs and collected the eggs, releasing barely a dozen eggs from the hens. Christine returned to the cottage, "I think the weather is too cold, Mary."

"I think you're right. I hear the tractor. Donald must be coming from across the field," Mary commented.

He came into the cottage, "Blimey, it's freezing across the field, the winds cutting right through the hedge; from what I can see in the dark with my torch, all appears to be okay. Mum, will you check when it's daylight, please?"

"Don't worry, Donald, I'm a farmer, sit down and have your breakfast, the pair of you," she smiled.

Christine stared at her breakfast in disbelief. Two eggs, fried bread, bacon, sausage, tomatoes, "I'll never eat all this; I usually have a piece of toast."

"Not here, Christine," Mary insisted, "You will eat properly. You could do with a few pounds on you to keep the cold out."

"I hope your father mends quickly. I will spend most of my time trying to lose weight in the gym," she chuckled, enjoying her breakfast immensely; everything tasted absolutely fantastic. "You can use my bedroom Christine to change."

Both Christine and Donald changed, walking down the drive together.

"Thanks, Christine; it takes a load off me."

The coach arrived, stopped at the end of the drive, and they boarded, seeing Michael sat at the back with his arm in plaster. "What happened, mate?" Donald asked, concerned.

"Embarrassing, I fell over my girlfriend's dog; I haven't phoned you, Donald. I'm not right-handed, and you two have some explaining to do by the looks of things," looking at their expressions. Christine turned slightly red-faced, "Nothing to explain. I'm helping Donald while his father recovers from his broken back. Don't have any silly ideas, you dirty-minded old dog."

Michael smiled.

"Would you like a broken leg to go with your arm," Christine glared.

"Okay, okay, calm down," Michael trying not to grin. Donald looked puzzled by the whole conversation deciding to ignore Michael's comments.

They barely arrived at school. Donald was summoned into the head teacher's office. "I'm sorry to hear about your father, Donald; you must be having a challenging time on the farm."

"We're managing, Sir, thank you; I'm concerned about sitting my exams."

"I've spoken to the governing body; quite happy under the circumstances to allow you to sit when you can, sooner rather than later, Donald. Do you think you could take one after assembly? I believe you have a free period and another one this afternoon, or do you think it's too much?"

"Yes, if convenient for you, Sir, I only have two more to take after Christmas in my final year."

"That's correct, Donald; that reminds me. The game master spoke to me; he feels you are extremely talented on the rugby pitch and could possibly be signed to the local club in the first instance if you are interested. I know it's the last thing on your mind now; there is time."

Donald smiled; he enjoyed playing rugby something else for him to think about, "Something to consider, Sir."

"Quite possible, Donald, you could make a successful living playing rugby."

"Thank you for your vote of confidence, Sir," Donald expressed warmly. "Which classrooms for my exams."

"My office, I'm teaching."

"Okay, Sir, thank you." Donald left with a broad smile, wondering if he could combine rugby and the farm. He wouldn't mention any of the conversations to his father for the moment.

Donald finished sitting his last exam five minutes before the school bell rang, wondering if he'd answered the questions correctly. He grabbed his briefcase and headed for the door stepping aboard the school bus; much to his surprise, Christine was on board. He sat beside her, asking, "Isn't your mother collecting you this evening?"

"No, I have animals to feed," she replied indignantly.

"Oh, I thought you were only helping me out in the mornings."

"No, it won't take long. My father said to give him a ring, he will collect me," she smiled.

Michael sat on the opposite side, "Must be serious," he grinned, seeing Christine stare at him. If looks could kill, he'd be dead.

Donald obviously hadn't heard. He's leaning with his head against the seat with his eyes closed; shattered from the day's events feeding animals early in the morning is one thing, but sitting for two exams is another. Christine asked, concerned, "How did you cope with sitting two exams in one day?"

"Okay, I suppose if I pass, I pass. If I don't, I don't," Donald shrugging his shoulders, "Nothing I can do about it now." They both jumped off the bus walking up the driveway. Mary opened the door to greet, already having coffee on the table. They both immediately changed. By 5 o'clock, the animals were fed. Mary suggested, "I'll take you home, Christine."

"No, allow father to collect me, please. My mother has no idea; she thinks I'm taking additional studies."

Mary sat down, realising Christine's life wasn't so charmed as she first thought, "You sure you should be helping us, Christine? Don't cause grief with your mother."

Christine sighed, "Mother doesn't live in the real-world Mary. She keeps trying to force me to go out with high society guys. They only want one thing; she's trying to make an arranged marriage for me to secure my future. We fall out all the time. If it weren't for my father standing by me. She'd have me shipped abroad and married in a foreign country; she doesn't care whether I like the person providing he's filthy rich. That's all that matters to her."

Mary made another coffee, concerned. Donald shook his head in disbelief at what he'd heard. "Neither of you, please repeat what I've said."

"Not on your life," Donald promised. "You can rely on mum to say nothing."

"I suppose you heard around the village my brother was prosecuted twice for drug-taking; he's an absolute waste of time costing a fortune to keep at University."

Mary nodded, "There has been talk," holding Christine's hand. "You are always welcome here, Christine. If you find you have a problem you want to talk about privately, come and see me."

Christine immediately embraced Mary, appreciating her support. "I don't have any female company at home to talk to other than mother; she only has one thing on her mind money."

"I owe you an apology, Christine," Donald remarked. "I have really misjudged you. I'm finally learning what a lovely person you are," he smiled.

Gerald entered the yard in his Range Rover. Mary walked out to meet him, slipping on her face mask, "Thanks, Mr Gibbs." Mary suddenly remembered him from a young farmer's dance years before marrying Martin. The next minute, he suddenly vanished into thin air; she heard he was with Josephine.

"Gerald," he smiled. "Mary, Christine speaks highly of you. No need to wear a face mask."

"Come, Gerald, coffee before you go home."

"A quick one," he smiled, recalling Mary at the dance many years ago.

Donald offered his hand, "Pleased to meet you, Mr Gibbs; thanks for helping."

"Gerald, I'm not helping my daughter is. I won't worry about a tractor and plough and bit of diesel compared to my wife's shopping bill," he frowned, glancing at his daughter. Christine suspected her mother spent a fortune on something ridiculous they could hardly afford or totally unnecessary, showing off to her friends in London. She would spend three or four days in her flat, which her parents purchased for her when she was single. Gerald hastily finished his coffee, "We must go, Mary. I have a few headaches to solve at home by the text messages I'm receiving."

"I'll see you in the morning, Donald." Christine smiled, leaving with her father in haste. Mary and Donald watched Gerald and Christine drive out of the yard at high-speed. "Something definitely has happened." Mary commented, "I wouldn't bank on seeing Christine in the morning; it sounds like her mother's been up to something." She sighed, realising how lucky she is to have a wonderful son and a loving husband without the drama of pretending to be something you're not.

***

"What's mother done," Christine asked nervously.

"Gambling again lost over ten thousand pounds on the roulette table."

"Oh my god," Christine voiced, "Doesn't she realise we can't afford sums like that?"

"She's showing off to her friends; she also gave two thousand pounds to Dixon. He said he's short of money! Yes, for drugs," he frowned.

Gerald's mobile rang; he pulled over to the side of the road. "Yes, that's correct. My name is Gerald Gibbs. Yes, I'm married to Josephine Gibbs! Who is speaking?"

"I'm phoning on behalf of the Metropolitan police; your wife was admitted to the hospital intoxicated. She was found in possession of drugs after being knocked down by a bus."

"How serious?"

"I suggest you make your way to the Royal London Hospital at your earliest convenience." The call ended abruptly.

"I'll stay at home and look after the estate; you go on to London. You drive careful," Christine smiled briefly, observing as they entered the drive; three police cars and two vans, officers everywhere. Gerald was greeted by an officer passing him a search warrant. Gerald and Christine both provided a statement. Mr Gibbs was released to travel to London to be with his wife a short while later. Christine stayed at home; she wanted no more to do with her mother and her crazy brother. Suspecting her mother wouldn't be carrying drugs unless they were for him. Christine anticipated in the papers by morning, glanced at the time 10 o'clock in the evening. The officers found nothing of interest, leaving a mess to tidy.

Christine phoned Mary in tears. "Stay here, Donald," Mary expressed earnestly, "I shan't belong." She ran out to the Land Rover, driving over to Gibb's house greeted at the door by Christine. They set about rectifying the mess, talking things over, Christine explaining how she felt, and Mary advising her not to worry. She's always welcome at their farm, and to ignore the gossip, it will fade into history.

Gerald phoned Christine, "Quite serious, love, the doctors, are investigating her injuries. I'll stay here, Christine, if you can manage?"

"Okay, father, Mary came over and helped me tidy the house. I hope you don't mind; she'd find out sooner or later on the news."

"I'm not worried, love. Thank Mary for me; I'll be home sometime in the morning when your mother regains consciousness. She's under arrest for possession of drugs; I've cancelled her credit cards under the pretence they're stolen."

Mary placed a reassuring arm on Christine's shoulder, "If you don't want to stay here tonight, Christine, there's room at the cottage," she suggested with a warm smile.

"Thanks, Mary; I prefer not to be alone tonight in this house."

"Grab some clothes, and we'll go home."

Donald's stood in the doorway, spotting the headlights of the Land Rover turn into the yard. Donald eagerly approached the Land Rover wondering why Christine had returned; he carried her suitcase into the cottage. "A few problems, Donald son; don't nag Christine for an explanation. We'll have a good night's sleep; nearly two in the morning." Mary showed Christine into the spare room. Donald retired to his own room full of suspicion.

5 o'clock soon arrived. Donald's out of bed, first dressed and made the coffee. Donald said nothing to Christine; he could see she'd cried; her eyes were slightly red and puffy. They fed the animals and returned to the house for breakfast. "I suggest neither of you goes to school today Friday, have a long weekend. How do you feel this morning, Christine?" Mary asked, concerned.

"Happened before; I'm okay, Mary," Christine said timidly.

Donald sat quietly listening and wondered what had happened. Christine turned to face him, "My mother was caught possessing drugs last night in London. She was blotto and hit by a bus. Fathers in London trying to clean up the mess. I phoned Mary last night to help me. The police searched our premises for drugs," she burst into tears.

Donald didn't hesitate; he moved to her side of the table, embracing her, "Don't worry, Christine. I'm sure your father will resolve any issues. You can stay here as long as you want, can't she, mum," Donald looked to his mother for reassurance.

"Of course, Donald, I suggest Christine take a shower or jump into bed and grab some sleep." Christine kissed Mary on the cheek, running off upstairs.

Donald sat at the table, holding his head, "We thought we had problems, mum."

"See, Donald, you should never judge a book by its cover."

"I'll have a piece of toast this morning, mum. I'm not hungry, really."

The paper arrived around 9 o'clock with the postman. Mary placed on the table opening barely mentions a tiny piece about Mrs Gibbs, the main story about a riot in Luton. Mary breathed a sigh of relief. Christine came downstairs into the kitchen. Mary smiled reassuring, "Barely a mention, Christine, look." Christine held her long light-brown hair out of the way, reading the small block smiling. "Right young lady, what would you like to eat?" Mary asked seriously.

"A piece of toast, please, Mary. I'll have to go home and see if there are any issues; my father's detained in London."

"I'll come with you for support if anyone wants to give you any trouble," Mary insisted. Christine smiled with appreciation. Mary slipped on her coat and boots. They jumped in the Land Rover and drove to Strawberry Estate Christine's house; a staff member approached the Land Rover to see Christine jump out. "We've had a few problems, Stephen; father's dealing with them now. Your plans for today are?"

"We've heard Miss Gibbs. We haven't planned anything; we were waiting for instructions, about to finish laying the hedge on-field thirty-seven," he advised lighting a cigarette.

"Move on to field forty-six. I think we should lay that one, Stephen; any decent timber can come to the house for firewood; what do you think?"

"Yes, Miss Gibbs, the hedge needs laying before the birds start to nest. I'll instruct the others," he advised walking off.

Mary and Christine entered the house finding the housekeeper lighting the fires that her father customarily performed. "Sorry, Susan, we've had a few problems," Christine sighed.

"I know Christine, your father is on his way from London, he phoned." Susan lit the living room fire. They retreated to the kitchen for a coffee. Susan smiled, "I was dreading what I'm facing this morning after the police paid a visit; you've obviously worked hard tidying the place, thanks."

"Wasn't just me, Mary helped," giving Mary a hug.

"If you're okay, Christine, I'll make my way home; otherwise, my son will think I've left the country."

Susan smiled, "Of course, you're Mrs Selwyn, Donald's mother. I'm sorry to hear about your husband. You won't want for anything when Donald's signed by a major league to play rugby."

Mary stared in disbelief. "Where has that information come from, Susan?"

"You don't know, Donald hasn't told you?"

"Obviously not!"

"Me and my big mouth, from what my daughter Teresa said over breakfast, it's all around the school. Apparently, a club wants to sign Donald; that's all I know. Aren't you please for him?"

"Of course." Mary is suspicious of the information. "I must go, catch you later; ring me, Christine, if you need me." Mary ran out and climbed in the Land Rover, heading home. Donald sat in the house drinking coffee; hearing his mother return home, he poured her a coffee sitting at the table. She sat beside him, "You have something to tell me, Donald?" she asked calmly.

"I don't think so, mum. The animals are fed. I can't do much else outside in this weather. Christine said she'd plough the fifty acres. I'm not sitting on an old tractor freezing to death trying to plough myself."

"Nothing to do with the farm Donald directly."

Donald shrugged, "I don't know what you're implying, mum, explain?"

"Signing for a major rugby team, and why haven't you mentioned it to me?" She asked, becoming annoyed.

Donald laughed, "More gossip, mother; apparently, the games master thinks he can have me signed by a local club to play rugby. I haven't mentioned it because I haven't made up my mind. Before making any decisions, I want to ensure the farm can run smoothly while I'm away. I don't see the point in causing more stress with you worrying and dad over something that might never happen."

"Oh, that will teach me to open my mouth before I have all the facts," Mary sighed, rubbing his hair.

***

Gerald returned home to Strawberry Estate, greeted at the door by Christine; they went into the kitchen Susan made coffee. "How bad is the situation, father?"

"Your mother was charged with possession with the intent to supply. Dixons arrested and charged with possession of cocaine," he sighed.

Susan sipped her coffee, "I think sent down this time Gerald, Dixon, especially."

"Bloody good job if he is, that boy is always a pain in the arse. Just a waiting game now. I see the press barely covered the incident; I suspect they'll go to town next time," he sighed.

"I've ordered Stephen to lay the hedge in field forty-six with the other men. I hope you are okay with that, father."

"Whatever you do, sweetheart is all right with me, you know that. I understand you stayed at Mary Selwyn's cottage last night, kind of her," Gerald smiled.

"Yes, father, she helped me clean the house; Susan would have never coped today."

Gerald phoned the workshop, "Johnson, I want you to check my new John Deere and plough, fill with diesel, out tomorrow working, thanks." He dialled another number. "Stephen, how do you feel about working on a weekend?"

"I wouldn't mind at all, Sir. The extra money would come in handy," Stephen replied eagerly; he'd worked for the farm for twenty years and enjoyed a better position than most.

"I want you to load a hundred bags of spring barley on the Ivor Williams trailer. Leave it parked in the barn; I'll collect in the morning. Attach the power harrow drill combination to the Ford with the flotation tyres. She won't compact too much. I'll pay you in cash, so you don't have to pay tax." "Thanks, Mr Gibbs, Sir."

"No need to start until 8 o'clock in the morning. I'll see you in the morning, Stephen, thanks."

"That's very generous of you, father," Christine smiled.

"Friends will be hard to come by soon, I fear, when your mother is finished and that idiot son," he remarked, walking out of the kitchen. Half an hour later, Gerald entered the sitting room seeing Christine reading a magazine.

He smiled, sitting beside her, enjoying the warmth from the open fire. "If we leave about seven in the morning with the John Deere and plough, I'll escort you, although I don't suspect any traffic on the road along the back lanes. I'll tow the Ivor Williams and leave it by the field. Stephen will pop along; I should imagine around 9 o'clock when he joins you to start drilling; use the set aside to turn on, shouldn't be much of a headland to cultivate."

Christine kissed her father on the cheek, "That's great, father. Mrs Selwyn will wonder what's invaded tomorrow," she grinned. "I haven't said anything to either of them, I thought to surprise."

***

At almost ten o'clock, Donald sat at the kitchen table with a cheese and pickle sandwich and a mug of coffee. Mary is eating a packet of crisps. "I wonder if Christine is ploughing the fifty acres, mum?"

"Don't you dare mention Donald? The poor girl has enough on her plate without worrying about us; we'll manage; your father will soon be out of hospital. The nurses can't wait to get rid of him," she smiled, "Apparently, he's his usual pain in the arse," she chuckled?

Donald smiled, "I'm off to bed, mum," kissing her cheek.

***

Christine and her father had an early breakfast, driving in his Range Rover to the grain store. They attached the Ivor Williams trailer loaded with bags of barley seed. They continued along the track to the enormous machinery store, sliding the doors open, waiting for Christine, the new John Deere and ten furrows reversible plough. "Be careful, Christine; you can do damage with this tool."

She smiled, "I know, father, you drive ahead; I'll follow." She started the engine turned on the lights, and gently drove out of the shed, leaving the cab and closing the shed doors behind her.

She climbed aboard, placing her flask in the holder; the whole machine illuminated almost resembled a spaceship. Mary heard a machine passing the buildings. She left the house to see what was causing such a loud noise; standing by a shed, she saw Gerald's Range Rover towing a trailer closely behind Christine. Mary, not believing what she observed, the machine was enormous. Donald came running from the barn. Christine waved, smiling from her heated cab that resembled a computer workstation more than a tractor.

Christine continued to the field, struggling through the narrow gateway when she finally achieved. She dropped the plough to the ground and started ploughing. The machine flew across the field as if cutting through butter.

Gerald stood proudly watching his daughter perform; she's proficient, he thought and very proud. Donald and Mary drove down in their Land Rover, standing by Gerald, watching Christine ploughing.

Donald asked, "What's the trailer for?"

Gerald lifted the sheet. "Barley, the drill will be leaving the yard in the next twenty minutes. I've to advise Stephen where to come and will have this planted by the end of business today, providing nothing breaks down," he smiled.

In shock, Mary put her hands to her mouth, "Gerald, this is far too generous."

"Don't be ridiculous; you help Christine; that's more than most would do. I'm so proud of her," he smiled, jumping in his Range Rover and suggesting to Mary, "Coming for a ride and a chat?" Mary smiled. "Donald, take the Land Rover home. I shan't belong." Gerald headed home, leaving the trailer. Stephen's waiting for him. "Morning Stephen, drive to Crabtree Farm fifty acres to seed. I dropped the trailer off; Christine is there ploughing, I'd like you to drill, and I'll settle up with you later."

"Very good, Sir," Stephen replied with enthusiasm. He'd already heard about Martin, and his broken back suspected Gerald's trying to help him. After 9 o'clock, Stephen arrived at Crabtree Farm, making his way to the field where Christine was ploughing.

Gerald escorted Mary into the house, commenting, "I didn't realise you married Martin Selwyn Mary." Making them both a coffee, finally sitting at the kitchen table.

Mary could feel herself blushing, "Small world, Gerald, I've just discovered. I think only we two remember; keep it that way," Mary smiled.

"Yes," Gerald agreed. "I have enough problems in life without looking for any more. Josephine convinced me at the outset I was the father of Dixon. Then things got complicated, so I never bothered to contact you again."

"Several stories were circulating. I didn't know what to believe. Although we'd only seen each other a couple of times," Mary grinned. Mary finished drinking her coffee standing. Gerald approached, kissing her tenderly on the lips. Mary clothes her eyes, remembering the last time they met and what he'd done to her at the back of the hall in the mowing grass, and that was their last meeting until now. Mary whispered in Gerald's ear, "We can't, Gerald, we mustn't." Gerald didn't relent, encouraging Mary upstairs to his bedroom, continually kissing her neck, nibbling her ear. Before Mary realised she was topless, Gerald was on top of her within seconds. Mary had never been so excited for years. He caressed every part of her body. She's trying to control the way she's feeling. Finally, they dashed into the shower laughing, watching Gerald wash her large breasts. They quickly dried, not saying a word until they sat in the Range Rover, where reality returned. "Gerald, this never happened. We must continue as if we don't really know each other. Otherwise, a lot of people will be hurt," Mary cautioned.

Gerald smiled, commenting, "I agree entirely, Mary. My fault I couldn't resist you, and by God, you have developed into a beautiful woman. I should have married you and ignored the richest shoved under my nose," Gerald sighed. Gerald drove Mary home, dropping her some distance from the house, quickly turning around, leaving.

Mary prepared meals for Christine and Stephen; she was determined to show her appreciation. She carefully drove her Land Rover to where they were working at lunchtime. Stephen stopped. Mary passed him a plate. "Thanks, Mrs Selwyn; I hope your husband recovers soon," he smiled.

Mary made her way across to Christine. Christine jumped out of the cab sitting in the Land Rover, "That's great, starving," placing the plate on her lap and quickly eating.

"Steady on," Mary advised, "You will have indigestion."

"I want this finished by 5 o'clock. I presume we have to leave set aside, Mary?"

"I presume I'm unsure of the latest rules. We'll play safe. Yes, just the usual. Perhaps if you go along with your plough tidy-up, you can turn this monster on the headlands safely."

"Easy to drive Mary' like a car; you should come across the field with me once and see what it's like yourself."

"Okay, I will."

Christine finished her drink and climbed back aboard the John Deere with Mary sitting in the buddy seat. "High up here, blimey look, it's all computers."

On one of the monitors, Christine pointed out the speed she was travelling, the fuel consumption, and what gear she was in the list went on. "I won't dare ask what one of these would cost Christine."

"An awful lot we haven't paid for this one yet," she frowned. "Everybody thinks we're rich when you have machines costing over four hundred thousand pounds. You have to look after them; some of our drivers need sacking. Stephens, okay, he looks after everything. Some we've employed in the past are not worth mentioning," she sighed.

Mary jumped out of the cab waving to Christine; she slid in on the seat of her Land Rover, returning to the farm; after collecting the plate from Stephen, grateful for the food. Donald's sat at the kitchen table, mopping his plate with a piece of bread, refusing to leave a spot of gravy behind. Mary commented, "You're better than the dishwasher," rubbing his hair. "Finished by 5 o'clock, son." "joking, mum," he exhaled, looking from the hallway window, "You're right. She's flying across the field; nothing stops you when you have 600 horsepower."

Christine wasn't wrong. She left the field at 5 o'clock, met by her father, who escorted her home, leading the way. He returned sometime later, attaching the Ivor Williams trailer and tying down the empty paper sacks. Observing Stephen leave the field. Gerald walked over to the cab door. Stephen stopped the engine. Gerald removed one hundred and fifty pounds from his pocket, "There you are, Stephen, nice job, thank you for working on Saturday."

"My pleasure, Sir, the Selwyn's are a respected family. I knew the father awarded the Victoria Cross for something in the war; he'd help anyone out in trouble."

Gerald stepped back; Stephen started the tractor heading home. Gerald headed home pleased with what he'd achieved and felt good for a change helping someone out, costing a fraction of what his wife would waste in a year on clothes, jewellery, and gambling; he sighed.

Christine removed a meal prepared by the housekeeper from the oven before she left. She sat at the kitchen table, wondering how long they could survive with her mother behaving like she does. She loved her mother and wished her mother realised her behaviour made her look silly and the rest of the family.

The phone rang in the house. Christine answered the Metropolitan police. "We are trying to contact Mr Gerald Gibbs; his mobile appears not working?"

"I'm Christine Gibbs, his daughter. Can I help?"

"No, I'm afraid we must speak to Mr Gibbs personally. Could you please ask him to ring as soon as he's available?"

Christine wrote down the number. "Hang on, he's come in. Father, the police want to talk to you," passing him the receiver.

"Yes, Gerald Gibbs."

"Do you know the whereabouts of Dixon Gibbs, your son? We released him earlier today after questioning and formally charged to appear in court date yet to be set?"

"Ask his mother I have no idea where he'd be other than University," Gerald sighed. "If he contacts me, I'll notify you immediately. Goodbye," Gerald slammed the receiver down, fuming.

The doorbell rang. "Bloody hell will no one leave me alone," Gerald shouted. Christine ran to the door opening, finding two police officers standing, male and female.

"Can we come in for a moment, please, Miss? We need to speak to your father and yourself."

"Father!"

He came down the hallway, "Yes, officers!" He frowned, frustrated with the situation.

The male officer spoke nervously, "I'm afraid we have some bad news."

"I doubt," Gerald voiced. "My life can't become any worse, I don't think."

"Unfortunately, Sir, your son Dixon was found dead; we believe an overdose of heroin."

Gerald staggered backwards, sitting on a chair in the hallway. Christine placed her hand to her mouth in shock. The female officer moved swiftly into the kitchen, making a drink for them both; the male officer assisted Gerald to the kitchen.

"How! What happened?" Gerald asked calmly.

"A little sketchy at the moment, Sir; I presume you were aware your son was gay?"

"Honestly, officer, nothing about Dixon would surprise me," Gerald exhaled, holding his bolding head. "Sorry for my attitude, officer. My life hell the last few days."

"We understand, Sir, your wife in hospital and your son," the officer said.

Christine sat at the kitchen table drinking her coffee; she didn't know what she felt at this precise second, wondering how her mother would take the news, suspecting she would be devastated. Dixon was the blue-eyed boy. He could walk on water, unlike her.

CHAPTER TWO

THE SECRETS UNFOLD

Gerald held his forehead, glancing at Christine, "You knew Christine he's gay?"

"Yes, father."

"You knew I wasn't his biological father?"

She nodded slightly, "I thought it prudent to stay silent; we have enough problems without me making matters worse," she sighed.

Gerald poured two whiskies' passing one to Christine, "I think we need something a little stronger than coffee, love," he smiled briefly.

"I heard my mother talking on the phone to Mrs Montague about Dixon; that's when I discovered you weren't his father. I wondered if I should inform you at the time, then decided you weren't stupid, and you probably knew anyway," she frowned, sipping her whisky from a crystal glass.

"I knew the minute you were born, Christine; you would be the brightest star in my life, and you've never disappointed me," he smiled. "I'd better pack a bag and head for London; I wonder if Mary would help you while I'm away. She's the salt of the earth sort of person. A pity I didn't marry someone like her," he sighed. "I'll grab some clothes and call in at Crabtree Farm; I'll have a quick word with Mary. We can trust Donald; can't we too stay silent?"

Christine smiled, "Definitely, if you ever saw him play rugby, father; anyone upset him is facing a charging bull. He's unstoppable, especially when he's angry."

Christine and Gerald drove to Crabtree Farm. Mary glanced from the window, surprised to see them, and opened the front door, greeting them with a broad smile, "I'm pleased to see you both come in," she embraced Christine.

"I wonder if I could have a word with you and Donald, Mary. There are some rather serious developments, which must not leave this kitchen." He emphasised, "Total secrecy for the moment, please," he stressed.

Donald glanced from the farmer's weekly, closing the magazine and now paying attention to what was about to be said; he could gather from both their expressions something serious had happened.

Mary quickly poured them a coffee while sitting at the large oak kitchen table. Gerald took a deep breath, "My son Dixon has died. Police believe an overdose of heroin. I must travel to London to see my wife. I'm unsure if she's informed or not? Mary, if you could assist Christine with any issues on my estate, it would be appreciated while I'm away. She will probably manage anything that crops up; I like to be prepared for the unexpected, you know what I mean."

Mary sat in shock with her hand on her cheek, "You don't need to ask Gerald. No harm will come to Christine. I'd like to see anybody get past Donald."

"You can count me in," Donald expressed with determination written across his face.

Gerald smiled with relief, "Thank you both; difficult times ahead, I suspect. I don't know how many of you are aware, Dixon wasn't my biological son," he sighed.

"To be quite honest, Gerald, everybody knows around the village; talk a long time ago, everyone believed you were used as a scapegoat."

"You are correct. Without going into detail, Dixon's father is almost Royal, if not Royal from what I understand."

"People in high places could make your life miserable, Gerald, if you're not careful," Donald suggested.

Gerald stared in amazement, "Your right Christine. No flies on, Donald."

"This reminds me of the Diana episode," Donald commented. "I can't believe the way she died never have," shrugging his shoulders.

"Would everyone forget what's said around this table tonight, please? Carry on like nothing's happened for the moment; we'll have to see what transpires. Hopefully, Dixon will be buried, and life will return to normal, I should imagine. My wife won't see the inside of a prison with her connections," he sighed. "A month or two inside would shake her up and probably do her good," he remarked. "Thanks, both once again; I must make tracks."

Christine kissed her father on the cheek, "Drive steady, father, please."

He smiled, "You can count on that, Christine, and thank you both again, Donald and Mary; I don't know what I'd do without you pair at the moment," he remarked, dashing out of the door.

Donald didn't know what to say or do, opened his farmers weekly and continued reading.

"You're staying here, Christine, while your father's away."

"Thanks, Mary."

Mary and Christine retreated into the lounge, watching television. Donald stayed in the kitchen, unsure of what he was facing. He walked to the gun cabinet, loaded two shotguns with cartridges and locked the cabinet. He smiled, thinking a little drastic; he had no idea what could happen next.

**

Gerald arrived in London, finding somewhere to park; he dreaded what was coming next, making his way to the hospital. "I've come to see my wife, Josephine Gibbs."

Gerald was escorted into an office which he thought somewhat strange. Stood impatiently tapping her cane, Mrs Montague, in her travelling suit, looked at him as if he were dirt. "Josephine is convalescing on my estate in France." She spoke directly with a purpose in her tone. "Dixon will be buried there in a private ceremony. The newspapers silenced by the Prime Minister; too much has been said already," she assured with piercing eyes. "I suggest Gerald continue running the estate you were graciously gifted through marriage with your daughter; ask no further questions. I think that concludes our business today," Mrs Montague stepped out of the office like a peacock. Gerald followed, seeing a Royal limousine parked outside with tinted windows, which she entered and swiftly driven away.

Gerald didn't know whether to jump for joy or be extremely worried. He slowly returned to Strawberry Estate, arriving home at three in the morning tired and concerned, wishing he'd said nothing to Mary and Donald. Although pretty sure they wouldn't say anything, who would believe them anyway. He retired to bed absolutely shattered; he would continue along the lines of his wife residing in France to recover from her injuries.

In the morning, Mary drove the old Land Rover transporting Christine home to check the house on the farm, surprised to see Gerald's Range Rover parked. Gerald sat at the kitchen table drinking coffee. Christine asked cautiously, "Everything okay, father," surprised to see him.

"Yes, we decided your mother should spend some time in France recovering from her injuries."

"What about Dixon and the funeral arrangements."

"Taken care of love, Dixon will be buried in France on our other estate."

"Oh, I see, father."

"A very private affair as if it never happened."

Mary realised someone extremely high up had jumped in to resolve any issues. Mary smiled, changing the subject. "I'd hate you to lose any weight; I'll cook breakfast before I go for the pair of you," finding her way around the kitchen like a professional. Christine smiled, "Father, you must try one of Mary's breakfasts; it will last you a week," she chuckled.

"He's a grown man; he needs his strength like you, young lady. Boys are not always attracted to a matchstick," she laughed along with Gerald and Christine.

"No chance I'll be a matchstick if you stay here too long," Christine grinned.

Mary produced two of her famous breakfasts. Gerald stared in disbelief, "Would you like to move in permanent, Mary? I have never had breakfast like this for as long as I can remember."

"Right, I'm off; you know where I am if you need me," she smiled.

"Thanks, Mary," Gerald voiced along with Christine as Mary left the house.

"So, we won't be attending the funeral, father?"

"I don't think it really matters, love; you never liked Dixon, and neither did I. Shame I would have liked to pay my last respects. Politely advised to leave things alone; otherwise, the estate could vanish, and I want this place for you."

"Oh well, stick to the storey mothers in France to recuperate, father?"

"Yes, and Dixon went with her."

***

Mary entered the cottage. Donald could see her expression of concern, "Where's Christine?"

"With her father at home, he came home in the early hours. His wife and Dixon are now in France, not to mention it again, and I mean Donald again under any circumstances. These people deal with anyone; they could ruin your life in seconds, above the law when talking about Royalty."

"I know what you mean," moving to the gun cabinet, ejecting the cartridges from the guns.

Mary stared in horror, "When did you load the guns?"

"When you and Christine were watching television."

"Sometimes, Donald, I wonder where your brains are. You wouldn't stand a cat in hell's chance against these people; now put the guns back, close the cabinet."

"Back to school tomorrow; I wonder if Christine is coming to help with the animals."

"Ring and find out her father could have breakfast here; the least we can do after what he's done for us, don't you think, Donald?"

Donald nodded, ringing Christine on his mobile. She answered, " I'll be there in the morning," she laughed.

"Mum said to advise your father breakfast will be here in the morning."

"Oh, that's great, thanks; I will inform him. Father prepare to pile on the pounds or book a place at the gym. Mary is making your breakfast in the morning. See you, Donald."

Gerald laughed, "I'll be the size of a battleship. The woman doesn't understand small portions."

"What about me? Don't dare ask for toast; she'll go mad." Both smiled at each other, realising they had a friend.

5 o'clock in the morning, arriving at Crabtree Farm, Gerald knocked and entered the house; Mary had already prepared his breakfast. She removed it from the oven and placed it on the table. He stared in disbelief, "I hope that's for all of us?"

"No, yours, I'll deal with the other two when they come in. Sit down, no arguing," passing Gerald a large coffee. Christine and Donald ran out of the cottage giggling. Christine ran off to milk the cow, and Donald fed the animals across the field. By the time they returned, Gerald had finished eating, releasing the buttons on his waistcoat, trying to breathe.

Mary removed two plates from the oven and placed "You two breakfast," pointing to the table. Christine knew pointless arguing; she would never starve here. Gerald stood, "I must go, Mary, thanks; could I have half of that in the morning, please," he smiled.

"You enjoy Gerald?"

"Absolutely nothing wrong, perfect. I have to work."

Christine burst out laughing. Donald commented, "Only a snack."

"That's my boy," she smiled, patting him, "Get it down, you son; when you play rugby, they run into you; you're a brick wall. You're unstoppable."

"Gerald, tea's at 5 o'clock," Mary insisted.

He shook his head, laughing, walking out the door, saying, "You're a menace woman."

Christine and Donald attended school. Apart from a few snide remarks from his best friend Michael, nothing was said at school about anything. Christine is grabbed by Kevin and manoeuvred into a storeroom, and without delay, he kisses her softly on the lips. She grinned, "What are you up to, Kevin?"

"After our last conversation, you made me think, I've never asked you out on a date; you think that would be inappropriate, Christine?"

"I think of you more as a friend Kevin; I've never considered you a boyfriend. The answer is I don't know. I have to admit you kissed very nice; you should try again," she smiled reassuringly.

Kevin held her close, kissing her lips and neck. Christine dropped her briefcase, embracing Kevin. She's rather enjoying the experience, although it seems strange kissing him. Kevin remarked, "This is odd, Christine; any other girl I'd know what I'm up to with you, it's different."

The bell rang. They peered out the storeroom stepping into the corridor before they were seen smiling and laughing; Christine boarded the coach with Donald.

Gerald arrived at 5 o'clock, apprehensively knocking on the door. Mary opened smiling; he looked at the display on the table, almost a banquet. "Normal, father," Christine commented.

"No wonder Martin has a bad back carrying his belly around the farm," Gerald remarked.

"Don't be rude about my cooking Gerald; take a seat and help yourself plenty to go around."

"There's no doubt in my mind," he exhaled.

"Donald, don't forget to load the lambs in the stock trailer tomorrow; I'm taking the lambs to market."

"I'll do that for you, Mary," Gerald offered.

"Perhaps not, Gerald. We don't want to start tongues wagging, do we; your wife away gossip around here travels like wildfire. It doesn't matter that you are eating here; nobody knows, and it doesn't matter that Christine is helping Donald. If you started helping, people would really talk, don't you think?"

"You're right, Mary; although an innocent gesture would give ammunition to those who want to cause trouble, that's the last thing I need," he smiled in appreciation.

"That reminds me, Gerald, can Susan be trusted to keep her mouth shut?"

"She'd better, out of a job else part of her contract anything she sees or discusses in the house is not permitted to leave or disclosed elsewhere."

"Blimey," Donald expressed.

Mary smiled, "I hope she honours her contract. I think the worst that can happen is the kids at school, and the parents might think Donald and Christine, you know what I mean, which is okay, would be considered normal under any circumstances."

Donald started choking. Gerald patted his back, laughing, "I don't think you have anything to worry about, Mary or you, Christine. Donald would prefer a rugby ball any day, sensible lad."

Donald ran to the sink drinking a glass of water. "The first person suggests something will have no teeth. I've heard Michael make a few remarks; I've ignored him."

Christine looked at Donald's expression, slightly red-faced and feeling herself blush, he returned to his meal. Gerald and Mary looked at each other and grinned approvingly. The day finished without any further dramas.

Early the following day, Donald ran outside, hitching the livestock trailer to the old Land Rover heading across the field with Biscuit. He parked the livestock trailer at the end of the fencing, quickly sorting through the lambs and selecting those with a red mark; he started loading. Christine came across, "You okay, Donald."

"Yes, thanks, bloody sheep I hate the animals." He jumped in the old Land Rover along with Christine and steadily drove to the farm parking by the buildings, ready for his mother to take to market. They both entered the house to find Gerald and Mary laughing while enjoying breakfast.

Christine scolded, "You could have helped, father. You need to lose some weight; your fat." Both Gerald and Mary burst out laughing. "I'll drop you two off at school on the way to the market," Mary advised.

"I'm not going in that dirty old Land Rover with my school clothes," Donald commented.

"Okay, catch the bus, son," she advised, not bothered.

Donald and Christine walked down the drive to catch the bus; Gerald returned to his farm. Mary drove to market with their lambs reversing up to the pens like a professional. She walked to the office in the market and produced the correct paperwork, parking her Land Rover out of the way with the trailer. Watching a policeman look over the vehicle. She's waiting for him to start moaning about the state of it. Instead, he walked away; she breathed a sigh of relief; she knew the tyres were close to the legal limit; the last thing she needed was to lose her license. Mary stayed to watch the sale of her lambs. They fetched one hell of a price more than they had in the past by a considerable margin; perhaps now, out of the EU, prices may improve. She drove home a pleased woman avoiding the canteen where she usually met the other farmer's wives. She didn't want to become involved in any gossip, especially involving Gerald and Christine.

Mary phoned the hospital, informing Martin what they'd fetched. He's extremely pleased and relieved for once, the lambs made serious money, something they were always short of as a rule.

***

Three weeks passed uneventfully, just the usual routine. Donald and Christine had worked together, and Gerald piling on the pounds around his waist. Donald's concerned he's running out of silage thanks to the drought during the summer. "Mum, I think we have to sell some of the bullocks from their condition; I'd say a dozen we could sell. What do you think?"

Mary grabbed her coat, walking across the field with Donald. She glanced at the silage stack of round bales. "If we cut back on food, they will lose weight, Donald; you're right. I'm not prepared to purchase any more concentrate that's pouring money down the drain. I agree to send twelve. What's the swede situation?"

Donald sighed, "Not much better, mum. Could you buy in some stock feed carrots or potatoes?"

"Not really, Donald, the transport costs are horrendous, send a dozen to market of the best see what price we achieve. We keep the others. There should be enough grass in the field to help maintain them, soon start growing again," she smiled confidently. Mary phoned the hauliers arranging for a lorry Thursday morning.

***

Christine Gibbs left the house driving her father's quad bike toward an old shed on the estate. She'd secretly meet with Timothy Brocklehurst from school after receiving a text message; he's certainly no rugby player, although brilliant and could match her own grades. Christine would prefer to see Donald if she could coax him into asking her out. She felt she was gaining some headway with him but would make do with Timothy for now for fun.

Christine parked the quad bike out of sight, seeing Timothy approach from the woodland with a beaming smile. Timothy lit a joint and entered the dilapidated shed, sitting on an old box. Christine joined him, "I wish you wouldn't smoke around me, Timothy; I don't want the smell lingering on my clothes. If my father detects the scent of drugs, he will go loopy."

Timothy extinguished the joint, "Sorry, I keep forgetting, bloody freezing out here. Anywhere warmer, we could meet on the estate?"

Christine received a text message from her father: "Gone for two hours on business catch you later."

"I agree. Too cold here. I've received a text from my father; he's out for a couple of hours; jump on the back of the quad bike, we'll go home, have to be careful," she expressed with concern, although enjoying the excitement of the challenge outwitting everyone.

She slowly headed towards Strawberry Estate house with Timothy gripping her waist, appearing slightly scared. Christine parked the quad in the garage, checking her father's Range Rover's gone. She indicated with her hand to run. Timothy followed to the rear of the house, where they entered through the kitchen back door. "Certainly, warmer in here," he commented. He stepped forward, blowing on his hands for a minute and cautiously kissing Christine. She didn't object. Christine knew most of the girls at school were desperate to have a date with Timothy. Christine smiled, enjoying the moment permitting Timothy to continue kissing her. She had to admit she was aroused by his attention, accepting his hand on her blouse and cringed as his cold hands touched her bare back as he eased her blouse from her jeans; he could undoubtedly kiss. She felt him release her bra. His hand slowly manoeuvred to the front, holding her breast and squeezing gently. Christine wondered how far she should allow him to continue, feeling the top of her jeans released. She knew what was coming next; there was no going back once she'd lost her virginity. Although most of her friends were way past that stage, enjoying frequent sex with boys at school. Christine determined not to be like her mother and become pregnant through a stupid mistake in the heat of the moment. She felt Timothy's hand inside her knickers. Christine gently removed his hand, kissing him passionately, pulling away slightly, saying softly, "not yet." Christine pressed a button to close the blinds in the kitchen to prevent prying eyes.

Timothy smiled, anticipating what was to come, carefully easing his erect cock from his jeans, watching Christine's expression of shock. Christine realised Timothy expected a lot more than she was prepared to give at the moment. Not wishing to ruin any chance

Christine had with him, she continued to kiss him holding his cock firmly. He teased her nipples, driving her slightly crazy. She wanted to lay on the floor and experience sex. Timothy had already taken the initiative easing her down on the tiles. Reality returned hearing the doorbell ring. Timothy looked alarmed, running out of the kitchen door, trying to dress, glancing back, "I'll see you at school," he said, panting

Christine nodded, tidying herself and heading for the front door only to discover a package delivered by courier. She moved into the living room, leaving it on a table for her father, considering for him. Christine's somewhat relieved circumstances have dictated that nothing else happens between her and Timothy for now. She suddenly realised she may have made a stupid error. If Timothy spoke to Donald about her, she concluded that any chance she had with him would be gone forever, somewhat annoyed with her stupidity.

***

Donald and Mary, Thursday morning, loaded the best dozen bullocks and sent them off to market. Mary stood in the marketplace, wishing Martin was here to help. The cattle fetched an excellent price fat cattle had gone out of fashion these days. She returned home feeling somewhat deflated. She phoned Martin explaining what they'd had to do and hadn't informed him in advance, in case he lost his temper. "The right thing, love; I wish I were there to help," he sighed. "Hopefully, I'll be home in a couple of weeks; I know I'll only be able to moan, but better than laying here."

"I do miss you, Martin."

"Donald certainly turned out to be a man," Martin suggested with pride.

"You can say that again, Martin. Donald's a rock, not forgetting Christine, of course, and her father Gerald; assisted us over the past few weeks."

"I can't wait to meet him and thank him personally," Martin suggested.

***

Donald and Christine arrived at school, each attending their respective lesson. Christine watched discreetly from a classroom window. Donald charged across the rugby pitch with the ball tucked under his arm; no one seemed to want to block him. She watched the other girls shouting his name and waving.

"Miss Gibbs, when you've finished observing the rugby team, could we possibly have your attention on the board, please," the teacher advised. Christine turned bright red, embarrassed; the other girls laughed at her, suspecting she had a soft spot for Donald like most girls in the school. They boarded the coach at the end of the day. Michael commented, "I have an itch underneath this plaster driving me crazy," trying to relieve his discomfort with a ruler. "Father's thinking of having sewage sprayed on the grassland free fertiliser; using an umbilical cord system, not tankers, so the compaction problem should be minimal."

"That's not half a bad idea, Michael," Donald expressed with interest, "Anything that saves us money."

Christine advised, "Sounds good in theory; you'd have to make sure no adverse chemicals, after all, coming out of the drains, not only the sewers," she advised cautiously.

Michael remarked, "That had never crossed my mind, Christine, until you mentioned it could be anything in that."

"I suspect tested Michael," she advised, "Wouldn't be allowed to spread in case of contaminating the food chain."

"Would you consider some Christine?" Donald asked.

"Had some in the past on a trial plot not having any adverse effects on the field or crop, and they came back and tested," she advised. "Mother wouldn't allow us to spread anymore because of the smell father had to give in to her wish."

"See you tomorrow, Michael," Donald smiled, leaving the bus with Christine. They slowly walked on the cobbled drive. Christine commented, "The teacher caught me watching the rugby match from the classroom window during a boring mathematics lesson; the girls looked at me embarrassing."

"Don't worry, Christine," kissing her on the cheek, surprising her. "Not in your league," he continued walking.

They entered the house, finding Mr Gibbs sitting by the hearth reading the newspaper with a cup of coffee. Christine placed her hands on her hips, "You leave this morning, father or sat there all day."

He grinned, "Helping a friend out, that's all; your father's home, Donald. An ambulance brought him home this afternoon. I helped your mother rearrange the bedroom."

Donald grabbed Christine's hand, "Meet my dad."

Donald knocked on the bedroom door. "Come in," Martin said brightly, laying on his back on a board, "I can't move much, son, don't jar me, for christ's sake." He smiled, looking at Christine, offering his hand she held in hers. "You are the wonderful girl who kept my son in check and my farm running."

She smiled, slightly embarrassed, "I only helped Mr Selwyn."

"Martin please; we're way past formal. You better see to the animals," he advised watching them leave the bedroom. Both Donald and Christine carried out their evening chores, returning to the house; Gerald was already tucking into his tea. Mary came in from outside after taking a dish of food out to Biscuit. She always saved the scraps, especially a good bone, and was partial to crackling.

Mr Gibbs removed a letter from his jacket, passing across to Christine, "From your mother, I think," he sighed. She placed it in her jacket pocket, deciding to read after they'd finished eating, and sat quietly drinking her coffee. Gerald remarked, desperate to find out, "The letter, love, I'm dying to know what's inside and if we have any more problems to face."

Christine studied the letter, "My mother is apologising for her behaviour. Dixon cremated; I'm welcome to join her in France if I wish; the weather is far more pleasant." She passed the letter to her father he scanned the contents.

"Before you ask, father, I'm not moving to France; I'm staying here where I'm loved and have friends," glancing at Mary and Donald.

"Wise decision," Mary commented. "From what you said happened in the past, it could be a ploy to remove you from the country."

"My exact thoughts, Mary," Gerald advised.

Donald sat quietly, listening to the conversation. Christine looked across at his expression, wondering what he was really thinking. Did he have any feelings for her? Her secret desire.

Gerald and Christine left, heading home slowly. "Christine, what's on your mind?" Gerald asked, concerned.

"Nothing really, father; I'm definitely not travelling to France if that's what's worrying you."

"Somethings changed, Christine?" he asked, puzzled, considering Donald may be the problem. "Anything to do with Donald?"

"Sort of father, I'm asked out by a boy at school most weeks. Donald hasn't approached the subject," she frowned, puzzled.

"What's the actual problem, Christine? Do you feel insulted? The boy's a gentleman because he's only a boy. You're only a girl; you have plenty of time to consider boyfriend and girlfriend situations. You shouldn't rush matters."

"I suppose you wouldn't approve anyway, father; you want me to marry some rich boy with the brains of a dog."

They walked into the house, sitting at the kitchen table. "Whatever gave you that idea, Christine, my background is much like Donald's; my parents had not many acres. I don't know why she picked me other than that your mother was pregnant. That's the only reason we have this farm, or should I say an estate of this size; otherwise, I'd still be on my father's farm," he frowned.

"Oh, father, sorry, I didn't mean to be rude. I suspected you were similar to my mother. I don't know why your nothing like her in attitude."

"Perhaps I should prevent you from travelling over there. You seem to be confused."

"No, please, father, don't; I'm impatient. I suspect you are correct. What's the rush? I'm nearly 17, the same as Donald. He said something strange tonight; I expressed being caught watching the rugby team from the classroom window by a teacher; the girls were laughing. He remarked they're not in your league, don't worry."

"My clever daughter, you are really thick sometimes. Analyse what he said. I'm in the sitting room with a glass of whisky; enlighten me when you've decided what the answer is. You can't go over to Crabtree Farm again until you give me the right answer, silly girl," he muttered.

Weren't many minutes before she came running into the room, "He likes me; he's saying he's not interested in the other girls," she beamed excitedly.

"Finally," her father exhaled. "Donald will move at his own pace, don't try forcing him because you will lose; he's a decent lad. His grandfather was awarded the Victoria Cross for bravery during the Second World War."

"No, father, let's look on the computer and see what he'd received it for," she smiled, grabbing her laptop beside her father. She searched the Internet, "Look, father, look!" He read the page. "Smuggling people from France to England during the night and running the farm during the day; they estimate he saved over two hundred lives. You must remember Christine, Donald's from the same stock. Someone you can trust, remember that if you start flirting with other boys when he walks away, there will be no second chances; bear that in mind, Christine."

"I don't flirt, father, thanks," insulted by his comment leaving the room and climbing the oak stairway to her bedroom, feeling slightly guilty. However, she wasn't seeing Donald officially.

***

Mary helped Martin into the living room to watch TV; Donald joined him with a broad smile. Mary came in with a tray with three mugs of coffee, passing one to Martin. "You wouldn't believe how good it is to be home," he commented.

"Your own fault, Martin," she scolded. "How often have I asked you to take Biscuit to keep the sheep away while placing the food in the troughs?"

Donald grinned, "You should have stopped in hospital, dad, with those pretty nurses."

"I'm beginning to think you're right, Donald, I haven't been here a day, and she's at me. Okay, Mary, bad judgement on my part, the real reason too bloody lazy to bend down to unchain him."

"I'm phoning our local sewerage works tomorrow and have a hundred acres treated, using an umbilical cord and a tank, only slight compaction, no damage to the grass. What do you think, dad?"

"Free fertiliser."

"Christine said they've used it and found it quite effective."

"May stink to high heaven, son, but the word free always makes me smile. What do you think, Mary?" glancing at her, she quietly smiled, proud of Donald and how he's showing an interest in the farm and trying to solve problems. She shrugged her shoulders, "I'm not worried about the smell. Can't be any worse than you in bed at night, Martin."

Martin grinned, "I can produce some right crackers even worse now I don't move much," he chuckled. "Pass me the phone, son." Martin dialled a number, "Mark, Martin Selwyn, Crabtree Farm."

"Sorry to hear about your back, Martin; I hope you recover speedily."

"Thanks, Mark. Sorry to disturb you at home. Donald mentioned that you were spreading sewerage again using an umbilical cord this time, is that right?"

"Yes, Seven Trent put the contract out to tender. I was going to speak to you anyway. We could do with land to spread on; can I interest you."

"Yes, I'd like a hundred acres treated if you have enough."

Mark laughed, "The way people eat curry around here will always be enough," he laughed. "I'll come around tomorrow morning. You can show me which fields; thanks for phoning, greatly appreciated; start this Wednesday."

"A hundred acres," Mary frowned.

"How many would you allocate, Donald," Martin asked?

"Hundred acres, dad. We need the grass desperately, and the faster we can push it on, the better not forgetting the price of fertiliser these days."

"That reminds me, Donald, the fifty acres will have to do with barley this year if we can afford the seed," he frowned.

"You missed the excitement, Dad."

Martin looked worried, "What's happened?"

"When you were in hospital with your back, you know Christine's helping me; she came with her John Deere tractor and ten furrows reversible plough. Gerald came with his combination drill and planted the seed which he provided. I hope you're not angry."

"You're joking. I don't believe Christine ploughed the field; she's no older than you and a girl."

"She actually won a ploughing competition father in the next County. Her father has a brand-new 600 horsepower tracked John Deere the size of a house."

Mary commented, "I went across the field with her; it's like a luxury Rolls-Royce inside, heated cab. I'm surprised there isn't a television, although could be one, and I never noticed," Mary smiled.

"Bloody hell, that's definitely a shocker; she's only a slip of a girl, comes across as Miss prim and proper, to be quite honest," Martin expressed.

"You're not the only one that thought that, Martin," Mary advised. "We all did; she's a lovely person and her father."

"How much do we owe them, Mary? It can't have been cheap; the tractor alone would drink diesel like it's out of fashion with an engine that size plus the seed," he sighed.

Donald smiled, "Mum covered the price with her cooking; she almost killed the bloke and Christine. They are not used to wholesome cooking; dad like us," Donald smiled proudly. "Gerald wants nothing. We helped him out."

"I must go into hospital more often," Martin commented, looking at the smug expression on his son's face and Mary's.

***

Strawberry Estate housekeeper Susan's tidying the kitchen. Gerald's sat reading the newspaper. "You haven't said much about Josephine lately, Gerald."

"No, nothing to say, really. Josephine is in France on the other farm; she prefers the weather out there warmer."

Susan frowned, "What happened about the drugs?" she asked cautiously.

He shrugged, "Nothing ever happened; I've heard nothing."

"What about Dixon?"

"Not interested. What's the sudden curiosity, Susan?" Gerald lowered his paper.

"Nothing, oh nothing, making conversation, sorry I asked."

He sighed heavily, "I will remind you, Susan! Remember what's in your contract if you wish to stay working here," Gerald folded the newspaper, leaving the house. He jumped in his Range Rover, driving across the three-thousand-acre estate, coming across Stephen walking along the old farm track. Gerald lowered his window, "Jump in a moment, Stephen."

Stephen jumped in, extinguishing his cigarette outside. "You have worked for me for some time, Stephen."

"Yes, Sir."

"Gerald will do, not Sir seems ridiculous to me," Gerald smiled. "We have three members of permanent staff. What's your view on each one?"

"Johnson in the workshop is excellent. He is always helpful and does his best to repair the machinery, although I wouldn't give some drivers a wheelbarrow to play with."

"What about Thomas?"

"Like me conscientious, and so is Jake. When we're harvesting, you have all those idiots here; they don't give a damn about the equipment, Gerald, if you want my honest opinion."

"I can't be everywhere at once, Stephen."

"I'm aware, Gerald. We know you've had a few problems; I hope they are soon resolved. Miss Gibbs is knowledgeable and knows her own mind; she's never frightened to ask or take advice I've discovered over the years." Stephen smiled nervously, "I hope I'm not speaking out of turn, Gerald."

"No, you've made my day. How would you like the position of working foremen? I can give you a small pay rise, and if you run the old Land Rover to Johnson, ask to check it over; you can use that around the estate on red diesel. Stephen, before you purchase anything, come to me before you do, is that clear."

"I don't know what to say, Gerald. The last thing I expected to hear today, thanks very much for the opportunity."

"One last thing, Stephen. If you find someone abusing my equipment, report to me immediately, and I'll dismiss them; everything is about pounds, shillings and pence, as you know. I've just had the bill for that new John Deere; I'm going grey," Gerald smiled.

Gerald dropped Stephen off at the garage. He jumped in the old Land Rover, waving as if he'd won the lottery, taking the vehicle to the workshop. Gerald made his way over to Crabtree Farm at almost 5 o'clock; he wasn't missing his tea for anything. Everyone else sat around the table, including Martin. Gerald knocked and walked in, removing his jacket, hooking on the peg behind the door, releasing the buttons on his waistcoat, and making everyone laugh.

He sighed heavily, "Please don't take what I'm saying the wrong way. I'll be sad when I don't come here in the evenings and morning."

Martin voiced, "Either of you will always be welcome here; you don't need an excuse."

"I second that," Donald grinned.

"That reminds me, Mary, we have a shoot next week probably be at least fifty birds a deer or two; have you a large freezer big enough you might as well have the surplus birds, rather than go to waste. If you want Donald, you can come on the shoot as my personal guest."

"I haven't any fancy clothes, Gerald; I'd look out of place."

"Don't be silly, Donald," Christine voiced, "You're a friend. Come in a dress as far as I'm concerned." Which made everybody laugh, and Donald turned bright red.

"I do have a spare freezer, and Martin has nothing better to do so he could prepare the birds at the kitchen table and freeze. You and Christine could come and help us eat them," she smiled. Martin looked horrified, "I'm incapacitated, wife," he protested.

"Nothing wrong with your hands." Donald laughed.

"Actually, Donald." Gerald sat in thought. "I may have old shooting clothes in my wardrobe at home; I'll bring them over. I'm sure your mother will alter for you," Gerald suggested. "Blimey, we're almost the same size. You're only a teenager, will fit without alterations."

"Thanks," Donald answered, unsure he wanted to attend.

"That reminds me, Christine, I've promoted Stephen to the position of Foreman; he looks after the place better than most. Give him another fifty pence an hour on his salary. What he will save us in repairs on machinery will be well worth the expense, don't you think, daughter?"

"Yes, father."

"Thank you once again for a lovely meal," Gerald voiced.

"Yes, thanks, everyone," Christine smiled.

"Thanks for keeping our farm together while Martin's in this shape."

Donald and Mary watched Gerald and Christine leave in his Range Rover. Mary sighed, "I'll have to clean the old freezer out in the cellar. We'll have to hang some; looks like we're going to be swamped in pheasants," she grinned, looking at Martin's expression.

"Mother, I don't know whether I fancy really all snobs hoity-toity people," he frowned.

"The only difference between them and you; is they have more money."

"Yes, don't be silly, Donald," Martin voiced, "You're as good as them, if not better most of them were born with a silver spoon in their mouth and never had to work for a penny."

***

Christine, at home, made a coffee in the kitchen, "Do you think sensible father inviting Donald?"

"I thought you'd be please, Christine," glancing at her, somewhat surprised by her response.

"Sort of. Am I on peg seventeen again? If so, perhaps Donald should stay with me; I don't want him to feel like a fish out of water," she expressed concern.

Gerald shook his head, "I don't think anyone is coming to the shoot; Donald couldn't sit on their arse; you noticed the size of his hands like anvils," Gerald expressed.

Christine smiled, "Is Copthorne attending this year, father? I hope not," she sighed.

"No, they weren't invited, only a select few. I don't need the headache; I dismissed the gamekeeper and prefer to see the birds running free around the estate. I want the birds around here to be wild and free, not lined up as cannon fodder; half the beggars can't shoot properly; in fact, this may be the last shoot solving the problem altogether."

"That's a good idea, father; we don't make any money, quite the opposite. Perhaps we should just hold a private shoot for a couple of friends and the staff thanking them for their service during the year."

"I agree," Gerald smiled, sipping his coffee.

"My gun dog Badger looks like a battleship; Susan's overfeeding him again; she has a thing about that bloody dog," Gerald smiled.

"Changing the subject, father, you think it would be prudent to write a letter to mother wishing her well and speedy recovery?" Christine asked, deep in thought.

"Yes, a good idea keeps the wolf away from the door," he suggested. "Don't forget to send any correspondence registered post; we don't want any correspondence suddenly missing, do we? I would suggest email, but you don't know who's hacked into your account," Gerald frowned.

"I understand, father. We don't want to upset the apple cart. Don't forget to look in your wardrobe, see if you have anything for Donald."

"Don't panic, daughter, I'll make sure your prince comes to the ball," he chuckled, watching Christine's expression turn slightly embarrassed.

"I'm off to bed, father, thank you," kissing him on the cheek.

***

Donald and Christine caught the bus the following day after completing their farm duties. Michael was sitting at the back, looking worried.

"What's up, mate?" Donald asked.

"Peggy's pregnant; mother went absolutely ballistic. Her fathers banned me from the house. Dad said he's taking me to be castrated; I should have more sense and self-control."

Donald exhaled, "I don't know whether to congratulate you or offer to break your neck because somebody will."

Christine asked cautiously, "You're standing by Peggy, Michael, your fault."

"Of course, we plan to marry when we're eighteen; school sweethearts for as long as I can remember."

Christine sat back in her seat, realising her father's saying, don't rush into anything and push Donald. He would come to her when he was ready.

Michael remarked, "At least you two haven't made the same mistake."

"I think you should be careful, Michael," Donald expressed. "You're pushing our friendship a little too far. Nothing is going on between Christine and me. She's merely helping me out as a good friend, and that is that. You get the message!"

Michael lowered his eyes, "Sorry, I didn't mean to imply."

Christine reached across, squeezing Donald's hand; he smiled. She realised he was protecting her honour; she never needed to be afraid in his presence. He would be there, her knight in shining armour.

During assembly, the headteacher announced. "I would like to introduce Mr Davies; he's travelled from Cardiff, especially to see Donald Selwyn play this afternoon against a formidable team; we've never beaten. Donald, come to my office after assembly, please."

Christine watched Donald make his way to the headteacher's office suspecting Mr Davies wanted to sign Donald for a rugby club. She knew he wouldn't until the farm was safe and he'd discuss matters with his parents.

Donald knocked on the headteacher's door and entered. Mr Davies explained he's a scout for various clubs, always looking for talent.

"I haven't discussed with my parents Mr Davies whether I will continue playing rugby just become a farmer or perhaps I could combine both. I don't know," Donald replied honestly.

"That's fair enough, young man. I'll see how good you are this afternoon. I watched the videotapes of other matches. You appear to be the strongest player in the team, showing great potential. You realise you can make an excellent living out of playing rugby, Donald."

"Probably until I'm thirty and the old bones start falling apart." Everyone smiled.

Donald left the office. Christine's waiting for him along the corridor, "You okay, Donald? You don't look thrilled."

"I'm okay, Christine. Honestly, I'm concerned about Michael and his girlfriend, Peggy."

"Why," she asked, surprised, "He could have taken precautions."

"I suppose you're right; I didn't think Michael's that stupid," Donald frowned.

"What happened in the office, if you don't mind me asking."

Donald grinned, "Don't worry, Christine, your breakfast is secure for some time," he chuckled, kissing her on the cheek, which shocked her, especially in school, watching him walking off along the corridor. She carried on to her lesson, feeling quite flustered. Unlike other boys trying their luck, he's patient, not forcing her; as her father had said, he never took liberties.

Donald ran out onto the rugby pitch, limbering. The game's master switched on the floodlighting, illuminating the overcast pitch. Christine sat in the cafeteria by the window with her coursework, watching the game. She could hear the shouting from pupils who ventured outside to watch in the cold. Donald's flying across the field like an unstoppable bulldozer on a mission. The opposing team were left in shreds; they had nothing to stop him. Christine could see Mr Davies videoing events, occasionally lowering the camera, shouting, that excited. Finally, the whistle blew. Stratford Academy had beaten the opposing team for the first time, the school in an uproar.

Christine had never seen the headteacher so excited about the outcome. She considered going out herself standing on the side-line cheering for Donald. Still, she thought that could make life complicated for them both, not wanting to ruin a good relationship. Christine sat on the bus. Donald joined her, "Good game, Christine, we overcame and conquered."

"Sorry I didn't watch; busy with my coursework."

"That's okay."

Michael stared at Christine; he'd seen her from the playing field in the cafeteria window; she placed a finger to her lips, and he said nothing.

"If you're in trouble, Michael, phone me. If you wish to find somewhere with Peggy, I have savings if you're both thrown out by your parents. I know your father can be strict sometimes."

"Thanks, Donald mate, both families, are meeting over the weekend to make decisions," Michael sighed.

Donald and Christine left the coach walking to Crabtree cottage; they quickly changed, attending to the animals. Christine walked into a building she had never entered, switching on the light with curiosity. She guessed this must be where Donald worked on the machinery. They had a Ford County, with the engine in bits.

Obviously, the machine is being overhauled and already re-sprayed and looks new. Everything else in the building is worse for wear, the combine harvester an old Massey Ferguson without a cab. She couldn't imagine driving something like that, inhaling the dust, your eyes soar from the chaff.

She looked in the far corner noticing the old green reversible plough. Donald wasn't joking when he said the mouldboards were thin; they were almost like paper. Close by an old New Holland round baler, she wondered if it still worked so dilapidated and a Massey square baler beside. In the other corner, power harrows needed a new set of tines. She smiled; seeing an old grain drill, she remembered they had one themselves in the barn at home specially made to go behind the Ferguson 20. Donald came in, "What's up? I must finish rebuilding the engine on the County, then we'll have at least 116 horsepower. Until she started burning more oil than diesel, a brilliant tractor, the rings are knackered."

Christine realised how lucky she was, no comparison to the equipment they had on their farm. They both made their way to the cottage finding her father sitting at the table with his waistcoat buttons released, Martin on the other side of the table. Donald and Christine took their places. "Father," he glanced up to Christine, "I'd like to borrow Johnson for a few days," she smiled. Gerald was somewhat puzzled.

"Why?"

"Perhaps he could help Donald; rebuild the tractor engine; all the parts are there. He could service the other equipment while he's here. We have a mobile workshop, so he won't be short of tools."

"No, Christine," Martin voiced quickly. "We can't afford it; that's why everything's how it is. We don't want to be in debt if we can help it. I can't afford new mouldboards for our plough; the power harrows need new tines," he sighed, "The list goes on, love. When my father suddenly died, I had to pay death duties destroyed our savings."

"Who normally carries out the repairs?" Gerald asked.

"Donald's a dab hand with a spanner and parts manual," Martin voiced proudly.

"No, you mustn't do anything else, Gerald," Mary suggested, "You're too generous."

"Let me see," Gerald removed his notebook. "If we said fifty pounds each for our meals, Christine, would you agree?"

Knowing what her father was planning, she smiled, "Yes, that's right, father, you wouldn't receive such good portions in a restaurant."

"We've eaten here for at least six weeks, so we owe you, Mary, by my calculations."

"Your impossible, Gerald," she smiled.

Martin frowned, "If we thank you for the next year, it won't cover the cost of the equipment you've used and the seed, Gerald."

"It might have fallen off the back of a lorry," Gerald laughed.

Christine commented, "The seed cost absolutely nothing, over purchase on my part. We would have to discard it. We don't keep old rubbish, do we, father."

"No, daughter," he grinned.

"Excuse me a moment," Gerald remarked, removing his mobile. "Johnson, do we have any leftover spares from when we had Dowdeswell ploughs?" Gerald placed his phone on speaker so everyone could hear.

"Yes, Sir, I have mouldboard skimmers discs; I think I could build a new plough from the spares. I was going to ask should I scrap; we are never likely to buy another plough these old things would fit."

"Tomorrow morning, come to Crabtree Farm with the plough spares. There's an old plough here they might fit. Look at the tractor. The engine wants reassembling. That reminds me, have we any power harrow tines Dowdeswell?"

"Yes, Sir."

"Throw them on as well; thank you, Johnson, goodnight. That should make some room in the workshop for him." Everyone else was silent around the table, just looking at each other they had never known anyone this generous. Gerald looked down the front of his waistcoat, "I spilt something," he looked.

Mary asked Christine, "Have you ever considered taking your father to the doctor; you realise all those parts are worth hundreds of pounds, Gerald. We will have to pay."

"I agree; I'm actually eating here for the next six months," he laughed.

Mary scurried down into the cellar, returning with a large jug of cider. Gerald stared as she poured him a glass and Christine, herself, Donald and Martin. Mary raised her glass, "Too good friends," she smiled, looking at Gerald, remembering the time in his bedroom, wondering if the opportunity would arise again.

Gerald took a large drink lowering his glass to the table, "My god, woman, what have you put in that? Its dynamite."

"You won't catch a cold drinking that, Gerald."

Christine's holding her throat, "Tastes almost like pure brandy."

Gerald emptied his glass, "Christine, home; otherwise, we'll be sleeping in the barn tonight if we drink any more of that stuff."

Donald watched from the door as Gerald and Christine vanished into the darkness. He returned to the table, sipping his cider, "I had a visitor at school today, a talent scout from Cardiff; he thinks I have potential. I explained to him the farm comes first. He seems to think I could earn a lot of money dad, would be beneficial to the farm if we can slot it in somehow; what do you think?"

"Your future Donald, I can't advise you what to do. I suppose you follow your heart."

"I want the farm; I may never be rich, but I'll be happy. I thought we could go all arable if I were signed by a major club. I'd be earning sufficient money to keep you two, and what the farm earned would be a bonus."

Mary and Martin looked at each other, "You have been thinking, haven't you, son."

"What happens if you're injured playing rugby?" Martin asked seriously.

"I'll be insured if I can't play again; I'll be worth millions," he smiled smugly.

Mary chuckled, "So what you're saying, Donald, you're in a win-win situation."

"Yes, if I go down that road, nothing settled until I decide to sign on the dotted line. We'll leave things alone; stay as we are, don't you think?"

"One or two things you haven't considered, Donald," Martin suggested. "As you mature, you will probably find a girlfriend marry and have children."

"I hope so. I can't see how that will affect the situation, one step at a time. You never know, I might be gay." Donald chuckled, drinking another glass of cider, looking at his mother and father's expression of shock at his remark.

Mary smiled, "I don't think so, Donald, how you and Christine look at each other."

"Not for me, mother; I want an ordinary girl. I can't imagine Christine ever interested in me."

"Is he really my son Mary? I was beginning to think he's bright; now I'm unsure."

Donald looked puzzled, "What do you mean?"

Mary shook her head, "You have no idea, son."

Donald shrugged his shoulders, "Christine and I are good friends; I've kissed her on the cheek a couple of times in a friendly manner. I'm not like Michael; Peggy's carrying his child. He's in trouble up to his neck."

Mary placed her hand to her cheek in shock, "Your joking Donald. That's not funny. No wonder Peggy's mother hasn't phoned me lately."

"I don't know about that, but from what Michael said on the bus this morning, all hell broke loose they're having a meeting the weekend, I think to discuss what's to happen."

Mary poured herself another cider, sitting quietly, wondering if she should leave things alone and not bother to make contact.

"Seven Trent starts spreading Donald tomorrow; wait for the complaints and the smell," Martin grinned.

"I think Thursday the rest of the cattle should go to market. I haven't many round bale's left of silage, and we'll want those for the ewe's dad."

"I wish I could see to make an assessment myself; it's too risky for me. Mary, will you have a look tomorrow?"

"Yes," she smiled.

Donald and Mary helped Martin to the bedroom. Donald retired to his own room and was soon asleep.

Christine and Donald completed their duties the following day, preparing to catch the bus and board. Michael sat at the back with a black eye and a cut lip.

"Who's responsible for that?" Donald asked, annoyed.

Michael sighed, "Peggy's brother. He said break my other arm if I come near his sister."

"I don't think that's fair," Donald voiced calmly, "Striking a man who can't defend himself. Ring me if he comes after you again; I'll sort him out," Donald assured.

"Don't become involved, Donald," Michael insisted. "Not your fight; it's my mistake."

Christine remarked, "It takes two to tango, Michael. You are only half to blame. Donald's right to hit someone who can't defend themselves is out of order; as much as I detest violence, phone me, I'll embarrass him. I'm a black belt in judo; I'll sit him on his backside."

Donald stared, "I didn't know that!"

"Me neither," Michael exhaled. "We will have to be careful what we say to you." They laughed.

Michael looked from the coach window, "Bloody hell, her brothers here," Michael sighed, suspecting another slapping.

"He's mine," Christine voiced, "Don't worry, Michael, he won't bother you after I've finished with him. I presume everyone knows around the school about Peggy's condition." Michael nodded. "Right." Christine left the school bus, passing her briefcase to

Donald, standing close by. Peggy's brother tried to sidestep her to grab Michael.

Christine grabbed his hand and threw him on the floor, "What's the matter, little boy throwing your rattle out of the pram. Your sister is pregnant. It takes two to tango, so why don't you ask her why she wasn't taking precautions before slapping someone with an arm injury that can't retaliate. Try me; you'll visit the hospital, I promise you."

Peggy's brother stood in shock and walked out onto the road. "Blimey," Michael expressed, "I wish you were my sister."

Donald passed Christine her briefcase expressing, "have you ever considered playing rugby."

She smiled, jabbing him in the ribs and walking into school. Michael's summoned into the headteacher's office. He explained what had happened and how Christine had protected him from a further beating. The headteacher phoned the police; he's not having this sort of behaviour and violence against one of his students regardless of the reason. Christine watched Michael driven away in a police car, suspecting he was taken home. She's quite surprised she wasn't summoned to the head teacher's office; she made an error of judgement showing off, especially on school property. She could be expelled for violence, although preventing against another pupil.

On the way home in the evening, Christine explained what she'd seen to Donald, and that's why Michael's not on the coach. Donald turned on his mobile, seeing a message from Michael. "Don't worry, everything's okay and thank Christine for saving my skin." Donald smiled, showing the text to Christine, who grinned.

They walked along the drive together; Donald noticed the lights on in the shed where he stored the equipment, hearing a six-cylinder engine start his County four-wheel-drive tractor. He couldn't stop grinning; he dashed into the house, running straight to his bedroom to change, dashing out of the house to the machinery store introducing himself to Johnson.

Johnson explained she's now fully serviced and operational. He showed Donald the plough, which looked almost brand-new, with no worn part on the machine. New tines on the power harrows and serviced both balers and combine explaining; he'd repaired the hole in one of the feeders to the tank letting grain out onto the floor. Donald shook his hand with gratitude, "Thanks for helping us."

"My pleasure, young man. Mr Gibbs covered the costs."

Donald ran back into the house. "Mum, Dad, you should see the equipment brilliant." Excited, he lifted Christine, kissing her on the lips and quickly putting her to her feet. "I'm sorry, Christine, I shouldn't have done that. I'm excited and thank you and your father for everything," drinking his coffee, ready to feed the animals. Christine smiled. From the expression on her face, Mary could see she had no objections to him kissing her.

The two ventured out to carry out the feeding duties.

Mary sat beside Martin, "A good son Martin. I think he's been quietly worrying, trying to find the time to make the repairs to the equipment and carry out his other duties."

"I know, love, I'm no bloody help like this. My back hasn't felt this good for ages," tickling her playfully.

"You're not fit for that, Martin," moving away, pouring another coffee. Gerald knocked and walked in. "You smelt the coffee pot, Gerald."

He smiled, "While the kids are not here, I'd like to talk to you both. You probably know I have a total of three thousand acres. Five hundred is down to woodland and conservation. Hopefully, Christine can drive one of the Claas Lexion combines; I hope you'd allow Donald to drive the other. I will pay him, of course. I wouldn't have to employ bloody strangers who wreck my equipment. With my daughter and your son driving, the combines shouldn't take too long to cut the two thousand five hundred acres. I know you have a hundred acres here. I thought perhaps we could drive a Lexion over here. We could cut a hundred acres in a few minutes and send the trailers; what's your view on the idea?"

"It's up to the kids; I have no objections," Martin voiced. "You, Mary?"

"Not really at least we'll have more corn in the tank than on the floor."

"Yes, I've talked to Johnson; your combine harvester isn't in the best health. He has made several repairs. Without a major overhaul, it won't go on much longer, outweighing its value by thousands of pounds."

"I guessed as much, Gerald," Martin frowned. "Father bought that one many years ago. The wheels were falling off then. We only harvest a hundred acres a year of cereals. Some we sell, some we keep depending on the livestock situation, which Donald is desperate to dispose of."

Christine came in, sitting at the table and Donald a few minutes later. "I can't thank you enough," he voiced joyfully. "Johnson has made a marvellous job of our machinery. You are a generous person Gerald and you, of course, Christine."

"I have a question for you two," Gerald looks seriously at them. "Christine, you drive one of the Class Lexion combines this year and the other one, Donald. Don't worry, I will show you how she works; come over here and cut your corn; it won't take many minutes when it's ready. What do you two think?" Gerald searched their expressions, trying to ascertain their views. "Providing okay with everyone, yes, I'd love to learn," Donald expressed.

Christine smiled, "Yes, our combines won't be bent or abused."

"That's settled," Gerald smiled, relieved his combines wouldn't be destroyed by idiots.

Donald commented, "Christine is one brave girl! You remember I said about Michael Pearce and Peggy Mum. When we jumped on the school bus this morning, Michael had a black eye and cut lip. Apparently, Peggy's brother thumped Michael for her condition; he couldn't defend himself because he's one arm still in a sling. When we arrived at school, Peggy's brother waiting for Michael. Christine stepped in and sat him on his backside. So funny you should have seen her in action."

Gerald smiled, "I'm pleased I made you have those self-defence classes at a professional club. After all, they came in handy, daughter after disposing of the Copthorne brothers."

"Yes, father. They took Michael away in a police car. I think home, we will see whether their parents resolve their differences or not; Donald said he'd help if he could."

"We have old cottages down the bottom, Christine, not lived in for a couple of years; I don't like renting. The last lot we had in there was bizarre and took some moving. But if push comes to shove, they could temporarily live in one of those until they sort their lives out."

"Why is Biscuit barking?" Donald ran to the gun cabinet, grabbing two shotguns, passing one to Gerald and a box of cartridges. "Dogs amongst the sheep. Will you come with me, Gerald, please?" Donald asked.

"Absolutely, we'll take my Range Rover, go anywhere."

They ran out of the cottage releasing Biscuit. Biscuit tore off across the field in the darkness. Gerald drove across the grass field like the wind, spotting Biscuit fighting with a dog in the headlights. Donald jumped out of the Range Rover cocking his gun; he shouted, "Here, Biscuit." Biscuit released the dog, and Donald discharged both barrels into the animal, killing instantly.

Donald opened the tailgate on the Range Rover, and Biscuit jumped inside, sitting quietly. He'd suffered a few bites; besides that, he appeared to be okay. Gerald drove to where the dog was lying. Donald jumped out, slinging the dead dog on the tailgate. They scanned the whole field with Gerald's headlights discovering no dead ewes; it may be another story by morning.

Gerald commented, "A bloody good shot in the dark. Is the dog wearing a collar? We can report to the police and prosecute if any ewes are injured. I know an excellent solicitor to deal with these people; bloody townies are all the same. I have the same problem on my estate people hunting at night, you hear the gunfire but no way of finding them," Gerald sighed.

"Thanks for your help, Gerald; it's too dangerous to bring my mum out here at night. You never know what you're bumping into."

They made their way back to the cottage. Donald removed the dead Alsatian from the tailgate, throwing it on the cobbles. "Biscuit in the house. Mum, look at Biscuit," Donald called out.

Mary grabbed Biscuit at the door, taking him inside; he was bleeding from the neck but nothing that wouldn't heal. She grabbed a basket from down the cellar. "You're staying in here tonight, Biscuit. You earnt a warm night's sleep for sure."

Martin asked, "How many dead?" in a disheartened tone.

Gerald smiled, "None from what we can see. Biscuit was on the ball taking on an Alsatian, and Donald shot him."

Gerald and Donald returned outside to look at the Alsatian; they knew the dog was wearing a collar, hoping to discover an owner's name. They had barely reached the animal when a police car entered the yard. Two officers left the vehicle approaching shining their torch on the Alsatian, advising, "One of our dogs."

Donald swallowed hard, suspecting he was in trouble up to his armpits. "Not your fault; he went rogue, bit his handler and a child, lost the plot, and don't know why. We traced him here by his tracker." The officer inquired, "Anyone injured by him?"

Gerald suggested, "There may be sheep we won't know until morning; the sheepdog is injured. Biscuit was bitten by your animal. I assisted Donald to prevent your dog from causing any more harm."

"Mr Gibbs from Strawberry Estate," the officer asked.

"Correct, officer."

The officer exhaled, "If any of your stock requires attention or your dog, phone the case number." The officer grabbed the Alsatian's collar throwing the animal in the boot of their car. Mary and the others watched from the cottage front door seeing the police officer's leave.

Gerald advised, "At least your covered, Donald. If any old ewes die overnight and any veterinary bills, the police will pay."

"I would have preferred not to have the problem, Gerald. Nevertheless, we are safe." They both went inside.

"That reminds me, Donald, have you tried on the old shooting clothes. I say old they were brand-new," he chuckled, looking to Mary.

"Yes, thanks, Gerald; Saturday?"

"Yes, come to the house at about 8 o'clock. You can stay with Christine at her shooting peg; beaters start around 9 a.m. Christine will have her gundog Scooby-Doo; what a name to give a gundog the poor animal," Gerald frowned. "He will retrieve, providing it isn't a deer, collect later," he smiled.

Christine smiled, "Friday tomorrow Donald. You forget, father. Donald can travel with us Saturday morning after feeding the animals. You put on another few pounds eating a gorgeous breakfast," she grinned. Watched her father look somewhat embarrassed, trying to hold his stomach in without much success.

Christine and Gerald left. "Come on, everyone," Martin voiced, "bed."

Mary commented, "If you keep stinking the bedroom out at night, I'll put you in the spare room; your stomach must be rotten."

Donald laughed, heading for his bedroom; he couldn't wait for the season to change. He was fed up working in the dark in the morning and at night, never having a chance to study the animals, and relying on his mother to check over the winter months.

Donald woke early, taking the Land Rover across the field using the headlights to see if they had any injured or dead ewes. Much to his surprise, nothing. Biscuit must have arrived in time, distracting the Alsatian from the sheep. He returned to the yard, parking the Land Rover, running in to have his cup of coffee, seeing Christine had already arrived. Mary is sitting at the table stroking Biscuit.

"What's our losses, son?" she asked cautiously.

"Nothing as I can see, mother, thanks to Biscuit."

Mary smiled, gently patting Biscuit on the ribs.

"You okay, Christine?" Donald asked.

"Yes, thanks, Donald; I used to look forward to the shoots, not anymore."

"Why not?" Donald asked curiously.

Christine sighed heavily, "Mother used to try and introduce me to what she considered suitable males. Almost trying to sell me to any rich farmers who were invited, embarrassing."

"I'll give a fiver for you," Donald joked.

Christine grinned, "Is that all."

"Times are hard Christine for us, small farmers," he grinned, "We only purchase bargains."

She poked her tongue out at him.

"I wouldn't worry about anybody pestering you, Christine; Donald will deal with them. You have trained anyway." Mary smiled, "Great thinking on your father's part. At least you're always safe. Off you go; you two feed the animals. You will be late for school," Mary smiled.

CHAPTER THREE

PERSISTENT WEATHER

Donald and Christine ran out of the house, laughing. Donald feeds his sheep, and Christine milks the cow and deals with the chickens and pigs. Both sows had given birth to half a dozen piglets; she left them in the sty with the heaters. Approaching Christmas, the weather is all over the place. One-day sunshine, the next freezing cold with a bitter wind cutting across the fields. Donald kept the rest of the cattle for another week; he wanted to try and fatten them a little more, although he could barely see what they looked like in the dark.

Christine returned to the cottage carrying a tray of eggs; a warm couple of days had improved the hens' laying. She opened the door. Mary grabbed the tray of eggs, "That's an improvement, Christine."

Christine sat at the table, starting her breakfast, commenting, "Donald's a long time this morning, Mary?"

"I thought that myself, Christine, I'll try his mobile if he remembered to take it. Switched off, that boy," Mary exhaled.

They heard Donald cleaning his boots on the scraper outside the front door; he walked in, removing his coat and bobble hat quickly. "Problem this morning Donald," Christine enquired.

"You sound just like mother, nag, nag."

Mary grinned, "I'm not like that, son," she emphasised. "Eat your breakfast."

"An old ewe, her head trapped in the pig wire, I had to try and release her," he sighed.

They caught the school bus, and Michael was not on board, much to their surprise. Donald asked, "Has anyone seen Michael?" His closest neighbour hadn't seen him since yesterday.

Donald dialled Michael's number, "Where are you?"

"In hospital, the police have arrested Peggy's brother Frederick; he hit me again last night and broke two of my ribs. The police are prosecuting him for GBH," Michael sighed, "That will improve the situation. I didn't want to press charges. You know what other people are like."

"Okay, mate, stay safe. I wish he'd come to school; I'd show him how to break ribs," Donald disconnected the call looking to Christine, who'd heard the conversation shocked. "I feel sorry for Michael; he doesn't deserve that treatment."

"No, and I can't see improving the disagreement between the two families; I was hoping for an amicable solution. That's not likely to happen now if the police are involved."

"No," Christine agreed.

The rest of the school day passed uneventfully apart from Christine, grabbed by Timothy and taken into a storeroom. "Not at school, Timothy," Christine giggled, protesting. Christine dropped her briefcase to the floor. Timothy, kissing her; in seconds, Timothy had opened her blouse, lifting her bra over her ample breasts' caressing her nipples, driving her crazy. She wanted to go all the way, suspecting it would be marvellous from what she'd heard from other girls. He started kissing her on the lips. "I must go, Timothy; I'll be late for my next lesson. Come on, not here," she stepped away, realising Timothy had other ideas placing her hand on his large erect cock. She quickly removed her hand, tidying her blouse, "Definitely not here," she insisted. She peered cautiously from the store cupboard door to check no one would see her leaving. Stepping out into the corridor, not noticing someone had seen her and taken a photo with their mobile of her and Timothy leaving.

Christine joined Donald boarding the coach and returning to Crabtree Farm in readiness to look after the animals. Christine commented, "I have really enjoyed the time I spent here with you and your family," placing her arm in his.

"We've enjoyed having you," kissing her on the cheek, "You've helped save the farm. I've learnt a lot. We always thought you were a stuck-up little bitch, but that is not the case; you are a lovely person. It shows how you can misjudge people," Donald remarked.

"Thanks, Donald; I can't help my parentage; it's not my fault father has three thousand acres, just the luck of the draw."

"It doesn't matter what you own, Christine. Only your personality counts. You could be penniless as long as your you. That's all that matters." She kissed him on the cheek.

Her father's Range Rover is already in the yard. He's sat in the kitchen discussing things with Martin and Mary. Mary glanced at the expression on Donald's face, "What's happened? I know that look," she frowned.

"Poor Michael," Christine sighed, "He's in hospital with broken ribs. Peggy's brother to blame the police are prosecuting him for GBH," she sighed heavily.

"Oh, that's great," Mary voiced. "Why do people have to be like that; what's done is done rectify the mistake and move on."

"What do you think will happen now, kids?" Gerald asked.

"I suspect Michael will be thrown out. His father won't take this sort of crap. I shouldn't think Peggy's in much of a better position, although I really don't know her parents that well, mum does though," Donald glancing at her.

"I've heard nothing on the grapevine. Everybody's staying quiet; I hope they're not forcing her to have an abortion that would be criminal," Mary voiced.

Gerald sighed, wondering if it had been better if Josephine had gone down that road, although he wouldn't have had the farm or Christine if she had.

"Donald, we've discussed the best way forward for the farmhouse here, fourteen bedrooms we haven't lived in for years."

"I thought pretty obvious dad renovate when we have sufficient funds into holiday flats. You could charge a fair whack if you made seven self-contained good rooms out of fourteen. I'm sure the bank would loan against that, income all the year-round probably, not so much in the winter the summer should see people constantly."

"And who's running that?" Mary glared at him.

"An agency, they'd run the whole show for you. Of course, they take a cut for their services unless you run yourself, mum."

Gerald, Martin, Mary, and Christine glared in astonishment at Donald. "You worked this out, son?" Martin asked, surprised and delighted.

Donald shrugged his shoulders, "I thought it obvious I was waiting until I left school before starting the project," he sighed. "Pity, Michael's in a mess; he's excellent at building work and carpentry; there's nothing in the building trade he can't do. He constructed pig pens for his father, did the lot himself over two years."

Gerald smiled, "Our answer, friends, if Michael's interested, he could rectify my two cottages and live in one. He can move on to your farmhouse here and rectify with a little help." They all looked at each other, smiling.

"He may want to go to university. Anybody considered that?" Mary asked.

Donald burst out laughing, "That won't happen. Michael's brilliant with his hands, a bit like me with his brains not in gear half the time, especially when exams. He certainly won't want to go to university, may attend college, but that's it."

"You're not stupid, Donald," Mary jumped in, "You always come away with a B on your exam papers."

"If you want to see brains, father, look to Christine; she has distinctions, the girls a walking genius."

Christine smiled, "Thanks, Donald, for the comment, I study hard, and I have more time than you and Michael; plus, I appear to be able to grasp answers where others struggle. I've always been that way."

Gerald smiled, "That's from your mother's side, not mine; your mother's a genius; she went to a school for young ladies in London hence the flat. What happened to her Range Rover? Will, it still be in London, or have they transported to France," he asked the question aloud, deep in thought.

"There's one way to find out, Gerald; phone the Metropolitan police."

Gerald removed his mobile, finally connecting. "I'm trying to trace my wife's Range Rover, Mrs Josephine Gibbs; her black Range Rover has a private registration J B G DC 22."

"The vehicle is in our compound Mr Gibbs after your wife's accident, transported here to check for drugs. The matter has since been closed. No further action will be taken. You can collect at your earliest convenience."

"Okay, thank you very much; I'll be in touch shortly."

"I thought she would have taken it to France with her," Gerald expressed, "I'll have to make contact and ask what she wants me to do with it," he frowned.

Christine remarked, "Couldn't you have it brought home on a transporter, father, save you the problem?"

"That would be the best solution, Christine; otherwise, I have to find another driver. You know what London's like a bloody nightmare."

"Sorry about that folk's got side-tracked." Taking another mouthful from the plate, he grabbed a slice of freshly cut bread and mopped his plate.

Mary commented, "You know someone who does that, Martin." Everyone looked at Donald.

"Waste not, want not," he smiled.

Mary descends into the cellar returning with a jug of cider. "This should help you sleep, Gerald." Pouring him a glass and the others. Gerald and Christine gingerly consumed this time; otherwise, would blow their heads off if not careful. They said their goodbyes leaving.

Donald went to his bedroom, phoning Michael, "You okay, Michael?"

"I think so, Donald," he sighed heavily.

"Has your father calmed down?"

"I hope, Donald; mom suggested I leave. I'm an embarrassment."

"Don't take this as gospel Michael. I may have accommodation for you and Peggy plus employment. You have no more than six months left at school; you could leave now."

"What do you mean, Donald," Michael excited.

"If everything goes pear-shaped on your end, I think you can possibly reside on Strawberry Estate; they have two cottages, and they haven't lived in for a couple of years. Mr Gibbs suggested that you could live in one if you did them up."

"That sounds great, Donald."

"Wouldn't get too excited, Michael; no one knows what condition therein now. They could be absolutely knackered. For the next project, the old farmhouse at our place too expensive for us to live in. We're having converted into seven self-contained holiday flats. I told mum and dad, you were great at building work; you think you could handle it? Obviously, we'll pay you."

"Sounds great in theory. I must have a look, cost materials and labour for you properly. I couldn't do things like electric and gas; I don't have certificates."

"That's not a problem, Michael; we want you to handle the basic work, perhaps be the project manager. If nothing else, that should keep you out of mischief for a couple of years while you and Peggy get your life in order. Of course, this is all hypothetical and depends on what happens between the two sets of parents."

"I know Peggy's brothers in jail; they locked him up because of his aggressive attitude towards me. I don't know why we used to be friends, not as if I'm deserting Peggy because I'm not Donald. I've been in love with her for years, and her with me just one mistake that could happen to anyone," he sighed.

"I understand, Michael; I'm surprised her brother has behaved in such a way; perhaps he will realise his errors if he's locked up for a few days. Of course, he might know something you don't. Have you considered that possibility Michael?"

"Peggy and I were thinking about running away, Donald eloping."

"No need, Michael, we'll sort this out, maybe rough for a while; we'll win, you'll see," Donald assured.

"I must go now, Michael, speak to you soon. Take care," Donald rang off.

He returned to the kitchen. "How is Michael?" Mary asked, smiling.

"How did you know I was speaking to him, Mother?" Donald asked, puzzled.

"Listening at your door," she grinned. "You gave sound advice. That's a true friend to be there when no one else will stand by you. You make me so proud, Donald."

"Thanks, mum; I'm off to bed. I've had enough of today; goodnight."

***

Michael is released from the hospital; he caught a bus taking nearly an hour to return to the village. He walked along the public right-of-way on Gerald Gibbs's estate to the cottages. Apart from the brambles, the windows were still intact and shut; he squeezed his way through to the doorway. The doors were locked, a good sign; he peered through the windows, cobwebs everywhere, and the furniture looked worse for wear. He walked away from the buildings looking at the tiles on the roof all in place, present and correct, which meant no roof leaks.

He started conjuring a plan, not realising Gerald's walking up behind him. Michael jumped, "Sorry, Sir, I don't mean to be on your property. I came along the public footpath and saw the two cottages."

"Michael Pearce, I believe," Gerald smiled, holding his hand out for Michael to shake. "We have a mutual friend Donald Selwyn," Gerald smiled. "You'd better make your way home, Michael. We have a shoot starting any minute. I don't want you to be caught in the crossfire; that's why I'm here checking the footpath. We will discuss the properties later, I'm sure," Gerald smiled.

Michael grinned, "Appreciated, Sir, Mr Gibbs, they look in reasonable condition. They only need a little attention here and there," Michael smiled, quickly walking up the footpath to the road and removing his face mask.

Gerald ran to his Range Rover, returning to Strawberry Estate house. He left his Range Rover seeing Christine and Donald walking down the track heading for peg seventeen with Scooby-Doo following closely.

Donald and Christine positioned behind the bales specially placed, looking over for birds coming in their direction. Donald felt an absolute prat the way he's dressed; he would have sooner been in his jeans and wax jacket. The first two birds flew over. Donald allowed Christine to take the first two shots, she missed, and he dropped both birds. "Scooby-Doo fetch," she ordered.

12 o'clock. Donald and Christine had ten pheasants and two Partridge, shot by Donald. Christine looked furious, "Must be something wrong with my gun; I've never been that bad at shooting." Donald grinned; she thumped him on the arm. Gerald drove alongside, collecting what they shot, "Not bad at all," he voiced.

Donald looked on the tailgate of the Range Rover, at least fifty pheasants and two deer already gutted. "How many you shoot, Christine?"

"Don't ask, father," she suggested sliding onto the back seat of the Range Rover.

"Oh, it must be the sights on your gun, love," Gerald remarked, trying not to laugh. The one thing Christine struggled with was shooting; she shot absolutely nothing last year.

"We will take this load to Crabtree Farm; I think it will give Martin something to do rather than sit there bored," Gerald suggested. Donald sat quietly in the front seat, not wishing to cause any rift.

Mary came out of the cottage, "My goodness, you have been busy." Donald carried the deer one at a time on his shoulder, hanging in the cellar, helping take the pheasants and place them on the kitchen table. "There you are, dad, if you are bored this afternoon."

"I love you too, son," he frowned.

"You're quite Christine; you're not happy, love," Mary asked.

"I'm okay, Mary; my shooting a little off today."

Martin commented, "At least Donald had the prettiest girl on the field to look at. Must be a bonus." Christine grinned at the compliment.

Donald remarked, "She will make a great conservationist! She hit nothing." She turned quickly on her heels, lashing out at Donald, and slapping his face. She placed her hands to her cheeks, realising what she'd done and ran out of the cottage. Gerald stood there shocked, "I didn't see that coming; she must apologise. I'm sorry, Donald."

Donald started laughing, much to everyone's surprise. "She'll be no good at rugby; she doesn't slap hard enough." Everyone burst out laughing in the kitchen. Donald cautiously ventured out, seeing Christine sitting in the Range Rover crying. He opened the door, "What's the matter? Only having fun with you, Christine."

"I'm sorry, Donald," she sobbed, "I shouldn't have hit you."

"Is that what you call hitting? Oh, I must remember; ouch!" She laughed, placing her arms around his neck and giving him a cuddle; the others watched from the front door. "Come on, coffee time," lifting her out of the Range Rover and placing her to her feet. She stood with her head bowed, "I apologise to everyone for my behaviour."

"The only person you hurt, my love, is yourself. Donald thought hilarious," Gerald smirked, "That's the end of the matter."

"Right, I must get back to the shoot," Gerald suggested feeling his mobile vibrate in his pocket. "Yes, Susan."

"Copthorne's arrived."

"He wasn't invited; okay, on my way."

"I'm staying here, father. I want nothing to do with that man," she suggested looking fearful.

"I understand, love. I will deal with him," Gerald assured, leaving the cottage.

"Need support, Gerald?" Donald asked.

Gerald smiled, "No thanks, Donald. I can deal with that piece of scum myself; you stay here to look after Christine for me," Gerald remarked, climbing in his Range Rover.

Donald could see from the expression on Christine's face; that she absolutely detested the man.

Mary could see her trembling slightly; she made another coffee. "Come with me," they both went into the lounge, "Explain what's happened if you want to?"

"A long time ago, Mary. Copthorne's an animal. I was thirteen; he tried to molest me. He was supposed to be training me in martial arts with his brother until my father discovered what was happening. He dealt with the situation and sent me somewhere else to be professionally trained to be a black belt in judo. Father said no one would ever touch me again without my consent; he'd make sure of that," she smiled.

"A good job; Donald didn't hear this conversation; he would beat him within an inch of his life."

"So nice to have someone to talk to like you, Mary; I could never sit down with my mother and hold a conversation like this."

Mary patted her leg reassuringly, "We'll go back into the kitchen; otherwise, they'll wonder what's going on."

"Where is Donald?" Mary asked.

"He had an errand; he said he wouldn't belong; he's taken the Land Rover."

No one realised Donald had listened at the door. He was livid when he arrived at Strawberry Estate. Gerald's already in a heated argument with Copthorne pushing Gerald.

Donald didn't speak; he hit Copthorne under the jaw. He's on his back, knocked out. Gerald stared in disbelief. "He won't want to assault Christine again," Donald advised firmly. Gerald wanted to do that himself; he may be a little old to take on a twenty-one-year-old man who spent most of his time in the gym trying to look pretty. The rest of his family was always that way inclined. They were notorious; sons were always playing the field. Copthorne struggled to his feet. Donald stood prepared, and Copthorne took a swing. Donald clashed fists with Copthorne, shattering the bones in Copthorne's hand and again a right hook under his jaw. Copthorne dropped to the ground in extreme agony, holding his wrist, shouting, "You've broken my hand." He jumped to his feet. Donald punched him on the nose. "I've broken that, free of charge!" Donald replied calmly, "I'll break your neck if you ever come here again, get in your car and piss off before I lose my temper."

Copthorne jumped in his Jag and drove off. He's no match for Donald, whether he's fit or not. Donald is solid muscle from years of hard work, with no part of his body that wasn't toned.

Gerald couldn't stop laughing, "My god Donald you're like a brick wall. I've never seen anyone lifted off their feet before with a punch under the jaw."

Donald smiled, "I didn't want to leave him in doubt about what he'd face if he ever returned." Donald jumped in his old Land Rover, cutting across the fields and down the narrow lane for a mile to his own drive, guessing he would receive a roasting but well worth it in his book.

Mary came dashing out, "Where have you been, Donald?"

"Unfinished business, mum," he smiled.

"Why is there blood on your knuckles? Have you been fighting?"

Christine's talking to her father on her mobile with a broad smile, "He didn't. Okay. Mary, he's been a naughty boy for all the right reasons; Copthorne will remember him for some time."

Mary grinned, "I suspected as much."

Martin's plucking looking extremely miserable, "You have all the fun, son," he chuckled.

Donald sat down and started to pluck a pheasant, feathers everywhere, especially when Christine and Mary joined in. By 5 o'clock, the birds are in the freezer. Mary's frantically trying to clean up before making tea while the kids feed the animals.

Christine and Donald came in hearing Gerald's Range Rover come into the yard. Donald glanced, realising another deer on the tailgate. He went out; Donald carried the deer on his shoulder. Gerald and Christine carried in another twenty birds. Mary gasped,

"Not more," taking them down into the cellar to stay cool overnight. Gerald smiled, "I provided a brace for each of the staff with our compliments; thank god that's over for another year; the shoots from now on will be for private friends and staff."

"That reminds me, Donald," Mary scolded, "Stop listening to private conversations."

"That works both ways, mother; you were listening to me speaking to Michael through my bedroom door the other night; I learnt from the best," he smiled smugly.

Mary turned bright red, pouring the coffee; Martin laughed.

"I've arranged for your mother's Range Rover to be collected early next week. A chap at the local garage taking a car to London suits him well to have a return vehicle," Gerald smiled.

"Brilliant father, another problem solved."

"Right young lady, home," Gerald suggested.

"One moment, father," Christine held Donald's hand heading along the hallway; she turned and kissed him, "That's for righting a wrong."

Donald stood shocked, watching her leave through the front door; he came into the kitchen. Mary grinned, "Who's a lucky boy then," watching him turn bright red with embarrassment.

"Red lipstick does suit you, Donald," Martin teased.

"Will you two pack it in? Nothing going on, and won't be," he assured, less than confident with his own assessment.

***

Christine entered Strawberry Estate house, finding Susan feeding Badger, "Don't overfeed him, Susan; he struggled to run after the pheasants today."

Gerald passed Susan fifty pounds, "Here's a bonus for you," he smiled.

"Thanks, Gerald, greatly appreciated."

"Don't forget to take a couple of braces of pheasants home with you, Susan; we'll never eat this lot."

"Thanks, I'll go now, Gerald, Christine. If there's nothing else, you want?"

"No, we'll be fine; the last shoot won't be any other than for close friends and staff."

"That's great," Susan expressed. "Horrible to see the birds bred to be shot; they have no idea what's happening and haven't lived long enough."

"My sentiments exactly, Susan," Gerald expressed.

They heard Susan drive off. Gerald placed his arm around Christine's shoulders, "I'm shattered, love?" Watching her nod in agreement, they both retired early.

***

Donald lay on his back, looking at the ceiling in his bedroom, and felt his mobile vibrating to see Michael's name. "Hi, Michael, how are things with you?"

Michael exhaled, "Peggy's brother has a court order against him not to come within fifty meters of me, or he will go to prison for two years. I will explain to father I'm leaving home and want no more aggravation, Donald. Peggy's told her parents the same they are over sixteen. Social services have jumped in with both feet trying to dictate what we do. Any chance you could talk to Mr Gibbs concerning one of the cottages. I had a look today; he caught me down there. He said he'd sort of spoken to you. I looked through the windows, not bad cottages Donald with some work."

"What about the furniture?"

"Some in the old cottages, how good I can't tell at this time, Donald. I have about £5000 in savings. We'll have to skimp along."

"Leave it with me, Michael. I'll speak to you in the morning."

Christine arrived at five in the morning; Gerald parked his Range Rover coming in for his breakfast with a beaming smile. Donald explained the conversation he had with Michael.

"When you have fed the animals this morning, Donald, we had better look inside the cottages; asked Michael to meet us there at 9 o'clock."

Donald texts Michael, not expecting a reply at this time in the morning; he'd barely finished drinking his coffee. Michael replied, "Okay, thanks."

"That's Michael; he will be there."

"Off you go, you two, earn your keep while I struggle to eat my breakfast," Gerald grinned.

Christine commented, "Some people."

A short while later, Christine and Donald returned, enjoying their breakfast. They left in Gerald's Range Rover, cutting across the estate to the two cottages only about a mile from where Michael lived on his father's farm.

They cut their way through the brambles using garden shears to the door; brambles were everywhere, a bonus in some respects, keeping unwanted visitors away. Gerald unlocked one front door; the place stunk after being left for so long. Michael arrived, and Peggy was with him, much to everyone's surprise. Christine immediately embraced her, seeing the remains of a black eye where her brother had struck her. "Look around, Michael, advise me what you think," Gerald suggested.

"I think the place needs a good airing." They entered next door, in the same state that needed cleaning and airing. "We appreciate your help, Mr Gibbs."

He smiled, "I presume Donald has briefly explained you can live here rent-free; in return, you repair next door and the property you live in. I will pay you to repair buildings around the estate, and I believe Donald has a project for you. This should give you a good start and an income." Michael shook Gerald's hand eagerly, then Donald's and hugged him. "You don't know what this means to me; you saved my skin and Peggy's. We can start a life together, although not the way we'd intended; nevertheless, we will be together; that's the most important thing to me," he expressed.

"You haven't said much, Peggy," Gerald suggested, "What's your view?"

"I can continue my studies from home; once our child is born, I can acquire employment, perhaps in accounting. I have distinctions in all my grades."

"Of course, you go to college; you're slightly older than Michael."

"Yes, the year above him, eighteen next week; hopefully, Michael will have this ready for us to move into by Christmas," Peggy looking at him.

"Yes, Peggy, I will, I promise."

"You realise not long away, a week or so."

"I know, better than home with that bunch."

"The furniture in the old house at home may be useful to you two; you are welcome to have a look with my mother. We can transport over with the stock trailer," Donald suggested.

"I may have some furniture at home," Christine voiced, "You can have it if you're interested, Peggy; take a look."

"Thanks, Christine." Peggy felt quite out of place and slightly embarrassed she had really hoped for a better start to married life than this. Realising beggars can't be choosers at the moment, she thought, praying Michael would never discover her secret. Gerald passed the keys to Michael; much to everyone's horror suspecting trouble, Peggy's mother arrived in her Subaru fitting her face mask.

She introduced herself to Mr Gibbs. "You've obviously heard what happened, Mr Gibbs. I deeply regret what her brother administered to Michael wouldn't solve anything; I'd like to help you two. Your father, Peggy, appears to have a short memory. The same happened to him and me. Barely sixteen when your brother was born, which I had to remind him of yesterday. I can't thank you enough, Mr Gibbs, for helping these two; you need to find employment Michael," she suggested.

"He already has," Gerald advised, "Working for Donald and me on building projects; he will have his own successful business within twelve months."

She stared in disbelief. Gerald suggested, "You throw out the furniture you don't want, Michael; I'll have it collected tomorrow; I'll speak to my farm Foreman. One last thing," Mr Gibbs remarked, "Your brother is not permitted on my estate under any circumstances. I find it very distasteful that he would strike someone with a broken arm. From Peggy's eye, he obviously hit her, Mrs Sanderson. Any problems Michael, contact me, I'll leave you to sort out what you want and the cottage you wish to live in. Repair the other."

Gerald climbed in his Range Rover along with Donald and Christine driving away absolutely fuming. "How could her brother strike her," he muttered under his breath.

Christine commented, "You see the look on Michael's face when Peggy ordered him to have the property ready before Christmas. I hope he's not making a mistake, Donald," she sighed.

Donald grinned, "That's the trouble when you go with older women; they rule your life." Gerald burst out laughing. "While this far down the estate, I want to look in the old building. I can't remember what's in there; it borders on our conservation section. You two don't mind," he smiled.

Christine commented, "We might be worth millions you've forgotten about, father." They left the Range Rover struggling to open the shed doors packed with old strawberry boxes. They worked their way to the back. Discovering a Massey Ferguson articulated tractor on blocks was forgotten about for years. Gerald scratched his head, "I don't remember buying that." Stephen entered the shed to ascertain who was on site. "Great, Stephen, you know anything about this old tractor in here? I don't remember purchasing."

"A gift from Massey Ferguson for permitting testing their tractors on the estate in secret. Mrs Gibb's parents had the tractor parked here some years ago."

"Oh well, that's all in here apart from strawberry boxes from when the farm produced strawberries during the war?"

"Yes," Stephen remarked, "I suspect your grandfather Donald would come across and pick a few trays. You must remember the people your grandfather rescued hadn't enjoyed a strawberry for years."

"Okay, leave the doors shut on the place; for now, we'll decide what we do later," Gerald remarked, already deciding in his mind what's happening to the tractor. He dropped Donald off at home, returning to the farm. Gerald smiled, realising Sunday and Stephen still riding around the estate; obviously checking the place was secure, making him smile; his investment was worthwhile.

After visiting Crabtree Farm Monday morning, Gerald made his way to the workshop. "Johnson," Gerald smiled, "Come with me."

Johnson climbed into Gerald's Range Rover parked outside the shed where the Massey Ferguson is stored. He showed Johnson, "You think this will run again? I'd like to give it to someone as a Christmas present, say nothing to anyone about it." Johnson quickly looked in the cab, "Only two hundred hours on the clock shouldn't be a problem, Sir."

"Right, leave it with you. Wait until everybody's gone home before moving to your workshop to service; leave at the back where no one will notice." Gerald dropped Johnson off at the workshop and continued home, observing his wife's Range Rover outside the house.

Gerald ran indoors, finding Josephine sitting at the table talking to Susan.

Josephine smiled, "Aren't you pleased to see me, husband?"

"Of course," kissing her on the cheek.

"I thought you were staying in France?"

"I popped over to fetch one or two things and my daughter, a better environment for her in France."

Gerald laughed, "I'd like to see you persuade Christine to move to France."

"I've heard Susan has explained; she's associating with some inappropriate boy, a commoner."

"I can't wait for you to advise her," Gerald grinned. "My dear wife, I suggest you pack your things and return to France while I'm in a good mood. You upset Christine; I will bury you myself," he glared. Josephine stared in disbelief at the way he spoke to her. Susan quickly left the kitchen, her position at risk for opening her mouth.

"My estate Gerald, not yours," she glared.

"Perhaps if you spent less time on your back in London, you could run it; no, you'd sooner ponce around and make yourself look an idiot than do a day's work."

All the time Gerald and Josephine were married, he had never spoken to her that way. She frowned, "I see you won't be reasonable, and I suspect my daughter will have your attitude. I'll return to France on my own and let her become involved with commoners. I heard what happened to Copthorne, a lovely man good breeding."

"You should know Josephine; you slept with most of the men around here." Gerald watched Josephine jump to her feet, "How dare you speak to me like that," she slapped his face, and he slapped her back. She stood absolutely stunned, walking out of the kitchen, grabbing her two suitcases, throwing them in the back of her Range Rover, and driving off.

Gerald shouted, "Susan come here," she walked into the kitchen calmly. "What have you said to that woman about Donald's family?"

"I didn't have to, Gerald. She already knew; she wanted confirmation her information was correct. I didn't say anything hadn't a chance, you returned I was making her coffee."

"If she comes here, you phone me immediately, Susan, you understand," Gerald glared. She nodded. Gerald ran out of the house, jumping in his Range Rover and heading for Crabtree Farm, suspecting his wife wouldn't quit that easily. He knocked on the cottage door and walked in; Martin and Mary were plucking pheasants. They looked at his expression. "What's happened?" Martin asked suspiciously.

"Josephine has returned attempting to persuade Christine to live in France," he expressed out of breath.

"I don't think she'd attempt anything at school too closely guarded, Gerald. Christine would embarrass her on purpose; the headteacher certainly wouldn't release her under those circumstances." Mary removed her mobile and texted Donald and

Christine, hoping they had their mobiles turned on against school regulations.

Christine felt her mobile vibrate in her pocket; she was in the common room and went to the loo. She read the message from Mary with horror. She quickly texts, "thanks, message received."

Martin's now moving about more freely; he poured Gerald a whisky, "Looks like you need one of these, mate."

"Thanks, Martin, the last thing I expected to happen this morning."

Gerald finished his drink and left, heading back to the estate, wondering if Susan's in league with Josephine; how well-informed would she be otherwise. It crossed his mind the house could be bugged, perhaps not recently used in the war for intelligence gathering. Josephine's relations would know that for sure. Gerald started laughing at his ridiculous thoughts. He walked into the kitchen, seeing Susan washing up one or two items, not bothering to place them in the dishwasher.

"She's not trying to take Christine, Gerald," Susan suggested nervously, attempting to cover her tracks.

"Who knows what Josephine's conjuring in her little mind," he sighed?

"To be quite honest, Gerald. Donald and Christine are well suited. I hated functions here; the so-called gentleman always pinched my backside their disgusting."

"I didn't know that," Gerald glanced up, "You never said anything."

"I have to, Josephine, she would laugh. Saying who's a lucky girl, you know where the spare bedroom is."

"You What!"

Susan took a deep breath, "I know she's been there herself with the Copthorne brothers when we had other shoots; I'll gather my things and leave. If you give me a reference, Gerald would appreciate it."

"Are you resigning, Susan?"

"I've broken the terms of my contract by disclosing information about Mrs Gibbs," she sighed.

"No! Thank you. That's a real eye-opener, so she's still playing the field, and we're married," he sighed, realising he now had proof. However, only from an employee who may be trying to save her own skin, and he'd recently misbehaved himself.

"I'm pleased; I discreetly asked for a blood test on Christine. I know she's definitely mine," he smiled.

Susan passed him a coffee pouring one for herself, sitting beside him. Gerald patted the back of her hand. "Thank you for the confirmation. You're a brave woman to say that, and you're certainly not dismissed; thanks for your honesty."

"I don't want Christine to go abroad; Josephine would destroy her. She's not fit to look after Badger, sorry I shouldn't have said, Gerald."

Gerald commented, "Neither are you; he's a battleship. You spoil him to death." Susan grinned. Gerald removed his wallet, passing her twenty pounds. "Buy a box of chocolates," he smiled, standing and walking out of the kitchen, deciding to collect Donald and Christine from school just in case Josephine's there.

***

Christine walked along the main corridor, confronted by a boy brandishing his mobile. Christine stopped in her tracks, studying the picture of her leaving the storeroom; she watched the boy grin. "What's it worth to destroy the picture, Christine Gibbs?"

"That proves nothing, so I came out of the storeroom, proves nothing," she said, trying to bluff her way out of the situation.

The boy grinned, "Perhaps more interesting, to Donald Selwyn or the headteacher, interested in seeing you and Timothy leaving the storeroom almost together and Timothy's zip undone."

Christine panicked, "Here, five pounds, now destroy the photos and go away."

"No thanks, that's not enough bitch. Besides, I'm not interested in money. My parents are loaded."

"How old are you?" Christine asked. "You're certainly not in my year, that's for sure."

"I'm fifteen a year below you; follow me if you don't. You know what will happen," he grinned smugly, walking off.

Christine reluctantly followed him to the rear boiler room, somewhere unfamiliar. Christine nervously descended the stairs, wondering what she was letting herself in for, although she had suspicions. She needed to grab his mobile and smash it to pieces, and the evidence would be gone forever. Christine stood in the dim light asking, "You sure the caretaker won't appear; we'd really be in trouble," she expressed nervously.

"He won't. He is detained elsewhere; he's a friend of mine."

"How convenient," Christine folded her arms. "What's your name," she asked, racking her brains for a solution. "Gypsy," he approached Christine standing beside her, flicking through photos of her friends appearing in the same place, standing almost naked. Christine couldn't believe Jackie would even entertain such a thing; he must have had something substantial on her to make her comply. "How did you convince Jackie to comply with your perverted wishes Gypsy?"

"Caught her with the student-teacher giving him a blow job," he grinned smugly. The student-teacher pays me forty pounds a month not to enlighten certain parties." Gypsy scrolled through one or two short movies, "This one should interest you, Christine," he smiled. Christine stared in horror, recognising her mother's voice bent over a table with someone thrusting into her, screaming at the top of her voice. Gypsy switched off his mobile, placing it in his jacket pocket. "I guess you realise who that is, and the man giving her one, my father. Bitch you'll do as you're told like her; she often comes and sees him. He'd do her a favour and have a fuck." Gypsy, with short red hair, spotty complexion and exceptionally well-built, moved towards Christine. Christine dropped her briefcase, preparing to defend herself. Gypsy grinned. "I wouldn't if I was you bitch.

I'll burn your farm to the ground," he advised calmly, removing a six-inch blade from his inside jacket pocket. Christine froze to the spot. The last thing she needed was to be stabbed or scarred, and she definitely didn't want the farm burnt to the ground. Gypsy placed the blade against her chin. She could feel the cold steel against her skin. "Remove your blazer. I'll teach you bitch who's in charge."

Christine knew she could disarm him, but that wouldn't stop her farm from being destroyed by the gipsies. Trying to stop trembling, Christine slowly removed her blazer, discarding to the floor, hearing someone coming down the metal stairs into the boiler room, suspecting she was about to be saved, only to observe Gypsy grinning. A man stepped into the light she didn't recognise. He certainly wasn't on the school staff. He was way past retirement age, suspecting a Gypsy by how he's dressed. Christine really wanted to escape weighing up her options. She would hate to explain why she's in the boiler room to the headteacher, her father, and Donald when he found out. He would never forgive her. Christine couldn't imagine the scandal. She probably expelled, deciding she might be able to fight one but not two people, especially one with a knife. Then have to explain her actions. Gypsy removed his knife, stepping back and speaking, "This is her, the bitch Josephine's daughter."

The man nodded, steadying Christine with his glazed eyes, "My present?"

Christine's horrified at the conversation, lashing out at the old man knocking to the floor and Gypsy. She's about to run, grabbing her briefcase and blazer, only to be confronted by a female student teacher on the metal staircase. Christine suspected she was in trouble up to her neck standing on the concrete floor at the bottom of the stairs. Gypsy assisted the old man to his feet, hearing the student teachers say calmly, "What's going on here?" Seeing Christine is about to speak, "Silent Miss Gibbs."

Gypsy and the old man approach brushing off their clothes. Gypsy slapped Christine's face firmly, taking her by surprise and thrusting his knife under her chin. "You hurt my grandfather, your pay bitch I promise you." Christine is confused. Why hasn't the teacher intervened? What's going on? "Miss!" Christine said, alarmed. Christine is escorted to the rear of the boiler room where the old coal store used to be many years ago. Gypsy advised, "Sandra won't say anything she owes me, and you're saying nothing either bitch; stand on the table under the light. Go on now!"

Christine stood on the small coffee table looking at the student-teacher she thought was her saviour. Christine sighed heavily, petrified. She watched the old man remove his limp cock only to be held by the student-teacher. Christine couldn't imagine what Gypsy had on the teacher to make a perform; it must be something dire. Gypsy grins watching his grandfather playing with the student teacher's tits while she wanked him. Gypsy reached up. Christine watched him unbutton her blouse. She pushed him away, re-buttoning her blouse. Gypsy removed a small handgun from his pocket. Christine panicked; there was no way she could beat a bullet. She tried to think of a way out of the situation, "If I give you one hundred pounds cash, no questions asked will you destroy the photos, please?"

"No, money isn't an issue. You will be more useful in the future. Father advised me to be careful; he knows your Guardian Angel, and if she's pissed off, we're all in trouble. Nevertheless, this will be a lesson to make you more careful in the future."

"Come on, Gypsy, what exactly do you want?"

Gypsy approached Christine; she watched Gypsy grin. He held her hand, moving her under the light where it's brighter in the boiler room. Christine hadn't realised she was filmed. Christine looked at her wristwatch, "I haven't long. Hurry up, let's get this over with, pervert."

Gypsy kissed Christine. He moved away, "strip, strip!" Christine slowly removed her blouse and bra. "And the rest Gypsy grinned." Christine took a deep breath. She thought she had no other choice; if there was any suspicion, she wasn't a good girl, and the information escaped to her parents she be finished. Christine removed her skirt and knickers. Gypsy dropped his trousers, holding his erection;

he approached Christine. "I'm not having sex with you, Gypsy that's final!"

He placed her hand on his cock, which she considered quite a handful; commenced to masturbate him; he put his hand on her fanny, gently teasing her, which she permitted. Gypsy finally come. He stepped away grinning; she quickly dressed, determined to destroy the photos he possessed. With one swift movement, he was on the floor, knocked out. She grabbed the mobile, throwing it through the boiler inspection cover, watching it melt into history. Gypsy's grandfather is occupied with the student-teacher having sex in the corner of the old store, thankfully recently whitewashed, cleaned, and used for storing old school furniture.

Christine ran out of the boiler room, catching Donald in the main corridor; she linked her arm with his, dashing outside both climbed into her father's Range Rover, looking everywhere for any signs of her mother. "I think she's returned to London Christine with any luck. What's that dirty mark on your chin?"

"Probably from the storeroom when I collected paperwork. I hope mother has returned to France father," looking out for signs of her mother's Range Rover.

Donald suggested, "You could stay at Crabtree Farm; Biscuit is an excellent guard dog, anyone he doesn't know, always barks." They arrived at Crabtree Farm, changing and feeding the animals. Donald instructed, "Biscuit protect Christine." Christine was surprised the dog understood the command. Biscuit didn't leave her side once; she patted him. She saw Biscuit look into the darkness by one of the buildings and start to growl. "It's me, silly dog," Donald laughed. Biscuit ran over and jumped into Donald's arms. Christine commented, "I'll have to try that."

Donald chuckled, "You'd hurt my back." She punched him in the ribs.

"You bully," he laughed. He picked Christine up, throwing her over his shoulder, playfully smacking her backside, and lowering her to her feet. She kissed him on the cheek; walked into the cottage sitting down to their tea. Christine commented, "I've gained a stone since coming here, and I'm working twice as hard as I ever have in the past."

Donald expressed, "I want meat on my woman." Christine stared at him, open-mouthed; Donald winked. Mary grinned; Martin and Gerald smiled at each other, and Christine continued to enjoy her meal.

Gerald's mobile rang. "Excuse me," moving away from the table. "Gerald, Mrs Montague. Josephine's in France; I thought you'd like to know she will not attempt to accost Christine again. Good day."

Everyone can see the relief on Gerald's expression. "Josephine's in France and will not be returning to collect Christine." Mary eagerly descended into the cellar returning with a jug of cider from a different barrel. "We think it's about thirty years old some Martin's father made; he said to use it for exceptional occasions, and I think this is one of those occasions." She poured everyone a glass. Gerald took a drink, "What's in that! I wish I could breathe; I'd enjoy the taste more," he spluttered.

Christine carefully took a sip, "That's lovely, oh dear," feeling her face burn. "You sure it's not paint stripper, Mary." Everyone laughed. Donald emptied his glass in one go everybody sat waiting for a reaction; he shrugged his shoulders. "That son of yours is not human, Mary," Gerald professed, finishing his drink with Christine, "We must go, thanks for everything."

Christine commented, "Whatever is in that barrel, father is powerful. I think you could run the tractors on that," she laughed.

"Yes," he smiled, wondering if he'd ever see Josephine again. Is that her last attempt? Convinced Christine's smitten with Donald, a good choice for her. Whatever happened, he'd protect her?

After breakfast at the Selwyn's the following day, Gerald drove to the cottages, finding Stephen loading old furniture onto a trailer. Somebody had gone around the two cottages cutting down the brambles and pushing the hedge back. "Who's tidied around the property Stephen?"

"Me, Gerald, I thought to give the boy a fighting chance. I didn't see you objecting to me bringing the flail hedge cutter over; it only took a few minutes to push the hedge back and daylight into the building." Gerald patted him on the shoulder, "You're a good sort, Stephen. Find somewhere discreet, set fire to this rubbish, then sort out the scrap if there's any," Gerald smiled. "How are they getting on?" Gerald asked, looking through the window.

"All right, by the looks of things, Gerald, the lads here virtually every day and night, that girl is cracking the whip something fierce. Her mother's not much better, excuse me for saying."

"I bet Michael wished he'd been more careful," Gerald chuckled, observing a Subaru coming along the track with mother and daughter. He walked off to his Range Rover, not wishing to engage in conversation. Gerald had no time for the mother with her attitude and wasn't impressed with the daughter Peggy. He didn't know them that well; perhaps he shouldn't judge. Gerald drove to the workshop finding Johnson. "Would you like to have a look, Sir, at our project?"

Gerald nodded and smiled, walking past tractors and machinery to the back of the building. Parked a gleaming Massey Ferguson 1805 almost looked like it had come off the assembly line. "Cleaned up okay, Johnson."

"Only has two hundred hours on the clock, done nothing."

"What horsepower Johnson?"

"According to the manual 192, everything works perfectly. She hasn't autosteer or any of the modern stuff, a reasonably horse-powered tractor; it's good."

"I suppose it cost too much to update to modern tractors spec?"

"Yes, she would have been brilliant in her day, but not now with all the electronics and the new models. She sat there for at least twenty years, started straight away with new batteries and fuel filters."

"You made an excellent job of that, Johnson," Gerald looking in the cab, climbing down, passing Johnson twenty pounds, "have a drink on me."

Gerald returned to Strawberry house. Susan had made him lunch, a light salad, "I hear I have competition," she grinned, "You're having breakfast and tea at Crabtree Farm? At least it saves me a job; I can attend to other duties around the house."

Gerald smiled, "A light salad will suit me fine; I'm piling on the pounds; Mary doesn't understand the word small portion."

"That's why Donald's the size he is; he's not fat. My daughter watches him play rugby, frightening like a building charging toward you. She said some players confessed they're frightened of him."

"What do you know about Michael Pearce and his girlfriend Peggy?" Gerald asked.

"Not a lot, Peggy Sanderson. Butter wouldn't melt in her mouth. How she became involved with Michael, I don't know. I wouldn't have thought he'd be her type."

"That's my assessment; the mother isn't much better either, from what I can see."

"The mother owns three hair salons and doesn't she charge; no wonder she can run an expensive car. Peggy's father is a keep-fit instructor. He also trains boxers for the ring."

"That explains why Michael had such a hammering; he didn't stand a chance against a professionally trained person like her brother," Gerald sighed. "I'd like to see him go up against Donald," he laughed.

"Me too," Susan agreed. "Donald would knock nine bells out of him, trained or not."

"What's your husband's profession? I don't think I have ever heard you mention him," Gerald asked.

"Dead now; he never saw his daughter born; on the way back from Scotland with a load of steel during the winter in a massive pileup."

Gerald stopped eating, "I never knew that I'm sorry, so sorry for asking," placing an arm around her shoulder.

"Josephine suggested I go upstairs with the Copthorne brothers; they are definitely not my type," she frowned. "Once my daughter was born, I started working here; thankfully, Josephine found me acceptable."

"You were here all that time, and I never knew," he sighed, "I must know my staff better if you have any issues, Susan, talk to me, please."

"Yes, Gerald, thanks." Feeling more secure in her job and one step closer to her plan, Susan had now expressed her thoughts and feelings about situations.

Gerald finished his lunch, realising only three days before Christmas something he could celebrate this year with his daughter; he decided he would give Susan a hundred pounds as a Christmas present. Money would be far more helpful to her than some silly present she probably didn't want in the first place.

The Massey Ferguson tractor, a gift to the Selwyn family at Crabtree Farm, cost him nothing and certainly wouldn't fit in on their farm now, with all the technologies the other equipment possessed. Plus, the Selwyn's could further their decision to go all arable. They would have a tractor to last for years, capable of handling the workload and more, avoiding the purchase expense. Gerald allowed Christine to drive the tractor to Crabtree Farm on Christmas Eve.

Gerald finally made his way over to Crabtree Farm at 5 o'clock for his tea. Martin greeted him, "You're having Christmas lunch with us, Gerald, only you and Christine."

"No, thanks, Martin. You must have some time to yourself as a family without strangers."

Mary insisted, "You will be here at twelve noon if I have to bloody well fetch you and Christine," she voiced with determination. Gerald held his hands up, "Okay, I surrender. I thought you'd like some time to yourselves."

Martin commented, "If he annoys me, I will send Donald to fetch him and Christine. He can carry one under each arm."

Christine and Donald came in for their tea. "You and your father here for Christmas Day lunch, Christine, no arguing."

"I wasn't going to," she smiled. "I know it's pointless," looking at her father. After tea, Gerald drove onto the workshop showing Christine what he was planning. She hugged him, looking over the machine herself. She glanced around the cab, "Won't be as quiet as our tractors, probably have to wear ear defenders, should operate anything they have at the moment."

***

Mary is curious why Donald spent so much time in his bedroom instead of watching television with the rest of the family. She knocked on his door. "Just a moment." She could hear shuffling around, wondering what was happening; she swiftly opened his door. "What's that you're trying to hide? Appears to be a portrait, not nude women?"

"No," he shouted. "Don't you dare say anything, mother; I'm trying to finish for Christmas for Christine. Your opinion would be valuable; what do you think?" placing the portrait on the easel.

"I didn't know you enjoyed painting Donald. I thought you were studying; that's beautiful, Donald. Martin, come here," Mary insisted.

Martin slowly made his way to Donald's bedroom, "What's up?" he asked, catching sight of the portrait, "Blimey son, you're wasting your talents on the farm."

Donald had secretly taken a photo of Christine and Gerald with his hand on her shoulder, using his mobile as a reference copying to the canvas in oils. "You think rubbish, dad?" he asked, concerned. "Mother, what do you think?"

"I'm jealous," Mary remarked, "I'd have thought you would have painted one of father and me." She noticed in his cupboard another portrait covered.

"Not until Christmas," seeing her move to have a look. She grinned, rubbing his hair, "I can't believe your hands can hold a paintbrush. I thought they were only designed to destroy people." Martin smiled proudly, "If they don't appreciate that portrait, Donald, they don't deserve anything as a present."

"Please, mum, dad, say nothing. Allow me to finish first. I thought I could present Christmas Day," he smiled.

"We won't say anything, son," Martin assured.

***

Christmas Eve. Donald and Christine finished feeding the animals and had their tea. Gerald and Christine went home to the workshop where the Massey Ferguson's sat waiting. Christine climbed aboard, starting the engine quite noisy in the cab compared to what she's used to driving. Nevertheless, she slowly made her way escorted by Gerald to Crabtree Farm. Donald, Mary, and Martin gazed from the kitchen window seeing an enormous tractor enter the yard. Christine stepped from the cab. They walked outside, wondering what it was about and why she was there? "Merry Christmas to you all," Gerald smiled, "this is yours."

Donald explained, "That's the one we found in the shed; it looks almost brand-new now it's clean." Christine kissed him on the cheek, "Only has two hundred hours on the clock; the reason the tractors on our farm, under secret testing for Massey Ferguson. We have plenty of equipment and wouldn't suit what we do, so we decided to give it to you for Christmas to start you on your way to becoming arable."

Donald picked up Christine in his arms, kissing her warmly. Everyone watched.

"What about me, Donald," Gerald asked, laughing. Donald gave him a hug.

"Right, we'll leave you in peace now if you can find a shed big enough to store in Donald," Gerald laughed.

"I think now is the time, Donald," Mary smiled, "Come inside the pair of you, please." Christine and Gerald looked at each other, wondering what's happened.

"A surprise to you and Gerald, as to Martin and me, we had no idea what Donald was achieving in his spare time."

Donald carefully left his bedroom, placing the portrait on the sideboard. Gerald and Christine glared in disbelief, portrayed in their shooting attire, Gerald's arm on his daughter's shoulder. Gerald shed a tear; he'd never seen anything so beautiful; Donald had captured the moment. Gerald removed his handkerchief, and Christine dabbed her eyes, "I don't know what to say," Gerald smiled.

"There's nothing to say, Gerald," Donald suggested, "If you're pleased with my amateur attempts, that's what matters."

"Amateur! Come off it. I have paintings at home by famous artists, not a patch on your work."

Mary asked, excited, "Donald, can I see ours now? I'm desperate."

Martin looked surprised, "He's painted a portrait of us."

"Very well," he returned from the bedroom with the same sized portrait. This time, his mother and father, with Martin's father standing behind them with Biscuit, sat beside Martin's feet.

The tears ran down Mary's cheeks, "Son, you've done me proud." Martin stayed silent.

Donald carefully wrapped the portrait for Christine and Gerald, placing on the back seat of his Range Rover. Gerald and Donald hugged each other. Gerald drove off steadily. "I think you can safely say that was a success, son," Martin voiced proudly, staring at his portrait of himself, his father, Mary, and the dog.

"How long, Donald, to produce one of those portraits?" Martin asked curiously.

"Yours and mothers nearly six months. Gerald and Christine about four weeks, the photo I originally took was in their general work clothes. I looked for shooting attire deciding to change the scene. I would have to work until nearly two in the morning most of the time. Otherwise, they wouldn't have been finished, especially theirs."

"How long have you enjoyed painting Donald?" Mary asked, surprised by the whole episode.

Donald shrugged, "Always, I suppose; finding the time is a problem." He sighed, "So relaxing painting. You can drift into another world away from everyday problems and place all your dreams and aspirations on canvas."

"Where shall I put our present, dad? On the Internet, this tractor is 192 horsepower a monster, and for us," he grinned. "I was there originally when discovered in the back of an old shed," Donald commented. "I'm off to bed, mum, dad."

"You're not Donald, not until my pictures hanging in the front room." Donald collected his electric drill and gently drilled into the wall, locating a wall plug; he hooked the picture frame onto the screw. They stood back in the front room. Donald finally smiled as he looked at the picture he'd produced, realising he'd done his best.

"The tractor won't hurt there tonight, Donald. It's a dry night; just take the keys out of the ignition if we have any crazy people trying to steal stuff; they will have to escape Biscuit," he chuckled.

Donald's up bright and early Christmas Day, feeding the animals. He'd text Christine advising her to stay in bed; he could manage, see her at lunchtime.

***

Gerald had forgotten to give the hundred pounds he promised to Susan. He sat and wrote a cheque for her and fifty pounds for the remainder of the staff. He quickly visited each staff member, leaving Susan until last. He quietly knocked on her door. She opened her council house front door, surprised to see him. "Is there a problem, Gerald?" she asked.

"Merry Christmas," passing her the cheque.

"Would you like to come in, Gerald?"

"No, I'm fine. I have things to do, love; I'll see you after Christmas. You have a break, and thank you for all your hard work," he remarked, returning to his Range Rover. She waved as he drove off. Gerald returned home. Christine quickly made a little breakfast toast and marmalade two coffees, their old routine. She'd already fed the dogs.

***

Donald's sat in the new tractor reading the handbook, finally starting the engine, gingerly reversing into where they store the equipment, towering above their 1164 County. He attached the refurbished plough to the Massey Ferguson switching off the engine on Christmas Day. Still, he's determined next week to try out.

Mary prepared lunch. Everyone would have a choice, duck, goose, pheasant, or venison, not forgetting the traditional turkey. Her Aga is working overtime along with their other cooker. She's determined a Christmas Gerald and Christine would remember for many years to come and quietly prayed Donald and Christine would seriously fall in love. Martin's becoming quite mobile with a walking stick; at least he could move around if only to criticise everyone else.

***

Gerald gathered a few bottles of wine to go with lunch. For the first time in a long time, he hadn't stayed at home for Christmas lunch. In some ways, he missed Josephine; he recalled what Susan told him Josephine is nothing but a high society tart with the morals of a dog. Gerald loaded the bottles on the back seat of his Range Rover, dressing casually for a change. Christine wore her jeans and blouse with a suede jacket. They slowly made their way to Crabtree Farm parking in the yard. Warmly greeted at the door. Mary had already laid out the table; everything in serving dishes as usual banquet style. "This took you hours, Mary," Christine commented. Mary smiled. Gerald popped the corks on a couple of bottles of wine to allow for breathing before serving.

After an hour, Gerald professed, "I can't eat another mouthful; I will explode."

"Me neither, father," Christine said, watching Donald and Mary clear the plates away only to return with Christmas pudding; each portion was set alight with brandy. "I thought we were friends, Mary," Gerald commented, "I think you're quietly trying to kill me." Watching Mary pouring thick cream from a large jug. Donald glanced to the window, "Snowing."

Christine watched Mary approach with her dish of Christmas pudding. "Please, Mary, no more," Christine pleaded as Mary poured a large helping of cream, extinguishing the brandy flame.

"Get it down, you lass. Your boyfriend will never find you; you're that thin," she chuckled, looking at Donald.

Gerald and Christine not escaping Crabtree Farm until midnight. They had never eaten so much in their lives. They retired straight to bed, the snow falling heavily by morning, several centimetres on the ground.

***

Donald the following day travelled across the field on his Ferguson twenty with the sheep rations with Biscuit riding on the trailer. The ewes fought to have their heads in the troughs; the hay rack was empty. Donald placed two bales to replenish and a few swedes on the ground. He made his way across the other field. They only had five bullocks left, a scrawny bunch; Donald hoped to improve their condition now there wasn't so much competition for food. He placed a bale of hay in their rack and concentrates in their trough, slowly driving to the farm buildings. He put the tractor in the shed feeding the chickens and pigs, finally milking the cow, not expecting Christine to turn in today.

There wasn't much to do anymore, although he had a strange feeling of missing her and Gerald. He patted Biscuit, watching his mother leave the house with a bowl of warm food placed by his kennel.

Donald walked inside and sat down to his hearty breakfast, feeling very content with his life. "We have some decisions to make, son," Martin expressed, "We have 500 ewes in lamb that should start dropping any day, and we can't leave them out in this weather; you'd better prepare the barn."

"Already have, father."

Martin looked surprised, "You ever sleep, Donald," Martin smiled.

"I was thinking dad fetch in after breakfast."

Martin smiled, "I could drive the Land Rover if you can walk with Biscuit, I won't be much help, son, but I'll try."

"You won't, father; you stay in the house. You only need to slip once, and you'll be back where you started; mother will drive the Land Rover, and I will walk with Biscuit."

She smiled, agreeing with his decision.

"Our own fault." Martin expressed, "Mixing up the dates for the ram; maybe our last lambing if resorting to arable."

***

Christine forgot to set her alarm, and so had Gerald. They both woke around 9 o'clock, meeting in the kitchen. "I just want a coffee, father. Donald will have to manage; take me a day to recover from last night," she professed.

"I agree, daughter. I'm absolutely shattered; I don't think my stomach will recover. He hasn't many animals now, only the ewes and a couple of scrawny bullocks. I'm surprised Mary hasn't phoned roasting our ears, not in time for breakfast," he smiled.

***

Donald and Mary persuaded the old ewes to go into the barn; they immediately started steaming. Donald glanced across to the other dutch-barn hoping the hay would last. Almost immediately, the old ewes started lambing, most having twins. Donald made small pens out of hay bales to keep the mothers and lambs together. He marked each one with the corresponding number. Christine phoned inquiring, "Donald, you managed okay this morning?"

"Yes, I've had to bring the ewes in and started lambing."

"You need me," she asked eagerly.

"Any help is appreciated when lambing. Entirely up to you, Christine. You've done enough for us in the past few weeks; you rest if you want, I'll manage."

"I'm coming," she insisted.

"Wear your old clothes, Christine, and wrap up warm."

It wasn't long before Christine's with him, carefully helping the ewes lamb.

She helped place in pens by the end of the day; a hundred had lambed; unbelievable, Donald had never lambed so many so quickly, which is a miracle. Mary came with mugs of hot coffee. "Blimey Donald, the old ram must have been keen this year," she chuckled. Christine laughed.

"You stay here until midnight, Donald; I'll take over," Mary insisted, "Until 6 o'clock."

"Okay, mother or I can have my sleeping bag out here, and you stay with dad; I don't mind, really."

"You grab something to eat, Christine," Donald suggested, hearing her father's Range Rover arrive, suspecting it must be teatime.

"If you're staying out here tonight, so will I," she insisted.

"No, you'll distract me," Donald professed, making Christine smile, realising she had some effect on him. "Okay, I won't argue." She grinned, kissing him on the cheek and heading for the cottage. When Christine entered, Mary, Gerald, and Martin sat at the table talking. "We messed up this morning, daughter. Donald could have really used your help fetching in the ewes."

Martin smiled, "Don't scold her, Gerald. If she wasn't here, we'd have to manage."

Mary assured, "If my crazy husband had remembered to take Biscuit, he wouldn't be out of action either."

"You won't allow me to forget that wife," Martin frowned. "I see the specialist next week. Hopefully, I can start and do something around here." Martin sighed, "I hate feeling bloody useless."

Mary made the tea and sandwiches for Donald, who didn't want to leave the ewes. He'd never seen so many lambs in his life in such a short time, not wanting to let one of them die because he wasn't there. He sat in his sleeping bag, keeping the cold off him, watching the snowfall. He didn't bother with the cattle across the field. He knew they had enough food for tonight. Christine would milk the cow and see the other animals around the yard, taking the pressure off him to concentrate on the job.

CHAPTER FOUR

SPRING APPROACHES

Gerald and Christine had gone home. Donald sat in the barn almost like an on and off switch. The ewes had decided lambing's over; that's it for tonight; no more showing any signs. The bitter wind howled around the buildings rattling every loose piece of tin. No chance of sleep, that's for sure. Michael phoned, a pleasant distraction; Donald smiled. "Hi, mate."

"Hi Donald, the cottage we selected cosy; made me sweat to prepare for Christmas, but I managed; what you up to?"

"Sat in the barn watching old ewes."

"Oh, I wanted to phone, say thanks, Donald, you saved my skin. Gerald came down and fetched Peggy with Christine to see if there's any furniture we'd like from their house going spare, nice I thought."

"Yeah, I presume you won't be returning to school, Michael?"

"Under the circumstances, no, to be quite honest, never any good in exams. I have work with a list from Gerald as long as my arm. He is presently sourcing me a vehicle to drive around the estate to carry my tools and ladders, the guys, great."

"Yes, very generous treat him right, Michael, and he will look after you," Donald cautioned.

"I hear what you're saying. No worries, bye for now. I have to sit by this roaring fire, and blimey, it's so hot," he chuckled.

"You know what you can do, Michael," Donald grinned.

***

Christine's upstairs where her father stored spare furniture in one of the many bedrooms, Christine asked. "You enjoy living with your boyfriend; no parents breathing down your neck?"

"I suppose I wish turned out differently, shocked to find myself pregnant; in several months, we'll find out what I'm carrying."

"I'd thought you would be on the pill, Peggy?" Christine asked.

"Perhaps I should have," she sighed, "Too late now; I suppose it's one way of forcing the issue of living with your boyfriend. We first met when I was four, and he was two." Peggy selected two armchairs that weren't antique, an old sideboard and a mirror. "My mother's help considerably, and Michael has purchased the essential washing machine cooker, bedding, and beds. My mother has given us money to have a new sofa." Gerald dropped Peggy off at the cottage, the snow blowing across the fields the crops covered, keeping snug while this weather persisted.

***

Mary came out to the barn, "Okay, Donald, I'll take over."

"Not in these conditions, mum; you go back to the house with dad."

"You sure, Donald, you've been out here all day. You must be freezing?"

"No, I'm fine, mum; I'm behind a stack of bales and out of the wind."

Mary admired his dedication to duty returning to the house. Martin looked worried, "Mary, I'm not happy with him alone in the cold."

"I shouldn't think the sheep are impressed, although it's better than in the field," she sighed heavily. "I noticed Donald's wearing the thermal underwear we purchased for him; he should be fairly warm. I'll check on him about three in the morning. Come off to bed, set the alarm, and give your back some gentle exercise," she grinned. Martin had never moved so quickly to the bedroom for months. Mary commented, watching him undress, "I see you didn't need asking twice," removing her clothes lying on the bed. She now remembered why she married him, bad back or not. He could perform better than she'd ever remembered feeling slightly guilty for sampling Gerald. However, it brought a conclusion to a nagging intrigue.

Donald could smell burning; he jumped out of his sleeping bag and ran into the neighbouring shed. He switched the lights and saw smoke from around the Massey Ferguson tractor cab. He quickly searched in his pocket; luckily, he had the key. He started the tractor, drove away from the building, and ran back inside. He grabbed a pair of pliers and cut through the battery cables, ensuring no power to the wiring. He waited for half an hour; the smell had dissipated. Looking in the cab, breathing a sigh of relief, everything appeared to be okay; he was fortunate he was in the barn; otherwise, he'd have lost the farm.

Donald shut the doors of the machinery shed. He realises if the Massey decides to burst into flames, she's far enough away from the buildings and inflammable material not to hurt anything else. He returned to attend to the ewes finding while away, three more ewes had lambed on their own.

At 3 o'clock in the morning, Mary came into the barn carrying a hot mug of coffee. "Hi mum," Donald smiled, pleased to see her.

"Why is the new tractor outside?" Donald explained. She's horrified, realising if not for him and his quick thinking, they could have lost the whole farm; they couldn't blame Gerald or anyone, just sod's law. She'd known neighbours having tractors catch fire before now wasn't such an uncommon thing.

"You grab a couple of hours sleep, Donald; I'll stay here," she smiled, patting him on the shoulder. "Are you sure, mum?"

"Yes, go on. I'll be fine; it won't be the first time I've sat out here all-night lambing," she smiled.

Donald eagerly went to bed, woken by his father at 5 o'clock. Gerald and Christine had arrived; Donald quickly made coffee for everyone and explained what had happened to the tractor. Gerald's horrified to think he'd allowed something onto the farm, potentially a fire hazard. He immediately removed his mobile at 5 o'clock in the morning or not, livid. "Johnson the Massey you prepared nearly burnt the farm down. I want explanations. I want you out at first light. I want to know what went wrong," Gerald switched his phone off.

Martin suggested, "I wouldn't blame your mechanic at the moment; see what he finds, that tractors stood for some time, Gerald."

"Yes, father," Christine agreed, leaving the table with Donald grabbing the milk bucket and heading out into the yard.

Mary came in, and Donald took over, looking after the ewes. By 8:30 a.m., Johnson had arrived finding Donald, "What happened?" he asked, extremely worried.

"I could smell burning wire. I ran around to the tractor shed, saw smoke coming from the tractor and drove outside, severing the battery cables praying she wouldn't burst into flames."

Johnson returned to the Massey tractor, replacing the battery leads and opening a side panel; he saw the problem straightaway a wire had rubbed on the chassis by the engine. Gerald walked over, "What coursed the problem, Johnson?"

"Wasn't my fault. You wouldn't notice a wire pinched and rubbed through; it looks as if there's nothing wrong until you try and move the wire you realise trapped."

"Okay, good job, rectify whatever is wrong, Johnson and don't miss anything, please."

Gerald returned to the house and explained to everyone what they'd found.

Martin commented, "I'm surprised the tractors haven't set fire to the place by now, half the wirings hanging and shouldn't be Mary," he sighed.

"Not any more, Martin. Johnson checked; he'd fix if something wrong those were his instructions," Gerald smiled.

Johnson knocked on the cottage door. "Come in," Mary voiced, pouring him a coffee, "You must be freezing stood out there?"

"Thank you, Mrs Selwyn. Won't happen again," he remarked, drinking his coffee. "An isolation switch, very handy fitted at some time by the batteries, turn the switch off, and no power around the machine at all."

"You show Donald, please, Johnson, before you go?" Mary asked calmly.

He nodded, "Thank you for the drink, greatly appreciated," leaving the cottage, finding Donald showing him the isolation switch, and drove off, heading to Strawberry Estate.

Gerald and Mary came out to see Donald. "Mum, we need bags of lamb creep-food. Can you nip into town and purchase? Half a dozen bags will do for now."

"I'll fetch those. I can take Martin with me, take him away from the house; I suspect he's sick of these four walls."

"That would be great, Gerald, thanks," Mary voiced, brightly returning to the house with Gerald. Christine made her way to Donald. Gerald and Martin set off for town.

Christine sat on a bale of straw by Donald; he wrapped his sleeping bag around her. "Sorry about the tractor, Donald. We were trying to help you, not destroy your farm," she sighed. Donald shrugged his shoulders, "Things like this happen. It could have been any one of our tractors. Even brand-new machines set fire these days, I've seen many times on television, especially combines."

They cuddled close to each other; Donald gently kissed her lips. She thought her mind would melt; he kissed her again, holding her close. She smiled, hoping to start a relationship that would last for the rest of her life. Christine decided to take the initiative encouraging Donald to be more forward, cuddling close to him and kissing him passionately, pressing his hand onto her covered breast. She could feel his hand gently moving over her jumper from one breast to the other. Christine decided not to take things any further, plus it was too cold out here, but at least she knew he was interested.

An hour later, Gerald drove around the rear of the buildings with his Range Rover. Donald unloaded the pellets inside the barn to keep dry. Martin stepped from the Range Rover looking at his ewes, the first time he'd seen them since his accident. Martin inquired, "How are we doing, son?"

"All twins at present. I hope it stays that way. We don't want any triplets; they're a pain. I estimate three hundred and fifty lambed," he smiled, seeing three more in labour. "I don't know what we fed our ram on this year; lambing could be over within a few days; no wonder he sat on a chair in the Bahamas resting." Everyone grinned.

Christine kissed Donald, sliding into her father's Range Rover. Donald helped Martin to the house, not wanting his father to catch a chill. His health improved by the day, but he still wasn't fully fit. Donald sat at the kitchen table, drinking a cup of coffee. "I'll take over for a while, Donald. You grab some more sleep," Mary suggested.

"Okay, mum."

***

Christine commented, "A narrow escape father for the Selwyn's. The place could have burnt down if Donald wasn't out there." Gerald nodded in agreement, "Essential, we have insurance, love. Any one of our tractors can go up in flames or combines," he sighed heavily.

Christine asked, "Are you and mother divorcing?"

"I shouldn't think so, love; why do you ask?"

"Who actually owns the farm, dad?"

"Both of us, I suppose and you, why do you ask?"

"I wondered if mother would try and ruin everything for us with her connections."

"If they didn't want us living at Strawberry Estate, we'd be long gone; they have the power, the money and the contacts, I can assure you. You must remember Christine; you are of her blood as much as she doesn't like the direction you're taking. I don't think she'd trash your life out of spite. They have more money than they know what to do with," he explained, trying to reassure her.

Christine smiled, "I hope your right, father when I marry Donald," she realised what she was saying.

Gerald smiled, "You have made plans, daughter."

She grinned, "A long way off, father. Would you approve?"

"Yes, I think Donald is a wonderful person. Don't force the situation, Christine; you will lose. I noticed the detailing he put into painting you, not a hair out of place. You didn't see what he'd faintly written on the reverse of the portrait, have you?"

Christine stared, "What?"

"I'll show you. Don't you dare say anything; I think Donald forgot to remove."

Gerald removed the portrait showing Christine what was written in light pencil. "The girl in my dreams."

In shock, Christine placed her hand to her mouth, "I didn't think he felt that way about me! Wow, that's wonderful," running upstairs.

Gerald rehung the portrait, smiling, suspecting his daughter's future was secure. Gerald's mobile rang the local garage. "Mr Gibbs, we have located a tipper transit three and a half-ton five thousand pounds plus VAT in excellent condition."

"Okay, if there's any logo, please remove it. It would be appreciated if you could put Strawberry Estate on the doors."

"Perfect, Mr Gibbs, with you in a couple of days."

Gerald drove to the workshop finding Johnson. "I don't know whether you are aware of the situation Johnson concerning Michael living in the cottage."

"There's talk, Sir."

"You use this building attached to yours for storage."

"No, I have enough room where I am now, thanks."

"Michael will use it for storing his ladders and other building equipment; can you weld a clasp on the door, then we can secure it," Gerald smiled.

"Okay."

Gerald jumped in his Range Rover and returned to the house, phoning Michael. "Michael, I have purchased you an estate vehicle. I will take you to purchase equipment tomorrow if convenient with you from the wholesalers; set up an account so they will deliver your

116

materials until you pass your test. Then you can fetch them yourself. The vehicle will not leave the estate until you pass your test."

"I don't know what to say, Sir, Mr Gibbs."

Gerald smiled, "Don't worry, I'll recover my money; I'll phone you in the morning."

Michael couldn't believe his luck; Peggy had heard the conversation. "Everything is coming together. We'll soon have a daughter or son, so cosy living here, never thought it would be." She smiled, turning to her computer, carrying on with her work, hoping her secret would never be revealed.

Christine made lunch for herself and her father, a light salad. She spent some time in the fitness room, trying to lose the stone she gained. Gerald entered the kitchen and sat down for his meal, "That looks lovely, Christine, thanks. I'm organising transport and equipment for Michael; his arm should be out of plaster in the next few days. I think he's keen to start work he must have struggled to prepare the accommodation for Christmas. I don't think he would have if it weren't for his friends helping."

Christine smiled, tingling from the thought Donald wanted her, realising; she would have to contain her excitement, so Donald didn't realise she knew how he felt.

***

Donald came staggering out of his bedroom midday, "You should have woken me, dad. I hope Mum's okay."

"She has her mobile, Donald; you must remember we were lambing long before you were born," Martin smiled.

Donald grabbed his mug of coffee and headed out to the ewes seeing his mother carrying lambs placed in a pen and the mother. "I can't understand Donald had over fifty ewes give birth this morning, and we still haven't lost a lamb, touch wood."

***

Finally, the sun started to shine. Gerald looked from the front door to the trees planted on the lawn many years ago, noticing the snowdrops coming through the turf and daffodils progressing under the snow. He thought how strange the sun always makes you feel optimistic. He slowly drove around the estate and saw the snow had already melted from some areas. He could see the slugs appeared to be attacking the oilseed rape. He immediately reached for his phone, smiling, seeing Stephen with the quad bike with slug pellets ready to treat the affected area. He noticed Jake in the field beyond, finishing off laying the hedge.

Gerald drove into town to the local garage, noticing the new transit for the estate presently having the Strawberry Estate logo placed on the door in strawberry red. He jumped out of his Range Rover, checking around the vehicle, extremely pleased with what he could see. The vehicle wasn't battered, and the garage proprietor shook Mr Gibbs's hand, "We'll deliver this tomorrow morning Mr Gibbs. I hope you'll be pleased with your purchase."

"Looks good," Gerald smiled, climbing back into his Range Rover, noticing Susan walking from the shops carrying her shopping. He pipped his horn, parking by the curb, "Here, I'll help you. Where is your car?"

She sighed, "In the garage, fifteen years old trying to get through the M O T for me."

"Come on, I'll take you home," Gerald smiled, helping her into his Range Rover with her shopping. "Back to work next week," he remarked after unloading her purchases. She grinned; he guessed she was worried about the car. Gerald dashed back to the garage, asking, "What's the problem with Susan's car?"

"The long explanation or the short one," the mechanic asked sarcastically.

"The short version please," Gerald frowned, not impressed with his attitude.

"The car is worth one hundred pounds, cost three hundred to repair, waste of bloody money."

Gerald walked away, realising Johnson could have made the repairs costing a fraction. Gerald looked along at the cars for sale. Ford Fiesta, two years old, sat on the forecourt, the same vehicle she presently owned, only a lot younger model. He spoke to the proprietor, "That Fiesta, incorporate in the Ford transit price, I can run it through the books," he grinned. "Take the Ford Fiesta to Susan. Don't charge for those crappy repairs you carried out if you wish to continue doing business with the estate."

"I hear you loud and clear," the proprietor shook his hand, "A pleasure doing business with you, Sir." Gerald climbed in his Range Rover. He phoned Susan, "Hello Susan, a surprise for you at the garage. See you soon, bye."

"Gerald, Gerald," she realised he'd cut her off; she shrugged her shoulders two hours later received a phone call from the garage; closed her eyes, dreading the bill, "let me hear it," she sighed.

"I need your insurance details. I can send the logbook off and tax the vehicle."

"What are you talking about? My car is insured and taxed."

"Your new one isn't."

"You what! I can't afford a new one."

"Here and paid for."

She now realised what Gerald had done; she couldn't resist smiling. "I'll be there in a minute," she ran to the garage arriving out of breath. "This is for me?"

The proprietor nodded, "I need your insurance details, I can tax, and you can take it home; no bill for the work carried out on your old one. We'll dispose of it for you. You might get a couple hundred quid for it in the auctions." Susan was absolutely stunned; she gave him her details. He taxed the car for her; passing the keys, she looked around inside the car spotless, driving home. She realised she'd misjudged Gerald. What she was told by Josephine is rubbish, nothing like she described. She had a suspicion from the start, absolute proof; he's a gentleman of better breeding than Josephine by a mile. Although she may be in too deep and would have to be careful.

Susan sat in the kitchen at home feeling as guilty as hell realising Josephine had her watch Gerald's every movement believing him to be an animal. He wasn't, she concluded. She knew the truth; she set about making him a lovely cake and taking it to the farm. She entered through the front door seeing the portrait of Gerald and Christine hanging in the hallway. Gerald came to see who had entered the house. "Whoever painted that Gerald, wonderful; the likeness is good."

"Not half as good as that cake looks," he said eagerly, taking it from her hands. "I presume that's for me," he grinned, noticing Susan's blouse hardly buttoned, giving him a view of her bulging breasts trying to escape her black bra. He'd never seen Susan dress so revealing.

"Yes, and this," she kissed him very tenderly. "Boss, I will never be able to thank you for your help," Susan realised he'd seen what was on offer should he choose to venture.

Gerald grinned, "I don't know, Susan, that went down very well," he laughed. "Just remember I didn't purchase the vehicle, stay very quiet, please; otherwise could cause me problems."

"I understand, Gerald; I shan't say a word," she kissed him again, pressing her breasts against him.

"Okay," he laughed.

Christine came into the kitchen suggesting, "Susan put my father down," she smirked. "He's already explained. I suggest you fasten your blouse; otherwise, my father will go blind," she laughed, smiling, watching Susan fasten her blouse above her bra.

"I believe you're still on holiday. Go home, woman; we'll see you soon. Oh, that reminds me, Susan, when your car needs a service, talk to Johnson; he will service it for nothing or if you have any issues."

"Thanks, Gerald, Christine, see you in a few days," Susan smiled, running out of the door. Gerald's walking around the kitchen like he'd won the lottery, he hadn't been kissed like that for years, and he hadn't realised Susan's so well blessed. Christine grinned at his expression.

Christine and Gerald made their way to Crabtree Farm. Finally, there were some signs of lighter evenings, not by much, though. Christine milked the cow, seeing to the chickens and pigs. She made her way to Donald, looking after the ewes, "How many Donald?" she asked.

"I think there's only two hundred left to lamb, ridiculous; we've never had lambing go so quickly. The old ram must have been on Viagra."

Christine sat beside him on a bale of straw out of the wind. He placed his sleeping bag around her shoulders, kissing her softly on the cheek; she's now convinced it wouldn't be long before official; they were a couple. She stayed with him for half an hour. Donald commented, "You'd better have your tea, Christine. Mum will bring mine later," he smiled. She couldn't resist. She bent down, holding her fragrant hair out the way, kissing him on the lips, "Catch you later," she smiled, returning to the cottage.

Mary had made venison sandwiches. "Martin," she commented, "Gerald, this venison is excellent. You know some of the best we've ever tasted."

Martin smiled, "Hospital tomorrow; I want to return to work. Although I may have to attend physiotherapy, I thought I could have made myself fit enough at work."

Christine remarked, "Take it easy, Martin. We don't mind help-ing," she assured. Everyone grinned, suspecting her real reason for coming here; plain to everybody, Donald and Christine would become an item short of a disaster.

"I must say, Christine, since you've looked after the pigs, they're far better. Soon have pork ready for the table. We have to take them to the abattoir to be killed."

"I have a licence, Mary; my father had a small farm and a butcher shop at the back, so when they are ready, contact me," he smiled. "That's where I worked on weekends. Josephine used to come with the chauffeur for joints of meat for the house," Gerald sighed, ven-turing down memory lane in his mind for a moment.

Martin smiled, "That means we can slaughter a bullock and hang it in the cellar, Mary. Gerald could dispatch, and I suspect you know how to joint him properly, unlike us amateurs."

Gerald smiled, "I have slaughtered a few in my time."

Mary walked out to the barn with sandwiches and coffee for Donald. "Thanks, mum, greatly appreciated."

"You stay until midnight, Donald, then I'll take over," she smiled. Mary returned to the cottage.

Gerald and Christine had already left for home, finding a limousine parked outside the house. Gerald glanced to see the driver reading a newspaper using the interior lighting. Gerald suspected Josephine's in the house. They could hear voices in the lounge walk in to find Mrs Montague and Josephine. "I thought you advised Mrs Montague; that Christine would not be bothered again," Gerald expressed firmly.

"That is what I said, Gerald," Mrs Montague replied. "However, Josephine wants a private conversation with her daughter; she may reconsider her position," Mrs Montague glared, shrugging her shoulders in disbelief.

Christine folded her arms, "If you two think you could change my mind, you are in for a shock after setting me up with the Copthorne brother's mother," Christine glared. "I think the short version; bugger off a couple of old tarts, nothing better to do than cause trouble for ordinary people. Why don't you two share the Copthorne brothers? I wonder if your husband is aware, Mrs Montague, of your behaviour."

Mrs Montague, shocked, "I have never associated with the Copthorne brothers; thank you," she insisted.

Christine laughed, "Would your husband believe you? Jump in your car and piss off. Take that witch of my mother with you." Josephine moved to cuddle Christine.

Christine stepped aside, "Don't you touch me, you old witch." Josephine and Mrs Montague left without saying a further word. Gerald stood shocked; he didn't know his daughter could behave that way and unleash such language. He couldn't imagine Christine having the better of Mrs Montague. Christine had hit her in the wallet by suggesting she would talk to Mr Montague.

"I think you can safely say, Christine, they have the message this time. You're a braver person than me, that's for sure."

"My mother has nothing better to do. Let them stew. Mrs Montague won't want me to phone her husband, suggesting she flirted with the Copthorne brothers. Suspicion is worse in some cases," she grinned.

"Okay, daughter, calm down," placing an arm on her shoulder, feeling her tremble. Gerald poured them both a whisky.

"I feel sorry for Donald if he's to marry you. God help him. You've a tongue like a razor blade. You really shouldn't have made an enemy of Mrs Montague," Gerald suggested.

"You're probably right, father; nevertheless, I wasn't leaving them in any doubt I wasn't interested in France."

They both rose early the following day, heading for Crabtree Farm. Donald sat having breakfast, "lambing is finished," he remarked. "Absolutely ridiculous lambing normally goes on for weeks; I thought we'd achieved a perfect count. Unfortunately, we lost one lamb deformed."

Everyone finished their breakfast, and Christine and Gerald returned home. They weren't there long before the Ford transit arrived for Michael. Gerald drove down to the cottages; Michael glanced out of the window, excited, running out with a beaming smile. Gerald ordered, "jump in; let's buy you some tools," it wasn't long before at the wholesalers, "Spend wisely; I'm watching," Gerald advised. Michael purchased nails, bolts, screws of varying sizes, and drills and saws. Michael suggested, "If we have to work on a roof, we can use the JCB loader safer to operate than ladders."

"Smart thinking Michael. We have some ladders on occasion; you need them for painting."

"I'm sure you know Michael Pearce; he is authorised to spend one hundred pounds here without authorisation from me, or you stand the loss. I'm not made of money," Gerald insisted, exhaling. "What have we spent so far."

"Three thousand pounds Mr Gibbs,"

"Okay, that will do to start him in the right direction."

They loaded their purchases on the back of the transit returning to the farm parking by the workshop. Gerald introduced Michael to Johnson and showed him the shed to store his equipment. "Keep the shed locked at all times," Gerald insisted. Michael couldn't stop smiling. Gerald parked the transit by the workshop. "That's bloody clever," he said aloud, grabbing his mobile. "Christine, drive my Range Rover to the workshop, please."

"Yes, father," she smirked, realising what he'd done. She drove steadily along the track to the workshop, sliding across the passenger seat, grinning. "Okay, smarty-pants," Gerald chuckled. Christine didn't say anything, and neither did Michael dropping him off at his cottage. "How long before your arms out of plaster?"

"Next week, they had to reset after the cast was damaged. I want to start work, please, if I can?"

"Goodbye for now," Gerald and Christine both smiled, waving. Gerald's phone rang Mrs Montague. He sighed heavily, "Yes, what can I do for you, Mrs Montague?"

"Josephine feels you owe her five and a half million if you wish to buy her share of Strawberry Estate, worth considerably more. However, you are looking after her daughter."

"She's saying she wishes to have a divorce?" Gerald asked cautiously.

"I suppose reconciliation with your attitude and Christine's out of the question." Christine's about to speak. Gerald placed his finger to his lips.

"Allow me to speak to my solicitors. I have to take advice on the situation. Her immoral behaviour must be considered, plus maintenance for Christine until she's eighteen. Her university fees will be horrendous, not forgetting the scandal when the Copthorne brothers are named publicly. I don't understand why she needs the money because she doesn't? Josephine was left twenty million when her parents died and the estate in Scotland unless she squandered from her private account."

"Josephine's hoping this could be handled privately, not involving solicitors, and she certainly doesn't want to involve the Copthorne family."

Christine mimed, raising two fingers and whispering, "Two million take it or leave it," her father grinned, placing his finger to his lips.

"I agree it would be easier to settle rather than drag everybody's name through the mud. If Josephine is prepared to accept one million, we will say no more, but we will require it in writing from Josephine; she has turned over her estate shares to her daughter Christine."

Christine had both her hands over her mouth, trying not to laugh. A long pause. "Josephine feels one million five hundred thousand pounds is a fairer settlement."

"I can't afford that; keep the farm running. The crops aren't growing very well this year. I have salaries to pay, definitely not. Josephine can take it or leave it or run it through the courts. Allow the newspapers to print the separation and pictures of the Copthorne brothers," he suggested grinning.

"A moment, I will discuss with Josephine." Another long pause. "Reluctantly, she agrees to one million. You will say absolutely nothing to anyone concerning her or myself, is that agreed, Gerald?"

"Providing you keep your side of the bargain. Otherwise, I will open the gates of hell on the pair of you. I'm sure Christine would join in for good measure. I will send Josephine one million when the deeds are turned over to Christine, naming her a Strawberry Estate shareholder. You agree, Mrs Montague?"

"Agreed, Mr Gibbs, good day."

Christine smiled, "That will dent the bank balance, father."

"No, it won't. She's never known, or you, where I've hidden the money. She believed she squandered it over the years. Whenever she went to London playing on the roulette wheels and paralytic, I shifted money to a secret account. Over the years, I've moved three million from our private account, which we share. She knows we have one million two hundred thousand pounds between us in our joint account, that's what she's hoping to bleed me dry of, and the farm at the same time, we've prevented," he smiled.

Christine stared, "You sneaky devil father."

"Don't smile until we prove you own the other half of Strawberry Estate, were not home and dry yet, love. Say nothing. Keep your fingers crossed and watch the post," he grinned.

"You really think ahead, father," she said, kissing him on the cheek as they strolled into the house; he smiled. "I'm determined; whatever happens, we would win. If we lost this property by some twist of fate, I would have sufficient money to buy somewhere else not so big; you'd have a farm, something you can call your own," he smiled reassuringly.

Much to their surprise, they found Susan making lunch. "You're not due back until Monday, Susan," he remarked, looking out the kitchen window and seeing her car parked around the back.

"I think the least I can do for you, Gerald, Christine, under the circumstances. I received compensation for my husband's death, but nothing can last forever. I wanted to invest some in my daughter's future," she smiled. "To be quite honest, Gerald, I was panicking. I didn't know how I could afford to replace the car; that's why I kept repairing, and you save the day because I haven't any spare money." They both sat down to a beautiful salad. Susan had made another one of her marvellous sponge cakes; she knew Gerald enjoyed it immensely. She smiled, "See you two Monday and thank you both very much again," leaving the house. Gerald watched from the window as a bird pooped on her car; Suzan removed a tissue wiping it off. He laughed, realising how proud she was of her new car.

After lunch, Gerald and Christine drove around the estate, checking the crops, realising they would soon have to apply fertiliser to increase the growth. Christine made a note on her mobile of the field number they were inspecting and the amount of fertiliser they thought needed, realising they'd have to spend at least 100 thousand on fertiliser. Prices had soared; lucky still have some left from last year.

The oilseed rape looked a little worse for wear, usually at this time; the pigeons had a field day. They bumped into Stephen coming along the track with a tractor and trailer. "Stephen fertiliser Monday, please, come to the office, and we'll give you the amounts per field depending on the mapping." Stephen nodded. "Oh, that reminds me, any staff with gun licences have permission to shoot the pigeons and rabbits. Leave the other wildlife alone for the moment; if they come across a fox, I don't mind you shooting that," Gerald smiled.

"Thanks, Gerald. I'm sure they will be interested. I know a few people from the gun club; they'd be only too pleased to walk the fields and shoot the bloody pigeons."

"Very well, but they must all wear orange vests, so we know where they are and only shoot pigeons and rabbits. They are not to enter the reserve; please make it plain, Stephen, to everyone."

"Okay, Gerald, thanks."

"As an afterthought, I want the names of every person who comes onto the estate with a gun. And checked by the police first as a precaution they comply with the law." Stephen nodded and drove off.

They continued driving towards the cottages where Michael lived, seeing him outside arguing with someone. Christine voiced, "Quick, father Peggy's brother who hit him last time," Gerald accelerated. Christine jumped out of the Range Rover. Gerald phoned the police. Fredrick aggressively moved to slap Christine. She dropped him to the ground. He tried to stand; she kicked him in the balls, and he rolled about in the vegetation screaming in agony.

Michael holding his shoulder from where Fredrick punched him. Peggy's leaning against the doorframe crying wasn't many minutes before the police were there and arrested Fredrick after taking statements. Gerald and Christine helped both into the cottage. "What's his problem?" Christine shouted, puzzled by his persistence. Peggy sat down sobbing, "I don't know. Mum will go mad; he will be detained for two years."

Christine made them both a drink looking around; they had really changed the appearance of the inside of the cottage, "looks great full marks, Michael. You completed a marvellous job here; the place looks charming," Christine voiced.

"Thanks; I wish I knew why he keeps coming after me, no real reason. I'm not bothering him," Michael sighed.

Gerald looked to Michael, convinced he knew nothing about why he would be attacked, suspecting Peggy's the key. "I think you should come clean and explain the truth to Michael, Peggy; you know something, don't you?"

She sighed heavily, "Fredrick wants me to go with one of his friends. Apparently, he had a crush on me for years. I started seeing him and realised I loved Michael more," she paused. "Sorry, Michael, only a brief affair, perhaps a week. We went our separate ways when he discovered I'm pregnant and Michael's the father."

"Fredrick doesn't believe Michael's the father does he, Peggy?" Gerald surmised.

Christine and Gerald watched the tears run down Michael's cheeks; he had stood by her since they were toddlers; cheating on her had never crossed his mind. "That's why you wanted to go with your brother to Devon on a boxing tournament for a fortnight."

Peggy nodded, "A stupid fling I regret more than you will ever know, Michael." Gerald sighed heavily, not expecting his day to end on this note.

Christine advised, "You're unable to discover at the moment who's the father."

"Not yet. Graham used protection every time he made love to me, so I'm sure it's not his."

Mrs Sanderson entered the cottage frowning, "I think you better come home, Peggy. If everybody had been honest and upfront initially, your brother wouldn't be facing a two-year prison sentence. Fredrick phoned me from the police station; your father is absolutely livid. Graham's no longer a member of the club." Mrs Sanderson turned to face Michael, "I didn't know until an hour ago; I couldn't understand Fredrick's persistence. Now I understand why he's trying to split you two and make Peggy confess the truth."

Peggy glanced at him, "Sorry, Michael," walking out the door. "I'm sure it's yours."

"Where do we go from here?" Gerald sighed heavily.

"I can still live here, can't I Gerald on my own?"

"You don't seem overly upset, Michael," Gerald asked, puzzled.

"No, she talks in her sleep; I've listened to her talking to someone called Graham most nights. Right, what they say, Gerald, you don't know anyone until you live with them. I'll be ready and willing to work once this plasters off in the next few days. My education is finished anyway. I want nothing to do with my parents after how they treated me. I think the word is they can kiss my arse."

Gerald chuckled, rubbing Michael's red hair, "Good for you, lad. You will make something of yourself, and we will help you." Christine smiled as they left the cottage, climbing into the Range Rover and heading for Crabtree Farm for tea.

They sat around the table. Gerald and Christine explained about Michael and briefly about Josephine. "You two really live exciting lives," Mary commented, pouring everyone another drink.

"Hopefully, everything will calm down in the next few months and be normal, whatever normal is," Gerald grinned.

***

The following day after breakfast, Donald and Biscuit took the sheep to a new pasture; although still chilly, the old ewes enjoyed fresh grass that had regenerated while in the barn giving birth.

Martin is mobile, slowly building his strength without placing too much stress on his repaired back, continuing to use a walking stick as a precaution for the moment. Donald and Martin walked across the fields to see the barley growing nicely.

Martin commented, "Could do with a little fertiliser, son. Do we have any in stock?"

"I think so, dad, a few bags; I'll put the fertiliser spreader on the Massey and apply some later today." They slowly walked to the farm buildings. Donald commented, "I've been thinking, dad, rather than play rugby, I'll paint landscapes, less stressful than charging around a field after a ball and certainly less painful. What do you think?"

"We need an expert to assess your skill; our portrait is wonderful, and I know Gerald feels the same about his. However, what the real world thinks may be a different story," Martin sighed.

Donald nodded.

"The person to speak to is Gerald. I'm sure he has contacts in that circle of people; ask him tonight."

Donald fitted the fertiliser spreader to the tractor, filled the hopper, spending the next three hours applying fertiliser to the barley. Checking the wheat in the neighbouring field seemed to be progressing nicely. However, fertiliser wouldn't go amiss if they had any spare. He applied to both areas by teatime to see Gerald and Christine enter the yard. "Gerald, can I ask you a serious question," Donald enquired nervously.

"Sure what!"

"Do you have any contacts in the art world who could assess my artwork and see if it's good enough to sell rather than play rugby? I can stay home and paint landscapes in my spare time," Donald smiled nervously.

"No problem, you're good enough; we have to find the right outlet to maximise your earnings, which I will gladly do. I'm sure Christine would assist."

"Thank you both. I have one more question; would you have any objections if Christine and I became an item?"

Christine stared in disbelief; that's the last thing she thought he would ask, if ever. Mary ran down into the cellar. She couldn't believe her ears and never imagined Donald would ask anybody, especially a parent, if he could go out with their daughter in a million years.

"Is this what you want, Christine?"

Christine tried not to grin, "I don't know, father; do you think he will look after me?" Christine remarked, trying to stay calm.

Gerald laughed, "You ask the silliest bloody question; stop teasing the boy. At least he had the courtesy to ask me first; anybody else would have you in a haystack and sod the parents."

Martin clapped his hands, "Nicely said Gerald, that's a fact. Mary, wouldn't you say," he laughed. "I was dragged in a haystack once by a wild farmer's daughter and trapped ever since." Everyone burst out laughing.

"Donald, I have no objections whatsoever. I thought you'd never asked; she didn't either, by the look on her face. Oh blimey, the cider headache time," Gerald muttered. Mary filled the glasses, "Who's going to chaperone these two? You can't be left alone together, asking for trouble."

"We have a long way to go before that stage," Donald insisted. "I wanted to ensure Christine's interested in a steady, good relationship. I've seen enough disasters to last me a lifetime. I don't want to be included as one," he expressed firmly.

Donald drank his cider-like water, topped up, and consumed another glass of cider straight back. Everyone else drunk there's steady as usual. "I see the paint stripper hasn't improved Mary," Christine laughed, trying to catch her breath. They chatted for another hour and were about to leave the cottage. Christine grabbed Donald's hand, taking him down the hallway, kissing him softly on the lips, "That's nice, boyfriend," she smiled, running back to the door past her father, jumping in the Range Rover. "Come on, father," she smiled.

Martin commented, "I think we have two happy teenagers; hope it remains so." They agreed.

Gerald and Christine drove off. Martin turned to face Donald, "Excellent son, wise choice of girl. You have the manners and decency to ask her father first, although, in all honesty," he grinned. "We thought a foregone conclusion knowing you, we could have been wrong."

Mary kissed Donald, "I'm so happy for you, son."

***

Gerald's grinning steadily driving home, "You have what you wanted, daughter."

She smiled, "Yes, father, I've trapped my security," she grinned.

Gerald glanced at her, "I think you have your mother's cunning."

The doorbell rang, and Christine signed for a large envelope addressed to Gerald Gibbs. He opened cautiously with a knife inside a letter, a deed of ownership; Christine Gibbs was entitled to 50% ownership of Strawberry Estate when she reached twenty-one. Mr Gerald Gibbs would continue to manage Christine Gibbs's portion of the farm until she reached the said age, where she would contribute to the running of the estate in full.

"I'll have our solicitor look at the document, Christine. I don't trust your mother or her friends."

"I agree, father. I wasn't expecting that," she frowned.

"Sounds reasonable. Perhaps worried your dash off marry some raving lunatic and squander the money, I certainly would be concerned."

"I find that rather insulting, father; I've hooked Donald. You might as well start and look," she grinned. "I don't think so one Josephine in a lifetime is enough."

"I think Susan has a crush on you since you purchased her a car. There are no airs and graces about her. What you see is what you get, and she's offering you quite a substantial amount from her ample cleavage."

"Will you stop trying to organise my life, Christine, please," Gerald trying not to smile.

Christine chuckled, "We will see, father."

"Right fertilising, office." They both went into the office, switched on the computer, and displayed a farm map. Deciding what fertiliser to be applied, placing the information on a memory stick for Stephen to use for the fertiliser spreader to save wastage. They'd had the fields mapped many years ago, so they knew where less profitable areas were that required attention.

Gerald drove around to Stephen's house, passing the memory stick, "You know the routine, Stephen. Any issues, phone me, and have Jake bring the fertiliser to you on a trailer will save you running about speed up operations. I presume the chariots made ready?"

"Yes, Gerald," Stephen advised.

"Try not to make too much mess; there are one or two soft spots, but you must stick to the tramlines." Gerald smiled, "I'm sure you will do your best."

Stephen smiled, "You can guarantee that, Sir."

The next few days passed uneventfully; other than fertiliser spread everywhere around Strawberry Estate. Gerald contacted a friend in London asking for an assessment of Donald's painting skills to ascertain whether he thought he could make a living painting?

***

Donald enjoying the limbo period, which didn't often happen, decided to paint a landscape of the lambs and ewes in the field for his next project. In two more days back at school and Christine.

He took several photographs with his camera returning to his bedroom; he downloaded the photos to his computer and enlarged. Applying paint, losing himself in his own mind.

***

After breakfast, Christine and Gerald drove home, finding Susan in the kitchen. Christine immediately noticed Susan's dressed slightly different with makeup. Her hair was not out of place, her dress slightly shorter and a lower neckline; she thought her father may go blind if Susan leant forward.

Christine tried not to grin entering the office, checking the differences between Susan's age and her father, realising some difference. Some women liked older men, which is okay in her book. She didn't feel threatened by Susan; she wanted to see her father happy. Christine returned to the kitchen to see Susan and her father chatting, dashing upstairs, not wishing to interrupt. She heard her father coming upstairs half an hour later. She descended, seeing lipstick on his cheek, not commenting he'd be a free man in due course. Why should his life be ruined by her mother?

Christine jumped on her father's quad bike, deciding to see how Michael was coping. She slowly rode down the farm track to the two cottages, suspecting him to be upset, although probably putting a brave face on things. She knocked on the door. Michael opened the door, tidying himself, "Hi," he smiled, looking flustered as if a naughty child caught with his hand in a sweet jar. Much to Christine's surprise, one of her best friends from school Pamela Robinson sat on the settee drinking coffee; her father owns a chicken farm on the other side of town. "Would you like a cup, Christine?" Michael enquired with a slightly embarrassing smile.

"Yes, please. Pamela, I didn't expect to find you here."

"All over the village, what happened to Michael. I thought he might need a friend to talk to. Mother dropped me off this morning while she went shopping."

"Oh! should have phoned me. I'd have come down sooner," Christine smiled, realising her friend lying through her teeth. Pamela tidied her blonde hair standing to look in the mirror over the fireplace, checked her make-up and discreetly slid her bra under the settee with her foot, hoping Christine would not notice. "Back to school soon," Pamela trying to make conversation and not feel awkward. Christine sat quietly, drinking her coffee. Both Pamela and Michael continually glanced at each other, giving the impression they were praying Christine would hurry up and leave. Christine stood, "Must go things to do." Christine climbed aboard her quad bike, surprised by what she'd seen.

"That was close," Michael expressed.

"Doesn't matter, Michael, you're not with Peggy now you're with me," kissing him, "lucky old me," she grinned, retrieving her bra.

Christine's puzzled, wondering why Pamela had not phoned her, not believing in her wildest dreams Pamela's like that. As far as she knew, Pamela and Michael were barely acquaintances at school, and she couldn't imagine her venturing that far on a first meeting. Christine shrugged her shoulders, parking the quad bike by the house, noticing a Ferrari parked by her father's Range Rover. She ran inside to see who, bumping into Jack Potter, who owned an art shop and small gallery in London, studying the portrait Donald had painted of her and her father. Gerald removed the painting for Jack to examine more closely. "Recent work, Gerald, not old with very fine brushstrokes, especially on Christine, the artist, must be in love with her." Jack smiled, glancing at Christine, who turned bright red.

"Any talent in your opinion, Jack; could he make a living. Would you be prepared to exhibit his art on your premises?"

"I need to see more of his work," Jack advised passing the painting to Gerald to hang.

"Jump in my Range Rover, Jack; I'll take you to Crabtree Farm to meet Donald. I will see what other artwork he has so you can assess it better. No good, trying to drive there in a Ferrari, wouldn't survive the cobbled road," Gerald assured.

The three climbed into Gerald's Range Rover, arriving at Crabtree Farm in time for elevenses. Mary displayed a large cake centre of the oak table. Donald came in and introduced to Jack along with everyone else. Jack's shown a portrait in the lounge Donald painted of his parents and grandfather with Biscuit, the dog. "A different painting style again; you are multitalented, Donald. You'd make a marvellous forger," everyone smiled. "You have anything else, Donald?"

"My doodles, but I wouldn't think they'd interest you," he sighed.

Jack smiled, "I'll be the judge of that."

"Take a seat, Jack."

"No, I want to see where you hide; I can judge their importance by how you handle them." Donald sighed, leading Jack into his untidy bedroom. Donald apprehensively walked to his cupboard, slowly passing out half a dozen paintings. "Good gracious, look at that," Jack laughed. "Perfectly captured the night sky and the stars. Donald, I'm taking this one to London; I will frame it. I can see everyone fighting to purchase from my gallery."

Donald shrugged his shoulders, "I painted that one last summer, sat on a stack of bales watching the night sky. I had to be quick because everything kept changing and finished from memory over the next three or four weeks."

They returned to the kitchen. Mary poured a cup of tea for everyone passing Jack a large slice of cake. "Don't argue, Jack. You won't win when it comes to food in this house."

Jack had never seen the sky painted the way Donald had betrayed.

Donald had to ask, "What do you think it's worth, Jack?"

"The start price will be five thousand. You have an exceptional talent Donald and a way to transmit to canvas, and I meant five thousand in your pocket; I'd make mine on top of that. Don't be surprised if that figure doubles; I'm not here to swindle anybody. I'm a multimillionaire in my own right. I do this work for the love of art, not the money. Keep painting, Donald; I can't wait to see what you produce next. Think out-of-the-box as you have with this portrait," Jack smiled encouragingly. Jack stood, "Must love and leave everyone; transport me to my chariot, Gerald; I can't wait to return to London."

Christine kissed Donald on the cheek. Jack commented, "Marry him while he's still available, Christine, mark my words. This lad will do fine if he continues along these lines, and I discovered him," Jack shouted, almost losing his trilby.

Gerald and Christine returned to Strawberry Estate. Jack embraced them both, "Thank you for contacting me, Gerald; I owe you one. That boy will be fine; you mark my words." Turning carefully slid the artwork into his Ferrari, tearing down the drive like he was on a mission.

***

Donald sat at the kitchen table, bewildered, "What's just happened, mother."

"I know, son sounds exciting; keep your feet on the ground. Be yourself; that could be the biggest bag of wind you've ever heard in your life. I can't imagine anybody paying that money for a picture."

"Hey, steady on Mary," Martin expressed, "Artwork fetches enormous prices."

"Yes, it does, Martin, for a well-known artist," Mary glared.

Donald grabbed his cap and walked out of the door and across the fields sitting on the hayrack stroking the old ewes surrounding him. Donald felt his mobile vibrate realising Christine. "Hello, girlfriend," he smiled.

"Would you like to hear some juicy gossip, Donald?" Christine asked, barely able to contain herself.

"You're as bad as my mother," he laughed, "Go on, I'm listening."

"I went to see Michael this morning to ensure he's okay after what happened between him and Peggy."

"Go on, I'm listening."

"Guess who was in the cottage with him?"

"Haven't a clue. I'm sure you'll enlighten me."

"My friend, Pamela Robinson."

Donald shrugged his shoulders, "Why is she there?"

"A good question her explanation, she felt sorry for him and wanted to give him her support."

"I bet!" Donald falls off the hayrack, laughing.

"She tried to conceal her discarded bra under the settee with her foot."

"Is that all she'd taken off? I bet Michael's disappointed."

"You're not surprised, Donald," Christine asked, somewhat puzzled.

"You must have led a sheltered life, Christine; she keeps the rugby team happy," he laughed.

"You haven't! Not with my friend; she's not like that, Donald, is she?"

"I haven't tasted the goods I think most others have."

"Oh! that rather takes the wind out of my sails. You wouldn't go with her, would you, Donald? You're on the rugby team if she offered?"

"Don't be silly, Christine. I could have the prettiest girl in the school with my looks."

"You pig!"

"Why I have the prettiest girl in the school, talk to you later; bye, for now, Christine," he rang off laughing.

Christine stood grinning; he thought she was the prettiest girl. The sun shone quite brightly. Christine released Scooby-Doo, her favourite dog walking along the track. She'd covered quite some distance noticing the daffodils were coming into bloom; everything was lovely in her life. She looked across the fields seen the crops progressing nicely, catching sight in one of the willows; a cuckoo had arrived; one bird she wouldn't mind shooting, not impressed with the way it laid its egg in somebody else's nest.

She continued strolling, staying out for almost three hours before returning to the house. She watched Stephen go down the road with the sprayer and another tractor pulling a water tank.

Christine walked into the kitchen, making a coffee; her father came carrying papers. "I've heard from the solicitor Christine concerning your entitlement to Strawberry Estate. Appears the paperwork is in order. Your mother has signed over the deeds of ownership to you, admittedly not until your twenty-one. I have spoken to Mrs Montague and electronically transferred a million pounds to your mother's account in Switzerland, which should conclude our business with her. Your mother has removed herself from our joint account and hasn't taken any more money, which surprised me."

"Perhaps a little good in the old witch after all," Christine laughed. "You have to call me Miss Gibbs, father; I'm a lady with prospects," she giggled. Susan came into the kitchen. Christine couldn't refrain from smiling, noticing Susan had selected a lower neckline dress, applied makeup again, and wore expensive perfume. "I think I need to go upstairs," Christine commented, running out of the kitchen before bursting out laughing.

***

Donald and Martin removed the last five bullocks from the field they wanted to plough, placing them in an adjacent field. "Careful that tractor is bloody powerful. Don't bend the plough remember, she's articulated or perhaps you should use the County that's in working order now."

"No, I want to try this monster," he grinned.

His father watched him drive off into the twenty-acre field. Donald set off steadily at one side of the field close to the hedge, making his first cut into the turf, which folded very neatly. He could smell the earth; once he'd set the plough, he opened the throttle, no holding back. The tractor pulled the five-furrow plough like it wasn't on the back.

Martin and Mary watch from a discrete position, so they can't be seen watching Donald travel across the field. They hugged each other proud of everything they'd achieved, especially their son Donald. Mary and Martin returned to the house. Donald continued ploughing; he wore his ear defenders, although he enjoyed listening to the sound of the engine. He knew it would eventually damage his hearing, chuckled realising he wouldn't be able to hear Christine shouting at him when he was old, which really brought a smile to his face.

***

Michael had visited the doctors and had his plaster removed; he could finally scratch his arm with relief. He wasn't in the cottage long before his father arrived. Michael invited him in, "Would you like coffee, father?" he asked, trying to be civilised.

"Thanks, son; I've come to apologise. You're not to blame for the situation, are you?"

"Nobody knows for sure; father could be my child," passing his father a coffee.

"You certainly made this place look nice, Michael."

Michael smiled, "Father, I'm not coming home. Mr Gibbs has set me up; I have a vehicle. I have tools. I'm starting my own business, working for him and the Selwyn's."

"That will teach me to open my big mouth before I have all the facts."

"Still could be my child father. Whether or not Peggy and I won't be getting back together. I stayed loyal to that girl, and she couldn't return the compliment; if she strayed once, I'm sure she'd do it again," Michael sighed.

His father held his hand, "I hope we can stay friend's son, and you'll visit our farm occasionally. Your mother and brother will be only too pleased to see you." Michael watched his father sigh heavily, leaving the cottage and removing his mask.

***

Mary made sandwiches and a flask for Donald; she knew he wouldn't want to stop for lunch. He never did, taking out to the field; by 5 o'clock, the field almost ploughed apart from the headlands and a short piece in the far corner. Donald parked the Massey Ferguson in the shed isolating the electrics, seeing Christine and Gerald arrive in their Range Rover. Christine kissed him on the cheek, "Hello, boyfriend," she smiled. Donald picked her up in his arms, throwing her over his shoulder, carrying her into the cottage as if she were nothing.

"Put her down, Donald, behave." Christine smiled, and everyone sat down to enjoy tea.

Donald commented, "Gerald, that tractor you gave us is marvellous to drive. No problem pulling the plough."

"Great, Donald, I'm pleased to do you a favour; how's your painting coming along, young man?" "Slowly, I have other duties to perform. Back to school tomorrow," Donald sighed.

"You have to finish your education, Donald," Martin insisted. "Whether you play rugby, paint portraits or run this farm when your mother and I kick the bucket," he smiled. "Education doesn't hurt. You won't go far wrong with Christine's support."

Christine and Donald glanced at each other, grinning, "She won't have the time, dad, with the ten children." Martin choked; Mary gently patted his back. Donald's laughing, and Christine. Gerald remarked, "I know the way, Mary, I'll go," running down into the cellar coming back with a jug of cider, pouring a large glass for Martin, trying to recover from the comment. He finally caught his breath, "Why ten children, son?"

"Quite simple, father, we'll all be using horses again soon when oil runs out. The labour cost these days, never afford to run the two farms," everyone's laughing, although he could be right. No one knows what the future holds for anyone.

"Don't I have a say, Donald?" Christine asked, grinning.

"Of course, Christine," Donald smiled.

Gerald commented, "That reminds me, thanks, Donald; our diesel tanks are low. Christine, better order five thousand gallons tomorrow, please."

Martin stared, "Five thousand gallons, Gerald?"

"Yes, if we buy now, the prices are usually lower at this time of year and hopefully will see you through to the end of harvest. The new John Deere tractor we purchased can use four hundred gallons daily, and the combines will burn the same at least."

"Thank god we don't have bills like that coming in," Martin sighed.

"Horses for courses, if you are as big as we are, you'd think that quite normal," Gerald expressed, placing a piece of venison on his slice of bread, butter on the other, adding lettuce and tomatoes, a few onion rings. Christine burst out laughing. "What's so funny, Christine?" Gerald asked.

"You have no idea how to make a sandwich, father."

"I'm old school, love. As long as it goes down doesn't matter in which order it ends up in the same place in my stomach."

Mary laughed, "You can kill a pig when you're ready, Gerald. In fact, kill two, then you can hang one at home, and we'll hang one here; the price of pork in the market isn't worth the diesel to transport. We might as well enjoy them here."

"Thanks, Mary; I haven't had home-cured bacon for a long time that will put hairs on your chest, daughter." Donald obviously saw the funny side of the comment and burst out laughing. He leant so far back in his chair he fell over. He scrambled to his feet, looking embarrassed. "While you're doing that, we might as well take one of our bullocks, slaughter. You have half of it, and we'll have the other half here."

"Very generous of you, Mary," Gerald expressed warmly.

Martin commented, "That's paid for the wheel nuts on the Massey tractor."

"Definitely," Gerald remarked.

***

Gerald and Christine travelled home; she thought the evenings were slowly becoming lighter. Christine decided to go for a walk with Scooby-Doo taking her torch, excited about her life. She hoped nothing would go wrong returning home, leaving Scooby-Doo in the kennel realising school tomorrow, not for much longer. She had to decide her future, attend university, which she'd readily be accepted for, or stay on the farm close to her father and Donald. She loved the man in her life. She wondered, is this what she really wanted? She could go to parties every night, take drugs, have sex like the rest of her friends and end up like her mother. She sat up quickly on her bed, feeling a cold shudder run down her spine; the thought of that destiny was definitely not on the cards to try.

She looked out of her bedroom window, seeing a pheasant and two partridges in one of the security lights bringing a smile to her face; how could she ever improve on this life other than with the boy she selected. She realised her mind is sometimes confused and must be because of her immaturity, she suspected. She's sure things would become more apparent to her; she must take one step at a time as her father advised. After all, he's obviously very clever; he'd outwitted his wife, her mother; otherwise, they would be probably broke if it wasn't for his foresight.

CHAPTER FIVE

FORGING AHEAD

Everyone had decided that Martin had recovered adequately; there was no need for Gerald and Christine to come over so early for breakfast. They could have an extra hour in bed before breakfast at Crabtree Farm. Christine would catch the school bus with Donald, and Gerald could continue to work. Mary looked out the window, watching Donald and Christine walk out of the yard holding hands. She thought it rather sweet.

After registration, Christine and Donald ventured to their different classes. Jackie sat by Christine, looking less than happy. Jackie discreetly removed her mobile. Christine stared in horror, seeing a picture of her in the boiler room with Gypsy; her heart sank, realising must be another camera somewhere taking photos. Jackie whispered, "You fool Christine, you shouldn't have hit him; he said if you don't come to the boiler room at break time with me, he's showing Donald the film he took of you performing."

"What can we do, Jackie. I certainly don't want Donald to find out or anybody else. If the headteacher found out, we might be expelled; my father would go loopy," Christine expressed, disheartened.

Jackie shrugged her shoulders, "I'm trapped; you know my parents are Jehovah's Witnesses, and I'm supposed to be one. If Gypsy exposes the truth, I'll be disowned, and the student teacher's career finished. I shouldn't have allowed it to happen, rather carried away at the time."

"Perhaps we should ignore him altogether. If he dared say anything, Donald would probably beat him to death. The trouble is if he saw what I'm performing, I'm finished along with my reputation."

Jackie exhaled, "We'll have to go; Christine, at least we're together." The class finished. Jackie and Christine reluctantly made their way to the boiler room finding the lights on, and slowly descended the stairs. Christine wondered whether better to confess; regardless of the consequences, at least Gypsy would be finished, unable to bribe anyone else, although she suspected her farm would be in flames the same night.

Gypsy appeared from the shadows frowning, "Nice try, Christine; your attempt to destroy the information failed miserably. At least you had the common sense to listen to Jackie's advice." Gypsy passed a packet to Jackie, "I will supply you, Jackie. We don't want any unwanted mistakes, do we."

"No," Jackie replied nervously, fearing what was to come. Christine realised the packet contained the morning after pill; must be at least a hundred pills in the box.

"I hear your father's permitting shooting on the estate; one of my brothers will take the occasional deer left by the top hedge to be collected later. I'm mentioning to you to make sure he's not inhibited; we like fresh meat on the camp, don't worry, we won't shoot pregnant deer, only the stags, rabbits, etc. On my brother's fluorescent jacket, to identify a circle like a bull's eye from the others. He won't want to be seen if possible; however, if one of your employees interferes, I expect you to intervene, Christine."

"Okay, explain to him to stay out of sight would be the solution. I'm not worried about the odd rabbits or deer missing; I'm sure you've harvested our estate for many years."

Gypsy smiles, "You are correct in your assumption. Jackie strip," Gypsy smiled, enjoying having power over someone. Jackie never muttered a word, slowly removing her clothes. Christine watched her remove her blazer, knickers and blouse, releasing her bra patiently waiting; she presumed Gypsy would assault her. "You can go in a minute, Christine. You are mine. I have film safely stashed away," he smiled. "One last thing, Christine, I know you are a black belt in judo. If you ever touch me again, your life will end in so much misery you couldn't comprehend." Gypsy removed a knife glaring at Christine, "You will learn Christine to do as you're told or else." Christine watches someone else come down into the boiler room. She's petrified, suspecting the caretaker only to discover someone she didn't recognise. "Meet my brother Christine," Gypsy smiled. Christine thought she was in real trouble, desperate to escape, not wanting to be scarred by a knife. She watched Gypsy's brother approach, grinning; he had the same colour hair as Gypsy, red, only taller in stature, far more muscular; he kissed Christine. She didn't flinch. He squeezed one of her covered breasts, lifted her skirt, sliding his hand inside her knickers, grinning. He moved away, laughing, dropping his trousers; she watched him ease Jackie down onto a table and thrust into Jackie, lifting her legs in the air. Gypsy's laughing, "You will do as you're told from now on, Christine or face the consequences. We are Gypsies. We do what we like, take what we want, now fuck off."

Christine said nothing, attempting not to hyperventilate, walking towards the boiler room stairs. She glanced back, observing her friend Jackie, shared by gipsies' brother and violently thrusting into Jackie, which she thought must be uncomfortable. Christine turned and ran up the stairs, convinced he would rape her. Christine stepped into the corridor, breathing a sigh of relief. She wondered if she could kill him without anyone finding out and end the misery for everyone. However, his father would still have the photos and film.

Christine could see from the window around 11 o'clock a van had arrived with BBC written on the side; a cameraman and interviewer stepped out. The headmaster ran out to greet the television crew; Christine watched the art teacher and headmaster interview. Donald joined Christine looking out the window. "What's going on, Donald?"

"I don't know; the headteacher has asked to see me."

The headteacher came running into school and down the corridor to Donald. "I had a phone call at 8:30 something to do with a painting you submitted to a gallery," he asked, bewildered. "I explained you attended art classes here. You know what this is really about, Donald. Are you happy to be interviewed? I haven't had a chance to talk to your parents."

Donald sighed, "Must be something to do with Jack Potter, the art dealer; he's raving about one of my paintings he took with him, Sir."

"Come and speak to them, Donald. Good for the school publicity, one of our students was noticed by an art dealer."

"Come along, manager."

The headteacher glanced at Christine, asking, "You are his manager?"

"Apparently so, Sir," she smiled, checking her reflection in the door before stepping outside. The headteacher hadn't realised not only a film crew but the press had arrived, half a dozen photographing Christine and Donald. Reporters shouted, "Smile, your girlfriend."

"Yes, and my manager," he replied.

Christine was annoyed; questions were fired in every direction before she could answer one or Donald. She shouted, "Quiet, please, one question at a time." The headteacher stared at her bold outburst. Nevertheless, had the desired effect. "Your name?" A reporter asked. "Christine Gibbs."

"You're the daughter of Josephine Gibbs. You are a distant relation to the Royal family." The cameras flashed even more.

Christine responded swiftly, "Rubbish."

Another reporter asked, "What inspired you, Donald? You have a name for your artwork everyone is talking about."

"The inspirations relaxation; if I were to give the piece in question a title: Where god Resides."

Jack Potter's running around his gallery like a headless chicken. The phone was red-hot, the press had photographed the painting, and the camera crews visited. He just received a phone call from a reporter stating Donald named the portrait "Where God Resides."

Jack looked at an offer from America for over $200,000 for the picture. He knew the artwork was good, but Donald was unknown to the art world; he never imagined reaching such a price, and sure, that's the end of the bidding. He'd made his commission on top.

"How long have you known Donald Selwyn, Miss Gibbs? Will he be painting you nude?"

Christine responded, "That comment does not really deserve a response. Get your mind out of the gutter; I will not be posing. I've known Donald for some time. We have become very close friends."

"Your father owns Strawberry Estate is that correct, Miss Gibbs."

"That's correct, along with me."

The reporter lowered his mobile after receiving a call. "Donald, are you aware your painting has reached the sum of $200,000?"

"No, I had not! If you gentlemen would excuse us, we are here to learn." Gerald arrived in his Range Rover, speaking to the head-teacher, "I think in light of what is happening, I should take these two home and allow the school to calm down."

"That would be very kind of you, Mr Gibbs; I didn't think the press would be so unreasonable and persistent."

"Donald, Christine in my Range Rover now, please." They both climbed in; Gerald drove off quickly, returning to Strawberry Estate. Everyone silent during the journey; no one had expected Donald's painting to cause such an uproar. He'd imagined fetching a couple of hundred pounds perhaps but nothing else.

"Come on in, Donald, don't stand on ceremony I don't at your place," Gerald smiled; Christine glanced at her mobile, receiving a message from her mother, "Well done, have him in bed. He'll be yours; he's a hunk. If you don't want him, send him to me, he's gorgeous."

"What's wrong?" Donald asked, looking at the expression on Christine's face; she showed him what was written; Donald smiled, kissing her on the cheek, "Don't worry, Christine; I won't attack you this week," he chuckled.

Gerald looked at the message sighing heavily, "I think that says it all, don't you, daughter?" She nodded.

They sat around the kitchen table. Susan made everyone a coffee; Gerald received a phone call from Jack. "I'm sorry, Gerald, things are rather out of hand from what I can see on the news; I didn't give his name or the school he attended. Somehow someone found out, and I want to know how," Jack said, annoyed.

"I will convey what you've said, Jack, to Donald; he's here with me now."

"Thanks. Since he's named his painting, the price is surprising, even I don't believe $250,000 plus my commission. The Americans have more money than sense. Still, help Donald on the farm, buy himself a new tractor or something," he suggested, "Bye for now."

Gerald smiled, "Price is now $250,000, Donald. I don't think you'll have trouble buying the new combine."

Susan jokingly placed her arm around Donald, "Are you looking for an older woman in your life," kissing him on the cheek. Everyone laughed.

Donald sat, astonished his life was changing. He's determined he would not; he loved his mother, father, and friends. "You must let me know how much I owe you, Gerald; all thanks to you and your generosity," Donald exhaled.

Gerald smiled, placing his reassuring hand on Christine's shoulder. "I think if anybody tried to harm Christine, you would break them in half; that's the reward; I'm looking for nothing else, Donald." Donald smiled, "let anyone try," Donald replied, glancing at Christine; he meant every word. To everyone's surprise, Martin and Mary came over in their Land Rover, invited in by Susan. Mary looked extremely worried, holding Martin's arm, glancing up at Gerald and Christine's portrait hanging above the archway. She paused, "My God, does it look good, Martin?"

"I told you, Mary, there is money in paint."

Gerald said, "Don't stand on ceremony; I don't in your place," he smiled. Susan made everyone a coffee, joining them at the table.

"What have I done, mum? I wish I'd never started painting; I don't want all this attention," he sighed.

"We had a phone call from Jack explaining where you were, and he apologised; he's trying to find out how they found out who you were so quickly. He thinks it's something to do with Josephine, but how would she find out?" Mary asked.

Gerald glanced at Susan. "Nothing to do with me, Gerald; honestly, check the phone calls to the house or check my mobile. I want nothing to do with that woman anymore, thank you," standing about to leave.

"Calm down, Susan," Gerald said, placing his arm on her shoulder, "Everyone's jumpy the minute Josephine's name is mentioned. I still think this place is bloody bugged." Everyone laughed.

"Sorry Susan, I wasn't accusing you, accusing anybody because I haven't a clue who's to blame. You're now worth $250,000, Donald," Mary smiled.

"I don't think we have to worry about anything now, Dad."

"Right, this is Susan's kitchen," Mary smiled. "We'll have an early tea, then go home and feed the animals, Donald."

"I haven't enough food to cater to everyone," Susan said, looking somewhat embarrassed, "Usually only Gerald and Christine."

Mary sighed, "Okay, Susan, to my place. You can help me with tea, have some yourself, and put some meat on the bones; otherwise, Gerald has nothing to chase around the kitchen." Susan stared, not believing what she'd heard. Christine placed her hand over her mouth, trying to stop laughing. Mary's already heading for the door. Gerald turned bright red like a beetroot. "No good you, telling me porkies Gerald, I know the signs."

"My god is your wife a mind reader too; on this occasion, she is way off the mark," Gerald spluttered, seeing Susan running for her car. Christine and Donald climbed into Gerald's Range Rover. Mary and Martin returned home in their Land Rover, followed by Susan in her nice car.

Donald and Christine sat in the back seat, staying very quiet. She's trying not to grin at her father, glancing at her in the rear-view mirror. "Nothing is going on, Christine, honestly."

"Does it really matter, Gerald," Donald unconcerned, "Your life?"

"My sentiments exactly, Donald," Christine remarked, holding his hand.

To Donald's surprise, Michael came out of the old farmhouse with his notepad jotting down what would need altering to turn the premises into seven holiday apartments. He joined them in the cottage sitting on a stool at the edge of the table. Mary made everyone a drink and started cooking with Susan assisting. "Make sure you do enough, Susan; you can take some home for your daughter," Mary smiled, "You can bring the dishes back another day. Better still, fetch your daughter; you are only down the road."

"Are you sure, Mary? You don't mind."

Mary shrugged, "Why should I mind, and no one else will."

"Thank you," Susan dashed out of the cottage jumping in her car to collect her daughter.

"Come on, I can work and listen at the same time. I'm a woman; I can do two things simultaneously," Mary laughed.

"Michael, give us the bad news," Martin voiced.

"No bad news, everything is badly organised for what you intend to use the property for now. Most of the heavy work Donald can assist me with." Michael sketched out roughly on paper, "You could have two bedrooms and bathroom the kitchen by knocking down three walls, not load-bearing, so no issues there. You can have four on the ground floor and three at the top. We can utilise some of the attic space."

"What you estimate, Michael, if everyone chips in."

"About £90,000 the walls can be breeze block; we can utilise the floors that are already laid, beautiful timber just needs cleaning, of course, the whole place will have to be rewired which I can do and requires tested by a professional electrician to ensure it complies, and I've made no mistakes, you don't have gas?"

"Yes, we do, Martin. You pass more gas than anyone else I know!" Mary advised everyone grinned.

"The sewage system is already in. I can handle the pipework; not a problem. The roof is sound the guttering requires cleaning. I would leave the exterior of the building. It gives an old farm appearance for these holiday families, who want to come, see old and goldie on the outside but want modern conveniences on the inside. I would also suggest you make signage with no-go areas around the farm. Smoking must be strictly prohibited anywhere on the property."

Gerald clapped, "What a presentation you can work for me anytime, lad."

"I think when I've received the money for my painting that will hopefully cover the renovation cost, let's do it," Donald smiled.

Martin glared at him, "Donald, that's all your money."

Donald shrugged, "Investing, father, and hopefully, you won't have to work so hard anymore. We can go arable; I'll have to have my paintbrush working."

Mary smiled with pride, "I don't think we could wish for a better son, Martin; he's so unselfish."

"Start as soon as you can, Michael," Martin confirmed, "We'll pay you as we go along."

Michael smiled.

Mary walked into the cellar, "Just a small one while the food is cooking." They had a small glass of cider. "I'll give you a lift home, Michael, after having tea with us."

"I can't stay. I have a visitor coming, thanks, Mary."

Donald and Christine grinned. "Pamela, by any chance?"

"Yes, we appear to be getting along; her mother is dropping her off and collecting later," he grinned.

"Jump in the Land Rover," Donald suggested, "I'll run you back. I could nip across your estate. Gerald, would you mind?" Donald asked, looking at him.

"No, carry on, stay on the old tracks," he smiled, watching Donald and Michael leave the cottage.

Susan returned with Teresa, looking very nervous. Mary placed an arm around Teresa, sitting at the table with the usual loving temperament. "You're amongst friends here, Teresa, no worries. I love the way you platted your beautiful brown hair." Teresa smiled, feeling very out of place. Christine asked, "Where are you studying?"

"College for a year, then I'm off to university in Edinburgh specialising in genetics in the hope I can cure illnesses," she smiled.

"Excellent," Gerald remarked, "We need more people like you."

Donald came running in, stopping in his tracks, spotting Teresa; he held out his hand, "Pleased to meet you and welcome to our home." Christine looked at the expression on his face; she felt threatened for the first time. "Why don't you three have a wander around the farm and check the stock while we finish preparing your early tea," Mary suggested.

"Good idea, mum," Donald smiled, helping Teresa with her coat and Christine, if looks, could kill Donald in serious trouble. Christine quickly asked, "You have a boyfriend, Teresa?"

"Oh yes, he's coming to Edinburgh with me. We are studying the same subject," Christine tried not to grin, thinking that trashed your ideas, Donald Selwyn. Christine started to relax, the threat passing; Christine milked the cow, talking to Teresa. Donald walked off to feed the other animals on his own.

They all enjoyed a lovely meal. Susan and Teresa left along with Gerald and Christine.

"You, really sure, Donald, you want to use your money for the alterations on the old house?"

"I suppose I can go out and buy a Lamborghini, but that would be an absolute waste of money and wouldn't earn me anything. At least this way, I am investing for the future if we charge around three hundred and ninety-nine pounds a week or something along those lines, in midsummer for each apartment, perhaps three hundred pounds during the winter," he smiled.

Mary smiled, concerned, "Do we really want strangers wandering around the farm, Donald?"

"Quite simply, mother, they wouldn't be allowed in the building where machinery is stored as long as we have the correct signage. We shouldn't have anything to worry about."

"What happens if it turns out to be a white elephant," Martin suggested, "Nobody comes."

"You could cut down the number of bedrooms in each apartment and have no children's policy."

"I'm beginning to think," Mary sighed, "We haven't thought this through properly, have we?"

Donald rang Michael, "Hello mate, delay any work here for the moment; we are having a rethink; we'll go ahead just deciding one or two options."

"Okay," Michael answered, "That sounds rather ominous. Let me know what you decide. I have plenty of work on Strawberry Estate at the moment. I'll speak to you tomorrow bye."

Martin smiled with relief, "Yes, I was a little hasty. Step back and rethink the project; sleep on it for a few days."

Donald smiled, "I'm off to bed; folks see you in the morning; good night."

Mary made another coffee. "I'm not so sure, Martin. I like things the way they are; I don't want people wandering around the farm," she sighed, feeling Martin's hand on the inside of her leg, making her smile, anticipating what he was after.

"I suppose you're right. Should be no need, really, if Donald keeps painting and making money like that, or just a one-off," shrugging his shoulders.

***

Christine made two coffees after arriving home; her father sat at the table. "Perhaps we should let the cottage next to Michael once he's renovated; what do you think, Christine?"

"An income father everyone we employ as their own house, better if it's lived in."

"I suppose," he smiled.

"I'm off to my bedroom, father," Christine kissed his forehead, slowly ascending the stairs.

Martin received a phone call from Gerald; he would dispatch the pigs and bullock in the morning if that's okay.

Martin replied after speaking to Mary, "Why not." In the morning, Instructing Donald to separate the worst bullock and place in an old stable, Martin and Donald separated two pigs, placing them in another stable before breakfast. Gerald and Christine arrived in his Range Rover. This is a part of farming Christine had never experienced; she'd never been to an abattoir. She had dispatched birds and the odd monk-jack on shoots. This would be a whole new situation for her.

They sat around the kitchen table at Crabtree Farm, having breakfast. Gerald came with knives and a gun to shoot the animals.

Christine asked, "Do you mind if I don't watch father, please."

"No, not everyone's cup of tea."

They went out to the first stable; Gerald loaded his gun. Donald turned Christine into his chest, placing his hands over her ears, two shots. "Over, Christine," Donald said calmly. Martin operated the JCB loader, hanging the two pigs while the blood ran out into buckets. Gerald set about preparing, first burning the hair off skinning, removing the chitterlings and other succulent organs to be consumed later.

Christine ran over to a drain, violently sick. Mary guided Christine into the cottage sitting in front of the television. "Stay here. We'll deal with this; you have nothing to be ashamed of."

Mary ran outside; it wasn't many minutes before Gerald had prepared both animals, slipping one in the boot of his Range Rover and Donald carrying the other down into the cellar where it would hang. Gerald loaded his gun again, the bullock dead hanging from the JCB loader.

Gerald gutted the animal saving all the organs to be used. Anything suitable for the dogs was chopped up into plastic bags and dated they could consume later. Gerald cut the carcass into manageable joints. Donald carried half down into the cellar hanging, placing

Gerald's in the boot of his Range Rover. Gerald smiled, "Not a bad animal, Martin, that should feed us both for some time." Martin nodded, "Yes."

Gerald washed up, placing his knives back in the box. Donald went in to see how Christine was; she looked at him with eyes of sorrow. Donald sat beside her, "Come on, Christine, it's not my cup of tea either."

Gerald came into the room, "You okay, Christine? We'll make our way home, don't worry, only joints in the Range Rover, nothing gross to observe." Christine kissed Donald on the cheek. Gerald and Christine waved, driving out of the yard.

Mary commented, "Poor girl."

Donald sighed, "Yes," hoping she'd be okay.

When Gerald and Christine reached home, he quickly placed the joints in the cellar to hang, a place he hadn't visited for some time, although he had hung the pheasants there in the past.

***

The following day Donald opened the post finding a letter addressed to him from Jack; Donald sat down in his chair. There in front of him was a cheque for £191,000. "Mother, father, look at this." Martin came into the kitchen, and Mary came from the living room. "My giddy aunt," Mary expressed, placing her hand to her mouth, "Far more than I imagined."

Martin poured himself a whisky and one for Donald, "I think you earned that, son, good gracious. Best place in your savings account, son," he said, holding his forehead, not believing the figures.

"A letter here from Jack. Dear Donald, I hope you're pleased with the outcome. I look forward to selling your next piece of artwork. Here's my email address; if you photograph what you're working on, I can assess it from here and decide whether it has any real potential. Please produce something magical, best wishes, Jack."

Donald smiled, entered his bedroom, sat down with his easel and canvas, continuing with the portrait of his sheep and lambs. Suddenly, he was urged to incorporate a starry-lit sky and the old ewes' eyes reflected in the Land Rover's headlights. The scene looks eerie at one stage, with the blood-red sky in the background behind the faraway hills. He looked at his watch, realising 3 o'clock in the morning. Carefully placed the portrait under a sheet and slid into bed. He awoke at 5 o'clock in the morning, dashing out to make coffee. Martin joined him outside, releasing Biscuit, determined not to make the same mistake twice. "We'll take you into the bank; today, Donald, you can deposit your cheque," Martin smiled.

"Thanks, Dad; I have unfinished business in my bedroom. I'm working on a painting; you have a look when I'm happy with it," he smiled.

"It appears you could paint an old sock be worth a fortune," Martin laughed.

They finished the animals seeing Gerald and Christine come into the yard. Donald thought, thank god for the teacher's training day. Christine ran over and kissed him, "Good morning, boyfriend," she smiled.

"Morning, your ladyship." Everyone went inside to sit down for the usual breakfast. After Gerald and Christine had left. Donald returned to his bedroom, carefully uncovering what he'd been working on; he took a photo with his phone, emailing Jack; suspecting he would be waiting until at least 10 o'clock for a response. Within seconds Donald's phone is ringing Jack.

"I'm coming to see Donald. I don't know how you're achieving such splendour; I've never seen artwork like that before; I must see it."

"Jack, you can't come up the drive in your Ferrari; it won't survive."

"I realised that last time I came with Gerald, I purchased myself a new Bentley SUV 4-wheel drive, like a tank," he chuckled. "I'm on my way. Don't breathe on that artwork; I will frame it if good enough," Jack ended the call.

Donald walked into the kitchen. "Jack's driving from London to see my latest artwork; he must be crazy," Donald frowned.

"Can we see, please, Donald?" Mary asked.

Donald shrugged his shoulders, "Nothing special, mum welcome to look."

Mary and Martin entered Donald's bedroom. "You'll have to tidy, Donald pigsty," she frowned.

"The boys an artist," Martin laughed, "They're all like that; I don't bloody care the bedrooms upside down. He's making money."

Donald uncovered his painting. "Pretty Donald, look how the night skies capture the sheep's eyes in the headlights of the Land Rover; mind you, it doesn't matter what we think. It depends on what Jack thinks you must give it a name."

"Wonders of life."

Martin smiled, "I see our sheepdog Biscuit in this one."

"I hadn't noticed," Mary smiled.

Within two hours, Jack had arrived. Mary made him a coffee while Donald carried his canvas into the kitchen. Jack studied, "The oils are barely dry. I'll frame. Oh, I see. That's worth a few quid, mind you. I said that about the last one. Look at the price it fetched far more than I ever expected, Donald; a real surprise pleasant one, mind you." Jack turned to Mary. "By any chance, Mary, you have any of that cake I had last time I was here?"

"Yes, I make it frequently."

"How much would you charge me for one to take home?"

Mary laughed, "I'll give you one; I can soon make another. I'll place it in a large tin."

Jack smiled, "You are wonderful. Something strange happened to the portrait you produced. Although paid for in dollars, it stayed in the UK and went to someone very influential, so I was told."

"You know who purchased in a roundabout way?" Mary voiced, "I bet something to do with Josephine."

Jack laughed, "That would be a turn-up for the books." Donald carried the painting to Jack's brand-new SUV Bentley, carefully placing it in the large boot. Mary put the tin on the front seat,

"Drive careful," she remarked, closing the door and watching Jack drive out of the farmyard. Donald returned to his bedroom, phoning Christine. "Jack has collected another piece of artwork."

"Great, Donald, we'll talk later, boyfriend," she advised, more concerned with looking at her figure in the full-length mirror for imperfections, deciding whether her breasts are well proportioned.

Donald attached the muck fork to the JCB loader and the Massey Ferguson muck spreader to his County. The first time the County tractor had worked since repaired. He wanted to see how she performed, although only muck spreading. Donald started removing the muck from the barn; although very fresh, he hoped the beaters would smash it. He spent most of the day emptying the shed for once; everything was working perfectly; by 5 o'clock, he was reversing into the shed as Gerald and Christine arrived.

She entered the building, kissing him very lovingly, "Hello, boyfriend."

"Hello, your ladyship," seems to be his favourite saying.

"You smell rather strong; I'm not impressed with your aftershave." Donald grinned, picking her up in his arms, threatening to lower her head into a water trough. She started screaming, "Don't you dare. I will never forgive you," he threw her over his shoulder like a sack of potatoes carrying her to the cottage. "Put me down," she ordered. "Otherwise, I shall be forced to defend myself."

Donald laughed, "Do your worst, woman." Christine tickled him; he put her to her feet, "Cheating," he protested, watching Christine run into the cottage. Mary smiled along with everyone else. "Okay, calm down," Gerald advised, "You should never play in the kitchen."

They enjoyed their meal, and Donald's phone rang, "Hello, Jack."

"I'm ensuring your hands for a million pounds," Jack laughed.

"Why?" Donald asked curiously.

"The oils are barely dry your latest creation bidding has reached £10,000 and climbing steadily." Donald flopped back down into his chair, easing Christine onto his knee and placing his arm around her waist. "I'd better acquire a good accountant. I'll be paying the government a fortune in tax."

"Talk to Gerald; I'll help you out finding the right person, don't forget to keep every receipt you can offset against the tax. You could probably use the farm as a tax loss and pay nothing. I'll keep you advised, or better still, log into my website, WW crazy Jack and his art.co.uk. Bye for now."

Everyone looked at Donald; Christine sat on his lap, cuddling up to him. Mary looked to Martin, "We allow this behaviour at the kitchen table Martin."

Martin grinned with his mind wandering down memory lane, "When we were their age, we did a lot worse."

Christine asked quickly, "Do tell."

Mary blushed, "Don't you dare, Martin."

Gerald's splitting his sides, laughing, "I don't care what mood I'm in when I arrive here. I always go home happy," he smiled. "On a more serious note, Martin, have you started placing shares in Donald's name?"

"Yes, make sure he doesn't end up in the same mess as when my father left it a little late, and we had to face a nightmare."

"In which case your tax shouldn't be much; keep a record of all your income and outgoings on paints, electricity everything, canvas all tax-deductible and pay yourself a reasonable wage."

Donald frowned, "What about the old house? I suggest we convert as planned, having seven apartments, I will have two, a wonderful art studio and the other one to live in on the top floor. We will rent the other side as self-contained holiday lets for adults only; that way, we won't have to worry about children running around the farm getting into mischief," Donald suggested.

Mary and Martin looked at each other. "We have to do something with the place before it falls down. Explain why you want to live there?" Mary asked suspiciously.

"Peace and quiet, work on my art somewhere I can entertain, a place Christine and I can have special moments together in the future."

Gerald looked away, grinning; Mary and Martin looked at each other. Christine tried not to smile.

"We appear to have a plan, Martin, with our son," Mary remarked, making everyone a coffee.

"I think, send the four remaining bullocks to market this Thursday, dad. I will plough a further hundred acres; that way, I should leave a hundred acres to grass; buy a few store cattle and feed them on barley, put them in the yard to overwinter to fatten. Perhaps have a couple more pigs," Donald smiled.

Martin and Mary looked at each other. "Sound like a plan, son; you're not putting all your eggs in one basket," Martin suggested.

"No, we could convert part of the barn into a grain store; I will purchase a good second-hand combine for the two hundred acres plus a couple of trailers. Donald glanced at Gerald, "I'm not ungrateful for your offer to use your Lexion combines; however, if we have a bad season, the last thing you'll want is to move one of your combines over here and permit your crop to be ruined. Now I have sufficient funds, it makes sense."

Gerald frowned, "You're galloping on ahead here, Donald everything you said makes sense; I'm not offended by your comment. Have you any idea how many acres our Lexion combines harvest in a day? You can't spend, spend, Donald; you must always have reserve finances for the unexpected disaster, and there's usually a few you should know that."

Mary remarked, "listen to Gerald, Donald and your father before spending your hard-earned money. It may not come so easily in the future; besides, by the time you've finished paying for the alteration on the old house, you won't have a lot left, I shouldn't imagine. I can tell you something for nothing, Donald; you are not placing this farm in debt when you've earned the money you can spend," Mary glared.

Donald turned on his mother, "Look what your penny-pinching has achieved! My father with a knackered spine, old before his time, and you're not in much better condition, mother."

Mary rose to her feet, enraged slapped Donald's face hard, "How dare you speak to us like that? Get out until you come to your senses, boy."

Donald rose to his feet, saying nothing to no one walking out of the door. Christine jumped to her feet, running after Donald.

"A smart move, Mary," Martin voiced, disheartened.

"He will not speak to me like dirt, and I'm not borrowing money your father never did, neither did mine. We manage until we have sufficient funds."

Gerald sat quietly, thinking everything Donald said made sense. The way his artwork was selling, he could easily afford his plans, which Mary hadn't appropriately considered. Gerald sighed, "Time to go home," standing up from the table, "Thank you both for a lovely meal," he walked out of the door.

Christine and Donald sat on a bale, mopping the blood from his nose. Mary had struck Donald with some force. "You okay, Donald?" Christine asked.

"I guess not; nothing turned out the way I planned."

"I have to go, Donald," kissing him on the cheek, running and jumping in her father's Range Rover. Gerald and Christine glanced at each other, "Very uncomfortable, love," Gerald commented.

"Yes, poor Donald. I think Mary misunderstood Donald, saying he's using his own money, not theirs."

"That's how I understood to love. I think Donald is working on the principle he would sell more paintings to cover the cost as they went along; he wasn't saying rush down the bank and take out a loan."

"I don't think she should have hit Donald like that; admittedly, his comment was harsh. Unfortunately, the truth they work themselves into the ground running the farm. They have nothing to show for it really other than Donald."

"I think that's a fair assessment, Christine, like me, old school, don't like to borrow. Farming can be so unpredictable. You never know what's coming around the corner to bite you in the arse," Gerald smiled. "Like your mother for instants." Christine smiled as they returned to Strawberry Estate. Susan's busy tidying the kitchen. Christine ran upstairs, pausing so far up, glancing through the window into the kitchen, seeing her father place his arms around Susan's waist, kissing her on the neck. She placed his hands on her covered breasts permitting him to fondle for a moment easing out of her bra altogether. Christine hadn't realised the relationship was progressing so rapidly.

Christine wondered when he would say anything to her. She smiled, continuing to her bedroom, not wishing to see anymore. Christine sat at her dressing table for a moment, deep in thought, deeply concerned about the film taken of her in the boiler room, trying to think of how she could destroy the evidence. She glanced from her bedroom window to the dog kennels seeing her father and Susan in the feed store. She guessed her father hadn't realised; he was in direct sight of her bedroom. Curiosity is killing her as much as she didn't want to watch her father perform; she couldn't look away. Christine hadn't realised how large Susan's breasts were until she watched her father unzip Susan's dress, laying her on the straw; he's certainly taking his satisfaction without any protest from Susan, who wrapped her legs around his back.

***

Donald released Biscuit from his chain, walking through the ewes and lambs, trying to decide what he wanted. He could so easily rent a flat and paint and give up the manual labour, sending most of his family to an early grave if they weren't careful.

Donald removed his mobile, taking interesting shots of rabbits playing on logs. An enormous buzzard swooped down and snatched an unsuspecting rabbit flying away.

That put everything into perspective. Here one minute gone the next, simple as that, life is like Russian roulette for everyone despite the technology. He slowly walked to the farm, chaining Biscuit; he ran inside his kennel, laying down on his warm blanket.

Donald walked to his bedroom, not speaking to anyone locking his door. He started painting the scene of the buzzard snatching the rabbit and turning the sky dark in his portrait. Not a moment to be celebrated. He tried extremely hard to capture the intricate feather structure; the bird struggled to fly away, carrying the squealing rabbit.

Mary knocked on Donald's bedroom door, "Lunch will be ready in ten minutes, Donald." He didn't bother to reply, engrossed in his painting. "Donald," his mother shouted again, "Come along, Donald."

He took a deep breath and walked into the kitchen, sitting quietly at the table, eating his meal. When he'd finished started heading for his bedroom. Martin asked, "When are you ploughing the other field?"

Donald shrugged his shoulders, continuing to walk to his bedroom, locking the door behind him. Martin looked to Mary, "You really put a spanner in the works, Mary."

She shrugged, "I don't care; he will not speak to me that way. Who does he think he is?"

"You appear to forget Mary; Donald can walk out of the door and not look back, he has sufficient money without us, and I can't run this bloody farm on my own. If you hadn't been so quick off the mark, you would have realised what he's saying as he earns money for his paintings; he would improve the farm. He wasn't asking us to run off down the bank and borrow money. You didn't like it because he spoke the truth, his father's a wreck, his mother's not much better, your hips will fail in due course." Martin walked out of the cottage to the machinery shed, taking out the Massey Ferguson and plough, enjoying the solitude and starting to plough a ten-acre field.

Donald was engrossed in his painting by 5 o'clock, tea on the table. Martin was already ploughing in the dark, not wishing to return to the cottage.

Mary sat patiently at the table, looking from the hallway window and seeing Martin ploughing a job Donald usually loved to do. She's surprised Gerald and Christine hadn't arrived; they were generally on time for meals. Mary knocked on Donald's door, saying softly, "Tea is ready, Donald," he didn't reply. Mary returned to the kitchen and poured a cup of tea.

Gerald and Christine walked in the atmosphere thick; you could cut it with a knife. Sat quietly eating their tea. Donald came from his bedroom, sitting by Christine, squeezing her leg under the tablecloth. She grinned. "I'm painting another picture," he smiled.

Gerald said, "At the risk of ending a good friendship, will you grow up and start talking, resolve the issue. Donald had merits, and you, Mary, for christ's sake, if you expect me to come here in this atmosphere, you're joking," he said, standing. "Christine, in my Range Rover now!" She kissed Donald on the cheek suspecting Mary would explode any minute. They passed Martin in the doorway; he guessed something had happened by the expression on everyone's faces. Martin sat at the table, "Oh wonderful, I should have stayed on the bloody tractor less troublesome than the sulky wife and son."

Mary reiterated, "I will not be spoken to like dirt Martin. I won't take it from either of you two."

"Okay, mum, I'm sorry," Donald said, frustrated. "I'll solve this problem once and for all. I will move out in a few days; find somewhere. You can have this farm and choke on it." Donald rose to his feet. Martin stood, "Calm down, son, think about what you're saying."

"I have dad all afternoon; I want a life of my own I don't intend to end up as a cripple over a farm if I were you, dad. Sell the lot and get out while you can walk."

Donald returned to his bedroom, losing himself in his artwork.

Mary and Martin sat quietly, looking at each other, realising they may have ignited a situation they couldn't defuse. "Give him a few days to settle down," Mary suggested.

Martin laughed, "I think you really put your foot in it. He's leaving; I saw that look in my father's eye when he meant something," Martin sighed. "Your only hope Christine, she may be able to turn him around; I'll speak to her," Martin suggested, dialling a number.

"Hi, Christine; Martin, big favour love. Mary's dug her heels in so has Donald. Donald threatens to leave and throw the towel in. Could you possibly talk to him?"

"I will try Martin, bye."

Christine phoned Donald, "Hi, boyfriend," she grinned.

"Hi, your ladyship," Donald smiled.

"You realise, Donald, you haven't taken me out all the time we've been together, not to a restaurant to the pictures, shopping perhaps," she advised.

"Be ready in half an hour; I'll change, go into town, your ladyship."

"See you in a minute or two, don't keep me waiting," she laughed.

Donald's phone for a taxi changed quickly; without speaking to his mother or father, he walked out of the cottage and climbed into the taxi. Mary and Martin looked out the window, seeing him disappear. "Pray Christine can turn him around, or we're in deep trouble," Martin frowned.

Gerald asked, "Where you going?" seeing her dressed to kill, looking absolutely gorgeous.

"Trying to prevent Donald from walking out on the farm for Martin."

Gerald laughed, "looking like that, you should be locked up," he smiled, seeing her slipping on her denim jacket. "Don't be late home, young lady, midnight or else."

Donald arrived in the taxi. Christine ran out, sliding on the back seat with him, heading for town parking in the centre. Donald paid; they started walking around, entering a coffee shop. Much to their surprise, Pamela and Michael sat at a table. Michael waved they joined them. "You appear to be enjoying life, Michael," Donald suggested, looking at the beaming smile on Pamela's face.

"Life couldn't be better, mate; I live on my own I have my own business, thanks to Gerald. I have a girlfriend, and so do you, by the looks of things." Donald nodded, placing his arm around Christine's waist, which she enjoyed immensely. " I've fallen out with my parents," Donald expressed, explaining events to Michael and Pamela.

"Oh, that's terrible news," Michael said. "What are your plans?"

Christine spoke, "He has no plans; he is staying at home; he will calm down and give his parents a chance to catch up with his ideas, won't you, Donald," Christine glared.

"You heard her ladyship." Christine placed her hand on his leg and squeezed gently.

"I think Christine is giving you good advice, Donald. I wish I'd have thought things through better than I had, although I enjoy living independently. I'm fortunate my father came around, and we made friends."

"Yes, I suppose you're right. Everything exploded, probably my fault," Donald sighed.

"Doesn't matter who's to blame," Christine assured, "No real damage done; kiss and make-up and move forward," she said, kissing him.

They spent the next two hours wandering around town with Michael and Pamela, looking in jewellery shops and pausing for what Donald considered unreasonable amounts of time. Staring into clothes shops, looking at the latest fashions that were of no genuine interest to him.

Christine noticed how Pamela's dressed; she wasn't leaving much to the imagination. Christine thought she had pulled it off wearing a miniskirt and extremely tight blouse making sure all her attributes were on show. Unlike herself, she preferred her warm jeans blouse and jumper with her denim jacket and a comfortable pair of shoes.

11 30 p.m. Caught a taxi sharing the cost dropping Michael and Pamela off at the cottage before continuing to Strawberry Estate. Donald quickly kissed Christine, watching her run into the house, and proceeded home to Crabtree Farm, settling upon arrival. He entered the house, finding his mother and father sitting at the table. "I hope you enjoyed yourself, son?" Martin asked hesitantly.

"Yes, thanks; I shan't be moving out for the moment. Is that okay with you? I would like to press ahead with the alterations to the old house. I will cover the cost, and then I'll have a decent studio to work in and live there." Mary made him a coffee, kissing him on the cheek. "You'll have to excuse me, mother father; I have a painting to finish, school in the morning," he sighed.

Martin and Mary were relieved their son wasn't leaving. Donald had explained to Michael how he wanted the two rooms upstairs laid out, one for his studio and his own apartment. Donald continued working on his painting until 4 o'clock in the morning; he couldn't put his paintbrush down. He realised he could do better with professional equipment and would ask Jack for advice on what to purchase to produce marvellous paintings. He needed the best equipment and suspected it wouldn't be cheap, especially the brushes and oils.

Donald ran around feeding what few animals were left in the morning with Martin. He made his way to catch the bus missing Christine. He boarded the bus; she was not on board arriving at school. Christine stepped from her father's Range Rover, greeting him with a kiss on the cheek. "I see I'm not good enough to travel with woman," Donald smiled.

"I have an extra half-hour in bed if my father transports me to school," she smiled.

Christine asked with curiosity, trying to ascertain Donald's thoughts, "You see how Pamela's dressed, Donald?"

"Yeah, I wonder how long before she's pregnant, she's certainly displaying what's on offer," he grinned, receiving a jab in the ribs.

"You're not supposed to look, Donald."

"Why! You girls do that to entice boys, so don't play sweet and innocent with me."

"I have never done anything like that," she protested earnestly, "Always dressed appropriately."

"I'll give you that, Christine. You always look like an old granny," he smirked, running off laughing, suspecting she would be furious at his comment.

Donald phoned Jack explaining he had a painting ready and could he send canvases, paintbrushes and oils. "I'll be down by 5 o'clock this evening," Jack replied, "I'll transport what you need. Could you possibly ask your mum to make me one of her cakes, please?"

"No problem, Jack, bye."

Donald texts his mum, explaining Jack's coming at five and will she make him a cake; Donald puts several kisses at the end of the message to ensure his mum knows he loves her. Seeing the exes, she saw the message, which brought a broad smile, noticing Michael come into the yard on Gerald's quad bike.

Martin came into the cottage. Michael unrolled his plans for the old house on the kitchen table so they could see what he'd planned in detail. Mary made Michael coffee cutting a large piece of cake, making him smile. "I presume we can keep these drawings Michael to show Donald?"

"Certainly, and if you are all in agreement, I will start work Saturday morning. Donald is desperate to have his studio built. I can understand why. Have you seen the newspapers?"

Mary and Martin looked at each other, "No!"

"You remember the last piece of artwork caused quite a sensation; I think the one up for sale is excelling." Michael took the newspaper from his jacket pocket several pages inside, a picture of Donald's painting with the caption: "Is this the next Vincent Van Gough?"

Mary placed her hand to her mouth. Martin remarked, "That boy is talented. Yes, press on, Michael; if everything is agreed with Donald, his rooms ready first, you can work on the others later, can't you?"

"Yes, I've catered for two more builders in my quote to speed up the process," he smiled.

***

Donald and Christine strolled into assembly. The headteacher requested, "Could Donald Selwyn come onto the stage, please."

Unsure of what was happening, Donald climbed the steps at the side of the stage and made his way to the headteacher. "I would like you, students, to realise your full potential; if you turn around to face the back wall, you will see what Donald Selwyn has achieved." Displayed on a large screen were his two paintings. "Not only is

Donald an excellent rugby player, but an artist, taking you from one extreme in life to the other. I hope this makes you students realise anything is possible. We each have a talent, and Stratford Academy is here to help you realise your full potential. If you want to talk to Donald, he would only be too happy to assist. Thank you, Donald." Donald returned to Christine feeling the skin melting off his face with embarrassment.

Gypsy had slipped a note into Christine's hand; she quickly read, ripping it into small pieces gripping tightly in her hand. She left assembly, heading for the boiler room, discarding the note in a wastepaper bin. Christine quickly descended into the boiler room twenty minutes before she had her first lesson in mathematics; the teacher wasn't tolerant of late students. Gypsy stepped from behind the boiler into the light. "What do you want, Gypsy! If I'm late for mathematics, I'll receive punishment."

"Father wants a hundred gallons of diesel red diesel. We can take the colour out at our campsite."

"How am I supposed to hide a missing hundred gallons of diesel Gypsy?"

"My brother said the bowser was filled the other day on your farm. We know everything that happens. Make sure the shed door is unlocked; leave the lock in the clasp, and we'll snap it shut, Christine."

Christine took a deep breath, "Okay, I'll unlock the storeroom at 8:30 p.m., leaving the padlock for you to fasten after you leave."

"Good, your learning Christine," he gently patted her cheek; she didn't flinch. He moved closer to her kissing her on the lips. Christine did not react, although she wanted to break him in half, fearing that she and Donald would be finished if she had. Her life is finally coming together apart from this problem, which she would have to resolve one way or another. Gypsy left the boiler room. Christine followed shortly after.

At the end of the school day, Donald watched from the coach window as Christine climbed into her father's Range Rover heading for home, not bothering to wave to him, which he thought strange.

The bus started with a jolt, finally pausing at the bottom of his drive. Donald stepped off, walking to Crabtree Farm. Much to his surprise, Jack's there unloading his Bentley, filled to the brim with art materials; they greeted each other. "How much do I owe you, Jack?"

"Four thousand pounds for the materials; I'll deduct from your painting which has presently reached fifteen thousand pounds, bidding a lot slower on that one. Quickly show me what you have for me," he said, excitedly rubbing his hands together.

Donald dashed into his bedroom, uncovering his latest artwork. Mary stood in the doorway, remarking, "That's real, looks alive; about to fly off the canvas, Donald."

Jack stood spellbound, "I have never seen work like this before; you'll be a millionaire by the end of the year; mark my words. The oils aren't dry the bird is almost frighteningly alive. You feel the eyes looking through you. Be very careful when you place it in my boot Donald; I will frame it." Mary followed Donald outside, carrying a cake tin with Jack's cake; she placed it on the front seat taking the empty one he had returned. "I must go. You are astonishing, Donald, astonishing."

***

Christine ran upstairs feeling somewhat depressed; she wasn't with Donald. She released Scooby-Doo from his kennel, quietly walking along the lane, wondering whether she dare walk over to Crabtree Farm. She carried on along the tracks passing the cottage where Michael lived. She peeped in the window to see if anybody's home. To her surprise, Pamela and Michael were making out on the carpet by the fire. Christine could hear Pamela shrieking from outside; she suspected Michael well blessed or experienced in lovemaking. She watched for a few moments. The speed he's making love to her is unbelievable; he certainly didn't have a bad back. She stepped away quickly, not wishing to be seen, shocked; Pamela was no older than her. Christine strolled to Crabtree Farm, wondering if Pamela's mother knew what she was involved in. Christine wondered if she was jealous; she's of legal age to have sex. Nothing stopped her, only herself control; it crossed her mind that Donald wasn't finding her attractive, or perhaps she wasn't enticing him. He'd commented she was dressed like a granny made her smile. Christine sighed heavily, walking across the road and up the drive to Crabtree Farm, placing a lead on Scooby-Doo, not wanting her dog and Biscuit to fight.

She tied her dog to the barn door, knocked on the cottage door, walking in. Mary grabbed her. Martin explained, "You had a word with Donald; he's in his room painting."

"Mary, can I have a quiet word with you first, please?" Mary could see Christine's somewhat troubled inquiring calmly, "What's the matter, love? I'll see if I can help?"

"I don't know, Mary, what to do. It appears most of my friends my age are experimenting with sex. I walked past the cottage where Michael lived and looked in the window, and Pamela and him, well, you know, I step back quickly, so they didn't see me," she sighed heavily.

Mary made them both a coffee expressing, "I don't know whether you've heard the expression peer pressure. You see what happens with sheep one goes; they all follow regardless off a cliff. You don't have to do anything you don't want to do or feel you are not ready. I hope Donald doesn't pressure you; I'll kill him," Mary frowned.

"No, nothing to do with Donald; he's never laid a hand on me other than to kiss me, which is fine. I don't want to rush into anything."

"You answered your own question, don't, and if he doesn't like it, tough luck, it wasn't meant to be, do whatever you want to do, Christine. You will have my full support," Mary said, kissing her cheek, "That's it, smile. Eighteen before I allowed Martin to touch me, that wasn't until I had an engagement ring on my finger."

Christine laughed, "You're so good to talk to Mary; I wish my mother were like you."

"There's an old saying Christine, wish in one hand, poop in the other and see which weighs the heaviest." Mary laughed, seeing Donald coming into the kitchen, immediately smiling, seeing

Christine. He picked her up in his arms, "Kiss my ladyship," he smiled. "Michael starts work on the old house tomorrow; my art studio soon and accommodation. Once that's finished, your surprise will come," he grinned.

Christine looked at him, "What, surprise?" Donald shrugged his shoulders, "Wait and see. You can come to watch me paint if you like."

"I can't. I have Scooby Doo tied up; I walked over here."

"Too dark to walk home; I'll take you in the Land Rover."

"You be careful, Donald crossing the road; we don't want any accidents or trouble with the police." "Okay, mum," he said, kissing her cheek.

Christine placed Scooby-Doo into the back of the Land Rover, and Donald drove off.

***

Susan's busily tidying in the kitchen. Gerald came in, sitting at the table reading the newspaper. "Would you like a coffee, Gerald."

"Might as well you know where Christine is by any chance?"

"She went for a walk with Scooby-Doo, dark out there, Gerald. I hope she won't be much longer." Gerald rang her number, "Where are you? Dark outside."

"Donald's driving me home in the Land Rover. I walked over to Crabtree Farm."

"Oh, okay, love, see you in a minute or two," he smiled, realising that everybody was friends again. Susan kissed Gerald on the cheek, "I'm going home now, Gerald; I'll see you tomorrow morning."

"Okay, Susan, thank you very much. Susan, I'm off to Gloucester Sunday morning. Would you like to come, just you and me?"

"Okay," Susan replied, trying not to look too excited. "What time."

"I'll collect you from home about nine; no better still, you come here; prevent any gossip." She nodded in agreement and walked to him, kissing Gerald, patting his cheek, and leaving.

Donald dropped Christine and Scooby-Doo off at home, parting with a loving kiss. Christine looked at her wristwatch at 7:30 p.m. She would have to put her skates on. She quickly kennelled Scooby Doo running into the house, shouting in the direction of the kitchen, "Homework, do not disturb, please, father."

She heard him reply, "Okay, you should have completed it earlier."

Christine locked her bedroom door, quietly opening the window and shuffling along the window ledge to a large drainpipe. She carefully climbed down, checking she had her torch and keys in her pocket for the store. She glimpsed through the kitchen window seeing her father sitting at the table. She's away from the house, along the track to the building, an eerie place in the dark tin rattling and hooting owls. She could see no one around. She found the key for the padlock unlocking the store. Christine turned about to leave, confronted with a torch shining in her eyes. "Do you mind," Christine protested, petrified? Christine immediately recognised Gypsy's voice. He removed the keys from her hand, lowering his torch to a piece of clay, taking impressions of the store key. "We can come and go as we please until somebody realises what's happening, and of course, you won't say anything, Christine will you."

"No, give me my keys, and I can go home, please."

"You haven't met my father, have you, Christine." She's pushed inside the store, and the door shut. "No," she answered, panicking. Gypsy switched on the light in the store; Christine found herself in a heap of trouble. She could probably fight her way out, but that still wouldn't solve the issue of pictures and films. Gypsy's father was similar in stature, only with more muscles. "So, your Josephine's daughter, I have fond memories of her before she moved to France; perhaps I will have fond memories of you in the future," he smiled, leering.

"Over my dead body," Christine expressed firmly. Christine watched the door open four other men entered, carrying jerry cans filling with diesel from the bowser. "Over your dead body, you say, that can be arranged, Christine, although your mother wouldn't be impressed, and if something happened to cause your death, the back-lash would outweigh the gains." Gypsy threw the keys to Christine, standing aside along with his father. Christine left the store shining her torch, running for her life in the direction of home.

***

Donald steadily drove, returning to Crabtree Farm, looking forward to using some of the new oil paints Jack had supplied along with the paintbrushes and canvas.

Donald ran into his bedroom, sorting through what Jack had delivered, looking on his mobile at the pictures he'd taken of Christine. He sketched her on a large black stallion, searching the Internet for a suitable model to copy, coming across a horse called Jerusalem.

He thought what a lovely name and a beautiful animal checking on the Internet to select the suitable clothing, his surprise for her, using his skill with background and vibrant colours. He imagined the mountainside in the distance with lightning striking the fore-ground. He spent two hours perfecting her eyes the way he wanted her to look, the woman in control of his life.

He made a sign sticking on the outside of his door do not dis-turb. He worked until 5 o'clock in the morning like he was pos-sessed; the girl drove him crazy, and he had no idea why. He's pleased in some respects; she hadn't realised how much she meant to him. She could so easily make his life a living hell. Donald grabbed an hour's sleep, waking still in his pyjamas. He continued to paint; he spent hours ensuring her hair, every single strand, was in place, a test of his skill to the limit. The biggest canvas Jack provided, swallowing paint like it's out of fashion; Donald not caring.

Mary had seen the notice on his door and guessed it must be something important. As much as she disliked him not having break-fast, she realised he was making money to secure the farm, their live-lihood and future. Gerald and Christine arrived at 5 o'clock for tea, after Mary had phoned them concerned. If anyone could approach Donald, Christine, without causing a blazing argument, she hoped.

Mary kissed Christine on the cheek, "I have no idea what he's painting. I'm extremely worried, Christine; I wonder if painting drives him insane."

Christine smiled, "No, he's concentrating, Mary." Christine walked to his bedroom door and quietly knocked, "Donald, it's me, Christine. Can I come in, please?"

"No! Not yet, give me an hour," he said calmly. Christine was surprised by the response, and she returned to the kitchen. "He wants another hour; Mary must mean an awful lot to him. I can't wait to see what he's working on."

Gerald remarked, "Something to do with you, Christine; otherwise, he'd have let you in."

"He wouldn't paint nudes of me," she said, looking shocked.

"Mary smiled, "No, he wouldn't dare; he knows that would really upset you, must be patient. Be worth the wait." They sat quietly, eating their tea.

Donald finally staggered from his bedroom, exhausted. "Coffee, please, mother and something to eat; I'm starving." Everybody laughed, seeing him plastered in oil paints on his hands, face, and hair.

Christine asked, "What are you painting?"

"Look, but don't touch. I haven't finished; I shouldn't allow you to see; I have some minor adjustments to make."

Christine rushed to Donald's bedroom door and stared in disbelief. She screamed, collapsing to the floor. Mary joined her, not believing what she saw, followed by Gerald and Martin. Christine broke down in tears, "My mother's horse Jerusalem. I remember her purchasing him; she used to let me ride him; he died of a sudden heart attack, broke my mother's heart, how you know of the horse you've never seen him," Christine cried.

She glanced at Donald's computer seeing the horse on the screen. Gerald assisted Christine into the kitchen; tears ran down her cheeks in astonishment. Gerald offered, "I will give you a hundred thousand pounds for that portrait, Donald."

"Sorry, Gerald, not for sale."

Christine looked at him, "You painted that for me?"

Donald smiled, "I wanted to show you how much you meant to me; that's why it must be perfect before you have possession. Give me another day, and you can have teatime Monday."

"My god Christine I must contact Jack to frame," Gerald insisted.

"Not for sale, Gerald, no matter what anyone offers," Donald assured. "I hope you feel the same way, Christine."

"I promise you I will never sell my painting," she dashed back to the bedroom, standing in the doorway staring in disbelief, wondering how Donald could have made her look so perfect and Jerusalem. He'd never seen her on a horse or Jerusalem, for that matter, in the flesh.

"I apologise, mother, father," Donald said calmly. "I couldn't stop painting; I felt almost compelled and possessed. Excuse me, everyone, I'm going to my room," he said, leaving the kitchen after finishing his tea.

Christine ran over and kissed him passionately, "I love you, Donald," releasing him to continue his work.

Donald smiled; hearing those three words, he glanced back, "The feeling is mutual, Christine," he closed the door quietly. Christine looked at her father and smiled. "Mary, your advice is sound. You don't have to be like everyone else to achieve what you want."

"That's a fact, young lady," Mary went down into the cellar, returning with a jug of cider. Christine laughed, "We must celebrate with paint stripper."

***

Early the following day at Strawberry Estate house, Christine had made breakfast for her father and herself the usual marmalade on toast; he took a deep breath, "Off to Gloucester today, taking Susan with me."

Christine grinned, "What a surprise," she said sarcastically.

"Just so you know, Christine, I've signed over the estate lock stock and barrel to you when you reach the age of 21 like your mother, so whatever happens, this will be yours," he smiled.

"Oh. Thank you; suppose something happens in the meantime?"

"I've had a quiet word with Mary when you weren't in earshot, giving her and Martin power of attorney until you reach 21. God forbid that situation ever arises."

"Brilliant father, the one person you can trust is Mary. She's helped me out no end of times with decisions."

Gerald stared, "Really."

Christine nodded, "Women's things, none of your concern."

"Oh, okay," he smiled. "That reminds me, keep this information to yourself. If something should inadvertently happen to me, notify my solicitors. They will start the ball rolling, so the place runs smoothly until you take full control."

"Thanks, father. What you intend to do with Susan, Mr, and Mrs Smith situation," she chuckled, "Bed-and-breakfast or hotel."

"Nothing of the sort. A pleasant day out slowly is the keyword, and cautiously," he remarked, seeing Susan park her car jumping in the Range Rover. Christine commented, "Have fun," winking at her father, making him blush; he set off for Gloucester.

***

Jack arrived at Crabtree Farm to collect the painting for framing for Gerald; he didn't look pleased. "I'm a little disappointed, Donald, "he smiled. "You know how much your last painting has reached?"

"No, you mean the one with the buzzard and rabbit?"

"Yes."

"Five thousand pounds," Donald replied.

"One million five hundred thousand pounds so far, the bidding is open for another week on my website. I want to see what you're giving away," Jack remarked, walking to Donald's bedroom.

"Oh my god, I anticipate that's worth two million if not more; just look at those brushstrokes. You should be locked up; artists out there would kill for half your talent," he professed. Jack returned to the kitchen table. Mary poured Jack a cup of coffee, cutting him a large slice of cake. "May I make a suggestion when your latest painting dries? Would you allow me to make prints, say a limited edition of 1,000, so others can share this beautiful portrait, still not for sale?"

"I don't own it. Speak to Christine."

Christine entered the door after parking her quad bike around the back. "Ask Christine what, Jack?"

Jack explained; Christine looked to Donald. She held his hand, "Okay with me, boyfriend, if okay with you? At least that way, others will see your beautiful talent; could you send one to my mother, Jack, please."

Jack smiled, "Absolutely, young lady, my pleasure."

Donald asked, "Would you send me more paint, Jack?" He smiled, devouring the slice of cake on his plate, "You could name this portrait, Christine, if you wish," Donald kissed her cheek.

"Can only be called Jerusalem; there is no other fitting name," Christine remarked, drying her eyes.

CHAPTER SIX

What are the secrets

Donald carefully loaded his artwork into the boot of Jack's Bentley, and Jack drove off towards London. Christine turned to face Donald kissing him, and glanced over to the old farmhouse seeing builders frantically renovating for Donald to move into soon. Donald jumped on the back of Christine's quad bike, riding with her to Strawberry Estate and sat in the kitchen drinking coffee. Josephine walked in displaying her warm, inviting smile, dressed in a pink skirt with a cream blouse, short but not distasteful; she looked beautiful.

She held out her hand, which Donald accepted nervously, anticipating a blazing argument by the look on Christine's face. "You must be Donald," Josephine expressed with an inviting smile.

"I'm pleased to meet you," Donald responded likewise.

"Coffee, daughter, please. You're the young man the art world is raving about. My daughter has made an excellent choice; I have seen most of your artwork outstanding," she smiled.

Donald commented, "You are like your daughter in appearance."

Josephine blushed, "You flatter me, Sir. I believe you have discovered my horse Jerusalem on the Internet?"

Christine looked astonished, "Nobody knows. How can you possibly, mother?"

"Jack sent me a photo of the portrait, graciously presented to my daughter by you, Donald. You, Christine, asked Jack to send me a copy which I look forward to receiving."

That made sense to Christine but not why her mother was here. "I can see the question in your mind, Christine; why am I here?"

"Yes, mother, why are you here?" Christine observed her mother displaying most of her thigh to Donald, ensuring her attributes were on show.

"I miss you. I know we don't communicate hospitably, daughter; I am still your mother. I was in London; I thought I'd pop down on the off chance you'd be civilised to me."

"I'll leave you, Christine, to have time together with your mother."

"You will not, Donald Selwyn," Christine glared.

"Oh," he half-smiled, feeling awkward.

Josephine patted the back of Donald's hand, "You'll become a custom to her sharp tongue Donald. On the off-chance, Donald would you consider creating Jerusalem in oils with me on his back," she smiled invitingly. "Apart from my daughter, the horse is the only thing I really loved," she smiled.

Donald stood, stepping back, taking several shots with his mobile. Josephine's quite happy to sit and be photographed. She stood seductively, smiling, unbuttoning her blouse, "Would you like to study my vital statistics closely, Donald? I'd hate you to have my measurements disproportioned."

He grinned, watching Christine glare. "Mother!" Christine protested, watching her mother tidy herself, smiling. "I should imagine your vital statistics similar to your daughters. You are both beautiful, so that will be fine," Donald tried not to smile, realising Christine's livid.

"I misjudged you, Christine," Josephine kissed her daughter on the cheek. "You certainly know how to select a man. Jack is of the impression that the portrait you refused to sell of Jerusalem would venture over two million," smiled. "Don't worry, I shan't sell mine either. Where is your father, Christine? Is he on the estate somewhere I can see Susan's car! You're joking," Josephine remarked as she realised what was possibly happening. "With her of all people, I suppose beggars can't be choosers," she frowned.

"Not what you think, Mother," Christine assured, glaring.

"No peace for the wicked off to France, of course, Christine, you know I own an estate in Scotland. You should take Donald there may give him some fresh ideas for a painting," she remarked, patting her daughter's cheek.

"Thanks, Mrs Gibbs," Donald replied to the invitation, "Very kind of you."

Josephine remarked, "Donald, we'll soon be related," she grinned, lifting her eyebrows.

Josephine walked over, kissing Donald on either cheek. Once on the lips. "Scrumptious daughter, bye for now," she grinned, commenting, "I look forward to seeing my painting of Jerusalem."

Donald called out, "How shall I contact you when finished?"

"Inform Christine; she'll contact me." Christine and Donald followed Josephine out to her Range Rover. Christine kissed her mother on either cheek, "Nice to see you when you're sober."

"I'm pleased to have met you, Josephine, have a safe journey," Donald smiled warmly.

"Won't take long, Donald, these days on the shuttle. If you ever become bored with England and fancy spending some time in France, I'm sure some interesting things to paint over there." She grinned, kissing him once more on the cheek, climbing into her Range Rover, waving, smiling as if she'd had the cream off the milk, heading down the driveway, excited by the sparkle in Donald's eyes.

Christine turned on her heels, pushing Donald, "You enjoyed that, didn't you," Christine shouted. Donald started laughing, "Enjoy what?"

"Don't look innocent, you pig." Christine stormed to the house. Donald sighed, heading for home. Christine realised he wasn't following her. Livid and decided not to run after him.

She sat drinking coffee, thinking how ridiculous she behaved; her boyfriend presented her with a portrait valued at over two million pounds, worried about his sincerity. She noticed Oliver standing at the door. She quickly ran, looking somewhat flustered. "Why are you here, Oliver?"

"Having a walk, I haven't seen much of you at school. You appear to be avoiding me," he suggested.

Christine grabbed his arm and closed the front door; she went to the stable block. "You can't be seen here. My father will go mad," she professed, worried.

Oliver started kissing Christine; she didn't resist. She'd had feelings for him for some time. Most of the girls liked him. She could feel his hands wandering as he passionately kissed her. She allowed him to continue for a while, realising she was cheating on her boyfriend and would be classed no better than her mother. "No, Oliver," she said, tidying herself. "I have to go my father's due home in a minute. Don't allow him to catch you here; I'll see you at school," she fastened her bra, removing his hand from her knickers. Christine hurried off to the house. She realised her blouse was grubby. She'd acquired dust from the old stables; she looked at her bra, in no better condition. She would have to change before her father came home but enjoyed Oliver holding her immensely. Christine's aware many girls at school had sex with him, determined not to be a pushover.

By 3 o'clock in the afternoon, Gerald had returned. Susan stepped from the Range Rover, jumped in her car and drove off.

Christine came out to greet her father, expressing, "Guess who visited today."

"Not Josephine," the smile left his face.

"Yes, she met Donald and commissioned a painting of Jerusalem; she's all over him like a rash." Gerald laughed, "Your jealous daughter; she doesn't stand a cat in hell's chance with Donald."

She stamped her foot. "I scolded him; he walked off," she sighed heavily.

"Jump in my Range Rover, you silly girl." They drove over to Crabtree Farm. Mary had made coffee already, laughing. "I heard I don't blame you, Christine. Donald thought, hilarious the expression on your face when your mother kissed him."

"Where is he, Mary?"

"Trying to find somewhere to hide in his bedroom, starting on the portrait for Josephine, you might as well stay for tea. How is Susan, Gerald?" Mary grinned.

Christine grinned, "I didn't say anything, father," she expressed, trying not to laugh.

"Most of her lipstick is on your neck, Gerald."

Gerald ran to the mirror, "Damn, I thought I'd wiped everything off," he expressed, embarrassed.

"I suspect in a gateway somewhere, Mary." Mary started laughing. Gerald ran to the bathroom. Christine and Mary sat down almost in tears laughing at Gerald's embarrassment.

Martin came in after feeding the animals, "At long last, you can see in the evening; summer will soon be here and more hard work."

Mary patted him gently on the back, "Come on, old man, I'll make you a coffee," she smiled.

Gerald returned, "I'm rather concerned about Josephine suddenly arriving unannounced. Of course, she could be telling the truth. She wants to see her daughter!"

"More like she wanted to see Donald in the flesh," Christine expressed.

Donald came out of his bedroom. "I thought I heard your voice, Christine. September father, mum, I'm finishing school. I don't see the point in continuing; I don't need the qualifications. I have work to do here," he said, looking at their expressions.

"I suppose," Martin said, "I would have liked you to continue your education, Donald. However, your future is pretty secure."

Gerald asked, "Christine, what are your plans?"

"I'm not attending university, father; I don't need the education; I have the estate to run with ten children to raise." Everyone burst out laughing. "I'll stay on in school until I'm eighteen, perhaps see how it all pans out. I'm beginning to think Donald is ashamed of me, father; he hasn't taken me out," she grinned.

"Right, finish eating, and off to town, your ladyship."

Gerald laughed, "Just like her mother always has her own way."

"Oh, I'll have to go home and change Donald," Christine professed.

"No, you won't."

Gerald gave them a ride into town. "I want you home by midnight, young lady," Gerald cautioned, driving off.

Donald grabbed Christine's hand, taking her by surprise. Never expected him to hold her, especially if anyone saw them from school. Much to Christine's astonishment, Donald escorted her into a jewellery shop. "You buy what you'd like, Christine."

She stared, totally surprised, "What a beautiful gold necklace and earrings, blimey! Look at the price, two thousand pounds."

Donald placed his credit card on the counter, "I'll take that, please." Christine immediately put her hands to her cheeks, saying, "No, Donald, you mustn't," Christine watched the jewellery packed in their individual boxes.

"You didn't have to buy me anything, Donald, although beautiful," she smiled; Donald grinned, placing his arm around her waist. Christine thought about purchasing a ring and decided not to force the commitment issue in case Donald felt pressured. Donald stopped in his tracks, noticing the television shop window displaying his portrait of Jerusalem and Christine. They both stared, unable to hear the sound gathering from the picture, Jack Potter's art gallery broken into. Christine phoned her father, "What's happening, father? Have you seen the news?"

"No," he said, switching on the television, "Somebody has broken into Jack's art gallery and stolen Jerusalem. The police think that's all they came for, cash left untouched and the other paintings."

"Okay, father, speak later. They stole my painting, Donald," Christine sobbed.

Donald sighed, "I would immediately blame your mother, but she commissioned her own work."

Christine noticed a text message on her phone from her mother. "Don't worry, Christine, my friends and I will recover your artwork. Leave the problem with me," finishing the message with several kisses.

Christine showed Donald the message suspecting the portrait would be returned anonymously. Christine and Donald waved down a taxi heading for home. Donald dropped Christine off at home, and he continued to Crabtree Farm. Mary and Martin sat at the kitchen table, "We've heard, son."

Donald shrugged his shoulders, walking off into his bedroom to continue his commissioned work for Josephine, sitting quietly applying oils to the canvas. The following day after breakfast, Donald caught the school bus. Donald's surprised to see Christine hadn't arrived by 9 o'clock. He phoned her, somewhat concerned. "Hello, boyfriend. I forgot to mention the dentist this morning; no worries, I love you; Donald, don't worry, my mother will find my portrait with her contacts."

Donald's not feeling quite his old self. However, he played in a rugby match only to find himself waking in the hospital, a surprise nothing ever stopped him as a rule. His mother sat beside him, worried. Donald smiled, "What happened?"

"Good question, Donald. You collapsed. You're not a girl. You don't faint; you crush people," she smiled.

"Mrs Selwyn, could I have a word with you, please?" the doctor asked, walking away from Donald's bed.

"We need to run more tests to confirm what's on Donald's lung. We'd like to keep him here for a few days and carry out further tests, it may be nothing, but it's better to be safe than sorry."

"Whatever you say, please save my son," Mary expressed, petrified, fearing cancer.

The doctor asked, "Has anyone in your family or your husband suffered from cancer?"

"No, neither of us," she confirmed.

"That's good news," the doctor and Mary returned to Donald's bedside. He looked at their expressions. "Cancer?" he asked.

"Not confirmed a spot on your lung; we are trying to ascertain what it is, don't jump to conclusions. You will remain here for a few days while we conduct tests." Donald nodded, accepting his fate.

Mary slowly returned home. Martin stayed on the farm, suspected broken arm or something silly, and rugby was a brutal full-contact sport. Martin saw the expression on Mary's face as she poured two coffees. "What! What's wrong with him?" Martin asked suspiciously.

Mary burst into tears, "They found something on his lung, unsure if it's cancer, keeping him for a few days for tests."

Christine phoned Crabtree Farm, "Donald's mobiles turned off. I can't reach him, Mary; I've been home all day."

"He's in hospital, Christine; the doctors have discovered something on his lung."

"I don't know what to say! Mary, maybe nothing; I hope it's nothing. There'd better be nothing wrong with him." Christine burst into tears ending the call. Dropping in the armchair, Gerald came running over, kneeling beside her, "What's the matter, Christine?"

Christine explained. Gerald poured two drinks, "I thought life was going too well for us. Let's hope nothing," he sighed, expecting the worst.

Christine ran to her room, lying on her bed; all her hopes and dreams were wrapped up with Donald. If he perished would be destroyed. Christine quickly ran downstairs, "Father, will you take me to the hospital? I want to see Donald please?"

Gerald looked at his wristwatch, "They won't let you in, my love, until 6: 30"

Christine sighed.

"Only an hour, my love. Be patient." She ran upstairs, carefully placing the necklace he purchased around her neck and attaching her new earrings. She looked at herself in the mirror, deciding that life was sometimes too short and unfair.

Gerald and Christine drove to the hospital, seeing Martin's Land Rover parked. They slowly made their way upstairs, stopping at reception. "Where is Donald Selwyn? We are good friends."

The receptionist answered, "He has a private room over there." Christine knocked and went in; massive and had every convenience you could imagine. Donald's parents are already there, sitting around a large table. Donald smiled brightly, seeing Christine and Gerald.

"My word, this room, Donald," Gerald voiced.

"Nothing to do with me, Gerald or mum and dad; Jack has arranged for a private specialist to see me in the morning, carry out a few more tests and hopefully, I can come home."

The television was on, although the sound was turned down; a picture of Jerusalem and a reporter suddenly appeared. Mary quickly increased the sound. "Donald Selwyn's portrait entitled Jerusalem discovered today by special branch about to board an aeroplane for the United States. The man and woman involved were international smugglers wanted by police for many years. An anonymous call from France to the police led to the arrest, detained at Scotland Yard for further investigation. The painting will be returned to Jack Potter; its value has reached four million dollars and is rising by the day since its disappearance. We believe the artist is presently in hospital undergoing tests."

Jack came into the picture, "I would ask the press to leave Donald alone. He needs to rest. I've had over a million well-wishers on my own computer. Thank you all."

A nurse knocked on the door, walking in, "Mr Selwyn."

Donald and Martin both answered, "Yes," making everyone laugh.

"We are swamped with well-wishers sending flowers."

Donald spoke, "Share them around the wards, especially with the elderly; please, nurse, I'm sorry I'm causing you a problem."

She smiled, "You're no problem, Donald Selwyn," she winked.

Christine felt her mobile vibrate in her pocket, "Damn, I didn't turn my mobile off." Christine studied the text from Josephine, "Said we'd find it!" She conveyed with kisses; Christine showed her father and then Donald. Christine texts, "Thank you, mother," with kisses.

Christine commented, "You're enjoying yourself, Donald; I saw how that nurse looked at you, buster."

Donald grinned, "You have nothing to worry about, Christine; a little treatment if actually cancer, making sure I have no secondary infections around my body."

After an hour, heading for home, Christine felt more relaxed now she'd seen Donald in the flesh. She wondered how her mother traced the portrait; royalty had their own contacts and network. If one wanted the portrait, it would never have been seen again. She couldn't believe how her mother was behaving, going out of her way to help Donald and her.

Finally, peace and quiet. Donald contacted the horse breeder he'd spoken to for the last couple of days, trying to trace any mare or stallions sired by Jerusalem, the horse Christine and her mother loved. "Hi, Donald, I hope you're feeling better; all over the news, the painting you produced of Jerusalem is the spitting image of his son, The Rising Sun. Apparently has a good temperament, is easy to ride, and was used to sire one or two mares. According to the vet, he has no heart issues they can find, like his father. Everyone believed bad luck for a better reason for him suddenly dropping dead. To be quite honest, Donald, you couldn't separate The Rising Sun and Jerusalem in likeness."

"What's he worth."

"The Rising Sun's stud fees plummeted since Jerusalem, his father struck down. They were over a hundred thousand; now, around ten thousand pounds. People are very wary of unexplained death in animals. To be quite honest, Donald, I think if you offered twenty-five thousand pounds for him, you'd be in with a chance."

"Could you handle it for me, Derek, please? If you're successful, arrange for transport to Strawberry Estate; the new owner will be Christine Gibbs."

"She must be exceptional, Donald, for you to lash out that sort of money and give away a portrait worth two million, if not more."

"I don't know how much time I have left. I was delaying the purchase until I asked her to marry me; I'm moving everything forward in case, you know what I mean," Donald sighed.

"Don't worry, Donald, you'll recover. I'll be in touch."

Two days passed, and Donald was undergoing test after test; he felt almost like a pincushion. Donald received a phone call from Derek, "Your lady is fortunate; she is now the proud owner of The Rising Sun, the son of Jerusalem. I will arrange for delivery Saturday morning at Strawberry Estate. I take it you want to be a surprise."

"Thank you so much, Derek; what's the damage?"

"They were happy to settle for twenty-one thousand five hundred pounds. I won't charge my usual fees. You're a pleasure to work with transport fees are a thousand pounds, travelling in style," Derek smiled.

"Do you want me to pay you over the phone, Derek?"

"No, okay, Donald, I know you're good for the money; how long are you in the hospital for."

"They reckon another two days, I may have to start treatment," he sighed.

"I'll pop round. You're only a hundred miles from me; come down with Jack, old mates. If you are one of Jack's friends, you must be something special."

***

Early Saturday morning, Christine replenished the birdfeeders on the lawns; she loved to sit on her windowsill watching the little birds come down for the seed.

Gerald's in the kitchen reading the newspaper. Christine watched an enormous horsebox turn onto the drive; she suspected the driver must be lost. Gerald came out hearing a vehicle approaching.

Christine approached the driver's door and electrically operated his window; he smiled politely. She asked, "Are you lost?" Joined by her father.

The driver smiled, "Strawberry Estate and you are Miss Christine Gibbs, I presume?"

"Yes," Christine answered, puzzled; the driver passed her the paperwork.

Gerald stood behind her, reading over her shoulder, "My god Christine, Donald's lying in the hospital, and all he thinks about is you. You own the son of Jerusalem." They watched the driver slowly unload; you couldn't distinguish between The Rising Sun and Jerusalem.

Christine hugged the horse's neck. The driver spoke, "A beautiful horse with great temperament. You have all his medical reports and stud fees; my employer Derek Baldwin asked me to give you this letter."

Christine examined it quickly, placing her hand to her mouth. Gerald gasped himself.

"Please don't repeat to Donald; the reason you have the horse now is in case he doesn't recover. He'd planned to give you on the day he proposed to you, Christine. May you have many years of enjoyable riding; the Rising Sun is a beautiful horse."

Gerald made the driver a drink before he left for Somerset, where the horse had resided for three years. Christine led her horse to the stables at the back of the house. Found bales of sawdust and hay to ensure The Rising Sun was comfortable for his first night on Strawberry Estate.

Christine returned to the house sitting at the kitchen table, not believing what Donald had gifted her. Gerald sat at the kitchen table, "That boy astounds me; he showers you, Christine, with every gift possible. You realise Christine, you are worth over three million in gifts alone?"

"I know, father, he doesn't have to."

"He knows Christine because he wants to, oh that reminds me. The Rising Sun's saddle, bridal and blankets are in the hallway. You'll have to tidy the tack room Christine, not used since Jerusalem died." Christine finished her drink heading outside.

Susan commented, "Donald's really serious about Christine, isn't he, Gerald."

"Yes, of course, and I think you can safely say the feeling is mutual," he smiled. "You know something I don't, Susan?" Gerald asked cautiously.

"No, I think he's putting all his eggs in one basket, both very young. You know your own mind at that age, Gerald?"

"I thought so when I first saw Josephine. God, the woman, gorgeous; she could melt my socks any day," he smiled, reliving events in his mind.

Much to everyone's surprise, in walked Josephine. Susan moved and left the room quickly. Gerald turned to face Josephine. She kissed him very lovingly, expressing, "Hello, husband," she smiled, sitting on his lap, placing her arm around his shoulders, and kissing him again. "Do you remember Gerald, when I used to sit on your lap before Christine was born, and you carried me upstairs to the bedroom?" she smiled.

Gerald couldn't help but laugh. "I bet you couldn't do that now," she grinned.

He picked her up in his arms, carrying her up the stairway. Susan had listened to the conversation and was not impressed. She thought she had one foot in the door and was unsure now.

***

At Crabtree Farm, Martin and Biscuit had rounded up the remainder of the breeding ewes to be transported to market. Finally loading the lorry, saying goodbye to a bad back, and watching the ewes head off for the market. As soon as the lambs were fat, it would be the end of sheep on Crabtree Farm. Martin reached down, patting Biscuit, "Whatever happens, Biscuit, you're staying."

***

Donald started to dress, the spot on his lung something he'd inhaled while driving the combine harvester without a cab. He breathed a sigh of relief; it could have been worse. Donald thanked the doctors and nurses for their kindness walking out of the hospital. He climbed into a taxi, not bothering his mother and father, too much to do on the farm.

***

Gerald and Josephine came laughing and joking downstairs, heading straight into the kitchen to make coffee. Josephine commented, giggling, "You're in good working order, husband."

"Thank you, I'd forgotten how good you look. We seem to spend too much time arguing," he grinned, slapping Josephine's backside as she tidied her mauve dress and matching jacket.

Gerald made coffee, glancing at the window to see Susan had gone shopping. Christine came running in, stopping dead in her tracks and looking at both their expressions, suggesting, "You've either been fighting or upstairs. Your hair is untidy, unusual for you," she commented, wondering what's going on, nothing making sense.

Gerald laughed, "You remind me of the old matrons in the hospitals. They were tyrants forever cracking the whip."

Josephine walked over, cuddling Christine, "lovely to see you, Christine; I said your portrait would be found."

"Yes, thank you, that is appreciated; I suppose you already know I own The Rising Sun." Her mother stepped back in shock, "No, I didn't know he's the son of Jerusalem."

"He arrived this morning. Donald purchased him for me as a present because he knew I loved Jerusalem like you."

Josephine grabbed Christine's hand, "Show me," running out of the house together, laughing. Gerald sat at the kitchen table smiling; mother and daughter both enjoyed horse riding.

***

Donald arrived home, greeted by his mother's loving arms. "What the doctors say?" she asked eagerly.

"Inhaled something while combining without a cab; years ago, I think they called it farmers lung not wearing a mask."

"You are not using that bloody old combine again. Have a new one, a good second-hand one with a cab," she insisted.

"How is the renovation progressing, mother?" Donald asked eagerly.

"Come and see," they walked over to the old house, carefully climbing the stairway to the upper floor. Michael busily installed the plumbing the area vast. Michael stopped work, wiping his hands, "Pleased to see you, Donald; yours as soon as I finish, about two or three weeks, and you can move in. Unfortunately, you will have to put up with the noise below while continuing the renovation."

Donald smiled, "I'm sure it will be great when you finish, Michael. How are you and Pamela?"

"That's over with; I'm afraid when I saw her step out of an old boyfriend's car," he sighed. "Apparently, I'm the child's father, a boy," he smiled. "Peggy phoned me yesterday offering the DNA results. My family think I should give her another chance," he said, shrugging his shoulders.

Donald patted him on the shoulder, "I'm sure you'll make your mind up, don't rush into anything, Michael; I'm here if you need me," Donald smiled.

"Thanks, mate," Michael returned to his plumbing.

***

Josephine patted The Rising Sun's neck, "Beautiful animal, Christine."

"Yes, wonderful mother, I haven't phoned Donald and thanked him. How rude of me, I've become lost in recent events, the horse arriving, my mother turning up. What a wonderful morning," she expressed, smiling.

"Why don't you ride him to Crabtree Farm? Allow Donald to see you on him."

"I thought perhaps allow him to settle for the day, mother."

"No, he'll be fine like his father, Jerusalem."

Josephine helped Christine saddle. "Go steady and make sure you keep your hardhat on, no showing off."

Christine smiled, "Thanks, mother, I love you."

Christine slowly rode The Rising Sun across the fields crossing the main road without any issues, entering the yard at Crabtree

Farm. Mary glanced from the kitchen window and told Donald, "You have a visitor." Donald came from his bedroom seeing Christine on her horse; he immediately greeted her. He helped her dismount, and she removed her hardhat, kissing him passionately.

"You are a crazy man. Thank you so much for my present you're spoiling me, Donald. What have the doctors determined?" she asked, concerned.

"Nothing really; I inhaled something probably harvesting without a cab, disease farmers used to have many years ago called farmers lung. Thankfully doesn't happen very often these days, and I'm perfectly okay," he smiled reassuringly.

Christine tied her horse to the railings holding Donald's hand. They went into the cottage; Mary embraced Christine. "A beautiful horse."

"Yes," Christine responded, "and one fortunate girl."

"Come watch me paint if you wish, Christine."

"Okay, I can't stay long. I want to ride my horse around the estate and show off," Christine smiled. Donald and Christine entered his bedroom. Donald picked up his paintbrushes and continued working on the portrait he started of Josephine sitting on Jerusalem.

Christine removed her riding jacket, observing Donald placing his brush.

Mary entered carrying two mugs of coffee left on the table beside Donald, leaving his bedroom, shutting the door quietly.

Christine's unsure of what to do. She wanted Donald to kiss her and show him she cared for him. She's grabbed by other boys before and immediately shunned their advances apart from the unfortunate instances she's involved in, out of her control. Christine sat sipping her coffee, watching him paint. She kissed him on the cheek, his concentration not wavering; she kissed him again. He smiled, "I do love you, Christine."

She smiled, realising he wasn't expecting anything from her, quite the opposite. He wanted to be with her. "I must go, Donald," Christine advised, kissing him.

"Okay, if you see your mother inform her that her painting will be ready in two days, she will have to arrange to frame herself, sure she won't mind," Donald smiled.

"No, that's fine, Donald; thanks once again, boyfriend, for my beautiful present," she kissed him lovingly on the lips, feeling his strong hands grip her waist. If he threw her on the bed at this precise second, she would not resist him in the slightest, she thought, leaving the bedroom.

Christine mounted The Rising Sun, trotting out of the yard and crossing the minor road onto Strawberry Estate. Allowed her to study the crops in more detail; the horse caused minor damage. She could see Stephen spraying in the distance; the oilseed rape had recovered from the winter and was growing rapidly. The harvest approaching wouldn't be many more weeks now. Christine finally returned to the stables placing her saddle in the tack room and brushing down her horse. Feeding and watering ensured he had plenty of wood shavings to lie on rather than the old straw method.

She started walking towards the house, glancing through the lounge window and seeing her mother and father behaving like teenagers on the settee making love. She stepped away, wondering if the relationship was on again. Christine considered Dixon's why her mother initially misbehaved? Perhaps feeling guilty, but she couldn't imagine her mother feeling guilty over anything.

***

Donald continued to apply oils to his canvas thinking about Christine; he realised if he'd stopped painting when she kissed him, he wouldn't be able to let her go. He wanted to make love to her but would only do so on her terms. Besides, Donald didn't know if she was taking any precautions. The last thing he needed was to be irresponsible in the heat of the moment and ruin everything he had. Donald heard the clock chime at 4:30 a.m. Leaving his bedroom, venturing outside to help his father feed the lambs and the pigs.

Donald released Biscuit. He ran around like a charging bull, excited to see him. Donald started walking across the field, meeting his father returning with the Ferguson 20; he jumped on the trailer for a ride. Martin put the tractor in the shed. "The grass is growing, son. We'll have about fifty acres to bale this year, fifty acres of milling wheat to cut and fifty acres of straw to bale."

"Something else we could consider having veal calves only raising to twelve months. We could buy cheaply from dairy farmers as they are considered a by-product in many cases."

"That's not half a bad idea, son, have to work some figures out at home. Don't forget we could have barley beef if we wanted," Martin smiled.

"You can do whatever you want, father providing my paintings continue to sell; we will have money to play with."

"Your money Donald; I know you spent a considerable amount on Christine. Don't try and buy her son. It won't work," Martin cautioned.

Donald nodded, "Crossed my mind; I went a little wild."

Martin smiled, "You sort of paying them back for their kindness several times over. " Martin grinned, providing us with the tractor, planting the crop and their encouragement turning you into a wonderful artist," Martin grinned. "Sort of swings and roundabouts, Donald."

"Mother won't be thrilled with me Monday," Donald sighed.

Martin stared, trying not to grin, "What have you done, son?"

"I sold the bloody old combine and purchased another second-hand one, only one year old and something for you and mum personally."

Martin gently smacked Donald behind the head, "What make of Harvester Donald?"

"International with a forty-five-foot header."

"Good make, son."

"Comes with warranty, dad."

Martin smiled, "Clever lad, we have an agency less than five miles from us, so they're on the doorstep, and why you purchased from them."

Donald nodded, "Plus, it has all the latest gizmos, which I will need a degree to understand," he grinned.

"What have you purchased for mother and me?" Martin asked cautiously.

"Not saying you two have to wait until Monday morning, delivered along with the combine."

"Donald spent most of Sunday finishing off the portrait of Josephine on Jerusalem in front of Strawberry Estate house. Donald attended school, as usual. Monday morning, seeing Christine dropped off by her father. Donald walked over, "Morning Gerald, Josephine's portrait is ready for collection. If you see mum, she'll give it to you," Donald smiled.

"Okay, have a good day," Gerald drove off.

Christine kissed Donald on the cheek, expressing, "I don't know quite what's happening at home. Mother and father seem to be sociable, which I find strange," she advised looking puzzled.

"Well, face it, Christine, your mother, is a stunning woman like her daughter," Christine grinned, not saying anything continuing to her classroom.

During the first two periods, Donald's playing rugby back to his usual self. Doctors had placed him on a course of cholesterol pills saying his cholesterols off the scale and may have resulted in him collapsing.

***

At Crabtree farm, Martin and Donald had decided the old sheep barn would be converted to store grain. Martin spoke to Michael, "could you lay a concrete floor here so we can store the grain? Make sure the fall is to the door. We don't want water running into the grain."

"Okay, should have all the accommodation finished by the end of June, then I'll concrete the floor here, Martin."

***

Susan turned into work, surprised to find Josephine still there. Josephine made coffee, making sure Gerald was not in earshot. "Susan, you will not have my husband," she expressed with a purpose in her voice.

"You'd led me to believe Josephine you finished with him?"

"Not quite yet, I'm undecided, young men okay; usually all over in a flash, hardly worth the trouble," she smiled, drinking her coffee.

Susan nodded, saying nothing, wondering if she should say anything to Gerald and would he believe her or conclude sour grapes.

***

Gerald called in at Crabtree Farm. Mary made him a coffee. "I suppose you've heard Josephine has returned home for how long, I don't know," he sighed. Mary sat down, holding her cup, "What's her game, Gerald?" Gerald stared at Mary. "I know what Josephine was like before you married her, Gerald. She nearly robbed you of everything you work for, including your daughter Christine; she suddenly returns sweet and innocent. She has an ulterior motive, Christine. She stated; clearly, you weren't good enough the first time around. What's changed?"

Gerald stared, "You don't mince words, Mary. You think she's up to something?"

"I wouldn't be surprised. I suppose I could be wrong. Have you considered how poor Susan feels? That may be why she's returned; there's more than one way to skin a cat." Mary glared, "Maybe her intention to separate Christine and Donald was her original plan to take her abroad. She knew Christine wouldn't leave Donald. However, Christine might change her mind if Josephine could rock the boat. There's food for thought, Gerald."

"I'm an old fool, Mary," he sighed. "I don't want to cause any unnecessary unpleasantness."

"Put bluntly, Josephine wouldn't give a shit if you drop dead tomorrow, as long as she could achieve what she wanted. She's unconcerned about what damage she leaves in her wake, how you think people like that made their money years ago, Gerald bred into her. Look at your history with her. Come on, man, wake up, for christ's sake."

Martin came in, "I can hear you halfway down the yard, wife, now you see what I have to put up with Gerald," Martin duct as Mary hits him with her towel.

Mary made Gerald another coffee along with Martin. "Just when I thought life's turning around for me," Gerald sighed.

"If anybody else Gerald other than Josephine, I would have said good luck. Susan is less devious than her, although she has a few skeletons I've checked with my friends," Mary grinned smugly.

Gerald and Martin sat patiently, waiting for her to continue talking. "Come on, wife, spill the beans; you've perked our interest."

"No, I'm saying nothing."

Martin laughed, "That will be a first," finishing his drink and running out of the door, laughing

Mary entered Donald's bedroom, carefully carrying out the portrait of Josephine sitting on Jerusalem. She placed it on the sideboard. "Look at that woman Gerald for a moment. Donald has captured every feature, including her bloody-mindedness. You can see by her expression; that she would cut you in half and not think twice. Unlike the portrait of Christine, they may seem similar, but they're not. You have a look when your home Gerald, you will see exactly what I'm saying. For a boy to pick that up, and he's only ever met your wife once saying something, isn't it."

Gerald nodded slowly, "I've seen that look before; I suspect I've messed things up with Susan by now, permitting Josephine to stay in the house and other things." Mary carried the portrait into Donald's room, followed by Gerald; Mary turned to face him. He kissed her lovingly on the lips. Mary smiled, watching him place his hands on her large, covered breasts. "No, Gerald, no more," she walked past him out of the bedroom, looking in the mirror and tidying her hair.

Gerald loaded the painting into his Range Rover, "Thanks, Mary, for straight-talking. I've looked through tinted glasses again, not facing the truth." Gerald climbed into his Range Rover, heading home slowly, trying to decide the best course of action.

10 o'clock when Martin heard an engine; he looked down the drive seeing the International Harvester combine approaching the buildings. He ran into the house, grabbing Mary by the hand; she placed her hand over her mouth, "When you buy that?" she scolded.

"I didn't. Donald has sold our old combine."

"Looks brand-new and cost a fortune."

Martin shrugged his shoulders, "Donald purchased, not me."

For the first time, he wasn't having the blame for something. The combine parked on the side of the drive-by the buildings. Within a few minutes, a brown Range Rover came up the drive, followed by another vehicle. The Range Rover was parked by Mary. The driver jumped out, holding a bouquet of flowers, "Mrs Mary Selwyn?" passing her the flowers.

"Yes," she said nervously, "Your birthday tomorrow, I believe, a present from Donald Selwyn," he passed the keys.

Mary looked at the registration plate, "Brand-new!"

"Yes, our demonstrator with every extra you could think of and carries a full-service package your find there are only fifty miles on the clock."

The guy ran off, jumping into a waiting vehicle. Mary dried her eyes, saying, "I'll kill that little bugger wasting his money," she grinned, sliding into the luxurious front seat, feeling the heater warming the vehicle, unlike their old Land Rover. Martin heard his old Massey combine start and gently drive out of the shed heading down the drive. Martin asked, "Have you left anything cooking, love?"

"No, I haven't started, Martin."

"Good, take me for a spin, wife," he fastened his seatbelt. Martin realised he'd forgotten Mary's birthday in all the mayhem over the past month. "Take me into town, wifey," he grinned.

Martin never saw Mary smile so much in his life apart from when Donald was born. They parked in town, Mary still in her slippers, guided by Martin into the jewellery shop. "Choose something, wife." The salesperson looked at her standing still, wearing her pinny and long hair in pigtails. She selected earrings for fifty pounds.

"That's all you want, Mary?" Martin asked.

She nodded, "I will remember this day for a long time Martin." She smiled, left the shop, and climbed back into her Range Rover, enjoying driving home feeling the warmth instead of a draft. She parked her Range Rover by the kitchen window where she could study, removing the key she locked. "You can use the bloody old Land Rover. I want my Range Rover kept clean," she smirked.

***

Josephine met Gerald at the door seeing him carrying her portrait, "Let me see, let me see," she asked excitedly. Gerald placed it on the kitchen table. Susan glanced, walking off to do other duties. Josephine studied every detail, "Gracious, that boy is talented. I look beautiful Gerald on Jerusalem; I must have it framed. I'm off to London, Gerald; I'll see you soon."

Gerald placed the portrait in Josephine's Range Rover. She ran upstairs, returning a short while later with an overnight bag; she kissed Gerald on the cheek, "Bye for now."

"Susan," Gerald called out; Susan came into the kitchen. "I suppose you think I'm a rat?"

She made two coffees, "I think a rat has more morals than you, Gerald, to be quite honest," she suggested expecting to be sacked any minute.

"I had that coming," he frowned, "You know what she's up to; this is too lovey-dovey. She must be up to something, Susan. You know anything?" He asked with authority in his tone.

"If I say anything, Gerald, you will accuse me of sour grapes, so I will say nothing."

Gerald grabbed both her arms, "Help me out here, please," he emphasised.

Susan could see he was desperate and genuine. She took a deep breath, "She is up to something I don't quite know what yet; Josephine said you were her husband, and she's rather tired of young men all over too quickly."

"Bloody hell, I scored some brownie points," he laughed, "Thank you for the update," kissing her very lovingly on the lips.

"I hope you don't expect me to continue with you, Gerald, while sleeping with your wife. I'm not somebody's bit on the side for amusement."

"I agree entirely unfair on you, never meant to be that way; I had no idea she was returning. My only concern is she still may be after Christine and will somehow try to split Donald and Christine, and Christine would want to leave the area."

Susan suggested, "if you want real proof, Gerald, why don't you hire a private investigator and have an independent report? No one can be accused of having an ulterior motive," Susan smiled, patting his cheek, leaving.

Gerald looked through the Yellow Pages finding a company specialising in surveillance. If Josephine ever found out, he suspected she would shoot him. He took a deep breath giving names and addresses of her apartment and places she likes to visit.

The company promised to provide detailed conversations where possible and video footage. Gerald hired the private investigators costing ten thousand pounds. Gerald's mobile rang Christine, "I'm glad I have a friend's father leaving your daughter stranded at school."

Gerald glanced at the clock on the wall at 3:45. "I'm sorry, love."

Christine laughed, "Doesn't matter; Mary's bringing me home in her new Range Rover."

Christine slid onto the back seat by Donald. "You might as well come home for tea Christine. You're looking thin," Mary smiled.

"I'll be having a conversation with you shortly, young man wasting your money on a Range Rover and a new combine." Donald tried not to grin. He knew his mother wasn't angry.

He remarked, "This must be the only vehicle we have not covered in cow muck." They arrived at Crabtree Farm; Donald went off to change. Mary held Christine's hand, "I want a private conversation," Mary asked seriously. "Your father and I suspect your mother may be trying to part you and Donald."

Christine glared, listening intently. "You know her real reason for turning up on your doorstep again?"

Christine shrugged her shoulders, "To be quite honest, Mary, suspicious myself. One minute, she doesn't want to be with father. The next minute she's all over him like a rash, at least with Susan; you know what she's after," Christine sighed.

"I don't mean to be horrible about your mother, Christine; look at all the facts before deciding regarding her. I'm advising you as a friend to be very careful. Your mother is so used to having her own way that failure is not an option in her book; come along, have tea," Mary suggested.

"Have you spoken to my father, Mary?"

Mary nodded, seeing Donald return to the kitchen, making tea for everyone. Christine commented, "I must go. I have my lovely horse to tend to, acquired by my lovely boyfriend," kissing him. Mary grinned.

"You don't kiss me like that," Martin suggested.

"No, Martin, you didn't buy me a harvester or Range Rover." Everyone burst out laughing. Mary transported Christine home in her new Range Rover she loved to drive, the first new vehicle she'd ever owned. Christine kissed her father on the cheek as he came out of the house looking at the new Range Rover Donald had purchased for Mary. "Would you like to come in, Mary," Gerald offered? "No, I'll get home."

"Mary, I've hired private investigators to watch Josephine; she's returned to London, hoping they can discover what's transpiring," he frowned.

"Maybe money well spent. Gerald had a quiet word with Christine advising her to be careful about her mother. I hope you are not annoyed. I really don't want to interfere." Gerald kissed Mary on the cheek. "I shall have to help you more often, Gerald," she smiled.

Gerald ran around to the stables helping Christine finish off her horse. "I thought it was too good to be true, father; mother had changed."

"She would never change, too used to the high life, Christine. I've upset Susan in the process. She suggested I have fewer morals than a rat."

Christine laughed, "She's right, father; you can't blame the woman."

"I'll enlighten you, Christine. You must not repeat to anyone; otherwise, we are dead in the water. I've hired a firm of investigators to follow your mother in London to see what she's planning. I know it's underhand; sorry, I don't trust her."

"Oh, whose idea, Mary's?"

"No, strangely enough, Susan, no one can dispute the evidence. They are totally independent and have no ulterior motive, which makes sense. What do you think?"

Christine shrugged her shoulders, "Private investigators don't come cheap."

"No, you won't have much change out of ten thousand pounds."

"The same price as her gambling debt for a visit to the roulette wheel," Christine sighed, patting The Rising Sun on the neck. They both returned to the house.

***

Donald sat at the kitchen table with Mary and Martin looking through catalogues and selecting furnishings for when the conversion was finished in the old house. The weather had turned seemed to be no consistency in anything anymore. Donald could remember the six-week school holiday would be dry and weren't far away; barely a month at least, the grass would grow. "Father, mum, we need a new round baler one we have is knackered; I would suggest a large square baler; the problem is when it rains, the bales are wet quicker than round bales, at least it runs off. If we have a bad time, we can at least make silage out of the bad hay."

"You better start painting, son. You're spending money like it's out of fashion and may come back to haunt you."

Donald checked his bank account on his mobile showing his mother and father. "How much!" Martin gasped. Mary stared in disbelief. "I'm not buying a brand-new one. We have better tax relief if slightly used," he grinned. "We'll have a look after school tomorrow, dad; you can collect me in the old Land Rover. I don't want to give the impression we have money."

Mary laughed, rubbing his hair, "No flies on you, son," she smiled. "Everyone knows you, Donald. We will go in my Range Rover; I like to pose these days," she said, imitating a posh voice holding her teapot with her little finger prominent.

***

The following day, Donald and Christine were at school and kissed in the corridor, going their separate ways to study. Christine felt someone pat her backside. She paused, instantly discovering a new coloured boy nicknamed Jamaica by everyone standing beside her. Christine smiled, "You're presumptuous, Jamaica." Christine looked up, tall, towering above her.

He grinned, displaying his perfect teeth," Gypsy suggested...."

Christine immediately placed her hand over his mouth, "Be quiet," she said, looking around, making sure no one had heard. Guiding him into a storeroom, quickly closed the door switching on the light. "Gypsy said what," she asked in a panic?

Jamaica grinned, "He said you'd be nice to me or else; I'm one of his friends."

Christine sighed. Would this nightmare ever end? She could lose everything her horse, her boyfriend, her future. "What you want exactly." She watched him grin, carefully removing his erection.

Christine stared in disbelief. He reminded her of a horse. Surely no woman would be interested in something that large; he placed her hand on his cock. He commented, "You know what to do, drop your knickers; I paid £10 for the privilege, my first white girl."

Christine froze on the spot, hearing the fire alarm. "On the playground quickly before discovered here, we'll both the expelled," she panicked, running out of the store cupboard and leaving him. She didn't care if he was burnt to death. Somehow she would have to resolve the issue with Gypsy. He's going too far.

School finished, and Mary arrived to collect Donald with Martin; he ran over and kissed Christine as she climbed into her father's Range Rover. Everyone waved and went their separate ways.

Mary pulled outside the Massey Ferguson dealership looking at the second-hand round balers. Chris popped out of the office, "I hear you purchased an International axial flow. What's wrong with Massey Ferguson?" he inquired.

"Couldn't agree on a price your guys wouldn't budge, so I achieved the best deal possible."

"Who were you dealing with?" Chris asked cautiously.

"Jacko," Donald replied.

Chris exhaled, "I've told him repeatedly that we have to make a little profit. It's no good trying to be extortionate; people go elsewhere. Sorry about that, Donald, it won't happen again. You talk to me and me only when you want to purchase," he smiled. "What are you exactly looking for?"

"I want a round baler."

"We have nearly new depends on what you want to spend Donald, this is a new one, I say new used last year to demonstrate she's a continuous baler, you don't have to stop. You could net wrap, plastic wrap, and string comes with a two-year warranty because your farm is only three hundred acres."

"Will a Massey 165 drive it?"

Mary intervened, "That tractor is to be sold." Donald stared and Martin. "My son is not driving old tractors anymore. What horsepower is that one over there?"

"175 hp four-wheel-drive Mary, ample to drive the baler, yes and more."

"How old is the tractor?"

"Only a thousand hours on the clock looks brand-new, doesn't she."

"Donald, how many hours on our Massey Ferguson 165 at home."

"Nine thousand hours."

"We'll see how good you are, Chris. Give it your best shot. Otherwise, we're down the road," Mary said firmly. "I want that baler that tractor, and I want to part exchange our round baler and Massey tractor. Let me know in the morning before 10 o'clock. Thank you, Chris," she said, walking off.

Donald shrugged his shoulders; Martin, following Mary to her Range Rover, jumped in. "You, my mother or a bloody alien, landed and took her," Donald asked. Mary tore off down the road, leaving Chris, the sales rep standing open-mouthed. He'd never known Mary to be so resolute with her instructions; Donald and Martin sat quietly in the Range Rover, trying not to laugh. "What! What's wrong? Not having Donald in the dust or you, for that matter, Martin. How much is that tractor?" she asked, rather timidly.

"God knows the baler will be horrendous," Martin sighed.

"At 10 o'clock the next morning, Chris drove to Crabtree Farm, shown by Martin the two pieces of equipment to be sold. They both entered the cottage. Chris carefully wiped his feet on the coconut mat. Mary invited him to sit at the table, pouring the coffee. "You already know the two machines you have basically scrap; however, you could have the two we discussed, the tractor and round baler, for one hundred and ninety thousand plus VAT, and I can't better the price," scribbling his quote out on a piece of official notepaper.

Mary texts the figures through to Donald. He texts back, "buy mother," with a few smiley faces attached. Mary smiled, "Okay, thanks, Chris," shaking his hand, "I presume the tractor will come fully serviced?"

"You need to ask that Mary from a company like us, will have a twelve-month warranty. Thank you very much for the drink and the business," running for his car, trying to stay dry in the torrential rain.

"You know we are bloody crazy, Martin," Mary confessed. "Donald has a bad effect. We used to be so thrifty."

Martin glanced out of the window, "I wonder if we'll have any corn to cut, the way the weather is performing," he frowned.

***

The end of June approached, and it continued to rain. Everything was sodden pointless. Applying fertiliser would simply wash off the field. Gerald looked out of his bedroom window across the estate seeing many fields had water standing absolutely waterlogged. He came down for breakfast by 9 o'clock, knocking at the door. Susan discovered someone extremely official in his black camel hair coat and trilby. "Could I speak to Mr Gibbs," passing his card, saying safe and secure surveillance cameras?

Susan called out, "Gerald."

He came from the sitting room. "Could you possibly make two coffees, Susan?"

Gerald offered his hand. The man looked at Gerald with beady eyes, "We'll say my name is Thompson. I can't give information away that could cost our lives."

"Can I take your coat and hat?"

"No thanks, I shan't belong." Gerald, leading the gentleman into the sitting room with him wearing a mask he almost looks like a bank robber Gerald concluded.

"What have you discovered?" Gerald asked eagerly.

"A moment, Sir," Thompson stood holding a device that clicked like a Geiger counter. "This old house used to be bugged in the war, deactivated now." Thompson moved over to the television plugging in the device and a plug to the mains.

Susan came in with a tray, "You can stay, Susan. I shouldn't think this will be news to you." She sat quietly in the armchair.

"We have had your wife under surveillance virtually from the moment you phoned; she's an easy lady to follow; she believes her connections protect her. Unfortunately, they could also destroy her. As you can see, the dates are displayed on the screen. Monday evening, she's at the roulette table wearing one of her notorious dresses, almost everything visible. Later, she returned to her flat, where two men joined her, the Copthorne brothers. They spent the night with Mrs Gibbs playing various games, as you can see from the footage."

Susan placed her hand to her mouth in shock, never believing Josephine still like that. She didn't love anyone other than herself, Susan concluded. "Mrs Gibbs, over the next three days, appears to visit different gentlemen; as you can see from the footage, what happened. I don't think any explanation is needed," Thompson said.

"Could I have a copy, Thompson?"

"Once we receive payment, yes, Sir."

"I'll pay you now," Gerald said, becoming angry. Thompson contacted the office, transferring Gerald's card details, passing him a memory stick from his coat pocket. "Everything is on here, Sir, and thank you for your custom; we are happy to do business with you again should the need arise." Thompson left.

"What happens now, Gerald?" Susan asked, sitting by him.

"Nothing, I will have to show this to Christine," he said, "She's of age she can understand."

"The best ten thousand pounds I've spent this week," Gerald concluded. The rest of the day he spent around the estate instructed his men to use the JCB digger to ensure all the ditches were clean to help the water off the fields. Gerald collected Christine from school. "What's happened, father?" She asked, seeing the expression on his face; he didn't answer.

They arrived home. "Come with me." Christine followed him into the office. "You remember I hired private investigators? Here's what they found." Gerald loaded the memory stick into the computer. Christine sat watching her mother perform; remembering the Copthorne brothers and what they tried to do to her; she sighed heavily. "I'm sorry, Christine, you had to see for yourself. I wouldn't expect you to believe anything I said without evidence" he sighed.

"So, this is what she does every time she goes to London, staying in her private flat. She has no intentions of trying to repair the marriage and become a mother to me; she's after me. Let her try!" Christine glared.

Gerald made several copies of the memory stick as a backup in the safe; the combination changed, and Josephine couldn't gain access.

***

Donald eagerly entered the old farmhouse to inspect what Michael had achieved. The studio is a blank canvas with easels, tables, and a few discarded chairs. Donald walked through the dividing door to his apartment, which is almost the size of a cottage. The furnishings fitted quite luxurious, everything he would want to move in and live there. Deciding the weekend, he would set up his studio. Donald looked from his elevated position across Strawberry Estate to see the house nestled amongst the trees. He realised Christine and him spending less time together, excluding school; perhaps they were drifting apart, he wondered, sighing heavily.

Donald ran downstairs, finding Michael, "That's great upstairs, Michael; how long before you finished down here?"

"A couple of weeks, I'll have to quickly move on to the barn. Otherwise, you will have nowhere to store the grain if it stops raining," looking out the door to overflowing guttering on the stables.

Donald returned to the cottage, realising he should make more effort concerning Christine. He ran out of the cottage jumping in the old Land Rover, struggling to drive across Strawberry Estate; mud was everywhere. Donald knocked on the door. Christine seeing him through the glass door she opened, kissing him, "Lovely to see you, Donald, other than at school, why have you come over?" she asked.

"To see my girlfriend, I hope," he replied cautiously. "I presume you are still my girlfriend?"

Christine shook her head in disbelief, "I'm not my mother, and of course, you're my boyfriend, come on in, Donald." They walked through into the kitchen.

"Where is your father?"

"Solicitors on business," Christine made Donald Coffee, "We've been a little preoccupied the last few days," she sighed.

"Your mother?" Donald asked.

"Yes, unfortunately."

"Would you like me to leave Christine? I don't want to be in the way."

"No, don't be silly. Whether you're here will make no difference to the situation," holding his hand and taking him into the lounge. Christine wondered whether she should show him the memory stick of her mother or keep it quiet. Donald started kissing Christine on the lips; she felt exhilarated by his touch. "I have to breathe, Donald," she smiled.

"Sorry."

"I'm not complaining," she grinned, sitting on his lap, "That's more comfortable."

Christine heard the front door open and close. She jumped to her feet, quickly fastening her blouse, checking nothing was out of place, expecting her mother or father. Instead, Mrs Montague with her chauffeur-bodyguard.

"Go home, boy. This doesn't concern you," Mrs Montague ordered. Donald's about to start dealing with the bodyguard in Christine's defence. Christine grabbed his arm, "They won't hurt me, Donald."

Mrs Montague smiled, "Chivalry isn't dead after all. Unfortunately, my bodyguard, young man, would break you in half; I can assure you no harm will come to Christine. I need to talk to her privately. I've seen the portrait of Jerusalem and Josephine. I may commission you myself for a portrait of one of my horses. You are an excellent artist, good day." The bodyguard opened the door.

Christine called out, "I'll ring you, Donald," watching him leave the house, and to her relief, her father's Range Rover parked. He quickly asked, "What's happening, Donald?"

"Don't know, Gerald was ordered to leave by that woman. I wanted to thump the bodyguard; apparently, he could break me in half; I'd like to see him try."

"You did the right thing, Donald. Leave these people; you really don't want to mess with them. I'm here now, thank god," he said, rushing indoors.

Gerald hurried in; Donald headed for home. Mrs Montague walked through into the lounge; her bodyguard poured her a large whisky she sat by the fire. She took a deep breath advising, "Josephine has behaved inappropriately, as you are aware, a shrewd move on your part having private investigators follow her every movement. She originally advised me she's only after Christine, which I explained a fruitless endeavour she would fail." Mrs Montague smiled, "Donald looks like a very nice young man Christine. Obviously, he's quite prepared to take on the world in your defence; there are not many people like that left in the world today."

CHAPTER SEVEN

NEW SITUATIONS

"You obviously know what I want, Gerald. Bluntly we're not leaving without the evidence. You will not be permitted to destroy Josephine; she can do without your assistance. We have considered Josephine unstable and committed for psychiatric evaluation in France. Christine, you will take over the running of Glencoe Estate. You are seventeen in a couple of weeks; in the interim, we have placed a manager there who will liaise with you on the slim chance your mother recovers. We had planned for Dixon to live there without embarrassing the rest of us with his inappropriate behaviour. Since he is deceased, naturally become yours when you reach the age of twenty-one like the other properties," Mrs Montague smiled. "I have to say, Christine, I am proud of you. Your behaviour has been exemplary; you are fit to be a Royal connection. You have caused the family no concerns, unlike some. Donald Selwynm, however, a commoner, has never broken the law or caused his parents' undue concern or any member of your family. We can safely say his future is assured in farming and the art world."

Mrs Montague paused while her bodyguard whispered something in her ear. "Really!" She smiled, "The painting of you and Jerusalem, Christine, has reached six million. Your refusal to sell makes it a more attractive proposition, clever girl. We can safely say money will not be an issue for you, your future husband, providing you are not so stupid as your mother; you could live a charmed existence.

One last thing, Christine regrettable accident Gypsy and his relatives' caravans caught fire nothing survived what a shame."

Christine approached Mrs Montague, kissing her softly, "Thank you for the information; what a shame no one survived."

Gerald hadn't a chance to say a word. He wasn't about to take on Mrs Montague's bodyguard; he walked over to the safe, removing a memory stick and placing it in her hand. "Thank you, Gerald, wise decision, good day to you both," she said, leaving the room. Gerald and Christine followed her, speedily driven away in a black limousine with tinted windows.

Gerald grinned, "I still have a memory stick."

Christine smiled, "Careful, father, we have everything. Don't be too clever; you don't know surveillance has been deactivated. I wouldn't trust her?"

"Who knows, we'll say no more on the subject," Gerald suggested.

***

Donald had arrived home, explaining events to Mary. She made coffee sitting at the table, seeing lightning strike a tree across the field from the kitchen window. She shook her head, "Will this weather ever relent." Mary cut a large piece of cake, passing to Donald, and taking a slice for herself. "I wouldn't be overly concerned, Donald. Mrs Montague is not interested in Christine; she's merely interested in protecting the Royal family's credibility. I suspect Josephine's been a thorn in her side for many years. If Christine has not phoned in the next ten minutes, we'll phone her to ensure she's okay." Mary smiled, patting the back of Donald's hand, remarking, "You're moving into your studio tomorrow, will be independent, son," she smiled. "less for me to do."

"What do you mean, mother?" Donald asked curiously.

"If you're living over there, there's no need for me to wash your clothes, cook, tidy; you have the facilities. Why should I do it?" She grinned.

"Oh," Donald's shocked, not expecting a response like that from his mother. "I'll have to employ someone I won't have the time; I'll be too busy to do those sorts of chores," he said, trying not to grin.

Mary stood, placing the cake back in the cupboard. "1 hope she can make cakes like your mother." she stormed off to the living room.

Donald popped his head around the door, "You could have the job, mum. I'm quite happy to pay."

"I want ten pounds an hour and paid holidays." they both laughed, hugging each other. "You must try and help yourself a little, Donald," Mary advised.

Donald slipped on his raincoat, venturing outside, finding his father standing in the shed in his wellingtons plastered in mud. "I've tried to open up some of the drains to help the water away. Trouble is the ditches are full, too wet to take the Land Rover across the field. Even the lambs aren't doing so well now."

Donald's mobile rang, Christine. "You, okay?" he asked, concerned.

"Yes, everything's okay, Donald; I'll help you move into the studio tomorrow after seeing my lovely horse. Bye."

"Dad, have the lambs in; I suspect they have foot rot by now. They won't be worth much; it wouldn't hurt to have them in before Michael starts concreting the floor in the old sheep shed."

Donald ran out into the pouring rain, releasing Biscuit; within minutes, the lambs inside; steam rose like a thick mist from the hot animals. An old weighing machine didn't accurately indicate the lamb's weight.

Donald ran them through the machine. Martin checked the scales marking each one with a red spot that would make the grade in the market, totalling up to a fifty-fifty split. "Leave all the doors open, Donald. We don't want the lambs too hot; it's a risky move I wouldn't normally consider," Martin suggested. "Half for slaughtering the other half stores on Tuesday. Come on, then that's the end of the lamb problem."

"That's a gamble, dad."

"They're doing no good in this weather."

"I'll fetch the troughs, dad, from across the field with the Ferguson 20."

"Okay, son, make extra rations, and when we weigh them at the market, we might discover we have better lambs than we think."

Donald smiled, dashing to the tractor, placing a plastic bag across his legs to stop his trousers from becoming wet. He quickly threw on the metal troughs and hay rack, heading back to the buildings slipping and sliding everywhere. A good job they were ploughing this field, considering the ruts he's making.

Martin and Donald set up the troughs, and the hay rack, the lambs, enjoyed being inside and ravenous. Donald emptied an extra bag of concentrate in the troughs, so they settled. "I phoned for a lorry, Donald; collected Tuesday morning." They both ran into the house. "Pointless trying to clean this floor," Mary scolded. Martin explained their plan. Mary looked over her glasses, going through the accounts while she had five minutes spare, "If it weren't for Donald, the place would be sold; we can't rely on the farm for an income," she sighed.

Donald kissed his mum on the cheek, "You have nothing to worry about, mother; we own everything," he smiled.

"You haven't painted lately, Donald. Why?" Mary asked.

Donald laughed, "An artist can't rush these things, mother." Christine's birthday shortly seventeen, Mary realised, sliding the books under Martin's nose, "You can do brain of Britain," she chuckled. "Donald and I are off shopping in my new Range Rover." Donald's somewhat puzzled went along all the same. Mary parked in town. "I think it's time you showed Christine your genuine intentions, seventeen shortly. You need to buy her an engagement ring and perhaps marry in a couple of years."

Donald stopped in his tracks, "I can't, mother; I'm not ready for commitment."

"You're not going to slaughter, Donald; you're showing your intentions are serious," Mary insisted.

"What happens if she says clear off?" He frowned.

"Christine do that," she laughed, "Come along, Donald." He reluctantly entered the jewellers. "Could I see your selection of engagement rings, please?" Donald asked nervously. "I can't see anything of interest, mum."

"We can make something," the manager advised.

"Donald glanced across, "I suppose you don't have any black diamonds in stock?"

"We have one very expensive," the manager showed him, "The current value is twenty thousand pounds because of its unique structure. If you look carefully, you can see the picture of a black horse in the diamond. It could be made more prominent with a little work and surrounded by other diamonds to set it off. The total bill would be thirty thousand pounds and must be paid in advance. When would you want the ring completed by?"

"You have two weeks."

Mary stood open-mouthed she wanted him to buy a lovely engagement ring, not spend the earth. "You sure, Donald?"

"Yes, can you also engrave in gold, The Rising Sun, her horse's name? If she doesn't want to marry me after that, I give up," he frowned.

The manager recognised Donald, "Of course, you're an artist in your own right. I admire your talent, Mr Selwyn, and your portrait of Jerusalem. I presume the lady riding him will be receiving the ring? Now I understand why you want the horse made prominent in the stone. What a lovely gesture." Mary took a deep breath watching thirty thousand pounds taken from Donald's card in a flash. "Don't worry, Mr Selwyn, we have Miss Gibb's ring size on record from when she's purchasing rings for herself."

They left the shop, Donald smiling and Mary looking like she was shot. "Donald, you spend money like water," Mary complained.

"You only live once, mum."

Early the following day, after feeding the lambs, Donald started moving his art equipment to the old house, setting out everything how he wanted. Gerald dropped Christine off after she'd finished seeing to The Rising Sun. "Good morning, boyfriend."

"Morning, your ladyship," he smiled.

"Blimey! How much room do you need to paint," she said, glancing out of his window and seeing the top of Strawberry Estate house, "Now I know why you wanted this room so you can spy on me," she grinned.

An hour later, a van arrived carrying more art equipment sent by Jack, approximately five thousand pounds worth of blank canvasses. Jack didn't send over framing equipment. He would prefer to frame himself to make sure it's done correctly. Christine opened the adjoining door entering Donald's apartment. She asked, "Coffee, Donald?"

"Yes," he answered. Christine removed her shoes lying on his bed; he found her; She looked somewhat guilty and kissed him passionately. She sat up quickly with all her emotions running wild.

Mary came in, "Wait, please put a ring on your finger," Mary cautioned, laughing.

Christine grinned, "I'll be an old maid before he does that, Mary."

"Be careful what you wish for." Christine stared at the expression on Mary's face wondering what was planned by Donald. She quickly stood, finishing making the coffee. Donald moved his easel, trying to find the best place in the room and the sort of light he wanted. Donald had taken several shots of his mother in the kitchen when they were lambing; he wanted a lovely portrait of her, hopefully without her finding out initially.

Tuesday morning, the lorry arrived; the lambs were loaded and sent to market. Donald travelled to school, praying they would have a good result. Mary and Martin travelled in her Range Rover to market; she felt quite the lady now she had her own vehicle. Martin had friends at the market who realised some of his lambs were selling as stores were fit to go to the butcher.

They swapped the lambs around before he arrived; they explained what they'd done, and he thanked them. A real gamble placing nearly a thousand lambs in one market. Somehow the buyers found out and must have been relatively desperate for lamb; bidding took off rapidly. He'd never known lamb prices soar the way they had;

one pen of lambs made the highest price at the market and was applauded by other farmers.

Mary and Martin entered the Cafe to celebrate a successful gamble. Mary texts Donald about the outcome while Martin purchased two teas and beefburgers with onions. They sat quietly at a table, enjoying, realising they wouldn't be so lucky when it comes to harvesting; the rain persisted, which could wipe out the crops completely. Martin remembered towing the combine one year with the tractor stuck in the mud, trying to salvage a barley crop, making it appear that someone had rolled the crop flat.

**

Christine walked down the corridor; she had a free period heading towards the library to carry out additional studies. Oliver tapped her on the shoulder. She smiled. He grabbed her hand, guiding her downstairs to the underfloor storage room below the stage. She laughed, "What do you want?"

"I thought we should talk or perhaps," he smiled, kissing her.

"I have a boyfriend, Oliver."

"I have a girlfriend doesn't mean I can't fancy you," he smirked. "You must like me; otherwise, you wouldn't be down here, Christine."

Oliver kissed her again. Christine placed her briefcase on the floor, watching Oliver unbutton her white blouse. She was excited and fearful, not really understanding what she wanted. Remembering she was mauled by the Copthorne brothers, not informing her father of the whole truth of what actually took place and, of course, the Gypsy incident plus Timothy.

Reality returned to her mind realising Oliver was taking a photo of her with his mobile, standing topless with her skirt and knickers around her ankles. She lashed out, pushing him away quickly, dressing. "How dare you take a photo of me? You'd better destroy that Oliver, you promise?"

Oliver pretended to delete the photo, moving closer, fondling Christine; she's enjoying, realising wrong. Oliver had removed his cock, attempting to insert; Christine becoming excited, he ejaculated prematurely before penetrating her. Christine stepped away, relieved nothing had happened, quickly replacing her knickers, correctly adjusting her black bra, leaving the storeroom and returning to the main corridor when no one's insight.

***

Gerald's sat at the kitchen table reading the newspaper. Susan had barely spoken to Gerald since the Josephine incident. Curiosity is killing her, "How is Josephine these days, Gerald?"

"I have no idea; I suspect she's somewhere in France enjoying herself. Why do you ask?"

"Oh, would you like a coffee, Gerald?"

"Yes, it would be nice, thanks. Have you forgiven me?"

"Not really trying to be sociable. If you wish me to resign, I will," wishing she kept her big mouth shut sometimes.

"No, it's fine if you want to sulk. I can't help what's happened. As long as you haven't put rat poison in my coffee, that's fine," Gerald remarked.

Susan thought, what the heck? Live dangerously, she's getting on in years, and the chances of finding someone better were slim to none. She looked at her wristwatch. Christine wasn't due home at least for two hours. Besides, Gerald would collect her. She passed him his coffee kissing his neck; he tried not to grin, realising he was forgiven. He smiled, observing Susan releasing the buttons on the front of her dress. He grabbed her hand, rushing upstairs. Soon she's naked on the bed.

***

Michael's busy working at Crabtree Farm, clearing the old sheep barn and preparing for concrete if the lorries don't get stuck in the mud. His phone rang. "Hello Peggy," he said calmly, sensing she was crying. "Michael, I miss you terribly. Can't we patch things; I don't want our child not to have a father. Surely you still love me?"

Michael sat down on a hay bale, realising he'd been with another woman, so he's no better than her, neither of them happy. "I'm swamped now, Peggy, I'll meet you in the Rose and Crown in the village later, say 8 o'clock, and we'll talk, bye."

Michael carried on until 5 o'clock. He could be pouring concrete within another day. Using Gerald's quad bike, he dashed back to the cottage washing and changing, only a mile into town, so he decided to walk. Michael purchased a bar meal, watching Peggy enter looking radiant, even pregnant. "What would you like to drink, Peggy? Can I buy you something to eat," he offered, eagerly feeling emotions for her he hadn't felt for some time. She smiled sweetly, "A coffee, please."

"How are you, Peggy? You look radiant, if I'm honest."

She smiled, "Thank you, you've gained some muscle since I last saw you. I suppose it's all the hard work."

Michael nodded, "Yes, I haven't had five minutes of peace, but I can't complain. Gerald and Donald and everyone else want me to succeed."

"That's good; How would you feel if we started dating Michael again? I can't undo what happened; we'll have to live with my mistake; it won't happen again. You've always been good to me."

"Looking at you walk through that door is like the first time you walked into my life all those years ago; I suppose I still love you," he sighed, "if I'm honest. I suspect you heard about Pamela?"

Peggy nodded, "Both made mistakes, nothing that can't be repaired with a little effort. We could have such a good life together, Michael, three of us your son due shortly, he needs a father, I need a husband, loving husband," she emphasised.

"You're welcome to move into the cottage Peggy; we can give it a try providing you stop talking in your sleep about your ex-boyfriend."

Peggy put her hand to her mouth, "I don't, do I, how horrible, I'm so sorry, Michael."

"What about your brother?"

Peggy shrugged her shoulders, "The solicitors think he may have to serve a year max. My father will kill whoever comes near you. You wouldn't believe how ashamed everyone is, including me," she sighed.

Michael passed her the spare key to the cottage, "Move in when you're ready after discussing what we've said with your parents and make sure it's what you really want, Peggy. You want me to walk you home?"

"No, I'll be fine," Peggy softly kissed him, trying not to grin, slowly walking out of the pub. Michael wondered if he'd made the right decision; he didn't want anyone else raising his son. He thought that was his job, smiling and walking down the lane towards the cottage.

***

Donald breathed a sigh of relief no more school; he's finished apart from picking up his exam results later. Donald loved his new studio; he could see the stars through the skylights on clear nights. The meteor strikes, scarring the moon observing with his telescope, realising so much he didn't know and probably never would. He sketched what he could see on canvas through his telescope and quickly painted. Realising if he grouped the stars together, he could create a mystical dancing lady keeping her almost transparent to the rest of the scene. Still painting by the time the sun started to rise. The first time he put a brush to canvas in weeks, other than doodling, some people were deeply concerned he'd lost the gift.

Mary phoned, "You haven't slept in your bed, Donald. Where are you?"

"Painting, you cook me a lovely breakfast, mother," he suggested.

"Yes, I will bring it to you if you are busy, Donald; I don't want you to stop."

"No, you stay their mother; I'll come to you and dad, then I'll finish my painting," suspecting she wanted to see what he's creating.

He ran downstairs and across to the cottage sitting at the table, smiling and splashed in oils. "You manage to cover yourself in paint." Martin asked, "You roll in it and then on the canvas?"

"All in the wrist action, father," he laughed.

"All in, who's going to bloody wash your clothes more to the point," Mary scolded.

"Yes, that's my fault, mum. I didn't change into my overall I hadn't intended to start painting; however, a certain scene presented itself, and I thought now or never. That's it! Now or never, the title of the painting," he jumped to his feet, kissing his mother on the cheek.

Donald quickly finished his breakfast, dashing across to the studio. He sat comfortably painting the final touches to his work, taking a couple of pictures with his mobile, and sending Jack the title. "Now or Never!"

Donald received a text. "On my way," Jack made Donald laugh, realising the woman's outline amongst the stars resembled Mrs Montague, the old dragon who threatened him with her bodyguard. Donald burst out laughing, thinking that's the best place for her. Much to his surprise, Jack's there within an hour usually, two hours with the London traffic.

Jack came running upstairs, followed by Mary and Martin, desperate to see what Donald had painted. Jack stood gazing at the brushwork, the whole scene drawing you into the canvas miles into the stars. The depth made you believe you are floating in space with the woman. "I don't know how you do it, Donald; that's brilliant; I love the title. What's that?" Jack asked, setting up two easels quickly, "You've been doodling and not told me." No one had realised Donald had never stopped painting, carefully removing the concealed paintings.

The first one is Donald's mother preparing food at the kitchen table. Mary gasped, "You're a sneaky devil," she scolded. Jack placed the other on an easel falling over. Donald had painted Jack outside his art gallery wearing his trilby and suit, blue velvet cape, and walking stick. "That's thanks for helping me in hospital; not that good, but I hope you approve." Mary ran into Donald's kitchen, pouring two small whiskies for herself and Jack.

Donald hadn't painted Mary in fancy clothes, just like she is, a genuine farmer's wife struggling with the day's toils. Jack sat on the floor drinking his whisky; he dried his eyes. "The reason I'm early dropping off Christine's portrait. You realise I've had offers of nearly six million. I've instructed Gerald to insure it immediately. I was calling round to see you kick your arse because you weren't painting, and you are. I have a painting; I'll have to pay for myself because it's gorgeous."

"Jack, for you," Donald expressed quickly. "I don't want anything; what you do with it is up to you."

"I settled up with Derek on your behalf for the horse," Jack cuddled Donald.

"What do I owe you, Jack?"

"I'll take it out of the next painting, which I should imagine will be sold in ten minutes. It's absolutely beautiful."

"Jack," Mary asked calmly, "Would you frame the portrait of me, please?"

"My pleasure."

Mary smiled, "I have a cake in the kitchen, Jack."

Jack linked his arm in Mary's, "Take me to your kitchen; I'm all yours. Donald, wrap the paintings carefully. I don't want watermarks on them," Jack instructed, running downstairs and laughing with Mary. Martin stayed to help Donald.

Martin and Donald carefully placed the artwork in Jack's Bentley. Jack came out of the house clutching a tin with a cake as if fine art; he sped off into the distance, and normality returned to Crabtree Farm.

***

Gerald hung Christine's painting high up in the hallway; anyone who wanted to steal it would need ladders. They walked into the kitchen. Gerald asked, "What would you like for your birthday, Christine?"

"Driving licence and lessons, I won't have to pester you when I want to travel, father."

"Anything else, Christine?"

"I don't think so; I have everything. I have you, I have Donald."

"You want a quiet dinner, a party, help me out here, daughter. I know your mother would go to town," he smiled.

"I'd like you to invite the Selwyn's to a nice restaurant where we can celebrate my 17th birthday in lovely company."

"Your wish is my command, your ladyship."

Christine burst out laughing, "Donald always says, your ladyship."

Gerald rang Mary, "A taxi is collecting you, Donald and Martin, at 7:30 on Christine's birthday. You are joining Christine and me to celebrate at the Hilton."

"We don't go places like that, Gerald," Mary panicked.

"Rubbish, you're coming; we don't care how you dress. I'm sure Christine won't. If you don't come, you will offend Christine and me. You don't want to be on the wrong side of her," Gerald grinned.

"Thanks very much for the invite," Mary said, lowering the receiver. Donald and Martin sat at the kitchen table. "The Hilton 7:30 p.m. To celebrate Christine's 17th birthday, best bib, and tucker folks," she chuckled.

Mary, Martin, and Donald dashed into town the next day. Mary selected a new dress, Donald and Martin a new suit and shoes. Donald paid with his credit card for everyone. They weren't prepared to look like the village idiots, especially in the Hilton. Donald made his way to the jeweller's, looking at the ring design he was presenting to Christine. Donald studied the ring closely. You could now see the outline in black of the horse with diamonds surrounding, almost as if planned by a higher power, especially for Christine. The engagement ring was placed in a velvet box with a lovely bow. Donald left a thrilled; he thought the skill of the jeweller outstanding, even the engraving of The Rising Sun in the gold band.

***

The following two days passed like wildfire. Donald changed into his new smart suit, Mary into a lovely dress and evening jacket, Martin in his grey suit. Mary checked everyone's labels were removed, locking the door on the cottage as they sat in the taxi. Donald checked he had the ring in his pocket and, after thirty minutes, sat in a cab and finally reached the Hilton Hotel. They cautiously entered the plush establishment, somewhere they would never visit in a million years under normal circumstances.

Christine caught sight of Donald, relieved, panicking for a moment they wouldn't come. Gerald had invited Susan to join him as company for the evening, almost going blind looking at her low-cut evening dress. Everyone had a few drinks at the bar, waiting for their table. Donald remembered work from the outside with the cutlery; he thought he could make a ploughshare out of the amount of steel on the table.

Christine wearing a beautiful evening dress sparkling under the lighting, applied a little makeup. Her hair shone in the light. Donald thought, now or never, over with before they started the meal. Mary tapped Gerald's arm, watching Donald stand. Christine looked at him; he had a strange expression on his face. She saw him remove a small box from his pocket. The moment she'd waited for. Donald went down on one knee, no, changing his mind; he's fully committed, or he'd look a right idiot.

Christine placed her hand to her mouth time seemed to stop. He offered her the box; Christine quickly untied the ribbon, carefully opening the box and staring at the ring. "Christine Gibbs, I would like to offer you this ring as a token of my love and affection for you. Would you consider becoming engaged to an unworthy person like me?"

The whole dining room had gone quiet watching Donald. "Yes, yes, yes; oh yes, please," she hugged him. Gerald and the others rose to their feet, clapping and the rest of the restaurant cameras flashing. Donald and Christine hadn't realised who was there, only a local press member taking several shots of Donald, proposing. Donald removed his handkerchief and wiped his brow.

Gerald received a phone call from Michael informing him police were everywhere. They had called at the cottage advising Michael to stay inside while tracking criminals trying to steal equipment. "I explained to the police officer they might want to check Crabtree Farm."

"Thanks, Michael, of all days," Gerald sighed; Gerald looked at everyone around the table. "I think we'll have to cut the celebration short. Michael phoned a robbery taking place. The police are there trying to catch the perpetrators. Michael suggested they check Crabtree Farm, maybe a target." Everyone quickly stood from the table. The restaurant manager came rushing over. Gerald gave him a fifty tip, "Nothing to do with the food; we have to return home; urgently." Gerald sped off in his Range Rover with Susan and Christine, admiring her ring. Donald and his parents climbed into an awaiting taxi and speedily drove home, dreading what they might find.

Finally dropped off in the yard, Biscuit came out of his kennel. Realising who, he went back inside. Mary breathed a sigh of relief when she unlocked the front door, finding nothing. Donald quickly slipped on his wellington boots, grabbing his torch. He checked the machinery; everything appeared to be present and correct. He slowly returned to the cottage. Everyone changed out of their new clothes, jumped in Mary's new Range Rover headed towards Strawberry Estate, parking by the house. In time, to see Susan in handcuffs and placed in the back of a police Range Rover. A police helicopter scanning the fields could see two low-loader lorries further down the lane, obviously come to load some of the equipment while they were away.

Gerald came out, inviting Donald and his parents into the house. Christine changed and checked her horse was okay; they sat around the kitchen table. Gerald explained, "Thanks to Stephen, none of the equipment was stolen; he realised something untoward seeing headlights coming along the track. He can see part of the estate from where he lives in his elevated position." Gerald chuckled, "Good job, I don't run down the track naked; Stephen can see anyone approaching the buildings. Anyway, he phoned the police, and all hell broke loose. One man is on the run hence the police helicopter. I wouldn't fancy his chances out there," he smiled.

"Excuse me for asking Gerald. I saw Susan led away in handcuffs?"

He sighed heavily, "Oh yes, gullible old me believed Susan's story. Her husband was killed in a lorry accident in Scotland. Yes, he was involved in an accident and spent five years in prison transporting stolen farm equipment. Susan had divorced him. However, they were still in touch because of their daughter. The police believe she may have been involved in supplying him information, making it easy for him to steal equipment from here and have the perfect alibi with me."

Mary jumped to her feet, "What have we in the fridge; where have you hung the pork and beef, Gerald? We have potatoes and vegetables; I just need meat, and we're in business. We'll have to celebrate here," Mary professed.

Gerald smiled, "That's a good idea, Mary. Should have done this first," he said, leading Mary down into the cellar.

Martin shouted, "Careful with my wife down there, Gerald."

Mary said, "lucky old me." Everyone laughed, watching them disappear. Mary and Gerald looked at each other in the dim light in the cold cellar. Gerald quickly stole a kiss. Mary shook her head in disbelief at his persistence. She kissed him, saying quietly, "No, behave," trying not to smile.

Christine helped Mary prepare the food. Donald stood in the hallway studying the paintings produced by famous artists. Gerald and Martin sat in the lounge, drinking whisky.

"If the police can't find any evidence of Susan involved, Gerald, are you keeping her on?"

Gerald took a deep breath, "The honest answer is I don't know; I'm not impressed with the sob story, that's for sure."

Martin shrugged his shoulders, "Perhaps too scared to expose the truth; she certainly doesn't give you the impression she's loaded. I would certainly use the explanation my partner is dead to protect my child from an embarrassing time at school."

"Valid point Martin. Perhaps she used the same explanation elsewhere. Mary will know," Martin expressed.

They went into the kitchen. Martin asked, "You know Susan's husband was still alive, Mary?"

"I suppose the story was he had an affair, and Susan didn't want her daughter affected at school, so she killed him off when her daughter was born. That way, no one will ask probing questions. I would have done the same to protect my family," Mary voiced calmly. "However, I didn't realise imprisoned, and why, if I'd known, I would have informed Gerald."

The doorbell rang. Gerald ran to the door, a police officer. "Mr Gibbs, we caught one on the run and everyone in the gang, with any luck, we'll have their mastermind shortly," the officer expressed. "Millions of pounds worth of farm equipment has vanished over the years finally, we know where. Thank you very much. Goodnight."

Everyone sat down to a beautiful meal. Donald sat by Christine, grinning, looking at her ring. Mary advised, "Christine, put it on your insurance policy; it's a very valuable one-off. I was there when Donald chose for you. The chances of another diamond exactly alike, I should imagine impossible."

When everyone had finished eating, Mary stacked the dishwasher, starting. "Good gracious midnight," she expressed, "We'd better leave you in peace, Gerald," Mary smiled.

Donald kissed Christine, "Happy birthday," heading for the door. Donald and his parents return to Crabtree Farm.

***

Early the following day, Gerald summoned Stephen to the house. Stephen stood nervously at the front door removing his cap and extinguishing his cigarette. Gerald greeted him with a smile,

"Excellent, Stephen, thanks to you, they were caught. What's the damage to our equipment, if any?"

"We've lost a few padlocks where they used bolt cutters; Johnson is checking each piece of equipment to see if they were trying to hot-wire so they could move it. The police had made a mess of the track moving the low loaders. They had come fully prepared; I think they were after the Lexion harvesters or perhaps the John Deere," Stephen shrugged his shoulders.

Gerald passed him a hundred pounds, "A bonus for you," Gerald smiled. Christine came running downstairs. "Good morning Miss Gibbs; I understand congratulations are in order from the newspapers. You're on YouTube and the news from what my son said." Christine stopped dead in her tracks. "Why are the media so interested? I'm shocked; thanks for enlightening me, Stephen, a good job last night. You have saved us a fortune."

Christine ran upstairs, switching on her computer, finally seeing herself standing and Donald proposing videoed by someone using their iPhone; they'd already had ten thousand hits, making her chuckle.

She glanced at the clock 8 a.m. She switched on the news in a shot again with an iPhone. The presenter said, "We wish them both every happiness." Gerald had gone into the living room and turned on the television.

Christine came downstairs having to make breakfast. Susan's obviously still detained or had decided to quit.

Gerald went to the safe, realising Josephine's memory stick was gone; he knew Christine wouldn't touch it. Susan didn't have the combination; Gerald suspected Mrs Montague was responsible. Nothing else was touched, only the memory stick missing. Gerald smiled, shrugging his shoulders, closing the safe; it didn't matter. Mrs Montague and whoever she's really working for didn't want Josephine as a problem either.

Finally, stopped raining. "Father, The Rising Sun is desperate for exercise; I'm riding to Crabtree Farm. Will you cover my ring on the farm policy, please," she smiled, kissing him on the cheek and continuing out the door. Gerald phoned the jewellery shop where the work was carried out on the stone. The manager answered, "Good morning Mr Gibbs. From what I understand, your daughter is extremely pleased with the ring?"

"I think you can safely say that. We need to insure. Can you give me an insurance figure, please, to make sure it's properly covered?"

"If you insure for over fifty thousand pounds, that should cover, never be a replacement, one-of-a-kind, and to be quite honest, I undervalued the black diamond at the time of sale."

"Thanks." Gerald rang off, sitting down in a chair, wondering whether Christine should wear the ring other than on a special occasion.

Christine was about to leave the stable her mobile rang. "Where are you, Christine?" Gerald asked.

"By the stables, father, why?"

"I'll come to you. Don't move," Gerald hurried round to the stable block. Christine dismounted, looking at his concerned expression. "What's the matter, father?"

"I phoned the jeweller who made your ring. It's one of a kind. He advised me to insure for over fifty thousand pounds. In light of that information, should you really be wearing other than for special occasions; don't you think should be in the safe, Christine?"

"You will take this ring off my finger over my dead body, father. Donald bought it for me to wear, and I'm going to, more to life than money."

Gerald put his hands up, "Okay, don't say you weren't warned. You'll be heartbroken if you lose, can't be replaced," walking off less than impressed with her attitude. "I've sent your application for a provisional driving licence, Christine."

She ran over, kissing him on the cheek, "Thanks, father," running back, mounting The Rising Sun and trotting off along the lane. Christine checked the wheat; the rain certainly swelled the grain. However, it would have to dry out before harvesting over the next month.

Christine felt her mobile vibrate. She removed it from her pocket, seeing a picture of her minus her head, topless, her skirt around her ankles and someone's hand inside her knickers. She didn't respond, realising if she had, that would give everyone proof it was her. Christine's livid with herself to start with, and then Oliver; he promised to remove. She studied the photo again, realising she had a gorgeous figure, if nothing else.

She finally trotted into the yard at Crabtree Farm, releasing The Rising Sun in the stable where he could enjoy some hay. She could see the lights on at the top of the old house, suspecting Donald's painting; running upstairs, she entered the studio quietly, observing Donald sitting painting. "Appears we made the news again, Christine," he casually commented.

"I know. Shall I make the coffee, Donald?"

"Good idea Christine; I could do with a coffee."

Christine sitting beside him, "I'm applying for my provisional driving licence. Donald, once I pass my test, we can go anywhere we want, even to the estate in Scotland, now mine or will be when I reach twenty-one."

"We can't go anywhere, Christine, until after harvest. I'd like to go to Scotland; I've never seen other than pictures on television, that's all."

"You'd like Glencoe Estate; only twenty-five thousand acres, some woodland for shooting gentry if they want to pay silly prices for fishing and shooting, I don't mind."

"Twenty-five thousand acres!"

"Yes, not breaking even at the moment. We do have wedding functions there occasionally. I'm not sure about five hundred acres of cereals and two hundred acres of hay. Donald Macpherson is managing on my behalf, so I'd like to visit as soon as possible once I pass my test."

"If you remember Christine, you promised your father and mine we would drive the combines this year for both properties. I think Mrs Montague has eyes and ears everywhere. She's on the ball;

nothing will escape her. If there's something she doesn't like, all hell will break loose," Donald smiled.

"Okay, then Donald, we'll wait until the harvest is finished, and you can come with me, boyfriend, fiancé, I can't say, lover," Christine grinned.

She saw Donald lower his paintbrush. Christine jumped to her feet in a panic, dashing out of the studio downstairs, screaming with laughter. Mary came out of the cottage slightly alarmed, "What you two up to?" she grinned.

Christine caught her breath, cuddling Mary. Donald grinning. "My fault Mary," she said, "I challenged him; I stated he's my boyfriend, fiancé, I couldn't say lover yet."

Mary smiled, "Don't tease Christine. That's naughty," Mary smiled. "I have to admit I drove Martin crazy sometimes," she remarked, reminiscing, clearing her throat, walking into the cottage, making two coffees, passing two slices of cake.

"Where's dad, mum?"

"Having a look at the new grain store Michael's finished, he's returned to Strawberry Estate carrying on the work there for Gerald. He may be back with Peggy; they've been discussing things."

"Do you think it will work this time, Mary?"

"Good chance, Christine, the girl realises she really messed up. Michael is willing to forgive and forget, well, forgive, he definitely won't forget the incident," she sighed.

Christine kissed Mary on the cheek and Donald on the lips. "I'm off on my wonderful horse," Christine smiled, trotting out of the yard. Donald ran upstairs to his studio.

***

Gerald looked out of the front door seeing Susan's car had gone; he suspected the next thing he would receive would be her resignation. The woman was totally embarrassed; the police notified him that she was not charged with any part of the raid some hours earlier or her ex-husband.

***

Much to Donald's surprise, his mobile rang; not recognising the number, he answered, instantly recognised the clear and precise voice. "Donald, Mrs Montague, I walked past Jack Potter's art gallery and noticed your latest work. My dear lad, you are so talented. If I didn't know better, I would say that's myself, betrayed as a mystical lady; you've incorporated into the heavens. I have to ask, am I correct?"

Donald suspected his ears were about to be burnt, "Yes, Mrs Montague, I don't know quite how it happened. I apologise if you are offended; not my intention."

She grinned, "Not in the slightest; Donald and I also wanted to compliment you on how you offered the engagement ring to Christine. You don't belong in this time zone Donald; you are a chivalrous person worth knowing and included as an acquaintance."

"Thank you, Mrs Montague," he replied quickly. "Would you be offended, Mrs Montague, if I painted a portrait of you in suitable surroundings?" A silence Donald's hoping to make everyone friends with everyone, although he may have overstepped the mark.

"For me, personally or to sell?"

"For you personally, what you do with it is your affair. I would not sell any artwork betraying a person without their consent."

"In that case, yes, when you have completed, contact Mr Jack Potter; he will frame and convey the artwork to me; good day Donald," she discontinued the call.

Donald turned on his computer looking up Mrs Montague, finding she was closely related to the Queen. There weren't many official photographs of her. He managed to take one with his mobile on the one occasion they met at Strawberry Estate. He came across a picture of her property in France, an enormous castle with undulating grounds surrounding the property. Donald started to sketch, letting his mind run wild, hoping the perfect setting would come to mind.

He settled for her, sitting on a wooden swing amongst red roses, enjoying the sunshine in front of her property. Within three days, he'd finished, dressing her in white embroidered lace of the finest quality and suspecting her favourite attire when at home. He carefully incorporated a lovely wide-brimmed raffia sun hat shading her eyes. Donald had noticed her eyes were a beautiful ice blue and paid particular attention to removing at least ten years off her age. He thought it would put him in good stead. Donald entitled the painting "A Moment for Reflection."

He removed his mobile, taking a shot of the portrait and sent to Jack. Within ten minutes, Donald's mobile rang Mrs Montague. "For once, I am lost for words, Donald; you are an outstanding artist, and the title is superb. A moment for reflection. You have transformed me and my property into something wonderful. My husband is ecstatic, which I must confess never happens; he is the most settled person I know. Mr Potter is on his way now to collect your work. I can only say thank you, Donald. I can assure you your artwork will be displayed in the most prominent place in my home. Good day." Donald breathed a sigh of relief. He didn't know Mrs Montague at all; however, he suspected she could be a nice person under the right circumstances.

***

The sun had finally shone for three consecutive days. The weather report, in general, improving the rain and sheep muck had encouraged the grass to grow. Donald found his father in the machinery shed attaching the mower-conditioner to the new Massey tractor they'd purchased, which looked an overkill considering the horsepower. Nevertheless, they should be able to cut at high speed. "You are mowing tomorrow, father?" Donald asked.

"Yes, they can't guarantee the weather for more than three or four days. We may have to settle for silage this year, son."

"At least we have the equipment to cater for whatever conditions arise," Donald smiled.

Martin grinned, "You carry on with your painting; I can manage. My back is excellent touch wood. You can help with the baling. We still have half a bay of small bales of good quality hay from last year."

Donald smiled, "I should imagine grain prices will be good this year; yields down." Martin nodded in agreement stopping the tractor and removing the keys. They walked to the cottage together. Martin commented, "Thanks to you, son, I have a decent tractor to drive, and that one has a heater and air conditioning."

***

Johnson at Strawberry Estate prepared the two Lexion combined harvesters, ensuring he'd greased and no worn parts. He could see this would be a challenging harvest from the weather. Essential the two harvesters perform to their full potential; speed would be of the essence. The four sixteen-ton grain trailers were attached to the JCB fast-tracks for moving the grain to storage. The shed is cleaned out, ready to receive whatever's coming this year. The most expensive piece of equipment in the store, the dryer costs an absolute fortune to run and swallows the profit of the grain, as a rule. In some cases, cheaper to leave the crop in the field than try and dry with high diesel prices.

***

After breakfast the following day, Gerald drove to Crabtree Farm to find Donald to show him how to operate the Lexion combines. All combine's virtually the same, only these two are massive. Donald jumped into Gerald's Range Rover, meeting Christine, where the Lexions are stored. Gerald spent an hour starting and operating one of the machines, so Donald's familiar with the controls and understood what he had to watch for on the panels. "These particular Lexion are the top of the range you press a button. They drive themselves, controlling everything, including the forward speed, so the combine's always working at maximum capacity." Christine and Donald held hands, walking to Strawberry Estate house. "Fathers purchased a Range Rover for when I passed my test," she smiled, "Plus, I can drive around the estate and gain more practice, not as if I need any," she smiled.

They noticed Susan's car parked at the rear of the house. Christine remarked, "I suspect she's handing in her notice; she must be terribly embarrassed. I feel sorry for her."

Donald sighed, "Makes you realise how lucky you are; I suppose I do anything to protect my kids if I ever have any," he smirked.

Christine paused, "What are you implying, Donald Selwyn," she asked abruptly.

Donald shrugged, "Nothing, Miss Gibbs, your ladyship."

"I'm certainly not ready to breed with you or anyone else; I'm too young," she scolded.

Donald turned on his heels; he was in no mood for confrontation, especially for a jocular comment she took the wrong way, feeling no reason for her to respond. She stood in the doorway, watching Donald walk down the drive; he didn't glance back. Once, she thought about what she said, realising her mistake. She sighed heavily, walking into the kitchen and finding Susan and her father sitting around the kitchen table drinking coffee. Christine half-smiled, exhaling. "What have you done, daughter?" Gerald asked.

"Upset, Donald, my mouth is working before my brains in gear, father."

"Thanks, daughter probably buggered up the harvest completely; like your bloody mother, you have a big gob. Christine ran upstairs, realising her fault; she created the situation herself and needed to rectify somehow. She rang Donald's mobile number he wouldn't answer, that's a first. She switched on the television fuming with herself, astonished to see a portrait of Mrs Montague in her stately home in France. Donald's popularity rising in the art world and with influential people, the presenter interviewed Mrs Montague. "Thank you for the interview, Mrs Montague. You have seen the artwork, the portrait Donald Selwyn has painted of you."

"Yes, he is an artist of outstanding ability; he captures magical scenes other artists fail to observe." Donald walked into the yard at home only to find photographers and cameras flashing in his face. Christine watched on television. Mary and Martin stood proudly at the door of their cottage. "Donald," one reporter asked, pushing his microphone almost up Donald's nose. "Are you aware a painting Jack Potter has in his art gallery now reached fifteen million in bids, Donald?"

"No, that's news to me," he smiled, "I can afford another tractor," he grinned, feeling more comfortable with the cameras. "Where is your fiancé, Christine Gibbs?" the reporter asked.

Donald shrugged, "Who knows, probably polishing her nails." Mary realised immediately something was wrong. The reporter asked, "You still engaged?"

Donald shrugged, "I'm not certain of anything, to be quite honest." Gerald had seen the interview on television. He's absolutely fuming with Christine.

"We understand you painted a portrait of Mrs Montague, a personal friend of the Queen."

"Yes," Donald replied, "Very astute woman, has an excellent bone structure easy to paint."

"What are you painting next?" The interviewer asked.

A reporter from the back shouted, "Over between you and Miss Gibbs?"

"Who knows! Thank you," Donald remarked, making his way to his studio and shutting the door.

***

Gerald's horrified, Christine's in tears. "What the bloody hell you say to him, Christine?"

"Basically, I wasn't ready to breed with him or anyone else."

"Oh, wonderful, pestering you for sex?"

"No, he never has, never laid a hand on me."

"You realise that women will be crawling out of the woodwork after that interview," Gerald sighed. Christine's phone rang Mrs Montague. "I've seen Donald's interview; what's going on, Christine?

When we originally tried to take you to France, you refused; stating Donald's the one you wanted. You've terminated the relationship. Is that correct?"

"No, I haven't terminated anything!"

"You've obviously upset the apple cart somewhere; you're like your mother your end up the same as her if you're not careful, girl."

"What's it to do with you, Mrs Montague! Keep your nose out of other people's business," Christine advised.

Mrs Montague replied swiftly, "Anyone who has connections to the Royal family; is my business. If you'd like to visit your mother and disappear, keep going the way you are, young lady. You're starting to become a concern. Donald has offered you everything giving you more than most would, and asked for nothing in return; you ungrateful girl, good day."

"That was stupid, Christine; I could hear her from here."

***

Mary made her way across to Donald's studio, making coffee, "Spill the beans, son."

"I had a disagreement with Christine."

"What about explain to your mother," she frowned.

Donald explained what he'd said. Mary burst out laughing, "Is that all? That's not a disagreement."

"Mum may be best if we don't see each other for a while. Dad said something a few weeks back that made sense, you can't buy someone; I showered Christine in gifts most people couldn't afford; perhaps I'm only a gravy train to her," he sighed.

"I think you're blowing this all out of proportion, Donald. Christine's merely stating she doesn't want to have children too early with you or anyone else. She's not saying I don't love you; she certainly wasn't saying take a hike. I don't see what your problem is other than your own insecurities, which are unfounded."

Donald nodded, "You're probably right, mum." She kissed him on the cheek and left him to paint. Donald found himself sketching

Christine; he continued to draw to see where it led him. Before long, the paint's flowing Christine's in a long velvet blue dress and jacket, seated under an oak tree on her front lawn, reading a book displaying her engagement ring on her finger.

***

Christine's determined she wasn't running after any man regardless of her feelings for him. Gerald's tearing out his hair, talking to Mary, trying to decide the best way forward to make the two stubborn idiots realise they'd fallen out over nothing. Susan had returned to work promising never to lie again. Gerald couldn't see any chance of a relationship with her venturing further than the occasional kiss and cuddle.

***

Donald photographed his painting, sending a picture to Jack entitled: "My Future." Jack knowing the situation sent a picture to Christine; he climbed in his car heading for Crabtree Farm. Christine screamed with excitement. Gerald came running from the kitchen as Christine ran downstairs, "father, father!" Gerald saw the picture on her mobile. "Blimey! I must see that," grabbing Christine's hand, dragging her to the Range Rover, driving over to Crabtree Farm. Gerald holding her hand, continued up the stairway to Donald's studio. Donald's surprised to see Gerald never bothered to come before.

"Where is it, Donald?" Gerald asked quickly.

"Where is what?"

"The painting of Christine."

"I scrapped; I didn't like it in the end," he said, trying not to laugh.

Christine glared, "Pig, you don't love me," she shouted.

Donald uncovered the portrait as Mary and Martin came upstairs. "My giddy aunt," Mary expressed, "That is one portrait; I think that's the best you ever painted, Donald."

Christine slapped Donald's face, "That's for lying," then kissed him.

Gerald held his forehead, "I don't remember courtship being like that, Mary?"

Martin commented, "I do; you used to beat me with a stick," receiving a backhander from Mary.

"You liar, I wasn't that bad." Everyone laughing.

Jack came upstairs looking, "Outstanding portrait Donald, as usual. It beats me how you can complete so quick; anybody else, I'm banging on their door for a month to start sketching."

Donald exhaled, "The difference is, Jack, I paint for relaxation, not the money."

Jack smiled, "I can see that nothing is too much trouble. Every detail is important to you; you don't give a damn what anybody else thinks. That's the way it should be. Mrs Montague sent a private plane for her portrait. You have a terrible effect on people, Donald; you appear to bring the best out of them even if the situation is dyer at times. I presume you want this sold out of the way, Donald?" Jack asked, already suspecting the answer.

Christine glared at him. Gerald jumped in, "I'll pay you a hundred thousand pounds for that, Donald. I've never seen Christine look so beautiful."

"What do you want me to do," Jack asked?

"You will have to check with the owner first," Donald smiled, looking to Christine, who realised what he'd said.

"As Donald's manager girlfriend, fiancé, the painting is not for sale," she grinned smugly. "Send me the bill for framing Jack; I want it in the hallway at home."

Mary remarked, "I think you two need to sit down, talk to one another, and stop winding each other up. Otherwise, one of you will say something you really regret." Mary pointed at them both, displaying a stern expression.

Donald and Christine were left alone in his studio; they laughed, realising the whole situation had been blown up out of proportion. Christine took a deep breath holding Donald's hand and taking him into his apartment. "Obvious what you expect of me, Donald, from your last remark." She started to unbutton her blouse. Donald, transfixed to the spot for a moment seeing Christine's breasts, turned his back, "Don't Christine, you're not ready, and I don't think I am either this has to be more than sex. I want you to really love me and want to be with me the rest of your life."

Christine reached for his hand; he slowly turned around to face her, picking her up in his arms and kissing her passionately. "I do love you, Donald, and I want to make love to you at the right time. You're seventeen shortly; I would like to be married on my Scottish estate perhaps early next year if you have me." She smiled with anticipation, "That doesn't mean we can't cuddle each other time soon flies when you're in love," she smiled reassuringly.

"Whatever you say, your ladyship." Both climbed into bed, still dressed, kissing and cuddling. Both Donald and Christine fell asleep holding each other. Gerald and Mary entered Donald's flat, seeing them in bed together. Gerald commented, "Inevitable, Mary, they want to be together."

"He could have waited, Gerald; men are all the same. They put a ring on your finger and think that entitles them to every privilege." Donald and Christine jumped out of bed dressed apart from their jumpers, jackets, and shoes. Gerald laughed, "We automatically jump to conclusions, Mary."

"Me to Gerald, sorry, kids."

"Father, Mary," Christine said thoughtfully, "Next year we are marrying on my Scottish estate in the New Year when neither farm is busy. Within a couple of months after the set date, we'd be eighteen anyway and can please ourselves if you object," Christine smiled. Donald stood unsure of what anyone's response would be.

"Where are you two living?" Gerald asked curiously.

"Here would be the obvious choice because of Donald's painting. I can travel to Strawberry Estate, and by that time, father, we should have you married off with any luck."

Mary burst out laughing, looking at the expression on Gerald's face of absolute shock.

"Who am I marrying, daughter?" he asked, bewildered.

"Well, we thought if you can't find someone, we'd talk to Mrs Montague. She must have a list of free women suitable or desperate," Christine giggled. Donald couldn't help himself; he dropped to his knees in stitches at Christine's comment.

Mary had both her hands over her mouth, trying not to laugh. Gerald wanted to jump out of the window with embarrassment.

Christine turned to face Donald, scrambling to his feet, "Thank you, kind Sir, for the cuddle. We must do it again sometime," she grinned.

Donald bowed, "Thank you, your ladyship, my pleasure to be of service." Everyone went downstairs; Christine and Donald kissed each other, and she left with her father.

Jack arrived at his gallery; he displayed the portrait of Christine like every painting Donald had produced, the bidding crazy.

***

Christine received her latest portrait, which her father displayed in the hallway. Christine had taken a week's course driving and passed her test with flying colours. She's free to go anywhere she wants in her white Range Rover.

***

Donald ploughed the remaining pastureland on Crabtree Farm to be cereals next year using the Massey Ferguson articulated tractor. He nipped to the local Massey Ferguson dealership with his father. They looked over the drills, selecting a nearly new one which meant Martin could quickly drill a hundred acres a day. The seed corn could be delivered in ton bags which Martin could move with the JCB loader; the same applied to the fertiliser. Martin could never remember when he had it so easy on the farm. The most challenging thing he had to do was milk the cow. Everyone decided when she was too old wouldn't be replaced and have milk from the supermarket delivered.

***

Finally, the grain harvest would begin. Christine drove to Crabtree Farm, collecting Donald around 9 o'clock in the morning. "Hello, boyfriend."

"Morning, your ladyship," he chuckled. Christine drove them over to the combines; they each started their machine in contact with two-way radio. "Follow me, boyfriend," she said, laughing. Gerald intervened with his two-way radio, "Remember, we can hear your conversation, daughter."

"Sorry, father." The combined headers were fitted to each machine. Christine led the way, and Donald followed some distance back, trying to stay out of the dust as much as possible. They were harvesting the oilseed rape first, which he didn't have to cut too low to the ground to harvest. By the end of the day, nearly midnight, five hundred acres cut by the two machines, Gerald checked the moisture content at 10%, which is a little high. Nevertheless, the crop is already sold and in lorries tomorrow morning. Donald stepped from the cab, enjoying the day immensely; sandwiches and drinks were made for Christine and Donald, not stopping during the day. Both combines' back in their shed without a scratch on either. Gerald applauded, "Excellent, you two; along day, unfortunately, the oilseed rape in the store, I have to dry slightly."

Christine kissed Donald on the cheek, "I'm off to have a shower; father will run you home, see you tomorrow, boyfriend," she patted his cheek.

"Very good, your ladyship."

Gerald laughed, watching the two tease each other, taking Donald home and dropping him off in the yard returning to Strawberry Estate. Donald went inside the cottage and had a shower and something to eat his mother had already prepared. Martin inquired, "What's it like driving a combine with a cab?"

"Wonderful, dad, no bits," both smiled. "You have the same privilege, dad; our combines sat waiting for you or me."

Donald soon retired to bed. Donald thought he'd never master the art of emptying the combine grain tank on the move; thanks to the skilled tractor driver, it was easy. Gerald's over the moon. He hadn't needed to call in extra drivers; the only person on the farm was Donald, everybody managing.

Donald lay in bed listening to thunder and lightning, rain pounding against his window. He surmised that the combines will undoubtedly stay in the shed tomorrow, if not for the rest of the week.

CHAPTER EIGHT

FIGHTING TO COMPLETE THE HARVEST

Gerald rose early, looking from his bedroom window to the thousands of pounds of grain growing in the surrounding fields, wondering how much he could salvage. By 10 o'clock, he could see the lorries transporting the oilseed rape to a processing plant, some consolation.

Christine dressed, checking on The Rising Sun feeding him and mucking out before returning to the house for breakfast, which consisted of her usual piece of toast and marmalade since they'd stopped visiting Crabtree Farm so often. She missed and especially Donald in some respects.

***

Donald dressed, had his breakfast and returned to the studio, thinking about what he'd like to paint next. He looked through his skylight in the direction of Strawberry Estate, seeing a rainbow engulfing the house; he quickly sketched, remembering the sequence of colours. He started painting and soon realised the painting would have no value; nothing was dramatic or spectacular about a rainbow other than its existence and personal enjoyment. He put the canvas to one side standing up using his binoculars, scanned in every direction, looking for something to inspire him; he sighed deeply. The farm seemed sterile without sheep and cattle, although he didn't miss venturing out in lousy weather to feed.

***

Christine jumped in her Range Rover, heading for Crabtree Farm, arriving to find Donald talking to Biscuit. They greeted each other with a loving kiss entering his studio and his private apartment, where Christine made both a coffee. "You enjoyed combining yesterday, Donald?"

"Yes, great fun, lovely combines to drive comfortable like driving a car," he smiled.

***

Gerald had started his second cup of coffee; seeing Susan coming through the back door, she placed her handbag on the sideboard, frowning. "What's the matter? You don't look pleased, Susan?" Gerald asked.

"My daughter with her father; he takes her out drinking. It worries me," she sighed.

Gerald shrugged his shoulders, "If she didn't want to go, Susan, she wouldn't. Teresa is old enough to make her own decisions."

Susan smiled, "Can't stop worrying. I suspect you were fed up with the bloody rain last night. I never thought it would stop."

"That's farming for you," he frowned.

***

Christine kissed Donald goodbye leaving him in the studio to paint. She drove into town, finding somewhere to park, unbeknown to Christine; Gerald had a tracker fitted to her Range Rover as a safety precaution, disclosing to absolutely no one. He knew Christine loved her new Range Rover and hated driving through the mud. She would sooner grab his.

Christine had purchased one or two products for herself and headed home, driving along the side of the estate. She noticed a van moving along a side track that leads only to the reserve and the disused sawmill. Christine exhaled, reversing up the road, slowly turning onto the old path and realised the van must be four-wheel-drive; otherwise, it would never progress in the mud. The van had finally come to a halt by the old sawmill concealed by a brick wall. Christine jumped out, ensuring she had her mobile. She slowly walked through the mud looking in the van windows, trying to find the owner, not realising he concealed himself behind a large oak tree. Christine knew it couldn't be any of Gypsy's family disposed of by Mrs Montague. Christine is confronted by a man wielding a shotgun. "You realise you're on private property." Christine voiced, pressing one button on her mobile, instantly ringing her father and the record button simultaneously, trying not to look nervous. The scruffy young man stood weighing up the situation, "You can piss off to start with, bitch or I'll put both barrels in you; no one would find you down here for weeks," he advised speaking in an Irish accent.

Gerald realised something wrong, Christine, her phone; he could hear the muffled conversation. He looked on his mobile, realising where Christine was and suspected poachers.

Gerald ran for his Range Rover, grabbing the keys from the sideboard and phoning the police simultaneously.

Christine folded her arms, absolutely petrified, watching the man approach slowly. She's fully trained in martial arts; nevertheless, he's a big man. He came within a few feet of her, "Move your vehicle; I'll be on my way, girl, not even a woman."

"Okay." She grabbed the gun barrel, kicking the man between the legs; he dropped to the ground in agony. She hit him with the butt of the shotgun and placed the barrels against his grubby ear. "You move, and you'll see daylight." Christine glanced up quickly, seeing her father's Range Rover coming, followed closely by the police.

The man was initially arrested on a poaching charge, also carrying a shotgun they suspected he had no licence for since he's a traveller from an encampment along the road; they arrived a few weeks ago, causing problems in the town. Christine gave a statement cuddling her father, and the police officers left.

"Whatever possessed you to take on someone on your own could have so easily shot you love." Christine glared, "Is this a woman thing again; listen, you had me trained to look after myself; now you're saying I can't," she frowned.

"Okay, be careful, Christine." Gerald sighed, suspecting he wouldn't win the argument.

"While we're here, father," Christine exhaled. "I'm plastered in mud in my best clothes; look at the state of my Range Rover. We'll have a look at the old sawmill. I think we can utilise this," she smiled, walking through the brambles, followed by her father noticing everything was here. Needed tidying and servicing with a few roof repairs here and there. Michael could do; even the old petrol-paraffin engine that drove the sawmill and generator for electricity is still here.

"What's the point?" Gerald asked.

"We will have to diversify, father; we have plenty of trees on the estate sold to another sawmill, and they make money. We can start a small operation here and open it to the public during the summer. People go mad for these events, watching how things are processed and manufactured years ago," she smiled.

"What about the cost?"

"Yes, we probably have to employ two foresters and purchase a forestry tractor and trailer. You could have a little café people could buy drinks and must have a loo, make wooden fencing, benches, all sorts of things from the timber."

"How would they travel down here?" Gerald asked, looking at the waterlogged track.

"Simple, I'll contact the local authority and purchase road plainings. We only want a track wide enough for one car with passing places to look authentic. I'm sure Michael could handle this operation," she smiled confidently.

"You appear to have a plan, daughter," he said, unconfident with her idea. "I'll talk to Michael for his evaluation and costings."

Gerald returned to his Range Rover, carefully turning around and heading home. Christine followed. Susan observed Christine's state of dress while Gerald explained what she was involved in. In disbelief, Susan moved her head slowly from side to side, commenting,

"Bring those jeans back down with you, Christine; I'll put them straight in the washing machine; I think you can safely say your pumps are scrap."

"Stick them in the washing machine with my jeans and blouse."

"You can't do that," Susan exhaled.

"I would have," Christine smiled.

"I pity your husband. I'll have to train you how a washing machine works," Susan laughed.

***

The sun shone for the rest of the day, although the ground was still wet underfoot; by midday the next day, Gerald's prepared to risk cutting. Christine had collected Donald advising him not to cut too low to the ground. They were unconcerned with the straw; the less damp straw they put through the combine, the better the seed would be. They started cutting the moisture content 19%. As the day progressed, it came down to 15%. Gerald's running the dryers, seeing his wheat's profit vanishing into thin air.

Michael had suggested Gerald invest in solar panels. Plenty of roof space would lessen the electricity bill if nothing else.

They had cut two hundred and fifty acres by the end of the day. The ground was very wet. The two Lexions struggled to travel in places. If not on rubber tracks, they wouldn't have cut. The tractors carting grain had to be towed off the field with the articulated John Deere tractor on rubber tracks.

The next day went a little better. They managed to cut over five hundred acres, and everything was cut within the next three days.

***

Martin at Crabtree Farm ventured out with the new International Harvester Donald purchased. Thank god that's on rubber tracks; otherwise, he would have never moved; he couldn't have the trailers in the field and had to empty his grain tank over the hedge. Mary transported the grain to the shed using the County on one trailer and the Massey Ferguson on the other. Martin managed to cut the fifty acres of barley that resembled a bomb site. How they would ever bale the straw; he didn't know it depended if it ever dried out.

Martin moved onto the wheat; the weather's improving. Donald helped him. Donald left him driving the combine; his father smiled in a dust-free environment. Gerald had sent over two of his JCB fast-tracks, sixteen-ton trailers and one Lexion. Their acres vanished within hours. Donald sat there laughing, seeing Christine exit from the cab of the Lexion and jumping into his arms. She had grease on her cheek; he gently removed it with his handkerchief. "Thank you, your ladyship, for your help."

"You are welcome, boyfriend," kissing him once more on the cheek, climbed back aboard. At the same time, the other team members released the header on her combine and slipped the header trailer underneath the rear to transport it. She backed up carefully, the header trailer attached to the combine. She steadily drove to Strawberry Estate, towing the header trailer.

The next day, Donald attached the new round baler to the Massey tractor and round baled the barley straw. He moved on to the wheat straw, and round baled, realising next year will be another one hundred and fifty acres, almost like a trial run.

Martin never remembered a time when life was so pleasant, spearing the straw bales placed on a trailer transporting to the yard for storage. Martin's unloading finding Gerald stood in his grain store with a device checking the moisture content in the grain.

"Martin," Gerald called out.

Martin came over.

"Good enough for milling and pretty desperate at the moment because of the poor harvest; prices are high," Gerald grinned. "I have someone looking at mine tomorrow. Would you like me to invite him here to see if I can sell the wheat?"

"I think this deserves a celebration," Martin advised.

Gerald grinned, "Why not," they made their way into the kitchen. Martin ran down into the cellar returning with a large jug of cider. "I don't know what this one is like," Martin remarked, "I've only just tapped," they both emptied their glasses.

Gerald expressed, "Beautiful Martin, smooth," pouring another large glass and himself; by the time they'd emptied the jug, neither could stand.

After taking sandwiches to Donald, Mary came into the kitchen. Discovering Martin and Gerald grinning. Martin staggered to his feet, "Give me a kiss, wife and a cuddle."

Gerald giggled like a girl; Mary pushed him. He fell over. Mary called, "Christine, your father is rather intoxicated. He can't drive; I need help with him to your place." Christine laughed, "I'll bring some help. Susan, in my Range Rover, we need your help. We have a problem with my father."

Susan ran for the door, "How serious?" she asked, worried.

"Not as serious as in the morning; he will have one stinking hangover," Christine laughed. Susan smiled. They arrived at Crabtree Farm. Susan and Christine helped her father into the passenger seat of his Range Rover. Susan tried to fight off his wandering hands; they finally strapped him in. Mary was in stitches, laughing. "Drive carefully." With Gerald's wandering hands, Susan struggled to control the vehicle, finally arriving home with Gerald trying to kiss her neck.

Mary and Christine hugged each other. "You want me to help you with Martin?" Christine asked.

"No, he can stay on the kitchen floor, and I can kick him occasionally makes me feel better." Mary chuckled, "You get off home."

Christine waved as she left the yard when she arrived home; Gerald was no longer in the Range Rover or Susan. She could hear them upstairs and the occasional slap her father received from Susan.

Susan came downstairs, re-buttoning her blouse, "I never knew your father was like that; he has more hands than an octopus," she said, trying not to grin.

"I hope you will remind him in the morning how badly behaved he's been, Susan," Christine advised. "You will have a nasty mark on your neck in the morning, I suspect, Susan." Christine tried not to laugh, knowing that Susan had enjoyed every moment of her father's attention. She saw Susan run to the mirror to make out she didn't know.

***

Donald came into the kitchen, discovering his father on the floor, "What happened?" he asked cautiously, noticing the empty jug on the table. "Mother, you and father, partying?" Mary lashed out with the towel, "No, we have not," she emphasised.

Donald smiled, leaving the cottage and running upstairs to his studio, remembering the story Christine told him about her encounter with the traveller and how she dealt with him. He decided to sketch Christine in similar attire to superwoman; he spent a couple of hours sketching out and applying the paint, trying not to laugh. He wondered how she would feel about the painting. He continued the rest of the day, enjoying every brushstroke on her exposed flesh, leaving Christine in hot pants and slightly exaggerated bust size. Her cape blew in the wind with a gun broken in half-lying beside the traveller, looking petrified. He wondered if he dared send a photo to Jack or would Jack think he'd lost his marbles.

Donald stepped back from his work, taking a shot with his mobile and sending it directly to Jack, entitling the portrait, "My girlfriend." Jack's on the phone, Donald barely made himself a cup of coffee, "I want! Shows a different side to you, brilliant I'm on my way." He could hear Jack chuckling as he lowered the receiver.

Just for the hell of it, Donald sketched Gerald and Martin blotto at the table with his mother beating them with a rolling pin. He had difficulty painting, laughing, and keeping his hands steady. By the time Jack arrived, Donald had finished the second portrait. The fastest artwork he ever carried out, although it looked terrific. Donald entitled "Harvest." Donald could hear Jack running upstairs; he stood in the doorway, laughing. "That's great you applied the paint like a muck spreader, so bad it's brilliant; I can't wait to frame that one and sell it in my gallery." Jack looked at the portrait of

Christine in her superwoman outfit. "That's lovely. Donald again has a humorous side. Your title is apt. My girlfriend," Donald and Jack loaded both portraits in Jack's Bentley very carefully because of the wet paint. Neither Mary, Gerald, nor Martin had seen what Donald had produced, not forgetting Christine.

Within a couple of days, the portraits were displayed. Mary was on the Internet checking Jack's gallery; she didn't recognise herself until she saw Martin and Gerald. She placed her hand to her mouth, thinking ring that little bugger's neck, continuing to scroll along the artwork, coming across the one of Christine remembering the story Gerald had told her.

Mary phoned Christine, "Have you looked at Jack's website lately, Christine?"

"No, Mary, why?"

"I've had a shock, and I suspect you're going to."

"Okay, thanks. Bye."

Christine quickly switched on her computer, calling her father to the kitchen table. "What's the problem," he asked, sitting beside her. She scrolled through the portraits, first coming across Gerald, Martin, and Mary. "The little devil," Gerald exhaled, "Be careful around him. You never know what he's going to paint next." Christine continued through the paintings. She stopped dead in her tracks. "I will personally kill him," jumping to her feet.

Gerald's grinning, "Not that bad, daughter; you have outstanding attributes according to his paintbrush."

Gerald received a sharp jab in the ribs. "Not funny, father, which reminds me you've finally recovered from whatever you were drinking with Martin; fancy being in that state, and you remember what you did to Susan?"

Gerald glared, "I remember having a drink. The rest is a little vague, as you can see; I wasn't in the best of state."

"Neither was Susan when you finished with her; fancy giving her a love bite at your age, father."

"I certainly didn't. I haven't touched the woman," he remarked, scratching his head, not remembering.

Susan came in through the back door; he noticed the plaster on her neck. "Have you injured yourself, Susan?" he asked, concerned.

"I'm not speaking to you; Gerald, I have to wear a plaster. My daughter thinks it's disgusting at my age. I didn't realise you were that sort of man." Susan could no longer keep a straight face and laughed, removing the plaster. "You're responsible for that mark, Mr Gibbs, and you have more arms than an octopus when you've had a drink."

Christine laughed, "Perhaps my mother is not guilty of anything, father," Christine muttered. Gerald turned, glaring at her watching her smile with satisfaction; he was embarrassed beyond belief.

Susan made everyone a coffee sitting on Gerald's lap while Christine was there. "If there were any secrets around here, you exposed them a few hours ago, Gerald. I take it you have no objections to your father and me, Christine?"

"No, not in the slightest you could eat each other alive if you like."

Gerald stared at Christine, watching Susan look at the portrait of Christine's superwoman's outfit, commenting, "I wouldn't mind a figure like that, Christine," Susan smiled. "You can see what's on that boy's mind."

Christine took another look at the portrait, smiling, "I suppose you're right. I do look rather stunning."

***

Jack phoned Donald, "I hope you've followed the bidding Donald on these two portraits?"

"Not really, your side of the business. I enjoy painting and, of course, spending the money. A problem, Jack?"

"A problem?" Jack exhaled, "The portrait entitled Harvest was so badly painted. Reached ten thousand dollars. The other one, My girlfriend, has reached over a hundred thousand dollars. The Americans are going wild, bids changing by the minute. I think you could paint in cattle manure, and they'd still buy," Jack chuckled, "Bye, for now, Donald."

Donald walked out into the yard, filled the Massey Ferguson tractor with diesel and started ploughing. He ploughed throughout the night, occasionally stopping to take a night sky photo when he saw something of interest.

Mary realised he hadn't been to bed. She looked out of the window seeing him ploughing the bottom field. Martin quickly had his breakfast driving down in the old Land Rover, taking diesel with him for the tractor. "Morning, son, fill up, and I'll carry on; the sooner this lots ploughed, the better; how's it going?"

"No problem, dad," Donald smiled, climbing into the Land Rover and heading home, finding Christine sitting at the table eating a hearty breakfast. She glanced at him, "I don't know whether to hit you or kiss you over that portrait."

"Kiss would be better; I haven't been to bed, having my breakfast catching some sleep," he finished his food running over to the studio. Christine went with him; he showered and climbed into bed.

Christine slid in beside him, still dressed, pressing the button, drawing the blinds on the windows. Donald cuddled up to her, and they both fell asleep. Christine's intrigued, wondering what it would be like to sleep with him, only to discover he snored like a tractor. At times, he almost crushed her with his enormous hands, which didn't stray, which surprised her considering their position.

She felt him move and jumped out of bed, making coffee for them both. He opened his eyes smiling, "Hello, your ladyship, absolutely wonderful cuddling you." She grinned, realising it could have been much more with encouragement from her.

Christine pressed the button the blinds retracted. She looked at her wristwatch at almost 5; Donald went to shower. Christine sat in the studio looking at all the doodles Donald had stacked in the corner of unfinished work.

Donald changed, entering the studio and placing his arm around Christine's waist. "September, your birthday, Donald."

"Yeah, seventeen, I can start to take driving lessons and pass my test," he smiled.

Christine made her way home and decided to take an evening ride on The Rising Sun.

Gerald came out to find her, and she smiled. "I thought you'd like to know Christine. I've spoken to Michael he thinks your idea is brilliant; resurrect the old sawmill not only for producing timber for our needs but also to sell. He also suggested we should open up the reserve for people to walk through as an added bonus," he said, shrugging his shoulders. "What's your view, daughter?"

"That would make more of a day trip for someone to visit. We could have a little café and toilet facilities by the sawmill. The reserve is right next door; it makes sense and make a few pounds."

Gerald watched his daughter ride off towards the reserve in the cool evening air; a couple of hours of daylight left, he thought, seeing her trot on.

Christine paused outside Michael's house, dismounting. Michael opened the front door, offering, "Fancy a coffee, Christine. I'm on my own, I'm afraid."

Christine nodded, smiling, entering, and removing her riding jacket. Michael made the coffee, passing a mug to Christine, asking, "You and Donald, okay, he's certainly making money. I wish I had his talent?"

"Yes, don't we all. "Christine started to cry, placing the mug on the draining board. Michael moved to comfort her, gently placing his hands around her waist, asking, "What's the matter, Christine?"

She exhaled, " I don't know. I'm all confused. I think I have everything straight in my mind, and the next, I'm panicking. I wish I was like Pamela. I happened to see you on the carpet wondering if I should venture down that road or wait; so many unanswered questions I don't know what to do for the best?"

Michael thought for a moment, "I can't really advise you. I started having sex when I was 11 with Peggy. She was my first girlfriend. I hadn't planned to try anyone else until circumstances changed.

I wouldn't worry. Donald loves you, and he will look after you, Christine."

Christine produced a glimmer of a smile, "I wish he'd be more assertive. Perhaps he doesn't think I'm pretty enough, and he can do better," she frowned.

Michael cuddled Christine kissing her on the cheek. She drew away, taking Michael by surprise and kissing him. He stood there momentarily, realising this was his best friend's girlfriend. "I'd better return to work," he said quickly. He owed Donald everything. He wouldn't be where he is today without Donald's support. He certainly wasn't going to shag Christine while she's feeling so vulnerable. Christine smiled, slightly embarrassed, slipping on her riding jacket and leaving.

Gerald returned to the house; seeing a letter which had fallen off the sideboard, he retrieved it, opening it with a knife; much to his surprise, divorce proceeding for him and Josephine to separate legally. He sat a moment, staring, reading the content, the reasons stated irreconcilable differences to sign and return.

Gerald felt a pain in his chest. Susan came into the kitchen, realising Gerald was about to have a heart attack. She phoned for an ambulance as he collapsed to the floor, placing a pillow under his head. She immediately called Christine. She came galloping on The Rising Sun, guiding him in the stables leaving.

Christine rang Mary crying down the phone. Mary grabbed Donald jumping in her Range Rover. They ran into the house on Strawberry Estate. Donald administered CPR, finally restarting Gerald's heart. The ambulance arrived, and they took over once they had him stable, taking him to hospital, and Christine travelled with him.

Mary asked, "What caused that? She retrieved a piece of paper from the carpet and opened reading. "That's what," passing to Susan.

Susan sighed, "He's a lovely man; thank god you managed to keep him alive, Donald. I panicked."

"We are trained at school on the rugby team."

Mary patted him on the shoulder, "I think a strong cup of tea is in order." The three of them sat around the kitchen table. Susan put a nip of whisky in each cup. "I need something," she said, sobbing.

Mary patted the back of her hand, "The same thing happened to Martin's father. He didn't read a letter, he suffered a heart attack, and that was it; hopefully, Gerald will recover."

An hour passed, and Christine phoned Mary. "He's okay, Mary; he needs to rest. Other than that, he should make a full recovery."

"I'll come and collect you. Which hospital?"

"Coventry, I can come home by train if you want; I don't mind. Damn, I haven't any money, and I suspect Susan hasn't been paid either. If you can scrounge together three hundred pounds and give it to Susan, that would be appreciated, Mary."

"No worries, I'm on my way to collect you, Christine."

Mary conveyed the conversation to Susan. "I can wait to be paid."

"No, you won't," Donald expressed, opening his wallet and counting out three hundred and fifty pounds, "A bonus for making Gerald happy."

Susan hugged him, "I can see why Christine loves you," she said, walking out the door. Donald's mobile rang. "Yes, Christine."

"Donald, do me a favour. I left The Rising Sun in his stable, must be frantic by now still saddled."

"Don't worry, I'll deal with the situation. You go, mum, collect Christine; she shouldn't say here alone."

"My thoughts Donald, she'd drive herself insane with worry."

"I'll deal with The Rising Sun, lock the house, and walk home not far," Donald smiled.

Mary patted his cheek, heading for Coventry. Donald went to The Rising Sun's stable, removing his saddle and then his bridal as if the horse knew Donald. Donald brushed, watered and fed him, cleaned out, and checked his hooves, no stones trapped inside, causing discomfort. Donald's inspecting, The Rising Sun's front leg, The Rising Sun turned his head, nibbling Donald's trousers, making Donald laugh.

Donald patted him on the neck, "You're a scoundrel." Donald returned to the house, checking everything's secure, ringing Christine, "You're staying with us tonight. Can I have permission to drive your Range Rover home, and what is the code to set the alarms on the house? If you don't mind informing me, change in the morning."

"You could drive my Range Rover home across the estate tracks. You will have to wash if you get dirty," she cautioned, "The alarm code is 2717. Enter the code; listen to the intermittent beeps. Close the front door lock."

Donald climbed into Christine's plush Range Rover, driving steadily. Donald came across Stephen in his Land Rover. Stephen looks suspicious, seeing Donald in Christine's Range Rover.

"Don't panic, Stephen. Gerald's in hospital; he's had a heart attack; Christine is with him; he's okay."

"Thanks, Donald, for the update; I'll keep my eye on the place tonight." Donald continued home. Mary had already phoned Martin to explain the situation. After what appeared to be an eternity, Mary and Christine returned to Crabtree Farm. Christine ran over, cuddling Donald. She had never felt so alone as she had at this precise moment.

No one was interested in eating; they all settled for a slice of toast and a cup of tea. Martin commented, "I think your father arranged a meeting with someone tomorrow who wanted to purchase the wheat for milling, offering mine at the same time and seeing what sort of price we can achieve."

"Thanks, Martin. I haven't had a chance to speak with my father. He never mentioned," Christine smiled, realising if you don't take every opportunity in life, you may not have another. Donald kissed Christine on the forehead, "I'm off to the studio to paint or go to sleep," he exhaled, wishing he could make things better for Christine.

"I'll come with you," Christine expressed, kissing Mary goodnight on the cheek. Christine sat in his apartment. Donald offered, "I'll sleep on the settee if you like, Christine."

"There is no need, Donald; I want you close to me. I feel safe when you're near," she smiled, watching Donald continue painting. Christine undressed and entered the studio standing beside Donald. He glanced at her lowering his paintbrush. She sat on his leg, encouraging his hand onto her breast and kissing him. She could tell he already had an erection ensuring his interest. Christine gently pulled down the zip of his trousers, holding his erection. She repositioned on his lap, parting her legs. Christine could feel him kissing her back and neck, holding her breasts in his hands. She slowly eased his cock inside her. Now she knew what she'd been missing all these years.

To start with, quite uncomfortable, she thought until she relaxed then fantastic. Donald picked her up in his arms, carrying her into the bedroom and throwing her on the bed. She couldn't help but grin. He almost tore his clothes off. Gently laying on top of her. Now, she felt his power. He thrust like a wild man. She could barely catch a breath.

Both finally fell asleep, Christine waking first finding herself in his powerful arms. She didn't care. He brought meaning to her life with every special touch, so gentle yet, he could crush her in his hands. Finally, both smiling at each other, realising what happened, went to the shower together; no more hiding the truth is out. Christine lay on the bed, and Donald immediately obliged, sending her wild inside. She couldn't get over the way he held her; those enormous hands of his knew precisely how to caress her. Christine dressed in her old clothes she would change when she returned home shortly.

Mary rang Donald, "Breakfast is ready."

"Thanks, mum, we're coming." Donald put his hands on Christine's waist, lifting her to his lips; she placed her arms around his neck, whispering, "if you only knew how much I loved you, Donald."

Donald smiled, "I think I do, Christine." They ran downstairs like naughty schoolchildren who'd stolen a packet of sweets running into the cottage sitting at the table.

Mary grinned straightaway; she knew what had happened, "You will have to cover that nasty mark on your neck Christine before we see your father," Mary advised, trying not to laugh, realising Christine had consented and on her own terms.

Donald turned red with embarrassment, realising everybody knew.

Christine asked, "You have time to come to Strawberry Estate this morning, Mary, so we can sort out sensible grain prices, please?"

"Of course, your father is not so stupid not to prepare for every eventuality; I will accommodate anyone looking for trouble this morning," Mary assured.

Donald wondered what they meant while eating his breakfast, "You want me to come?" Donald asked.

"No, your mum and I can organise, Donald. You stay here."

Martin remarked, "I don't interfere, Donald; those two are dangerous enough on their own together, bloody lethal," he chuckled.

Mary took Christine home in her Range Rover. Susan had already let herself in; she had her keys, made the fires and sat drinking coffee at the kitchen table. "Your father rang, Christine asking me to prepare a bed; he's coming home in the morning."

"Nice of him to inform me," Christine remarked, less than impressed with her father. The doorbell rang, and Susan answered. She called, "Christine, gentlemen here to see your father about grain."

"Yes, I will deal with him."

"Are you sure, Christine?" Susan asked.

"I'm sure," Mary said, pushing past Susan. Christine trying not to grin. Mary would be like her son, an unstoppable bulldozer if you made her angry.

Christine took her father's Range Rover; they drove to the grain store. "Of course, you realise you'll have to cover the transport cost."

Christine shrugged her shoulders, "Normal."

"I'll offer you eighty pounds a ton."

Christine laughed, "You won't be having any; I'd sooner let it rot. Goodbye."

Mary's impressed, watching Christine close the doors on the grain store and lock it.

"Hundred and no more," he said, tidying his leather jacket.

"Come on, Mary, he's wasting my time; let the other company have it." Christine climbed into her father's Range Rover. The grain purchasing agent advised, "Don't be so hasty," he cautioned.

"While you're wasting my time with disgraceful prices as far as I'm concerned, the grain can stay in the store for another year. It will make no difference to us not desperate for money."

"My best offer is three hundred and fifty pounds a ton."

"I will think about it. I want you to look at my friend's wheat, follow me." He jumped in his car, following Mary and Christine. Mary patted Christine on the leg, "That's one hell of a price, Christine."

"I know father said they were desperate for decent milling wheat the other day." They arrived at Crabtree Farm, the agent for the mill took samples. Martin and Donald join them in the yard; the agent shrugged his shoulders, "One hundred and twenty pounds?"

Martin is about to speak. Mary glared at him; he knew that was a sign to stay quiet. "I expect the same price for theirs as mine. Take it or leave it and you can pay for the transport," Christine stared at the agent. Donald thought she was about to thump him for a moment.

She watched the agent exhale, "We have a deal, Miss Gibbs," taking her hand. "My company will be in touch shortly, thank you." They watched the agent drive away.

Christine remarked, "I should have made him pay more, but father said he wanted it out of the way if we could achieve a reasonable price. Now I must go home and change," Christine smiled, "And see my horse. He will think I've neglected him."

Donald scooped Christine up in his arms, "What about your future husband."

She grinned, "You had far more than you are entitled; so, think yourself lucky," kissing him on the cheek and lips.

Christine's mobile rang her father. "I've talked to the agent from the mill. He said you were rather abrupt with him, Christine."

"Perhaps I should have sold your grain for eighty pounds a ton, father, and why didn't you contact me before Susan. You intend to spend all day in bed with her when you come home from the hospital."

"Don't be so bloody rude, Christine," Gerald scolded. "What have you finally settled on."

"Three hundred and fifty pounds a ton, and he's paying for the transport."

"That's a good price. Well done."

"Your home in the morning, father?"

"Yes, hopefully, although my blood pressure is off the scale."

"Good, I can plan to go to Scotland with Donald; see what the Glencoe Estate Manager is up to and work out why the property doesn't make more money."

Mary and everyone else listened to the conversation. Nothing frightened Christine, bloody-minded to a fault.

Christine turned to Martin, "Can you manage for a week without Donald? I want to take him to Glencoe Estate and see if he sees anything I don't; where money could be made in the future."

"We can manage. We have all the equipment we'll need here," Martin suggested.

"Mary, would you watch my father and Susan? I don't trust her completely."

Mary nodded.

Christine jumped in the Range Rover, heading home to Strawberry Estate; a black limousine parked at the front when she arrived. She sighed heavily; running inside, Mrs Montague sat in the living room drinking coffee with her bodyguard. Mrs Montague rose to her feet and embraced Christine, much to her surprise. "We are sorry to hear about your father's condition; I understand he's home tomorrow from your servant?"

"Yes, then I'm off to Scotland. I'm not convinced the estate is run properly; with all the activities should make more money."

Mrs Montague smiled, "No flies on you, Christine; I have suspected as much for some time. However, you couldn't rely on your mother to sort anything out, including her own life," she briefly smiled. "Talking about your mother, we are arranging for a very private divorce. I think your father has earned after Josephine's behaviour." Mrs Montague paused, holding Christine's hand, looking at the engraved black diamond ring. "You are so fortunate, Christine, to find a genuine man like Donald; I can ascertain he is well rewarded for his loyalty from your neck" she frowned. "I would suggest avoiding liaising with Oliver. I appreciate what you think is amusing. If Donald discovers he will leave you, don't behave like your mother. Oliver's mobile was conveniently destroyed. However, we cannot detect where all the photos were sent."

Christine exhaled, "Thank you," somewhat relieved and wondered how Mrs Montague knew! "Donald and I are marrying next year at Glencoe Estate. We are both eighteen, not as that really matters."

"Excellent," Mrs Montague smiled, "Today's turning out to be wonderful so far; I would ask a favour. Would you allow your wedding ceremony to be videoed so your mother could view it? It would be most awkward if she attended; besides, I would prefer her not to return to the UK."

Christine sighed, "Never crossed my mind, Mrs Montague. Yes, I agree with your thinking. We could have a copy of the video."

"Elizabeth R has asked me to extend her best wishes for your future, how high up the ladder you are watched, Christine. That includes Donald, who I have to say is exemplary in everything he does. Donald managed to encourage the Royal household into laughter with his portrait entitled girlfriend and the other one, The Harvest.

"Christine smiled, "Donald is very special to me."

"A word of warning, Christine, your servant, be careful," Mrs Montague smiled, standing to hug Christine. "My husband gazes at the portrait Donald painted of me every morning before breakfast; he is an unbelievable artist. Good day to you, Christine."

Christine ran upstairs to see the end of the limousine, leaving the drive from the landing window. She showered and changed. Susan's in the kitchen, "What would you like for lunch, Christine?"

"I'll grab a quick sandwich; thanks, Susan. You could have the rest of the day off."

"What does she want?" Susan asked, concerned.

"Family business," Christine commented, walking away.

Christine ran out to her horse saddled, riding across the estate, coming to Michael working on the old sawmill to return it to its former glory. She dismounted, tying her horse to a nearby post. Michael came over smiling. "How's everything progressing, Michael," she smiled.

"Wonderful should be ready for next year shortly after Christmas. Johnson looked at the old engine and is acquiring parts. He doesn't think it would be much trouble to have her running again; actually, an old tractor engine converted."

"Good news, how are you and Peggy getting along?"

"You mean Peggy and my son," Michael smiled.

"I'm sorry, Michael, I forgot; I've had a few issues."

"Haven't we all," Michael smiled, "He's a month old now, Charlie; that's what we call him because he's such a character."

"Perhaps in time, you and Peggy will marry."

"We planned to marry when she's in shape and Charlie's settled."

Christine hugged him, "Donald and I plan to marry early next year at Glencoe, my estate in Scotland. I hope you will come. I suspect Donald will ask you to be best man; I can't wait to see you in a kilt Michael."

They both laughed. "We will pop around one of these evenings and say hello if that's okay, Michael?"

"Absolutely, Christine; I'd love to chat with you. Perhaps Donald will be my best man."

Christine remarked, "I can guarantee that for you," she smiled, mounting her horse. "What's happening about the road plainings Michael?"

"Delivered next week, Christine. Everything is taken care of; I'm sorry to hear about your father." "Thanks, Michael."

Christine rode off, seeing Stephen in the new John Deere ploughing the harvested rape field. Christine saw the two JCB fast-track ploughing with Christopher and Arnold operating across the harvested wheat fields, taken on as new employees after Stephen caught the other two less than honest. Christine smiled, realising Stephen was an asset to the farm. Nice to have someone they can trust. The two new operatives appear to be toeing the line under Stephen's supervision. She returned The Rising Sun to his stable, brushing down, tending his needs cleaning out his hooves to prevent discomfort.

Early the following day, Christine drove to Coventry Hospital by 10 o'clock on her way home with her father. He continually shut his eyes at Christine's driving, convinced he would end up back in the hospital. "Father, I'm off to Scotland Saturday morning with Donald. You think you can manage. I will arrange for Mary to keep an eye on you."

Gerald smiled.

"Mrs Montague came to see me."

"I know Susan told me."

"When?" Christine asked, annoyed.

"We talk on the phone. She doesn't abandon me in hospital; I was neglected by my daughter."

Christine didn't respond.

"Come on, Christine, what did Mrs Montague have to say?"

"No, I thought your spy would have been listening."

"This is unlike you, Christine; what's happened?"

"Sorry, father, I don't trust Susan. Neither does Mrs Montague; you're only interested in having her in bed to give you another heart attack," Christine suggested.

Gerald went silent, "Am I wearing dark glasses again, daughter missing something regarding Susan? If you don't explain to your father, how would I understand what you're implying."

"Mrs Montague said to be careful of her. Have you ever known that bloody woman to be wrong? She wants me to have my wedding videoed so my mother can watch, which I've agreed to. That way, you won't be confronted by her. Mrs Montague doesn't want her in this country, which is understandable from what I understand."

"Back to the Susan bit, what do I need to know about?"

"You know as much as I do, father. Mrs Montague didn't elaborate. I suspect she thinks it's pretty obvious. We're too dim to realise what's happening, similar to the other two staff. Stephen saw straight through what's happening, and you sacked them."

"I take it you and Donald have actually," Gerald paused.

"Nobody's business what Donald and I do together," she smiled.

Gerald grinned, "Inevitable, anyway, Christine, you remind me of a tarantula which has sex and then kills her mate, poor Donald," he sighed.

"I'm not that bad, father, provided he does what I want," Christine smiled.

***

Donald eagerly packed his suitcase Friday night, under the supervision of Mary making sure he'd correctly packed ready for him to depart early Saturday morning.

Christine pulled into the yard at Crabtree Farm at 5:30 a.m. Saturday morning. Donald loaded his suitcase, hugged his father and kissed his mother on the cheek. Christine drove off, heading up the M6 towards Glasgow. Christine complained, "Should have come on my own, your falling asleep."

Donald chuckled, "Very difficult to sleep. I'm excited about the trip, my first adventure and seventeen shortly; by now, most kids have travelled halfway around the world with their parents."

Christine smiled once they passed Glasgow. The scenery was spectacular. Donald's camera working overtime.

Christine hadn't notified the Estate Manager she was arriving. She wanted to catch everybody unawares. She had her private apartment, her mother's, so accommodation shouldn't be a problem. They travelled along a winding driveway, shrouded in trees, parking outside an enormous house, almost a castle. Donald carried the suitcases, and Christine opened the door, surprised she was not greeted. Apparently, everyone was still asleep and nearly midday. She could hear voices along the corridor. She walked down, finding herself in the kitchen still with no staff. She sighed heavily, returning to reception, cracking the fire alarm glass on the wall. Donald stood in amazement; he wouldn't want to be in anybody's shoes at this precise moment with the expression on Christine's face. The staff poured outside, some half-dressed. Christine determined that no guests were there because there were no vehicles. "Leave the suitcases there, Donald."

A staff member came running in, "Outside, Lass, fire!"

"Who are you!" Christine inquired abruptly.

"I'm the manager."

Christine opened the door aggressively. "Right, you can come inside, no fire; although maybe shortly, I suggest you tidy yourselves and meet me in the drawing-room where we will discuss your future on my estate," she glared.

She heard Donald Macpherson mutter under his breath. "Bugger."

"That's an apt phrase, Mr Macpherson. You are in it right up to your neck. I've driven several hours to inspect my estate. I could have robbed the place, no fires lit, no staff on duty."

"Who do you think you are! Coming here telling me how to do my job?"

"I own the estate; wash your bloody ears out! My name is Christine Gibbs. I'm the daughter of Josephine Gibbs." Christine watched him turn white even if he was supporting an enormous beard.

"We had a party last night with guests leaving," he spluttered.

"That won't happen again. You're dismissed," Christine advised, rubbing her hands together. "Who's next on the list?"

Mr Macpherson made the mistake of grabbing Christine's shoulder. Donald launched his enormous fist; Mr Macpherson, on his back, knocked out. Christine smiled. The other staff members came running in, standing in a line, seeing Macpherson on the floor. Christine asked, "Does anyone else want to join him," she glared. "The holiday camp is over! Anyone not pulling their weight here will be dismissed instantly like the manager. Will somebody turn the bloody fire alarm off; where is maintenance," Christine shouted.

A man in overalls entered, seeing Christine standing in front of the other staff. He immediately replaced the broken glass, reset the alarms, and joined the line. Three members of house staff, not including the chef and his team. Three external estate staff which she had yet to meet. Christine suspected mobile phones would be red-hot by now, warning of her presence. Macpherson struggled to his feet, leaving the room with his head bowed. A few minutes later, he left carrying his suitcase. "Who keeps accounts here?" Christine asked. The maintenance man stepped forward in his late fifties, the eldest. "We each keep a book, Miss, presenting to the manager every month of expenditure and requests for purchases every department from the farm to myself." Christine smiled, "Good system, like that," she grinned, "We obviously don't have any paying guests at the moment."

The maintenance guy stepped forward, "My name is Justin. I've worked here since I left school, madam. I presume you are the daughter of Josephine Gibbs. You have her look," he half-smiled.

"And where were you, Justin, when I arrived?" Christine asked.

"In my workshop at the rear madam where I repair the furniture or anything else relating to the estate buildings. I live here in my cottage provided by the estate."

"I suspect you've seen some changes, Justin, over the years?" Christine asked.

"Yes, some good, some bad, and the estate has employed some cowboys, such as the one you've sacked," he frowned.

Christine turned to face the remaining staff, "One mistake, you're gone, or you can leave now; I don't care either way," Christine voiced with authority. "Glencoe will pay its way from now on, no wastage or partying by the staff. My mother may have turned her back. I will not! I am not my mother; you're dismissed. Go to your duties. I will check on you individually. We are staying here for a week to ascertain the alterations that need to be made and staff changes."

"Justin," Christine smiled. "You come with me around the estate and bring me up to speed on what's happening. I would be interested to hear if you have any suggestions you think could be made to the property." Justin smiled, feeling more secure than he had ten minutes ago, suspecting he would be out of the door his age against him. They went outside, climbing into Christine's Range Rover, stopping at one of the farms. Christine stepped out, looking at the machinery immediately confronted. "What's your business around here, Lass?" A tall, bearded man asked.

Christine held out her hand, "My name is Christine Gibbs. I own the estate; I'm your boss."

He chuckled for a moment, "You're serious," seeing Justin in the back of the Range Rover.

Justin stepped out quickly, fitting his mask he forgot earlier in the commotion, "Careful Robbie, how you address this young lady? The manager lost his head; she owns the property. Treat her with respect; she's not stealing."

Robbie turned, fitting his mask, an authentic Scottish lad in his kilt. "Pleased to meet you, Robbie; nice to find someone awake on this estate and looking after the property."

"My pleasure, Miss Gibbs, hard enough to acquire new equipment if we ever do; we have to look after what we have; otherwise, it will walk."

"You suffer much from thieving, Robbie?"

"I. We do some sheep from deer to grouse, if not on the ball. They took my Molly last year, a Highland cow I reared."

Christine exhaled, "I didn't realise that bad. If you have any suggestions, Robbie, on how we can improve security, I'm here for a week assessing the property. Come and see me," she smiled warmly. "I'll do that, Miss Gibbs."

Christine jumped in her Range Rover, continuing across the estate. Absolutely stunned, the fences appear in shambles, not repaired since World War II. "Suggestions, Justin?"

"The bottom line is we need more money to repair the fencing. We spend more on maintenance; spare parts for old tractors and machinery than the cost of a new one. The lads on the farm look after the machinery as if it's their own, the only way we can survive, everyone wants to keep their position, no one dare speak out."

Christine stopped looking directly at Justin, "If you have something to say, Justin, say providing constructive, I'm here to listen. My fiancé and I are marrying here next year," she smiled, "And I want this place running smoothly and efficiently. That doesn't mean I have to go around with a hatchet disposing of loyal staff. The estate must pay its way, you understand, Justin."

Christine watched Justin smile. "I've just realised you're Donald Selwyn, the artist. My wife and I have seen your portraits on television. I knew I'd seen you somewhere before, and you're marrying here, Miss Gibbs?"

"Yes, if I can salvage the estate from bankruptcy, not breaking even, nothing to invest, that's the problem."

Donald remarked, "I can put half a million to improving the farm equipment isn't a lot, but it's a start; I want to spend some time here painting."

Christine chuckled, "You will not spend any of your money Donald until we are married. I might dump you and run off with Justin."

Justin's more comfortable as they looked over the land, the estate generally, and at the sawmill allowed to decay. Donald commented, "Have that operational, Christine, make our own fence post, sell the timber processed directly from the estate."

"Yes, I agree, Donald. I'll have to cost first," she frowned.

They returned to the house. Christine asked: "What's the state of the property? I mean, the house?"

" No real issues, only general wear and tear with the building," Justin expressed.

"You know anything about farming, Justin?" Christine asked.

"Yes, my father was a tenant farmer until he passed. The estate had the farm back under their control; I've worked for the estate ever since."

"Good, I think you have a good heart and want this to work. You obviously know how the house works; we need to generate more income and decide who stays and who goes; all rotten apples down the road, Justin, you agree?"

"I. lass, before we go completely bust, it'll not happen not in my lifetime," he sighed. "We've seen good intentions, usually all talk and no action."

"Hey Justin, that's unfair," Christine said, annoyed. "I've been here five minutes. This place will be right in the next couple of years, or you can come and say, I told you so. Now, new manager, off your arse and sort this place out. I will leave you my contact numbers, you report any issues to me, and we can decide over the phone together. I will visit here regularly to check on you; I'll make you earn your money," she scolded, watching a broad smile come to Justin's face, the last thing he expected today.

Christine walked inside the hotel, someone in reception. "Notify all staff members; Justin is now the new manager of my estate until further notice."

"Yes, Miss Gibbs."

"Justin, Monday morning, nip into town and purchase a nice tweed suit; you're the manager. Look like one, please. I presume we have an account somewhere?"

Justin smiled, "Yes, thanks for trusting me and giving the place a second chance to return to its former glory before I die."

Christine smiled, patting his cheek, "Dying is not in your contract, and if you die before the job is completed, I want my money back," she smiled.

"The chef came running into the reception, "Miss Gibbs, what would you like for lunch."

"Have venison. I can assess your ability," Christine watched the chef scurry off.

Donald commented, "Okay, Christine, I think you made an impression. Calm down; you will have nobody working for you."

"Yes, I think you may be right, Donald. I don't want to be poisoned while I'm here." Christine looked out of the window seeing a helicopter land on the pad with the Royal crest. Much to her surprise, Mrs Montague walked into the hotel-entering the lounge. Donald stood. Mrs Montague commented, "I don't know where you learnt your manners, Donald, impeccable."

"You wish me to leave you and Christine to talk, Mrs Montague?"

"No, Donald, thank you and please don't keep hitting people; I know you're only defending Christine. What have you found out, Christine? You've been here at least an hour; problem reports I'm receiving leaving no stone unturned? I appreciate you sacked the manager."

"Yes, I placed Justin in charge for the moment; he seems genuine, has his heart in the place."

"A good decision should have thought of that one." Mrs Montague frowned, "What're your thoughts on the estate?"

"Rundown lack of capital, Donald offered to put money into the estate himself, which I refused until we are married."

"What is your view, Donald?" Mrs Montague turned to face him.

"I agree with Christine. However, jumping up and down on genuinely loyal staff badly managed is not the solution. They should be given some leeway to adjust to the new management."

"A wise head on young shoulders. Listen to him, Christine; he will be your anchor in life like my husband is with me. I was like you once Christine hot-headed, knew everything," she smiled reassuringly.

Christine smiled, "I didn't suggest I'm perfect; I will not be ripped off."

A waitress approached, "Will you be staying for lunch, Mrs Montague?"

"Yes, I think I will. I'll have the same as Christine and Donald. I suspect you have venison." Christine grinned, "No flies on you,

Mrs Montague. You can help me decide whether I keep the chef or not," suspecting the information would be relayed to the kitchen.

Mrs Montague grinned, "You have a wicked streak in you, Christine."

Lunch is served at noon in the dining area on a large, highly polished, banquet oak table that could seat a hundred people. Everyone was on their toes, the cutlery laid out and the place absolutely gleaming since Christine arrived. They sat quietly at the table the soup served. Donald felt out of place; enough weaponry on the table to start a war, let alone have lunch.

Dessert served strawberries and cream they'd barely finished eating when the chef approached the table. "I hope everything met with your approval, ladies, gentleman," he asked, looking extremely worried.

Mrs Montague looked to Christine, "Pleasant."

Christine remarked, "I'm here for a week. I will make my final assessment then."

Mrs Montague put her hand to her mouth. Christine's taking no prisoners. She didn't care much like her mother, who trampled everyone underfoot. The chef scurried off to his kitchen. Mrs Montague finished her glass of wine, "The food was excellent, Christine; I enjoyed every mouthful, don't be too harsh. Listen to Donald, please," she emphasised.

Mrs Montague holding Donald's hand, made her way to the helicopter. Donald assisted her aboard; she commented, "If I were only younger, Donald," patting his head, "Good day." Donald stepped away from the helicopter, watching her fly away. Donald noticed how much cooler the air was in Scotland to home.

Christine entered the office examining figures while Donald walked along the many trails leading from the house. He looked in the farm sheds at the dilapidated equipment realising they struggled like him to survive until he became an artist. Donald sat on an old tree stump, watching a Kingfisher on the embankment. He'd taken five hundred photos and already absolutely adored the estate, so different from home, wild and untouched.

The rest of the week was very much the same; Christine spent time with Justin discussing the best way forward. Donald left her to ride around in the estate Land Rover. Finally, he comes across a majestic stag standing on a hillside surveying his domain, quickly taking photos.

Christine and Justin had placed several adverts promoting the estate for weddings: advertising in magazines. The house had forty bedrooms which took some maintenance. Christine decided to take on an apprentice for Justin to supervise maintenance. Hopefully, the apprentice would stay, taking most of the work off Justin. Christine realised they needed more staff; they needed to generate more income; a vicious circle to have more staff. She couldn't have one without the other. Friday morning, Justin came to the hotel wearing his new tweed suit and hat. Donald commented: "That looks uncomfortable, Justin; once you've worn a while, I guess it'll give."

Justin smiled, "Never so proud, Donald, as I am today."

Christine came out looking at him, "Wonderful, my new manager, about your business and make me money" she smiled, linking her arm in Donald's, leaving the hotel and walking alongside the stream running by the house. Once everybody realised Christine's boss, only when necessary and most of the time, she's a lovely person, everyone settled down proud to work for Glencoe Estate. In seven days, Christine had turned the place around with the help of Justin, looking forward to the future and seeing what materialised.

Christine shook everyone's hand before she left. "We will be back in a month to see how things are progressing. If you have any problems, talk to Justin, or if you need to speak to me personally, my number can be found at reception, don't be frightened to phone. I'm here to help you as you are here to help me. We will make this place special once again." Everyone stood at the front door, watching Christine and Donald drive away.

"Well, husband-to-be," she smiled, "Hope you enjoyed your time here?" She asked, looking at the smile on his face.

"How could you not enjoy the place, god's country, the wild friendliness of the people outstanding?" Donald suggested, "You know what's on the way home, Christine?"

She looked at him, puzzled, "What?"

"Gretna Green!"

"We can't, Donald, we mustn't," she chuckled, excited by the thought. "My father would kill me and your parents."

Donald shrugged, "You have a property in Scotland you own."

"Your wicked Donald, and I thought I'm the bad one."

"Think of the money we could save Christine, have a lavished do; at Glencoe Estate," he grinned.

Christine and Donald pulled into Gretna Green, entering the old blacksmith's shop; they were approached. Christine asked, "Can we be married here?"

"Only if you have resided in Scotland for nineteen consecutive days?"

"My name is Christine Gibbs, the owner of Glencoe Estate, and this is my fiancé."

"Oh, you have your birth certificates with you." Donald went into a cold sweat looking through his wallet, coming across a copy of his birth certificate.

"You need two witnesses."

Christine ran outside, grabbing two gentlemen on the way to the pub, "Fifty pounds if you're witnesses to my marriage."

The two men laughed, taking the fifty pounds standing in as witnesses. Christine and Donald looked at each other as they were married. "You now may kiss the bride." Donald kissed Christine carrying her to the Range Rover, "Now we are really in trouble, Christine," he laughed.

"Not half as much as I am, Donald," she said, starting the Range Rover and continuing homeward.

"Why?" Donald asked, puzzled.

"You know you said you wanted ten children?" Christine watched the smile vanish from Donald's expression. "Yes," he replied cautiously.

"You remember what happened in the studio and what's been happening at Glencoe Estate every night? I will add sometimes twice, you beast."

"Yes," he replied cautiously.

"I think I'm pregnant. I haven't taken precautions," Christine grinned, "I hadn't planned; certainly not sleeping with you in the studio, a spur of the moment thing; of course, now I've sampled the sweets I can't stop eating, I discovered."

Donald laughed, "Who's going to tell who when we get home; I think the best solution would be to turn around and return to Glencoe Estate, build a fence around it quickly. Your father will kill me, and my mum and dad will certainly blame me," Donald expressed.

CHAPTER NINE

RESCUING GLENCOE ESTATE

Christine and Donald had travelled for about an hour, deciding to take a break and eat at a motorway station. Donald entered the cafeteria to order, and Christine nipped to the loo; she returned, looking somewhat disappointed. "What's up?" he asked.

"I'm not pregnant. I suppose it's a godsend; we have enough to deal with now," she smiled briefly.

Donald shrugged his shoulders, "I wouldn't have cared either way. Whatever you decide, we have plenty of time ahead. We can have another marriage to please everyone," he smiled.

Christine grinned, realising how much Donald loved her; they finished their brief snack and continued their journey home, heading straight for Crabtree Farm. Christine had decided she would stay here, guessing all hell would break loose when her father found out. By 9 o'clock in the evening, they pulled into the yard. Mary and Martin came out to greet them both. Mary immediately noticed the gold band on her finger, "What have you done, Christine?" Mary exhaled disappointingly.

Donald jumped in, "Don't blame Christine. My idea to visit Gretna Green."

Martin and Mary burst out laughing. "You must be joking; one thing Gerald will be pleased it will save him a fortune on arranging the wedding."

They walked inside the cottage sitting around the oak table. Christine explained what transpired in Scotland, and Mary admitted they hadn't seen much of Gerald. Christine commented, "We must see my father, Donald; I need to collect my clothes. We'll have to face the music sooner or later." Donald and Christine headed for Strawberry Estate only to find Mrs Montague's limousine parked. They walked into the house, finding Mrs Montague and her father in the sitting room. Mrs Montague stood immediately smiling, "According to my sources, congratulations are in order, a romantic gesture on your part, Donald." Christine looked at the expression on her father's face. Donald stood in front of Christine, "I'm to blame my idea a spur of the moment thing," Donald expressed, watching Gerald burst into laughter along with Mrs Montague.

"You're not married," Gerald finally managed to say. Christine, annoyed, produced a marriage certificate. "Doesn't count; Donald has not resided in Scotland for nineteen consecutive days, although you own Glencoe Estate, Christine. Mrs Montague covered the incident for you, so it doesn't become an issue. Marrying next year, not long."

Donald commented, "Oh, blimey! Divorced already," which made everyone laugh even more apart from himself and Christine.

Mrs Montague sat down, trying not to grin, "Your trip to Glencoe Estate was very fruitful, Christine; your choice of Estate Manager wise. Justin knows everything about the estate. I can assure you from my spies that he is working extremely hard to rectify the mess left by your mother and other managers."

Christine flopped down on Donald's lap, "Fortunate I'm not pregnant. Donald would have had a bigger mess to deal with," she frowned.

Mrs Montague insisted, "You must take precautions. We don't want any inappropriate mishaps like your mother," looking to Gerald. "Your mother couldn't have found a better husband under the circumstances. You have turned out certainly to be a wonderful daughter."

A faint knock at the door, "I suspect your mother, Donald," Gerald advised, checking. Mary came in, introduced to Mrs

Montague and politely left with Donald; he glanced at Christine with a hopeless expression on his face of pure disappointment.

"I made a mess of that mother," Donald suggested on the way home.

"Not really, son, at least I have a wedding to attend," she said, patting his leg. Donald smiled, heading to his studio.

***

Early the following day, Christine's out on The Rising Sun, a lovely horse, suspecting Susan had fed him by the expression on his face of disappointment with the amount served. Susan came to the stables, "A lovely horse, Christine. I have enjoyed riding him. You must go away more often," she grinned.

Christine noticed another love bite on Susan's neck, "My horse isn't the only one receiving extra rations," she grinned.

Susan turned slightly crimson. "Well, you never know what life will throw at you. You have to take every opportunity. I heard what you and Donald were up to on the way home from Scotland," she smiled sympathetically. "How romantic. Breakfast in half an hour, Christine."

"Thanks," Christine smiled, riding off.

***

In his pyjamas, Donald sat in his studio, looking at a blank canvas deciding to paint the worst storm he could ever imagine, sweeping across the heavens in vibrant colours. He wanted people to feel his pain and sorrow. The paint flew in every direction; he applied thick and fast the first time he used a knife, almost like a builder exposing his love and hate of life.

Donald stood and walked away from the canvas, considering it a disaster. He realised that he could see his life on canvas, although to the untrained eye would merely appear as a mistake. Donald took a deep breath and snapped several shots with his mobile, sending them to Jack.

Donald showered and changed, nipping across to the cottage in time to see the last lorryload of wheat leave the farm. Donald sat down at the kitchen table. Mary could see he was upset about the situation between him and Christine. She suspected he realised he's controlled and Christine by a greater power you'd be ill-advised to cross. Donald's phone vibrated with a message from Jack, "I'll be there shortly."

Mary asked, "like to talk things over, Donald?"

"Nothing to say, mother; I sort of used to the idea of married on the way home, and then everything we wanted, stamped on," he sighed.

"Not really only delayed, and you probably thank everyone in the end. I was your age once impulsive inpatient," Mary advised, kissing his forehead. "We all go through these moods every generation," Mary suggested. Martin came in. Donald asked, "What's happening today?"

"Nothing odd jobs have to arrange for Gerald to kill two more pigs," he smiled.

"Are you having any animals, dad?"

"I suppose, although I've had an offer on the barley. Apparently, fit for malting, I was waiting to talk to you. This year-round, we should sell for malting at a good price and perhaps look at animals next year after harvest."

"You'll be bored, stupid dad," Donald chuckled.

"No, I won't. That reminds me, the four-holiday apartments are completely booked for the next six months." Donald stared, astonished. "Thanks to you, son and your reputation. You haven't noticed the old front garden, we put one parking bay for each apartment. Michael thought it would be a good idea, then no chance of cars clashing with farm equipment."

Donald ran outside the cottage, the main house front garden missing. Donald suddenly found himself with people and cameras taking a picture of him, famous whether he liked it or not. He waved politely, returning to the cottage.

"Doesn't pay to go away for a week," Donald smiled.

"You realise what you've achieved, Donald. I can take your mother away on holiday, something we only dream of; you've made possible for your mother and me," Martin smiled.

Mary grinned, "You know where we're visiting for our first holiday."

Donald shrugged his shoulders, smiling.

"Glencoe Estate, Christine offered us a room for a couple of weeks. Her ulterior motive is to see how the place is run and would provide her with suggestions for improvements."

"Who's running the farm and the holiday lets?" Donald asked.

"You," Mary suggested, "The agency if any maintenance issues phone Michael, he will deal with it. I think you can manage to feed the pigs and Biscuit," Mary smiled.

"When are you leaving?"

Mary looked at her wristwatch, "In a couple of hours, Gerald offered to watch things for us."

Donald sat down, "Blimey! I have a yuppie mother."

Jack arrived, parking by the cottage. Donald came out to greet him both ran upstairs to the studio. Jack commented, "Fascinating piece, Donald, not your usual style, difficult to assess from a photo." Jack is barely in the doorway. He stared, seeing the sunlight strike the canvas through the skylight. Jack sat in a chair, staying very silent.

Christine ran into the studio and paused, looking at Donald's artwork. Jack commented, "I've never seen the heavens torn apart with such ferocity. A million soles are bleeding, and the world is crying through your brushstrokes. An artist committed suicide, unable to control the pain inside," Jack sighed.

Christine asked, "The artist committed suicide in the end?"

Jack nodded.

Christine sighed heavily, "I hope you're not planning anything so stupid, Donald; we have a life to live together," she hugged him.

"That wasn't even on my mind, I don't think," Donald sat in thought. "I was angry, that's all; I feel a failure sometimes."

"You realise, Donald when I hang this portrait in my gallery, the bidding will start at two million-plus. You have excelled to a higher understanding of life than most people can reach. Few people worldwide who will understand the meaning and want to possess are those with bottomless bank accounts."

Christine and Donald helped Jack load the painting into the boot of his Bentley, watching him drive off carefully.

"Changing the subject, Donald, father's coming this afternoon to dispose of the other two pigs. Mary will be on her way to Scotland with Martin. I'm living with you while they're gone," she grinned.

"What about The Rising Sun?"

Christine pointed to the far stable; Donald smiled. Christine and Donald ran to the cottage. Christine advised, "No time limit. If you want to stay for a month, please do. All your expenses are paid for," she advised calmly.

Mary looked at her, "According to the brochure I found in this fancy magazine, the rooms start at four hundred and fifty pounds a night. If meals are to be included, that's six hundred and fifty pounds. Drinks are charged as an extra."

"You were family yesterday until Mrs Montague put a spanner in the works," Christine expressed. "I still think of you as my family; you will be family next year."

Mary smiled, "If the service is any good, we'd like to contribute. If it's rubbish, I will be phoning you immediately, young lady; I will expect you to rectify it. You will have to sharpen your claws to run an estate," Mary advised.

"Excellent," Christine grinned, "Just what we need the wicked witch of the west to turn my business around." Everyone laughed with Mary pointing her finger at Christine for being so cheeky.

"Oh yes, I have one present for my darling son before we go." She handed Donald a packet of condoms. Christine put both her hands to her mouth in shock, Donald's glowing red with embarrassment. "I want no mistakes while away," Mary said, earnestly looking at them.

Martin, in stitches, looking at everyone's expression, received a jab in the ribs from Mary, "You should be loading the Range Rover Martin, or I'll leave you here," she suggested.

Everybody took a photograph every time the Selwyn's stepped out of their cottage. Mary glanced back, commenting, "Hard work when you're famous." Donald could never remember a time when his mother looked so happy, not worrying about money or him. She wasn't worried about the farm anymore.

Donald and Christine watched his mother and father leave for Scotland, calling in at a Travel Lodge on the way to break up the journey.

Gerald arrived, helping Donald separate the pigs to be slaughtered; they could see the residents in the holiday flats watching. Gerald advised Christine to explain what was happening. It was advisable not to watch unless they had a strong stomach. Christine knocked on every door, explaining, hearing the first shot and then the second. To her surprise, everyone wanted to watch; some videoed the process. She went inside, not in the slightest interested. She couldn't make up her mind whether it was a fact Donald's there or they enjoyed the process of preparing an animal.

Donald threw one pig in Gerald's Range Rover, and the other he carried down into the cottage cellar throwing the odd bits to Biscuit, who thought his birthday. Gerald washed his knives and drove off home after having a cup of coffee. Gerald couldn't remember a time when he felt so contented; he wished things had turned out better for him and Josephine. He's unsure of Susan deciding it would be okay to enjoy each other's company; he could not take it further. He didn't want to jeopardise anything for his daughter Christine.

***

Jack phoned Donald around midnight waking both him and Christine. Christine slipped on her dressing gown to make a coffee. Donald placed his phone on speaker so Christine could listen. "What's the matter, Jack?" Donald asked, laughing.

"I suspect I've woken you, haven't I?" Jack exhaled, "I couldn't resist phoning you, thank god, for quick-drying oils. Your latest composition will be heading to Germany bidding has reached four million. Now five," Jack shouted.

"Calm down, Jack," Donald advised, "You'll give yourself a heart attack."

"How can you possibly be so calm, Donald?" Jack asked, bewildered.

"You must remember Jack only fun for me; admittedly, the money is great. I'll be seventeen soon and have to buy myself a nice motor or perhaps a tractor," he laughed.

"You don't need a tractor Donald just a paintbrush," Jack expressed.

"You must remember, Jack, none of this would have happened if it wasn't for the farm giving me the insight into life."

"My god, you're a bloody genius." Jack shouted, "The title of the painting. Insight into Life. The Internet is wild, Donald, seven million since I've added the title."

Christine's laughed at Jack's excitement, realising her future was assured with Donald; money appeared no longer a problem. He had sufficient funds to buy Strawberry Estate or Glencoe and still had change. Now no one could accuse him of chasing Christine for her money, as suggested by some people at the outset of their relationship.

Donald suggested, "Jack, take two aspirin and go to bed before you have a heart attack."

"I have personally made over three million commission in the short time I've known you," Jack expressed.

"Our relationship will not continue, Jack; if you're dead, rest," Donald insisted, disconnecting the call. Donald slipped on his dressing-gown, kissed Christine on the forehead, and took his cup of coffee into his studio, switching on the lights. One o'clock in the morning by the time he'd managed to remove Jack off the phone. Donald remembered the stream strolling along at Glencoe, visualising the Kingfisher. He started sketching, applying a few oils deciding the Kingfisher should be perched on Christine's shoulder. Christine went to bed. She's worn out, drifting off to sleep, leaving Donald to pursue his passion. By 5 o'clock in the morning, Donald had created from memory the scene with Christine sitting on a large boulder looking at a brown trout with the Kingfisher surveying from her shoulder and the stone footbridge in the distance. Donald never understood how he could paint so quickly. Was it his youth?

Christine came wandering in carrying a cup of coffee for him; she stared in amazement, noticing the painting was of her and Glencoe. "I'm hanging that at Glencoe you're not selling Donald; please, we don't need the money."

"I'm donating to Glencoe. When sold, Justin could use the money to buy new farm equipment to improve the estate; our future is not a waste of money."

"Oh, very well, beast, your hearts in the right place," slipping off her nightdress and sitting on his lap. She stood for a moment removing his erect cock, gently sitting on it, gasping as he kissed her back and neck, gripping her breasts with his large hands and gently twisting her nipples. She couldn't help but make a noise and couldn't move fast enough. She couldn't have enough of the sensation. Christine was beginning to understand why her mother enjoyed sex so much, wondering whether she should experiment no longer, a virgin? Donald wouldn't know who she slept with. She suspected that was her mother's conclusion with Gerald, her father.

Donald smiled, heading for the shower. Christine made breakfast, which consisted of her usual marmalade on toast. Donald returned after dressing, observing what was on his breakfast plate, eating the toast with one hand switching on the frying pan, grabbing a pound of bacon from the fridge, sausage and tomatoes and a couple of slices of bread. He wasn't starving, girlfriend or not.

Christine glared, "You're not having breakfast like that. More cholesterol in that concoction," she said, placing her hands on her hips.

Donald grinned, "If I'm going to die, I'm dying with a smile on my face; I'm not turning into a scrawny old chicken."

Christine punched him, "You're suggesting I'm a scrawny old chicken?"

"Of course not. Would you like me to cook you breakfast, Christine?" he grinned and winked.

"No, toast is adequate for me, thank you. I'll feed my horse," Christine said, poking her tongue out and heading for the door. Donald took a photo of his latest artwork, and within minutes, Jack was on the phone. "You go from one extreme to the other, Donald; that's so serene and beautiful. You have so many sides to your character. You will discover ten million transferred into your account this morning as I predicted your latest portrait on its way to Germany."

"Thanks, Jack, for all you do for me; I'd be lost without an agent like you," Donald professed.

"The pleasure is all mine, Donald; not only do I have the best artist in the world. I have the enjoyment of surprised by every picture you paint. My insurance company has also insisted I upgrade my security. It's like living in Fort Knox here," he chuckled.

***

Martin and Mary turned into the enormous Glencoe Estate driveway shrouded in trees. They headed down the drive seeing the hotel set out before them as they crossed the bridge. They parked the Range Rover; staff were out to greet them, assisting with their luggage to the best room on the property, actually Christine's.

Justin knocked on the door, fitting his mask. Mary invited him in, adjusting hers. "I'm the Estate Manager; my name is Justin. I've had the pleasure of meeting your son Donald and his future bride Christine Gibbs, my employer. If there's anything you need night or day, ring reception or my personal mobile number," he said, passing his card. "If you wish to see the estate, please feel free to drive anywhere. Although I would advise taking myself with you or the gamekeeper, so easy to become lost in twenty-five thousand acres of trees and hills."

Mary and Martin shook his hand, impressed with how he presented himself and offered the hotel services. Mary and Martin decided to rest for a while, notified by a receptionist at 7:30 p.m.

that dinner was about to be served in the dining room. Martin and Mary were not alone. The advertisement campaign organised by Justin and Christine before she left is working; they had not a spare bedroom. The guests sat around the hundred-seating banquet table laid out to perfection. After the soup moved onto the main course, grouse, and venison, some guests had wine with their meal and others a glass of malt whisky provided by the local distillery.

Justin made sure Mary and Martin left in no doubt they were special. Martin whispered in Mary's ear, "I could get used to this way of life, love, couldn't you," he suggested.

Mary smiled, "I'm trying to find something to complain about; I can't." Surprised to see a large bouquet of flowers come into the dining room carried in by a staff member. "With the compliments of the management, may you enjoy your stay."

After dessert and coffee, the setting sun slowly disappeared behind the mountains in the distance; Mary and Martin walked along the stream embankment leading to the abandoned sawmill.

After a short while, they returned to their room, realising the air was cooler in Scotland than at home. At 8 o'clock in the morning, breakfast is served with a menu of eight selections, from egg and bacon to a mere toast and marmalade. Someone had obviously phoned the chef. Two large breakfasts appeared placed in front of Mary and Martin. Christine would not be beaten; she's not receiving a complaint. Other guests looked at the enormous breakfast Mary and Martin were consuming. A guest asked, "Is that special?"

The waitress remarked, "Yes, Sir, only made on request. It's affectionately called the Selwyn breakfast; not many can master the beast from what I understand from my employer. Sir, the chef, will willingly make you one if you are inclined."

The guest smiled, "No, I don't think so; I couldn't handle that, I don't think many people could," returning to finish his bowl of cornflakes.

The chef came from the kitchen, "May I ask Mrs Selwyn, have I made the breakfast correctly? Have I missed anything?" he asked nervously.

"Should be three slices of fried bread, two eggs, not one, four rashers of bacon, not three, four sausages and two slices of black pudding, other than that perfect well done," she smiled, clearing her plate, watching Martin do the same.

***

Christine at Crabtree Farm returned from her ride on The Rising Sun. The Rising Sun appeared to enjoy a different location, especially the carrots provided by the visitors. Jack arrived dashing upstairs in his usual, I have six places to be at once attitude, looking at the composition of Christine, and the Kingfisher sat on the boulder by the stream, watching the brown trout in clear water. "I wish I knew how you made everything look real, Donald. You almost feel like they are alive."

"I know just a talent I have," Donald grinned.

"I must ask your mother for a cake, and now she's in Scotland, I can't."

Donald smiled, looking in a cupboard, "Mum thinks of everything there you are," he said, passing Jack a tin. "I think you only come for the cake, not my portraits," Donald grinned.

He carried the portrait to the Bentley, carefully slipping in the boot. "Just for curiosity, Jack, what do you think that portrait is worth?"

Jack shrugged his shoulders, "Nothing wild or dramatic; about six hundred thousand pounds wouldn't go amiss."

"Don't sell Jack, frame for me, please. It can go to our Glencoe Estate so everyone can admire my beautiful wife and hang in the hallway along with the other frosty old portraits, which should add some life to the place."

Christine stood behind him, feeling threatened, "Since when do you make decisions about Glencoe Donald?"

Donald exhaled, "Sell the bloody painting Jack," walking off, releasing Biscuit from his chain, walking through the recently drilled crops his father had planted before going on holiday.

"Jack," Christine instructed. "Please send the portrait to Glencoe if you could frame it for me. I'm only teasing him. Donald's desperate to help everyone."

Jack nodded, "Careful, Christine; I'd hate to see your relationship explode in your face; some artists are extremely temperamental, especially concerning their work."

Jack jumped in his Bentley, heading for London. Christine mounted The Rising Sun, galloping off to find Donald. He was discovered on a bench by his grandfather's ashes underneath the old crab apple tree, the only one remaining on the farm. Christine sighed heavily, dismounting, "Have I upset you again, Donald?"

"Not really I thought we were a partnership; apparently not, that's okay." Donald went to walk away. Christine grabbed his arm, "What do you mean by that remark?" she asked firmly.

"Nothing, simply stating the obvious; I presume we'll have to have a prenup before marrying?" He asked suspiciously.

Christine stared in shock; the thought had never crossed her mind. "Why, do you want one, Donald?"

"I suppose I will have to protect myself from you if we marry with your money and power. I could lose everything; I'm not giving up the farm, married or not. I want something for my children other than to be swallowed up by an estate management team."

Christine jumped on The Rising Sun's back, riding towards Strawberry Estate. She'd opened another can of worms for herself making Donald think about insignificant things at this time. She didn't care whether he had half of her estate; it had never crossed her mind. All she was interested in was marrying him, becoming less likely by the minute.

Christine placed The Rising Sun in his stable on Strawberry Estate, trying to calm down and think sensibly after all that's said. Gerald saw Christine entering the house. He realised immediately something had gone wrong, "What's happened, Christine?" he asked, deeply concerned.

"Nothing, father. Would you give me a lift to collect my Range Rover?"

"Yes." They climbed in his Range Rover Christine collected her clothes from Donald's studio, driving home to Strawberry Estate. She ran straight to her bedroom, was she acting too hastily. Donald's only trying to raise money for her estate, which is in a mess and had a mountain to climb to recover if it ever did. She'd slammed the door in his face by reminding him who owned what.

Gerald sat in the living room, sipping his glass of whisky. Christine is seventeen and could please herself more or less; he wasn't interfering unless she asked his opinion, although highly tempted.

***

Donald came home with Biscuit realising Christine had gone. Pleased in some respects, he hadn't donated any money to the Glencoe Estate would have been a bad investment. Donald checked his bank account, realising twelve million, more than most people would ever dream about having. He sat quietly watching television; his mobile vibrated, mother. "Hi, mum having a good time?"

"Wonderful Donald, like a different world, put Christine on."

"I can't; she's in the shower, you enjoy yourself, mum say hello to dad for me, bye."

Mary looked at Martin, "Something's happened. I could tell by the tone of his voice," Mary rang Christine. She answered. "Come on, who said what or did what?"

"What Donald say?" Christine asked cautiously.

"He didn't say anything apart from you were in the shower; I know when my son is lying, it's plain that something happened, Christine."

Christine explained.

"You're both right and wrong; you must decide whether you want a prenup to protect your estates. Donald shouldn't presume what is his when it isn't. We'll pack and come home in the morning," Mary sighed.

"Don't you dare, Mary! Donald would never forgive me; I will never forgive you. Enjoy your holiday. I'll sort this mess out myself," Christine sighed.

***

Donald sat quietly, thinking the bottom-line money. Everything revolved around money. A few months ago, he was a poor struggling farmer; he's now a millionaire thanks to his gift with a paintbrush. Donald decided to ring Jack, "Hi Jack, I want to donate 10% of whatever my paintings make to help the less fortunate. Can you arrange that for me?"

"Yes, Donald and I will add 10% of my takings. They will have 20% such a giving person. You have never been selfish, Donald. I'll make arrangements; you realise Christine has instructed me to send the painting of her and the Kingfisher to her estate."

"I own the painting. She may own estates, not me," he said firmly, gritting his teeth, "How dare she presumes she controls my every movement. I want the portrait auctioned off and the total earnings to go to the charity you choose; those are my instructions, Jack, please."

Jack was silent, "let's not be too hasty here, Donald, don't do or say anything you may regret in the future."

"Why should I regret anything? She's quite happy to explain how her estates were nothing to do with me, so why is my artwork anything to do with her?"

"Point taken, Donald, see what the bidding produces before deciding."

"Okay, as you wish, Jack, please remember any decisions concerning my art must be approved by me, no one else. Bye."

By 10 o'clock in the evening, all over the news, the artist Donald Selwyn is donating 10% of his earnings from his portraits to assist the less fortunate in life. The portrait of his last painting, Christine and the Kingfisher, the price had already reached one and a half million pounds.

***

Christine stared in disbelief; she was under the impression the portrait was heading for Glencoe Estate. Obviously, Donald had blocked her instructions; she sat quietly, fuming, realising she had no control over his artwork. Similarly, he had no control over her estates, Christine thought, serves me right. Gerald approached Christine, "At the risk of told to keep my nose out, what's happened?"

Christine explained. "Oh, a simple term of expression. I'll have a word with Donald and explain that he must always say Christine's estate or Christine's Range Rover, or Christine wants her arse kicked, stupid girl."

Christine stared at him, not believing he would criticise her. "Miss, hi and mighty, I presume any children you have, if anybody will have you, will be continually reminded who owns what." Gerald's so angry he throws the newspaper at her. Christine turned on her heels. "I will teach you a lesson, Christine, you won't forget. I will leave my shares of Strawberry Estate to Donald Selwyn to solve the problem of who owns what. Glencoe Estate has always been run as a tax loss. It will always be a bloody tax loss unless you get off your arse and fix the situation. You realise, Miss high and mighty, you are already one million in the red, and you will not use my farm to prop your business failings like your mother."

Christine was speechless; she had never known her father to explode in such a manner. "I've spoken to Mary and Jack; how dare you instruct Jack to ship Donald's artwork to Glencoe Estate without his consent. You know the irony of it all, girl; he gave you the bloody portrait to raise money for the farm anyway." Gerald, absolutely fuming, "He treats you like a Princess. You suck every drop of blood you can out of him; you are worse than your mother," he said, slamming the door as he left.

Christine burst into tears; she could feel herself trembling with fear. She could never remember when her father lost his temper with her, and she read things into situations that didn't exist. So many unanswered questions ran through her mind.

Gerald jumped in his Range Rover and drove to Crabtree Farm. He ran into the studio and found Donald painting a portrait of Biscuit rounding up the sheep.

"Hi, Gerald, I guess you've come to burn my ears, probably all my fault the situation anyway; usually is," Donald expressed downhearted.

Gerald removed a bottle of whiskey from his pocket and the other two glasses, "That makes two of us, mate," Gerald smiled. "I've given Christine a roasting long overdue. I've allowed her to get away with everything, my fault. She thinks she's god's gift to the human race like her mother; she's just landed on her arse," he said, taking a large drink from his glass. Donald burst out laughing, drinking his. Donald put his paintbrushes down, "A warm evening, Gerald fancy going slightly wild?" Donald grinned.

"What do you mean," Gerald chuckled.

"How do you fancy a late-night barbecue in the yard? The holidaymakers here can join in. Give them something to remember, and we can have a laugh at the same time."

"I didn't believe you were crazy. I do now, come on," Gerald laughed.

They set up the large barbecue made from old oil drums using torches and floodlights. Gerald and Donald piled on the timber lighting with a splash of diesel to get things moving rapidly. Donald visited each apartment, inviting everyone who was staying to join in. Donald suggested, "Why don't you phone Susan? She could pop over and help?" he grinned.

"Good idea," Gerald said, drinking from the bottle of whisky, trying to stop catching fire, "She could nip home and bring a case of whisky and wine. We could really let our hair down." Donald shrugged his shoulders, "Go for it, brother."

Gerald rang Susan. She had already gone to bed, "What Gerald, what you, suggesting," she frowned, "At this time, okay," Susan laughed, dressed, heading for Strawberry Estate to collect the alcohol. Everyone started dancing, bringing tables and chairs; four couples stayed in the apartments, enjoying the event. One asked Gerald, "Countryfolk do this all the time?"

"Yes, and worse, we usually chase maidens across the field with a pitchfork," he laughed.

***

Christine came downstairs hearing a commotion in the kitchen, finding Susan. Christine folded her arms, looking suspiciously, "Are you robbing us now?" Noticing Susan dressed in a short skirt and an extremely low-cut top, obviously, she wasn't wearing a bra.

"No, Christine, I'm off to a party Donald's holding and your father. Gerald phoned me to join in collecting a few bottles of whisky and wine, which were my instructions." Christine frowned, realising Donald had not invited her. Watched Susan load the two crates. She ran off upstairs, changing into jeans and a jumper, slipping on her denim coat and following Susan down the drive. Weren't many minutes before they were parking outside the floodlit yard of Crabtree Farm. Christine couldn't believe she could see Donald dancing with a strange woman. To make matters worse, her father did the same until he saw Susan grabbing the crate of wine and returning to her boot carrying whisky.

Christine stepped out of her Range Rover into the light. The music is loud playing from the stereo in the studio. Biscuit's hiding in his kennel; he wanted nothing to do with the affair.

Christine grabbed a glass of red wine, standing in front of Donald. They grinned at each other. Donald removed the glass carefully from her hand, kissing her passionately. They started to dance to the music, everyone helping themselves to the pork on the barbecue along with the baked potatoes wrapped in foil. No one was in charge of the cooking; everyone seemed to jump in and help. Christine watched her father dancing, realising Susan's earlier statement her father had hands like an octopus was not exaggerating. By 2 o'clock in the morning, everyone is off to bed apart from

Gerald, who's absolutely plastered; helped into the spare room in the cottage by Susan, who didn't return, staying with him for the night.

Christine carried on Donald's shoulder upstairs to the studio. He threw her on the bed. She "laughed," watching him collapse beside her, snoring moments later.

Early the following day, Mary phoned Gerald, surprised, answered by Susan, lying beside him. "Could I speak to Gerald, please?" Mary asked.

"He's asleep, Mary, after the party Donald threw here at Crabtree Farm last night. I hope you're not annoyed we sort of borrowed your spare room. He's too far gone to make it home."

Mary laughed, "What's this about a party?"

"I'm not quite sure how it all came about; I was phoned by Gerald at 10 o'clock in the evening to fetch wine and whisky from Strawberry Estate. I don't remember much after that. Apart from old octopus hands here, everyone joined in, including the guests in your apartments, having a whale of a time. The last conversation I remember clearly is one of your guests asking Gerald if this is a custom. He replied, we have many customs especially chasing young maidens across fields with pitchforks," Susan grinned.

"Where is Donald?"

"Last I saw of him heading up to the studio with Christine over his shoulder, don't worry if any mess I'll clear up before I go home," Susan promised.

Mary laughed, "Everyone's happy. That's the main thing."

Susan remarked, "I certainly am after last night. I can assure you, Mary, I'm not often invited out these days; bye for now."

Susan made coffee staggering outside. No real mess, only the barbecue and table to pack away. Everyone is still asleep in the apartments. Gerald came staggering out, grabbing Susan around the waist, kissing her neck passionately taking her back inside.

By 9 o'clock, Donald's dressed, drinking his first coffee. Christine was asleep; he came downstairs and started clearing away; an hour later, Gerald came to assist Susan. Donald checked the barbecue was cold, packing away for another day. Gerald patted Donald on the shoulder, "One hell of a party. I haven't felt this good for years," Gerald grinned.

Donald smiled, watching Susan quietly slip into her car and drive away. Donald jabbed Gerald in the ribs, "You're an old dog." Gerald turned bright red, not expecting a comment like that from Donald. He was about to finish clearing seeing Christine coming down into the yard, trying to brush the knots out of her hair. She kissed Donald on the cheek, "I must go, my horse, boyfriend."

He smiled, "Okay, your ladyship," smacking her backside. Gerald realised the relationship was now back on track; he would say no more and jumped in his Range Rover, heading home. Donald nipped into the cottage, grabbing dried food for Biscuit; he stood in front of the kennel for a moment expecting Biscuit to jump out at him. Donald went into a cold sweat and knelt, easing Biscuit from the kennel he'd passed on.

Donald carefully held Biscuit in his arms, grabbing a spade from the shed with tears streaming down his cheeks, feeling someone had ripped his heart out. Biscuit, a faithful friend for many years, and now gone.

Donald had decided Biscuit should be buried by his grandfather's ashes. He slowly dug the grave, gently placing Biscuit's body in the grave, carefully replacing the soil. Donald walked to the yard, making a grave marker out of timber burning Biscuit's name into the oak board. He returned to the graveside with a sledgehammer; he drove the stake into the ground, spending a few moments in silence before returning to the farm.

Donald ran upstairs to his studio, where his half-finished painting of Biscuit rested on his easel. No matter how many times his mobile rang, Donald wouldn't answer. He continued painting the portrait of an animal he really loved.

Christine tried most of the morning to contact Donald without success; by 3 o'clock, she was really worried jumping in her Range Rover. She came over to Crabtree Farm, running up into the studio. Donald is painting, crying, broken-hearted. She looked at the scene and immediately realised Biscuit was dead.

She quickly made coffee with a nip of whisky and kissed Donald on the forehead, placing the mug on the table beside him. Christine reflected how she felt when they found Jerusalem dead in the stables some time back, almost like your heart had been stamped on, ripped out and thrown away. She remembered crying for the whole day along with her mother for the loss of a lovely horse and friend. Christine realised it didn't matter what she said or did; she couldn't ease his suffering and sat quietly in a chair looking out of the window at Biscuit's old kennel.

Donald took a deep breath standing some distance from his portrait of Biscuit, and collapsed in tears, crying inconsolably. Christine encouraged Donald to sit in an armchair, sat on his lap, and brought a brief smile to his face; they cuddled each other. Donald kissed Christine on the forehead, "I do love you, girl," he smiled, easing Christine to her feet, leaving the studio and into the yard, taking a sledgehammer. He smashed Biscuit's old kennel to pieces, not wishing to be reminded that he had lost his best friend every morning.

Christine joined him moments later, holding his hand, "You remember the old sawmill on Strawberry Estate? Michael has worked extremely hard along with the new Forester father's taken on; would you like to come and see? Donald no good moping around here, as harsh as that may sound."

"I know, Christine, come on, we'll go," sliding into the seat of her Range Rover.

Christine drove on to Strawberry Estate, parking by the renovated sawmill. Donald's surprised by the place, giving the appearance never ceased working. Heard the old petrol-paraffin engine burst into life. Douglas, the new Forester employed by Strawberry Estate, tested the saw blade on a piece of old pine tree trunk, checking no failures one more time. Douglas switched off the old engine approaching Christine and Donald. "Douglas, I'd like you to meet my future husband, Donald Selwyn."

Donald greeted Douglas warmly, surprised by how Christine had introduced him. Douglas, in his late fifties, moved into the adjacent cottage to Michael with his wife. Douglas remarked, "I've seen your artwork, Donald, marvellous," Douglas smiled warmly.

"Douglas," Donald asked politely, "Would you mind standing by the saw blade for a moment so I can take a photo? Would it make a marvellous painting?"

Douglas smiled, "You'd be better off with your future wife in the picture than me," he remarked, standing by the saw and part of the old tree trunk.

Christine and Donald returned to Crabtree Farm; she's determined to stay with him and ensure her future husband eats properly and has someone to talk to. Donald ran upstairs immediately, covering his artwork of Biscuit and placing it in the corner of the studio. He selected a new canvas transferring the photos from his mobile to his computer and transmitting the information to a large screen on the wall so he could see every detail. Christine set about making dinner while Donald sketched the old sawmill. He decided not to notify his parents of Biscuit's demise, not wanting to ruin their holiday.

Donald had finished painting by 9 o'clock in the evening. Christine had fallen asleep on the settee in his adjacent apartment. Donald entered the room seeing Christine curled up asleep; he carried her gently to the bedroom, slipping her beneath the duvet; returning to his artwork, making sure everything was perfect before he sent a photo to Jack with the instructions, "Make a thousand prints then placed the portrait up for sale, please."

Jack replied almost immediately, "Will do."

Although a lovely portrait, there is nothing dramatic in the scene, although the way Donald's artworks sell, he could walk on water as far as the art world is concerned.

Donald realised he would be seventeen next week; he only had to pass his driving test and be mobile. Donald wondered what sort of vehicle he would like; virtually nothing he couldn't afford; the obvious choice would be a Range Rover. Decided how boring. He didn't often go off-road, even with the farm's Land Rover; most tracks around Strawberry Estate were passable with any four-wheel-drive.

Donald's rather taken by Jack's four-wheel-drive SUV Bentley. Maybe a little extravagant, he thought at least; he would have the ability to travel anywhere plus ride in comfort. Definitely, plenty of room to carry his art equipment should he wish to park somewhere and paint rather than have to take pictures and return home.

***

Blissfully unaware of home events, Mary and Martin at Glencoe Estate have a wonderful time in Scotland. Every morning served the Selwyn breakfast, which caused such a stir that some other guests had tried it even if it cost twenty pounds each. Glencoe's finally making money; everyone adored Mary and Martin, invited to houses around the estate for a few drinks and a haggis. Martin noted the problems after talking to each farm staff member; their suggestions for a cure boiled down to a lack of investment. Although one or two suggestions were a matter of implementation to make things run better.

Finally, they're last night at Glencoe Estate. They danced until eleven in the evening, which Mary had loved doing as a child. She remembered Martin taking her to several dances when they were courting. Everything flooded her mind realising Donald made all this happen for them both, life beyond the farm.

They waved goodbye to everyone early in the morning, heading home, deciding to travel the whole journey in one day, arriving at their cottage around seven in the evening, much to Christine and Donald's surprise. Mary looked at the expression on Donald's face, "What's happened, son!" Donald couldn't speak; he pointed. Mary placed her hand to her mouth, "Oh no, not Biscuit."

Donald walked away. Christine explained to Mary and Martin. Mary commented, "That old dog helped Donald as a young boy; he used to be picked on at school. When Donald came home, he would sit by Biscuit's kennel, explaining to Biscuit his troubles until Donald grew in size and flattened everybody who was nasty to him," Mary smiled.

Christine had no idea how vital Biscuit was to Donald; she now understood why he was so upset he'd lost his best friend.

After making coffee, Mary, at the kitchen table, told Christine what a wonderful time they had in Scotland on her estate. "What do I owe you?" Mary asked.

"Nothing; if you enjoyed yourself, that's payment enough," Christine smiled.

"Don't be a silly girl; the place has to make money. It won't survive else. After talking to the staff, Martin made a list of the urgent problems."

Christine sighed, "Father reminded me Glencoe Estate is a million pounds in debt, and I couldn't use Strawberry Estate to prop up. He threatened to give Donald his shares of Strawberry Estate for my arrogant behaviour."

"I know he told me," Mary frowned. "He won't; it's your breeding Christine your sort of aristocracy. What they wanted came first, and the ordinary person could take a hike for a better explanation."

"Yes, I've made some right blunders; I almost wrecked my relationship with Donald."

Martin walked down to the corner of the field where the crab apple tree and his father's ashes were scattered. He saw Biscuit's grave and a bench Donald had made for the family to sit on while they considered their thoughts. Martin sat beside Donald, "The best place for him. I remember my father buying that puppy for you when you were one year old," Martin smiled.

Donald grinned, "You enjoy your holiday, dad?"

"Great son, a holiday we won't forget, the staff from the farm to the hotel were very polite. We visited many of their homes having a private party; at least I had a chance to talk to some farming staff and find out what was really happening."

Donald lent back on the bench, "Give me the lowdown, dad."

"I thought our equipment was knackered. You want to see what they have to use, for me to call something junk; I think you have the picture. They're still driving old power majors. The newest tractor they have there is an old Ford 4000. They have an old 3C JCB for handling the bales and everything else. The muck spreader, if that's what you could call it, is one of those old Russian machines, and that's about where it belonged in Russia. Combine an old Massey Harris, the baler new Holland what's left of it anyway."

"Thanks, dad, although Christine virtually told me to keep my nose out of her estate. I think I'll have to talk to her even if it does cause a blazing argument," Donald frowned.

They returned to the cottage. Donald grabbed Christine's hand; she looked pretty alarmed, throwing her over his shoulder, carrying her up into the studio, and gently placing her in an armchair. Donald took a deep breath, "Really none of my business; however, it may be next year Glencoe Estate is a mess, and you know it, don't you?"

Christine bit her tongue; she felt like saying, mind your own bloody business, realising that's not the way forward with her relationship and husband, she hoped. "Yes, doing my very best with the money I have available. Father said I can't use Strawberry Estate shares to help support Glencoe Estate; he's threatened to disown me in not so many words."

"Would you like me to purchase the whole estate off you, Christine?"

Christine stared in shock, "You can't be serious, Donald. I would never sell my estate. I'll make it work."

"Not with the equipment your staff have to use, still in the dark ages, worse than my farm was."

"What are you proposing, Donald? Cut to the chase," Christine asked, becoming upset.

"Are we to marry Christine next year? I'm not throwing money down the drain," Donald asked seriously.

"Well, yes," she said, feeling a cold shudder run down her spine of his uncertainty.

"Okay then, I propose I invest two million in your estate; I'm not sure of anything. I would expect the two million to be repaid to me if the relationship fails," he said cold-heartedly for the first time regarding Christine; he had his business head entirely switched on.

Christine sat dismayed, "I can't, Donald, accept your offer. I would rather struggle than place the estate in further jeopardy. Until I opened my big mouth the other day, you would have willingly given me the money," Christine stood. "I must go," she kissed Donald on the forehead, walking down the stairway from the studio, realising his attitude was her own fault, turning him into a calculating monster. His kind and loving heart she worshipped, destroyed with her own mean statistic attitude. Christine jumped in her Range Rover, heading for Strawberry Estate.

Gerald's in the sitting room, drinking a whisky. Christine sat beside him, suggesting, "For the first time, father, I'm unsure of Donald. I think I've changed him too much," she sighed heavily, bursting into tears.

Gerald poured Christine a small sherry, "What's happened, Christine?" he asked, concerned.

Christine explained.

Gerald took a deep breath, "To be quite honest, I wouldn't invest two million in a three-legged donkey either; perhaps you should have taken his offer and sold the estate to him. Although I don't think Royalty would have permitted it. You are correct, daughter. Your attitude has brought the situation to this. I warned you, it's obvious Donald is unsure of your intentions; he's wondering if he coughed up the money. Would you clear off dumping him once you have your own way," Gerald sighed.

Christine sipped her sherry and glanced at the clock on the wall at 9:30 p.m. Somehow, she had to convince Donald she was the same girl who loved him immensely and wouldn't betray him. She kissed her father's forehead, "I won't be home tonight. You deal with The Rising Sun in the morning, father."

He nodded, "Be careful, love, think about what you're doing before you destroy any happiness you could have had."

Christine drove to Crabtree Farm and ran upstairs to the studio, seeing Donald painting. She went into his apartment, removed her clothes, and walked in, standing beside his easel. "I want you to paint a nude portrait of me, Donald."

304

"Why?"

"A week ago, you would have given me anything; until I made a stupid comment, Glencoe is my estate, not yours. If you think I don't love you, I will run off if you invest in Glencoe without security. A portrait will be your security, for your investment," she said stone-faced with determination.

"No thanks, I'm not painting you naked. Hopefully, my future wife."

Christine grabbed his hand, "Come with me," she insisted. "If any doubt in your mind, Donald Selwyn, I don't love you, and you're so wrong," she expressed, laying on the bed, "Make me pregnant I don't care, you wanted ten children, be a man can you manage that?"

"I could, but I won't," he smiled, walking into the kitchen and switching on the kettle.

Christine sat up, dressing absolutely fuming as far as she's concerned, obviously didn't want her anymore; otherwise, she surmised he would have been in bed with her in seconds.

Donald came into the bedroom carrying two coffees, passing one to Christine and walked into the studio, sitting in an old chair. "Be honest, Donald, we're finished; you've had enough of me?"

"You don't get it, Christine. If I made you pregnant, yes, we have a lovely child. That doesn't mean to say we stay together." Donald shrugged his shoulders, "I could paint a portrait of you naked, and I'm sure it would make millions. That isn't what I want from you; I want you to understand I love you. You should trust me; I'm not trying to steal anything from you other than your love. You're destroying the relationship, not me, by your attitude and behaviour. Look at yourself before you look to me and make up your mind. Am I the person you are looking to share your life with?"

"I'd better go," Christine sighed, not knowing what to do next. She offered him everything she had, then realised he only wanted her love and trust, not her property. She remembered the way she loved him before he was famous. He had nothing to offer her, only love. Now he's a wealthy man in his own right. He could probably pick from a hundred women, yet he stays with her. She'd been such a fool.

Donald grabbed her hand, "You're going nowhere, your ladyship," pulling her down onto his knee and making her grin. She felt his powerful arms embrace her. She jumped to her feet, "Return to Glencoe Estate and spend some of your money. Give the place a fighting chance. Will you help me, Donald, please. I'm sorry I'm arrogant; sometimes, I've had to fight for what I want."

"We'll go, girl. You better phone your father first, explain we'll be gone for two or three days. I'll leave a note for mum; I have to be back here for Saturday, my birthday; otherwise, mum will have a fit," Donald scribbled a note. Christine phoned her father; he's trying not to laugh down the phone, realising his daughter had finally seen the light he hoped.

They decided to buy fresh clothes on the way. They would only need jeans, boots, and a rain mac, not forgetting a thick woolly jumper. They arrived at Glencoe Estate at 7 o'clock in the morning. They ran to reception, seeing a number ring if unattended. She rang the bell. Someone came into reception, staring in disbelief at Christine and Donald. The receptionist immediately phoned Justin, who came running from his cottage trying to swallow the remains of his breakfast, straightening his tie.

The chef came from the kitchen, "Miss Gibbs, Mr Selwyn, would you like breakfast?" Christine and Donald smiled; definitely, an improvement on their last arrival. "Yes, I think we will," she said, walking into the dining room. Christine looked at the new menu bursting into laughter, seeing a breakfast entitled. The Selwyn's special, and in brackets (be afraid.), "We will have two Selwyn specials, please, chef."

The receptionist entered the dining room, "Excuse me, Miss Gibbs, your luggage is missing?"

"Don't worry, we have eloped and run away from home," Christine joked, watching Donald laugh. "Don't worry, a spur-of-the-moment decision; purchase a new wardrobe later." It wasn't long before they sat down to a lovely breakfast. The chef had listened to everything Mary had told him about how the breakfast should be prepared. Finishing their coffee, when Justin approached, "May I ask Christine is there a problem? Haven't I run Glencoe correctly?" he asked, concerned.

Donald spoke, "To be quite honest, I don't know how you manage; my father explained what a wonderful holiday he had here and wanted to return. I have a shopping list that he made out for me. I'm about to make everyone's day, Justin," Donald smiled, kissing Christine on the cheek.

They entered the office following Justin. Christine showed Donald the books, and they went through the figures. "According to this, your nine hundred thousand pounds in the red. Since we visited, and Christine made a few alterations along with you, Justin, you recovered a hundred thousand pounds."

"Yes, Mr Selwyn, I'm doing my very best."

"I think that's brilliant," Donald remarked, "If I pay a million into Glencoe's account, that will leave you a little spending money." Justin sat silently, his jaw almost bouncing off the table in shock. "I'm off to buy equipment for the estate. You ever acquire a price on resurrecting the old sawmill Justin?" Donald asked, smiling.

Justin poured everyone a small whisky; his hands were trembling, trying to grasp what was happening. "Yes, Mr Selwyn, it will make a hole in sixty thousand pounds. I suspect if we want the sawmill to operate how it used to many years ago powered by a water wheel." He pointed to a map on the estate wall, "Used to be a large reservoir now overgrown and requires dredging in places and the water channel. The wheel needs unclogging, and the water wheel needs repairing along with the sawmill. Everything needs checking and testing. It would be more cost-effective, Mr Selwyn, to electrify the whole operation."

Donald grinned, "You will not," seeing Christine smile. "Visitors will be able to watch how things used to be. Water-free, electricity isn't! Okay, some initial costing. Once she's up and running and maintained, this problem won't happen again."

Christine kissed Donald on the cheek, "I thought I was the bully around here," she grinned. Donald asked, "Where is your nearest machinery supplier?"

"A few miles away from here, Mr Selwyn."

"Call me Donald. We're friends, Justin; we're on the same team. Where is Robbie? He seems to have a grasp of what we need. He can come as well."

"I'll try his mobile if he can receive a signal."

"Robbie, Justin. Miss Gibbs is here with Donald, her future husband. They want you to come to the office, change and make sure you look smart; wear your best kilt. You'll have to give him ten minutes to get here from where he lives," Justin said.

Robbie arrived wearing his best kilt built like Donald, not shy of hard work. Christine smiled, "You hold the fort, Justin; we won't belong." They headed for the dealership. Robbie showed them the way, quite excited about having modern farming equipment. "To be quite honest, we thought you were hot air Miss Gibbs. You've proved us wrong," Robbie smiled.

"Not me; you should be thanking Robbie, my future husband, Donald. He's the one with the money."

Christine parked her Range Rover and started looking around. Jock McKendrick came out from his office, immediately noticing Robbie. He laughed, "We have no rubbishy old machines at the moment for Glencoe Estate, Robbie."

"I'd mind your words, Jock. The future laird's here to purchase equipment."

Donald turned angry, "I take it we are a joke, McKendrick?"

"I apologise for my remark. I didn't realise."

Robbie expressed, "Don't you recognise the man; he's on the news often, the artist Donald Selwyn, future husband of Miss Christine Gibbs."

"Robbie," Donald asked, "Where's the next farm machinery dealership in the area?"

"A few miles from here, Mr Selwyn.

"Donald, Robbie, you don't have to stand on ceremony with me; I'm like you; I know hard work. I wouldn't piss on this place if it were on fire." Christine grinned, not believing the way Donald was behaving. She didn't argue. They climbed in the Range Rover, heading towards Inverness.

"Please accept my apologies," Robbie voiced. "Donald, Miss Gibbs, we are always treated like that," he sighed heavily.

"Not anymore, Robbie; I want you to hold your head high. We are turning Glencoe around, I promise you."

They parked in a tidy yard at a Massey Ferguson dealership with considerable machinery stocks. Hamish Mactaggart came from the office in his suit-wearing his face mask. "I'm pleased to meet you, Miss Gibbs," he said, holding his hand to Miss Gibbs and Donald. Christine looked puzzled, "How do you know me?"

"The phone lines are red-hot; the owner of Glencoe Estate and the famous Donald Selwyn was here; how can I assist you?" Hamish asked.

Christine smiled, "Talk to my future husband. He wishes to purchase one or two items for the right money, or I'll have the equipment shipped from England on a low loader; I don't mind either way." Donald almost splits himself laughing, realising what Christine's up to. Donald asked Robbie, "How many acres do you plough?"

"About five hundred, and we have at least three hundred of hay!" Donald asked the prices of several tractors, selecting one for a hundred sixty thousand pounds, not many hours on the clock, 190 horsepower. He selected a Dowdeswell six furrow plough. Robbie's amazed, not believing in his wildest dreams they'd ever have decent equipment at Glencoe. "I presume all your fields are sloped, Robbie?"

"Yes, some a bit fierce."

"I presume a big square baler would be better than round bales. At least they wouldn't end up breaking the fences?" Donald asked.

Robbie nodded.

"We will have that Massey Ferguson big square baler I want a season's warranty."

Hamish nodded, "No problem, all your equipment will come with a twelve-month warranty," not believing the sales. Donald purchased two-grain trailers. He looked at the Massey Ferguson combine climbing into the cab, only a thousand hours on the clock. Donald looked at the header wasn't bent or twisted, obviously coming from a good home, "I'll take this combine." Donald noticed a JCB. "Take that with a bale grab and muck fork." Donald climbed up in a second-hand muck spreader looking inside massive. Hamish advised, "Our demonstrator, I can give you a good price."

Christine asked, "How good considering the money we've spent here today?"

"An unbelievable deal," Hamish smiled, writing down the figure showing Donald.

"We'll take it. Who owns next door the plant hire firm?" Donald asked.

"That's mine as well. I operate two separate companies."

"I'm looking for an ex-hire JCB with a full range of buckets." Robbie couldn't believe his ears; he was so excited that he grabbed Christine's hand and started dancing with her in the yard, realised what he was doing, and stopped immediately. "I apologise, Miss; I can't remember a time like this." Christine laughed, "Should be dancing with the man paying the bill."

Donald laughed, "That won't be necessary, Robbie; you make sure this equipment is looked after, or I will be bloody angry."

"Have I missed anything, Robbie?"

"We could do with a couple of chainsaws and tools."

"Purchase what you want within reason."

Robbie selected two chainsaws and hand tools, "We could do with a new mower and Tedder." Donald chose and purchased, although the season is over, ready for next year like the combine, which is why he suspected he had it at the right price.

"Have I forgotten anything, Robbie?" Donald asked.

"We could do with another tractor Donald; it needn't be so big."

Donald noticed two more tractors at the back, about a hundred horsepower each, "How much for those two?"

Hamish wrote down the price, "They have 2000 hours on the clock roughly; comes with a twelve-month warranty. I stand by everything I sell."

"Right, we better total up. Don't forget to include the JCB digger; I want it less than twelve months old; I presume you will deliver free of charge?" Donald asked seriously.

"Definitely," Hamish smiled, "The bill comes to 1 million 700,000 plus vat." Donald removed his platinum card from his wallet. Hamish had never seen one before. "Can I offer you refreshments while you're here, perhaps a coffee?"

"Yes, that would be very nice. I'd like all the equipment on Glencoe Estate before the end of next week. We have many alterations to make," Donald smiled. "Don't forget to supply a VAT number; I want the VAT back," Donald insisted.

Robbie smiled, "I'll be marrying this Christmas to a bonny lass; I feel I can risk a wife now Glencoe's under new management."

"You'll be holding the wedding on the estate?" Donald insisted.

"Couldn't afford, Donald. We will have a quiet gathering in the village hall."

"You will not! I will personally cover the expense of your wedding Robbie. You're no less a man on this estate than anyone else here; you won't be treated like one."

Robbie grabbed Donald around the waist, lifting him from the ground. "If you kiss me, Robbie will be the finish of your employment." Christine's screaming with laughter. Robbie lowered Donald to his feet, "I've never met a more generous man. Thank you both."

"Explain to Justin Robbie when you intend to marry, and Justin will fit you in," Christine smiled.

"I have to ask Maggie first if she'll marry me; we've been courting for ten years, waiting until we've saved enough money. I hope she'll still have me." Everyone climbed in the Range Rover, heading for Glencoe Estate.

CHAPTER TEN

FORGING AHEAD

Christine drove to the reservoir on the estate, supplying the water to the sawmill to drive the waterwheel. The reservoir is approximately thirty acres and is fed by various streams from neighbouring hills that continually flow with fresh water. The overflow from the reservoir helps support the stream running by the house. They stepped from the Range Rover, looking over the spectacular site. At one end of the reservoir, the sluice gate controls the water leaving the reservoir. Thankfully made from steel, although slightly rusty. Robbie cranked the handle; much to everyone's surprise, the sluice gate worked. Robbie quickly closed to prevent unwanted water from reaching the sawmill for now.

Christine jumped in her Range Rover, following Robbie and Donald walking along the narrow channel that fed the sawmill. Donald thought the mill was about a mile from the house, so the noise interference would be minimal. However, in plain view, which would intrigue everyone's interest. By the time Donald had reached the old sawmill, he was plastered in mud and Robbie no better. They both continued walking around, impressed by its construction. "You realise, Robbie, a multi-sash sawmill?"

"I know she's old," Robbie commented. "With the new JCB, we should have no trouble clearing out the water supply to the wheel and clearing the channel to the stream for the spent water to return to the watercourse."

"Everything appears here, Robbie, a matter of servicing and repairing what is rotten, don't you think?"

"Yes, Donald, we have five thousand acres of pine trees; some will be due for felling this winter. We need a full-time Forester," Robbie suggested.

"What we need, Robbie is someone who knows how this works properly. I'll ask our Forester at home; in the meantime, if you can find anybody who understands how this all works, that would be appreciated. Also, mention to Justin." Donald jumped in the Range Rover along with Robbie. Christine complained about the state of their feet. "Don't worry, Robbie, her barks worse than her bite." Christine glared at Donald and drove Robbie home, dropping him outside his small cottage with his ageing mother. Christine went straight into the village, discovering a clothes shop open. She purchased them a couple of pairs of jeans, socks, and everything else they needed for a few days. They barely left the shop before Donald's surrounded by people wanting his autograph, mainly Chinese tourists. Donald couldn't understand a word they were saying. He stood, having his photo taken with various children and females. Taking the first opportunity to quickly jump in Christine's Range Rover heading for Glencoe Estate.

"I have a celebrity husband," Christine grinned. "I'll have to watch you very closely."

They showered, changed into fresh clothes, and ventured into the bar. Justin joined them, shaking Donald's hand, "I never thought I'd see Glencoe come alive in my life the way she used to be," he smiled. "We are booked solid, Miss Gibbs, I mean Christine, for the next eight months; many of the bookings are from abroad. All over the news, Donald Selwyn is staying at his retreat, according to someone called Jack Potter."

Donald laughed, "Crafty old Jack trying to help by listing this place as one of my retreats. He knows everybody will want to book on the chance they might see me here."

"Has Robbie spoken to you, Justin?"

"Has he spoken to me? I thought he was coming down the telephone to bite me! We have low loaders arriving with new machinery in a couple of days. You're repairing the sawmill dredging the lake?"

"No, you are, Justin, you are the Estate Manager; I put everything in place, no excuse for failure. You will have to control everyone; contact Christine if you're concerned. Next time I come, I want to see the sawmill either working or almost completely repaired. Failure is not an option. Justin head's will roll; I'm very sure of that," Donald advised glancing at Christine. She's grinning from ear to ear. "One last thing, Justin, any suppliers to Glencoe Estate who find it funny to take the mickey. Find new suppliers and advise to clear off."

Justin nodded, "I heard your hot gossip in the village; you advised McKendrick to take a hike. He's hopping mad when he discovered how much money you spent at the other dealership."

Donald grinned, "Perhaps you would send him a letter, ask him to shut any accounts we have. We no longer require his services," Donald watched Christine grin with satisfaction.

"I will spend some time here, Justin, painting once I've passed my driving test. I may purchase an RV to use as a studio. That way, none of the rooms will be occupied by me. We are here to make money, not to walk around like lady and lord muck that doesn't pay the bills."

Christine glared, "Where do I fit into your life, lord and master," she frowned.

"Christine, you realise eight stables at the back of this establishment. If we could find placid horses, we can offer riding across the estate where it wouldn't affect the wildlife; of course, we'll have to discuss with the gamekeeper."

Christine couldn't prevent herself from smiling. Justin sat in disbelief; he couldn't believe the discussion.

"I suppose none of you noticed the old waterwheel-powered generator. Obviously used many years ago when the sawmill wasn't working to provide power to the house, or perhaps capable of performing both operations simultaneously, I don't know. I presume there must be a cable leading to the house; it would obviously need testing to see if viable. We can create our own electricity and earn money by powering into the grid and selling the electricity."

Justin jumped off his stool, grabbing Donald's arm, "I know where that is down in the cellar." Christine followed, laughing, shaking her head in disbelief; her future husband was going wild. Everything he said made sense to have their own power supply knowing the electricity bill in winter. They descended into the cellar. A large panel on the wall needs updating, but there is no reason why the cable-laid underground wasn't still serviceable; it would require testing.

"Justin, you make sure they don't damage the electric cable by the waterwheel, have the generator serviced? If faulty costs a replacement to be driven by the wheel."

Justin's writing everything down in his notepad. If he smiled any more, he'd break his jaw. They returned to the bar to find a police officer holding his notebook. "I'll have your licence for permitting underage drinking; neither of you is eighteen."

Christine frowned, "These are my premises; I own Glencoe Estate, and what have you done about the animals and equipment stolen. I know it's been reported, and what have you done absolutely nothing?"

"I don't have to answer to a slip of a girl."

To everyone's surprise, Mrs Montague entered wearing her favourite travelling suit. She tapped the officer on the shoulder with her walking cane. He turned to face her, "You will answer to me, young man and your superiors, when Elizabeth R has finished with your employer. You'll be lucky if you can acquire a position sweeping the road. While on the subject, you find time to visit Nancy in the village? You don't have the time to prevent the thieving from this estate and others on your patch."

The officer turned white. Donald thought the young officer would wet himself the way he was trembling any minute. Mrs Montague pointed to the door with her ivory crested walking stick, "That's the way out; you can report whatever you wish to your superiors and watch it bite you in the posterior."

Donald placed his arm around Mrs Montague, kissing her on the cheek. She looked at him rather strangely, "Unhand me, young man," she insisted, trying not to grin. "I'm staying at Balmoral. Elizabeth R is in residence for a few days. I thought I'd check on my favourite couple," she smiled, "By the looks of things in time. Don't worry about him, his superiors looking to climb the ladder; he wouldn't dare upset Elizabeth R or me for that matter," she smiled. "Enlighten me," taking a drink from the bar sitting at a table, inviting Christine and Donald to join her. Christine explained what Donald had purchased and their plans.

"Excellent, well thought out, you have an excellent business head on your shoulders. I think the term used for your father Christine, octopus' hands, may apply to your future husband," she grinned, teasing.

Donald ventured to the bar returning with three more malt whiskies. "You wouldn't be trying to intoxicate me, young man." A new side to Mrs Montague having fun Donald didn't think in her criteria. They chatted for another hour. Mrs Montague rose to her feet, kissing Donald on both cheeks and Christine. "I must return to Balmoral." Donald opened the door for Mrs Montague. "Don't be a stranger," he smiled.

Mrs Montague grinned, climbing into her limousine. She waved as her chauffeur drove away. Justin commented, "That's lucky we must be more careful until you are of age; it never crossed my mind." Justin confessed, "You're more adult than many that visit this establishment."

Donald remarked, "Robbie intends to marry, the venue held here around Christmas; I'm covering the cost."

Justin smiled, "I know, Donald; Maggie is my daughter. The clothes shop you visited in the village I purchased for her is only a small affair. She gets by."

Donald remarked, "Robbie's marrying a woman of substance like me," kissing Christine on the cheek. Donald thought, "Do you have a recent photograph of Maggie and Robbie together, Justin?"

"That I do. We were at someone's wedding only a week ago," proudly removing a photo from his wallet with Robbie and Maggie dressed in their tartans. "Can I keep this one, Justin? I'll paint a portrait of them together in better surroundings for their wedding present?"

"No, Donald, you are covering the cost of their wedding," Justin expressed, excited at the thought.

"Our secret, Justin, inform no one," Donald cautioned.

"No, Donald."

"To business," Donald said, clearing his throat, "With Christine's approval, implement our plans, keep us advised of expenditure. If you have any questions, phone Christine or me; that's okay, wife-to-be," Donald smiled.

Christine shrugged her shoulders, "I suppose I would prefer you to contact me first, Justin, as a matter of courtesy."

Donald frowned, "Yes, her ladyship first, then me," he grinned, disappointed with Christine's remark. "I'm off to take more photos while I have a chance, Christine; I want to follow the stream. I haven't seen everything," he said, leaving the table. Christine, quite annoyed, gathered she'd upset him again, leaving the table. She ran to her room, looking at what she was wearing in the mirror. Christine smiled, deciding to be bloody-minded, changing out of her jeans into a short skirt, leaving her jumper on; cold outside, she chose to drive in her Range Rover around the property. Christine left a message at reception, "Inform Donald I'm inspecting other parts of the estate. I'll return in due course." Christine ran out to her Range Rover, driving towards the water wheel and the reservoir, not seeing anyone.

Christine left the main track; she cautiously drove along, stopping after seeing someone in the distance approaching. She removed her binoculars from the glove compartment realising Robbie. Christine sat thinking for a moment removing her jumper. She's still single; Donald doesn't own her. She released several buttons on her blouse, wondering if she dare could be fun. She almost jumped out of her skin after an enormous clap of thunder, and the heavens opened.

Christine started laughing, the perfect excuse to give someone a lift. Daring herself, she eased her skirt until she saw her knickers slightly, exposing more of her legs, advancing the heater. Christine speeded along the track to find Robbie standing under a conifer tree out of the rain. She operated her electric window, offering, "jump in, Robbie, you'll be soaked."

Robbie ran to the passenger side, quickly jumping in, closing the door, and clutching his walking stick. He promptly removed his handkerchief, wiping his face and walking stick dry to prevent it from dripping on the carpet. "Thanks for stopping, Christine; I'm far from home. He suggested, "I've had a few soakings since I've worked here. "I can remember one time with your mother...." Robbie realised he should have kept his mouth shut.

"Oh, Yes, enlighten me, please I'm intrigued."

"Often, I'd accompany your mother on walks; she used to enjoy the fresh air," he grinned nervously.

"Only walks Robbie? You're not unattractive, and I know what my mother is like. You might as well confess," Christine smiled.

"Nay lass, I'll not say anything against your mother, a beautiful woman like her daughter. I spent many hours walking around the estate with her. I'll not betray her trust."

Christine grinned. Robbie's eyes wandered from her short skirt to her pink bra, which could partially be seen since she'd released several buttons on her blouse. The rain's hitting the roof of the Range Rover no chance Robbie could walk home in this, and Christine realised Donald would be in the hotel. She had little to worry about.

"You won't be dismissed, Robbie; if you had sex with my mother, I wouldn't be surprised; she found you attractive as I do," she suggested, encouraging him. Christine watched Robbie laying his walking stick across his lap. Christine smiled, watching his stick touch the side of her leg. "Were you ever in a vehicle with my mother," she asked calmly.

"Many times, we'd come up here in her Range Rover. I've said too much already."

"Your, obviously not enlightening me; show me I shan't say anything," she smiled. "I'm intrigued. She obviously liked your walking stick," Christine grinned. "No one will find out Robbie our secret. Neither of us married we can please ourselves, not exactly cheating."

She looked at Robbie's expression. "You sure, Christine?"

"Yes, positive, show me what she liked," Christine's heart is pounding with anticipation.

Christine watched Robbie lift his stick, gently rubbing the inside of her leg, venturing further each time until he touched her black knickers, almost screaming with anticipation. The sensation is unbelievable. Robbie turned the walking stick end for end. He rubbed the inside of her leg. This time, he applied pressure, encouraging her legs apart until she couldn't part any further; one leg was now resting against the centre console and the other against the door. She allowed the seat to recline slightly.

Christine couldn't believe the thrill watching Robbie venture to the top of her knickers, easing the end of his stick inside and forcing down the front of her knickers. Christine asked, slightly hyperventilating, "My mother enjoys, Robbie?" She watched him nod as he concentrated on what he was performing.

She felt the large ivory nob on the walking stick venture inside her knickers. Christine tried to control her breathing as Robbie moved the stick gently; she thought sex with a man was good, but this was unbelievable. She released the lever on the side of her seat, allowing the seat to fold back, providing Robbie more access, quickly removing her knickers. She raised her legs, parting as much as she could, unable to prevent making a noise. Within a few minutes, Robbie was on top of her. She watched what he intended to insert into her from beneath his kilt; he's blessed beyond belief, she concluded, closing her eyes and feeling him sucking her nipples. He appeared to make love to her for hours. Finally, she felt him come.

She scrambled out of the Range Rover, taking a pee by the front wheel, leaving her knickers off. The rain had subsided. Robbie said nothing walking off with his walking stick. Christine quickly tidied herself and thought her mother knew how to enjoy life. Christine surmised as reality returned that she wasn't on the pill; something else to worry about now. After ensuring she looked perfect, Christine returned to the hotel before Donald; she quickly showered and changed. Played the loving girlfriend for the rest of the evening, making sure he had sex with her so she could compare the events.

Early the following day, Donald and Christine set off for Crabtree Farm. "Stop just a moment, Christine," Donald asked.

She pulled over to the side of the road in the village. Donald jumped out using his mobile and snapped several photos of the front of Maggie's shop, which he thought was an apt name. He ran over to the Range Rover and jumped in, "Okay."

Christine smiled, "You're up to something."

Donald shook his head, "No, making sure I have as many pictures as possible helps me remember when I'm painting." Donald inquired, "You okay with everything, Christine, me involved in your estate?"

"Yes, if you remember, I'm part of the team; I'm so used to being number one. Sharing the position doesn't come easy, Donald. If I started interfering in your farm, I think you'd find it difficult to start with."

"Point taken, Christine, everything is for our benefit and thank you for my birthday present last night. You were certainly wild," he grinned.

Christine smirked, "I must take contraception," glancing out the side window and seeing a woman pushing a pram.

"I thought you were on the pill?" Donald asked, slightly panicking.

"When I remember, I'll go to the doctor."

"What happens if you're pregnant? Are you really trying to hang me," Donald expressed, concerned?

Christine smiled, "A few weeks ago, you didn't care either way when you forced me to marry you at Gretna Green. Now suddenly, be careful. If I'm pregnant and you don't stay with me, I'll be able to glean millions of pounds from your bank account in maintenance," she said straight-faced.

Donald turned to face her, staring in disbelief, "So that's your plan?" Christine pulled over to the side of the road. "Get out now, Donald; I'm sure I'm pregnant. I don't need you anymore."

He continued to stare in disbelief. Christine finally laughed, driving off, "You are a fool, Donald. Could you imagine me doing that to you, the person I've loved for years at school? I finally convinced you to ask me to be your girlfriend. I throw it away. I don't think so."

"Christine, I thought you were serious for a moment."

Christine realised Donald had not seen the funny side of her joke. "Sorry, Donald, I didn't mean to upset you. I was honest about the contraception situation, one of those things I've meant to get round to. I'm not bothered if I'm pregnant; I'm safe with you. You're not like the other boys trying to seduce me, failing miserably."

Donald sat quietly. He'd rather hoped Christine had taken precautions. He didn't mind having a child, although later more practical with what was happening.

They arrived home at Crabtree Farm, greeted by Mary and Martin. Mary took Christine aside, "Are you taking precautions? Plenty of time for children, Christine; take the morning-after pill," passing one to Christine discreetly. Christine sighed, "I can't do that, Mary. If I'm pregnant great. If I'm not, I will go on the pill."

Mary kissed Christine's forehead, "You must love my son." They went inside the cottage to have a light snack before retiring. The journey was quite tiring, especially with one driver.

Donald woke, showered and dressed, peering out of the studio window into the yard, seeing happy birthday Donald in different coloured paper across the garage doors. Donald realised Christine was missing although her Range Rover was in the yard. He ran downstairs, greeted by his mother and father with a big hug. Christine's in the kitchen, helping prepare the day of celebration. Around 10:30, a lorry pulled into the yard. Donald remarked calmly, "My surprise to everyone." They followed Donald outside, overseeing the four-wheel-drive SUV Bentley reversed from the lorry, the Bentley a deep royal blue. Airbrushed into the passenger door Christine on her horse, the nearside rear door his mother and father, the driver's door his friend Biscuit, and the other rear door Gerald.

Everyone stood silent, glaring at the vehicle, which appeared to have gold in the paint. "My birthday present to me," Donald smiled, "Not a bad job," he said, studying the airbrushing. "I just have to pass my test." They helped the lorry turn around in the yard and watched him leave down the drive. Donald jumped in his new motor having a diesel engine extremely quiet considering the size. Christine sat on the passenger side, hugging him. Gerald arrived after having a wild night with Susan, looking at the artwork on Donald's Bentley and seeing himself airbrushed on the door.

The holidaymakers staying in the apartments came to survey the vehicle and cameras flashing. Mary burst into tears. She'd never been so proud of Donald. Whatever he did is for somebody else's benefit, not very often his own. Donald travelled up and down the drive a few times in his new motor. Although so silent, he didn't realise the engines running. Still, its appearance gave you the impression that you could plough through a hedge without stopping.

He applied for his driving licence, patiently waiting, studied the highway code until he knew it backwards, determined to pass his test within a week. Early the following day, Christine came trotting into the yard at Crabtree Farm on The Rising Sun. She placed him in the stable reserved for him, dashing upstairs to the studio and finding Donald painting a portrait of Robbie and Maggie. Christine kissed him very lovingly, "Guess what," she smiled. "The police have caught the rustlers on our estate at Glencoe. They shot a stag and carried it to their car, and further along the lane, a lorry with a dozen ewes on board, all with our ear tags." Donald lowered his brushes, standing up, "Brilliant," kissing Christine.

She looked at the portrait, remembering her time with Robbie. "Beautiful Donald standing in front of Glencoe by the bridge," she smiled. "You don't hold me so tenderly as he is in your painting," she lifted her eyebrows.

Donald, not needing encouragement, embraced each other with the passion of a thousand lovers. Christine made coffee, and Donald sat down, continuing his artwork. "I visited the doctors, Donald; he's given me pills to take."

Donald smiled, "We have a lifetime together, Christine and a mountain to climb with Glencoe. If you can control yourself until after we are married," he sighed. "Either way, I don't really care."

That's the Donald she remembered and loved so much. Donald's provisional driving licence finally arrived; like Christine, he booked a week's course and quickly passed his test. Costing him nearly two thousand pounds to insure his Bentley fully comprehensive. He dared not inform his mother or father. They would have advised him; that he'd been too extravagant in buying an unnecessary vehicle for showing off. Donald's first journey to Strawberry Estate. Christine came running out smiling, realising he'd passed. Donald jumped out, advising, "Pack a bag; we're off to Glencoe. I want to see what's happening," he remarked, looking forward to the journey.

Christine ran inside, kissing her father on the cheek, calling out, "Susan, will you look after The Rising Sun for me for a couple of days, please?"

Susan laughed, "Of course."

Christine came running downstairs with an overnight bag, kissing her father on the cheek. He'd never seen Christine so happy she's growing up quickly, seeing Donald wave.

Gerald realised Christine would be safe with Donald, especially in a car built like a tank. He dreaded the miles per gallon, even if a diesel; the engine dwarfed his Range Rover. Christine curled up and drifted off to sleep while Donald destroyed the miles, realising he was travelling at nearly ninety miles an hour at one time, quickly backing off, not wanting to lose his licence for speeding. By 10 o'clock in the evening, Donald parked at Glencoe, and someone came out to greet him. "I'm sorry, Sir, we have no rooms," not realising Donald. "You are welcome to stay for refreshment and a meal."

Christine was asleep. The staff member placed her hand to her mouth, "Oh, Mr Selwyn, I'm sorry I didn't recognise your vehicle." Justin came running out, realising Donald immediately. Donald laughed, "I presume Christine's suite is available; you haven't let that; I hope otherwise you will have your ears burnt," watching Christine move.

"Are we here, Donald?" she asked, stepping from the car, "I don't remember the journey so comfortable."

Donald insisted, "Come to check up on you, Justin."

Justin exhaled, "I'm glad you have; I'd like you to see our progress since your previous visit. I've never seen Robbie work so hard, making the other staff work hard. He will have nothing said against you, Donald, and anyone who dared would be on their backside."

Donald smiled, "He's a great mate. Come on, sleepy, let's have you in bed."

"Not in front of the staff," Christine laughed. They entered the reception area.

"My daughter Maggie," Justin introduced, "Helps in reception in the evening and saves employing a full-time staff member."

Donald reached across, offering his hand, "I'm pleased to meet you, Maggie."

"Likewise, Mr Selwyn; although I've seen you in my shop, my sales increased that day for a change."

Christine reached over, offering her hand, "lovely to meet you. Have you set a date for the wedding?" Christine asked.

"First of November, father advised he could slot Robbie and me in for a reception and a few of our friends," she smiled politely.

"Where are you staying for your honeymoon?" Donald asked.

"Can't afford a honeymoon, Donald."

He frowned, ringing his mother, "Do we have a spare apartment for two weeks from the first of November?"

"Why, Donald?" Mary asked.

"Robbie and Maggie are marrying on the first of November, coming for a two-week honeymoon at Crabtree farm. I thought you could clear a space." Donald listened to his mother flicking through the bookings.

"Yes, flat 4 is vacant that month."

"Book it for Robbie and Maggie. They can come to where I live for a fortnight," he smiled.

"No, Donald, we can't; how are we travelling? I have an old car, but she's not designed for that distance."

"Minor detail," Donald smiled, "I will see you at your shop in the morning. We'll see if we can generate custom. Leave everything to me, Maggie."

Justin said quickly, "Thank the laird, Maggie, you're not find a nicer man."

"Maggie has nothing to thank me for, Justin," Donald grinned, throwing Christine over his shoulder. "Put me down, Donald, you fool, not in public."

Early the next day, Donald and Christine sat at the breakfast table, enjoying the Selwyn special with a broad smile. Justin approached as they finished their coffee, advising, "The reservoir has had the rubbish removed. The new JCB excavator, I think Robbie sleeps with it," he laughed. "He cleared out the watercourse to the waterwheel, which has been removed and under repair. You heard about the rustlers caught?" Justin asked.

"Yes, I understand the police using a drone; it can scan large areas more effectively," Christine advised.

Justin nodded. Donald looked at his wristwatch. "I'm taking a walk to the sawmill, only half a mile; I want to see the progress."

"Yes, have an early morning walk, Donald, together," Christine suggested with a broad smile. They left the dining room following the narrow winding stream close to the sawmill. Donald was highly impressed with the progress; he looked at the enormous waterwheel, estimated twenty feet tall when erected. Many timbers were rotten, especially where they sat in the mud before removed and cleaned. "I can't wait to see this working," Donald commented. Christine smiled, enjoying his enthusiasm for the estate. They noticed in the distance a yellow JCB digger coming down the track, driven very carefully by Robbie, realising Maggie's in the cab with him. He parked by the waterwheel. Maggie climbed out, and he followed. "Nice to see you, Donald and Christine," Robbie voiced cheerfully, "Maggie informed me you arrived last night."

"I must go, Robbie; otherwise, I'll be late opening the shop; we need every penny we can save." "Where's your car, Maggie?" Donald asked, puzzled.

"Wouldn't start this morning; an old Morris Minor is usually very reliable," Maggie smiled.

"I'll give you a lift to work; I'm coming to your shop and boosting your sales," he smiled.

Christine linked her arm in his they walked off towards the house, leaving Robbie to continue the repairs. Maggie stared at Donald's Bentley. She walked around, looking at the artwork. Christine opened the back door, "Maggie and I will ride in the back; we have a chauffeur," Christine grinned. Donald started heading into the village only a mile or so, nearly 9 o'clock in the morning. Tourists were coming from God knows where, which Donald thought strange. He jumped out, entering Maggie's shop. She barely had time to turn on the lights and open the cash register before people bought most things, from postcards to tartans.

Donald felt his mobile vibrate text message from Jack, "We know where you are, ha, ha." Christine went behind the counter to help Maggie; she struggled to cope. Jack had commissioned a Donald Selwyn tartan arranging delivery to Maggie's shop in his wisdom understanding how Donald operated. Maggie noticed from the window a van parked outside; the driver fought through the tourists carrying in an armful of tartans. Maggie does not recognise the design, "I never ordered these," she said, looking at them and observing the label inside the band. Donald Selwyn tartan. She showed Donald. He shrugged his shoulders, "That's Jack!" Donald dialled Jack's number, "Brilliant Jack, send me the bill."

"I intend to," Jack laughed. "Marketing is my game; bye for now." Donald signed for the tartans passing the paperwork to Maggie to know what to sell to make a profit. Donald went to the changing room, slipped on a kilt, standing by his Bentley outside the shop. Tourists taking photos. Christine came outside, taking a picture with her mobile and sending it to Mary and her father. Donald's signed autographs for a few minutes and walked back inside to change.

Donald kissed Maggie on the cheek, leaving the shop. He could see that Maggie had a good morning by the empty shelves. Christine and Donald drove away. Christine's still laughing, remembering Donald dancing with the tourists. His interpretation of the Highland Fling left a lot to be desired.

They drove some way out of the village. Christine asked, "Where are we going?"

"To find Maggie a car." They drove some miles, finally coming across a garage selling various second-hand cars. Christine exhaled, "I think you may be interfering in people's lives too much, Donald, don't you think?"

Donald stared directly at her, "I'm only purchasing her a second-hand car costing a fraction of your horse; I can't quite see your concern?"

Christine bit her tongue. The last thing she needed was a blazing argument. Christine shrugged her shoulders, "Please yourself!"

"Come on, Christine, what's the issue? I could die tomorrow; what would happen to my money? Go to my mother and father, who would probably stash away in a bank and never spend a penny." Donald jumped out of the car, looking for something practical for Maggie and Robbie. Christine stayed in the car, deciding whether she was jealous he was buying another woman a present or just mean. Donald came across a Subaru Forester ideal, looking at the mileage of nearly fifty thousand miles. The salesperson came to Donald. Donald enquired, "The vehicle has a full-service history?"

"Yes, one owner from new."

"I presume it will be fully serviced an M O T before leaving here. Have a new cambelt fitted?" Donald asked politely.

"The cambelt isn't due."

"Will be in ten thousand miles, and the vehicles over four years old, the cambelt should be changed every four years, I think," Donald grinned.

"If we change the cambelt, that's an extra."

"Not at those prices, it won't; no worries, I can look elsewhere," Donald advised, walking off.

"Very well, we will service and change the cambelt."

Donald turned back, facing the salesperson, "The car will have an R A C inspection before it leaves here; make sure it's roadworthy," Donald asked. Donald watched the salesperson's expression turn white.

"That won't be necessary. We stand by our vehicles, delivered with a three-month warranty included in the price," the salesman replied, realising who he was talking to.

Christine had operated her electric window listening to the conversation. She quite expected Donald to buy some ridiculous flash car. He wasn't trying to impress Maggie, only to find something suitable for her to use.

Donald removed his platinum card. The salesperson looked astonished, realising whatever Donald purchased was covered by the card for a full refund. Donald paid for the vehicle passing the salesperson Maggie's business card, "When you've finished preparing the vehicle, notify this young lady, and you can deliver to her shop."

Donald left the garage jumping in his Bentley and tearing off down the road. He wanted to punch the salesperson, could see crook written all over his forehead. Now he had the money and the connections to make the guy's life miserable if he failed to produce the goods.

Christine stayed silent while they drove to Glencoe Estate. She realised she had a generous future husband, one you wouldn't want to cross and expect to escape reprisals.

Donald walked around the rear of the house, which resembled a castle, or hotel converted from a stately home some years ago. Christine followed, "What are you looking for?" she asked, concerned.

"The stables, I presume that's Justin's cottage beyond another farm; where are the stables, Christine?"

"In the undergrowth over there," she pointed. Donald picked her up, throwing her over his shoulder, trampling his way through the stinging nettles and brambles so she wouldn't be injured. He finally fought his way to stable blocks, eight stables in total. He lowered

Christine to her feet. She grinned. Donald laughed, "What's the matter?"

"If you'd have asked before attempting to find the stables. I would have suggested you come with a chainsaw and a slashing hook. I can never remember them being used, Donald. It would be more cost-effective to demolish and rebuild with pre-fabricated stables, don't you think?"

He took a deep breath, "From what I can see, yes." He picked Christine up, throwing her over his shoulder.

"I can walk, Donald, or you want to hold my leg," she giggled, "and smacked my backside. I don't mind, you Tarzan, me Jane, you realise we're watched from every window by guests."

Donald lowered her to her feet as they cleared the stinging nettles. "There you are, your ladyship, no damage from what I can see," he said, smacking her backside as she ran towards the entrance with Donald chasing her. They entered, advised by reception that lunch was served, walking into the dining room, enjoying wild boar followed by lemon meringue and cream. They could see from the window dark clouds gathering. Suddenly, the heavens opened with an almighty clap of thunder; Donald thought that was the end of any excursion today.

He walked down into the cellar to see if any progress was made regarding the control panel, regulating the electricity to the house from the waterwheel when finally rectified. He's pleasantly surprised all appeared to have been inspected, cleaned, and ready to work. Donald returned upstairs, finding Christine talking to the receptionist. She glanced to the front door seeing the sun's shining. Arm in arm, they ventured out together like an old married couple slowly walking along the stream embankment, inhaling the fresh air. They were both astounded observing three works vans by the sawmill. They observed that the waterwheel was back on its axle and repaired.

The electrician in another part of the building checked the wiring reconnecting to the generator. Robbie approached them both, grinning, "She'll be running in a minute. I mean the generator. The rest of the building will take a little longer," he beamed with satisfaction.

"That reminds me, Donald; thanks for helping Maggie this morning; she sold more when you were there than normally in a week. I'll be wearing the Glencoe's new tartan," he proudly voiced.

Robbie moved away, attaching the drive belt to the pulleys running along the oak beam and down to the generator. The electrician spoke, "Miss Gibbs, we are connected. Just a matter of trying the waterwheel, then we will test the electricity supply to the house with your permission."

Justin came in his Land Rover, jumped out, passing a two-way radio to Robbie, "Release the water slowly, Robbie and listen to the radio if we have a disaster down here; you need to shut the supply off quickly."

Robbie nodded, grabbing the two-way radio, climbing aboard his favourite JCB digger, and driving off to the reservoir. Justin ordered everyone, "Stand away from moving parts, please. We don't know what will happen until she's tested. We want no accidents."

Robbie radioed, "Justin releasing the water now." Robbie slowly lifted the sluice gate watching the water run down the narrow channel towards the sawmill listening intently in case he needed to shut it off quickly.

Everyone stood clear, seeing the water coming down the hillside in the channel, directed to the top of the wheel, watching it turn underwater power for the first time in many years. Christine's quite excited, running to the stream to observe the discharged water run under the old track and into the stream on its journey past the house. Justin voiced proudly, "I think should be the privilege of Christine Gibbs to switch on the main power to the house."

Donald concurred, "I second that." Christine's somewhat embarrassed at all the fuss, everyone has worked extremely hard, and she didn't want to disappoint. The electrician suggested, "I'll go to the house with Miss Gibbs and Donald when I phone you, Justin, throw the switch here. I will disconnect the mains switching to our own power."

Donald and Christine jumped in the electrician's old van returning to the house. Donald advised, "Notify the guests of a power change in a minute. Anyone using electrical equipment to turn it off for a moment while we swap the supplies." The receptionist immediately contacted everyone still in the building while the electrician, Christine and Donald descended into the cellar. The electrician shone his torch, "Place your hand on that lever there, Miss Gibbs. I'll disconnect the mains supply. Pull it down when I say, now!" The electrician disconnected the mains, and it was dark. "Now, Miss Gibbs." Christine pulled the lever down, suddenly lighting in the cellar, much to everyone's relief. They made their way to the reception. Donald advised, "Anyone who wishes to see the waterwheel working to generate the estate's electricity is welcome to view. They can see the building from their rooms in most cases and from the balcony." Not many minutes before, the guests with binoculars were looking toward the old sawmill. Thanks to the gearing, the waterwheel didn't have to turn quickly to generate sufficient power to drive the generator. Donald noticed Robbie returning, driving the JCB from the hills. Christine and Donald walked along the stream embankment, watching the wheel majestically rotate under waterpower.

The electric bill would be no more. Unless there was a failure in the water supply or some other catastrophe. They slowly walked towards the house, passed by visitors walking along the track to view the waterwheel, such a simple device. However, it would significantly contribute to Glencoe's future success.

Donald inhaled, "Somebody's muck-spreading," he grinned, dashing up onto the roof where a viewing point was built many years ago, allowing visitors to survey some of the landscape. Donald could see a muck spreader he purchased in the distance, one of the tractors spreading muck and someone else ploughing, preparing for next year's harvest.

Christine had gone into the office to check the accounts with Justin, discovering they were not overdrawn considering the amount of money spent. Glencoe is now booked over Christmas the only spare room is her own; she wasn't giving up to anyone.

"When the restoration is completed on the sawmill. Can you ask Robbie to demolish the old stable blocks? In the meantime, Justin priced prefabricated replacement stables, capable of handling eight horses for the next project on the list." She smiled, "Make nine stables and attack room. I may transport The Rising Sun, my horse," she grinned.

Donald came into the office, hearing the end sentence of the conversation, "Is my future wife sneaky," he grinned.

Justin smiled.

"No," she replied emphatically. "If I want to transport The Rising Sun, I can, my bloody property."

Donald started laughing, "Who's grumpy, now?"

Christine shook her head and started laughing, "Before you completely take over my life, my estate."

"I wasn't arguing with you, Christine. I think that it's very sensible to have an extra stable. Now I think about it. Why are we purchasing stables when we have all the timber in the world on the estate. We only need a craftsman to construct, save money, Miss prim and proper," he said, poking his tongue at her.

Christine tapped his cheek, "You're not just a pretty face." Justin's in stitches watching these two perform. Christine turned to face him, "Once the sawmill is in working order, Justin, and we appoint a new carpenter-sawmill operator, the problem should be solved."

"That's a fact, Christine. Robbie is good with his hands. He will construct something bombproof, spent some time working with a sawmill at another estate, aged fifteen for a couple of years until he's allowed to return here."

Christine asked, intrigued, "What happened, do elaborate?"

Justin took a deep breath, "Involve your mother. I think no more should be said about the matter everyone here ordered to remain silent if they valued their employment."

Christine and Donald both sat down. "I'm ordering you to tell me," Christine glared, deeply concerned, dreading what she might hear.

"Wasn't Robbie's fault a miserable winter's night, although blamed. Robbie was only fifteen at the time, just left school. He saw Josephine laughing, drinking from a bottle. She appeared to be pinned against the hotel wall by a man. Robbie's account: your mother is already topless. Robbie presumed, in the process, of being raped. He grabbed the man, not realising who he was and beat him. Your mother said nothing in his defence, running into the hotel. The man Robbie had assaulted was important. Robbie was given the option of leaving the estate. Or his mother and father would be evicted. Left with no real alternative; otherwise, his whole family is homeless. I cannot disclose the gentleman's name; your mother and he had liaised here for many years. I suppose you could call them childhood sweethearts. Josephine had seen him since she was twelve, if not before. She's always talked about. Robbie was unaware of the situation; otherwise, he would have probably ignored what he'd seen and walked away."

Christine sat quietly, suspecting the man was Dixon's father; they weren't far from another large estate. "Thank you, Justin; I think I know who you're talking about. Say no more on the matter and certainly don't mention to Robbie we know."

Justin sighed heavily, "The boy suffered while away. His father died, and I think that was one of the reasons leniency was shown, so he could work on the estate and look after his ageing mother."

Christine sighed heavily, leaving the office followed by Donald. Christine made her way to her private apartment, ordering two coffees, "My poor father, he had no idea what my mother was like before he married her. As my friends at school would say, she's an old bike."

Donald cuddled Christine, "Nothing we can do about the past, Christine. We must look to the future; Robbie is marrying Maggie. He's happy now; leave the past buried."

The waitress carried coffees into Christine's suite, leaving on the table. "I agree, Donald. Robbie's built like you; even at fifteen, I wouldn't want to fall out with him."

"No," Donald expressed, wondering what the future held for him and Christine. Will he always be able to trust her? He lay on his back on the bed staring at the chandelier for answers that didn't exist.

Eventually, Donald and Christine entered the large dining room for their evening meal. Donald's becoming used to eating like this, certainly a different lifestyle from home. He realised his life would change forever; he only had to set up on his own somewhere quiet. A member of the waiting staff came to his chair, whispering, "Someone to see you in reception, Mr Selwyn."

Donald left the table immediately, observing Maggie in reception. She didn't say anything. She kissed him on the lips, "Thanks, Donald, way too generous; not only have I excelled in my shop today thanks to you. I have a car delivered to my shop."

Donald smiled, "As long as you're happy, Maggie."

Christine watched from the doorway, everything taking place, although she couldn't hear the conversation between Donald and Maggie. In hindsight, she presumed Maggie's thanking him for the car and thought it a lovely gesture after what Justin had revealed, hoping Maggie would complete Robbie's life. She would reward him again if the opportunity arose.

She watched Maggie kiss Donald once more on the cheek and leave. She never really experienced jealousy, although she considered she may be now wishing to scratch Maggie's eyes out for kissing her future husband.

Donald returned to Christine, grinning. Christine remarked, "Could you possibly wipe her lipstick off your cheek, Donald," she folded her arms, returning to the table.

To everyone's surprise, haggis served a very Scottish meal with potatoes. Some of the holidaymakers look strangely at the parcel. Christine rose to her feet, "Ladies and gentlemen, those of you who have only heard of haggis, a staple meal for many Scottish residents years ago. I think it is only fitting that we should honour the Scottish people. You will be pleasantly surprised by how wonderful it tastes."

She sat down, cutting into hers, watching everyone else follow suit. After eating, Christine and Donald walked along the stream embankment towards the waterwheel, hearing the water against the paddles. The electrician was rather artistic; lighting the whole area, you could watch the waterwheel in action at night. Robbie had fenced the area off securely to prevent injury. They continued walking, following the water supply to the sawmill until they reached the reservoir, showing no signs of emptying. Thanks to the small streams from the mountain continually replenishing whatever's taken away.

Christine asked, "if you had a choice, Donald would you live here, at home with your mother and father, or Strawberry Estate?"

"I love my mother and father. I would love to live here; so much peace. I'll have to find a wife, and I can settle down." Christine was so incensed that she pushed him vigorously, and he fell into the reservoir. She placed her hands to her mouth, laughing, "Sorry, Donald."

"It's okay," he said, holding his hand out, freezing, pulling Christine in. She screamed at the top of her voice, entering headfirst into the cold water. To their amazement, the gamekeeper appeared in the evening twilight, not realising who they were to start with. He pointed his shotgun, "Out of there," discharging his shotgun in the air.

Within minutes, Robbie stood by the gamekeeper, "You're not shooting these two. The future laird, Jock, you'll be looking for a new position." Robbie held out his hands, easing Donald and Christine from the water, "A little cold to be bathing," he suggested straight-faced.

"I wasn't," Donald pointed out quickly, "Christine pushed me in." Jock burst out laughing.

Christine commented, "He pulled me in," she frowned. Jock walked over the ridge. They heard a motor start a Land Rover, and he returned. "Climb aboard. I'll give you crazy people a lift to the house," less than amused with their performance, especially in the evening twilight, could have easily been mistaken for poachers.

Both Donald and Christine slid into the front of the old Land Rover. Jock commented, "You'll be wetting my seats." Donald grinned and Christine.

Christine remarked, "You don't have a new Land Rover, Jock?"

"No, gamekeepers only have rubbish, always the same on this estate."

"What sort of vehicle would you like, Jock?" Donald asked.

"Something without holes in the floor, your feet freeze in the winter, and I could do with a new set of tyres, won't happen. I keep getting stuck."

"What do you think of the old sawmill restored, Jock?" Donald asked curiously.

"All right, for those tourist folks, I guess if what I hear is correct, powering the estate's electricity will save a few pounds. Probably end up in the laird's pocket, not spent on the estate."

Jock realised what he'd said, "I apologise I spoke out of turn," not wishing to be dismissed.

"Haven't you heard, Jock?" Christine asked, "My estate now and my future husband, we intend to make changes, hopefully all for the better. How do you feel about horses, Jock?"

"They're okay. Better for taking people around the estate in small groups. I prefer people to come to look at the birds and animals rather than take pot-shots. Half the time, they injure the creatures. I have to track them down, put them out of their misery," he frowned.

"That's what my father has introduced on Strawberry Estate; people can come and look at the wildlife and not shoot, although we may hold one shoot a year for staff only."

"Unfortunately, there has to be culling. I accept that fact," Jock sighed, parking by the front of the hotel.

"Thank you for the lift, Jock," Donald expressed, helping Christine out of the Land Rover. "We will talk more, Jock, about your ideas in the future," Donald smiled.

They slowly walked into the house like drowned rats, extremely cold. Robbie had already phoned. Justin placed blankets around their shoulders, "Take a hot shower and change quickly," he suggested. Christine and Donald went into the shower together and giggled at what they'd done. Donald remarked, "The gamekeeper takes no prisoners; that's for sure if he could shoot us, he would."

Christine smiled, cuddling close to Donald. Although Glencoe Estate felt like home, retiring to bed early, realising the last day here tomorrow. Donald kept having the same reoccurring dream he purchased a vehicle for Jock when he was last here.

By 3 o'clock, he sat by the fire, watching the flames lick the back of the fireplace. He glanced at Christine peacefully asleep in bed, hoping their life together would continue to be fun and not all business. Donald's looking forward to returning home as much as he loved Glencoe Estate; he wanted to have paintbrushes in his hand. He promised to buy an RV park on the estate to use as an art studio. Something for him to put on his to-do list along with solving the puzzle of a vehicle for Jock, who gave the impression he could be a mean old bugger.

Nevertheless, from the short time Donald had spoken to Jock, he appeared to have his heart in the right place. Donald fell asleep in the armchair, woken around 7 o'clock by Christine kissing his neck. "Why are you sitting here?"

"I was sure I purchased a new vehicle for the gamekeeper when we went on our shopping spree?"

"We discussed," she said, deep in thought.

Donald suddenly jumped to his feet, saying, "I have it." Christine dressed, wondering what Donald's up to now, what crazy idea is running around in that mind of his. Donald ran downstairs, stepping out of the building. He removed his mobile phone, asking Google search, "Where can I purchase ex-army vehicles."

"Forty miles from your location." Donald ran to his Bentley, tapping in the postcode. Christine came running out. "Explain, Donald, calm down, please, breakfast before doing anything. I want to know what you're planning," she said, searching his excited expression with her beautiful eyes.

Donald picked up Christine in his arms, carrying her into the hotel. "Put me down; everybody's watching Donald; you're a crazy man," she remarked, observing Maggie stopping and Robbie climbing out of her Subaru Forester. Donald had barely lowered Christine to her feet when Robbie grabbed Donald in his arms and kissed him on the cheek, dropping him to his feet. Donald stood, shocked, watching Maggie drive off laughing. "Thanks for your generosity Donald, the car is beautiful, but you've already been too generous."

Christine's screaming with laughter, looking at the expression on Donald's face trying to recover from a kiss by a wiry-faced Scott dressed in the new Selwyn tartan. Donald had failed to notice due to his shocked expression.

"I purchased the car so you would have no excuse; you couldn't drive to my farm and spend your honeymoon in a luxurious apartment," Donald remarked, recovering from the shock of being kissed by Robbie. Robbie patted Donald on the shoulder, heading for the waterwheel to continue his work. "You are one in a million, Donald," Robbie called back.

Christine asked, "What's it like being kissed by a big hairy man?"

"Not dissimilar to being kissed by you," he watched Christine glare.

"I'm not hairy," she whispered.

They went inside and had a hearty breakfast. "You still haven't explained to me what you're up to, Donald?"

"Come along, Christine, you'll find out. I think you will be pleased. I know Jock will, I hope." Donald drove the forty miles to the storage of old military vehicles, inspecting a troop carrier four-wheel-drive lorry already with seats in the back. However, they would be a little hard and may need a cushion. The roof tarpaulin could be rolled up so everyone could look in whichever direction they wanted and be closed, should the weather suddenly change as often would in Scotland. They'd have to manage, looking through the plastic windows.

"Donald, this is silly! Jock won't have a driving licence," Christine pointed out.

"Private estate," Donald shrugged his shoulders, "Not on the road; his old Land Rover never has. Think what you could charge for the excursions Christine to view twenty-five thousand acres of unspoiled beauty. The public would now have access to, including disabled people, which would be a bonus because the seating folding up, and wheelchairs could be loaded on board."

Donald only paid ten thousand pounds for the lorry. He looked in the cab, noticing it had a heater; Jock certainly wouldn't complain. The vehicle would go anywhere with a hi-low range gearbox and on all-terrain brand-new tyres with a six-cylinder engine. The vehicle sprayed for desert camouflage which Donald thought appropriate.

"Will you explain to Jock, or will I," Christine asked cautiously, "Because if he is unhappy, you will certainly know about it," she cautioned.

"I'll explain to him," Donald smiled, arranging for the vehicle to be delivered tomorrow morning, hopefully before they'd left for home. They returned to Glencoe Estate. Both entered the office grinning, which Justin knew meant trouble.

Christine grabbed Justin's decanter of whisky, passing everyone a small glass, "Could you summon Jock to the office, please, Justin?"

Justin glared in horror, "I'm aware Jock may have spoken out of turn yesterday. You're not to dismiss him; he's a damn good game-keeper, Christine, please?"

"Not even on our mind, Justin."

Justin rang Jock, "Can you come to the office, please. Christine and Donald wish to speak to you." "Am I to be sacked, Justin?"

"No, Jock, you can breathe a sigh of relief. Please come to the office they are waiting to speak to you. What's all this about, Donald?" Justin asked curiously.

"Wait and find out." Jock knocked nervously and came into the office, removing his deerstalker.

"The Land Rover you presently drive is worse for wear," Christine suggested. "Thanks to the generosity of my future husband, we have purchased you a new toy, which we hope you will look after. We listened to your complaints yesterday concerning the treatment of wildlife on the estate. We thought this was a golden opportunity to offer the guests a tour around the estate. You can explain everything you know about animals and their behaviour."

Jock stood in shock. Donald switched on his mobile showing him a picture of the vehicle arriving in the morning, "Before you complain, Jock, I checked a heater in the cab and no holes in the floor."

Jock smiled for the first time and walked over to the office wall to the estate map, explaining to Christine and Donald the roots that would be suitable and good places to view animals. Jock looked to Justin, "You are right about this pair; they're not all talk," Jock left the office.

"You actually made Jock smile," Justin commented. "A word of caution, please don't turn the estate into a theme park."

"Definitely not," Donald voiced firmly.

"Over my dead body," Christine assured. "We only want horses; that's the last purchase. Jock needed a new vehicle, and Donald thought it very apt to have a vehicle capable of carrying people safely around the estate. While we're on the subject of safety, Justin. I expect Jock's vehicle to be inspected by a fully qualified mechanic yearly before the public can travel in the back. Maybe prudent to have lap belts fitted. That way, no one can fall off the seats. A few cushions wouldn't go amiss. We don't want to give anyone a sore backside."

Donald embraced Christine, "As always, you put the final trimmings to a good idea."

***

Gerald at Strawberry Estate had purchased a horse to ride, accompanying Susan on Christine's horse, around his estate. He's becoming quite smitten with her; she made him feel twenty-one again. They often rode to the restored sawmill to check on progress and around the reserve, Gerald's conservation area.

Mary and Martin thought it rather strange that Gerald hadn't visited them for a meal, suspecting Susan had something to do with why.

***

Christine and Donald watched Jock's vehicle arrive as they left Glencoe Estate to head home. Watching Jock wave and smile. They finally arrived at Crabtree Farm in the early hours, thanks to an accident on the M6 causing massive tailbacks. They quietly entered Donald's apartment, sliding into bed absolutely shattered from the journey.

Martin left the cottage, spotting Donald's Bentley. He milked the cow fed the pigs and returned to the cottage; Mary's making breakfast, noticing the Bentley parked across the yard. She smiled, realising her son was home safely. She glanced at a picture on the wall of Donald in his kilt she had printed off. She phoned across to Donald's apartment, "Would you like breakfast, Donald, Christine?"

"We'll be across in a minute, mum," Donald expressed, scratching his head; both quickly showered, slipping on their clothes and heading for the cottage. Donald spotted the picture of him immediately in a kilt. He commented, "I have lovely legs." Christine grinned.

Over breakfast, Donald and Christine explained what had taken place at Glencoe. Mary advised, "I haven't seen your father since you left, admittedly only a couple of days. He is usually here for breakfast or tea unless he's found a new cook," she smirked.

Everyone looked out of the window noticing two horses come into the yard. Gerald in his riding clothes on a horse and Susan on The Rising Sun. "I think there's your answer, Mary; my father's been in the sweet packet again," Christine commented sarcastically.

"Not unlike his daughter," Mary smiled, watching Christine grin.

Christine stepped outside, followed by everyone else, giving her horse a cuddle. "I see you managed to return Christine safely," Gerald observed.

"Yes, father, thank you, and I see you've been spending. I presume this is your latest acquisition?"

"Yes, I haven't a rich boyfriend, so I had to buy my own horse," making Donald laugh.

Susan grinned, displaying some of Josephine's jewellery on her fingers. Christine realised the relationship had gone further than she'd anticipated. She surmised she would have to talk with her father privately, sooner rather than later.

"Oh well, back to Strawberry Estate, come along, Susan. Hopefully, you will find your way home later today, Christine?" Gerald asked.

"Definitely, father, I need a word with you," she said, glaring at him. He trotted off, followed by Susan. Mary noticed the frosty tone in Christine's voice, "What's the matter, Christine? You're not happy about something?"

"No, Susan's nosing in my mother's jewellery box. I recognised some of the rings; no chance Susan could afford them."

"Before you go off the deep end, Christine," Mary cautioned, "Calm down, finish your breakfast, and Donald will take you home. Check the jewellery is actually from your mother's jewellery box before you go on the rampage if you must. Does it really matter if she borrows jewellery, providing she doesn't intend to keep it? If your mother ever requested it returned, could it be a problem for you and your father?"

Christine sat quietly eating, "One ring alone is worth over two hundred and fifty thousand pounds, an heirloom, surprised my father allowed out the house."

Mary sat back in her chair, "Good gracious, that is an awful amount of money for such a little object."

Donald gave Christine a lift home. "You go, Donald. I'll be okay; I'll have to do some straight talking." Both Donald and Christine were surprised to see Mrs Montague's limousine park alongside Donald's Bentley. Mrs Montague stepped from the vehicle with her bodyguard, which meant, as a rule, she was prepared for trouble. Christine kissed Donald on the cheek, "Go home, Donald, I'll phone you," Christine assured, stepping from his car. Donald waved, driving away. Mrs Montague smiled, "I've come to collect Josephine's jewellery. It appears to be inappropriately used by somebody else," she grinned.

Christine's astonished, "I was about to confront my father concerning my mother's jewellery. How are you so well-informed, Mrs Montague, of events?"

Mrs Montague actually placed an arm around Christine's shoulder. "A Spy in the sky," she grinned. "Some devices can hear conversations; spy satellites have become very sophisticated, Christine."

"Mrs Montague," Christine gasped. "The government would never tolerate using a spying device for such a trivial matter."

Mrs Montague smiled, "I thought hilarious when you pushed Donald in the reservoir at Glencoe, and even more amusing to see him pull you in." Mrs Montague smiled, lifting her eyebrows.

"So, you monitor all of us; we're not that important, surely?"

"The incident on Glencoe captured by a drone monitoring your property and another acquisition by Elizabeth R . I must add, Donald has turned out excellently his intentions towards you, and everyone else is totally honourable, a rare commodity, in this day and age Christine, cherish him."

"You astonish me, Mrs Montague."

Gerald came out of the house, re-buttoning his shirt, looking extremely flustered. "No guessing needed, father," Christine voiced calmly.

"I'm over twenty-one, Christine. I can do what I like," he glared, annoyed.

"Unfortunately, you can't, Gerald. I'm here to collect Josephine's jewellery totals over a million," Mrs Montague removed her notebook. "I have a list. You will have to pay for anything missing," she advised without hesitation.

Christine stood with her arms folded to support Mrs Montague's decision.

Gerald realised he was in trouble. The jewellery belonged to Josephine; she had accumulated it long before marriage. Gerald sighed heavily, staring at Christine with disappointment, opening the front door and inviting Mrs Montague into the lounge. He ran upstairs, returning with Josephine's jewellery box. Mrs Montague's bodyguard poured her a drink placing it on the coffee table while she counted the jewellery, checking it was accounted for. "Five hundred thousand pounds worth of jewellery missing, Gerald?"

"Oh, wait a minute." He left the room, going into the kitchen. "Susan, I need those rings, please." She removed the rings from her fingers, looking angry and frustrated. Gerald returned to Mrs Montague, placing the rings on the table. She smiled, "Thank you, Gerald. Your mother Christine wishes me to convey these will become yours in due course at the appropriate time."

Susan ran into the room, "You spoilt two-timing bitch Christine; ask her about Oliver, Gerald," Susan shouted, slapping Christine's face hard. Christine grabbed Susan's arm, throwing her to the floor, preparing to administer a death blow. Mrs Montague's bodyguard blocked Christine from delivering the fatal blow. "Stop Christine," Mrs Montague ordered, "She's not worth the trouble Christine. Throw her out," Mrs Montague insisted, pointing to the door. Her bodyguard didn't hesitate to escort Susan to the door, pushing her outside. Gerald stood in shock, surprised at Susan's behaviour and remarks, wondering who Oliver was? Is Christine seeing him behind Donald's back?

Mrs Montague approached the trembling Christine, removing her handkerchief. Mrs Montague dried Christine's cheeks. "I'm sorry, Christine," Gerald finally muttered.

"I suggest you speak with Mary Selwyn; she will advise you on a suitable replacement for the refuge we've tossed out the door. Didn't you realise Gerald, a woman of her age with no prospects and a criminal record allowing a fifty-nine-year-old man to maul her, is up to no good? According to our observations, I think you should check; some of the silverware is missing," Mrs Montague advised trying to discredit Susan.

Gerald collapsed on the settee holding his head; Christine sat beside him. "I'm okay, father, shaken; I didn't see that coming."

"Neither did I. I thought she was really interested in me, not just my money. I warned myself not to become too involved at the outset," he sighed heavily.

"At least you have a horse now, father. We can ride together," Christine assured, trying to ease the pain of her father's suffering.

Mrs Montague indicated with her hand to her bodyguard they were leaving. Gently patting Christine on the shoulder, she didn't say anything, left the house-entering her limousine, and drove away.

CHAPTER ELEVEN

WHAT TO DO NEXT

Christine poured her father a large whisky from the decanter, leaving him with his thoughts; walking into the kitchen, she phoned Donald explaining what had taken place, holding her cheek still stinging from where Susan had struck her.

Donald's busy painting a portrait of the sawmill on Glencoe Estate. He found the old mill rather intriguing, deciding he would incorporate Robbie and Maggie in the scene in a romantic embrace, with the waterwheel turning in the background.

Martin came in, sitting beside Donald, listening to the rain hitting the roof, which appeared not to distract Donald. "I'm thinking, Donald, about purchasing a large set of Cambridge rollers to save so many passes across the field."

Donald lowered his paintbrush, "Coffee, dad?"

"Why not, son." They moved to the kitchen. Donald made the coffee, "Purchase what you need, dad. I'll cover the cost. Makes sense to me," Donald expressed, smiling.

"I wasn't begging for the money, Donald," Martin advised. "Simply trying to keep you advised the farm has sufficient funds to buy the roller without me begging."

Donald stared quite shocked by his father's comment. Deciding not to pursue the statement lowering his coffee cup to the draining board, he returned to his painting. Martin stormed out of the room, realising the wrong thing to say. Donald has supported the farm many times and wouldn't have the equipment today if it wasn't for his son. Martin paused at the bottom of the stairs, then continued to the cottage. He'd probably, make matters worse by whatever he said now.

Mary sat quietly, drinking coffee. She could see from the expression on Martin's face something had happened. "What have you done, Martin?"

He shrugged his shoulders, "I was explaining I wanted a large set of Cambridge rollers, and Donald said, buy them; he would cover the cost. Why does he think I need his money every time," Martin frowned. "Got my goat."

Mary remarked, "Men and the stupid way they carry on," she sighed heavily.

Donald continued painting, thinking about what his father had said, realising he didn't feel like a man, and perhaps he shouldn't keep offering him money. He decided that's not the way forward, and maybe he's a constant reminder to his father how hard he had to work for his money, unlike his son.

Donald finished his painting photographing and sent it to Jack. Although he felt it may fetch a few thousand, Jack was not overly impressed until Donald wrote "Precious Moments." The cash register rang in Jack's eyes, especially Donald Selwyn; writing those words meant so much more to many people. Jack phoned Donald, "Save my petrol bill, you can come to London, stay the night, as my guest. We can have publicity shots taken while you're here, Donald."

Donald thought for a moment, "I suppose. Give me your postcode, and then I can program my satnav. I suspect I will have to pay charges to enter London with this beast?"

Jack sighed, "I'm afraid so, Donald. We all have to bear the brunt of change. The government is slowly strangling London." Donald loaded the painting in the boot of his Bentley placing Jack's location in his satnav. He drove out of the yard without saying anything to anyone, which Mary thought strange on this occasion. She suspected Donald would read more into what's said than actually existed. He's at that sensitive age; she'd never known Donald, not at a sensitive period. He always took comments to heart instead of brushing them aside. Mary rang Donald's mobile; she knew he had hands-free so it wouldn't interfere with his driving. "Where are you going, Donald?" she asked calmly.

"London mum, I've finished a portrait."

Mary took a deep breath suggesting, "Take no notice of your father a man thing making him feel inadequate sometimes, totally stupid. He's gone into town to buy the new Cambridge rollers he wants; he will have forgotten the incident when he returns."

"He has a point, mum, I make my money so easy, and he's had to graft all his life, and me being there rubs it in his face. I may move to Scotland to Glencoe Estate for a while to give you two breathing space."

Mary shouted, panicking, "You will not, Donald Selwyn, you will not leave your mother your totally irrational as usual!" Donald disconnected the call. Mary rang time and time again, but he wouldn't answer. Martin walked into the cottage. Mary didn't hesitate; she explained the conversation. Martin looked worried. Mary's final comment, "If he goes, so do I, Martin, your bloody mess," she stormed out of the cottage jumping in her Range Rover and heading for Strawberry Estate. Mary parked outside the front of the house. Christine came running out to greet her. Mary immediately noticed a slight bruise on Christine's cheek, "I hope Donald isn't responsible for that, Christine?" Mary asked cautiously.

"No, Susan, she's gone. Don't worry. We won't be seeing her around here again. What's happened? You look worried, Mary!"

Mary sighed heavily, "Short version Martin and his big mouth have upset Donald. Donald is presently on his way to London with a portrait. Donald feels he's in the way and maybe moving to Glencoe; in fact, pretty sure he will."

"He hadn't better go without consulting me first," Christine voiced, worried. "Come in, Mary; we'll have a drink." They went into the lounge. Christine poured two small whiskies removing her mobile. Christine phoned Donald, and he answered. "What's this? I hear you're moving to Glencoe, my estate, without consulting me first, Donald."

He sighed heavily, finally answering, "Problems at home, Christine; I need to get away."

"Before you do anything, come and talk to me, Donald. I find it rather insulting you haven't consulted me, your future wife or have you dumped me?"

"Don't be silly, Christine, the furthest thing from my mind."

"When you return from London, I want to see you; Donald, come directly to Strawberry Estate, please, promise me?" She requested, crossing her fingers.

"Okay. I'm currently fighting through the London traffic, trying to find Jack's art studio. Speak to you later, Christine, bye."

Mary breathed a sigh of relief, "Thanks, Christine."

"I wouldn't worry too much, Mary; I know Donald had planned to buy an RV. One of his crazy ideas is to park on Glencoe Estate as an art studio rather than occupy any of the rooms," Christine smiled with confidence. "Besides, I'm pregnant. I keep forgetting to take the bloody pills. Donald doesn't know yet. Don't let on, please, Mary. I don't think he's going anywhere," Christine smiled.

Mary sat there, astounded, "How far along are you?" She asked eagerly.

"Only a couple of weeks, but it's enough to frighten Donald to death," she grinned.

Mary exhaled, "You don't care a damn, Christine. Any other girl of your age in that state would panic!"

"Why should I panic about a natural process. I've fancied Donald for years at school. When Martin injured his back, a golden opportunity for me to step in to help you and become closer to Donald. Hopefully, he would fancy me."

Mary sipped her drink, "My god, you are an intelligent young woman your father's right about you. You should come with a health warning. I should be livid, but I'm not. It will be you if anyone can control and look after Donald."

"Donald is exceptional, Mary. Mrs Montague said I'm fortunate. I didn't think he'd pay me any attention."

Gerald came into the room, kissing Mary on the cheek, sighing heavily, sitting in an armchair, "I presume you've explained to Mary, Christine?"

"No, we have another crisis I've resolved; hopefully," Christine smiled smugly.

"I don't know what Donald will say when he sees that mark on your cheek; I hope he doesn't strangle Susan," Gerald remarked, pouring himself a whisky.

Gerald spent the next ten minutes explaining events to Mary in detail about the situation with Susan. Mary sighed, "That does surprise me, Gerald; she actually hit Christine; lucky you didn't want to kill her, Christine," Mary smiled.

"I was, thankfully, Mrs Montague's bodyguard stopped me; in hindsight, it would have made a real mess of things if I had."

"I'll see who I know who may be interested in part-time work, Gerald and not come with a load of baggage around her neck. Perhaps we should consider someone from a farming background, so you both have a common interest," Mary grinned. "I think I know just the person."

Gerald smiled, intrigued, along with Christine. "We are looking for a housekeeper, not a pole dancer Mary," Christine cautioned.

"Not what I'm suggesting. Gerald may develop a relationship if the person I'm thinking of is interested. Christine, remember when you and Donald are married? Why should Gerald be left alone?"

"You call me intelligent Mary," Christine voiced, "and cunning," glancing to her father, who looked dumbfounded at the conversation. "Must go," Mary smiled, "I have plans to make and people to ring," she grinned, "I will leave Donald for you to sort out, Christine." Mary left in haste, conjuring a plan.

***

Donald finally arrived at Jack's art studio, parking around the back by Jack's Bentley. Jack looked at the artwork in Donald's Bentley, "Beautiful Donald." They finally walked inside. Jack studied the painting, "That is really beautiful, Donald," placing it on an easel in a temporary frame taking several shots to be transferred to the Internet. "Watch Donald," Jack advised, pressing the enter key. Donald stood in amazement. The painting, within thirty seconds, had reached over seven hundred thousand pounds. "You have followers, Donald; not many artists can boast of that. I've never known anyone like you in my life. You throw paint on like changing engine oil or mucking out a cowshed. People love you. You have a technique all of your own." Jack made a quick phone call within minutes cameraman taking pictures of Donald's new portrait. Jack stood beside him. A reporter asked, "What makes you get up in the morning, Donald and gives you the inspiration?"

Donald smiled, "The love of my mother and father, my girlfriend, and what the earth has to offer. So many beautiful things are ignored, people cast nature aside when in reality the only thing keeping us alive."

No one had realised someone was recording; within minutes, the information was transmitted to a news station and on-air.

Donald's comment played through the remainder of the day and into the late evening, seen by his mother, father and Christine. Donald stayed the night with Jack in his plush apartment above the shop. Donald preparing to leave after breakfast. Jack called him into the office, "Look, Donald." Donald looked at the monitor one million five hundred thousand pounds his latest artwork had achieved. Donald smiled, shaking Jack's hand, saying with gratitude, "Thank you for your hospitality, Jack. That reminds me, brilliant of you, working out what's happening at Glencoe. I love the tartan," Donald smiled, leaving.

Donald drove steadily home, often; people would wave, his car very distinctive. Donald's beginning to realise it could turn out to be a nightmare. Nevertheless, he had a good life, thinking his mother may be right. He overreacted to his father's comment. Finally pulled into Strawberry Estate. Christine's riding The Rising Sun came from around the rear of the house. She dismounted, kissing Donald affectionately, "We have to return to school next week, Donald. We both have exams to finish," she sighed heavily. Donald noticed the make-up on her cheek, unusual for Christine; he licked his finger and wiped, seeing the bruise as she flinched. "Who hit you?" His expression had turned into one of anger.

"Don't panic, Donald, Susan, a long story. Let me place The Rising Sun in his stable; I'll explain what happened." Donald followed her to the stables. Christine explained the events watching Donald calm down slowly. She couldn't imagine the damage Donald would do to someone if she'd ever been hurt by a man. Her final comment was, "Oh, yes, I may be pregnant. I'm sure I'm pregnant," she smiled, heading for the house, holding Donald's hand.

Donald sighed, "Christine," he emphasised. "You know I love you; do we need a baby so early in our relationship? We have Glencoe to sort out, which means a considerable amount of travelling," he exhaled.

"I'm only a couple of weeks late, it may mean nothing like last time, or you're a daddy." She grinned, running for the house. Donald followed her, realising that no matter what he wanted, she would have her own way in the end. He glanced across the field to see a monstrous John Deere tractor ploughing the remaining field before planting.

***

Mary walked into the cottage on Crabtree Farm. Martin eating a sandwich he made for himself. Mary commented, "If Christine can't repair the damage, you're making your own meals for the rest of your life," she glared. Martin glanced up; nothing he could do about the situation. He would have to grin and see what happened.

Mary made a phone call. "Cindy, how are you?"

"Fine, thank you, Mary; I'm making a sandwich. I find it strange, not on the farm with my hubby," she sighed heavily.

"How long now, Cindy?"

"Three years to this day; how strange I'd forgotten for a moment. He should have known better, Mary, to mess around with the trailer while the tractor engines running."

"They are all the same, Cindy; look at my Martin, who didn't take the sheepdog and broke his back. We were lucky this time; thank god the sheep are gone. I presume your son is running the farm now?"

"Yes, I have nothing to do with it anymore. He lives with his girlfriend; I don't think they will marry. More's the pity."

"Do you know Gerald Gibbs on Strawberry Estate?"

"I think we were at school together; yes, we were; he's nine years older than me. His father had a butcher shop and farm; he married Josephine Spires."

"That's the one. I hope you don't find this insulting. I wondered if you wanted to earn a little extra cash. Gerald's looking for a house-keeper; you don't have to do much. He has a daughter Christine; she's to marry my son Donald hopefully," Mary expressed calmly, crossing her fingers.

"Oh, I don't know. I suppose it would prevent me from becoming bored. What happened to the last one who worked there, and what about Josephine?"

"I can't go into too much detail. The wife has gone the house-keeper rather naughty, shall we say and dismissed," Mary trying to be vague in her explanation.

"I didn't like Josephine anyway, stuck-up little bitch; she wasn't at school long, then they moved her to a private school in London. I suppose no harm to look into the position," Cindy expressed cautiously.

"I know they have a couple of horses, and you like riding. Would you like me to introduce you to Gerald; he's a nice man, better than the bugger I have now, a pain in the arse."

Cindy laughed, "Oh, dear. Okay, I'm coming your way tomor-row. Shall I call in around 10 o'clock, Mary?"

"Yes, meet here first. If all is hunky-dory, we can go on to Straw-berry Estate."

"Great, bye, for now," Cindy rang off. Mary rubbed her hands together. Cindy was beautiful at school, with blonde hair, blue eyes and a marvellous figure. Mary had no idea what she looked like now; they rarely saw each other over the past three years or more.

Mary rang Gerald, "Be here at 10 o'clock tomorrow; you remember Cindy Crawford, Gerald?"

"No, I can't say I do, Mary."

"Her husband was killed three years ago by a machine he failed to turn the tractor engine off. The farm, her son, is running the place now. She has nothing to do with it, becoming rather bored, so you should have plenty in common and a farmer's wife. She won't be frightened of work," Mary emphasised.

"Okay, Mary, thanks very much; I'll bring Christine, essential everyone likes each other," he sighed.

The next day, Cindy arrived at 9:45 a.m., stepping from her gold-coloured Porsche. Mary stared in disbelief, not expecting to see Cindy absolutely gorgeous, with long blonde hair and blue eyes. You wouldn't have noticed if she had a child. She's slim, wearing her jeans and blouse with a denim jacket, slipping on a face mask from her pocket. Mary greeted her at the door, "Good gracious Cindy, you haven't changed. You don't need to wear a face mask here."

Cindy removed her mask, saying, "My hubby is well insured; that's the one thing he did right; protected my future. He ensured I would never be penniless. To be quite honest, I'm bored stupid." Cindy sat at the table; Mary poured coffees. Gerald and Christine came into the yard in his Range Rover, knocked, walking in with Christine closely following him. He paused in his tracks staring at Cindy. Christine commented, "Father, don't stare."

"I remember you from school, Cindy; vaguely, you just about started as I was leaving, I think." Gerald offered his hand to Cindy, which she accepted, with a smile melting his soul. Mary trying not to grin; she could see the attraction immediately.

Christine asked, "You have any experience in farming or interest; although the position we offer is merely housekeeping," she assured.

"My husband died three years ago; a trailer slipped off a jack wasn't properly fixed; he was crushed. We own five hundred acres, mainly cereals since my son's taken over the farm with his girlfriend, I'm no longer involved and, to be quite honest, rather bored."

"Oh, I'm sorry for your loss," Christine voiced calmly, feeling a bitch for an aggressive stance.

"You really want to be a housekeeper, Cindy?" Gerald asked calmly, "Surely you could acquire a better position with your intelligence."

Cindy smiled, "Why go looking for hard work when I don't need it. I have more than enough money to support myself. I can fly off to foreign countries, have a suntan, have a hundred and one gigolos that wouldn't make me happy."

Gerald sighed, "You are welcome to come and look at my house, perhaps go riding with me on Strawberry Estate. I have three thousand acres," he slightly boasted.

"No time like the present," Cindy suggested, standing. "Let's see what you expect of me," she smiled, winking, making Mary laugh; she couldn't control herself. Christine asked, "What's so amusing, Mary?"

"I'll follow you, Gerald," Cindy suggested, following Gerald out of the cottage. He climbed in his Range Rover, watching her climb in her Porsche Boxer, the same colour as her golden hair.

Christine stayed behind. Mary sensed she wanted to ask another hundred questions. Christine immediately turned to face Mary, "You're not trying to pair off my father, Mary?"

"I've known Cindy a long time. She was loyal to her husband, and I think it would take an extraordinary man to interest her in a relationship. I think you're worrying unnecessary, Christine," Mary assured.

Christine frowned. Donald came into the kitchen, "Who's Porsche? Your father certainly smiling, Christine," he teased.

"Oh, you're worse than your mother, Donald," Christine professed. Donald burst out laughing, kissing Christine on her cheek. "Have you told my mother; you know about what?"

"I'm not! A false alarm," Christine expressed.

"Go on the pill Christine," Mary suggested, "look what I have to deal with," she said, pointing to Donald.

Christine burst out laughing, "I see your point, Mary."

"That reminds me," Donald expressed calmly, "My latest artwork fetched two million. I've asked Jack to produce a hundred prints which I will sign and can be purchased from Glencoe Estate if anyone's interested; they can be purchased for five hundred pounds each apart from the one I give to Robbie and Maggie. The money can go into the Glencoe Estate fund," he grinned.

Christine pointed at herself, "Me owner, your boyfriend, talk to me, Donald, don't go over my head," she suggested as calmly as she could, biting her tongue.

Mary burst out laughing again, having a giggling fit. Christine stamped her foot. "What's so funny." Donald started laughing, watching Christine glow in frustration. He picked her up in his arms; she struggled to free herself and couldn't, his tight grip kissing her on the lips. "I have to breathe, Donald, please."

He lowered to her feet, "Sorry, Christine, I thought you would approve. I didn't realise I had to ask for your approval over every decision," he frowned, walking out of the kitchen door and heading to the studio.

Mary stopped giggling.

"Oh, damn, me and my big mouth," Christine shouted. "He has not an evil bone in his body; I'm jealous of everything," she sighed heavily.

"Mary poured two more coffees, "Between you and Martin, I don't know which is the worst. I can see him jumping on an aeroplane for Australia the way things are here." Christine ran out of the door up into the studio. Donald sat at his easel, painting a portrait of Christine in a white wedding dress. She stood in amazement, seeing herself standing by the bridge with Glencoe holding a bouquet of flowers in the background. "Beautiful Donald, I'm in a satin wedding dress. I can even see the pattern; I look alive." Christine ran off to make two coffees as Mary entered the studio carrying Christine's mug, "You only need to make one. Yours is still here. You didn't finish," she advised, noticing the portrait.

***

Gerald's busily showing Cindy around the house where everything is. She commented, "No shortage of modern conveniences here, Gerald. You sure you need somebody?"

"Not so bad in the winter; summer is mayhem with the harvest and everything else. Would you like to see The Rising Sun, my daughter's horse? I purchased myself an eight-year-old hunter the other week; I call him Pig," Gerald smiled.

Cindy patted Gerald's belly, "Looks like you could lose a few pounds too." Gerald was taken back by her boldness; she didn't care whether she had the position or not; wasn't necessary, and she certainly wouldn't steal from him financially secure in her own right.

They walked around to the stables. "Now I remember Donald Selwyn, of course, he painted that famous portrait Jerusalem all over the news for weeks, and this is the son of Jerusalem, The Rising Sun, which he purchased for your daughter, coming back to me now. Blimey, I am a dum dum at times," she expressed calmly.

"In all honesty, Donald is a godsend; Christine, she will want for nothing for the rest of her life. I suppose you already know about my situation?"

"Not interested," Cindy advised. "Mary's briefly brought me up to speed, and that's all I need to know, other than my salary you are offering me to work here and what are my duties?"

"Basically, run the house, washing, cleaning, cooking whatever needs attention at the time. Obviously, Christine and I chip in. I will pay you ten pounds an hour which I suppose is an insult, but it's the going rate, and if I pay you more, Christine will beat me with a big stick," he smiled.

"She's a smart girl. Shall we say a six-month trial, Gerald? That works both ways," Cindy grinned.

"If you wish, you can start tomorrow; how far away are you from us?" Gerald asked, concerned.

"About ten miles not far, don't worry. I use my Range Rover in the winter," she smiled, walking in front of him, fully aware that he was watching her every movement, which tickled her pink.

***

Donald finished drinking his coffee, placing the portrait he's working on another easel covering to protect against dust. Mary returned to the cottage. Donald gave Christine a lift home, intrigued to see her father's decision concerning Cindy, although suspecting he would take her on if only to watch her walk around the house.

Donald and Christine kissed each other warmly, said goodbye, and she ran into the house, waiting to find out what her father had decided.

Donald drove into town, calling in at the Massey Ferguson supplier. Selected a flail hedge cutter and a suitable second-hand Massey tractor to permanently attach to. Donald realised they couldn't keep cutting down the few trees remaining on Crabtree Farm; it would be better to purchase what timber they needed from the Forestry Commission or some other source. He spent some time deciding which wood processing machine he wanted and would fit on the back of one of their tractors, PTO powered and capable of taking large pieces of timber. Donald paid, driving home and running up into the studio. He searched on the Internet phoning the Forestry Department ordering a lorry load of second and first thinning's, which would be ideal for firewood, paid over the phone.

He ran downstairs, crossing the yard to the cottage finding his mother and father, taking a deep breath, and pouring himself a coffee. "I made some purchases," he said, holding his cup. "A new flail hedge cutter on a second-hand tractor and a new wood processor. I've already ordered the timber rather than destroy any more trees we have around here."

"Thanks for discussing with me, son," Martin voiced, annoyed. Mary glared at Martin. She could understand why Donald had made the purchases, although she realised he should have spoken to Martin in the first instance.

"Please explain why son"? Martin asked calmly.

"For years, we paid for a contractor to trim the hedges. Now there's no livestock; only sensible to have our own equipment, which means we can cut the hedges exactly at the right time and not be delayed, waiting for somebody else. Regarding the wood processor and timber I purchased. You're not a young man, dad. You've escaped the wheelchair once; your back will not take any more punishment; you've already suffered one major accident. You only need to load the wood processor you can perform with the JCB; the processor will do the rest cut into lengths and split into whatever size blocks you want. The timber is coming directly from the Forestry Commission. You only have to order if you require more or find another source."

Martin couldn't argue they haven't many trees left on the farm. He certainly didn't have any spare money to lash out on a hedge cutter and another tractor or a wood processor, for that matter. With his chainsaw, he would have had to cut the timber one piece at a time.

"The next thing I'm leaving school, the new term starts in a couple of days. I'm not continuing with my education. I don't quite see the point. I can play rugby or paint; the farm is secure. You don't need me anymore."

"What are you saying, Donald?" Mary asked.

"Nothing really, mum. I'd like to concentrate on my painting and spend some time in Scotland or travel around the country to see things I haven't seen before, other than on the Internet. I'm only a phone call away, not as if I'm leaving the planet," he smiled.

"Have you discussed your decision with Christine, Donald?" Mary asked.

" Nothing to discuss. I'm only suggesting I may decide to travel; no point upsetting anyone at this stage."

"I thought you were smitten with Christine; what's changed, Donald?" Mary asked suspiciously.

"Nothing! I appear to be controlled by everyone and always appear to be what they want instead of what I want," he sighed heavily, leaving the kitchen and returning to his studio.

Mary and Martin looked at each other. "I think that boys suffering from depression, Mary," Martin voiced concern.

"Yes, that's not the Donald I know, or perhaps he's growing up and wants his own space, who knows," Mary sighed heavily.

Mary phoned Christine to explain Donald's conversation. "I'll come and see him, Mary; some of this may be my fault," Christine exhaled, lowering the receiver, running to her Range Rover, coming over to Crabtree Farm, running up into the studio, finding Donald sat in an armchair watching television.

Donald sighed, "I suppose mum phoned you?"

"Everyone cares about you, Donald; explain what I've done wrong?" Christine asked, intrigued.

"You've done nothing wrong; I feel down and out. I want to run and hide somewhere. Perhaps I'm depressed, Christine. The thought of returning to that bloody school doesn't impress me. You might as well know; I'm leaving, not continuing with my education."

"I'm only staying for a short while, taking a couple more exams; always useful to have qualifications."

"You want me to collect you for school in the morning, Christine?"

"No, I'll go in my own motor if I'm delayed, or you're delayed," she smiled, kissing him on the cheek. "I'll see you at school tomorrow," she left the studio less than convinced Donald's okay, running over to the cottage. Mary eagerly opened the door. Christine shrugged her shoulders, "Maybe slightly depressed, I don't know. I think the thought of returning to school doesn't help matters, but he's leaving anyway now. I'm only staying to take two more exams than I'm finishing. I have too much to do on Strawberry Estate and Glencoe. I could do without having Donald to worry about," she said calmly.

"You find Donald too much trouble, Christine. Perhaps it's time you drifted apart and went your separate ways," Mary advised refusing to consider her son's a problem.

"Oh." Christine turned quickly on her heels, not saying another word heading home with the thought of separating from Donald; she had never considered the idea sending a shudder down her spine.

Donald was about to drive to school when he saw the Massey Ferguson tractor and flail hedge cutter delivered and a Range Rover with a trailer carrying the new wood processor. He pulled over, allowing him to pass, leaving for his father to sort out. He would be most likely to use the equipment, not him. Donald arrived at school. The girls were swarming around his Bentley, looking at the artwork. Finally, Donald made his way to the headteacher's office. He knocked, walking in, "Good morning, Sir."

"Good morning, Donald. I presume you are here to inform me you're not continuing your education," the headteacher smiled.

"Yes, Sir, I have so much work ahead of me. I don't think I need qualifications to hold a paintbrush," Donald smiled. "I would like to thank you for all the opportunities the school has afforded me, from rugby to art. I don't think I'd be where I am today if it wasn't for the encouragement of the teachers." Donald removed his cheque book, writing a cheque for two hundred and fifty thousand pounds. "Please accept, help fund children less fortunate than myself."

The headteacher collapsed in his chair, astounded by the generosity of a student, "You are most gracious, Donald. We are having financial issues with the budget, which will bridge the gap for this year," the headteacher exhaled, standing to shake Donald's hand warmly. "Please keep in touch, Donald; we will eagerly follow your progress on the television," the headteacher smiled and opened the door. Donald jumped in his Bentley, finally feeling free. Pleased, he donated money to help students less fortunate. He passed Christine coming the other way he waved he looked in his mirror she stopped, but he didn't he continued home. Christine rang his mobile, "You didn't stop, Donald. Why?"

"I have to work for a living now, Christine. I don't have time to flirt with a girl." Christine smiled, "Okay, boyfriend, speak to you later."

Donald changed into his work clothes finding his father looking over the wood processor and deciding where to place it so he'd have good access to feed timber into the machine. Martin put his arm on Donald's shoulder, "You don't buy anything by halves, son? We only have three or four fires; you can process enough with this machine in an hour to run Battersea Power Station," Martin grinned.

"I didn't want you to stand out in the cold too long," Donald smiled. "What do you think of the hedge cutter, dad?"

"Great, as you rightly pointed out, one less bill, and we could cut hedges when we're ready and beholding to no one." They glanced down the drive seeing an articulated lorry load of timber. With its own crane, the lorry removed, stacking neatly in a pile, Donald signed for the shipment, and the truck left. Mary came out, hearing the commotion and seeing the new equipment. She grinned, seeing Donald and his father laughing together. She hoped sanity had returned. Martin smiled, "I think we ought to test, don't you, Donald?"

Donald grinned, "Absolutely, dad." Donald started the tractor, increasing the PTO to 540 revolutions. Martin collected logs from the pile, slipping one on the feeder with the JCB. Martin jumped from the cab showing Donald, "We press that button, and the process is automated."

"We'll find out, dad, both pressing the button together, standing back, watching the timber cut into blocks and forced through a log splitter onto a conveyor belt. Donald quickly reversed the old Ferguson 20 with the trailer under the conveyor to catch the processed timber. They only had the machine running for fifteen minutes and had to stop. They'd buried the small trailer. Martin could barely keep up with the pace of the wood processor, stood, looking at each other and burst out laughing. The air filled with the aroma of processed pine trees.

Mary was carrying two mugs of coffee, suspecting they'd be there for hours, standing in shock, passing each a mug. "That load will fill the woodshed twice, Martin," she frowned, "And how's your back?" she inquired.

"Perfect Mary, the machine did everything. We have to find the buried trailer," he grinned.

Gerald walked around the rear of the building and saw what they were performing, studying Donald's equipment. "Having a little spend, Donald," Gerald smiled. "I see our timber isn't good enough. You purchased from elsewhere?" Gerald grinned.

"I didn't think you had any spare timber, Gerald. I suspect you would want for your own sawmill operation; hopefully, running shortly?"

"Won't be long now. Michael is finishing off a small café and toilet block. We'll open to the public; see if that's another white elephant enterprise," he remarked, less than convinced it would work.

"We are quite happy to purchase timber from you, Gerald," Martin suggested. "I suggest you have your winter wheat planted by the eleventh of October, weather permitting? We are oilseed rape this year, Martin," smiled.

"Finished in a couple of days," Gerald advised. "I think you ought to look at your oilseed rape at the bottom of the hill; you'll find slugs have moved in."

"I'll check," Martin said, rushing off, jumping on his quad bike with a slug dispenser attached, taking a bag of slug pellets with him.

"Coffee Gerald?" Mary asked, grinning.

"Thanks, Mary, I will."

Donald watched them walk off together, tidying up the mess and trying to stack blocks on the small trailer before taking them to the woodshed.

"You obviously want to talk to me, Gerald; what's the matter?" she asked, concerned.

"Yes, a couple of things, Mary; thank you for finding Cindy. I think she will be a great asset. She has her own money and no interest or ambitions conflict with Strawberry Estate. Secondly, what's going on between Christine and Donald? Something's not quite right; I sense it. I just can't put my finger on it. I dare not ask Christine; she would bite my head off and say, mind your own business could make matters worse."

Mary sighed, "Somehow, I don't think they will be together much longer; I hope I'm wrong. I'm not sure if there's anyone to blame or not. I know Christine doesn't care if she becomes pregnant or not. I know that worries Donald; he thinks plenty of time for children."

"I didn't know that," Gerald remarked, alarmed, "Isn't she taking precautions, Mary?"

"The doctor has prescribed pills; she seems to forget to take them whether, by design or accident, I can't comment."

Gerald sighed heavily, "Doesn't she realise they have a lifetime ahead? The chances of Donald leaving her is non-existent. However, I can understand his reluctance if she's behaving irresponsibly."

"We have no proof, Gerald. Please don't go on the warpath with Christine. I think, sit back, and see what happens; I would love to interfere. Christine commented yesterday that she had enough on her plate without Donald becoming a problem. I suggested they should separate. I think it shocked her and may have done some good."

Gerald smiled, "She hates if she doesn't think she's in full control. Christine doesn't like how Donald jumps in with both feet resolving issues. She can't afford to do it herself and has stopped using Strawberry Estate shares as security for Glencoe improvements. The only way forward is with Donald. If I thought she was using him for one minute, I would throw her out the house and disown her for disgraceful behaviour."

"Come with me. I'll show you something," Mary took Gerald into the studio, carefully removing the cover from the unfinished painting of Christine in a wedding dress.

"My goodness, beautiful, Mary, look at the detail. I'll have to talk to Christine. I can't allow this situation to continue; she could destroy him. She has her mother's attitude believing she can walk on water; I'm about to sink her." Gerald placed his arms around Mary, kissing her softly, "No, Gerald, please, not here."

Neither Gerald nor Mary had realised Mrs Montague had come into the yard with her limousine chauffeur bodyguard. He escorted her into the studio and stood in the doorway. Mrs Montague entered, "Excuse the intrusion," Mrs Montague voiced calmly, studying the artwork and glancing at Mary, "Your son is heaven-sent. Observe how he's made the embroidery stand out on the wedding dress." Mary's about to say what the bloody hell are you on my property for, then thought better of it and wanted to know why she's here. "Would you like a coffee Mrs Montague? We'll return to the cottage."

Mrs Montagu answered calmly, "Thank you," smiling politely. They entered the cottage, Mrs Montague instructing her chauffeur to stay outside. She sat at the kitchen table, casting her eyes around the rustic kitchen; remembering some of the equipment from when she was a child hanging on hooks from the oak beam made her smile.

Mary made Mrs Montague a coffee in a cup and saucer, not a mug she had for Gerald and herself. "To business," Mrs Montague suggested. "I know you are both concerned like myself concerning Christine and sometimes her erratic behaviour. We all agree it's far too early for her to become pregnant and unnecessary pressure on her life and Donald's. He has been exemplary in his behaviour towards her. He has spent considerable sums rectifying Glencoe Estate. One more project to finish the riding stables, I believe. However, Elizabeth R insisted and rightly so that Christine is married before she conceived her first child, which I think we would all agree on," Mrs Montague said, glancing at Mary and Gerald. "What I'm about to reveal to you both must never be spoken of again. Gerald, what you don't realise, Josephine is not a true Spires, conveniently adopted. She is of true Royal descent. Royal mistakes are concealed. Even Josephine doesn't know who her real parents are and believes she's a true Spires." Mary and Gerald stared at each other, a revelation no one had expected to materialise.

Mary exhaled, "Christine is of Royal blood, good gracious!"

"What neither of you know and not repeat, Christine has received an injection. She will be unable to conceive until the middle of next year when I believe the wedding is set around that period."

"How, when?" Gerald asked, concerned.

"She visited her doctor for contraceptive pills; the doctor advised she's slightly anaemic and gave her an injection. Nothing wrong with the child. She's fit as a fiddle," Mrs Montague chuckled, "She would breed like a rabbit if we didn't prevent."

Mary laughed, "I don't know who you are, Mrs Montague. You seem to know everything and take appropriate steps."

Gerald laughed, "I have to admit a load off my mind."

"I wish some way we could make Donald aware, and unfortunately, I'm pretty sure he would say something to Christine at least if he knew; he wouldn't be so stressed. I think that's causing the problem with their relationship," Mrs Montague surmised.

"We apparently all agree, Mrs Montague," Gerald exhaled.

"Mary, you have made an excellent choice of housekeeper for Gerald. I knew you'd find somebody suitable," Mrs Montague smiled, sipping her coffee. "The woman is of good breeding and a suitable candidate for Gerald to become involved with; she has no ulterior motives and is financially secure. What happens from now on is entirely up to you, Gerald. If I were you, I would take every opportunity to impress her? She would make an excellent replacement for Josephine without the expense," Mrs Montague smiled. "I must be about my business," she advised as Donald walked in. "My favourite artist," she said, kissing him on both cheeks. Brushing her pink suit before stepping into her limousine.

"I filled the woodshed, mum. What does Mrs Montague want?"

"Called in for a coffee. I'm high society now, son. You should know that the mother of the famous artist." Gerald smiled, watching Donald grin.

Gerald patted Donald on the shoulder, advising, "Hang in, their son. You have nothing to worry about."

Gerald drove home, wondering how Mrs Montague got away with whatever she wanted. She's almost like MI 5 on steroids. Mrs Montague knew everything; she corrected what she didn't approve of. Gerald realised he would have to treat Christine the way he always had; otherwise, she'd be suspicious of his behaviour. He certainly wasn't allowing her to destroy Donald.

***

Christine walked to her Range Rover; Oliver ran over. She glared at him, "You promised to destroy that photo, and you didn't, Oliver."

Oliver smiled, "Face it, Christine, your gorgeous unfortunately my mobile set fire and I lost everything, he lied. You can give me a lift home," he suggested, "I'm only ten minutes out of your way, then you can really see a posh house. My father owns a distribution company, you can see my car a Ferrari when I pass my test," he boasted.

Christine grinned, "I shouldn't; come on." Oliver gave directions to Christine parking in a driveway on a housing estate. The houses were large, at least 5-bedroom, with a red Ferrari on the driveway. " Have a coffee with me before you go home," he suggested. Christine sighed, walking into the house; everything was spotless. "I will put the kettle on," taking Christine's blazer, he kissed her gently on the lips. "I can't, Oliver; I have a boyfriend."

"Oh, what difference does that make, Christine," kissing her on the lips, she finished her coffee standing to place her cup and saucer on the table. Oliver eased her down onto his lap. Christine remembered one of her mother's men performing the same trick. Reality returned to Christine, realising Oliver attempting to slide her knickers off. She allowed him to continue feeling his cock slide inside her while she sat on his lap. he slowly unbuttoned her blouse, releasing her bra and playing with her nipples. She didn't care at this precise moment. He finally moved to lay her on the settee riding her like a wild stallion. She couldn't help but scream, penetrating substantially and obviously proficient at lovemaking. He seemed to last for ages before he came.

She quickly ran to the loo. Oliver took a Viagra, determined to have more of Christine. His cock almost immediately became firm. Christine was surprised to see him with an erection and quite shocked when he bent her over the table, thrusting into her again. She couldn't help but scream, climaxing several times, realising she had had sex for at least an hour.

He relented she ran to the loo. Returning dressing feeling well satisfied. They stood for a moment kissing before she left in her Range Rover. Christine parked in a lay-by trying to understand her own behaviour; she now appeared to have no self-control. Maybe the simple fact she's like her mother, enjoying different boys and men when the opportunity arose. Christine looked in the rearview mirror, noticing Jamaica, the coloured boy from school, running in his tracksuit. She had a brief encounter within the storeroom and managed to escape, thanks to the fire alarm interrupting jamaica's advances. Christine operated her electric window, "Hi, Jamaica." She removed £10 from her purse. "I'd hate you to be out of pocket because of the deceased gypsy," Christine smiled.

Jamaica took the money, panting. Christine passed him a bottle of water she had in the vehicle. "Thanks," he said, drinking heartily, quenching his thirst.

Christine inquired, "How far have you run?"

"About 5 miles on my way home."

Christine laughed, "You certainly won't have any energy left for anything else, Jamaica, and you need a shower by the looks of things."

He grinned, "You think so, give me a lift home. My parents are at work, and I'll show you who's tired."

Christine wondered if she should take the opportunity she'd never had a black boy new experience for her? "Jump in." Christine followed his directions; surprised by the size of the house, she parked her Range Rover following him into the house. Jamaica grabbed her hand, leading her upstairs, removing his tracksuit, standing naked and slowly removing her clothes. Christine is spellbound as she's encouraged into the shower with him. Jamaica dried her gently with a large towel taking her into his bedroom. He gently lifted her onto his bed. She screamed, feeling him penetrate; she could barely contain herself. He's enormous and certainly knew how to pleasure someone. Half an hour had elapsed, and he relented. Christine rushed to the loo, realising her mother was right. Enjoy the fruits of life, providing you are not caught. Donald would never know how many people she slept with.

Christine returned home, walking into the kitchen. Gerald poured her a coffee, "Sit a moment, Christine, we need to talk." She sat down, suspecting she already knew what the subject would be.

"What's going on between you and Donald? I've heard several versions, now what's yours, and if you say none of my business; there's the door, use it and don't come back," he glared.

Christine was shocked by his resolute instructions. She took a deep breath, "I keep forgetting to take my contraceptive pills; I shan't anymore; I've had a couple of close encounters. I'm not pregnant. I won't be pregnant until after we are married if we do. I'm not so sure anymore," she sighed.

"I suggest you make Donald aware you are now taking your contraceptive pills correctly, whether you are or not, that will ease the pressure off him. You will lose him, Christine. At the outset of the relationship, I warned you unless you want to become a prostitute like your mother." Gerald glared, seeing Christine's eyes fill with tears as she ran off upstairs, insulted by his remark. Understanding why he said it and remembered what had recently taken place.

Christine phoned Donald crying. Donald lowered his paintbrush, listening carefully to her, explaining she was sorry now taking her contraceptive pill correctly and wouldn't conceive a child until they both agreed. Donald breathed a sigh of relief, although deeply concerned. "I'm coming over, Christine; I'm not having you upset." Donald turned his mobile off, leaving the yard in his Bentley at high speed. Mary seeing him leave guessing something has really upset him, suspecting it had something to do with Christine. She quickly phoned Gerald, and he answered. "You have one upset boy on the way. Christine obviously said something to him by the way he's driving."

"I'll stay out of the way, Mary; thanks for the update. I don't want to be at the end of one of your son's punches. I'm too old."

Christine saw Donald skid disturbing the gravelled drive. She came running downstairs, jumping into his arms; he held her close. "Sometimes, Christine, you drive me wild with worry, be patient; I'm going nowhere. I love you," he assured, kissing her softly.

Gerald watched from the sitting room window, grinning, conveying a blow-by-blow account to Mary. "I think that's cleared the air, Gerald; now on the same page. That reminds me, Gerald. I think you should see the doctor; Cindy is younger than you. She might be too demanding."

Gerald heard Mary laughing down the phone. "You can clear off Mrs," he said, turning off his mobile. Gerald went outside, seeing Donald drying Christine's eyes. "That reminds me, Donald, a rake in the shed, please level the gravel before you go home; he turned his back, trying not to laugh, walking into the house. "Sorry, Gerald, I will," Donald expressed. Gerald watched Donald raking the gravel level from the sitting room window where his tyres skidded, leaving ruts.

Christine and Donald placed the rake in the garden shed and strolled along the track hand-in-hand, spending an hour together, finally kissing and separating at the front door. "I'll see you after school tomorrow. Christine, behave yourself," he smiled. Christine waved, watching him leave the drive. Christine ran upstairs, taking a shower looking at herself in the mirror, standing for several minutes admiring her figure, remembering how Robbie had touched her. She couldn't remove the memory from her mind. Jamaica was in a league all of his own. Christine smiled, wondering if she should try Michael, although she suspected he wouldn't be as good as Jamaica.

The following morning, Gerald woke to the doorbell ringing; he came dashing down in his dressing-gown, realising Cindy had arrived for work. He hadn't given her a key or the code to the alarm. He breathed in, opening the door, "Morning, Cindy."

Cindy smirked, "Toast and marmalade, Gerald?"

"Yes, please, thanks, Cindy." She went through to the kitchen, starting to prepare breakfast. She'd already removed her denim jacket, wearing her tight jeans and orange embroidered blouse. Christine showered and dressed, looking out the window and seeing Cindy's Porsche parked on the gravel at the front of the house. She wondered whether she should say anything and then decided against it. Did it matter? Gerald and Christine came down into the kitchen. Cindy had already disappeared; they could hear the hoover in the sitting room and the smell of polish, a rare occurrence these days. Cindy had made a list of things she needed in cleaning products. She approached Gerald as he read the newspaper at the kitchen table. He glanced up. She passed him the note, "Could you possibly acquire these products for me?"

He looked down the list, not understanding half of what they were but obviously required for cleaning the house. "You realise, Cindy, you also shop. I failed to mention that when we discussed the position?"

"No, Gerald, you never mentioned I have to purchase anything," she said, looking somewhat confused.

"I don't mean you have to pay. You nip into the village or the nearby town and purchase what you need on our accounts. You have an allowance at the local garage of ten pounds a week for petrol or diesel, whichever the case. That reminds me," Gerald said, exhaling. "I haven't notified our suppliers we have a new housekeeper." Gerald immediately removed his mobile phoning around the five suppliers used for the house, cancelling Susan's ability to place an order with Cindy Crawford. Each shopkeeper voiced cheerfully, "We know Cindy," making Gerald smile.

"Unfortunately, Gerald, my car can't be used for transporting goods which I don't own that would be called transporting goods for reward. I suspect your Range Rover is insured for any driver," she said, grabbing his keys and patting his cheek. Gerald smiled in disbelief at her forwardness, seeing her nip out the front door, climb into his Range Rover, driving off. Christine runs downstairs from the loo. "Father Cindy's in your Range Rover?"

Gerald explained. Christine laughed, "No flies on her father, and she is correct your insurance is invalid if your vehicle is used for hire or reward without notifying your insurers first." Christine ran upstairs, grabbed her briefcase driving off to school.

Christine sat in her first lesson, English, realising her youth is consumed with business affairs and Donald, deciding he is hard work at times. If it wasn't for his money, she wondered if she would still be interested in him.

She smiled, watching Oliver sit beside her, someone she'd fancied and sampled once. She's copying information from the screen on the wall, ensuring she has all the notes to assist in her exam. She suddenly felt something touching her leg; she noticed Oliver's hand sliding along her leg.

She felt exhilarated, thinking Donald would never find out. Oliver continued to stroke her leg while writing the information he required for the exam with his left hand. Christine couldn't understand why she was not feeling guilty. After all, she had a boyfriend planning to marry. Oliver whispered in her ear, "Meet me in storeroom five." Christine watched him leave, unsure whether she was trembling from excitement or guilt, wondering if she should take the offer. She sighed heavily, closing her briefcase and strolling along the corridor, wondering if her mother was like this in school.

She entered the storeroom. Oliver immediately kissed her; she felt his hands caressing her. She dropped her briefcase. Oliver switched on the light, astounded to see Christine stripping. She bent over a table. Oliver immediately dropped his trousers and pants thrusting into her and reaching forward, holding her breasts; far more than he expected to achieve with Christine; nevertheless, he's enjoying every moment, and from the sounds, so is she.

Oliver removed his phone, trying to take pictures of Christine when he'd finished; she turned to face him he snapped another shot. She quickly dressed, "You'd better delete those photos; otherwise, I won't let you touch me again, Oliver," she warned.

She pushed him away. Oliver left the storeroom without saying another word please with the photos he'd taken, which would give him bragging rights. Christine feels absolutely disgusted with her lack of self-control. She went into the girl's toilets, realising she had a mark on her neck she would have to conceal from Donald and everyone else.

***

Cindy's only shopping for about half an hour and returned, throwing Gerald his Range Rover keys, which he caught. She placed an arm full of products on the kitchen table and smiled politely, continuing her work.

Gerald grabbed his keys off the table, travelling to Crabtree Farm, sitting down to coffee with Mary, "That went better than I'd anticipated yesterday, Mary."

"Yes," passing him a mug. "Donald's in his studio busily finishing the portrait of Christine and her wedding gown."

Donald looks out of the window seeing his father trying to match the sprayer to one of their tractors. Donald lowered his paintbrush to the table and ran downstairs into the yard. He walked across to his father standing, scratching his head. "Donald, we have nothing the old sprayer will fit; all the tractors are too big. We would damage too much of the crop driving through on big tyres," Martin expressed.

"I can solve the problem, father, as long as you are not angry with me," Donald sighed. They both jumped in the Land Rover, driving into town to the Massey Ferguson depot. Mary looks out the window suggesting, "I suspect they've gone into town probably for spare parts," She commented casually. Gerald walked behind her placing his arms around her waist and kissing her neck. Mary sighed heavily, watching his hands slide onto her covered breasts, slowly gathering her jumper. "No, Gerald, please, I'm married. This isn't right. We shouldn't," quietly praying he wouldn't stop. She felt his hands inside her blouse, removing her breast from her bra and the second he touched her nipple, she thought her knees would give way. Without saying another word, she grabbed his hand and ran down the hallway into Donald's old bedroom. Locking the door, removed her clothes and Gerald likewise in a panic. Mary prayed she wouldn't be caught. Gerald didn't hesitate to pleasure her. She never realised her nipples were sensitive, perhaps because she was with a different man. Within 15 minutes, they'd finished and dressed. Quickly running back into the kitchen, Mary made another cup of coffee, looking in the mirror at her red face.

***

Donald and Martin observed a new sales rep appear from the office, "Good morning," he said brightly, offering his hand to Martin and Donald. "My name is John Roberts. How can I assist you? " John remarked, "Your Donald Selwyn, the famous artist."

"That self-propelled sprayer over there any good?" Donald asked.

"All our equipment comes with twelve months warranty. The sprayer has five thousand hours on the clock. It will be fully serviced before being released, powered by a Perkins engine, which is a bonus. All-wheel steer and hundred-foot spray booms are computerised. You have a set of narrow wheels as standard."

Donald glanced at his father, "Can you operate, dad?" Donald smiled.

Martin shrugged his shoulders technology advancing so fast these days. Gerald drove past, stopped, and reversed back, jumping out of his Range Rover, "You're not buying that, surely?" he asked, concerned.

John stepped back, realising Mr Gerald Gibbs from Strawberry Estate. "What's the problem, Gerald?" Donald asked.

"To start with, I have a perfect self-propelled sprayer; I have two. We can spray your farm while I have a coffee with Mary. Put your chequebook away, Donald; what do you think friends are for," he smiled, "Son-in-law to be. I'll have my crop walker check what needs applying; leave everything to me," Gerald laughed, jumping in his Range Rover and driving off.

Martin scratched his head and shrugged his shoulders, "Free is good, Donald," Martin smiled, gently punching Donald on the shoulder. "You hear that son-in-law to be!" Pinching Donald's cheek.

"No sale today, John, sorry mate," Donald advised slipping into the Land Rover with his father, driving to Crabtree Farm.

***

Gerald entered his house, the floor gleaming; he'd never seen it shine so clean everything smelt of furniture polish and barely lunchtime. Gerald called out, "Coffee, Cindy?"

"Okay, I'll be down in a minute." Cindy came running downstairs for a forty-nine-year-old woman. She's almost on steroids. She didn't look a day over thirty, Gerald decided. "One of your other duties, Cindy, you must come riding with me around the estate; we must keep the horses exercised," he grinned.

"Now you're teasing," Cindy expressed, slightly blushing. "You will have to ask Christine, her horse; I don't want to upset anybody," she suggested calmly.

Gerald sent a text message. Christine replied, "Okay, look after my horse." Gerald showed the text message to Cindy. She smiled, "Great." She slipped on her denim jacket they went out to the stables saddling both horses. Gerald named Pig his hunter and The Rising Sun; Christine's horse adored Cindy. They trotted off together towards the old sawmill along the track. Cindy's wearing Christine's safety hat and warm riding coat, her long blonde flowing hair reminded Gerald so much of Josephine. They reach the sawmill, watching Michael finish off the toilet block, trees waiting to be sawed into planks. Douglas, Head Forester, advised, "We're all ready to go, Gerald, as soon as Michael's finished. The coffee shop is up and running and tested. Everyone can stand and watch at a safe distance, walk through the reserve and observe the stunning wildlife. I've never seen so many wild birds until I moved here." Douglas smiled, "Thank you for the forestry tractor delivered yesterday;

she has everything I want winch, crane and trailer," he remarked, walking off.

Gerald and Cindy trotted around the reserve, checking the trails were safe for people to walk on. Douglas was meticulous, and Stephen made sure the walkways were clear of debris, and no branches would hit you in the face as you walked along. Cindy commented, "Beautiful Gerald," patting The Rising Sun's neck, he neighed in appreciation. Gerald's feeling like a school kid again with a crush which he thought ridiculous considering only the second time he'd met Cindy.

***

Donald returned to his artwork. Martin noticed someone walking across his field of oilseed rape; he walked over to investigate. The tall thin gentleman in his suit and wellington boots acknowledges Martin. "Sent over by Gerald to have a quick mosey at your crop of oilseed rape. I'm Mark. Gerald suggested because you both grow the same crops more or less, he purchased the chemicals for you simultaneously. Improves the deal, meaning you pay less for everything," Mark assured, showing Martin a list. "That looks expensive," Martin commented.

"Would be for a small outfit; you add two and a half thousand acres to your three hundred acres. See what I mean," Mark suggested, "Gerald's covering my cost," Mark smiled reassuringly.

Martin nodded, "See what you mean." Martin walked across the field to Mark's vehicle, watching him leave. Martin almost thought the farm was taken over by Gerald. Although he believed Gerald only had good intentions, he wouldn't want to jeopardise his daughter's future with Donald. Martin walked across the field, realising everything Mark said made sense.

Donald had finally finished the picture of Christine in her wedding dress, placing it on another easel and covering to protect it from dust.

***

Christine returned home from school, running into the house to find it empty apart from Cindy's handbag. She walked to the stables, both horses missing; she remembered her father's text at 12:30. She smiled, realising The Rising Sun would undoubtedly have some exercise today, noticing two horses coming along the track in the distance. She waited patiently for Gerald and Cindy. They dismounted; Christine cuddled The Rising Sun patting his neck. Cindy commented, "You have a beautiful horse, Christine; thanks for allowing me to ride him."

Christine smiled, "Any time he needs lots of exercise like my father," she grinned, watching her father turn bright red. Cindy commented, "A bit potbellied isn't he," making Christine laugh, realising Cindy didn't care what she said. She didn't need the work, so why worry about any dismissal.

"When you two have finished insulting me," Gerald commented.

"You can put the horses away, Gerald," Cindy suggested. "Christine and I will make the coffee." Christine glanced at her father; he couldn't stop grinning. If he wanted to tango with Cindy, he would have to get fit. Christine thought she wouldn't take any prisoners.

Cindy smiled, pouring the coffees, "You're marrying Donald Selwyn; Christine, you must be terribly excited?"

"Yes, he's lovely to cuddle, but I wish he didn't snore," she smiled, remembering what she'd allowed at school with another student and Jamaica.

"You wait until you've been married a while, and they start farting in the bed."

Christine almost choked on her coffee. Cindy patted her back, watching Gerald come in. He sat quietly at the table, looking somewhat depressed as the reality of his age and shape made him feel like Mr blobby instead of Steve McQueen. Gerald, feeling despondent, entered the fitness room looking at Josephine's brand-new equipment to keep herself in shape. The thought of jumping on a treadmill didn't impress him or any of the other machines. However, he realised he would have to exercise to lose weight.

Christine put her finger to her lips, indicating to follow me. Cindy followed, peeping through the door, and watching Gerald on the treadmill. To Christine's surprise, Cindy walked in, switching off the treadmill. Gerald looked puzzled. "Before trying to be Superman, Gerald, you must have a fitness plan. You can't jump in at the deep end could do untold damage."

Gerald frowned, "I'm too old and lazy," he sighed heavily.

"No, you're not. You need to eat properly and exercise. I will charge you extra if you're employing my skills as a fitness trainer," Cindy smiled, removing her blouse and jeans and stepping out of her shoes. The woman hadn't an ounce of fat on her. Christine stared in disbelief; this wasn't happening. Cindy jumped on the treadmill, cranking up to an unbelievable pace. Christine knew she couldn't match her. Gerald stood, holding his forehead.

"Easy, Gerald; once in the stream of things takes practice," she said, stepping from the treadmill and switching off, picking up her clothes. "Would you mind if I took a shower," she asked, heading into the shower and not waiting for a reply. Gerald and Christine looked at each other, wondering what they'd taken on. Gerald sat down on a chair; he was absolutely knackered. He'd done nothing.

A few minutes later, Cindy came out of the shower drying her hair. Gerald expressed, "You realise I'm fifty-nine, Cindy; I'm not a spring chicken like you," he emphasised.

"I see what you're saying, you can't be bothered, and you don't really care if you drop down dead before your daughter's wedding."

Gerald glared, "How dare you say that to me!"

"Why! Something special about you, Gerald? You're like all men, bone idle. I'm surprised you're still alive with the amount of fat you're carrying!" Cindy walked out of the door, jumped in her car and drove off.

Gerald sighed heavily, "She's right. The last time I saw the doctor, he said I should shed some weight; it wasn't good for my heart."

Christine's horrified, "You kept that a secret from me, father. You're stuffing yourself silly at Crabtree Farm; it wouldn't matter if you worked like Donald and Martin. Instead, you sit in your Range

Rover giving orders; no wonder you're piling on the pounds," Christine exhaled concern for her father's welfare. Christine telephoned Cindy, "Where are you, Cindy?"

"I guessed dismissed, heading home."

"You're not dismissed. I want you to knock my father into shape, the doctors already warned him. He's kept it a secret from me; he's confessed."

"If you're sure, Christine, I take no prisoners, and I don't like excuses. He will have to exercise properly under my control. I have seventy-year-old men that could run around your estate and not be out of breath. I'll see you in a minute." Cindy turned her car around, heading to Strawberry Estate.

Cindy removed a leaflet from her briefcase stating what Gerald could eat, and he's to purchase trainers and tracksuits. Cindy walked inside. Gerald had already made the coffee. "You can stop drinking that as well," she said, slapping the leaflet on the kitchen table, "Two coffees a day is fine; tea is far more rewarding." Gerald glared; not used to being told what to do; he bit his tongue, picking up the leaflet and looking at his diet. Christine surveyed, "I'll join you, father. I need to keep fit," she expressed, "Could be good fun," she smiled.

"I will prepare your meals. No snacking over at the Selwyn's. I will have to talk to Mary; he's far too heavy. Martin and Donald are okay because they both work hard, so they burn off the calories where I'm afraid Gerald and you, Christine, don't."

Neither Gerald nor Christine argued with her comments after seeing her figure on the treadmill, a gorgeous figure with no fat.

"Are you sure you can do anything for me, Cindy, at my age?" Gerald asked calmly.

"Of course, a matter of your willpower and diet is nothing magical. I will have those old joints more supple," she said, pinching his backside, making Gerald jump and Christine laugh. "If you're really a good boy, I might allow you to take me out for a meal one day," she grinned, teasing.

Although Gerald sat in shock, he relented to Cindy's every request; he didn't want to die before his time. Christine was determined not to be the same shape as Mary, although she loved the woman.

CHAPTER TWELVE

SECRETS

Donald had reversed the new wood processor into a small shed ideally for storing the machine. The new tractor and hedge cutter he placed with the other equipment. They had accumulated substantial machinery over the last year.

Donald strolled across the fields, checking the oilseed rape, progressing nicely. Although fertiliser wouldn't go amiss, he thought before too late to have any effect. Winter's approaching again in the middle of October, with the cold winds cutting across the field. Most of the farm machinery is now put to bed. Donald smiled, thinking no sheep. Donald's thoughts were disturbed by his mobile ringing. "Hi, mum."

"Can you come to the cottage Donald, please?"

"Okay, mum, on my way." Donald ran along the headland of the field, walking into the kitchen quite out of breath.

Mary and Martin stood, appearing concerned. "We have to make a decision, son. Do we replace the cow or purchase milk from the supermarket?"

Donald sighed, "Can't we put Geraldine in calf again, dad?"

"She's too old, son; that would be totally unfair on her."

"I suppose we could keep her as a pet; I really don't want to have her killed, dad."

"Come on, Donald, that's not practical," Martin frowned.

"Does everything have to be about money, dad?" Donald sighed.

"In this instance, yes."

"If you have Gerald slaughter her, I don't want to be anywhere in the area," Donald professed, "And don't you dare serve me any of her meat. I'd sooner become a bloody vegetarian than eat Geraldine."

Mary and Martin looked at each other. Donald walked out of the cottage. He decided to go for a run, feeling unfit and spending too much time in front of a canvas. He ran upstairs to his flat, changing into his tracksuit and trainers. He started running down the drive and along the lane; he continued running, feeling full of aggression. Realising after the money he'd spent on the farm, his parents couldn't be bothered to spare Geraldine. He realised that maybe a stupid sentimental thought and totally impractical. At least she would decide when she died; she would have the same privilege as anyone else. Donald slowed down, finally coming to a stop noticing he'd run over five miles, standing outside a rugby club of all places, laughed. He watched some old school friends practising under the floodlights bringing a smile.

Donald is about to turn around and head home, seeing someone wave beckoning him into the club ground. Donald walked in, discovering his old teacher. "Lovely to see you, Donald. Would you like to join the club? I know what you're like you're a bulldozer. Nothing stops you."

"I don't think I could commit the time. I have so many other projects at the moment, Sir."

"At least show these young men how they should perform before you go." Donald stepped out of his tracksuit, limbering. Stephane, the games master, shouted, "let's see who can bring Donald Selwyn down, then you know you've made the grade." Donald tore off across the field rugby ball under his arm. Everyone who stood in his way was trampled by a wild bull. Donald touched down with the ball laughing. He hadn't felt so relaxed for ages. Stephane ran over, "You are dangerous. I wouldn't want to stand before you," he smiled. "We train most Friday nights, Donald; come and join us if you can," Stephane suggested, passing Donald a carrier bag with team colours. "You never know. You might want to participate in a match we're not excelling at the moment."

Donald smiled, "Okay, if I can slot some time in, I enjoyed running across the field brought back so many simple happy memories," he smiled, running down the road holding a carrier bag.

Donald ran up the drive and into his studio. He glanced from his elevated position, noticing a wet patch on the floor in the yard under the lighting. A cold shudder ran down his spine, apprehensively walking downstairs with a horrible feeling, Geraldine's no more. He rushed across to her pen, seeing blood on the floor. Martin came from the cottage with Mary; he could see the expressions on their faces while he was away. They had instructed Gerald to dispose of Geraldine. Donald's outraged, hitting his father under the jaw. Mary stood in horror, watching her husband fly through the air, landing on his back. Donald stared at her, "You can go to hell," he shouted. Mary ran over to comfort Martin. Donald jumped in his Bentley driving off. He wasn't staying on the farm a day longer. Martin sat up, holding his jaw, "I didn't think he'd react like that, Mary; I thought we might have a few choice words," Martin frowned.

Mary's crying, "I've never seen so much evil in his eyes. If looks could kill, I'd be dead," she sobbed.

Gerald came into the yard with Christine in his Range Rover, seeing Martin on the floor. Gerald jumped out quickly, followed by Christine, "What happened?" Gerald asked, concerned.

"Donald, more upset than I thought he would be. Hence I'm on my backside."

Christine questioned, "He actually hit you, Martin, his father?"

"Yes," Martin sighed, "I don't think we'll be seeing that lad again; he told his mother to go to hell, and he meant every word. He has his grandfather's eyes when they turn evil; you're in trouble."

Gerald exhaled, "When he's had time to think things over and calm down, he will come to his senses."

"That's the trouble; he remembers everything and holds a grudge. Every kid that picked on him and teased him at infant school ended up on the end of his fist. Not one escaped reprisal when he was strong enough to take them on."

"Oh, dear," Christine expressed. "Another problem, I'll have to talk to him," she frowned. "All over a stupid cow," Christine muttered.

"Geraldine was sixteen years old, the same age as Donald and Biscuit." Mary said, "he treated them like family and should have realised."

Gerald helped Martin to his feet; they went into the cottage. Mary's about to make coffee. Gerald expressed, "I can only drink tea, Mary, without sugar or milk. I'm on a diet."

Mary smiled, "I forgot Cindy phoned me."

Christine phoned Donald he didn't answer, she thought out of character unless he's in an area the car can't receive a signal. She wondered whether he would venture to Glencoe phoning, advising to notify her if Donald arrived.

Over the next three hours, Christine tried several times to contact Donald and couldn't. She's starting to have a horrible feeling her plans would change if her loving boyfriend disappeared.

After three days, everyone is deeply concerned; no one can contact Donald; almost as if he had vanished off the face of the earth. Christine was surprised he hadn't bothered to contact her. Perhaps it was now over between them. She could barely consider the possibility of losing all that money. She'd heard nothing from Glencoe, so he wasn't there. She's pretty convinced he would run to.

Gerald exercises wearing his tracksuit and trainers under Cindy's control, making him run around the estate. Christine joined in some of the time worrying about where Donald had gone. A week had now passed. Martin, distraught, contacted the police; he's only seventeen and technically still underage. Considering a family argument, the police were not overly concerned, and Donald was seventeen.

"You think we'll ever see him again, Martin?" Mary asked.

Martin shrugged his shoulders, "You want to see him again after what he did?"

Mary shouted, "You're the one who instructed Gerald to slaughter Geraldine. Don't you blame me for your mistakes, Martin Selwyn; otherwise, you will be living on your own."

"The boy wants to grow up, Mary; he's always been too sensitive. Needs toughening up."

Mary's incensed; she picked up a saucepan and whacked Martin around the head, knocking him to the floor. She strutted into the bedroom, packing a bag. Donald's world, her son; he may not be perfect, but he had principles and stood by them. Martin tried to argue. Mary insisted, "Get out of my way, Martin, you make me sick," she expressed, jumping in her Range Rover.

Gerald came into the yard puzzled to see Mary driving out the end of the driveway at high speed, not even acknowledging him. Gerald knocked on the cottage door and found Martin holding his head. "Hi, Martin. Mary's driving like the wind; you know where Donald is. You hurt?"

Martin took a deep breath, "Mary's left me because I instructed you to slaughter Geraldine; she's blaming me for Donald leaving. The police won't inform us where he is if they know."

"Oh shit, what a bloody mess. I'm surprised Donald hasn't contacted Christine; you never know, he might have had an accident. He may not even be in the country. Although he'd have to acquire a passport from somewhere plus, he'd have to get around the coronavirus restrictions," Gerald said, racking his brains.

***

Christine's riding The Rising Sun, patting his neck, expressing her troubles. She couldn't work out why Donald hadn't contacted her. She couldn't be blamed for anything that happened or had someone from school said something to him, sending a cold shudder down her spine. She felt her phone vibrate in her pocket; she quickly dismounted, desperately trying to retrieve her mobile from the pocket of her tight jeans. Seeing a text message from Donald, "No worries, I love you, be in touch."

She couldn't prevent smiling, feeling the pressure lifted from her shoulders of uncertainty, relieved no one from school had said anything to him. She mounted The Rising Sun returning to the stable. After seeing to him, she jumped in her Range Rover driving over to Crabtree Farm, surprised not to see Mary, only her father and Martin. "Donald's contacted me. He said, " Don't worry, that's all," she smiled, "great news, where is Mary?"

"She has left me, Christine," Martin voiced.

Christine immediately texts Mary with the news.

***

Donald's staying with Robbie and his mother in their cottage on Glencoe Estate. Donald believed Robbie, a true friend, had said nothing to anyone; they'd hidden Donald's Bentley in one of the buildings.

Mary had driven all the way to Glencoe; she's spitting feathers. She could never remember being so angry. She's greeted at reception by Maggie on duty; almost eleven in the evening when she arrives. "You have anywhere I can stay?" Mary asked.

"You're Mrs Selwyn, Donald's mother. You can use Christine's suite; the other forty rooms are booked. I'm Maggie, by the way; Robbie and I are coming for our honeymoon at your farm," she smiled politely.

Robbie's walking past reception. He'd come to collect Maggie, so she wasn't walking home in the dark noticing Mary, he stopped dead in his tracks, turning bright red. Maggie looked at him, "You know something, Robbie, about the disappearance of Donald, don't you? You, not be lying to me?" Maggie glared.

"I gave me word lass to a true friend. You can't expect me to break my promise."

"Donald is here," Mary expressed, surprised.

"I. Donald wanted peace and quiet away from everyone. He's staying with Ma and me in our cottage. She's never had so much fun in her life. I've never seen Ma so happy."

Mary kissed Robbie, "I appreciate you looking after my son. I presume he explained what happened."

"I. he has. I understand how he feels. Someone stole my favourite cow if I could catch them," Robbie frowned, minding his language.

Maggie phoned Donald's mobile using Robbie's so Donald didn't realise it wasn't Robbie, "Hi, Robbie," Donald answered.

"You'd better bring your sorry self down to the hotel Donald, your mother is distraught, and she's left home. I think you punished everyone enough, Donald," Maggie suggested firmly.

Mary lifted her eyebrows.

"I, she has a fierce tongue on her," Robbie suggested. Mary couldn't stop laughing at how Robbie spoke, all sincerity in his voice.

It wasn't long before Donald walked into the hotel wearing his tartan, a deerstalker, and a beard that had grown considerably in the short time. Donald and Mary embraced each other. She sighed with relief. "I've left your father," Mary expressed. "Wasn't my decision to slaughter Geraldine, Martin's."

"Doesn't matter now, mother. I think father understood how I felt."

"Yes, that's the last thing he expected, you to sit him on his backside. I don't think he dared stand up if you hit him again," she advised.

Reception had phoned Christine. She threw a bag in her Range Rover and explained the situation to her father, heading for Glencoe. Driving through the night, arriving in the early hours. Mary's staying with Robbie's mother. Donald had moved to Christine's private apartment. Christine arrived, running up to her apartment, finding Donald snoring in her bed.

She grabbed a bucket of water and threw it over him, shouting, "You inconsiderate pig, I've worried for days about you, and you were here all the time." Donald jumped out of bed, about to defend himself. Christine punched Donald in the eye and kicked his feet from under him. He's on his back on the floor. He shook his head and started laughing, seeing a staff member come running into Christine's suite, wondering what the commotion was. Christine glanced at the female staff member, "Get out," she shouted. Kicking Donald in the testicles made him curl up in a ball, no longer smiling, in extreme agony. "I'm not here for your amusement, Donald. You dare upset me again," she screamed. By this time, most of the hotel is disturbed. Justin came running in. Christine glared, "Can't you bloody knock."

"Calm down, please, Christine. You're upsetting our guests; they're trying to sleep," he said calmly, walking out.

Christine stripped the bed, replacing the wet bedsheet and duvet. Donald stayed curled up on the floor. When Christine had finished making the bed and replacing the pillows, she knelt beside Donald. He grabbed her, placed her over his knee, spanked her backside, threw her on the floor, and climbed into bed. She stood, rubbing her bottom, realising if she touched him again, she would receive more of the same; it wasn't worth the effort; she'd made her point. Christine climbed into the other side of the bed, turning out the light. Both sleeping with their backs to one another.

Donald sat up in bed at around 7 o'clock in the morning. Christine's already dressed and gone, Donald glancing in the mirror to see he had acquired a black eye from Christine, and his testicles felt like they were run over by a ten-ton truck. He sighed, walking downstairs to the outside of the hotel. Donald wearing his old tartan, walked to the sawmill for the first-time seeing timber planks, concluding the waterwheel could cope with both operations running the mill and the generator. He noticed Christine's white Range Rover coming down the hillside in the distance, realising that his mother was in the front seat as it became closer. Donald continued looking around the sawmill, meeting the new Forester Justin had appointed. "You have a shiner, lad; I suspect the other person didn't fare as well," Nigel Blackmore said.

Donald smiled, "Actually, my future wife."

Mary approached Donald with Christine beside her; he turned to face them. Mary laughed, "You're the first-person Christine to give my Donald a black eye; you must have really walloped him last night," she continued laughing.

"Thanks, mum," Donald smiled.

Christine complained, "You're not the only one with a bruise Donald. You really hurt last night, my backside still tingling."

Mary commented, "Providing Donald only slapped your backside, we have nothing to worry about," she continued laughing.

They looked around the sawmill suspecting the planks were for the new stable block. They could see the JCB demolishing the old brick stables in the distance.

Christine commented, "Oh, I thought I should mention Robbie's mother's maid of honour at our wedding if I didn't kill you beforehand," she tried not to grin.

Christine and Mary drove to the hotel. Donald finished looking around, shaking Nigel's hand, "Brilliant job." Much to his surprise, he heard a set of Klaxons. Donald glanced to the hills observing an army truck descending; it had to be Jock with his new truck. Donald waited patiently for him to arrive. "Jock, you're actually smiling," Donald expressed.

"We've all heard Miss Gibbs has a fierce temper," he said, trying not to smirk.

Donald moved to the passenger side, climbing in, "Well, what do you think of her, Jock?"

"The envy of every estate. She's a beautiful beast. Goes anywhere I want to go. We installed safety straps on the seating. The seating now folds, and I can take wheelchairs. We place clamps on the floor to lock the wheels to give the disabled a safer ride. Thanks to Robbie; he has a keen brain on him." Jock dropped Donald off at the hotel. He went in to find Mary and Christine having breakfast with the other guests. Christine rose to her feet, "My future husband apologises for the disturbance last night and paying for your breakfast. Sample what you fancy," she grinned. Donald sat down with Mary placing her hand over her mouth, trying not to laugh. The guests rose to their feet, clapping in appreciation. Donald, tucked into his breakfast. After everyone had finished, Justin passed Donald the bill of slightly over three thousand pounds to cover the breakfast costs, including his own Christine's and his mother's.

Donald picked up the bill heading for reception, paying by credit card, not objecting. Christine joined him, "I hope you're not keeping that beard, Donald. I'm not marrying a hedgehog." Donald glanced at his mother, "Don't look at me, Donald, for support, between you and Christine. I've already hit your father with a saucepan, your Christine's problem."

"Can I have a dozen roses sent to Robbie's mum, please? Here, a thousand pounds if you could place in an envelope and make sure she receives for looking after me." The receptionist placed the money in a sealed envelope and ordered the flowers. Donald paid separately. Mary patted Donald on the back, "A very nice gesture, Donald. I suppose I could spend one more day up here," Mary sighed, jumping in her Range Rover and heading for Robbie's cottage.

Christine grabbed Donald's arm, "You're coming with me," he didn't bother to argue. She drove into the village, parking outside Maggie's shop. Maggie smiled, seeing them enter. Christine made several purchases kitting out Donald with a change of clothes. Christine asked, "I suppose there isn't a barber here?"

Maggie smiled, pointing to herself, "Step into the back here, Donald, if you can watch the shop, Christine; I'll soon cut his throat. Oh, I mean, shave him," she joked.

Donald stared in horror. Christine grinned. Donald sat in a chair nervously, Maggie lathered his beard, and with a cutthroat blade, she shaved him, splashing aftershave on his skin which made him protest. Maggie commented, "You're a big baby." Donald returned to the counter.

Maggie frowned, "See, no blood, you're still alive; I think you look more handsome with the beard Donald," she winked. Christine paid and left the shop with clothes for Donald returning to the hotel.

***

Martin at Crabtree Farm is sampling the cider most nights, feeling rather sorry for himself. He'd text Mary begging for forgiveness; in all the years they've lived together, the first time she'd been away from home for more than two days.

Gerald texts Christine advising her Martin is at his wit's end and deeply concerned for his welfare. Christine had phoned Mary to convey the information. Mary finally relented, suggesting to Martin, "Home in a few days. If I find the house untidy, I will turn around and drive away again," ending the call determined to make him suffer.

***

Gerald convinced Cindy specialised in torture and seemed to smile the more he suffered. She would make Gerald run through stinging nettles and around the reserve until he begged forgiveness. She would feed him less than a rabbit would have to eat. After every session, she would make him stand on the scales to see how much he'd improved. She had only worked on him for a fortnight; he'd already lost a stone. She would go on the treadmill herself, running for an hour at a time-stepping off, not even out of breath.

She shrugged her shoulders, "When you can do that, Gerald, you're on the way to becoming fit and living twice as long," she grinned. Gerald's too knackered to argue. He consumed his meagre ration, flopping on the bed.

***

Donald parked his Bentley outside the front of the hotel on Glencoe Estate. Donald ventured onto Christine's balcony, watching the illuminated waterwheel working, deciding, a real bonus to the hotel. Everyone's trying so hard to make Glencoe a success. Christine came in, standing beside him, watching the wheel. Donald commented, "I don't think we should purchase any horses until after Christmas, Christine; too late in the season now for anyone interested in riding, don't you think?"

"You're right; I've checked the books Glencoe is now holding its own. We are making a little money. Thanks to my lovely boyfriend's investment, we cover all our outgoing," she said, kissing him softly. "You realise, Donald, we haven't set a date for our wedding," she smiled.

"I think September," Donald commented.

Christine frowned, "Rather hoping for a Christmas wedding, although that may be impractical trying to transport everyone here, especially if we have snow."

"That's a fact, I wouldn't want anyone to be injured trying to drive here, and I suspect a lot wouldn't bother. You mustn't forget Christine, we have two harvests to complete, yours and mine. I want to drive the combine I thought most enjoyable."

"Yes, we had some fun, Donald, saved my father a fortune in repairs. I think we better go home in the morning, don't you? You make your peace with your father and don't hit him again."

"No, that's another mistake I made," Donald frowned. They finally retired to bed.

After breakfast, Christine advised, "I'm nipping to the top farm. I want to take a quick look around, Donald. I'll only be an hour or so if you want to set off ahead of me, you and your mother, I don't mind."

"Okay, your ladyship, I noticed the other week one of the buildings looked unsteady," he smiled, kissing her on the cheek.

Christine jumped in her Range Rover, driving along the stone track up into the hills; she knew Robbie would be checking the sheep. She noticed him in the distance by an old Crofter's house, the building looking worse for wear. Christine parked her Range Rover out of sight, jumping out. Robbie approached, "Morning lass, I fear the fog would be coming down. What brings you to this godforsaken place? You're certainly not dressed for cold weather?" Christine wore her short skirt and blouse with her denim jacket, "I haven't seen this place before; Robbie is still habitable?"

"Only used to shelter the shepherds, which is me," he grinned.

Christine walked into the old building run down, with an old table, a bunk bed, and an old rocking chair by the fire, which was lit, much to her surprise. An old-fashioned kettle in the hearth and two mugs, at some time a window fitted undoubtedly, wouldn't have been here originally.

Christine stood by the fire warming herself, feeling Robbie's walking stick on the back of her leg; she didn't turn around and stayed facing the fire warming. He gently moved his walking stick to the inside of her leg, lifting her short skirt as he ventured upwards until touching her knickers. Christine knew this was what she'd come for. She wanted more of the same as she experienced in the Range Rover with him. She felt the sensation of the walking stick rubbing between her legs; she wondered if her mother had been there.

Robbie gently placed his hands on her shoulders, easing her into the rocking chair, slowly sliding his hands along her legs, removing her knickers. Christine watched spellbound. Robbie gently held one leg, placing it over the arm of the rocking chair and then the other. He moved closer to her releasing the buttons on her blouse. She panicked for a moment watching him remove his knife, cutting her bra-free between her breasts. He used the knob on his walking stick, gently teasing her; Christine's going wild in her mind; no wonder her mother loved this place so much.

She couldn't imagine Donald performing like this on her, only plain old sex. Robbie removed his walking stick easing Christine to her feet, laying her across the table, lifting his kilt, thrusting into Christine, making her scream with extreme pleasure. Finally, he come. She dashed outside, peeing against the building. She tidied herself, removing her bra, casting it into the fire, and watching it burn. She looked out the window. Robbie was already walking across to where the sheep had moved.

Christine wondered if Robbie performed the same on Maggie and returned to her Range Rover. She checked in her mirror; there were no marks on her for Donald to see. She wondered when her fanny would stop tingling; he'd done something to her so different from other boys. Christine suspected her mother had spent many hours with Robbie and left feeling lovely and satisfied.

Christine returned to the hotel, surprised to discover everyone was waiting for her. Donald set off in his Bentley, and his mother,

her Range Rover, Christine, followed. Everyone set off in convoy heading for home, arriving safely some hours later. Donald had barely stepped from his Bentley before Martin embraced him, "I'm so sorry, Donald. I should have thought things through better."

"I'm sorry to dad for hitting you; everyone makes mistakes," Donald sighed.

Mary parked her Range Rover. Mary and Martin looked at each other and finally embraced. Donald ran to his studio, relieved to be home.

***

Christine arrived at Strawberry Estate and walked into the house, looking at her father, "You've certainly lost weight. How do you feel."

"Happy now your home. Has everyone made their peace?"

"I presume so, father. Donald and I are marrying at the end of September once the harvest is finished. You will be free, and so will everyone else to come to Glencoe for the wedding." Gerald smiled, hugging Christine.

"The white elephant appears to be paying off," Gerald smiled.

"You mean the sawmill, father."

He nodded, "We have taken over five thousand pounds in two days, not including the hot and cold drinks we serve; that's certainly paying its way now. Let's hope it continues. I've had several enquiries from schools for educational purposes. That could be another bonus, although I think we should run at breakeven cost; schools are under enough pressure now with their budgets."

***

Early the following day, Donald transported his portrait of Robbie, Maggie, and Christine in her wedding dress for Jack to frame. The London traffic hadn't improved, taking Donald longer to drive through London than to run twenty miles. After allowed through the security gates, he finally parked behind Jack's studio, a new addition to preventing theft. Donald explained the portrait of Robbie and Maggie needed to be at Glencoe on November the first, and the portrait of Christine could be returned to him for storage as the wedding wasn't until September next year.

Donald fought his way out of London on his way home. He couldn't believe how popular he seemed, from lorry drivers flashing their lights and coaches to children waving from the back seat of their cars. Donald had to smile sort of made your day realise your artwork was appreciated. Donald turned into the drive at Crabtree Farm, seeing his father operating the new flail hedge cutter, trimming the hedge with set-aside around the perimeter of every field, room enough to run the tractor without damaging the crop. Donald noticed a large self-propelled sprayer operating on the opposite side of his drive. Gerald was as good as his word, ensuring the pests didn't destroy the oilseed rape.

***

Christine and her father were running along the old cart tracks on Strawberry Estate with Cindy cracking the whip, making them maintain the pace she thought fitting for Gerald. She would make him go out regardless of the weather and complete a daily circuit. No doubt he's shedding the pounds, which he felt better for. They finally returned to the house, everyone taking a shower and changing. Cindy would start preparing the meals and keeping the house clean. Gerald and Christine decided Cindy wasn't human; she never tired working at a ferocious pace every day.

Christine made everyone a cup of tea. Calling out, "Cindy teas made." Cindy came running down the stairs. Gerald walked from the office; sat around the kitchen table. Christine suggested, "For a change of scenery, why don't you come to Glencoe; a different atmosphere there. Robbie's married on the first of November, you could accompany father, Cindy, what do you think?"

"Who's looking after the horses," Cindy remarked.

"Stephen the estate Foreman, only for a couple or three days. I know his daughter has a pony she keeps at the riding school." Gerald phoned Stephen asking the question, "Thank you, Stephen. Problem solved, he will come with his daughter; I think she's thirteen."

"You realise that's in three days, Christine," Cindy expressed.

"You must explain to your boyfriend Cindy; that you are away for a few days."

Cindy laughed, "Boyfriend, you're joking. I need one of those like a hole in the head. Besides, where are we staying?"

Christine phoned Glencoe, "Justin, will we have any spare room on the thirty-first of October until November second? No, make that the third."

"No, Christine booked solid other than your room."

"That's okay, don't worry; Justin put a spare bed in my room and make sure it's comfortable."

"You two will have to share; you heard the conversation. The hotel is solid. We haven't any spare rooms other than my suite. I'm sure you can behave like adults."

Cindy and Gerald looked at each other rather alarmed. "Where are you staying, daughter?" Gerald enquired suspiciously.

Christine phoned Donald. "Hello, your ladyship."

Christine smiled, "We have a problem, Donald. You remember you were purchasing an RV, one of those American things house on wheels. Now would be a good time no room at Glencoe my father and Cindy are sharing my room. I thought we could use the new RV for our accommodation otherwise we'll have to rent something in the village. I don't think it's wise to travel after the reception."

Donald frowned, "And you give me three days to solve the issue?"

"Yes, if you want to sleep with me," she grinned, watching the expression on Cindy's and Gerald's faces at her cunning behaviour.

"Okay, your ladyship, I'll see what I can do. Otherwise, we can sleep in my tent."

"You know what you and your tent can do, Donald; bye, boyfriend, inform me when you've organised," she turned her mobile off.

"I feel sorry for Donald," Gerald suggested.

Cindy folded her arms, "You're unbelievable, Christine. You any idea how much one of those things cost?"

"He can afford it; he only has to scratch his head and one million drops in his bank account, unlike the rest of us."

***

Donald jumped into his Bentley driving to Coventry, calling in at an RV Centre, quite a selection. The problem was he didn't have a PSV driving licence, stumbling across a fifth-wheel caravan attached to the back of a pickup truck. More sensible not only to have accommodation but a vehicle to drive around in some respects. Donald noticed at the other end of the showroom a Ford American Raptor pickup truck with a crew cab in black. He selected a pickup truck and a sizeable fifth-wheel caravan, giving a day to prepare for collection. The total bill came to just over one hundred and eighty thousand pounds with all the extras, including oversized tyres and two chromed exhaust pipes running up the crew cab that put a drainpipe to shame in circumference.

Donald phoned Christine. "Hello boyfriend, have you resolved the problem?"

"I've solved the problem and some," he laughed.

"What have you purchased, Donald?" she asked suspiciously.

"We can all travel together. I have plenty of room for everyone, including luggage." Gerald and Cindy were listening in on the conversation. "Cindy could leave her car at your place, and we can all set off from there."

"You're worrying me, Donald. What aren't you telling me?" Christine asked.

"Nothing, your ladyship, your carriage will arrive at 7:30 a.m. On October the thirty-first, bye, for now, your ladyship," Donald grinned.

As Donald's leaving the dealership, he watched the engineers scurrying around preparing his new Ford Raptor and his fifth wheel.

Time passed like wildfire, preparing himself for collection after struggling to find insurance for his new acquisition. He was excited and scared to death, all in one emotion.

Donald phoned for a taxi. Christine and everyone else was too busy to worry about Donald, preparing to travel for the wedding and organise Stephen with the horses. Donald's dropped off at the train station, caught the train for Coventry and found a taxi from the train station to where his new vehicle awaited him. Donald glared at the size massive, the same length as a juggernaut and almost as wide.

The suppliers had filled with diesel, ready for his journey home. For the first time, Donald felt afraid not of manoeuvring the vehicle, which was no different to trailers on the farm. The only difference is in the middle of a city. Donald walked around the vehicle, a stunning Ford Raptor, and he would have to master the steering wheel on the other side. Donald set off enjoying the automatic transmission. Finally reaching the bypass, apart from a few long blasts on the horn from upset drivers and the occasional hand signal, he'd escaped the city intact.

He settled down to drive in a straight line on the bypass, watching people stare as they went past. Because of Donald's age and inexperience, the outfit cost another two thousand five hundred pounds to insure fully comprehensive. He finally managed to turn into the drive on Crabtree Farm, parking around the back of the dutch-barn.

Mary and Martin had already set out for Glencoe staying with Robbie's mother in her cottage, helping with preparations for the wedding, totally unaware of what their son had purchased. Donald had barely reached the studio, noticing Christine entering the yard in her white Range Rover. She ran upstairs, entering. Donald poured her a cup of coffee. "Come on, own up, boyfriend; how are we travelling to Glencoe?"

"I'm not saying you wait and see otherwise; it won't be a surprise," he grinned.

Christine pulled a face, "I hope you know what you're doing, Donald; otherwise, I will make you phone for a helicopter. We won't be there on time."

"You worry too much, your ladyship; you be ready and waiting," he grinned.

Donald sat down at his easel sketching Christine; she glanced, "I'm nude!"

"I have to recover my money somehow, Christine; you're a very expensive girlfriend," he grinned.

"You will not, Donald Selwyn!"

Donald laughed, "Pulling your leg, that's all. One of the guests staying in flat three; comes up and poses for me nude. She wants a portrait for her boyfriend."

Christine glared in horror, "You will not! You hadn't better!" She watched Donald burst out laughing.

She went to punch him on the shoulder. Donald grabbed her, throwing her over his shoulder, taking her into his flat, enjoying each other's company until early evening. Christine concluded Robbie's okay for exhilarating excitement. Donald is more stable and predictable, although she wished he would venture further and experiment with her. She said, "I can't wait until we are married, boyfriend," she smiled, climbing into her white Range Rover and heading down the drive.

Finally, the day had arrived. Donald placed his suitcase in the locking box on his Ford Raptor truck, firing up the enormous diesel engine, which had a beautiful tone. He drove steadily to Strawberry Estate, heading down the drive. Christine glared from her bedroom, wondering what was coming.

Cindy had already parked her car. She opened the front door standing with Gerald trying to figure out the vehicle. Donald finally managed to turn the vehicle around without hitting anything, ready to leave.

He stepped from his new Ford Raptor truck. Gerald enquired, "Have you hired or purchased?"

"All mine," Donald grinned, watching Cindy look over the vehicle along with Christine, looking inside the fifth wheel, massive an understatement when the sides were extended.

Gerald stood laughing, "You are one crazy boy; you would have to be to become involved with Christine." They loaded their suitcases, setting the alarms on the house. Cindy and Christine sat in the back and Gerald in the front.

Gerald's horrified to sit without a steering wheel in front of him. Donald commented, "A little strange until you used to her, Gerald."

Gerald remarked, "Overtaking frightens the life out of me seeing other vehicles heading towards me." Once they were on the M6, the miles disappeared along with the diesel. Donald had to fill up halfway there; it gave everyone the opportunity for a break.

Christine phoned ahead, instructing Justin to ensure no vehicles were on the left-hand side of the hotel. She wanted an exclusion zone so Donald could detach the new truck from the fifth wheel. When they finally arrived. Donald's mother and father glared in horror, observing Donald's purchase. Donald carefully reversed the fifth wheel into its parking bay. Martin came over, helping Donald detach, "I'm not saying anything, son. I'll allow your mother."

"She annoyed dad?"

"No, son, she's not annoyed; she wants to strangle you. She thinks it's a waste of money considering it's yours."

Donald extended the slide-out sides, connecting the electrics, although he had a generator. Water supply from the hotel outside tap. Mary went inside the fifth wheel, astounded by the facilities that were better than any house you could purchase, sitting down on the settee and then on a swivel chair, looking at the shower units. The kitchen, the massive television screen. Mary patted Donald's cheek, " Useful son. You can transport to a campsite by the seaside. Martin and I can spend a week or two, very thoughtful," she walked away grinning. Donald parked his truck and seemed to draw more attention than anything else. Christine's already inside the fifth wheel, deciding how everything worked. Looking at the large bed she had to christen later with her future husband.

Cindy and Gerald were escorted to Christine's suite in the hotel; a single bed was placed. "The only way we can work this, Gerald, we'll have to change in the bathroom."

"Perhaps I should rent something in the nearby village, a bed-and-breakfast if you feel uncomfortable with me in here, which is quite understandable, Cindy," Gerald professed.

"No, I'm okay; thank you for the suggestion. Besides, you're in no condition to worry me," she grinned, "like your daughter, I am fully trained in the martial arts," she smiled smugly.

Gerald hung his suit, ready for tomorrow. Cindy had a shower; to Gerald's surprise, she left the shower with a towel wrapped around her. He immediately left the room, heading for the bar to have a small whisky.

Donald decided to go for a nice walk along the stream embankment to the sawmill seeing timber stacked in a neat pile. The water-wheel majestically turning, he smiled, looking forward to his own wedding next year. Donald walked towards the hotel and around the rear, noticing construction had already started on the new stable block. Robbie using the JCB had cleared away the old stables and graded the area so the stable block could be clearly seen from the hotel. No more shrubs stood in the way or old stinging nettles and brambles. Christine came out to join him, "We are getting their boyfriend; I've had a quick look at the accounts. Glencoe is holding its own thank god we're heading in the right direction."

They returned to the front of the hotel, glancing through the doorway, watching a guest fly through the air, and ending up on his back outside the front door. Cindy stepped forward, kicking him in the balls, "You pinch my backside again, and I'll break your arms," she assured. Christine intervened, "What happened?" Justin joined her.

Cindy explained, "In the bar having a drink came through to reception. This man pinched my backside, which I considered an assault, so I defended myself."

Christine asked Justin, "Which room is this gentleman staying in?"

"Number seven, Christine."

"Help him pack his bags and show him the door. We don't want people like that in my establishment." The female guests applauded her decision.

Christine asked, "Where is my father?"

"No one has seen him," Justin answered.

Cindy shrugged her shoulders.

Christine started to search, commencing with his room. Donald walked to the sawmill and waterwheel, finding Gerald enjoying a turkey leg sitting on planks stacked out of sight of the hotel.

"Who you bride for that, Gerald?"

Gerald put his finger to his lips, grinning, sucking the bone quickly, wiping his face throwing the bone over his shoulder, and noticing Cindy walking towards him with Christine.

Donald remarked, "Come along, Gerald, everyone's missing you," passing his handkerchief to quickly wipe the grease off his fingers.

Christine smiled, "At least your safe, father, no good you trying to blame the chef; you were seen leaving the kitchen with a turkey leg."

Donald burst out laughing. Cindy placed her hands on her hips, "Fortunate turkey is not fattening; that depends on how it's cooked." They slowly walked to the hotel. Cindy and Gerald go to their room. Donald and Christine, in his fifth wheel settling down to watch television, could receive a signal thanks to the satellite on the fifth-wheel roof. After a while decided to rejoin the party.

By 11 o'clock in the evening, everyone's dancing to the tune of bagpipes. Gerald had drunk more than his fair share of whisky. Martin helped him upstairs and into the large bed in Christine's apartment.

To Christine's surprise, Cindy wasn't too steady on her feet by 12:30 a.m., helping her upstairs. Mary and Christine placed Cindy in the small single bed where they could plainly hear Gerald snoring and Cindy giggling.

Mary commented, "Those two will have a severe hangover in the morning, Christine."

Christine smiled, "At least they enjoyed themselves, Mary."

"I suppose I better take Martin to the cottage. I don't want to disturb Robbie's mother by staying out too late."

Christine smiled, grabbing Donald's arm, "To bed now," she instructed.

Donald giggled, "Yes, mother."

Gerald woke first, holding his head. Cindy turned over, cuddling him. She opened her eyes, "Oh god, you took advantage of me, Gerald," realising she was naked under the duvet.

Gerald jumped out of bed, observing he was in no better state, grabbing the duvet and wrapping it around himself quickly. Christine knocked and walked in, closing her eyes, "You two dress now; breakfast in a few minutes or go without, and why are you in my father's bed, Cindy? That wasn't where we put you last night."

Christine walked out of the door closing behind her. Cindy stared at Gerald. He's like a Cheshire cat; he wasn't guilty. Cindy wrapped herself in the other duvet and grabbed her clothes, dashing into the bathroom. Cindy showered and dressed.

Gerald followed suit. They both came to breakfast, one after the other, sitting at the table. Donald grinned, observing the expressions on Cindy and Gerald. They finished their breakfast and coffee and headed upstairs, changing, ready to attend the wedding.

The portrait of Robbie and Maggie arrived by special courier. Donald immediately hung over the archway into the dining room, where everyone would observe. Robbie and Maggie were married in the local church in the village, returning to Glencoe Estate. They stood by the bridge and the entrance to the hotel, having photos taken professionally. Maggie threw her bouquet, and Christine dived, catching the bouquet and ending up in the stream; she didn't care. She caught the bouquet, and everyone laughed.

Donald helped her out of the water; she ran to the fifth wheel to change into something more comfortable. Maggie and Robbie entered the hotel entrance looking straight ahead. They immediately saw the portrait Donald had painted of them. They paused for several minutes, appreciating their pride of place in the hotel. Justin smiled, the proudest father in the world at that precise second.

Donald had spared no expense, the main dining room had the finest silver set out for the three-course meal, and the wedding cake was the pride of place, standing six tiers. Robbie's ageing mother, in her wheelchair, pushed in to save her from walking so far. She was seated at the far end of the table. Everything had gone off without a hitch apart from Christine falling in the stream. Once again, the partying commenced, and the whisky flowed like the stream outside. Christine and Donald watched Gerald staggering, trying to carry Cindy upstairs. Both grinned, hoping for a new relationship for Gerald and Cindy. Only time will tell. Thanks to an unreasonable guest, the spare room was given to Robbie and Maggie to rest before the drive to Crabtree Farm in the morning, followed by Mary and Martin.

Christine and Donald retired to the fifth wheel, enjoying each other's company watching the waterwheel turn, illuminating the surroundings, never missing a beat and the hotel supplied with free power.

Christine peeped through the bedroom window at 5 o'clock in the morning, seeing Gerald jogging towards the sawmill. Cindy following. Christine watched until they went out of sight, running up the hill to the reservoir. Donald's snoring, Christine jabbed him in the ribs, he turned over cuddling her, she didn't object.

Donald and Christine dressed, entering the hotel seeing Maggie and Robbie finishing breakfast, their car outside covered in spray and tin cans tied to the bumper. Donald removed his wallet, "You're on your way shortly, Maggie."

She immediately hugged Donald, "Thanks for a beautiful wedding. Robbie and I could never have afforded what you and Christine provided." Donald placed a thousand pounds in her hand, "Now there's no excuse not to enjoy yourselves." Robbie grabbed Donald before he could say anything. He kissed Donald on the cheek, "A true friend if I ever had one," lowered Donald to his feet, grabbing Christine and kissing her, which was a shock she hadn't expected.

Donald and Christine stood in the doorway and Justin, watching them set off on their honeymoon.

Justin shook Donald's hand, "I'll never be able to repay you, Donald, for what you offered to Maggie and Robbie. You have secured their future and made everything possible for Glencoe and the staff."

Donald commented, "giving Justin a bear hug, "Don't you go soft on me, Justin," Donald kissed him on the cheek, walking towards the waterwheel. Christine's in stitches, looking at the expression on Justin's face.

After jogging and showering, Gerald and Cindy returned, deciding to rest for a while, falling asleep. Gerald opened his eyes, glancing to his right, seeing he wasn't dreaming. Cindy's in bed with him; she smiled, "I think more fitness training is in order, don't you!"

Gerald immediately obliged.

Christine ordered breakfast in bed for Gerald and Cindy, toast and marmalade, and tea. The waitress knocked on the door as Gerald lay on his back, smiling. "Come in," Cindy said calmly. The waitress entered, placing the breakfasts on the bed on specially designed trays. "Miss Gibbs advised me to say enjoy your breakfast with her compliments."

The waitress curtsied. Gerald passed her twenty pounds from his wallet on the bedside table, "Thank you for the service," she left the room giggling. Christine could see by the expression on the waitress's face as she came downstairs that her father's having extra training.

By 10 o'clock, everyone dressed, had breakfast and looked more human after the celebrations. Donald had spoken to Jock, asking if he could provide a scenic tour for himself, Christine, Gerald, and Cindy. Jock parked his lorry outside the hotel. Donald explained to the others what he planned for their day; everyone wrapped up warm, climbing into the back of the truck using special ladders designed for the public. Donald had his camera determined to take as many pictures as possible of the outstanding unspoiled beauty Scotland offered to everyone, apart from where the wind turbines destroyed the landscape.

Jock set off steadily, ensuring he wasn't travelling too fast, making the ride as comfortable as possible. They passed the reservoir continuing upwards, hanging on for dear life. At one stage, the truck appeared to be travelling virtually vertical up the side of a hill. Sitting on the plateau at the top was the beginning of the five thousand acres of timber at various stages of growth. Some harvested, some just planted, and they continued their journey. Christine admitted, "I've never seen the whole estate only on a map."

Gerald laughed, "And you moan about Strawberry Estate and me."

Christine noticed her father and Cindy were holding hands under the blanket covering their legs. She immediately looked away, making sure they didn't realise she knew. Jock continued his route. Donald surveyed three hundred acres of cereals in one block, the grassland in another, suitable for tractors to work on without tipping over.

Christine glanced out of the rear of the truck, noticing a drone high up in the sky; she smiled, suspecting Mrs Montague's on the prowl, which brought a smile to her face. Jock drove through one farmyard. Donald noticed the new combine and other equipment he purchased neatly in sheds to protect him from the bad weather.

Donald thought he caught a glimpse of someone around the back of the combine. "Stop, Jock!" Donald ordered, patting the cab roof. Donald jumped off the back of the truck running behind the combine, only to see a man come running out. Donald could smell diesel, noticing a tin on the floor and a pipe. Donald gave chase using his skills as a rugby player; tackled, bringing the man to the ground. He pushed Donald off, standing. Donald jumped to his feet, hitting him once under the jaw sufficient to knock him out for the count. Jock came over smelling the diesel surmisings, "Robbing us again." They heard vehicles looking in the direction of the sound. A police Range Rover heading to their location, and a helicopter appeared from nowhere, landing on a flat piece of ground away from the buildings.

Jock remarked, "I bet travellers, parked on the top road for a week or two now. Most estates suffer when they are here poaching, stealing fuel."

Mrs Montague stepped from the helicopter wearing her tartan travelling suit with her bodyguard. Christine commented, "look, Donald."

Donald glanced, seeing Mrs Montague approaching. Donald explained to the police officer what he'd seen, showing him the five-gallon drum and the pipe leading from the diesel tank on the combine. The police officer asked Miss Gibbs, "Will you be pressing charges?"

"Yes," she replied firmly, watching the police officer lead the man away.

Gerald introduced Cindy, "Mrs Montague, I would like you to meet Cindy Crawford." They shook hands and politely smiled.

Mrs Montague kissed Donald on the cheek, "You fear nothing, Donald. You had no idea if he was armed or had a gun or knife charging in like a bull?" She smiled, patting his cheek.

"Christine, you're not the only estate to be robbed. I'm surprised he's operating in daylight. However, I shouldn't imagine many people come here without a vehicle, quite a walk to the top road." Mrs Montague's bodyguard whispered in her ear.

"The police have detained someone else further along on a side-track in a white van, obviously waiting for his friend to return with the diesel," Mrs Montague expressed.

Donald invited, "Would you be coming our way later, Mrs Montague, for refreshments, perhaps a meal, my treat."

"Control your future husband, Christine, prevent him from flirting with me," she smirked, walking to the helicopter.

Donald checked the combine harvester fuel tank was sealed before leaving the farm. Christine scolded, "Mrs Montague is right. You didn't know if he carried a weapon, Donald."

"I didn't care not stealing from my friends or me." They boarded the lorry, continuing their journey, passing Robbie's mother hanging her washing out in the garden; they waved and returned to the hotel finely. Justin came running out, "No one is injured, I hope. We heard the helicopter, and a member of the farming staff phoned me to explain the police presence."

Donald had barely stepped from the back of the lorry before the press arrived to take his photo, trying to interview him over the incident, which Donald dismissed as a trivial matter. Donald noticed another police Range Rover approaching the hotel.

Christine stood by Donald as the officer approached, "The travellers on the top road have vanished. They've hitched up and gone; we are tracking them down. They have designated sites, still refusing to use, and others aren't true travellers."

Christine smiled warmly, "Thank you for the update; appreciated."

Justin commented, "Robbie and Maggie have arrived safely at Crabtree Farm. They're having a great time; thank you, Donald, for your generosity."

"Very welcome, Justin. I like Maggie and Robbie, sort of people you can trust," Donald commented, walking towards the fifth wheel with Christine, who knows the truth, praying Donald would never discover what's gone on behind his back.

Donald and Christine lay on the bed, resting, watching the television and hearing a report. "Several police injured detaining travellers now facing charges of multiple thefts." The drone Christine had spotted following them in the lorry had obviously filmed Donald chasing the traveller and capturing, displayed on the television with the remark from the presenter, "One brave member of the public."

Christine asked, "You see my father and Cindy were holding hands under the blanket?"

Donald smiled, "Just think, maybe your stepmother shortly and to be quite honest, she has one hell of a figure for her age."

Christine grabbed a pillow placing over Donald's face trying to suffocate him, "Pig," she voiced, chuckling.

Gerald and Cindy were in the bar having a quiet drink. Gerald kissed her on the cheek and took her by surprise in public. Cindy whispered, "What are you after, Gerald?"

"Why, who cares."

"I don't want your daughter to think, gold digger after you for your money, everything happened so quickly, Gerald," she smiled. "You still have a stone to lose."

"Christine has her whole future ahead of her. I'm in the closing stages; I don't want to leave this planet a miserable, bitter old man. I've decided to grab every opportunity that comes along. We have the makings of a good relationship; let's see where the journey takes us," Gerald smiled reassuringly.

Cindy patted his leg, "You're nowhere near the closing stages if we remove that fat from around your belly. Although I must confess you were rather cuddly last night," she grinned. "Talk to Christine, be open and see her reaction to our situation."

Christine and Donald walked into the bar, grabbing drinks and sitting beside Gerald and Cindy. Christine looked around Cindy's neck, "You disappoint me, father, no love bites!"

Cindy stared in shock, Gerald held his forehead, and Donald laughed.

"Come on, you two," Christine said, smiling, "We're not blind. We saw you holding hands under the blanket in the back of the lorry; I caught you both in bed, whether by design or accident. Who cares as long as you're enjoying your lives."

Cindy expressed, "I thought you would think…."

Christine interrupted, "It doesn't matter what I think; you're old enough to make your own decisions. Father allowed me to make mine and has done so for many years and watched me make mistakes. Your relationship will either work or won't," Christine said, ordering drinks for everyone.

"Donald has already commented on your figure Cindy. The sooner father captures your heart, the better for me," she grinned, patting Donald's cheek with him turning red with embarrassment.

Cindy remarked, "Nothing planned, I had nothing planned. Christine, I can assure you, I've had plenty of offers from other men, I wasn't interested, or I wasn't ready. Your father is gentle and kind except when you order him around," Cindy grinned.

Christine smiled, "At least you'll keep him alive and make him lose weight."

"Definitely," Cindy expressed, "On his diet when we're home," she assured, relieved no one thought she was after Gerald's money. She couldn't understand why everything happened so quickly other than it had been meant to be. She wondered how her son would accept the news; she dating someone, another hurdle she would have to cross.

They set off for home early the following day, leaving the fifth-wheel caravan behind. Only taking Donald's new pickup, they made better time considering they weren't towing, reaching home early afternoon. Donald dropped off Christine, Cindy, and Gerald at Strawberry Estate. He drove onto Crabtree Farm, pleased to step out of his new pickup. He noticed his mother's Range Rover was missing, he opened the cottage door. No one was there; he suspected his father and mother had taken Robbie and Maggie out sightseeing. He ran into his studio to his apartment, falling asleep on the bed.

***

Christine quickly changed, running round to the stables checking on The Rising Sun and her father's hunter Pig. Both have been fed and watered the bedding clean. Indeed, nothing to complain about. The Rising Sun placed his head on Christine's shoulder, neighing softly. She patted his neck saddling, putting a halter on the other horse. She set off wrapped up warm, quite a chill in the air approaching the sawmill. She could see vehicles parked, hearing the sawmill working and Douglas explaining the operation.

Christine changed direction, not wishing to spook the horses enjoying an hour's ride before returning to the stable, bedding down before returning to the house. She noticed that Cindy's Porsche had gone; her father had made them a cup of tea. He glanced up from his cup, asking, "What do you think, Christine?"

Christine held her father's hand, "Don't be silly, father, you made my life perfect. Why shouldn't you make your own the same? I've had everything I want; you protected me from my mother. If you hadn't, God knows where I'd be now. You go for it, father, don't give yourself a heart attack. I wish you every happiness; besides, if she were up to no good, Mrs Montague would know before us." Gerald and Christine embraced each other warmly.

**

Donald woke and realised he had never noticed Maggie's car parked. He looked out his window it wasn't there, so Maggie and Robbie had obviously taken their car to wherever they travelled. His mother and father had gone somewhere else, he presumed. Donald looked at his wristwatch, now 5 o'clock. Donald checked his mobile messages finding one he missed from his father five hours ago, "Come to the hospital, your mother." Donald raced downstairs, jumping in his Bentley. He roared off down the drive running into the hospital an hour later out of breath. "Room six, Mr Selwyn" the receptionist had already recognised him. Donald knocked, walking in, seeing his father sitting holding his mother's hand. "Sorry, I just received the message; what happened?" he asked nervously.

Mary smiled, "A gallstone, if not two, the high life I live, Donald. The surgeon thinks he can fragment, and I should pass. I thought I was dying the amount of pain I've been suffering. I have to lose weight, Donald. I live too well; my son keeps treating me to luxurious holidays," she grinned in high spirits.

"Perhaps after you had the surgery, mum, I should fly you to Glencoe to recuperate for a month; I'll cover the cost. You go, dad; I can manage the farm."

Mary smiled, "I have to admit, Donald, I enjoyed myself immensely at Glencoe. I want to stay in your luxurious caravan, and the hotel wouldn't lose any money," Mary grinned.

"Of course, you could use my fifth wheel; she's parked. I'll notify Justin and arrange for a helicopter to collect you from here."

"Don't be silly; Donald would cost a fortune."

"No, it won't! Mum, come on, dad, pack some clothes for your-self and mum when mum's fit to travel, you can spend some time there."

"What will we do for a vehicle, son?"

"One there waiting for you to use; leave everything to me, dad."

Martin kissed Mary on the forehead, leaving the room. Donald said goodbye to his mother, leaving in his Bentley, immediately ringing Christine to explain what was happening. She's horrified at the thought of his mother's illness; she would meet him at the farm in an hour. Donald drove to Crabtree Farm, searched the Internet, securing a helicopter to take his mother and father to Glencoe. Donald phoned Justin explaining the situation and asking him to switch on the heating in the caravan. Justin advised, "Why doesn't your mother and father use Christine's suite?"

"Mum said she wanted to try my fifth wheel," Donald shrugged his shoulders.

Justin commented, "If she's uncomfortable, we'll move her to Christine's suite."

"Thanks, Justin."

Christine arrived, hugging Donald, "I didn't like to say anything, Donald, your mother's overweight. She would not have listened if I'd said anything," Christine sighed.

Gerald came running upstairs to Donald's studio, "How bad is the situation, Donald?" sitting down. Donald explained what he'd arranged. Christine smiled, "She could have my suite."

Gerald frowned, "If it isn't one thing, it's another. Cindy's talking to her son, explaining the situation regarding us. I hope he doesn't throw a wobbly throwing a spanner in the works."

Donald expressed, "You worry too much, Gerald; you are a really nice guy. You will help anyone out you can. God knows where we'd be today if it weren't for you, Gerald, pushing me with my artwork helping us out with machinery, and you've allowed me to go out with your lovely daughter."

Gerald said, "Thanks for your vote of confidence, Donald; at least my Christine will be safe with you. Although I don't know if you'll be safe with her." Christine jabbed her father in the ribs. Martin came into the studio, breathing a sigh of relief, "I packed two suitcases, Donald. I suddenly realised how unimportant the farm is when something like this happens."

Donald patties his father on the shoulder, "Spend what you want, dad. I will arrange for your Range Rover to be delivered to Glencoe, so you always have a vehicle, and when mum recovers, you can come home when you're ready. Advise mum that if she comes home too early, Cindy will be waiting for her to start her keep fit program."

Martin laughed, "That I would like to see."

Gerald patted his chest, "I'm losing weight, Martin. I'm not like you work all day."

CHAPTER THIRTEEN

RECUPERATION

Mary had her operation a success; she's to be discharged a day later. Donald arranged for a transporter heading for Scotland to collect his mother's Range Rover and deliver it to Glencoe Estate. Donald contacted the helicopter based at Birmingham Airport his mother and father were now ready for transportation to Glencoe.

Donald drove his father to the hospital with his suitcases observing the helicopter land on the helipad an hour later. Mary left the warm hospital, kissing Donald on the cheek, boarding the helicopter; her first flight ever and Martin's. Donald watched them take off, disappearing into the distance in a cloudy grey sky; they couldn't expect much else in November. Donald returned to Crabtree Farm, realising he hadn't painted anything for ages. Had he lost the gift?

He sat at his easel, trying to decide what he wanted to paint. By 10 o'clock in the evening, he hadn't placed a brush on the canvas; looking from his skylight, he could see the full moon shining through. He moved his easel and chair quickly to constantly watch the moon. He started painting, and the old thrills of painting rushed to his mind. His imagination took over once he'd finished painting the moon; he incorporated angels flying, meticulous in his betrayal. He'd finally completed by 4:00 o'clock in the morning. He couldn't decide whether he was pleased or not with the outcome, leaving for Jack to decide.

Donald took a photo text, Jack. Donald's convinced that Jack never slept. Within fifteen minutes, Jack's on the phone ranting,

"I want you to bring to London, I want in a minute, straightaway wonderful."

"Calm down, Jack," Donald advised, "Only a bloody painting and not that good, I don't think?"

"That is why you're the artist and me your agent; I know good when presented. That's the first painting you've produced in nearly a month. The art world is starving, ferociously hungry for something inspirational, and you never fail; don't keep me waiting, please."

Donald retired to bed, waking at 6:30 a.m. Only grabbing two hours of sleep, checking his mobile, a message from his mother. "We have arrived. What an experience to fly." With lots of kisses.

Donald smiled, nipping downstairs; he threw a bucket of pig nuts for the old saddlebacks. The stables running along the other side of the yard are now empty and not likely to be used again for their intended purpose. He realised they could make another four flats if they were converted.

Donald loaded his painting into the back of his Bentley, heading for London, a journey he didn't relish. He finally arrived at Jack's establishment at 9 o'clock, beating the early morning rush-hour traffic, which was a miracle. Jack came rushing out of his art studio, barely allowing Donald the time to open his boot, running the painting inside and placing on the easel. Jack carefully framed temporarily. "What are you calling this one, Donald?"

"Tranquillity. I wasn't bothering to name; I thought it too boring." Jack pushed Donald aside, pointing to the kettle, "Make the coffee while I photograph and place it on the web."

Donald's convinced Jack's taking speed; he's turbocharged. Donald made two coffees, passing one to Jack, grinning from ear to ear, pressing the enter button on his computer. Donald nearly fell over; within twenty seconds, the portrait had reached two and a half million pounds. "That's ridiculous," Donald concluded.

Jack pointed to himself, grinning, "Me agent, you artist, listen to what I say, Donald, you don't realise how good you are. You see through the crap and produce people's dreams and hopes; you are heaven-sent," Jack's final comment sitting down in his chair, watching the figures. They barely finished drinking coffee; the painting had reached four million.

Donald thanked Jack, fighting his way through the London traffic to escape, finally hitting the M40 and heading home. He hadn't realised his car was filmed behind by a television crew. Donald waved to the children, who acknowledged him in passing cars. He's only travelling at fifty miles an hour. He wasn't in any hurry to go anywhere. Some girls blew him kisses, and others lifted their tops, giving him a glimpse, which made Donald laugh. Since he's famous for his artwork, he realised that most girls driving a Porsche or Ferrari made sure he noticed them as they passed; he suspected gold diggers.

***

Christine's fuming watching the television at home and the camera crew filming relayed directly to a station. She watched the young girls in cars wave, flashing the goods at her future husband, and, to make matters worse, Donald waved. Donald suddenly noticed being filmed. He put his foot to the floor. His Bentley roared into life, leaving everyone behind. He turned off at the first exit from the motorway, driving across country, making his way home. Donald parked at Crabtree Farm, noticing Christine's white Range Rover with Christine leaning against arms folded.

Donald put his hands up, "Not my fault, Christine. I have to take my artwork to London."

"I could see you smiling and waving to the young girls flashing their boobs; how do you think that makes me feel, Donald?"

Donald sighed heavily, "I suppose it's my car, easily recognisable, especially because of the artwork on the panels. Perhaps when we're married, they won't bother?"

"Why should that make a difference, Donald?" Christine asked.

Donald shrugged his shoulders, heading up into his studio, followed by Christine. Donald professed, "I like my Bentley. I don't want to sell her be like disposing of you, unthinkable," he smiled.

***

Mary and Martin had settled into the fifth wheel. They noticed their Range Rover arriving as Donald had promised. Although they were not permitted to sample the Selwyn special, the hotel provided their meals. Mary's on a strict diet. Martin would join in now he wasn't involved in so much manual work he's gained a few pounds.

***

Gerald's sat at the kitchen table reading his newspaper, watching Cindy coming in; he wondered what her son had said about the situation. He made a cup of tea, standing to greet her. Cindy approached him, kissing him lovingly on the lips.

"Well," Gerald asked, concerned.

"He's of similar attitude to Christine. My life, make the most of it." Cindy smiled, relieved.

Gerald spilt his tea; that wasn't the answer he was expecting; picking Cindy up in his arms and kissing her. She grinned, "They say an equivalent to a five-mile run." Gerald carried her upstairs.

***

Robbie and Maggie entered the yard at Crabtree farm in their Subaru parking. They left the car arguing. Donald and Christine watched from the studio, the two shouting at one another. Donald commented, "Do you think they had any lessons from us!"

Christine jabbed him in the ribs, "Looks serious, Donald. You think we should go down?"

Donald exhaled, "We shouldn't interfere in other people's lives."

Christine burst out laughing. Donald realised what he'd said; he'd interfered in everybody's life for the right reasons, he hoped. Donald and Christine ventured downstairs, walking across to Robbie and Maggie; they stopped arguing. "What's happened?" Donald asked.

Maggie's almost in tears. "My fault, Donald." Robbie exclaimed, "She told me to look after her purse; I've lost it with all our money in," he said, leaning against the car.

"Where did you last see it?" Christine asked.

"We went to London sightseeing, stopped overnight, coming back this morning. I realised it wasn't in my pocket," Robbie frowned, "All our credit cards and cash."

Donald opened the car door on the driver's side, feeling underneath the seat. "You mean this," he grinned. Maggie and Robbie stared, "Your left pocket," pointed to Robbie; "No kissing me," throwing the purse to Maggie.

Robbie was dumbfounded, "I checked earlier. I checked several times it wasn't there."

"Which pocket do you use, Robbie, your left one?"

"I. I'm left-handed."

"The purse is trapped between the transmission cover and your seat. I've had it happen to me before. I never normally carry a purse, love! I'm more of a wallet man," Donald laughed, watching Robbie looking embarrassed and Maggie giggling. Donald smiled, holding Christine's hand and returning to the studio, relieved he could resolve the issue quickly.

***

The snow had started to fall on Glencoe Estate. Mary and Martin enjoying the extended break from the farm, no routines, no must-do; please yourself for a change. Mary starts losing weight, and Martin walks along the estate pathways for the public to use most days. They often sat and watched the illuminated waterwheel slowly turning, almost mesmerising. A week had passed in seconds. Most days, they would visit Robbie's mother, have a cup of tea with her, and chat.

They ventured in their Range Rover along the narrow tracks to Mrs McLaughlin's small cottage parking by the stonewall on Sunday morning. Mary knocked, walking in and finding Mrs McLaughlin Robbie's mother on the floor. She'd tripped and broken her hip Mary suspected, immediately phoning for the emergency services. Martin placed more wood on the fire. The cottage had gone cold because she was unable to move. A paramedic was there within fifteen minutes, immediately phoning for a helicopter; Mrs McLaughlin was taken away to receive medical attention.

Standing outside the cottage, Mary took a deep breath, trying to obtain a signal from her mobile, finally getting through to Donald. Donald's horrified runs to flat-four, explaining to Robbie and Maggie. They packed their belongings, heading for home, concerned for his mother's welfare.

Donald sat in his studio, staring at a blank canvas checking his bank account on his mobile, discovering he had over thirteen million in his account. He smiled, realising money didn't buy you happiness, although he wouldn't have to worry where the next crust of bread came from.

Donald sighed heavily, walking into the machinery shed, checking that every tractor had antifreeze in the radiator; they'd already had mild frosts. The last thing Donald needed was a destroyed engine. He went to his mother's cottage, lighting the fires to ensure the water pipes wouldn't freeze if left continually cold for weeks.

***

Gerald really making progress with his weight loss. Cindy's determined he must shed another two stone; none of his clothes fitted properly anymore, a good sign, she thought. Christine's out on The Rising Sun; she wrapped up warm, surprised to find the sawmill still attracting crowds.

Christine watched from a safe distance Stephen the farm Foreman laying another hedge with his two colleagues, sorting valuable timber as firewood. Some to be stored and some sold. She's extremely pleased with the efficiency of the estate for a change. Michael Pearce had become a godsend; he'd saved the estate a fortune in renovating costs and was happy living in a cottage with Peggy and his son Charlie.

***

Robbie and Maggie struggled the last fifty miles to reach Glencoe Estate; the roads had become quite treacherous. Unless you had a four-wheel-drive vehicle, you stood no chance of completing your journey. Mrs McLaughlin is eighty-nine years old, quietly passing away in her sleep while in hospital after an operation to repair her hip.

Maggie and Robbie are devastated. They never had the chance to say goodbye to their mother before passing on.

Mary sent a text message to Donald, explaining what had happened. He's devastated, wondering if interfering in people's lives is partially to blame. Donald realised he had pictures of Mrs McLaughlin. He placed her on his computer and on the large screen on the wall. He's determined that if this were the last painting he produced, it would be the best betraying Mrs McLaughlin sat by the open fire in her rocking chair, knitting her favourite pastime.

Christine phoned Donald, "I suppose you heard Mrs McLaughlin's passed away. How are we travelling for the funeral, Donald? Mary said, snow everywhere and ice; some roads were already closed. I think it's too risky to drive."

Donald sighed heavily, "I suppose we could fly Christine, although that may be dangerous. I'll have to check if a helicopter could make the journey. I'll have to ask mother to find out when the funeral is planned; I'll get back to you, Christine."

Donald phoned Birmingham Airport, the same company he used to transport his mother to Glencoe. They advised picking a break in the weather to ensure a safe journey. Donald and Christine would have to be prepared to fly at a moment's notice to ensure their safety. They would phone Donald as soon as they had a flight plan arranged.

Donald phoned Christine, "Be ready to travel at a moment's notice; the helicopter will pick us both up from your place. He can land on your lawn if your father doesn't mind."

"Okay, pack an overnight bag; I'll wait to hear from you, Donald. Bye for now."

Donald checked his wardrobe, finding a black suit he thought he'd worn twice. He tried it on to make sure it fitted. Carefully packed in the suitcase along with shirt and tie.

Donald phoned his mother, "Hi mum, I'll say this quick; Christine and I are flying for the funeral. You know when it is?"

"I think in about three days' time Donald from what I understand. Robbie's devastated, be careful around him. Maggie trying to console him." Donald losing the signal wasn't surprising considering the weather conditions.

Donald received a phone call from the helicopter firm specifying they would be at Strawberry Estate at 8 o'clock in the morning daybreak to ensure a safe landing.

"Okay, thanks very much. Goodbye."

***

Christine decided to walk with Scooby-Doo, her gundog coming across Oliver with a gun, which surprised her, "Why are you here with a gun? You don't have a licence?"

"My father is permitted to shoot on your land, and I borrowed his gun so I can have a go. We are shooting the bloody vermin."

"Don't allow my father to catch you; he'll have you arrested, Oliver," she smiled. They started walking along together, coming across the old strawberry box shed. Oliver opened the door entering inside; Christine followed. Oliver made a small fire-breaking a few damaged boxes sitting on two crates warming their hands. Christine couldn't understand why she was in here with him, her father would kill her for sure, and if Donald found out, they'd be finished. "I haven't seen you, Christine, since the storeroom. I thought you were interested in having sex with me again?"

"I have a boyfriend; cheating is unfair on him," she sighed. Oliver found a piece of old hessian bag lying by the fire. He encouraged Christine to sit by him, easing her down. He sat looking at her as she casually removed her clothes. She couldn't understand what she had allowed to take place. She had now betrayed Donald so many times, no better than her mother. The tears ran down her cheeks. She would have to live with the guilt, no turning the clock back now. She watched Oliver start making love to her, wrapping her legs around him and enjoying every moment as long as he lasted. She dressed quickly, watching Oliver pick up his gun and walk out of the shed without saying a word.

Christine sighed heavily, walking off with her dog feeling very despondent. Confronted by a staff member, an old guy they'd taken on for odd jobs, already receiving his state pension. He's holding his mobile showing Christine; she watched in horror, realising the old man must have been in the shed to have filmed her with Oliver performing. "I think your father would be very interested in seeing, don't you, Christine or perhaps your boyfriend Donald Selwyn at the very least, discover what a tart you are," he grinned smugly.

"What do you want, Josh money," she asked, stone face realising she's in it up to her neck.

Josh grinned, grabbing her arm and marching her into the old shed; he tied Scooby-Doo to a pallet. Christine stood with her arms folded, watching him place more timber on the fire she'd forgotten to extinguish when she left earlier. "What is good for him is good for me, Christine, your choice."

Christine approached the small fire looking at the expression on Josh's face. Christine wondered whether her mother had found herself in this position. She watched Josh approach until they were inches apart and contemplated whether a man of this age would have more surprises for her than she had already experienced with Robbie. Christine could probably kill him with one blow which would only cause more problems. Christine took a deep breath suspecting he just wanted to shag her, and that would be it if Josh could actually manage the process; Christine didn't feel threatened or scared. She could easily defend herself. She just didn't want the grief. Besides, she concluded one man was much like the next.

Christine looked down, her jacket already open, and the buttons were released on her blouse. Josh unfastened her bra in seconds, releasing the top of her jeans, sliding his other hand inside her knickers, teasing her fanny, driving her slightly crazy; the way he moved his hand gently around and especially the way he played with her nipples. A new experience, she concluded.

She thought all men would be the same, but that was not the case. She watched him kneel, easing her jeans and knickers down. She slipped off her shoes, stepping out of her jeans. She watched him remove something from his coat pocket, which appeared to be a sex toy, teasing her fanny with the object. She parted her legs, lying on the old hessian sack gasping. She couldn't remain standing.

Josh continued teasing her; she struggled to control her breathing, watching him unzip his trousers, suspecting the show's finale. Christine stared in disbelief. She thought Robbie and Donald were sufficiently blessed. How could a man of his age have something larger? Christine lifted her legs, excepting what was on offer, placing her hands over her mouth, not believing the sensation, better than Robbie, which she thought would be impossible to achieve. Josh is slow and gentle; she could feel every inch; she couldn't remember how many times she climaxed, biting her hand to stay silent, fearing she may be heard.

Josh finally relented, standing, holding his hand out for Christine, which she accepted, moving to the side of the shed and taking a pee before dressing. Josh approached, pulling down her jeans and bending her over. He thrust into her. Christine bit the back of her hand; the man is an animal, she decided, thankfully not lasting so long this time. She'd had enough.

She turned to face him, smiling. Josh kissed her softly on the lips, "You have a great pair of tits, Miss Gibbs and a superb fanny if you require servicing again. You only have to ask," he kissed her once more on the lips; his final comment shocked her, "You're as good as your mother any day," he kissed her which she found not unpleasant even if he is an old guy, he certainly knew a trick or two.

Christine watched him leave the shed. Checked she was tidy, brushed any dust off her from the floor, and released Scooby-Doo. Christine strolled towards home, realising she'd never had a cock that big before, which undoubtedly affected her. She'd never felt so content; even jamaica's not in his league.

Christine noticed Donald phoning her. "Tomorrow morning at 8 o'clock, I'll see you then. Could you please ask your father to feed the pigs while we're away, Christine?"

"Okay," she said, disheartened, "Bye." Christine breathed a sigh of relief Donald hadn't phoned while she was making love.

***

Early the following day, Donald's ready after throwing the pigs a few pignuts. He drove over to Strawberry Estate, greeted at the door by Gerald. "My goodness, Gerald, you are shedding the pounds."

"Thanks, Donald, don't worry, I'll look after the pigs; some of that bacon has my name when Cindy isn't looking," he winked.

Christine had made everyone a cup of tea, and Cindy sat at the kitchen table. Donald commented, "Now, which one is my girlfriend?"

Cindy suggested, "You need glasses."

Gerald remarked, "Hands-off, that one's mine."

Christine asked, "Would you like another black eye, Donald?"

"No, I'm okay," he kissed her.

They heard the sound of the helicopter approaching, watching it land on the large lawn. Christine and Donald carrying their suitcases ran and boarded. They were in the air within minutes, watching Cindy and Gerald wave goodbye.

The journey was relatively uneventful; you couldn't see much because of the low cloud. Occasionally, they hit turbulence, especially around the mountains. The journey taking approximately three hours, landed on Glencoe's helicopter pad, quickly disembarked, watching the helicopter take off, vanishing into the clouds. Greeted at reception by Justin, wearing a black armband in respect of Mrs McLaughlin. They went upstairs into Christine's suite. Christine commented, "I'm glad that's over with. I don't mind aeroplanes; helicopters frighten the life out of me; not normal to hover in thin air."

"My first time flying in anything," Donald remarked, "Glad to have my feet on the ground."

Mary and Martin knocked on Christine's door. "Come in." Mary and Martin entered, embracing Christine and Donald, "You two are losing weight, Donald commented, "I can actually place my arms around your waist, mother," Donald laughed.

"Don't be so bloody cheeky, Donald," she grinned. "I have to admit I feel no end healthier for losing a few pounds and not having the worries of the farm around my neck day and night for a change. I think Martin feels the same way."

Martin nodded, "Almost like we're courting again," he grinned, watching Mary blush.

"That's too much information," Mary glared at him.

Donald sighed heavily, "When's the funeral?"

"Tomorrow morning, you made it just in time. Justin gave Robbie permission to take the JCB onto the lane to ensure the snow wouldn't prevent the hearse from travelling to the village church. Mrs McLaughlin will be buried with her husband in the churchyard."

"Where is the wake held, mum?"

"Justin thought it appropriate for the hotel to cater for the event in light of the service Mr and Mrs McLaughlin contributed to the hotel and grounds."

Christine smiled, "Justin finally is making the right decision on his own without consulting me."

Mary remarked, "I don't know how much the funeral cost. The hearse's horse-drawn and transported from Edinburgh, especially for the funeral. I don't know whether insurance policies were in place to cover all the costs. Donald, I know Robbie wouldn't have to ask you for the money. You would willingly give it to him; however, on this occasion, don't, son, unless he asks, you may cause offence."

"I suspect Robbie's blaming me; he wasn't here when his mother passed away," Donald sighed.

"I don't think that's ever crossed his mind, Donald; he's not blaming you, so don't worry about that. I think around a hundred people are coming to the funeral. Mrs McLaughlin and her husband were well respected not only locally."

Justin knocked on Christine's suite door, and Donald let him in. "A sad affair, Christine," he voiced quietly.

"Don't worry, Justin; I'm aware of what you arranged; my future mother-in-law has explained you made the right decisions."

"That's a load off my mind, Christine. Thank you. I don't know whether you know Mrs McLaughlin was surviving on her pension; she had no funeral policies, couldn't afford them, and Robbie was in no better position. My Maggie has persuaded Robbie to accept donations towards the funeral cost from friends and relations."

"You know what the cost of the funeral is, Justin?" Donald asked cautiously.

"We do, and Robbie instructed me not to tell you. You have been more than generous."

Donald sat down at Christine's dressing table; opening his cheque book, he wrote a cheque out for ten thousand pounds to Justin. "Here, Justin," Donald said, ripping out the cheque. "I'm sure you'll see the money is spent where it needs to be to cover the cost without Robbie finding out it's from me."

"I can't accept that, Donald. Robbie will kill me if he finds out I've talked to you about the funeral costs."

Christine remarked, "Don't tell him that's an order. If you do, your dismissed," Christine said with determination. "Donald knew Mrs McLaughlin. He spent some time with her, and I will personally consider it an insult if you don't accept the money."

Justin exhaled, slipping the cheque into his wallet. "Can I speak to my daughter about the money?"

"If you must," Christine snapped, "You'll still be dismissed if he finds out from either of you. Now go," she said, pointing to the door.

Mary remarked, "That's harsh, Christine. Can't you see Justin is upset?"

"He needs to snap out of it, Mary; he's here to run my hotel. Whatever happens, it won't bring Mrs McLaughlin back; he'll have to get on with life and Robbie."

Donald's somewhat shocked by Christine's remarks. "Remember Donald, the aristocracy, they don't give a damn about people's feelings." Mary and Martin walked out. Christine realised she may have overstepped the mark with her attitude. Donald stepped out of the room and headed downstairs, finding Justin in his office, "Take no notice of her, Justin; she will sack you over my dead body."

Justin exhaled, "I'm afraid the lass is right. I'm an Estate Manager; I should act accordingly at all times; she's only saying for my benefit." Maggie came into the office, closing the door behind her, "You want to talk, father."

Justin passed the cheque from his wallet; she noticed Donald's signature on the bottom. "Maggie, you mustn't tell Robbie where the money is coming from; that's why Donald placed the cheque in my name. We raised the money through friends and relations; he needn't know anymore."

Maggie stared, "Donald, are you for real? You don't have to keep paying out, Donald; we'd have scraped the money together somehow."

"Mum warned me not to interfere if you wish to rip up the cheque; I'm not out to offend or upset anyone," Donald frowned about to leave the office.

Maggie grabbed his hand, passing the cheque back to her father, "Cash on Monday, father; I suggest you place it in our joint account; Robbie will never discover."

Donald left the office closely followed by Maggie, "Will you walk with me, Donald?" she asked, slipping on her sheepskin coat. "I haven't a waterproof jacket, Maggie."

She nipped into a storeroom returning with a fluorescent waterproof coat. Donald tried it on, much to his amazement, fitted. She grinned, "That belongs to Robbie for emergencies; I guessed it would fit."

They stepped outside into the cold air walking along the snow-covered track towards the water wheel. The further Donald and Maggie strayed from the hotel, the wind bitter, and by the time they reached the water wheel, they were pleased to hide from the wind in the workshop. Nigel, the Head Forester, had left heaters working to prevent freezing. They sat on the workbench, watching the water wheel.

Maggie remarked, removing her sheepskin coat and warming her hands on the electric radiator. "Robbie's drinking heavily; his mother was unwell for some time. You brought a sparkle into her life for a short period. She couldn't sing your praises high enough for helping her son and, of course, me."

Donald listened to what she was saying, wondering what difference it would have made if he hadn't helped anyone. Maggie approached him, kissing him on the lips. Donald placed his hands on her waist, enjoying for a moment and paused. "I can't; I'd be betraying a friend and my girlfriend."

Maggie stood with her arms draped around his neck, "You really think Christine is interested in you other than for your money, Donald. Mark my words; she will be gone when she's ready." Maggie continued to kiss him, and he responded. They stayed embracing for several minutes. Donald's insecurities had a field day in his brain, agreeing with everything Maggie's saying, although he had no proof. She kissed him passionately and moved away, slipping on her sheepskin coat, "We'd better go, Donald; otherwise, we'll be missed." She kissed him again on the lips removing her handkerchief; she wiped any traces of lipstick away, although he could still taste it.

They left the workshop together, closing the door to maintain the temperature. The snow fell quite heavily while returning to the hotel. Maggie placed Robbie's coat in the store cupboard and jumped in her Subaru, driving off. Christine came downstairs, "Where have you been?" She asked, folding her arms.

"Talking to Maggie, I went for a walk to the water wheel. It's freezing; I suspect freezing in the church."

Christine walked off suspicious of Donald. She had this strange feeling; she was losing her grip on the situation, not a sense she enjoyed or her guilt playing tricks with her mind. Christine remembered what happened to Robbie over her mother and another man. She sat by the fire, racking her brains who could possibly be competition for her, an unthinkable thought, concluding it must be Maggie if anyone would be competition. Suspecting Donald could be easily talked into anything with the right encouragement. She knew if she controlled Donald, her future would be secure. Yes, she loved him; she loved the money more.

Early the following day, preparations were made. The horse-drawn hearse led from Glencoe Estate with everyone walking behind, a mile to the church. By the time they arrived, everyone shivering from the cold, Donald especially without his overcoat. The service went without a hitch apart from everyone crying, Robbie inconsolably. They laid his mother to rest, walking back to Glencoe Estate. The fires were blazing, generating heat and everyone drinking whisky. Christine thought: thank god for Donald, writing out a cheque to help with the funeral costs; the whisky bill would be pretty high by the time the wake had finished.

Mary had suddenly had a wake-up call in her mind wondering what Christine's true feelings were for Donald. Mary discreetly watched her like a hawk. Is she really the sweet and innocent daughter she professed to be. Mary remembered how Christine had betrayed her mother as an evil person trying to make out; her mother manipulated her to secure wealth. The only person that would really know the truth would be Christine herself or Mrs Montague. Mary thought perhaps she was reading too much into things and blowing them all out of proportion like her son.

Mary stepped out into the hallway holding her glass of wine. She could hear someone in the store cupboard talking; she knew it wasn't Christine; she was with everyone else. She watched the door open; a waitress slipped out, quickly tidying herself, followed by a young man supposedly at the wake. Mary moved to the front door watching the snowfall gently, beginning to wish she was at home;

deciding you can have too much of a good thing, she wanted to be on her own property. Mary walked to the fifth-wheel caravan phoning Gerald. "Hi, Gerald, Mary; are you in a position to provide me with information, I've heard one story, and I'd like to hear what you have to say?"

"That sounds suspicious, Mary," Gerald remarked. "What are you unsure about?"

"Christine suggested her mother was trying to pair her off with the Copthorne brothers. You caught them apparently trying to take advantage of Christine."

"What suddenly caused you to ask the question? You're obviously suspicious of something, Mary?"

Mary explained how Christine had behaved with Justin. "She was cold and precise, Gerald, not an ounce of charm in her voice or compassion. She gave you the impression everything she did was planned. I'm not allowing Donald to become trapped if I can't find the truth."

"To be quite honest, I don't know the truth myself. I obviously love my daughter and will protect her. I can understand your concerns. If I thought she was up to anything or using Donald, I would be the first person to jump on her like a ton of bricks. In answer to your question. I remember the day you are referring to; the shoot takes place. I'm running around like a headless chicken trying to organise. Christine was thirteen at the time. The Copthorne brothers taught her karate, something Josephine had arranged since she was twelve behind my back. I was never there as a rule. If I'd known then what I know now, I wouldn't have allowed the lessons to continue. Although I have no real proof of what took place other than a couple of photos. Christine said she's nude some of the time, the Copthorne brothers said so they could see her joints were moving correctly."

"So, she wasn't telling me the complete truth when she said she hated the Copthorne brothers."

"She does now. Once she'd worked out what her mother was up to. I can guarantee you that's true with Josephine's high society friends. When I caught them, they were so petrified they handed over the camera and two photographs and left immediately, fearing I would involve the police. I would have done if it wasn't for the fact of causing Christine embarrassment."

"Oh, we won't speak of it again, Gerald, thank you."

Mary suspected she had misjudged Christine, perhaps. Mary remembered the old saying, no smoke without fire.

Finally, the last guests left the wake heading home. Donald came to the fifth wheel caravan knocking on the door, finding his mother watching television. "What's worrying you, mum? You were never this quiet?"

"If you must know, I don't trust Christine; after the way she spoke to Justin, she switched her charm off and started administering her authority, which I thought inappropriate under the circumstances."

"You're not the only one. After the way, she spoke to Justin with no compassion in her voice. I spoke to Justin afterwards and Maggie; they think she's only trying to help. I'm not so sure. Perhaps if I hadn't splashed out so much money on her, we might have seen her true colours if she wasn't genuine. I won't spend more on her now; although it may be too late, she has everything she wants."

"I can't go into detail, Donald. I spoke to Gerald concerning the Copthorne brothers. She wasn't honest but very close. Donald, can we go home tomorrow? Do you think the Range Rover would make it through these conditions? I want to be home in my own cottage. Glencoe Estate is losing its magic for me."

"Providing it doesn't snow anymore tonight; yes, I'm inclined to agree with you. I would prefer to be at home. I'll advise Christine if she wants to come; up to her," Donald said, leaving the fifth wheel caravan.

Christine sat at the bar, noticing Donald come in, "Where have you been?" she asked frostily.

Donald asked for a glass of coke, "We're leaving in the morning; mum's had enough, she wants to go home, and so do I," he said abruptly.

"Oh," Christine answered, somewhat surprised by his attitude. "I presume that includes me?"

"Of course, unless you want to stay here?"

Christine grabbed his arm, panicking, "What's going on, Donald? Is this all over what I said to Justin, my bloody hotel, I can say what I liked to people, and that includes you," she advised realising what she'd said. Donald threw his glass of coke in her face walking off. Christine was stunned, suspecting her own fault she had provoked the situation. Donald ran upstairs and packed his things, passing Christine as she returned to her room to change. Donald knocked on the fifth wheel caravan door walking in. Mary saw the suitcase closing her eyes, dreading what she would hear next. Donald explained. Martin commented, "Plenty of room here, son; leave her to stew."

Christine sat in her bedroom in a flood of tears. Every time she opened her mouth, she dropped herself in trouble. She wondered what possessed her to behave that way. She treated people like dirt. She packed her things, asking Justin to take her in the Land Rover to Inverness Airport, phoning her father to collect her from Birmingham.

Justin never said anything other than, "Are you sure this is the right decision, Christine?"

The reply was swift. "Yes, none of your business." Christine landed in the early hours. Gerald's there to collect her. She threw her bag in the back of the Range Rover and sat with her arms folded, fuming. "Yes, my big mouth again," she shouted, bursting into tears.

Donald ran into the hotel dashing upstairs to Christine's suite, discovering she'd gone her clothes, everything. He took a deep breath and ran downstairs, jumping in the Range Rover with Martin and Mary driving; they headed home. Donald noticed a text message, Justin explaining what time Christine had left.

The first part of the journey home was slow due to the weather conditions; finally, on the M6, they could gather some actual speed; arriving home at 10 o'clock in the evening, everyone shattered.

Early the next day, Donald framed the picture of Mrs McLaughlin for Robbie, packing it away securely, marking fragile the painting collected by 11 o'clock by courier service. Once realised that the artwork was valued at over two million, couriers would treat it with kid gloves.

Mary and Gerald talked over the phone, trying to find out the problem and why Christine is so aggressive other than her Royal connection, concluding, allow the dust to settle for a while and see what happens.

***

Gerald and Cindy went out for the day shopping in Birmingham. Christine is not interested, deciding to go for a ride on her horse, The Rising Sun. She'd wrapped up warm, extremely cold outside, wondering what to do regarding Donald. Was it over between them, or could she repair the damage? She realised Strawberry Estate is financially sound and Glencoe, thanks to Donald. She suspected everyone at Glencoe would hate her for how she treated Donald. She trotted around the nature reserve, finding herself by the old shed where the Massey Ferguson tractor had been stored for years, noticing the door slightly open.

She dismounted, tying her horse to a branch. She cautiously ventured inside, waiting for her eyes to adjust. Finally seeing the old strawberry boxes, she made her way to the back of the building, smelling something strange, discovering what she thought were two old tramps sitting around a small fire, with a rabbit on a spit roast, made from old pieces of steel. She's about to retreat and leave the situation for the police to deal with.

***

Donald in his studio suspecting Christine had done nothing wrong, unlike himself, allowing Maggie to kiss him the way she had. He's as guilty as hell. Thank god, he thought it didn't go any further. He was pretty convinced Maggie would have permitted, which he thought strange, considering she'd just married Robbie.

Donald looked to his mobile, seeing Christine's name displayed. He pressed the answer key, listening to her "screaming," the last thing he heard was, "The Massey tractor shed."

Donald jumped to his feet, placed his mobile in his pocket, drove his Bentley and headed to Strawberry Estate. He tried to reconnect with Christine, but there was no answer. He moved to the stables seeing Christine's horse missing. He stood wondering if it was a practical joke, but why would she mention Massey tractor shed when they didn't have any of those tractors? He suddenly suspected where she was talking about; he sped off at high speed along the track.

***

When Christine discovered the two men, she presumed tramps. She hadn't realised another one behind her. She immediately pressed the button on her phone, knowing it would phone Donald or somebody hoping they would hear her screaming.

The last thing she remembered was being struck on the head with a piece of timber. The old tramp tied her hands and feet, laughing and joking, finishing their rabbit before having fun with Christine. One of the three-spoke to the other two in a foreign language approaching Christine and preparing to remove her clothing.

The three-men pause hearing a vehicle jumping to their feet, grabbing pieces of timber hiding. Donald noticed The Rising Sun tethered to a tree; he cautiously entered, struck on the back of the head by one of the men not sufficient to knock him out. Donald jumped to his feet, punching the man in the face. He dropped to the floor like a stone. Donald could see Christine ahead of him, not suspecting anybody else to be in there. Suddenly finding himself with a tramp in front of him and one behind. Donald, wild with rage, picked up an iron bar and advanced, shattering the piece of timber the one tramp was holding in half, hitting him over the head with a steel bar; blood gushed everywhere. Donald turned; the other tramp ran. Donald launched the steel bar hitting him; the supposed tramp dropped to the floor. Donald dialled the emergency services requesting police and ambulance and his location.

Donald knelt down, releasing Christine; she had blood in her hair; he dared not move her if she was injured. Within a short while, the police and ambulance arrived. Donald explained what he knew, and the paramedic attended to Christine. She was taken away in the ambulance to scan for injuries.

Donald phoned Gerald explaining the events. "A miracle you answered the call. I know you too have had problems lately," he sighed heavily, "Thank you, Donald, I owe you one."

Donald gave a statement. One of the three tramps was taken away in the ambulance with severe head trauma. The other two were handcuffed in the back of a police Range Rover. Donald stamped out the small fire the tramps had made, noticing a partial burnt ID from his old school displaying a picture of Oliver, which didn't make sense, placing it in his pocket and closing the shed door. Donald tied The Rising Sun to his bumper using a rope from the boot of his car, taking him to the stables, bedding down.

He steadily drove home. Mary's waiting for him at the cottage door seeing blood on his hands and face. Donald explained the events to his mother and father. She made him sit down in a chair while dabbing his face and checked his head for any wounds.

***

Christine regained consciousness in hospital, finding her father and Cindy sitting by her bed. She started to cry.

Gerald cuddled her, " Donald saved you; he beat the crap out of the three. Arrested facing charges, one, if he lives. Donald hit him with an iron bar, defending himself against three people. How often have I told you not to investigate on your own, Christine? I dread to think what could have happened to you if Donald hadn't answered your call."

Christine nodded, "I do love him, father," she smiled, seeing Donald entering carrying flowers the nurse took from him, placing them in a vase. Gerald moved out of the way, "You'd better kiss her, Donald; otherwise, she'll burn your ears," he smiled.

"Hello, boyfriend. Thank you for saving me!"

"Hello, your ladyship, my pleasure as always."

The doctor approached, "Miss Gibbs, I'm pleased to inform you. You have no fractures. We will keep you overnight for observation, then home tomorrow after the doctor has seen you at 10 o'clock."

Gerald and Cindy left, along with Donald heading home. Everyone was relieved Christine had received no serious injuries. After visiting hours were finished. Mrs Montague visited the hospital and immediately entered a private room where Christine was moved on her instructions.

Mrs Montague's bodyguard stood outside the door to prevent anyone from entering. She sat by Christine's bed, "A narrow escape Christine, thanks to Donald's intervention. You're rather naughty with a boy called Oliver and Robbie, which we won't speak about and one or two others from what I understand. And you owe me a favour, young lady, for concealing your transgressions."

"Yes, Mrs Montague." Christine smiled, "luckily, Donald remembered where the tractor was stored; otherwise, things may have turned out very differently. I shan't make the same mistake again with Oliver or anyone else."

"What are your intentions with Donald, Christine?" Mrs Montague asked directly.

"I presume we will marry as planned? You know something I don't, Mrs Montague?" Christine asked, somewhat concerned.

"Of course, anything I disclose to you is strictly confidential. Christine, you must not repeat to anyone, you agree?"

"Yes, I understand completely."

"Good, Maggie was seen kissing Donald in a secluded place. It went no further; he didn't do what you permitted Oliver to do and many others. I would monitor the situation closely and wouldn't delay the marriage. He is your security financially. If love is included, that is a bonus, much like me. You understand, Christine, the men that attacked you were not tramps. I can say no more."

Christine didn't reply for a moment, wondering who was playing what game, the sort of thing her mother would say. "Thank you for enlightening me, Mrs Montague. I will monitor the situation."

"I have someone who would like to meet you, Christine, who may become good friends with you in the future."

"Do I know him?" she asked curiously.

"He's from France. Does the name Louis ring a bell; from the Royal Court, you had a crush on him once when you were eleven, and he was sixteen."

"He must be married by now," she said, sitting up in bed quite excited, "Yes, I'd like to meet him." "No one will disturb you, Christine, I can assure you. I would consider it a personal favour if you permitted him some liberties. No one will ever know, only me," Mrs Montague smiled.

"I understand. I owe you anyway."

Mrs Montague instructed her bodyguards Sid to escort Louis into the room without being observed.

Louis entered the room immediately, embracing Christine; they started conversing in French. Louis explained he was a doctor and would make sure she was okay.

Mrs Montague advised she was leaving for a coffee. They had thirty minutes, and Louis would have to return to his residence. Mrs Montague left the room. Louis started kissing Christine on the lips and neck; Christine didn't inhibit; within minutes, she was lying naked with him licking her all over, which she found rather erotic; finally, he climbed onto the bed, taking what he wanted. Louis only lasted fifteen minutes which she thought was a disappointment for a French man and wasn't that big. Louis kissed Christine on the lips leaving the room. She climbed out of bed, visiting the loo.

Christine quickly fastened her nightgown, suspecting this was what her mother would have planned for her. Mrs Montague returned, holding a cup of coffee, "Nice young man?"

"Only one thing on his mind, Mrs Montague," Christine glared, fuming with herself, allowing it to happen in the first place.

Mrs Montague kissed Christine on the forehead and left the room, and Christine's returned to the ward. Christine suspected the only reason she was allowed in the private room was for Louis to make love to her. She couldn't understand why she permitted. Christine hadn't seen him for years. Christine concluded Mrs Montague was mischief-making; she couldn't understand why. It wouldn't make sense for Maggie to be interested in her Donald after marrying Robbie. And for Donald to kiss another woman other than in a friendly manner wouldn't happen; he would sooner break their neck first. Why would he risk his own life if their relationship was so fragile to save her? She went further with Louis and Oliver; thankfully, Donald knows nothing about it or the others.

***

In his studio, painting a horrific scene of the three tramps attacking a woman, Donald was determined not to place Christine's face in the picture. He worked through most of the night, unable to sleep; he betrayed himself violently, killing the three men, unlike the actual outcome. At 6 o'clock in the morning, Donald sent Jack a photo of his canvas. Nothing had changed. Jack's ranted down the phone. He wanted the picture immediately, making Donald laugh. He loaded the canvas in the boot after a coffee and set off for London, finally entering the rear of Jack's art gallery after nine, thanks to the horrendous traffic. Jack jumped up and down, excited to see a different side to Donald again, placing the portrait in a frame and taking several photos while Donald made the coffee.

Donald passed Jack a cup, watching Jack press the send button on the computer. Donald's convinced a million robots paused, waiting for a portrait from him. Donald hadn't finished his coffee before his portrait had reached three million pounds. He thought it made an absolute joke out of farming or any other profession. Jack patted Donald on the shoulder, "You never fail, Donald, to produce something I wasn't expecting; I had heard what happened to Christine and your heroic behaviour. I never expected to see your version in oils."

Donald smiled, heading for home. Soon would be Christmas, and thankfully the snow had held off, although not the same could be said for Glencoe. Robbie rang Donald, "I've received the marvellous portrait of my mother. You captured everything beautiful about her; thank you. I hope to see you at Glencoe soon." The connection was broken; Donald suspected because of the weather.

***

Gerald collected Christine from the hospital. She's ordered to stay in bed for two more days before venturing out or participating in any vigorous activity. She phoned Donald. "Good morning, your ladyship," Donald laughed.

"Good morning, boyfriend; I'm restricted to bed rest for two days. You will have to come and see me; I feel neglected."

Gerald trying not to laugh.

"Okay, I'm on my way from London and about an hour from you. See you then, your ladyship, bye."

Christine rubbed her hands together, "That's a few more million in my bank account," she grinned.

Gerald refrained from smiling, "Christine, you are seriously in love with Donald; you're not after his money?"

"I thought you knew, father, all women are the same; they make sure their nest is well padded if they can catch the right husband," she smirked.

Gerald pulled over to the side of the road in a lay-by. "You are telling me Cindy's only with me because of my money?"

"Face it, father, you are a catch. Although she's already secured her nest with her first husband, you're a bonus," Christine grinned. She laughed, "Men, they're all the same, so gullible, joking, father."

Gerald parked in the driveway; Christine kissed him on the cheek, laughing, running for the stairs. Gerald's unsure of Christine and her real motives concerning Donald. She ran upstairs feeling fine. However, the thought of having a blood clot on the brain persuaded her to take a shower and rest as instructed and recover from her experience with Louis. She dreaded the thought of Donald ever finding out. She jumped into bed, waiting for Donald to arrive, churning over in her mind what Mrs Montague had advised. She had been tricked before and wasn't about to ruin her relationship with Donald over triviality.

Donald arrived, shown in by Gerald, who immediately embraced him, "Thanks for saving Christine Donald; before you see her, could I have a quiet word with you in the sitting room."

Donald perceived by Gerald's expression that something was bothering him. "What's the matter, Gerald? You look worried, mate?"

"How are things between you and Christine?"

"We have moments, as you know; usually row over something stupid. More often than not, it's probably my fault," Donald smiled, wondering where the questioning was heading.

"What I'm about to say to you, Donald is in strict confidence between you and me. Do not allow Christine access to your personal account; hide from her and never disclose your true wealth wherever you have money. I'm saying this as a friend, and it pains me to do so. I don't completely trust Christine."

"You're the second person to say that, Gerald," Donald frowned.

"Oh," Gerald remarked, surprised. "I presume your mother," he chuckled.

"No, someone I think knows more than they're letting on; possibly there again, I trust no one, doesn't take much to have my mind running around in circles," Donald frowned.

Neither Donald nor Gerald realised what they believed redundant spying equipment, updated, and activated. Everything Donald and Gerald discussed was transmitted to a secret location. Mrs Montague had authorised the work to monitor the whole household, especially Christine with her Royal blood connection. She also arranged for Crabtree Farm to be bugged along with Glencoe. A far more cost-effective way of surveillance than relying on agents. If she could hear what's discussed, she could determine by the tone of their voices how serious the situation is before taking any measures to rectify it.

Donald and Gerald had not realised that the three tramps were not really tramps, although they betrayed the part professionally. Mrs Montague realised Donald was an asset without causing suspicion of Christine's status. However, he wasn't a professional; he's solid and robust and would take some stopping if provoked.

Mrs Montague looking at the monitors, frowned, immediately using her walking cane, administered punishment to a surveillance operative striking on the head forcefully. "You are not here to watch Christine undress in her bedroom. If it happens again, you'll be sent to some faraway place where you will disappear," she advised with authority. The male operative held his head. Mrs Montague never spared the rod. Ensuring he realised the penalty for studying footage without her consent would only be permitted in a matter of Christine's security.

Mrs Montague's unsure of the operative she'd chastised, looking to her bodyguard, "Sid," she nodded. Mrs Montague, hearing the operative's neck snap, knocked on the chief officers' security room door with her cane. It immediately opened. She pointed with her cane, "Remove the rubbish and replace please," she continued out of the secure building not far from Jack Potter's studio. Mrs Montague walked casually along the street with Sid, her bodyguard a few paces behind; she paused, glancing into Jack's window and observing Donald's latest artwork, making her smile if he only knew the truth.

**

Donald ran upstairs to Christine's bedroom knocking on the door he walked in. Christine smiled brightly and immediately embraced, talking for over an hour about their forthcoming wedding. Donald finally kissed her on the forehead, "I'll talk to you later, your ladyship. Oh, here's a strange present for you," throwing the partially burnt ID of Oliver on her duvet. She stared, shocked, and quickly smiled, watching Donald walk out of her bedroom door. Donald wondered if he could see a faint love bite on her neck; at least now, she knew he was suspicious.

Cindy entered with a tray, toast, marmalade, and a cup of tea, "I thought you might need a light snack," she grinned.

"Aren't you confessing, Cindy?"

"What!"

"Fathers asked you to marry him, I don't know how you find the time to keep the house clean, and the only room you two seem to find is the bedroom," she implied straight-faced.

Cindy stared open-mouthed, "We don't," she turned bright red.

Gerald came into Christine's bedroom, glancing at Cindy. He exhaled, "You know, don't you?"

Christine smirked, "Of course, since you've lost all that weight, father, you put a rabbit to shame," she laughed, watching him cringe.

"And what about you, young lady? Your no goody two shoes."

"We'll have a Christmas wedding at Glencoe, you two, Donald and me?"

"That's not practical, Christine. The weather is terrible in Scotland," Gerald remarked, looking at Cindy grinning.

"The simple solution is to fly to Inverness and drive to Glencoe. Robbie would clear the roads with the digger if he had to."

"Daughter, I don't understand you-you are crazy. Gerald smiled, "The bang on the head has done you no good; what about accommodation? You haven't thought this out, Christine; I suspect Glencoe is fully booked. Where would guests stay?"

"Before you start panicking, father, I'll check Glencoe." Christine contacted Justin using her mobile, "Hi, Justin, what's the room situation at the hotel?"

"Only your suite and one other room; we had a cancellation because of the weather."

"How many people in the village cater for bed-and-breakfast Justin? You have any idea?"

"I think six I can ring and check if they have any spare accommodation. What are you planning, Christine?" he asked, suspecting this meant trouble.

"I'm trying to pull off a double wedding. Mine and my father's, need extra accommodation for the important people. I think Mr and Mrs Selwyn would stay with Robbie and Maggie; I'm sure they would agree. Cindy's son and girlfriend if they want to come and anybody special, father wanted to bring could stay in bed and breakfast."

"Can you give me half an hour, Christine, to ring around and see what's available? Changing the subject, your stable block is complete."

"Excellent, Justin; thanks for the update."

Christine rang Donald, "I thought I'd inform you, boyfriend, you're marrying me in the next few days at Glencoe. We're taking an aeroplane from Birmingham to Inverness, probably minibuses onto the hotel. We are setting up accommodation for your mother and father. Oh yes, I forgot to mention my father's marrying Cindy. We thought we'd make a family affair of it," she instructed. "Donald, Donald, you listening to me?"

"Yes, I think, so much for talking things over; okay, keep me appraised of your plans," he disconnected the call-in shock.

Gerald had already phoned Stephen to watch both farms and ensure the pigs were fed at Crabtree Farm and the horses on Strawberry Estate; the departure date is unknown.

Justin phoned Christine, "I can guarantee four bed-and-breakfast they will reopen; normally shut at this time of year. Robbie and Maggie will gladly have Mary and Martin. I reserve the room in the hotel for your father and his future wife, and of course, you will have your own suite. Jock has his lorry on standby to collect you from the airport; if the roads become impassable by ordinary vehicles, ensure you travel with warm clothing. We have a few inches of snow here on the roads. When can we expect your arrival."

"Saturday if I can book a flight, thanks, Justin. I'll keep you posted."

Cindy and Gerald stood, trying to grasp the situation. Christine's like a stampeding herd of elephants. Whatever stood in her way is demolished. "Smile, Cindy," Christine advised.

"I'm happy; I think Gerald only proposed to me an hour ago."

"I presume you said yes, Cindy?" Christine asked.

"Yes, we are very much in love like you and Donald. The only people I want to come, are my son and his girlfriend. I think I'm past the white wedding dress; a nice cream suit would do."

"Good, I'll dress. We'll go into town and buy something; you need an outfit, and so do I," Christine smirked, looking at her father's face of bewilderment.

Christine phoned Donald, "I hope to book seats for Saturday, your mother and father yourself, Donald you have any friends coming? Will you invite Michael and Peggy? You'll have to invite Jack. Without him, none of this would have been possible?"

"Christine, I don't know what you're thinking. I wish you'd slow down; your father, okay with everything?"

"Of course," she replied frostily. "You give me the impression…" not saying anything else, fearing she might upset the apple cart altogether. Determined to complete the marriage before Donald finds out about Oliver and Louis. "I'll ring Michael and Peggy and Jack, book seats anyway and pay if there's anything different. I'll sort it out, bye."

Donald reluctantly walked downstairs into the cottage, explaining to his mother and father, who looked deeply concerned; nevertheless, they agreed. Donald phoned Michael and Peggy, who decided to come and would leave their son Charlie with her parents. Donald called Jack, who couldn't stop laughing down the phone at the spur-of-the-moment decision made by Christine. Donald advised he would have to contact Christine for the accommodation; she was organising made Jack laugh even more.

Donald arranged for a courier to take the portrait of Christine in her wedding dress to Glencoe to be hung in the archway.

***

Christine quickly dressed, calling out, "Mrs Montague, you're invited to the wedding," suspecting the house was bugged regardless of what

Mrs Montague had assured. Mrs Montague smiled, realising no flies on Christine.

Christine and Cindy went into town they entered a bridal boutique. Christine removed her mobile, showing a picture of the wedding dress Donald had painted in the portrait. The lady in the shop searched, finally coming across something so close to a match could have been the same dress. The only problem was that the dress was five thousand pounds. She removed her credit card and paid with a cringe.

"You think Christine, I should buy a cream wedding dress. I'd like that one over there looks gorgeous," entering the changing room, stepping out a few minutes later, staring at herself in the mirror. "Oh god, I want this dress," Cindy looked at the sale tag for two thousand pounds; she gasped, passing over her credit card. She knew she could easily afford it; she questioned if spending that money was necessary. The dresses were placed in large boxes they moved on to a shoe store, spending another three hundred pounds on shoes. They both looked at each other, laughing, returning to Strawberry Estate.

***

Saturday finally arrived. Everyone gathered at Birmingham Airport, boarding a plane for Inverness. Only a short flight was very uncomfortable due to air turbulence. Justin, in his wisdom, had hired a four-wheel-drive minibus transporting everyone, dropping off individuals at their bed-and-breakfast and continuing onto Glencoe. Mary and Martin stayed with Robbie in the beautiful snow-covered hills. Gerald and Cindy were shown to their room, and Donald and Christine went to their suite. Christine looked from her bedroom window to the snow-covered stable block. Donald stood beside her, enjoying the view.

Christine had bribed the vicar with a case of malt whisky to perform the service at Glencoe Estate Sunday morning at 10 o'clock. Donald changed into warmer clothes strolling through the snow to the waterwheel, icicles hanging where water splashed. He took a photo to go on a portrait later.

Christine's in the office with Justin checking accounts. The hotel's performing exceptionally well since they'd made changes. Both agreed prices would have to increase in the New Year to maintain a steady profit. Since the poachers were dealt with, the estate is faring better with sheep and cattle, each section turning a small profit.

Mrs Montague stayed on a neighbouring estate in the security room where she could tune in to her surveillance cameras and audio devices for updates on events. She thought it wouldn't be wise to attend the wedding; otherwise, Christine would realise the house at Strawberry Estate was bugged. She had arranged for the wedding to be filmed for Josephine to watch. However, Gerald's not supposed to be involved. Nothing she could do about the situation.

Donald entered the bar after returning to the hotel, finding Michael having a beer. Donald joined him, "We don't see much of each other these days," Donald sighed.

"Can't be helped. I'm busy; you're busy. I have Peggy and Charlie to provide for."

"You don't sound over-enthusiastic, Michael. What's going on?"

Michael sighed heavily, "I don't know, don't trust her; I don't know why and probably totally irrational. She teaches people from home the rudiments of accounting because of Charlie she can't travel. She doesn't seem to want to know me, always too tired or has a headache," Michael shrugged his shoulders.

"Oh, perhaps you worrying about nothing, Michael; you still want to be the best man?"

"Of course, mate, sorry I'm on a downer."

Robbie's walking around the hotel, assisting with preparations for the wedding. Peggy's bored, strolling, looking down the stairway to the switch room, controlling the power to the hotel deep in the cellar. "Excuse me, Miss," Robbie said, "The public not permitted down there, and I don't know why the doors open."

"Sorry, I just wondered," she smiled encouragingly, "What's down there," looking at Robbie in his kilt. "Would you not consider showing me?"

Robbie switched on the light descending the stairway after closing the door so no one else would follow, "Nothing down here, Miss, other than switches for the electricity supply and old furniture."

"Why is it so warm? I would have thought the cellar cold. My name is Peggy, and yours?"

"Robbie. The reason so warm is we have underfloor heating to assist the fires; otherwise, the place would be freezing; we better go."

Robbie locked the door behind him. "Robbie, would you show me the waterwheel," she asked, zipping up her jacket.

"I." Robbie grabbed his coat, and they walked along the track to the waterwheel. Peggy started shivering, "Really cold." Robbie opened the workshop door, "Stand in here for a moment. The heaters are left on," he advised. Peggy warmed her hands, removed her coat, and approached Robbie, kissing him. He's shocked. Robbie stepped back, anticipating what was offered. "Peggy, I'm a married man."

"I'm a married woman. I like a handsome, strong man," she smiled encouragingly.

Peggy removed her jumper and blouse; it wasn't very long before they made love. Mrs Montague's shocked she's aware of Michael and Peggy's history and presumed that after her last mistake, everything is sorted. Obviously not, however, wasn't of any concern to Mrs Montague. She watched the pair for a short while, feeling sorry for Maggie, although her behaviour was not exemplary. She suspected if Donald had relented, he too could be sampling the fruits of infidelity.

Everyone is up early the following day preparing for the wedding. Donald kicked out of the suite using a spare room at Justin's cottage to dress while Christine and Cindy helped each other with their wedding dresses. Donald received a phone call from Jacob, a rugby player at his old school, "Hi, you still involved with Christine Gibbs, Donald?"

Donald tried to stay calm, "Yeah, why?"

"The story is she's sleeping with that prat Oliver. You know the kid thinks he's a lady's man."

Donald knew he'd found Oliver's ID card partially burnt on Strawberry Estate, "You have any proof or only hearsay, Jacob?"

"Oliver sent photos boasting he'd shagged her in a storeroom. I'll send it to you. You can easily see it's Christine Gibbs, her briefcases on the floor with her name. Admittedly, she has her legs wrapped around his neck, and you can hear her talking instructing Oliver to push harder. You look at her briefcase, her names on the handle. She's naked and enjoying herself. I thought you'd like to know. Sorry mate, you're conned; apparently, she's been with others."

"I owe you one, Jacob, thanks." Donald, trembling with anger, looked at the photos, no mistaking Christine. Jacob hadn't realised he'd sent one film taken on Strawberry Estate Farm, this time a movie with her and Oliver screwing each other stupid on an old hessian sack by a fire, where Donald discovered the partially burnt ID card. That's all the evidence he needed, no disputing. He definitely wasn't conned by his friend, who'd saved him from a catastrophic mistake. Donald entered Justin's office, linking his mobile to the printer. He printed off half a dozen copies of Christine in the storeroom and her naked in the old Strawberry shed.

The vicar arrived. The ceremony is to be performed in the large lounge. Martin stood in as best man for Cindy and Gerald, married without a problem standing aside to watch Christine and Donald. Michael is the best man for Christine and Donald. The vicar asked, "Is there anyone here who objects to the marriage? If not, stay silent."

Donald spoke up, "I'm not marrying this old tart sleeping with Oliver. She can go to hell," he produced a photo sent to him and passed it to Gerald, who stood absolutely shocked. Donald through the rest in the air, everyone silent. Mrs Montague spilt her tea on her dress; she hadn't expected that. Christine had fainted. Donald walked out of the door running upstairs, packing his suitcase.

Mary and Martin ran up to join him, "Pack your things now, mother and father, if you're coming with me." They ran downstairs, jumping in Justin's Land Rover, collecting their belongings from Robbie's cottage, and returning to the hotel as a taxi arrived. Everyone else was in turmoil; they had no idea what to do next. Donald and his parents left for Inverness Airport. "How you find out, Donald?" Mary asked, trying to recover from the shock.

"She picked the wrong guy to have a fling with Oliver; he thinks himself a lady's man and loves to boast. Jacob received the information a rugby player from school. Jacob phoned me, lucky I was changing for the wedding; otherwise, I'd have never known until it was too late," Donald sighed.

Mrs Montague sat at her monitor, realising she could not repair the damage. Christine had turned out like her mother gambling and would lose more often than she won.

Finally, Donald and his parents arrived home late in the evening; they retired no one wanted to eat or talk. Nothing was to be said.

Late morning Donald walked to the cottage. His mother removed his breakfast from the oven. Donald sighed heavily, "I should have realised when I found Oliver's ID. When Gerald advised me not to give Christine access to my accounts, everyone warned me I didn't read the signs."

The newspaper arrived all over the front page, "Donald Selwyn, famous artist, walks out on the bride after discovering she's having affairs behind his back." Showed a picture of Christine in the nude. "Christine Gibbs's whereabouts not known at this time."

Susan entered the yard and nervously stepped from her car. Mary opened the door. "Can I talk to you, please?" she said timidly.

"Come in, Susan," Mary sighed, "Things can't be any worse, I don't think."

"I thought you'd like to know Donald; your friend was correct. I knew about Oliver and someone else you should know about Louis; my friend told me from the hospital. She saw him arrive in Christine's room, he's from France. You can call me sneaky if you like. I used to read the messages on Christine's phone; that's how

I knew who she was seeing when I called her a spoiled bitch; she almost killed me."

"Thanks, Susan, it doesn't make me feel better," Donald professed. "Definitely something going on behind my back."

Mrs Montague's listening, absolutely livid, Louis, is mentioned. This could be a particularly dangerous time, although she suspected Donald wasn't interested in revenge, only moving on with his life. At this precise second, she couldn't see any way forward for Christine and Donald as much as Christine begged her to fix the problem.

CHAPTER FOURTEEN

THE NIGHTMARE

Donald and his parents were virtually prisoners on the farm; the press determined to have a story. The police moved the media off the property, and the reporters retreated to their camp at the bottom of the drive. Every day something different is in the news. "Glencoe Estate bankrupt everyone had cancelled their reservation disgusted at Christine Gibbs behaviour." The most disturbing part of the news. "Oliver took an overdose of heroin found by his parents dead in the garage."

Donald sighed heavily, accepting the crap had hit the fan; it takes two to tango, as Christine would remind him. Donald surmised that there was no need for Oliver to take his life; he wasn't solely to blame. Some report Christine Gibbs in a coma. Donald suspected that was bull. Besides, it wasn't his fault, although he thought he should have handled the situation differently. Angry, upset and hurt, why should he be the only one that suffered. He ran to his studio, receiving a phone call from Justin, which he thought somewhat surprising under the circumstances.

"Hi, Justin, what do you want!"

"I understand your anger, Donald; please don't blame the staff here. Everyone is dismayed by her behaviour; she had everything and threw it down the drain."

"I don't blame any of the staff; I'm sorry for my attitude," Donald sighed.

"Donald, please save Glencoe for the staff, not Christine; our bookings are gone. Everyone has cancelled and left. You were the attraction, their inspiration, not Christine."

Donald sighed, "I don't see how I can intervene; not my property, Justin, Christine's."

"You're wrong. Donald Glencoe Estate belongs to Josephine until Christine reaches twenty-one years of age. In all honesty, Josephine requested I phone you."

"Okay, I will see if I can defuse the situation, prepare the fifth wheel; I'll be there shortly."

"God bless you, Donald; I look forward to seeing you shortly."

Donald walked down the drive; the cameras and television crews were filming his approach. "I wish to make a statement." Everyone silent. "I'm returning to Glencoe shortly to continue my artwork. Miss Gibbs and I have gone our separate ways. However, Glencoe will remain my retreat and favourite place to visit in Scotland. I would urge all those who have cancelled their bookings to rebook, and hopefully, I will have lunch with them there shortly."

Reporters started shouting. Donald responded, annoyed, "Shut up, one question at a time, or I won't answer any questions," he glared.

A television presenter stepped forward, "Donald, you must be heartbroken; any chance you and Miss Gibbs will reconcile?"

Donald exhaled, "When you go home tonight and discover your wife's sleeping with your neighbour, would you reconcile! You've answered your own question."

Another reporter stepped forward, "Donald, would you mind explaining how you found out so our viewers know the truth."

"The truth of the story is, dressing for my wedding; a friend from school warned me, sending me a photo of proof. I'm sorry to hear about the death of Oliver. It takes two to tango. He wasn't solely to blame; he didn't deserve to die. My sympathies are with his parents."

The reporters applauded Donald's comment. "Excuse me, everyone, I'm now packing and heading for Glencoe. I have painting to catch up on and some dear friends to see," Donald smiled, waved, and walked back up the drive, wiping his tears.

Mary had watched on television with tears running down her cheeks, realising how painful it must have been for Donald to stand there.

***

Gerald's at home with his new wife, Cindy. The press had tried to acquire a story, and Gerald refused to comment. He couldn't believe Christine's behaviour; he warned her from the outset but still made no difference. She's too like her mother. They both sat watching the news listening to Donald's comments, bewildered.

***

Mrs Montague breathed a sigh of relief; Donald had shown no malice, not mentioning her or anyone else, only commenting on the situation, which is acceptable under the circumstances. Mrs Montague had taken Christine to France out of the way and under strict supervision, whether she liked it or not. She would not be permitted to cause any more scandal; admittedly, Mrs Montague is responsible for Louis, but not Oliver, now deceased. In some respects, she's pleased he could say nothing. She knew Louis definitely wouldn't. He'd returned to his wife in America out of the way.

***

Donald packed his bags, heading for Glencoe in his American Raptor, hoping to throw everyone off his trail, although pretty convinced he's followed. His American truck struggled through the snow like any vehicle, arriving at Glencoe at four in the morning. Justin, as good as his word, the fifth wheel was warm. Donald flopped on the bed, drifting off to sleep, not bothering to report to reception. Not a car in the car park, only his, the place desolate.

453

At 7 o'clock in the morning, Justin knocked on the door. Donald rolled over on his bed, "Come in." Justin entered, carrying a cup of coffee with a broad smile. "Our customers are returning, Donald, thank god and thank you; our bookings are back to normal since you spoke on television."

Donald sat smiling, "Everyone has a job, hopefully; who is running the place now, Josephine?"

"Josephine said, you were to give orders to me; you originally saved the place. I'm to ignore her daughter if she phones, which I doubt. Mrs Montague's on the warpath. I think Christine is under lock and key in some dungeon somewhere," he smiled.

Mrs Montague had bugged the accommodation, including Donald's fifth wheel. She listened intently to the conversation. "Oh," Donald expressed, "I can't stay for long, Justin; you have my phone number. You can always ring me," Donald smiled.

"I had a phone call from Mr Jack Potter; apparently, art materials will be arriving sometime today. Rather than wreck your new fifth wheel, I have a spare room in my cottage you can use as an art studio Donald, while you're here," Justin smiled.

"Are you sure, Justin; some of the materials I use smell."

"It won't matter; a computer is set up for you and a screen on the wall. Robbie has ensured you have everything you need under Jack's instructions."

Donald lifted his eyebrows, walking into the hotel, finding staff along the corridor applauding him and the waitresses insisting he gave them a kiss. He sat at the hundred seated table, remembering when Christine would sit beside him. Mrs Montague walked in. She was unsure how she'd be received; her bodyguard stayed in the doorway in case. Donald rose to his feet, pulling out a chair for Mrs Montague. She smiled, sitting; his manners were still impeccable, she thought, even under the circumstances. "I'll have trout," she ordered.

"I'll have the same, please," Donald advised with a smile. "Well, Mrs Montague, who is Louis when he's at home," Donald asked calmly.

Mrs Montague shrugged her shoulders, "I have no idea. I didn't know about Oliver; Christine kept everything quiet. After I interrogated her, this boy Oliver pestered her at school before you left; he told her you were having an affair with her best friend, which is why she had sex with him twice. Once at school and once on the farm, stupid idea to even the score in her mind." Mrs Montague thought this may put her in good stead and probably Christine if she could play her cards right. There was no one to prove anything different; she had to prevent herself from smiling.

"Are you serious, Mrs Montague! I had no affairs; admittedly, I kissed Maggie once and probably shouldn't have, went no further."

Mrs Montague knew he was speaking the truth.

"What about this Louis fella? What's her excuse with him?" Donald asked suspiciously.

"According to Christine, she went to a friend's party, and she had a little too much to drink and tried pot; the next thing she realised, she's having sex with Louis. You know what Frenchmen are like," she chuckled, " They won't see each other again. He's miles away and broke; he couldn't afford the airfare. We all make mistakes, Donald, and you certainly opened the gates of hell on Christine. I'm hiding her from everyone; most of the females in England want to lynch her."

"She should have owned up, Mrs Montague, then I could have beat the crap out of Oliver and Louis; I'd have felt better."

Mrs Montague chuckled, "They wouldn't have Donald! You'd probably end up in prison. You would have killed them; you are aware, of course, the tramp you hit over the head with an iron bar died. I covered for you," she lied.

Donald stared at Mrs Montague, who continued to enjoy her fish, realising she was almost home and dry with her plans, everything falling into place far smoother than she imagined. She would have to talk to Christine to explain what's said, so she didn't slip up when she met Donald again, which was her greatest wish. She wanted Donald, professing she loved him.

Donald shrugged his shoulders, clearing his plate, sipping his coffee, and looking at the snow falling on the stables beyond, "I can't see how you can repair the mess. I don't think I'd ever trust her again; I struggled the first time. I think I want to stay single."

Mrs Montague laughed, "You stay single with your looks. That will never happen, Donald. I could name a dozen high society females who would marry you tomorrow not because of your wealth; the way you behave is impeccable."

"Shall we elope, Mrs Montague," Donald joked.

She tried not to smile. "Would you be willing to meet Christine and discuss the issue shortly?"

"I suppose," standing, easing the chair back for Mrs Montague to clear the table, she kissed him on both cheeks. "Permit the dust to settle and see what happens," she smiled reassuringly.

Justin approached, "Donald, equipment in my cottage is set up. Your art materials have arrived."

"Thanks." Donald followed Justin to his small cottage, with only two bedrooms. Donald examined the equipment. Nothing was missing, surveying around the whitewashed walls for inspiration, watching a moth trying to escape. Donald immediately turned the room into a prison cell, and the moth clung to the wall with no escape. By the time he'd finished, Donald's convinced a bloody mess and couldn't understand his own composition. He snapped a photo with his mobile, sending to Jack, this would be the first time they'd spoken since Christine, and he had split. Jack text: "Bloody rubbish." That was a first, then Donald received a call from Jack, laughing down the phone, "I hope you haven't damaged the portrait. I want it," he chuckled. "A clear demonstration of your mind, you are confused like the moth in your portrait; you dare not fly to the light. I love it. You will find boxes designed to carry portraits amongst your special delivery packages. I'm not driving to Scotland to collect," he laughed. "By the way, I have ten steaming hot women here desperate to marry you. Are you interested!"

"No, bugger off, Jack," Donald laughed.

Donald left the art room, returning to the fifth wheel; he showered and changed, looking at his favourite waterwheel covered in ice. He watched Maggie park knocking on the caravan door; she entered, rubbing her hands together, "Cold out there, Donald."

Maggie kissed Donald, "Sorry things turned out the way they have, Donald, I warned you." She made them both a coffee sitting on the settee beside him. "What are your plans?"

"I haven't a clue; keep this place running if I can. Mrs Montague suggested Christine only slept with Oliver because she thought I was cheating with her best friend."

Maggie scoffed, "That's convenient, Donald. Oliver's dead. You can't find out the truth. The women you're dealing with are cunning Donald. I found out Robbie had sex with Peggy, your best friend, wife. I knew he's having sex with Josephine before I met him, and I wouldn't be surprised if he sampled the daughter, although I haven't pushed the question."

"How do you know," he asked, shocked.

"If Robbie's pushed, he speaks the truth; he is no liar, confessing, bedding her twice while she's here for your wedding."

Donald stared, horrified, "Does Justin know?"

"No, my dad would kill him. He's always been the same; he is loyal for all his faults," she chuckled. "I can control him when I shout."

Donald exhaled, "You can't live like that, Maggie. If you want to set up on your own and leave here, I'll arrange for you."

She patted Donald's cheek, kissing him, "I'll go before I jump into bed with you."

"Two wrongs don't make a right, Maggie, but I wouldn't say I'm not tempted," grinning, watching her smile. She sped off up the track towards her cottage.

Mrs Montague, listening surprised Robbie would own up voluntarily sleeping with Peggy. Now Donald's aware, she wondered what would happen. Mrs Montague is more concerned that Maggie knew about Josephine and suspected Christine.

Donald phoned Michael, "Can you talk, mate?"

"Yes, Donald, I would have never believed Christine's like that. We stayed and celebrated if that's what you call Gerald's wedding; after everyone found out what happened, it wasn't a celebration, more like a wake, and we flew home."

"How are you and Peggy getting on?"

"About the same, she's upstairs. She made me build her a sound-proof room; so she could see clients in the evening and wouldn't be disturbed by Charlie or the television down here. I thought during the day would be long enough," he sighed.

"I think you'll find she's having affairs. I have some information from a trusted source; she had sex with someone up here," Donald exhaled, "I would put Charlie in his playpen, nip upstairs and kick the door off its hinges. Probably catch her."

Michael paused, absorbing the information, "That explains every-thing; I'll ring you back, Donald; what you said makes sense."

Michael ran upstairs after placing Charlie in his playpen, listening at the door, hearing familiar sounds, stepping back, and kicking the door open. Peggy engaged in sex on the carpet with one of her clients in leathers and chains while being whipped by Peggy naked.

He walked back downstairs calmly, placed a coat on Charlie and went out to his small car heading for his parent's house. Michael's somewhat relieved the truth is out. He called in at his parents, explaining the situation. They were appalled, phoning Peggy's par-ents, completely shocked. Peggy's mother was on her way to see what Peggy had to say. Michael phoned Donald, "Thanks, Donald, you were right; you can't trust anybody anymore."

"Any problems, Michael, phone me. I'm at Glencoe now and for a while; however, I'm sure I can arrange anything from here for you, if necessary. Bye for now."

Mrs Montague sat back drinking her tea, realising the younger generation was far worse than hers; she felt sorry for Michael and Donald.

***

Gerald knew where Christine was and thought the best place for her was away from the press under the circumstances. Gerald hadn't spoken to anyone or the Selwyn's since what took place at Glencoe; he didn't know what he could say. He's pretty sure they wouldn't blame him for his daughter's behaviour. At least he thought his relationships on solid ground; admittedly, Cindy made his life hell if he didn't exercise properly.

***

Donald spent two weeks at Glencoe, convinced everything was back on track. The customers had returned. The hotel was fully booked again; he hadn't seen Robbie, suspecting he was ashamed of his behaviour and not wanting to face him. Donald packed his bags, leaving Justin in control, heading home slowly through the thawing weather, which he thought a godsend. He had intended to go there and remove his fifth wheel; however, he needed accommodation, so it would have to stay.

***

Christine's in France at Mrs Montague's residents completely bored, missing her horse The Rising Sun and Donald. She stared at her engagement ring, still not really understanding why she gave into Oliver and Louis. She had everything at her fingertips. She didn't know whether her father would allow her in the house; she'd not only ruin her own future but ruin his wedding at the same time.

Mrs Montague entered the lounge sitting opposite Christine. She listened intently, hoping for a glimmer of hope. "I've spoken to Donald. I have suggested that you were with Oliver because you were informed Donald's sleeping with your best friend. Regarding Louis, you were intoxicated and drugged at a party; Louis took advantage of you and was too scared to inform him. I also know Peggy and Michael have separated. Peggy was sleeping with Robbie and apparently with some of her customers at home, so one must presume she's become a prostitute for some reason?"

"Is Donald distraught, Mrs Montague?"

"What do you think, Christine! However, he has agreed to have a meeting with you that doesn't mean you're out of the woods. Your mother has taken control of Glencoe placing Donald in charge of the running and Justin. I'm surprised your mother is so upset; she appears to be gaining her faculties. She was an extremely intelligent woman before the Dixon incident; thankfully, it appears she may be recovering and her morals returning. Since Gerald found another wife, her behaviour has changed considerably; she thought no one would have him. Donald had the opportunity to sleep with Maggie, and he still refused. If I were only younger," Mrs Montague sighed, "He would be a dream husband. However, I mustn't complain. Mr Montague has afforded me every luxury I wish."

Christine asked eagerly, "When can I meet Donald," she expressed concerned.

"That is the next problem. I will arrange for Donald to have a passport. I think the safest place would be to fly him here for a few days or an hour. Christine; Donald, any mistakes will walk away; without some careful coaching, you will have to handle him with kid gloves; or your future is finished. You will become a high society prostitute. I assure you that no one would want to associate their name with yours. If Royalty ran the country, you'd be beheaded; that's how many people you have upset."

"I'm nothing like my mother. I can't see why everyone is so upset; I only had a few guys. They weren't that good either. Unfortunate, Donald or I weren't married before he found out," she frowned.

"You have no remorse, Christine; admittedly, Louis, my fault I shouldn't have brought him to see you. I think he's missing his wife until he flew home to America." Mrs Montague stood walking towards the door. "I'll see what I can arrange, Christine. With your attitude, I don't know," she sighed, leaving the room.

Mrs Montague flew to England, her first destination Strawberry Estate. Gerald came out to meet her, looking concerned, asking, "I hope Christine's, okay?"

Mrs Montague nodded. They went inside, entering the lounge, Cindy carrying a tea tray. Mrs Montague smiled, "One success and two disasters. I suppose you heard about Michael and Peggy." they both nodded. Gerald remarked, "I feel sorry for Michael. However, Peggy's gone to her parents; she doesn't want Charlie, so Michael's parents look after him during the day. Michael is taking over at night; full marks for the lad standing by his responsibilities."

"The situation between Christine and Donald. I have spoken to Donald he is prepared to talk to Christine. Christine believed Donald was having an affair with her best friend. That's why she went with Oliver. Louis, whom she met at a party, became intoxicated, and she sampled drugs. He took advantage of her; he is now in America and will never return to England. I can see from your expression that's the biggest load of rubbish you've ever heard!"

"Could you imagine Donald cheating on anyone, Mrs Montague?"

"If you want to see your daughter here, it doesn't matter what we believe as long as Donald swallows her excuse. Otherwise, I think you can safely say life will be difficult for Christine. She will always be known as Donald Selwyn's tramp and only sought out by men for one purpose like her mother many years ago."

Cindy expressed, "Where do Donald's feelings fit into this scenario; it appears Christine can walk on water, and Donald has to put up with whatever he receives. If she were my daughter, she would have the biggest hiding she'd ever had and thrown out. She's a tramp. Donald's a nice guy. He didn't deserve that from her, and I suspect you're to blame for most of the problems, Mrs Montague," Cindy glared.

Gerald stared at Cindy's stance; he realised what she said was the truth. "If Donald is gullible enough to believe that rubbish, he deserves to have Christine. If she wants to live here again, she will have to straighten her ways severely, or I will throw her out. She won't receive my Strawberry Estate shares until she learns to respect people."

Mrs Montague, surprised by their attitude, thought Gerald would be a pushover, but he stands by Cindy, who appears to be the strength in the house now. "Do you want me to inform your daughter she's welcome here or not; perhaps have a trial period?"

Gerald frowned, "We have lost our standing in the community; nobody wants to talk to us. We have not spoken to the Selwyns since the wedding. What other attitudes are we supposed to have? Oh, we love you, Christine. Come home, all is forgiven?"

Mrs Montague sighed heavily, "I will keep you advised of events and give you the option to meet your daughter and discuss a way forward if there is one," she said, disheartened; nothing is quite going to plan.

Mrs Montague drove to Crabtree Farm. Fortunate, Mary and Martin Selwyn were out. Donald came down to greet Mrs Montague, and they went upstairs into his studio. She passed him a passport, "This will permit you to my estate. The best place to meet Christine should provide peace and quiet without the risk of the paparazzi or press becoming involved. You can stay for as long as you wish as my guest. You will have your own private room." She passed him coordinates for his satnav if he wished to drive or fly his choice. She kissed him on both cheeks; he followed her downstairs, opening the door for her to climb into her limousine. She waved as she left the yard.

Donald phoned, "Jacob, is there any talk around school concerning Pamela and me ever having an affair?"

Jacob started laughing, "You do ask the silliest bloody questions, Donald, never. I see the other one's gone just in the nick of time. I'm sorry in some respects I didn't realise your wedding day. I should have phoned you before if I'd known the relationship was that serious."

"When Christine and I were together, Jacob, she ever, attended her best friend's party I didn't know about. You know a fella called Louis who was mentioned," Donald asked, confused.

"To start with, Louis is a French name, so what are the chances of her going to a party around here and meeting a French man unless prearranged. I can't think of any of her friends that had a party. I would have been invited to start with. You're not the only good-looking bloke at school," he chuckled.

"Thanks, Jacob."

"No problem, Donald, don't allow the bitch to beat you down; she isn't worth it, millions of women available; bye for now."

Donald sat in thought; he had the sneaking suspicion he was conned again. If anything had been said at school, Jacob would have found out. Like Oliver, most girls wanted to sleep with him; the only difference was that he wasn't a prat. He didn't need to show off. He was a damn good rugby player; Jacob's parents owned several restaurants. His father was a celebrity chef.

Donald noticed Cindy's Porsche come into the yard. He ran downstairs, greeting her with a kiss on the cheek, "lovely to see you, Cindy; I should have made contact before now," Donald expressed. They both went into the studio, Donald's private room, making tea. Cindy sat down, looking around the vast area. "I came because Gerald's too embarrassed; he thought you wouldn't hit a woman," she smiled.

Donald grinned, "Gerald isn't responsible; I think if he'd known what Christine's secrets were, he would have said and dealt with her. I'm pleased your wedding went ahead first; otherwise, a real mess, Mrs Gibbs!"

Cindy chuckled, "How do Mary and Martin feel about the situation, Donald?"

Donald shrugged his shoulders, "Never said much about it. I suppose allow sleeping dogs to lie is about their attitude. Mrs Montague suggests I meet Christine and see where it leads. I'm not sure it's a good idea they would lie through their teeth to achieve what they want."

"Mrs Montague has visited us suggesting Christine may come home. Gerald has really suffered. Most of his friends have deserted him, not wishing to associate after what happened. Although he can't be blamed for his daughter's actions. We haven't had our honeymoon; it didn't seem right."

"Gerald is not the only coward; I wanted to talk to you and explain why I did what I did. I suspected Gerald would support Christine under any circumstances plus blame me for ruining your wedding."

"I suppose you've heard about Michael's situation, Donald. They separated permanently this time," Cindy advised sipping her tea.

"What a mess," Donald frowned, "At least you two are okay."

"Gerald wanted me to make sure you understood. You are always welcome on Strawberry Estate, considered a good friend along with your parents."

Cindy stood embracing Donald, "Don't be a stranger and don't be fooled by Christine. Think carefully before making any decisions, Donald; you don't want a miserable life. I'm lucky I have Gerald, who is ageing by the minute with the stress," she smiled, jumping into her Porsche and driving off.

Gerald's stood outside with his hands in his pockets, watching a squirrel jump from tree to tree. Cindy parked, jumping out of her Porsche with a broad smile, "Donald's fine, Gerald. You have nothing to worry about; you still have a friend who doesn't blame you, and neither Mary nor Martin, I'm sure. Relax, calm down; otherwise, you'll have another heart attack."

***

Donald sat at his canvas, remembering something he hadn't done; he looked on his mobile for a picture of Gerald and Cindy together. Luckily, she's in her wedding dress and him in his suit. Donald smiled the moment his hands touched the canvas. The rest of the world disappeared and didn't count for anything. He spent the rest of the day on their portrait apart from having lunch with his mother, explaining what had happened while away. They were somewhat relieved the adults in this mess were friends.

Donald continued through most of the night on the portrait of Gerald and Cindy, not placed at Glencoe, outside the house on Strawberry Estate, not quite glamorous but less of a reminder of what took place a few weeks ago. At 6 o'clock in the morning, Donald set off for London with the portrait he would ask Jack to frame. Donald had parked at 9 o'clock. Jack came out to greet him, giving him a loving embrace. "Can you frame this for Gerald and Cindy? I'm sorry I left you high and dry at Glencoe Jack."

Jack shrugged his shoulders, "Better to find out before than after could have been a real disaster. I'm sure if she had her claws into your money, she'd have written you off. I was saving this for a wedding present; I'm glad I didn't give it to you. I set up a Swiss bank account when you first started painting. I deducted a certain amount from the sale price for each painting I sold. I placed it into a Swiss bank account as a nest egg, and your endorsements if you went silly. You never have." Jack grinned, "You presently have twenty-five million in a Swiss bank account; I shall continue to place money in that account. You make sure no one finds out. If you speak to Christine again, she must never know."

Donald hugged Jack, "A friend in a million, as Robbie would say. I don't know what's in my personal account now; I'll have to check when I get home." Donald removed the painting of Gerald and Cindy into the workshop for Jack to frame, which he would deliver directly to Strawberry Estate.

Donald started driving home; he's as popular as ever, receiving waves from people he never knew, children and pretty girls, as if he needed another headache. A film crew following Donald looking for a perfect story. Christine's watching in France, her almost-husband waving to everyone as they passed. Some women would sit in the middle lane blowing kisses at Donald. She wanted to scratch their eyes out, refusing to accept her relationship was finished. She would have him back one way or another, whatever it took.

***

Mrs Montague's somewhat concerned; she'd expected Donald to have visited France before now. She listened to what Cindy had said to him in the art studio. In fact, there wasn't any positive information to celebrate; she would give it a few more days, revisit Donald, and see if she could persuade him.

***

Much to his surprise, Gerald's Range Rover's parked in the yard alongside his mother's. Donald continued upstairs to his studio, not wishing to relive what happened anymore. He packed his suitcase, deciding he would make the trip to France and bring the situation to a close one way or another; although pretty convinced, he was wasting his time. He didn't really trust Christine before and now. Not saying anything to anyone, Donald jumped in his Bentley heading for Folkestone, driving onto a shuttle, a new experience for him. It wasn't long before he was in France, having to go on the wrong side of the road and navigate the roundabouts the wrong way, which didn't come naturally.

He finally headed out into the countryside. He travelled over two hundred miles. Eventually, the satnav indicated to turn left between two enormous pillars with the driveway at least a mile long to a vast castle, about the same size as Buckingham Palace. He's greeted by, of all people Mr Montague, slightly older than Mrs Montague. "Welcome to my home, young man. I must compliment you on your art; my wife's portrait hangs proudly; I study every morning before breakfast." Mr Montague spoke perfect English. His tone suddenly changed, shouting orders to someone in French to carry Donald's bags. The young man ran, picking up Donald's luggage and taking inside. Donald couldn't grasp the vast size, guided to a room through a maze of corridors with the most delicate art hanging on the walls. Donald entered a room allocated for him larger than his art studio. His bags were unpacked for him; clothes were neatly placed in the wardrobe. He walked out onto the balcony, looking across the vineyards appearing to stretch into the sky, the weather decidedly milder here. He noticed Mrs Montague on a horse accompanied by another female he soon realised was Christine. Mrs Montague paused, noticing Donald's Bentley. Christine took a deep breath. "You will only have one chance, Christine," Mrs Montague advised sternly.

Donald finally found his way to the ground floor after asking staff for directions, walking under the archway to the front of the house. Must be at least fifty acres of lawns, he decided. He certainly wouldn't want the task of mowing. Donald found a sunny place out of the wind sitting on a bench. Christine left her horse with a servant to deal with, dashing upstairs, having a shower trying to make herself as attractive as possible. Donald, with his eyes closed, was quite exhausted from the journey. The next time he looked, Christine stood in front of him. "Hello." Donald smiled. "Lovely to see you. You certainly look okay, that's for sure," he smiled, trying to control his feelings, noticing she's still wearing his engagement ring, specially made for her.

Mrs Montague watching from a discrete position. Christine sat beside him, feeling the sun's warmth on her face, not sure of what to say or wait for Donald to start the conversation, which she suspected wouldn't be very pleasant.

"You'll catch a chill out here, Christine; we'll go somewhere and sit quietly and talk." They both rose to their feet, headed indoors, entering the sitting room. Mrs Montague could now hear the conversation from her control room; like everywhere else, she had bugged to monitor staff and visitors. Christine and Donald sat by the wood fire. Christine took a deep breath deciding to take the lead, "Where do we go from here, Donald?"

Mrs Montague thought silence Christine don't force the issue.

"I don't know, Christine; I don't think there is a way forward. No one can undo what has been done. You deceived me. You were the love of my life. I would have given you anything," he sighed heavily, looking into the flames of hopelessness.

"You were having an affair with my best friend," Christine suggested calmly.

Donald glared at her with eyes of death, standing to his feet, "You dare to suggest I would cheat on you, Christine. I've checked with my friend at school, and no one mentioned me having a fling; all over the school in seconds, you can't keep a secret there, although you tried."

Christine bit her tongue, playing the miss innocent, "I made a mistake; he pestered me, talk about you and other girls," she protested.

Donald took a deep breath, "If what you're saying is correct, who is this bloody Louis and don't give me the bull shit about a party. I'd avoid your father like the plague. I think I'll order The Rising Sun to be shot," Donald said, becoming annoyed, snatching the engagement ring from her finger and throwing it in the fire. Mrs Montague's bodyguard ran in. Donald hit him once under the jaw and stamped on his kneecaps; he's out for the count. Donald ran upstairs, collecting his belongings, jumping in his Bentley heading home. Donald phoned Gerald, "I'm on my way home from France. Do you remember that surveillance firm you hired, have them check your house and Crabtree Farm? They are bugged; I'm convinced I will cover the bill."

Mrs Montague knew the games up now if Christine had kept her mouth shut. Christine phoned for a taxi, packed her bags, headed home and sod the scandal. She would live with it, not permitting her horse to be shot.

Mrs Montague threw her arms up in despair. She had lost control of the situation, her bodyguard in a mess, two broken kneecaps and a broken nose and lost a few teeth. She could never imagine Donald would overpower him; no one else ever had. He would now have to be replaced. His career finished.

Donald explained the conversation between him and Christine. Gerald sighed, "She's lying, Donald; she slept with those two people willingly: costing one his life. Cindy's phoning a company in London. They are coming straight down apparently with the deactivation equipment. God knows how that works."

"I threatened to shoot her horse; I ripped the engagement ring from her finger and threw it in the fire. I beat the crap out of Mrs Montague's bodyguard; that's how I knew the place was bugged. I'd barely touched the ring before he came in the room; he would never have known else."

Gerald laughed, "I would have loved to see you sit him on his arse; he frightens me. I bet you Christine is home shortly; she loves that horse. She won't want you to shoot it. I think you are only trying to punish her."

"I'm sorry, Gerald. I'm fed up with liars and people trying to deceive me. I probably wouldn't shoot the horse, Christine," he chuckled. "I'm afraid I exploded; I couldn't control my temper."

"How far away are you now, Donald? Call around if you wish."

"I've come off the shuttle about two hours from you, depending on the traffic."

Christine had landed at Birmingham Airport, catching a taxi heading for Strawberry Estate. She knew she could beat Donald there and determined to prevent him from shooting her horse; unless he phoned someone to do it for him in the meantime. She arrived at Strawberry Estate, stepping from the taxi and paid the driver. Gerald glanced from the sitting room window with Cindy seeing her arrive, not surprised by what Donald had said. The taxi driver removed her luggage and drove off. Christine stood staring at the front door as it opened, seeing Cindy and Gerald. She picked up her two suitcases and pushed past, heading upstairs. Gerald and Cindy looked at each other. Gerald commented, "Josephine all over again."

Christine changed into her jeans and jacket, coming downstairs. She walked into the lounge, "Come on, get it over with. Have your say about poor little Donald, how hard done by he is, anybody would think I'd shot him. I only slept with a couple of guys, for christ's sake."

Gerald jumped to his feet, slapping Christine's face as hard as he could, knocking her to the floor. "Get out of my house, you slut; you are definitely your mother's daughter."

Christine finally burst into tears, her hard shell now broken, realising her father no longer wanted her. The one person in her life she could always rely on. Cindy felt sorry for her kneeling down, dabbing her bleeding nose with her handkerchief, helping Christine to her bedroom, not saying a word, closing the bedroom door returning to Gerald downstairs, who is shaking in anger.

Donald parked at Strawberry Estate outside the house; he took a deep breath. Gerald and Cindy came outside to greet him. "As I suspected, she's here, Donald. If you want to shoot the horse, you can."Cindy stared in disbelief.

"No, definitely not; where is she?"

Gerald sighed, "In her room, I lost my temper like you and slapped her, advising she should clear off."

Donald, Gerald, and Cindy watched a television crew coming down the drive. Christine came to the front door, "I contacted the television station." Christine stood, watching the interviewer approach; she folded her arms. The interviewer asked, "You wish to make a statement, Miss Gibbs."

"Yes, I wish to apologise to everyone for my behaviour. I have caused considerable pain to my family, Mr and Mrs Selwyn and Donald. He would have been my husband if it wasn't for my foolish mistakes. No matter how I look at the situation, I only have myself to blame. I deeply regret what has taken place. I hope in time, everyone will find it in their heart to forgive me."

"Miss Gibbs, you've obviously cried and have a bruise on your face. Has Donald struck you?"

"No, I tripped on the stairs. Donald would never hit me," she briefly smiled.

The presenter immediately approached Donald, "Would you not consider giving Christine a second chance, Donald."

"And risk the same happening again," he said, looking at the female presenter's hand, realising she's married. "How about you and me nipping around the back? We needn't inform your husband." The presenter stared in shock. "How does your husband know what you're up to in the back of the van?"

"He trusts me," she replied indignantly.

"There you go, you answered the question yourself. All about trust. If you can't trust somebody, your life is finished, although I appreciate Christine's courage to own up at long last."

The presenter asked, "Where is your lovely engagement ring? Have you given it back to Donald? Is it really over between you two?"

"No, I lost it, unfortunately," she said, starting to cry, hoping that would gain her some sympathy. Donald felt sorry for her, removed his handkerchief, dried her eyes, and placed his arm around her, giving her a cuddle. He realised what was done was done. He couldn't change the situation; perhaps they should see each other, start over, and see where it led. He could feel Christine trembling. Donald commented, "I think the only way forward is to start over, see where we go if the relationship fails. That's it," he sighed.

The interviewer turned to face her camera, "You heard it here first. Good luck to them both."

Christine ran to her father, crying. She realised her final chance; she was genuinely heartbroken there must be no more mistakes. Christine ran around to the stables breathing a sigh of relief. The Rising Sun is alive; Donald hadn't shot him.

Donald entered the house sitting in the lounge, having a cup of tea with Cindy and Gerald. Gerald shook his head, "I love my daughter dearly, but I don't trust her, Donald. She has too much of her mother in her, the times Josephine would deceive me."

"I said I would give her one more chance if she makes the same mistake; that's it. Having an affair shouldn't be on her mind if she is in love with me."

The company arrived Gerald had used to investigate Josephine, they walked into the house walking around with devices, "I can advise you, Mr Gibbs, your house is bugged," venturing into the cellar finding the connection in the fuse box, only a professional would recognise, they immediately disconnected. Mrs Montague realised she could no longer listen. She would have to revert to the drone process if necessary. Gerald drove over to Crabtree Farm and explained events. The specialist investigator disconnected in the cellar, moving on to Donald's studio. He deactivated the devices severing the connection couldn't be reconnected. They returned to Strawberry Estate.

Donald asked, "Was I correct?" Gerald nodded. "What do I owe you," Donald asked.

" Five thousand pounds Donald." Donald passed him his credit card, and the agent phoned the office, deducting the amount from Donald's card. "A pleasure doing business with you gentlemen," leaving, passing Donald's card to him.

Christine came into the room, "We were bugged, weren't we?"

"Yes, daughter," Gerald said, bringing a smile to her face; she hadn't heard those words for some time.

"Come on, Cindy," Gerald said, smiling, "We'll go for our ride. Leave these two to talk," Gerald smiled, leaving the room holding Cindy's hand.

Christine moved, sitting on Donald's lap, placing an arm around his shoulders, kissing his neck. Donald was unsure how to react. He didn't feel anything at the moment, and his insides were turned inside out. Christine's phone rang. She answered Mrs Montague. "I thought you'd like to know, Christine, we have salvaged your ring; would you like to repair and return or sell the diamonds?"

"No, please repair. I love my ring, don't forget to have The Rising Sun engraved in the band. Thank you very much, Mrs Montague."

"Sorry, Christine. I was so angry," Donald sighed.

"If you, I'd have probably killed you; I don't understand myself; I love you so much," Christine sighed.

Gerald and Cindy were riding along the old track past Michael's cottage, noticing a brand-new mini parked outside; they could see a blonde female kissing Michael from their elevated position on the settee. Gerald chuckled, "That boy doesn't allow the grass to grow under his feet. I'm pleased for him; he deserves someone decent."

Cindy smiled in agreement and continued, crossing the road heading for Crabtree Farm. They entered the yard, warmly greeted by Mary and Martin. Mary commented, "All over the news, Christine and Donald are back together apparently, is that true?"

"I'm afraid so, Mary, Donald's decision. I have to give her credit for standing in front of cameras and owning up; I couldn't have done that," Gerald frowned.

Mary exhaled, "I suppose we all deserve a second chance. I can't believe she would do something like that having an affair; she doesn't look the type. She knows she's attractive, but you never saw her flirting with anyone."

"Who knows what goes through a girl's mind at that age," Cindy expressed, "Everything peer pressure, not like when we were at school."

Everyone entered the cottage. Mary had one of her famous cakes on the table. Gerald was already drooling. Cindy laughed, "I'll try a piece, Gerald; looks too gorgeous to ignore." Mary cut them a slice of cake each, smiling.

Martin asked, "Where are the kids now? They're not kids. I suppose almost adult hard to believe Donald's seventeen going on eighteen."

Mary surmised, "I don't think Christine will come and see us in a hurry after our talk; it makes what she said a joke."

"What was that," Gerald asked curiously.

"She was saying she didn't want to be pressured into having sex, I advised her to wait until she was married, and if Donald didn't want to wait, he's the wrong person for her."

***

Christine cuddled Donald, "Thanks for not shooting my horse, Donald. I love The Rising Sun as much as I love you." Donald smiled.

They heard the door open and close; Christine didn't move, suspecting her father and Cindy, much to her surprise, her mother, Josephine. Josephine smiled, looking at the pair, "You're a lucky girl Christine." Josephine poured herself a drink sitting in an armchair opposite. "You're all over the news; the pair of you, Glencoe, is booked solid thanks to Donald for clearing up the mess you made Christine. Just because your mother has made mistakes in her life, there is no need for you to follow."

Christine sighed heavily, "I said I'm sorry to everyone, mother. I can do no more. What do you expect of me; one minute, you're trying to sell me to anybody with money. You start preaching morals you don't have any of, mother."

Josephine jumped to her feet and Christine. Donald stood between, "Shut up, the pair of you," he shouted, pushing them. Josephine flopped in the chair and Christine onto the settee. "Can we change the subject? I am bored stupid; we can't change the past, only the future. Christine makes one more mistake. She's out of my life forever. I have no idea what you've done in your life Josephine, and it's none of my bloody business. You are a beautiful woman. I think you made a grave error by losing Gerald; he's a wonderful man."

"I won't argue with you, Donald. I saw the remains of Sid, the staff trying to remove the blood from the carpet; he's a trained killer. Special forces not expecting you to be that tough, Donald."

"Don't worry about Glencoe. I will support it, providing you keep your sticky fingers out of the bank account, Josephine; I'm not supporting your gambling habit, do you understand me," Donald glared.

Christine's trying not to grin, watching her mother torn off a strip. Josephine frowned, "For my daughter, although she doesn't appreciate anything I do for her."

Donald smiled, "She has your looks, nothing else she needs in life; she already has a farm, if not two." Josephine grinning, standing to her feet, kissed Donald on both cheeks and once on the lips and kissed her daughter. "I'm pleased for you, Christine, don't make the same mistakes I have; you have your whole future ahead of you if you use your brain and not your looks," her mother smiled, walking out of the front door and driving off in her Range Rover.

Donald sat down on the settee. Christine moved on his lap, cuddling close. She took the initiative kissing him on the cheek and slowly turning his face until she could kiss him on the lips passionately. He responded cautiously. She drew away, looking into his eyes, kissed him on the nose and then on the lips; he responded more favourably this time. Gerald and Cindy came into the house laughing, seeing the two on the settee together.

"You missed the excitement father, Cindy, mother was here, and Donald put her in her place, should have seen her expression. The minute she tries to take any money from Glencoe, Donald is finished with the project; he warns her he's not supporting her gambling habit."

Gerald exhaled, "I missed the fun. You will say for tea, won't you, Donald?"

"Thanks, Gerald."

Hearing a knock at the door, Gerald went to see a courier with a special delivery. The driver handed over the parcel carefully marked fragile; Gerald signed. Donald smiled. He knew what the consignment was, "Your wedding present from me, Gerald, Cindy, I hope you like."

They carefully removed the portrait placed on the sideboard. Cindy and Gerald stepped back, looking at themselves outside Strawberry Estate house. Cindy immediately kissed Donald, "So beautiful, Donald, thank you."

Gerald patted him on the shoulder, "Clever thinking, Donald, you didn't want to bring back memories, so you moved the location."

Christine started crying, "That could have been me in a portrait with my loving husband," she sniffled, hoping to impress Donald. He placed his arm around her waist, "Maybe one day, we'll see." She almost felt herself grinning but maintained her composure.

Donald returned home after half an hour of kissing goodbye to Christine on the doorstep. Donald sat in his studio, looking at the blank canvas. First, sketching a heart, not understanding what he's trying to create. He continued turning the sky into turmoil with a lonely heart sitting in the middle of the canvas, with blood dripping into a gaping mouth at the bottom of the canvas. Realising he may have made a severe mistake, only time would reassure him. Donald started panicking, hyperventilating, and feeling chest pains. He struggles to finish his painting, holding his chest with one hand. He finally belched and farted, his chest pain subsided, and he started laughing, realising he was suffering from indigestion and wind. He sent the photo to Jack. Jack phoned him immediately, " In your car, now," he shouted, "Oh my god! I can see the pain, the suffering; I want it now, Donald."

"I haven't had any sleep for twenty-four hours, Jack; I'll never stay awake at the wheel."

"Okay, I'll come to you. I don't care. I want it," Jack switched his phone off.

Already 8 o'clock in the evening, Donald flopped on his bed, immediately falling asleep. Jack turned into the yard at 10 o'clock. Mary looked out into the darkness, and Martin ventured to see who it was; they both laughed, realising Jack. "I've come to collect a painting Donald's too tired to drive. I want it now, and one of your cakes, Mary, please; I'm dying," he professed, kissing Mary on the cheek.

Mary couldn't stop laughing; Jack's a character. Jack ran upstairs, not disturbing Donald, removed the canvas placed in the boot of his car and went into the cottage. Mary poured him a cup of coffee. "Mary, I am concerned about your son. Gerald is one of my friends; I don't trust his daughter, though; why would any woman want to betray Donald," he sighed, especially after he gave her so many gifts; she treats him like dirt."

"She would be ill-advised to cross him again; my only fear is he would snap her neck like a carrot if he lost his temper, he'd be in real trouble." Mary cut a slice of cake for Jack already placed one in a tin for him. "Martin, this beautiful woman you are married to if you leave her, can I marry her, please? No other woman could make a cake like this," he professed, standing running out of the door, "Farewell, my friends," he voiced, jumping into his car and driving off. Mary's killing herself laughing, "At least I have a spare husband," she commented, "And with plenty of money."

By morning Jack had Donald's latest picture on the net bidding had already reached five million by midday. Jack phoned Donald, "You never gave me a title for your latest artwork.

"Betrayed Love." Donald heard him typing in the name. Within thirty seconds, the picture reached ten million. "Donald, I don't believe what I'm seeing. I have never had a painting jump five million in one go."

Donald switched the phone off. He wasn't concerned, glancing from the window and seeing Michael approach and his new girlfriend. Michael knocked on the door, entering Donald's studio, "I'd like you to meet my new girlfriend, Angela." Donald wiped his hands on a cloth, shaking her hand. Michael certainly knew how to pick an attractive young lady and could be a model. "Go through to my apartment away from the oils," Donald suggested leading the way. "How is Charlie?" Donald asked.

Michael smiled, "He loves Angela."

Donald grinned, making the coffee, "That's great, Michael, one less hurdle for you to jump."

"I saw on the news Donald, Christine apologising. Our friendship goes back a long way; Donald, are you sure you're making the right decision? Look what happened to Peggy and me; if you hadn't told me, I'd have never found out."

"That's what friends are for." Donald passed everyone a coffee leaving milk and sugar on the table so Angela could help herself. Angela dressed in a skin-tight mauve dress with blonde hair over her shoulders and beautiful brown eyes; her nails were impeccable, along with her cleavage, modestly displayed. Donald suspected she worked in an office; she didn't do anything physical. Donald joked, "You don't have a sister, Angela."

Angela smiled, "I do, actually; she attends your old school. She's in her second year. I'm a secretary at your solicitor's office, my day off."

"How did you manage to pick up an attractive girl like this, Michael. I want to know your secret," Donald chuckled.

"Quite by accident, Donald. Peggy's now decided she wants custody of Charlie; I'm fighting her considering her lack of morals. Angela in reception. The rest is history; we've seen each other now for a month; that's not quite the truth; Angela is living with me.

The old saying is Donald, one door shuts, another opens, I'm still waiting to wake up, I can't believe my luck."

"No, I'd have to pinch myself, Michael."

"Will you two stop, please," Angela smiled, patting Michael's leg. "All I would say, Donald, regarding your relationship with Christine, take it slow. Things on file I can't inform you about some of her family. That doesn't mean Christine's a bad person, but she's from the same bloodline."

"Thanks for your concern and advice, Angela."

Michael grinned, looking at Angela's expression. "Perhaps you could consider a portrait of Angela for me, Donald, something I can hang on the bedroom wall for private viewing."

Angela slapped Michael's leg. Donald tried not to look embarrassed, although he felt his face turning red. Michael and Angela left. Donald watched them walk downstairs and out to Angela's mini, which she carefully drove out of the yard. Donald thought Christine's pretty, but Angela was in a different league. Good luck to Michael. He felt he deserved some success in life. Donald phoned Michael, "if you need any money for legal fees, let me know; good luck to you and Angela, bye for now."

"Thanks, Donald, mate."

Donald checked his bank account. He now had thirty-seven million; he wouldn't have to worry too much about the electric bill, he laughed, sitting down at his canvas.

***

Christine had gone for a ride on The Rising Sun, staying on the estate, wondering whether she dare ride over to Crabtree Farm and what would be the reception from Donald's parents. She knew she'd have to face the music sooner or later. Christine noticed passing Michael's cottage, the new mini and Angela through the window she'd seen at the firms' solicitors on reception. She continued riding, pausing to cross the road to Crabtree Farm, sighed heavily, turning back; she wasn't ready for the inquisition she knew awaited her. Christine phoned Donald, "When are you coming to see me?"

"You know where I am, Christine. Come here. If on The Rising Sun the stables still there for him or come in your Range Rover," he expressed in a neutral tone.

"Maybe tomorrow," she said, disheartened, "I'm bored stupid. I feel like a prisoner."

Donald exhaled, "Okay, I'll collect you in about half an hour; we'll go out, Christine."

"Great, see you in a while," she disconnected the call.

Donald changed into something casual jeans, T-shirt, and a brown leather jacket.

Christine returned The Rising Sun to his stable, heading upstairs to change, deciding to be daring and encouraging Donald to show more feelings towards her. She wore quite a low neckline and a miniskirt with her suede jacket. Christine applied makeup and brushed her hair. Christine looked from her bedroom window to see Donald arrive in his Bentley. She ran downstairs, casually walking out through the front door. Donald had never seen her dress this way, like Angela in many ways. She slid onto the passenger seat, smiled kissed Donald on the lips. "Blimey, Christine, you're dressed to kill," Donald commented, making her smile.

Donald drove to the Hilton; he may not be formally dressed, but it didn't matter with his reputation. He thought he should be able to acquire a table. They were both greeted politely entering the restaurant. "Could we have a secluded table, please," Donald asked the waiter passing him twenty pounds?

"Certainly, Mr Selwyn, my pleasure."

They were directed to the far corner, where the light was dim and couldn't be observed from the rest of the restaurant. Christine was excited; she hadn't been out for months; she kissed Donald on the lips looking down the menu. "What shall we have, Donald?"

Donald shrugged his shoulders, "Have what you like I will settle for stake and all the trimmings." Christine had crab after their first course of soup. Donald summoned the waiter with a gesture of his hand. The waiter came over, smiling, "Yes, Mr Selwyn."

"Do you possibly have any non-alcoholic champagne?"

"Yes, I will have a bottle sent over immediately," Donald passed him another twenty pounds from his wallet. The waiter smiled. Donald's a good tipper.

Christine feels special, watching the champagne arrive in an ice bucket with two champagne glasses placed on the table. The waiter popped the cork pouring a little into Donald's glass first. Donald tasted, "Very nice, thank you." The waiter topped both glasses leaving the table. Christine's tingling all over treated like a princess.

They left the restaurant around midnight, steadily driving home. Christine kissed Donald on the cheek, "Will you take me to the studio, Donald, please." Donald smiled, continuing home, carrying Christine upstairs to the studio; she said she would break her heels on the uneven cobbles. She removed her shoes and the remainder of her clothes, jumping into bed. Donald joined her. Finally, they made love for the first time in ages. Christine finally thought her worlds coming together. The exhilaration of a fling with the other men was blown into insignificance when Donald held her in his arms. Donald's mobile rang at 8 o'clock in the morning, mother. "Is Christine staying for breakfast," Mary chuckled?

"Yes, we'll be there in a minute."

Christine had stirred, hearing the conversation stepping from the bed, holding Donald's hand, leading him into the shower with her. Christine realised she had old clothes here, not wanting to give the wrong impression; she dressed in her denim jeans, T-shirt and jacket and a pair of flat-soled shoes which she adored wearing. They went downstairs. Christine nervously entered the cottage. To her surprise, Mary gave her a hug, not a word about the wedding over breakfast. Christine stayed quiet, listening to the others talking about the farm. Donald and Christine were about to leave. Christine turned to face Mary, expressing, "Thank you for breakfast."

Mary realised Christine felt totally uncomfortable and embarrassed, sorry for the girl watching her and Donald returned to the studio. Christine collected her clothes she'd worn, and Donald drove her home so she could see to her horse. Gerald and Cindy were having breakfast seeing Christine come through the front door. They both grinned. "Where were you last night," Gerald asked.

"I went for a lovely meal with Donald. I stayed at the studio, having breakfast with Mary and Martin this morning. I felt out of place; I don't know why; perhaps it's my guilt. Mary's very kind to me," Christine ran off upstairs.

Gerald sighed, looking at Cindy, "I feel sorry for Christine; I hope everything returns to normal, whatever normal is." Gerald frowned, looking out of the window at the weather and seeing Stephen preparing to treat the oilseed rape in the sprayer. He had five hundred acres. Martin at Crabtree Farm had three hundred that Stephen would treat simultaneously.

Christine went out to The Rising Sun saddling him and setting off along the track; she realised tomorrow, if she didn't return to school, she couldn't sit her final exam. All her studying would be for nothing. The thought of facing that was certainly not appealing.

Early the following day, she showered and dressed according to the school criteria; taking a deep breath, she jumped in her white Range Rover parking at school. She stood in assembly. Nothing seemed to have changed; people knew what had happened, and they certainly weren't saying anything. Perhaps the headteacher had warned to say nothing. Much to her surprise, most of the boys would talk to her more than they had before, especially Tim Jenkins, which surprised her. He gently grabbed Christine's arm, "Talk privately." She looked concerned; nevertheless, they entered an empty classroom, standing away from the door so no one could see. "What's on your mind, Tim," she asked directly.

"I wanted to say how sorry I am you received a load of crap because of Oliver. Doesn't matter how many men you sleep with, your private affair; I think you were mistreated."

She smiled in appreciation, "Things are not the same for girls as with boys; you know boys are expected to sleep around, and a girl is instantly classed as a tart," she sighed.

"Anyway, good luck with your exams, you me and four others in the English classroom. Afterwards, everyone comes around to my house for a drink. You're welcome to come, Christine; you will be the only girl; it doesn't matter," Tim smiled.

"I'll think about it, Tim; thanks for the offer," wondering if she dared. The last thing she needed was more problems. She's only seventeen. Why shouldn't she enjoy life, her final exam? Why shouldn't she celebrate?

***

Donald sitting at his easel, thinking about Glencoe wondering if he should buy an estate himself as a retreat if things didn't work out with Christine. He's still very unsure of her; he moved away from his canvas, switching on the Internet, searching the Scottish Highlands for Estates sales in his price range. Although he thought it may be impossible to find something more spectacular than Glencoe.

***

Christine walked out of school, accompanied by the boys sitting for the same exam. Tim showed the way to his house not far from the school. Christine sitting on the plush settee offered a can of beer. "No, thanks, I'm driving." She sat quietly, drinking an orange juice and listening to the boys bragging; one of the boys kissed her. The other boys looked on; she didn't resist, quite surprising. The boys glared at each other. Tim asked, "You okay, Christine. Hey, lads, don't pester. She's taken some crap recently, as you all know."

Christine smiled in appreciation of his comment. "I didn't mind, I'm rather relaxed my final exam, and I suppose the final one for all of you. I'm looking forward to leaving school and working on my estate with my father."

Tim commented, "We can understand why Oliver chased you your attractive. I know talk around the school about you and Donald Selwyn. Most other boys wouldn't dare ask you out on a date suspecting the answer would be no."

Christine rose to her feet, "As a special treat and will probably never see each other again," Christine kissed each one lovingly. "You understand, boys, whatever happens here stays here. No photos or films of a private gathering, you agree?" She watched the boys eagerly nodding, Christine, rather thrilled she had so much power over people. She walked over to the light switch and closed the drapes. The boys seem to be spellbound, watching her every movement. Christine removed her blazer; she watched the boys swallow hard as she unbuttoned her blouse slowly. She could see what they'd like to do to her from the bulges in their trousers. She's no longer a virgin, so it didn't matter; no one would know. She finally released her bra.

Tim commented, almost stammering, "You have a fabulous pair, Christine, I would love to hold."

"Gently, Tim," she encouraged. She watched him approach. Tim spent several minutes holding and kissing her breasts while the other boys watched, anticipating they would receive a turn. Christine permitted the others the same privilege as Tim.

Christine suggested, "Why, don't you all step out of your trousers and pants? The one who has the biggest cock goes first." Christine had never seen anyone undress quickly; each boy stood there with an erection. She surveyed each cock; Tim had the largest. "Your lucky day, Tim, your first," she stepped out of her skirt and knickers, lay on the carpet, taking a pillar from the sofa to rest her head on, and as they say, the rest is history.

Christine realised Donald performed better; he's more loving. All these boys wanted was sex, and that's all it is, just sex Donald would never know or anyone else. Christine is beginning to think her mother's right enjoy herself to the full, providing you plan and make sure no one finds out. After a while, Christine dressed, waving farewell to the boys leaving the house. She returned to the school car park feeling a tart nevertheless great fun and who would ever know. Christine climbed into her Range Rover, hoping for more excitement none of the boys had anything to offer her. Obviously immature, she concluded. Christine steadily drove home, almost kicking herself; she'd walked straight into another stupid situation that she permitted to happen at least, no evidence this time.

***

Donald received a phone call from Justin, "Hi Donald, what's happening concerning the stables? Do you intend to purchase horses, or are we shelving the idea for a while?"

"What's the state of the accounts? Can Glencoe afford the horses, not forgetting the saddles and bridles. Has the farm sufficient food to feed the horses all year round."

"We have five hundred thousand since you saved Glencoe; we don't need anything special. Just good tracking horses, so they shouldn't be too expensive. We could increase the hay meadows by another two hundred acres this year now we have the proper equipment to cope with the terrain. As we stand at the moment, ample food supplies."

"Horses are a little out of my field of expertise, Justin. Do we have anyone there with sufficient knowledge?" Donald asked.

"No, we must take on a stable girl to manage the horses once they are purchased and maintain the leathers. She could be trained by Jock to take the tours; he wouldn't be overloaded with work."

"I think the solution is for me to come up with Christine; there isn't much she doesn't know about horses, and we can make the purchases. We can interview a stable girl at the same time."

"You realise, Donald, we are instructed by Josephine Gibbs to ignore any request her daughter submits; that decision is supported by Mrs Montague. I don't know how the staff feel she may receive a frosty reception after her behaviour."

Donald sighed heavily, "I understand, Justin. Please advise the staff to be polite and not provoke a situation. We must move on all of us. Hopefully, I'll be with you in the next eight hours. Bye, for now, Justin, thanks for phoning."

Donald phoned Christine. She'd step from her Range Rover arriving home, sitting at the kitchen table with Cindy drinking a cup of tea. "Hi, Donald, how is my lovely boyfriend," she smiled.

"Listen, Christine, I'm off to Glencoe; pack a bag we have to purchase horses and prepare for the approaching spring and summer holidays. We'll have to select a stable girl while we're there."

"Thanks for enlightening me, Donald, my bloody estate. Why am I not notified," she shouted?

"The truth, Christine; face the facts, girl. Your mother has stripped you of your powers of authority. Justin and I are running the estate on her behalf. If you can't deal with that, stay here, it's not my fault this mess was created."

Christine's shocked by his attitude realising she'd opened her big mouth. Cindy shook her head slowly from side to side at Christine's attitude. "I forgot, Donald, I'm sorry my mother is a bitch; she's been to bed with hundreds of men." Donald switched his phone off while packing his bags; he could see his phone lighting displaying Christine's name. He took a deep breath, answering, "Yes!" he said frostily.

"Can I come with you please? I'd like to be involved. I appreciate I'm not in charge anymore," she said, downheartedly determined to change the situation as soon as possible.

"Okay, collect you in ten minutes."

***

Mrs Montague had arranged for Christine's and Donald's mobile phone calls to be recorded along with anyone else of interest. Sent directly to her to monitor the situation without becoming involved. She's surprised at Christine's attitude and Donald's in some respects; again, she shouldn't be surprised after what had transpired. Donald had not elaborated on instructions of Josephine or herself concerning Glencoe Estate; if Christine didn't like it, unfortunate.

***

Donald parked outside Strawberry Estate house. Christine came from the front door carrying her suitcase. Donald opened the boot. She threw in, glaring at him, and kissed him on the cheek. Christine opened the passenger door and slid in, fastening her seatbelt; she sat like lady muck with an attitude. Donald waved to Cindy, who shrugged her shoulders, not suspecting the relationship to last much longer with Christine's attitude.

Donald drove off, and Christine curled up on the seat. They didn't speak for the whole journey; he might as well have come alone, he thought. She's no company. Donald parked outside Glencoe Hotel; he opened the boot. Christine grabbed her own bag, strutting inside, ignoring everybody heading for her private apartment. She threw her bag on the bed, exhaling; she was livid to be excluded from decisions. Donald carried his bag to his fifth wheel. Christine's puzzled as to why Donald so long. She looked out of the window seeing him walking around in the fifth wheel. She was annoyed. She ran downstairs, opening the door on the fifth wheel, "What's wrong with my suite?"

"Nothing, why I thought you'd want your own room, and I'd have mine. That's why the fifth wheel is parked here," he smiled, unconcerned at her attitude.

Mrs Montague, in her element Glencoe had not had her surveillance devices removed; she could hear and see whatever she wanted.

Christine sat down on the settee, bursting into tears, "If you don't want me anymore, Donald, say. I can't go on like this. You're so distant everybody's treating me like I have the plague," she sighed heavily.

Donald sat beside her, "Now I know what your game is," watching her stare at him, "You want my body."

She screamed in laughter, sitting on his lap, "If you don't come to my suite, I'm coming down here; I might be restricted in what I can do. Not with you," she grinned.

Donald lifted his eyebrows, "My place or yours."

She grinned, "Mine, a bigger bed."

Donald carried his suitcase, following Christine upstairs, unpacking in a familiar room. Justin knocked on the door. "Come in," Donald called out.

Justin entered, "Great to see you both; I thought I'd let you both know I've made some phone calls. Stables closing down have various horses and ponies to be sold. I thought it would be a great opportunity to source animals at the right price. One of the stable girls there would like to work for you, Donald; she's highly qualified."

Donald patted Justin on the shoulder, "I never needed to come, Justin. You solved all my problems," Donald chuckled. "How far away?"

"I don't know exactly to the north. I believe ten horses for sale and a couple of ponies."

"Would you phone Justin and advise that we will come first thing in the morning around 10 o'clock to see what's available to purchase? I expect you to come. Christine will be able to advise us if we hear a load of rubbish, won't you," he smiled, looking at her frowning.

"Hopefully, it may be advisable for Justin to arrange for a local vet to be there at the same time; he will see things we don't. The last thing we need is dodgy stock."

Donald kissed her on the forehead, "Not just a pretty face. Can you arrange for a vet to be there, Justin, please? Well done, by the way, for your efforts to resolve the issue." Justin smiled, leaving the suite.

Mrs Montague listened, quite impressed with Justin's efforts and Christine offering sound advice; she hoped the relationship would return to its previous status if Christine played her cards right. She could marry Donald within twelve months if she controlled her temper and behaviour.

After breakfast, Justin, Donald, and Christine set off to look at the horses and equipment for sale. The journey mainly along minor roads most of the time, finally arriving at the stables. Greeted by Mrs Montgomery, owner of the establishment. The vet already checking the horses selecting the best eight from the ten, not bothering with ponies. Donald and Christine looked at the saddles, bridles, and other equipment for sale, including barrows and a small tractor used for mucking out.

A young woman approached Donald and Christine, wearing her riding clothes. She offered her hand, "Mr Selwyn, my name is Sophie Mercantile. I believe you are looking for someone to look after the horses and assist with your new venture at Glencoe Estate. I would like to apply for the position, please." Passing her folder containing her history and qualifications. Donald invited her to sit in his car, "We can discuss things more privately while Justin and Christine decide what we should purchase." Christine frowned. Nevertheless, she bit her tongue. She would have the final say in whatever happened; she's sure of that concerning Sophie.

Sophie looked at his car, displaying artwork on the doors. She nervously sat in the front seat while Donald sat opposite, shuffling through her references and qualifications. "Excuse me for asking, are you the famous Donald Selwyn, the artist?"

Donald smiled, "I am he, for better or worse. You have some glowing references here, Sophie. You're qualified to train people to ride, which could be a bonus. You will be in charge of the stables and all the horses, from cleaning out to their healthcare unless they need a vet; of course, I will introduce you to Jock, our gamekeeper. He will assist in tracking around the twenty-five-thousand-acre estate. Your immediate superior Justin, the estate manager, should be consulted on all issues."

"You mean I have the position; you're not interviewing anybody else?"

"One last question. I presume you can drive a horsebox?"

"Yes, of course."

"One last thing, if I give you the position, you are not to become involved with Robbie. He's a bit of a lady's man. Otherwise, you will be instantly dismissed; no ifs or buts, the choice is yours," Donald expressed firmly.

Sophie looked at him strangely, "The oddest condition I've ever come across; I'm very selective, Mr Selwyn; I suspect you heard stable girls are a pushover. I am not, thanks," she expressed firmly.

"Good, you have the position." She stared in disbelief, suspecting she'd lost any chance of securing the position. "Sort your salary out with Justin."

Sophie, shocked, stepped from the Bentley. "Justin," Donald called out. He came over. Donald passed Justin, Sophie's qualifications, and references. "Excellent young lady, sort her salary, Justin. We'll say a six-month trial. What have you decided I should buy?"

"All the equipment there, the tractor and feed bins etc. The saddle's bridle's those eight horses unless Sophie knows some reason why we shouldn't," Justin commented.

"Those eight horses you selected have good temperaments and are used to having different riders, whether experienced or not. They are far from racehorses; steady and surefooted," Sophie advised.

Christine listened to the information believing it to be sound. Donald called over to the vet, "I'd like another horse. Which one."

The vet pointed to a horse; he's put with the others already selected. The vet passed Donald a report. The chosen horses were in good health; he could find no apparent defects. Most were eight years old and of sturdy build. Donald approached Mrs Montgomery, accompanied by Christine and Justin. "What's the asking price for what we've selected, Mrs Montgomery," Donald asked cautiously.

"Fifty-thousand is a fair price."

Christine laughed, "Twenty-thousand, more like, and that's generous, come on, home wasting our time here," Christine suggested.

"Twenty-five thousand," Mrs Montgomery sighed.

Donald looked at Christine and Justin. "We have a deal, Mrs Montgomery." Donald opened his wallet, "Cash or cheque, Mrs Montgomery."

She stood in disbelief at the question, "Cash would be excellent, Mr Selwyn, thank you."

"Obviously, I require a receipt listing everything I've purchased; with your permission Mrs Montgomery, my new stable manager, Sophie, will start transporting the horses we've selected for Glencoe Estate. Justin phone the insurance company and cover the horsebox; arrange for a transporter to move the rest of the equipment, now please," Donald ordered, taking Christine and Justin by surprise by his tone of instruction; no prisoners were taken today.

Christine went into the office with Mrs Montgomery, acquiring a list from her of everything they'd agreed to purchase with the price and signed by Mrs Montgomery. Donald walked to his Bentley and opened a locking glovebox removing thirty thousand in cash. Sophie watched him carrying the money into the office, excited to have the position guessing this guy didn't take any prisoners. However, it crossed her mind that he could take her as a prisoner, making her smile.

Christine stood with Donald watching him count out twenty-five thousand pounds taking the receipt signed as paid by Mrs Montgomery; they shook hands.

Sophie could only carry four horses maximum at a time. Donald walked over with Christine. He removed two thousand from his pocket, passing it to Sophie, "if you run into trouble or need fuel, use the cash," he gave his card with his mobile number, "Ring me any time."

Christine assisted with loading and shutting the ramp on the horsebox, an old Bedford well maintained. Everyone watches Sophie drive off carefully, heading for Glencoe; Justin approached Donald advising, "I have arranged for a transporter from the Massey Ferguson dealership. He will transport the tractor and all the equipment relating to it, the storage bins, etc. Sophie will take saddles and bridles with the last load."

"Good, home, guys," Donald smiled, satisfied with the business deal. They followed Sophie for a couple of miles seeing how carefully a driver she was. Donald overtook when wide enough, arriving at Glencoe. He walked over to the stables with everyone else. Robbie transported bales of sawdust from the mill, preparing the stables. Donald entered a stable, closing the door behind him with Robbie trapped inside. He turned on the light. Robbie looked at him. "I'm only saying this once, Robbie; you cheat on Maggie again, I'll break you in half."

Christine and Justin were listening outside the door. "I thought you were a better man than that, Robbie. If you don't want Maggie, then leave her. Allow her to find someone who loves her and doesn't mess about. I will destroy you." Donald hit Robbie under the jaw; he dropped to the floor and jumped to his feet, coming at Donald. Donald knocked him to the floor. Robbie kept getting up, and Donald knocked him down. Robbie's no competition for Donald. Finally, Robbie sat in the wood shavings with two swollen eyes, a cut lip and a bleeding nose. "Go home, Robbie, tidy yourself. Remember what I said. You're down the road next time, I promise you." Justin grabbed Christine's arm hiding in the adjacent stable, so Robbie wouldn't realise they listened. Christine placed her hand to her mouth, wondering how Donald had realised what was happening. Nothing will stand in Donald's way if he's upset.

Donald walked out of the stables heading for the hotel. He quickly went upstairs and showered, washing his face had a few bruises, but nothing like Robbie had suffered. Christine and Justin sitting on a bale. "My God," Justin expressed, "I knew Robbie was naughty. Maggie didn't think I knew; I dare not say anything to her."

Christine exclaimed, "I'd hate to be on the receiving end of Donald's punishment. You should have seen what he administered to Mrs Montague's bodyguard. He's crippled and will never work again; he's a trained fighter. I know I'm lucky to have him after my appalling behaviour," Christine sighed, realising Donald knew nothing about her and Robbie's affair.

Donald returned to the stables as the horsebox arrived. Christine helped Sophie unload, travelling with her to collect the next load of horses to speed the process.

Justin approached Donald, "I heard what you said to Robbie. Thank you for my daughter. You are right; she doesn't deserve to be treated that way. I know she would run away with you, Donald."

"I'm very fond of Maggie; I will not steal another man's wife. He'll not betray her again if he values his position. I would expect you to instantly dismiss him if you hear and have proof of another woman. I warned Sophie if she so much as breathes on Robbie, she's to be dismissed."

"I thought Christine's tough," Justin laughed, "You don't take any crap."

Donald and Justin watched the low loader arrive carrying the other equipment. The driver unloaded with his crane. Donald shook his hand and thanked him very much, watching him drive away. Christine returned with another four horses: Sophie and Christine, placed in stables, set off again to collect the final horse and tack.

Donald followed the stream to the waterwheel sitting on cut timber, and the Forester approached him. "You made a fine mess of Robbie. I hear he deserved it from talk! Maggie's a fine woman; perhaps you've taught him a lesson he won't forget," Nigel patted Donald on his shoulder.

Maggie skidded to a halt in her car, jumped out, slapped Donald hard across the face, and burst into tears. "You fool Donald," she kissed him. "He'll not forget you today or for the rest of his life; I don't think he'll screw Christine anymore. He's promised me faithfully he'll never step out of line." She jumped in her car, turned around, heading home to the cottage. Nigel laughed, "If that were a bloke, he'd be in a mess on the floor, a woman can slap you around, and you don't care a damn."

Donald started walking, chuckling; he was wrong no matter what he did. His knuckles were sore, the skin missing. He had really struck Robbie if he hadn't; he'd never have sat him on his arse, realising Christine had sampled Robbie, but in the past, and that's where he must leave it. He wondered whether it was worthwhile pursuing a relationship with her. Could he ever really trust her?

Exhausted, Christine and Sophie returned with the final load, bedding the horses for the night. Sophie handed one-thousand-five-hundred pounds to Donald. Donald smiled, "Keep, it's your bonus."

Sophie smiled, "Thanks, and thank you, Christine, for helping me. I'll unload the saddles in the morning. I've just realised," she laughed. "I should have asked you to drive my car, Christine still at the old stables."

Donald remarked, "Jump in my car; it won't take a minute."

Christine smiled, "I'm taking a shower. Don't belong, Donald," she emphasised.

Sophie jumped into Donald's Bentley, and they sped off to collect her car. Donald dropped her off, "Thanks, Donald, I presume I can call you Donald," she smiled sweetly. Donald sat watching her walk over to her old Ford Fiesta, which refused to start. Donald jumped out of his car, instructing, "Lift the bonnet, Sophie." He found a loose battery lead tightened down, and a wire had fallen off the distributor. "Try it now."

Started straight away, "Thanks, Donald," she drove off. Donald drove to Glencoe, parking outside the hotel and running upstairs. Christine sat on the bed with the towel wrapped around her. She immediately inspected him, "I'm checking for any female marks," she grinned, dropping the towel.

The following day, Donald took a walk to the sawmill and saw Jock coming down the hill stopping his lorry by Donald, "I hear the horses have arrived," stepping from his cab, "And I have an assistant to help?"

"Yes, her name is Sophie; she's the stable manager highly qualified impeccable references. I think you two will be fine, nip along to the stables, Jock and introduce yourself. Perhaps take the horses out and show Sophie around the estate."

Jock nodded, "Good idea; talk around the estate you gave Robbie a hiding yesterday. We all know why and agree with your decision. Maggie is a lovely woman and deserves to be treated better. I think she will from now on. You should see Robbie's face; it looks like a football this morning. He can barely see out of his eyes."

"Gives me no pleasure to hear Jock. I shouldn't have lost my temper; he will be sacked if it happens again." Donald watched Jock climb aboard his truck. He smiled, patting the cab door and driving off towards the stables. Donald sat on the cut timber, watching the wheel turn slowly. A while later, he observed Sophie, Jock and Christine coming toward him and three horses. The others were following tethered together, seeing how the horses really performed. Donald watched them ride past. Christine smiled along with Sophie; Jock's occupied patting his horse. Donald returned to the hotel finding Justin in his office, preparing an advertisement offering horse riding. Christine and Sophie had helped him calculate the cost per person for a track around the estate. Justin glanced up, "I apologise for my daughter's behaviour, Donald; she said to me she slapped you; God knows why you are trying to help her."

"I gave up trying to understand women years ago, Justin," seeing Robbie stacking hay bales in the end storage, transported with the tractor and trailer from the farm.

***

Mrs Montague was rather impressed with Donald's attitude and abilities. He appeared to have the necessary skills to organise any operation. Noticing on one of her monitors, Josephine had arrived, wondering why. Donald's about to leave the hotel, bumping into Josephine. She kissed him on the lips, "My favourite manager. I understand my daughter is spitting feathers; she's annoyed and serves her right." Josephine paid the taxi driver a hundred pounds from the airport to the hotel. Donald picked up her bag she booked in at reception, not heading to her suite; she had booked a guest room. Donald carried her suitcase to her room. "I've come to try out the horses you purchased and you if you're available," she grinned, making Donald blush. "I understand you gave Robbie a slapping your decision, of course. I have to say, Donald, I never thought I'd see this place on its feet, and you made that possible." Donald turned his back quickly as Josephine started to undress before him, slipping on her riding britches boots and everything else to keep warm. "You need not turn around, Donald. I'm not ashamed of my body," kissing him on the cheek. "Come and ride with me," she smiled.

"I don't ride horses; it doesn't interest me. Besides, I'm slightly over seventeen stone; I don't think the horse would appreciate me sitting on his back."

She grabbed Donald's hand, "You come with me." Justin watched from his office as they passed; he shook his head. Josephine would never change. The only thing she enjoyed in life was flirting and teasing every male she had the opportunity to. "Oh, the horses are gone," made Donald smile.

Donald watched the horses come into view. Christine noticed her mother stood by Donald; she dismounted about to speak. Her mother put her finger to her lips, "Careful with that tongue, daughter. You're on borrowed time. How're the horses, Sophie," Josephine offered her hand for the first time.

Christine intervened, "They're excellent, mother, for their intended purpose."

Josephine glared, "I didn't ask you, daughter."

"How should I address you, Miss Gibbs, Josephine." Sophie shrugged her shoulders.

"Josephine will be fine, Sophie; thank you for asking."

"In answer to your question, I have ridden these horses for two years. I know them all individually; they have excellent temperaments and will suffer inexperienced riders providing they do nothing foolish."

"We'll take a ride, Sophie," Josephine expressed. "You want to come, Donald?"

"No thanks, Josephine, you enjoy yourself," Donald smiled.

"You could be missing a golden opportunity, Donald. You could have an extra ride if you come along." Donald burst out laughing; he knew exactly what she was referring to. Christine's glowing like a beetroot. Sophie laughed, catching on to what Josephine was referring to. Sophie saddles two horses that haven't been ridden for her and Josephine. Josephine blew a kiss to Donald, "Love you, manager," she teased.

Mrs Montague had tuned into the external surveillance cameras watching Josephine perform, hearing what she'd said to Donald and Christine. She sat quietly drinking her tea, extremely amused and, in some respects, surprised Josephine would discipline her daughter, making her realise she wasn't top dog this time.

"Donald, remove my mother's lipstick from your face, please," Christine asked, annoyed.

Donald removed his handkerchief. Christine snatched it from his hand, licking the corner of the handkerchief and removing her mother's lipstick forcefully. Donald's trying not to grin. Christine's about to speak; he threw her over his shoulder. He hadn't done that since they were back together, smacking her backside, running upstairs with her throwing her on the bed. She couldn't stop giggling, quickly removing her clothes, watching him advance with anticipation. After a while, they showered together. Christine felt relaxed, convinced her mother hadn't made love to her boyfriend; his stamina didn't waver.

***

Mary and Martin were sitting in the kitchen at home, wondering how Donald's coping, beginning to wish he'd never become involved with Christine. Gerald arrived, knocking on the door, entering, sitting at the table, and watching Mary make tea. "I'm spraying your oilseed rape today, Martin," Gerald smiled. "Why do you two look so worried," Gerald asked suspiciously.

"We are worried about Donald," Mary sighed.

Gerald laughed, "I don't know why he can handle Christine, no flies on your son Mary. Christine phoned me yesterday; Donald had punched the living daylights out of Robbie for cheating on Maggie. Robbie's face resembles a football. Donald's a clever lad; you would have to rise early in the morning to have one over on him. Stop worrying about him, and enjoy your life. Honestly, I don't care what Christine's up to anymore. I have Cindy, time for me to enjoy my life before it's over."

Martin nodded in agreement, "You're right; Gerald, worrying won't make any difference only help us into an early grave."

"I'll catch you both later; bye for now," Gerald said, leaving with a spring in his step. Martin grabbed Mary's hand. She looked at

Martin suspiciously. "Come on, woman, have some fun equivalent to a five-mile run without leaving the house," Martin laughed.

Mary grinned, "If you can manage three miles, I'll think myself lucky." Martin looked shocked at her comment, chasing Mary into the bedroom as if they were teenagers.

***

Donald decided he needed some fresh air; slipping on his jacket, he walked past the waterwheel to the reservoir, seeing trout swimming. He followed the old track to the small plateau venturing into the conifer forest. He watched a pine Martin moving from tree to tree, probably after a grey squirrel. Walking deeper into the wood, Donald continued observing the wildlife. Pheasants were abundant. The remnants of shoots were discontinued on the estate. After some time, Donald appeared to leave the woodland onto an expanse of heather, hearing grouse realising he must be at quite an elevation suffering from the cold. Donald had no idea where he was. Wherever he looked, more mountains and hills. The ground is wet underfoot; he could be in serious trouble if not careful. He decided to follow the perimeter of the wood. He guessed it would be some distance to walk, remembering he's advised the estate has five thousand acres; nevertheless, he should see somewhere he recognised, giving him some direction for Glencoe.

Josephine and Sophie had returned to the stables. "Excellent, Josephine," commented, "You will do very well here; you certainly know horses inside out; it won't be long before you're taking tours around the estate," Josephine smiled, walking off, leaving Sophie to deal with the horses.

Christine's becoming concerned that no one has seen Donald as the twilight of the evening approaches. Christine walked along to the sawmill, hoping he's sat there in one of his favourite places. Nigel had gone home; she walked into the workshop sitting on the workbench, wondering where Donald could be, startled seeing the door open on the workshop and Robbie walk in. She looked at the state of his face, still very swollen; his eyes were black. "Have you seen Donald, Robbie? He's missing."

"No, Donald will be okay."

"Thanks for not mentioning our relationship Robbie; otherwise, I'd be in real trouble," she remarked, lifting Robbie's kilt.

"Nay, lassi were asking for trouble. Donald is aware of what happened some time ago. If he said nothing to you, let sleeping dogs lie."

Christine shrugged her shoulders, "he said nothing."

Christine stepped out of her jeans and knickers; she parted her legs smiling, lifting herself onto the workbench. Robbie lifted his kilt, thrusting his cock into her. She lifted her jumper, opened her blouse, and lifted her bra so Robbie could hold her breasts. Robbie stood at the edge of the bench, thrusting into her having her legs over his shoulders. She thought her eyes would pop out the man is undoubtedly well blessed and far superior to Donald. They spent half an hour before Robbie came. Christine looked outside, quickly finding a corner to have a pee, returning to dress. Robbie turned and walked out of the workshop, not saying another word, not wanting to associate with a woman, especially Donald's girlfriend. The last thing he needed was to be caught with her. Maggie's heading home observing Robbie leaving the sawmill; she naturally suspected he was up to no good. She parked; seeing Christine leave the workshop, they glared at each other. "Have you been with my husband, Christine, again? I can't wait for Donald to discover he already knows about your previous escapades with my husband."

Robbie's walking along the track towards Maggie and Christine. "Don't be absurd, Maggie. Donald is missing; that's why I'm here I don't know why Robbie's here?" She shrugged, "You think I would jeopardise my future with Donald by messing about with Robbie. Come off it, Maggie. I know you have been in here with my fiancé kissing him."

Maggie was shocked; she stayed silent. Robbie approached with his hands in the air, "Not guilty of anything, lass, neither is Christine. Apparently, Donald is missing. That's why Christine's here.

Maggie jumped in her car heading for home, leaving Robbie and Christine looking at each other. Christine realised if Maggie said anything to Donald, suspicion alone would be sufficient to finish the fragile relationship.

Mrs Montague had seen events and was quite happy to intervene if she had to on this occasion and lie for Christine. She would say she's using a drone, not wishing anyone to realise the sawmills monitored. Mrs Montague using a drone, had located Donald, realising he wouldn't make it to Glencoe before dark without assistance. The only safe way of travelling would be on horseback because of the terrain.

Mrs Montague contacted Sophie via mobile, explaining where Donald was and to take a horse for him; otherwise, he'd be trapped on the hillside for the night and probably freeze to death. Sophie didn't hesitate. She saddled two horses galloping off, surprising everyone, no one realising she was on a rescue mission. She could barely see where she was riding when she saw Donald sitting on a tree stump, looking bewildered and lost.

Sophie immediately dismounted, wrapping Donald in a thermal blanket to maintain his body heat for a moment, cuddling him inside the blanket to generate more warmth. His hands were frozen; she rubbed vigorously, improving circulation. She removed a small bottle of whisky. He took a few sips that started warming his soul. "Come on, have you home, Donald," standing packing the blanket away. She helped Donald mount the horse. Donald commented, "Poor animal, I'm too heavy for him." The horse neighed, "See, even the horse agrees," Donald said, making Sophie smile. Sophie held the reins of Donald's horse, slowly making their way down the hillside in the dark until they came onto the well-worn track, eventually seeing the hotel lights on Glencoe.

Mrs Montague, in her wisdom, had notified reception of what was taking place. Christine, her mother, and staff members were deeply concerned for Donald's welfare. Thankfully Sophie's trained in first aid and rescuing people.

Donald realised he'd taken on the right person; she would be a godsend in an emergency. The stables were floodlit, Christine and Josephine watching Sophie and Donald ride into the light. Sophie quickly dismounted, helping Donald off his horse; he's as stiff as a board from the mileage he'd walked and the cold. Sophie called out, "Christine, take him to the hotel to warm up quickly. He's freezing." Christine helped him into the hotel. Josephine approached, "Sophie, marvellous rescue Donald knew exactly who to employ, proud to have you as a team member," Josephine hugged Sophie taking her by surprise. "Before you go, come into the hotel, please."

Donald sat by the fire, shivering with the cold. Christine knelt before him, "Donald, I have something to say. You will have to believe my story; otherwise, I don't know what to do. We were looking for you. I walked to the sawmill looking in the workshop. Robbie arrived, we said a few words, and he left. Maggie returning from her shop, I presume and saw him coming out of the workshop, discovering me there. She put two and two together. She thinks, you know, I promise you I haven't."

Donald smiled, "That's okay. Sophie took all my clothes off, and we made passionate love on the hillside," he smirked, drinking a small glass of malt whisky and watching Christine's expression while she worked out; he's pulling her leg. "Pig, you do, believe me, Donald, please?"

"Depends on how much you warm me later. I'll know for sure," he grinned. Christine realised old Donald in action. Justin came in, in his usual, I'm on a mission stance, "I have ordered locators for every member of staff when they're out in the hills in case they are injured or lost. We will easily find anyone, Donald."

"Some people might object, Justin, may consider your spying. Have you considered the possibility?"

"The doors in that direction, if they object, have something obvious to hide; we don't need people like that working for Glencoe."

Donald and Christine looked at each other, "You had better have a drink, Justin; I don't think you're well you're frightening me making decisions like that," Donald laughed.

Justin grinned, "You don't change, Donald." Receiving a drink from a waitress. Sophie came in looking very nervous. "My hero," Donald expressed.

Justin asked, "Sophie, would you have an objection to carrying a tracker when you're out in the wilds."

"Not in the slightest. I know how to deactivate if I'm with a handsome man," she winked at Donald. He blushed; Christine saw the funny side of Sophie's behaviour, not suspecting her of anything. Justin smiled, "I see you're a bundle of fun; you'll be as bad as Donald and Christine."

"I think you're very sensible, Justin; I didn't think I'd become lost. Taught me a valuable lesson," Donald remarked, standing up and kissing Sophie on the cheek, "Thanks for saving me."

Donald retired to bed. Christine joined him, realising that's a narrow escape, not only for Donald but for herself if he hadn't believed what she'd said.

Donald's up bright and early, leaving Christine asleep in bed. He went to Justin's cottage, entering the spare bedroom allocated as an art room. He sketched with some vigour the scene of Sophie rescuing him in the freezing wind cutting across the hillside in the twilight of the evening. He spent most of the day using the photo he'd taken of Sophie for features. He would have copies made, one to be hung in the hotel with a plaque expressing her skill in rescuing him.

Donald parcelled the canvas by 7 o'clock in the evening, ordering a courier to collect it from reception, notifying Jack that a painting was on the way, transmitting a photo to him. Jack thought the scene was excellent; Donald's dramatic expression betrayed himself and Sophie. Donald never failed to produce a compelling portrait from a mundane setting.

Sophie had no idea Donald had painted her in a portrait. Donald left the room starving, heading into the hotel and sitting alone in the dining room, enjoying a meal everyone else had finished. Christine entered, "I guessed where you were; I can see by the paint in your hair; I thought best not to disturb you. How long are we staying here for Donald?"

"Quite honestly, I don't know. I'll have to check with Justin if there are any more issues," Donald smiled, seeing Justin coming into the dining room and sitting on the opposite side of the table. "We have bookings already for horse riding; I didn't think anything happened that quick. Once they knew Donald Selwyn liked horse riding, I used a little artistic license with my advertisement," Justin grinned.

Donald couldn't stop laughing, "You're worse than Christine," she glared at him, trying not to smile. "You require me here any longer, Justin? I think you have everything under control; you know the rules I've laid down concerning Josephine and Robbie. If either of them steps out of line, phoned me, and I'll be the hatchet man," Donald glared.

Mrs Montague's listening. Donald had changed; she admired his attitude. Failure is now not an option in his mind concerning Glencoe, and anything else could go to hell, which could also mean Christine if she wasn't careful.

Josephine wandered into the dining room, draping her arm around Donald's neck, driving Christine wild with jealousy. "I'm leaving Donald this evening. Could I have money please for a taxi fare to the airport from the Glencoe Estate account? I'm rather short."

"No, the agreement is you would not have your sticky fingers in Glencoe's finances. I believe a trust fund was provided for you by your parents. If you misspend your allowance, that's not my fault," Donald opened his wallet, "Two hundred pounds will cover the cost. You must have booked a return ticket to France so don't bull shit me, Josephine." Josephine struck him with her crop. Donald jumped to his feet, laying her on the table, spanking her backside until she screamed in agony. Christine stood holding her cheeks; she'd never seen anything like this. She wasn't intervening. Her mother had struck Donald first, not the other way around. Josephine stood shocked, "You're dismissed!"

"Good, I can go home! I look forward to purchasing Glencoe when you go bankrupt, Josephine. I will notify the press I have nothing to do with Glencoe Estate any longer." Donald walked for the door, followed by Christine, still in shock. Justin didn't know which way to go. Josephine rubbed her backside. "Donald!" Josephine insisted, "Okay, I won't touch the bloody money, you bastard," throwing her riding crop at him. Donald caught it in the air and walked towards her. Her eyes enlarged, suspecting he wouldn't dare. He pushed her over the table, whipping her backside twice. "Mess with me, woman, and you will pay. I could destroy you in the press in a second, be careful."

Mrs Montague watching from her concealed camera. No one had ever punished Josephine like that before and told her what she could and could not do. Mrs Montague's shocked. Donald's a force to be reckoned with, feared absolutely nothing, as her bodyguard discovered. She wondered if this might straighten Josephine further, realising she didn't walk on water and no one was there to protect her.

Donald shouted, "Christine pack our bags; we're leaving here permanently. Your mother is a drunk compulsive gambler. She dares to call herself your mother." Donald walked out of the dining room. Christine had never known him to be so resolute. Josephine sat at the dining room table, crying. Justin walked out. He knew without Donald, they were finished.

"Donald, please calm down," Christine asked, "I think you shocked the living daylights out of my mother certainly have me," she exhaled. "Give her a minute to compose herself. She will realise she's made a mistake. You gave her enough money for a taxi to the airport, and you're right. She does have a return ticket to France. Mrs Montague will be there to protect her; I'm surprised she hasn't arrived."

"Perhaps a little hard, but she takes the piss trying to flaunt herself around me to access the accounts; it won't happen, including you," he glared at Christine. Christine walked out of the room wondering if she had made a mistake with Donald; money was fine, but an aggressive boyfriend who laid the law down was not what she was looking for.

Christine found her mother in the dining room; she placed an arm around her shoulder, "Mother, I thought you liked being struck with a whip."

Josephine started laughing, "Daughter, what are you suggesting," drying her eyes. "Donald's right he worked so hard and you to salvage the messes I created. Now it's all gone. Donald won't help me anymore. I wanted this to be yours in the future; it's yours now if you hadn't been silly." Josephine grinned. "The other men any good?"

"I'm not answering that, mother," Christine turned crimson. "I can talk Donald around. He will continue to run Glencoe for us both; mother, don't worry, he gave you money. Here, another five hundred pounds from my allowance should see you to France," Christine and her mother hugged.

Donald's stood outside the dining room, listening to the mother and daughter's conversation and mentioning Christine's sexual encounters. He stepped away from the door heading for the stables stroking the horses with their heads over the stable doors. Donald wondered what he was trying to achieve. He had sufficient money to live a charmed life without becoming involved with complicated people who were determined to destroy him with their cunning, deceitful behaviour.

Christine saw her mother off in a taxi. She found Donald talking to the horses, "You will continue to run, Glencoe Donald, please?"

"Until someone has her sticky fingers in the accounts," holding Christine's hand, making their way to their suite.

After breakfast the following day, they packed their belongings, heading home after assuring Justin, Donald's still in charge, and Justin's to contact him for any reason. They actually make good time. It almost seemed as if Donald's Bentley knew the road and were home just after lunch; admittedly, he's bending the speed limit most of the time. Donald dropped Christine off at home and continued to Crabtree Farm, dashing up into the studio, flopping on the bed falling asleep.

***

The next day the postman delivered a registered parcel for Christine Gibbs. Gerald signed for it, passing it to Christine at the breakfast table. Christine smiled, "I suspect it's my engagement ring returned; Mrs Montague said she'd have repaired," she carefully opened the box; she studied it closely. You couldn't see any damage. The ring was perfectly repaired. She slipped on her engagement finger, feeling closer to Donald.

***

Donald's inspecting the fields, the oilseed rape in full flower, pondering what he should paint next. He returned to the cottage sitting with his mother, who passed his breakfast. "Donald, would you move the fifth wheel to Torquay so your father and I could nip down there for holidays. We've selected a camp-site, spoken to the owner we can pay the site fees, what you think?"

"Why don't I buy you a cottage in a seaside village. You wouldn't have any hassle; you'd have another home you could walk into and not share with anyone. I could easily purchase for about half a million," he suggested eating his fried bread.

Mary hugged him, "You are a wonderful son; you can have the property back when we pass away, so it's like an investment," she smiled.

Martin is already on the Internet, "Look at this place on the coast next to Torquay. We really don't want to be in a busy town, only five minutes drive from the beach, four-hundred and seventy-four-thousand pounds, three nice bedroomed and gardens, and look at the view."

"You better pack a bag and check it out." Donald phoned the estate agent, "My mother and father are interested in coming to look at a property; the name is Selwyn."

"You wouldn't be related to Donald Selwyn, the artist," the female estate agent asked.

"You are speaking to him," Donald heard a little scream in the background, making him chuckle.

"Right, Mr Selwyn," she cleared her throat, noting the property, "We look forward to meeting your parents later today. Phone the office when they arrive at the property only five minutes away. Thank you for phoning."

Mary kissed Donald on the cheek. "Don't buy rubbish, mother. Purchase what you want, look at something else, enjoy the journey," Donald smiled, watching his parents rush out of the house, jumping in their Range Rover.

Donald received a phone call from Justin, "I have some information come to me this morning. Robbie overstepped the mark by sleeping with Josephine. This liaison has gone on for years. Josephine thinks she can do what she likes, and so does Robbie. He's under the illusion he has her protection; as you can appreciate, Maggie's devastated. He actually boasted about it in the kitchen to her."

"Leave it with me, Justin; sit tight; I'll deal with the situation from this end and will be with you shortly."

Donald wasn't surprised to see Mrs Montague drive into the yard. She had a new bodyguard instruct him to stay in the car; Donald opened the front door, pouring two coffees into mugs. He's disillusioned with the so-called Royal connection. Donald pulled out a chair for Mrs Montague. She smiled, "I've heard Donald; Josephine has confessed to the liaison; the woman is a raving lunatic. I thought she was progressing nicely. Where do we go from here? We obviously don't want a scandal or Josephine's name mentioned? What you do with Robbie is your affair; from what I've heard of his behaviour after you cautioned him, he's not exemplary."

Donald took a deep breath, "Josephine is a bloody menace wherever she goes. Glencoe is her property, Mrs Montague. They are both over 18, so it is not as if they're breaking the law. Although I think the scandal would do you no favours if the press cottoned on, labelling Glencoe as a knocking shop."

"I can prevent her from coming to England. I wish I wasn't so lenient this time. I really felt she was trying to make amends for everything. I thought mother and daughter would be reasonable another mistake I made," Mrs Montague frowned.

"The solution, make Josephine send a letter directly to Justin and me stating she wishes Robbie to be dismissed. Robbie will realise he has nowhere to go other than leave peacefully. I'll be there to ensure he does; could you make that happen, Mrs Montague?"

Mrs Montague dialled a number on her mobile, speaking in French. From the tone of her voice, she was ordering somebody to do something now. She smiled, finishing her coffee, "The letter will be there when you arrive in Scotland, Donald. Thank you for your support in this difficult situation; of course, Maggie to be considered. She could always move in with her father, I suppose. You will want the property to take on another member of staff."

"We shall see, one step at a time, Mrs Montague." She rose to her feet, kissing Donald on both cheeks, "I hope Christine is not causing you as much stress, Donald; keep her in check, watch closely."

"Christine blows hot and cold you never know where you stand with her," he frowned.

***

Christine received a phone call from Tim, "I'm walking around the public footpath; you want to join me; Christine, have a chat. I'll allow you to kiss me if you smile." Christine burst out laughing. Tim's always good fun, and most girls quite liked him. "Okay, I'll meet you on the ridge in half an hour; bye." Christine hadn't realised her father caught the tail end of the conversation standing in the hallway.

Christine ventured out of the house, taking her dog Scooby-Doo walking along the track, it wasn't long before Tim, and she found each other on the ridge, quite a high spot you could see for miles. "You still with Donald, Christine," Tim asked, smiling. "By the way, my friends and I were impressed with your leaving present; no one will say anything, Christine; I promise you, and you have a marvellous body."

"Thanks, yes, trying to mend a few fences after what happened," She frowned.

"People have short memories," he placed his arm around her waist; she looked at him then decided it didn't matter; he kissed her on the cheek. They walked for some distance approaching the reserve; the heavens opened and started to rain. They ran into the old strawberry shed sheltering from the rain. Christine walked to the back of the shed, removing a box of matches from her coat. She lit one or two broken strawberry boxes making a fire; this brought memories flooding back of Oliver. She thought how strange to be in the same place. They sat on two crates warming their hands. Scooby-Doo had gone over into the corner, lying down.

***

Donald tried to phone Christine, but her mobile was off. He sighed heavily and jumped in his car, heading for Glencoe, wondering about the best course of action and feeling extremely sorry for Maggie. Donald arrived, resting in his fifth wheel. He went straight to sleep.

***

Tim kissed Christine on the cheek; she looked at him strangely, and then he kissed her on the lips. She couldn't resist; she felt him unzip her coat, easing her to her feet, holding her breasts, releasing her jeans. He removed a condom from his pocket. She knew this was wrong, and Donald would not forgive her. "No, Tim, I can't," she tidied herself quickly. "I've gone too far now."

Neither Tim nor Christine had realised Gerald had used the locator on Christine's mobile to find her. He quietly entered the shed and tried to hear the conversation watching Christine tidying herself, suspecting the worst. That's all he needed to see; carrying his shotgun stood glaring, shouting, making them both jump. "What the fucking hell are you playing at Christine? You boy off my property, and what's your name."

"Tim Jenkins." Tim ran for his life. He didn't want to be shot, hiding behind the shed if his father found out and probably be kicked out of the house. His father wouldn't accept any scandal whatsoever. Gerald pointed his shotgun at Scooby-Doo, instantly discharging both barrels and killing the dog. Christine screamed, crying, broken-hearted. Gerald walked out of the shed heading for home, leaving Christine crying. Gerald's determined Christine would learn the reprisals for inappropriate behaviour; cheating on Donald once bad twice is outrageous. Gerald walked into the house. Cindy looked at his expression, asking urgently, "What have you done?"

Gerald explained, "She's in the old strawberry shed with a boy, Tim Jenkins. I suspect Donald will know him, and if I were him, I'd leave the country, although I suspect Donald will throw the towel in this time. When I caught them, she's just easing her breast back in her bra." Gerald shrugged his shoulders, "She's worse than her mother."

Gerald texts Donald a message detailing what he'd seen and heard. Donald woke reading the info, realising Gerald hadn't said they actually were having sex. He knew Tim Jenkins, a lady's man like Oliver, but why is Christine in the shed with him?

Concerned, Donald entered the shower and changed his clothes, entering the hotel and sitting for breakfast. Justin joined, him holding a letter. Donald scanned the letter with the heading Josephine Spires, owner of Glencoe Estate, Josephine's using her maiden name. "I am instructing you to dismiss Robbie without further delay." The letter was signed and dated by Josephine Spires.

"You want me to deal with this, Justin, or can you?"

"I'm Estate Manager Donald, my responsibility if he gives me any trouble. I'll call you. To be quite honest, I think he will leave peaceably. Maggie has stayed at her shop in her one-bedroom flat."

"I didn't know. I was concerned about the accommodation problem. I intended to move my art equipment from your cottage to ensure she had room to move in with you."

"Look what's arrived, Donald prints of your portrait depicting your rescue, would you like to show Sophie. There are ten here, I presume one for the stables, one for the hotel and the others to be sold?"

Donald nodded, taking a print to the stables. Sophie was busy brushing a horse. Donald entered the extended tack room, which had been recently added. He used four drawing pins to fasten the print to the wall. Sophie came in to see what was happening, totally shocked, seeing herself in print in a rescue scene. "Now everybody knows your clever, this one, and one hung in the hotel with a plaque stating your heroic behaviour."

"Thanks, Donald; where's Christine? Is she riding today?"

"I wouldn't know; she's at Strawberry Estate on her father's farm, as far as I know," he said, less than enthusiastic.

"Oh, it's like that, sorry, life's a bitch until you die." She went to kiss him on the cheek, and Donald kissed her on the lips. They stood looking at each other for a moment. He kissed her again on the lips, she didn't say anything returning to continue working with her horse. Donald returned to the hotel, jumped in his car, driving to the village, deciding he was fed up taking the high moral ground; everybody around him appeared to be stabbing him in the back. He entered Maggie's shop; she was surprised to see him. "You were right about Christine," Donald showed the text messages he received this morning.

Maggie sighed, "Sorry, Donald, I don't know what to say. I guess you know Robbie and I are finished; staying here now. He confessed to having sex with Christine in the workshop. She's just like her mother."

"Yes, he's dismissed; your father's dealing with him; he wanted to as Estate Manager. Of course, Robbie could be boasting, trying to upset you, Maggie. Christine said nothing happened?"

Maggie cuddled him. Donald embraced for several minutes. They kissed once more, looking into each other's eyes. Donald left, returning to the estate and Justin's office. "He's gone, Donald; he'd already packed his bags. Silly man, he had good employment here, a good wife. I hope you and Christine have a success story."

510

Donald showed the text message to Justin. Justin put his hand to his mouth, passing the phone back. "What is the matter with people these days, Donald?"

"I'm off to your cottage, Justin, painting this morning to relax," he sighed.

After switching on his computer, Donald sat in front of the canvas, finding Tim Jenkins in the school photos. Now Donald remembered him. Donald depicted the old strawberry shed, placing Christine topless and Tim having sex with her in the scene. The first portrait he'd ever painted of a potential love scene, although it wasn't of particular interest to him. He suspected some people would recognise the pair, hopefully causing them embarrassment now and in the future. He painted away until 8 o'clock in the evening, finally completing, sending a photo to Jack. He almost went mad, shouting down the phone, "I want that portrait; worth millions; it looks great, transport to me Donald, what is the title."

"Betrayal."

"Oh my god! She hasn't? Not again."

Donald turned his phone off. Jack knew he was right; he could willingly shoot Christine himself, although she brought out the best in Donald with his broken heart painting. Donald carefully packed the portrait away for transport, and the courier collected it at ten in the evening.

***

Mrs Montague's absolutely fuming receiving Gerald's text message to Donald explaining what he'd seen Christine involved in. Mrs Montague held her forehead in disbelief; Christine would be so stupid.

***

Christine realised her dog was dead. Okay, she's a little naughty, not all the way, and her dog certainly didn't deserve to die. Tim had hidden behind the shed until he saw Christine's father leaving and heading along the track. "You okay, Christine? I'm sorry about your dog. I hadn't realised your father was in here."

Christine threw more old strawberry boxes on the fire; she's determined if she's blamed for something, she might as well enjoy the experience. Christine removed her clothes standing in front of Tim, "What are you waiting for, Tim," Christine lay on the old hessian sack. Tim didn't need asking twice soon making love. She suspected her relationship with Donald was over. There was no turning the clock back this time.

***

Donald sat in the lounge in the hotel, drinking malt whisky. Sophie walked in this time in a beautiful figure-hugging silver dress you wouldn't want to breathe in; there wasn't much left to the imagination. She purchased a drink. Donald said, "I'll pay for that," inviting her to join him.

She sat with her gin and tonic, realising she had caught Donald's attention. If he's now available, she's determined to state her claim. Not only is he good-looking, but wealthy, a rare combination these days. Donald commented, "Next time I want rescuing, please come dressed like that; you look absolutely stunning, Sophie."

"Don't drink too much, Donald. It won't solve the problem. You need a clear head; I wondered if you'd be over here tonight. I thought I'd keep you company for an hour. I've had someone break my heart in the past; I know the feeling too well, Donald. Ever since then, my true love is horses their loyal and trustworthy. I haven't worn this dress in three years; I'm surprised it still fits," she chuckled.

Donald smiled, "Oh yes, it fits fine," trying to put his eyes back in their sockets.

"Come on, Donald, you better return to your caravan before you can't walk anymore." She helped him out of the hotel to the caravan. "Would you like a coffee before I go, Donald?"

He laughed, quite intoxicated, holding her hand, sitting Sophie on his lap, kissing her neck softly and on the lips. "No, Donald, you are on the rebound. Asked me in a couple of weeks when you've had a chance to think things through; I'm not a pushover," she kissed him, and he placed his arms around her waist. She could feel the power of him pulling her closer, "I have to breathe, Donald. I must go." Sophie left content with the situation. Donald was confused at this precise second, although he had shown some feelings towards her. She wanted to make sure the real thing before committing to him. She realised her life would change forever if she were with him, her security secured.

CHAPTER FIFTEEN

NOWHERE TO HIDE

Donald stayed at Glencoe for two more days, the painting all over the news, "Over between Christine Gibbs and Donald Selwyn, has she betrayed him for the final time," the caption read. The newspapers were full of speculation. Christine hid in her bedroom. Whatever she watched on television or on the Internet showed Donald's artwork of her and Tim. Tim's parents realise it was him, and he's sent to America to live with his aunt for the moment to avoid publicity.

Mary and Martin Selwyn were oblivious to what had happened and could only say, "We have no idea or comment; we don't know where Donald is."

***

Mrs Montague's spitting feathers, she never expected Donald to destroy Christine; no way she could cover the mess too late. The only solution she could offer was to take Christine to France and wait for the dust to settle. She suspected no going back this time. Christine had really cooked her goose.

Donald couldn't prevent grinning, enjoying the misery he was inflicting on Christine. Why should he be the only one that suffered? The press approached him for a story. Donald stood in front of Glencoe Hotel. The reporter asked, "Could we have a comment from you, Donald, concerning Miss Gibbs and yourself."

"You are all aware that Christine's less than faithful before we were about to marry. Thanks to a friend phoning me, I discovered her deception. On this occasion, her father notified me of her indiscretion; you obviously can't marry someone like that. I can't."

"We understand Christine Gibbs's mother owns this property. Why are you still here?"

"I have made many friends here, which I will be sad to say goodbye to. However, I may have found my future wife here quite by accident. Early days."

"Will you give us her name? Who is she?"

Sophie rode past, taking visitors on a tour of the estate; she looked at Donald and waved. "Is that the young lady?"

Donald shrugged his shoulders, "Watch this space," he grinned.

Christine sat in her bedroom watching the interview on television, tears streaming down her cheeks. Her fault and Donald found someone else to fill his heart full of love. She sighed heavily.

The following day across the newspapers, Donald's portrait had reached fifteen million. Donald walked to the stables, finding Sophie, holding her hand, taking her into the tack room, and kissing her passionately. "I saw the interview on television. Donald, apparently, you have selected your girlfriend and wife; that's presumptuous. I haven't gone on a date with you." Jock came across to the stables patting Donald on the shoulder, "Sorry for your troubles, lad, sorry to see you go. If I had a better job, I wouldn't work for these bastards either."

"You're a good sort, Jock; I'll miss your happy smile."

That made Jock laugh. "Grab something to eat, the pair of you. I'll finish the horses."

Donald held Sophie's hand. "I have my sandwiches in the tack room, Donald."

"You won't be eating them today; you're coming with me." They entered the hotel into a private dining room; Donald had secretly arranged a lavish lunch for him and Sophie. She sat at the table, watching the food come in with a dozen red roses. Donald's pulling out all the stops, also a gold bracelet. Sophie didn't know what to look at first. He's lavishing every luxury he could think of on her. "My last night here before returning home, I will return with my American truck and remove my caravan."

"If you're serious about me, Donald, where do we go from here if you are no longer associated with Glencoe Estate. Neither of us could drive six hundred miles on the weekend and return for work."

"I may buy a property here, an estate if I can find one, I like, or purchase a farm anywhere in the country and see what transpires." Donald fastened the bracelet to Sophie's wrist; she kissed him on the lips, "You shouldn't waste your money, Donald." Sophie returned to work, and Donald tried to decide what to do next.

***

Christine went out to place flowers on Scooby Doo's grave. She saddled The Rising Sun taking a ride across the estate. Cindy and her father were not speaking to her. Christine wondered if she dared go to Crabtree Farm, suspecting the reception would be frosty. She'd performed nothing wrong to start with, then her pig-headedness compelled her to go all the way. How stupid.

Christine phoned Donald, he saw her name appear on the phone, he answered. "Yes!"

"I didn't have sex with him, Donald. I walked with Scooby-Doo and met Tim. We sat there talking because of the rain; from where my father was, it probably looked different from what had happened. I brushed my jeans, zipping my coat; I'm not guilty of anything. My father shot my dog as punishment. Will you come and see me when you return from Glencoe. I saw your nasty interview before you had all the facts."

"Okay, I'm a glutton for punishment."

"I love you, Donald, even if you are cruel to me." Christine disconnected the call laughing at the top of her voice, convinced she would have him back under her control. She'd switched off the tracker from her phone, so no one knew where she was.

Mrs Montague had listened to the conversation, wondering if Christine's deception would hold up under scrutiny, and gave the girl full marks for trying if nothing else.

Donald's in his motorhome watching television. He couldn't drink; he was driving early in the morning. Donald looked at his bank account forty-five million, a figure he couldn't even imagine possessing. A faint knock on the caravan door Donald opened. Sophie, he immediately smiled, inviting her in; she sat beside him on the settee, watching the television. She held his hand, leading him into the bedroom, slowly removing her clothes. Donald's eyes were transfixed as she released her bra lying on the bed. Donald couldn't control himself; Sophie is better proportioned than Christine any day. She's so different to make love to. She stayed with him until the early hours kissing him on the forehead as she left, realising he was all man and never held like that before, and he would be so easy to love. There wasn't an unkind bone in his body except if he was angry.

Donald awoke to have a quick coffee, threw his belongings in his Bentley, and headed home. A quiet and uneventful journey; he parked in the yard carrying his suitcase upstairs to the studio. Mary and Martin cautiously entered, Mary saying calmly, "We haven't bothered you, Donald, once we'd seen the portrait and what's said on the news. We guessed buying any property would be the last thing on your mind."

"You like the place?"

"Oh yes, you should see the views, Donald, and you're only five minutes from Torquay. Here is the estate agents' card."

"Donald dialled the number on the card. "Donald Selwyn, my mother and father looked at a property the other day still available? Good, I'll purchase please subject to a surveyor's report, can you arrange that for me please, thank you. I look forward to hearing from you."

Mary had made everyone a coffee, "What's happening between Christine and you," Mary asked. "We saw the news and the portrait you painted. She's a naughty girl, Donald?"

"Christine phoned me last night denying; she said her father had the wrong end of the stick, and from where he's stood, he wouldn't have been able to see. She's actually zipping her coat, that's all. She's there because she met Tim walking, and both went in there because it was raining her father, so angry shot Scooby-Doo."

Martin and Mary looked at each other. "I can't imagine Gerald mistaken; show me his message, son," Martin asked. Martin read the message, "According to this, he watched her put her breast back in her bra and retrieve her jeans from around her ankles. He'd have no reason to lie. I'm surprised he mentioned, knowing the outcome if Donald discovered; I call that a real friend."

Mary looked at Donald's neck, "You have a love bite, son," she grinned, "Where did you acquire that?"

"I've met someone; her name is Sophie. I employed her to work at Glencoe; the girl rescued me."

"Oh yes, we saw the portrait," Martin remarked, "Is she as good-looking as you betrayed her, Donald?"

"Yes, she's absolutely stunning."

"You've obviously tasted the goods by the mark on your neck," Martin smirked.

Donald refrained from replying. Continued to drink his coffee, deciding to return to Glencoe in the morning with his American truck and move the fifth wheel. He wished he'd met Sophie first rather than Christine. Admittedly Christine helped considerably with the farm when they were in trouble. He had to consider that he'd now been as naughty as her in some respects sleeping with Sophie. As far as he was concerned, he had nothing to hide if Christine noticed the love bite; that's okay in his book. Donald phoned Christine. "Hi, Donald, are you coming to see me?"

"Yes, I said I would."

"Don't come to the house. Meet me at the old strawberry shed, one or two things I want to show you without father butting in."

"Okay, if you insist, see you in ten minutes." Donald drove along the backtrack away from the house so he wouldn't be seen by Gerald and Cindy. He's prepared to give Christine every opportunity to prove her innocence. He parked by the building, watching her walk along the track. He stepped from his car. She held his hand, "Come with me," she insisted.

Christine lit a fire using old boxes, making Donald stand back in the shadows. Donald opened his mobile, reading what Gerald had described. She stood, zipping her coat, "What, you see."

"You, zipping your coat, Christine, that's all."

Donald showed Christine what her father had sent to him; she went into a cold sweat. How could she cover this up? "Perhaps he needs glasses."

"I don't think so, Christine." Donald started walking for the door, noticing a discarded condom suspecting belonged to Tim. "You'll have to give me time to think things over, Christine." Donald jumped in his Bentley, heading home as the heavens opened torrents of rain.

Christine is unsure what to do next, suspecting nothing she could do to salvage the relationship. Donald returned home feeling sorry for Christine and angry she found it necessary to sample other people.

***

Mrs Montague arrived at Strawberry Estate, greeted by Gerald; they went into the living room. Cindy made coffee for everyone. "Sad affair Gerald; I can't understand what possessed Christine to risk her relationship; in fact, her relationship is over, I'm pretty sure, with Donald."

"In some respects, Mrs Montague, I'm pleased Donald is such a nice lad. He would have done anything for her; all he asked for is her loyalty."

"I agree with you, Gerald; I think in light of what's happened, perhaps she should spend some time in France with me on my estate; she may meet Mr right over there. Who knows her motives? Moping around here will not improve the situation."

"What's happening to Glencoe Estate? I suspect Donald will have nothing to do with it now," Gerald asked.

"I know Donald is looking for property, an estate either in Scotland or here to purchase. He also has the makings of a new relationship, someone he's met. She's not the cause of the separation; Christine managed that alone."

"I hope it works out for Donald; he certainly doesn't need another Christine," Cindy professed.

"You know her, Mrs Montague. Is she a good person," Gerald asked.

"She's an adopted child; her mother originally worked at a stately home. She couldn't afford to keep the child, so she placed her up for adoption and went to a respectable family for safekeeping; accidents happen all the time, Gerald," Mrs Montague smiled.

Gerald suspected immediately another Royal mistake covered up; he didn't pass a comment. Christine came into the house realising Mrs Montague's here, she entered the room. "I presume you're taking me to France, Mrs Montague?"

Mrs Montague nodded, "Pack your things. Gerald and Cindy will look after your horse until you return; you never know, you might meet Mr right over there."

"I had Mr right and destroyed everything I wanted. The only solution may be to commit suicide, then I won't have to live with my guilt." Christine burst into tears running upstairs.

Gerald looked to Mrs Montague, who shrugged her shoulders slightly, "I don't know what to do, Gerald; I can't make Donald love her, especially after what she's performed with several men. We wouldn't be in this mess if you didn't send that stupid text message, just given her a roasting. I thought it rather cruel of you to shoot her dog; not necessary. She's suffering enough; I can tell you that for nothing."

***

Donald struggled to sleep, waking at 6:30 in the morning; he threw his suitcase in the back of his American pickup truck heading for Glencoe for the last time. He arrived late afternoon, reversing under the fifth wheel, ready to leave the next day.

Mrs Montague arrived, much to his surprise, by helicopter. "We need to talk, Donald. I appreciate Christine's less than faithful, and we can now add you to the list. However, I understand you have been extremely tolerant of her. Christine is presently in France, where she will stay for some time; give her a chance to grow up and not treat people like dirt. I'm here on Josephine's behalf. Would you please continue to run Glencoe? Marry Sophie if you wish. She's an excellent woman, and I'm sure she will make you very happy."

Donald was astounded by Mrs Montague's comments. "In all honesty, Mrs Montague, I want to run and hide. Regarding Sophie, she's a marvellous girl; I don't want to be responsible for ruining her life. I considered on my way here; am I the reason Christine looked elsewhere for companionship, or am I just a failure."

Mrs Montague hadn't realised how deeply affected Donald is by Christine and presuming he's like all other men, see a pretty woman and they're gone. "Absolutely nothing wrong with you; don't start looking for fault where there is none. No part of her actions can be contributed as a failure on your part. I can assure you, and I don't lie."

"I suppose it reminds me of Christine when I'm here; that's why I want to leave," he exhaled heavily, "You'll have to give me time to think things over, Mrs Montague. I don't know whether I'm coming or going."

Mrs Montague passed him her card, "If you need to talk to me, Donald, here is my number. I have grown very fond of you in the short time we've known each other." Mrs Montague kissed him on both cheeks, boarding her helicopter and flying away.

Donald entered the hotel, purchased two bottles of whisky, entered his fifth wheel, and turned on the television. He started drinking, then stopped realising it would solve nothing. Walking around the stables as Sophie returned with visitors from a tour of the estate on horseback. Her smile could have lit the sky when she saw him. Donald helped her down. She kissed him on the lips, "You've been drinking. Why?"

"Because I'm missing you," he smiled, tapping her backside.

The guests returned to the hotel. Donald helped Sophie remove the saddles, check the horse's hooves, and bed them down.

"Jock's looking after the horses for the weekend; I have a week-end off."

Jock came over. "Jock, you busy next week?"

He shrugged his shoulders, "Not, particularly why?"

"Would you do me a favour? Look after the horses next week; I want to take Sophie away."

Sophie looked alarmed, "Don't I get consulted, Donald. Who pays my salary? I have bills to pay like everybody else; you don't know I haven't planned my weekend away?"

"Have you planned something?" Donald asked curiously.

"No, apart from seeing if I can afford a new car on finance," she frowned.

Jock started laughing, "You silly girl, go with him. You're not finding a better man, I promise you, and he is always true to his word. I found that out the hard way, so have many others around the estate; I'll look after the bloody horses, don't worry."

Sophie stood, frowning, "Okay, where are you taking me?"

"Home to where I live and see if you like the area."

"Oh, Christine lives close to you. I don't want to bump into her; I hate feeling awkward, Donald."

"No chance. She's in France to stay with friends, so Mrs Montague informed me about ten minutes ago."

"That's okay if you're sure."

"Where are your parents," Donald asked curiously.

"I'm a reject. I'm adopted, and my foster parents have a small-holding in the Scottish Highlands north of Tain. My foster parents worked on an estate until they had saved enough money to buy a smallholding, and we moved there."

"Would you like me to meet your parents before I take you home? If they object, we won't go," Donald smiled.

"I'm over eighteen, Donald. I don't need parents' approval," kissing him on the lips. Donald held Sophie's hand, taking her into the hotel in her riding outfit. They sat at the dining table, enjoying a lovely meal. Justin approached, "You're not leaving us, Donald," he asked seriously.

"Not at the moment, but I'm stealing Sophie next week. Jock said he could cover and was happy to do so; I'll cover Sophie's salary."

Justin grinned, "Donald, my Maggie, has found a nice man; I think they will wed once she and Robbie are divorced."

"Good, I'm glad she's finally happy, Justin; I'll leave the fifth wheel here and my pickup truck. Can you book a helicopter to fly Sophie and me to Crabtree Farm, please?"

"No, I'm not flying. I tried once and hated it. We will drive," Sophie insisted.

"The lady has spoken, we will nip over to where you're staying, Sophie, and you can grab some clothes after we've eaten."

"Okay, I only rent a small room in a house, all I can afford; don't you start thinking I live in Buckingham Palace."

They travelled in Sophie's old car. It coughed and spluttered at every opportunity; finally, they came to a small village some ten miles away. She parked outside a run-down house. They entered the converted house, now four flats running upstairs entering her flat. The place looked like a bomb site; to be quite honest, how she could survive in these conditions, he didn't know. She packed her suitcase. A bang on the door, Donald opened. "Rent."

"How much?"

"Fifty and fifty in arrears."

Donald removed his wallet, passing a hundred pounds. "Receipt," Donald insisted. Sophie gave her rent book to the proprietor, who signed the book as paid and left. "I'll pay you back, Donald; sorry."

"No, you won't. You'll not return to this tip other than to collect your belongings; I'm not happy with you living in these conditions." Sophie locked the door and climbed into her old car, which coughed and spluttered to Glencoe. They walked to his caravan, the fifth wheel. "You sure you want to associate with a poor girl like me, Donald? Half my salary goes on rent."

"Money has nothing to do with what I'm interested in; I'm looking for that special person to fill my life and make me happy. I have more money than you could ever dream about. But that doesn't guarantee happiness, as I've recently learnt the hard way."

Sophie closed the panel taking a shower. She couldn't understand Donald's fascination with her; hundreds of pretty rich women out there who could cater to his every need.

***

Christine's bored stupid in France, missing Donald terribly. She couldn't stop kicking herself for making such a stupid mistake. She walked down into the cellar where it's cooler, finding three employees drinking wine and playing cards. They glared at her strangely; she explained bored when asked why she was here in French. They opened a bottle of wine, pouring her a glass; she suggested they play strip poker. The men laughed and started to play cards. After half an hour and several glasses of wine, she's beginning to feel slightly giddy, struggling to hold her cards groped by the men laughing and joking.

Mr Montague came down into the cellar, and the three men scattered, leaving the cellar by a different route. Mr Montague discovered Christine, "Why are you here."

"I came down here playing cards with three men; they poured me a drink," she slurred.

"Come along, young lady, to your room." He helped Christine up the cellar stairs and returned to her private apartment, sitting Christine gently on the bed. Christine struggled to her feet, "Am I pretty, Mr Montague, is there something wrong with me," she slurred, removing her knickers. Mr Montague, not bothering to look and left the room.

***

The following day, Donald detached the water and grey waste pipes and lifted the jacks. Sophie climbed into the front of the enormous truck, excited by the beautiful night they'd had together; she'd never felt so wanted. They set off for Crabtree Farm. The sun's shining soon be harvest time, and Donald wondering who would drive the combines on Strawberry Estate this year. By 9 o'clock in the evening, Donald parked the fifth wheel behind the barn. Donald carried the suitcases, Sophie close by. They walked the stairs into his studio. She gazed in amazement at his artwork and entered his enormous apartment.

Donald heard his parents on the stairs; they knocked and came in smiling, looking at Sophie. Mary immediately cuddled her, "Welcome to our farm and home, so you're the young lady that stole my son's heart."

"Apparently, so."

"Martin, my husband and I'm Mary, and you must be Sophie." Sophie smiled.

They sat around the table. "Have you finished with Glencoe now, son," Martin asked.

"Not quite; Mrs Montague came to see me yesterday and asked me very nicely on Josephine's behalf if I would continue to monitor, which I agreed to in principle; at least I have a decent reason to travel there now," looking to Sophie.

Martin asked, "Do you have a sister Sophie because I'm coming too." Martin immediately received a slap on the leg from Mary, "That's enough out of you."

"Plenty of food in the cottage if you'd like something to eat," Mary offered.

"No, thanks," Sophie replied.

"No, I have plenty in the fridge; I think mum, if I want a snack."

"I'll see you both in the morning for breakfast." Mary smiled, leaving with Martin, not wishing to question Sophie, making her feel like she was facing an inquisition.

Donald phoned, "Justin, I want you to find accommodation for Sophie on the estate, preferably free of charge. Her salary is appalling. I suggest you give her an increase with her qualifications; the estate can afford it."

"Okay, Donald, I'll sort something out by the time she comes home; I thought we were a little mean with the salary in the first place. That's my fault."

Sophie smiled, shaking her head in disbelief, removed her clothes, and walked into the shower returning sometime later, sliding into bed, patting the other side. Donald soon joined her; they ate each other alive, with real chemistry between them. Donald had never experienced more than sex. Now real love, both exhausted, they finally fell asleep.

Both showered and went for breakfast; Mary wasn't as generous as she used to be with food, understanding the problems it caused. Martin asked, "Can you manage the harvest, Donald, if your mother and I moved to the house you purchased for us near Torquay for a couple of months. You have to learn to manage sooner or later on your own."

"I presume you can drive a tractor, Sophie," Donald asked, panicking.

"Only for moving manure away from the stables."

"Don't worry, I can manage," realising he might have to call on Michael to help, he wouldn't be available to drive Gerald's combine this year.

Gerald entered the yard, knocked on the door, and saw Sophie sitting at the table finishing her coffee. "Quick question Donald will you be available to drive the Lexion this year?"

"Unfortunately, not Gerald, my parents are away on holiday, so I'm stuck with this place on my own."

"Okay," he sighed, "I was expecting that answer; good luck," he smiled, leaving.

Gerald realised he'd not only cut Christine's throat but his own in the process; obvious who the attractive young lady was with Donald. He could kick himself for being so hot-headed.

Donald thought it would only take half a day for the two Lexions to cut all the oilseed rape they were growing, three-hundred acres nothing for the two machines. He rang Gerald, "I might be able to help you, Gerald. You know we are oilseed rape this year. If we use your two Claas, Lexion's shouldn't take many minutes to cut three-hundred acres. Of course, I would be free for the wheat if you're interested; who will drive the other Lexion?"

"Good question; I'm hoping you and Christine worked so well last year; as you know, she's in France now, and I don't know whether I really want her home on the farm."

"Perhaps Michael would help, take him off building repairs for a while, only a couple of weeks, and we are done and dusted, Gerald."

"Thanks, Donald; I think that's a brilliant idea; if you want help with the cultivations and drilling, we have all the kit, as you know; bye, for now, Donald."

Sophie frowned, "I presume Gerald is Christine's father?"

"Yes, we are still friends. Christine and I are finished, and the likelihood of us seeing each other is slim to none," Donald assured. "I don't cheat; I don't expect my girlfriend too," he emphasised.

Sophie's quiet, assessing what he'd said, remembering what Jock told her about him and the rest of Glencoe. He's bomb proofed regarding relationships. Unless you cross him, then he will unleash hell on you.

Donald held Sophie's hand, "Come along, we are shopping,"

She looked at him somewhat puzzled, "For what?"

"Me to know and you to find out," he grinned, jumped in his Bentley, they sped off towards town, parking outside a car dealership. "Pick what you'd like, Sophie," she stared at him in disbelief.

"I haven't known you five minutes, Donald, and you're buying me a car?"

"I wouldn't worry about that if we were stood outside Mothercare, I'd be seriously worried," he laughed.

Sophie laughed, "You are a damn fool; how about that Suzuki over there. I don't like big cars to drive; look a mini, blimey look at the price, eighteen-thousand."

Donald opened the door. She sat inside, " lovely."

The salesperson came over. "We'll take this one." Sophie stared in disbelief.

"Only six months old, four thousand miles on the clock, that's all. She will come with a year's warranty, full roadside assistance and recovery."

They went into the office, and Donald paid with his card. Sophie spoke to her insurance company, and Donald paid the difference on the premium, fully comprehensive cover with legal protection. The salesperson advised it would be ready for Friday for Sophie to return to Glencoe.

Sitting in Donald's Bentley, Sophie turned to face him, "You are very serious about me, aren't you, Donald. No one in their right mind would spend that money on a casual romance."

"Would you like the good news now all the bad?"

She searched his eyes with hers, "I'll start with the good news."

"We are marrying next year."

"What's the bad news," trying to stop laughing.

"You'll have to learn to drive tractors properly and have babies."

"I can handle that, but I want my own horse," she grinned.

"You can have two if you want; you're the best thing that's happened to me."

They returned to the studio. Sophie held his hand, dragging him upstairs. She made two drinks sitting on his lap, "I had no idea this weekend would be so good; to think a few hours ago I had nothing; now I have a future," she said, kissing him. She placed her cup down on the table, holding his hand, leading him into the bedroom, where they stayed for some time.

After having an evening meal with Mary and Martin, they returned to the studio. Donald started painting, and Sophie stripped the bed, placing the old sheet in the washing machine. Donald realised Christine would never have done that. He could hear the vacuum cleaner and other kitchen appliances working. Mary stood out from her cottage door, listening to the appliances work in the warm evening air. Mary thought this must be the right girl, not frightened of housework.

Donald's painting a portrait of Sophie with her hair blowing in the breeze; she's standing by one of his stable doors stroking an Appaloosa, a horse he's purchasing for her. He decided to venture into the future, placing a young child in her arm and gazing at his mother's loving expression. Sophie came in to look; she stood there astounded, anticipating; what he had in his mind for her. She noticed on her finger a diamond ring, "I presume that's my horse and our child, we are married, Donald? I look stunningly beautiful."

"Oh yes, you do," Donald glanced from the portrait. "That reminds me, you never said yes to marrying me?"

She whispered in his ear, "Yes."

Donald smiled, making the finishing touches to his artwork, taking a photo sending to Jack. Jack phoned immediately, "You have a family already; she's beautiful, Donald. What's the title."

"True love."

"My art studio by 9 o'clock in the morning, please; I've had nothing from you for ages. This will show the world you can find happiness if you search."

"Okay, your lordship, we'll see you in the morning."

Sophie shook her head in disbelief, watching Donald carrying the portrait to his Bentley. He returned upstairs. They grabbed a few hours' sleep, cuddling in their warm nest.

Donald made breakfast while Sophie searched through her clothes, settling for jeans, a blouse, and a denim jacket like Christine would wear.

They set off, arriving at Jack's studio just after nine. Jack looked at Sophie, "You're right, Donald; the portrait doesn't do her justice." Sophie smiled in appreciation, following them through into the shop. She watched how carefully Jack fitted the temporary frame and photographed the portrait. One million five hundred thousand pounds in seconds on the web. Sophie stared at the figure. Jack commented, "The art world loves you, Sophie; otherwise, the portrait would not reach those figures. I will arrange for a camera crew and photographers, Donald. We have to keep the publicity train running, and if I were you, I'd run up the street to the jewellers and put a ring on Sophie's finger quick."

Donald grabbed Sophie's hand; she started giggling as they ran up the street, entering the jewellers. "Whatever you like, Sophie," Donald expressed warmly.

Sophie stared at what was on offer, a vast assortment. "Could I have a look at that one, please," she asked timidly.

The jeweller removed the ring, and she tried it on her finger. The jeweller checked, "Minor adjustment and perfect."

Sophie glanced at Donald, "What do you think, Donald? It looks expensive; I can pick something else."

"Don't be silly, Sophie, have whatever you want."

The jeweller carefully removed the ring from Sophie's finger, making a minor adjustment and slipping it on her finger.

Donald asked, "What do I owe you."

"Seventy-five-thousand, Sir."

Sophie stared, open-mouthed the sums of money Donald's spending on her were way beyond her wildest dreams. Sophie, without realising, had selected the same ring as Donald had betrayed in the portrait. They strolled hand-in-hand to Jack's art gallery, swamped by photographers noticing the ring. They entered the gallery, struggling past photographers photographing Sophie and the portrait. "Have you found true love, Donald," one reporter asked?

Sophie spoke, "Yes, he has! I love him immensely, look at my fabulous ring," the cameras went wild.

"Donald, when will you marry, have you set a date," a reporter asked, smiling.

"You will have to ask the boss," glancing at Sophie, still admiring her ring, trying to absorb the excitement of her and Donald together. Sophie glanced at the computer and noticed her portrait reaching three million; sums of money that didn't even venture into her thoughts. She realised she would be walking on water before long. Thanks to Donald, she would want for nothing.

Donald slowly drove down the motorway, children waving and some adults. Sophie couldn't understand the way everybody seemed to love Donald or his car. When they returned to Crabtree Farm, they went upstairs into the studio.

CHAPTER SIXTEEN

MAKE PLANS

Josephine in France with her daughter Christine sitting by the blazing log fire, discussing the best way forward and what to do with Glencoe. "I think we should dismiss Sophie from what I've seen on the news. She's in Donald's pants; it should be you, daughter, if you hadn't messed up, silly girl fancy caught. I managed for years having affairs, and your father never found out."

"I never wanted to have affairs mother or flings just happened my lack of self-control," Christine frowned.

"I'll fly over to Glencoe, Christine; I'll see if I can stir things to dismiss her out of the way. You might stand a slim chance with Donald. Harvest is due shortly. I suggest you fly to England to smooth things out with your father. He would sooner have you drive his combine than anyone else. I know from information received Donald's driving one. Maybe a golden opportunity to rekindle the romance. You should be financially right if you have a ring on your finger and you're married. Give him a child something to amuse him, then you can go wild with as many men as you like," she chuckled, "I have, Gerald never realised for years."

"I'm not like you, mother. I only want Donald," Christine assured.

"If that's the truth, Christine, why were you on your back with those other boys? You can't say you didn't enjoy yourself, especially for being sneaky; you liked the challenge."

Christine grinned, "Exciting at the time, someone different touching you is quite exhilarating, but I'd sooner not of bothered. Look where I am now; I don't have Donald."

"Leave to your mother. I'll fly out to Glencoe and see what mischief I can cause; once Donald's free of her, you'll be in with a chance; in the meantime, go home to Strawberry Estate. I'll keep you posted, daughter," they hugged each other warmly.

Mrs Montague entered the room, "Your plans will fail; they always do. Glencoe is surviving because of Donald Selwyn; bear that in mind, Josephine and you, Christine. The estate will soon be able to pay either of you a modest sum per annum if you don't interfere."

"I want Donald back," Christine voiced with determination.

Mrs Montague chuckled, "If I were single, I'd bed Donald be faithful and live a charmed existence; he has treated you, Christine, like a queen. You are a fool. You had everything, and you still have to play around like a common tart," Mrs Montague glared at the pair. "You are no better, Josephine. I wouldn't annoy Elizabeth R any further; she is not a patient woman. You create more scandal for the family. You will meet with an accident. Do I make myself plain, ladies?"

Christine exhaled, realising she would have to be careful with her mother; both seemed to be on borrowed time regarding patience from the Royal house. Mrs Montague left the room. Josephine patted Christine's cheek, "leave everything to your mother," she smiled.

***

Friday morning, Sophie's yellow mini arrived in the yard. She ran downstairs from the studio, signing for the vehicle. The driver passed the keys to her leaving in another car. Donald's in the studio painting, receiving a phone call from Justin. "Good morning, Donald. I've had notification from France that Josephine's flying over in the next few days. I find that rather suspicious; perhaps you should be here in case, you know what I mean. I'm worried about Sophie. You know what Josephine and Christine are like."

"I'll come with the fifth wheel; I can follow Sophie. I purchased her a new car, her old ones knackered."

"We know. We saw you on the news with your future wife; I suspect that's why Josephine's coming over to see what damage she can cause on her daughter's behalf. I'm afraid I don't trust any of them, Donald. A terrible thing to say," Justin sighed.

"No, it's the truth, Justin, don't worry. You'll have my full support. I wish I could purchase Glencoe, then they'd have nothing to do with the place."

Saturday morning, Sophie, in her mini, headed for Glencoe. Donald followed with his American pickup and fifth-wheel; both arrived at 9 o'clock in the evening, Donald parked his truck, and Sophie stayed with him for the night. After breakfast, Sophie and Donald walked around the stables. Jock had fed the horses. Donald passed him a fifty pounds, "Thanks, mate."

Jock smiled, taking the money. "Appreciated, Donald. We watched you both on television," Jock chuckled. "I bet Miss Gibbs is spitting feathers," he laughed, "Serves the bitch right."

"Be careful, Jock. You don't know who's listening; you don't know if the place is bugged," Donald watched the colour drain from Jock's expression realising Donald could be right, knowing Josephine.

Justin came out to greet them, "Sophie, you can take the horsebox to collect your belongings and move into Robbie's old cottage, rent-free."

Sophie hugged Justin, which he wasn't expecting. "Yes, well," he said, walking off liking Sophie, the more he saw of her believing she's the right woman for Donald.

Sophie drove the horsebox; Donald travelled with her to the rented room. She didn't have many things easily fitted in the back of the horsebox. They returned to the cottage; she's about to live in a still partially furnished accommodation, an estate policy. They lit the fire. Donald remembered spending many hours here with Mrs McLaughlin before passing away. "Come on, Sophie, we're going into town; you need new furniture and whatever else you wish to purchase."

"No, Donald, I can manage. Don't keep spending your money; it's unnecessary. Besides, I might sleep in the fifth wheel, maybe a strange man in there," she smirked, giggling.

"I'm leaving it there, and my truck, I shall fly to Crabtree Farm. Obviously, you can use my fifth wheel at any time."

***

Mrs Montague listened to the conversations realising everyone's expecting trouble from Josephine and Christine. She sighed heavily, wondering what the best course of action was. She certainly wasn't intervening in Donald's relationship with Sophie. Donald's excellent service to Glencoe Estate and the Royals absolutely adored him apart from his outburst over Christine, although he only spoke the truth.

***

Christine's wondering whether her mother's right; to enjoy life, marry someone, and then lead a separate life, more or less in secret. She had to admit that she enjoyed the thrill of the chase, almost like foxhunting. Never what you expected when you catch your prey, always disappointing.

Christine ventured outside in the warm sun, looking at the abundance of pretty flowers until she reached the rear of the castle where the horses were stabled. She observed a young man brushing a horse; she smiled, walking into the tack room, venturing out the rear door into the woodland beyond, following the footpath, smelling the remains of the fading bluebells. She could hear people laughing in the distance; she continued walking with curiosity stumbling across a waterfall with naked young men swimming. She sat watching intently, not realising someone was behind her. "You can join us," he said in French.

Christine moved her head slowly from side to side, "No, thank you, I could hear voices; just curious," she started walking away.

She heard him say, "You are so beautiful." She turned to face him; he gently removed her clothes, kissed her passionately, made love to her and eventually carried her to where his three friends were. Gently entering the water with her. They kissed, making love to her in turn. She thought her mind would explode; is this fantasy or reality? She didn't care; enjoying every moment, she finally left the water waving, dressing quickly, and making her way to the castle.

Josephine had already departed for Glencoe in a light, privately owned aircraft with an old lover. Christine sat on her bed, drying her hair. She had no reason to feel guilty; she wasn't attached to anyone. She's free and single and feels fulfilled. She secretly hoped her mother would succeed and have Donald under her control.

Mrs Montague's eating her dinner with her husband. Her bodyguard approached, whispering, "An unfortunate plane accident, madam, both embarrassments didn't survive over the channel."

"Thank you for the information, Derek; keep to yourself for the moment, please."

Mr Montague smiled, "What a shame," he said, sipping his wine. "A good year, I think."

***

Sophie's up bright and early, dealing with the horses and preparing for a group to ride with her around the estate. Donald's in Justin's office receiving a message, "Josephine Spires, and her pilot friend lost in the channel, a search is underway."

Donald exhaled, "She was a lovely woman, slightly scatter-brained; I wonder how Christine's feeling a love-hate relationship."

The newspapers arrived with pictures of a light aircraft Josephine flying in suddenly dropped off the radar smashing into the sea. No survivors were found. Justin remarked, "You know who owns the place now, Donald, Christine. We better batten down the hatches; god knows what devastation she will cause."

"I wouldn't be overly concerned, Justin. Mrs Montague controls those two; she won't take any crap from Christine. I think Christine is on borrowed time with many people."

"I hope you're right, Donald; we have everything running right for a change. I've never seen Glencoe in profit. Unlike some other estates, we have excellent equipment, good staff and an excellent future."

Mrs Montague had heard the conversation surmising Donald's astute in his conclusion. He realised she could control. The others were only puppets if she so wished. Josephine had overstepped the mark too many times. Christine had her last chance to prove herself. If not would be her demise.

Christine sat in her room. She'd shed tears for the loss of her mother, except she now owned Glencoe. Although suspected Mrs Montague could pull strings even after she's twenty-one. A week had passed they've given up searching for any bodies. They had found the aeroplane in bits and recovered some of the luggage. A short service was held for Josephine Spires at the castle. Christine had phoned her father, explaining she would be returning for the harvest. He reluctantly accepted her offer, trying to keep the peace. Mrs Montague gave Christine permission to fly to Glencoe Estate, left to her by her mother on the understanding she made no changes.

Christine booked a flight for Inverness Airport; she took a taxi arriving at Glencoe unannounced. She walked into reception on a mission. "Could you please contact Mr Selwyn and Justin to join me in the lounge in five minutes and provide coffees?" Christine continued upstairs to her private apartment. Donald and Justin received the message they'd been waiting for, anticipating conflict.

Justin and Donald sat around the table. Christine came in, taking a seat as the waitress arrived with coffee. "Good afternoon, gentlemen. To you first, Justin, what is the state of accounts?"

"We are sorry for your loss, Christine," Justin remarked.

"I have no time for sentimental claptrap; my property now, my mother is dead and buried, leave her there; answer my question, please."

Donald was surprised by her attitude; however, he didn't pass a comment wanting to see where this was heading.

"We have a million in credit; Glencoe's never so profitable thanks to Donald initially with the cash injection and careful management."

"I intend to make some changes. Dismiss Sophie. Jock can run both operations and you. Mr Selwyn is no longer required. Thank you for your service, and goodbye."

Mrs Montague choked on her glass of whisky, sitting by the fire, wondering if the girl had lost her marbles. She certainly hadn't discussed those plans, and she should have. Mrs Montague summoned her bodyguard, speeding off towards the channel tunnel.

Donald grabbed the poker from the hearth. Every picture he painted of Christine he destroyed. She stared in horror, realising they were his portraits. Donald continued walking out of the door. Jock was talking to Sophie; they could see by his expression something had happened. Donald explained. Jock opened the stable doors releasing the horses, "I'll not look after the bloody horses," he walked off and glanced back. "Lass, leave here now with Donald; you will not find another man like him."

Sophie quickly packed her belongings. What furniture she had left behind wasn't worth having. Donald hitched his fifth wheel to his American truck. Justin came running out, "I can't stay here, Donald; Christine's a raving lunatic; she'll wreck what we work for."

"Sit tight, Justin; I suspect Mrs Montague is on the way here. I can't stay, friend. If I buy an estate here, you'll be my first contact; you can work for me if you're evicted. You have my home number; I'll sort something out for you. That goes for the rest of the staff," Donald smiled, driving away, following Sophie.

Justin strolled into the hotel sitting in his office, realising his friend on the way home. Justin phoned Maggie, "Is there any way I could rent the flat above your shop, Maggie, now you're living with your new boyfriend?"

"Yes, why, father?"

Justin explained. "Listen to Donald, father. Stay where you are now; wait for Mrs Montague to arrive. I suspect Christine's feet won't touch the ground by the time that woman has finished."

"Okay, Maggie," Justin sighed, lowering the receiver.

Two in the morning, Donald and Sophie had arrived at Crabtree Farm.

Mary and Martin enjoyed an early retirement by the seaside, leaving Donald in charge.

Donald flopped on the bed, exhausted from the journey, a journey he's determined not to make again.

***

Christine looked out of her window, seeing the horses running free. She realised she had come down too hard on everyone; she'd cut her own throat, upset Justin and Donald. She disposed of the competition, including the man she wanted, excepting he would never come here again. She phoned for a taxi heading for the airport flying to Birmingham and catching a cab to Strawberry Estate. She carried her bag upstairs, flopping down on her bed, exhausted. Gerald and Cindy realised she was home, staying in bed. They would face whatever in the morning.

Justin phoned Donald. "You okay," Donald asked, concerned.

"Yes, shortly after you left, she packed her bag, heading for the airport. I don't know whether she's with her father or where she is. All I have here is a mess. I've had to persuade Jock to look after the horses if he can ever catch them again until I find a replacement for Sophie, which won't be easy. Be careful, Donald, if she's down your way."

"Thanks for the update, Justin. I'm here if you need me," Donald assured, livid with the situation.

***

Mrs Montague's notified that Christine's now at Strawberry Estate saved her some considerable travelling. Mrs Montague stopped for a few hours in Royal accommodation suitable for her standing and position. Arriving at Strawberry Estate at 8:30 in the morning. Her bodyguard stepped from the limousine; he opened the door for her. Gerald saw her arrival, suspecting something was terribly wrong. He opened the door. "Gerald, good morning to you. Could I see your daughter Christine, please, in the study?"

"May I attend the meeting, Mrs Montague?"

"You may not like what you hear, Gerald, but please don't interfere; way over your head," Mrs Montague warned.

Christine came downstairs, looking out through the balcony window and seeing the limousine suspecting Mrs Montague's here; she had a good idea why. Christine exhaled, guided into the study by Mrs Montague's bodyguard.

Christine stood defiant with her arms folded. "You know why I'm here, don't you, Christine," Mrs Montague asked.

"Probably because I dismissed the prostitute Donald's with, and I dismissed Donald suggesting he take a hike, I don't need him anymore to run my affairs."

"You are misinformed, young lady. Sophie has had one boyfriend other than Donald. Unlike a certain Miss Gibbs who slept around here and videoed in France having sex with four boys by the waterfall. Sophie has a good background. I think tart would be too good a description for you, Christine. I'm travelling to Glencoe to undo the mess created by you. If you make one more mistake, Christine, you will be with your mother. Don't try my patience."

Christine staggered backwards, dropping into an armchair, realising her mother's death was probably not an accident. Gerald's shocked; he knew the woman had the power to authorise operations, nothing like that.

Cindy came in, carrying a tray of tea. Mrs Montague sat down, "Thank you, Cindy." Christine didn't move or speak. Mrs Montague had made her point. Her next destination is Crabtree Farm. Informed Donald and Sophie were there. Christine stood, "May I be excused, Mrs Montague." She understood she was not in control. "Yes, think before you act, Christine. Any respect we had for you.

You have blown out of the window with your behaviour; you had the best boyfriend and lost him. You only have yourself to blame." Christine left the room, bursting into tears and running upstairs.

"I wouldn't blame yourself too much, Gerald, for her behaviour, from her mother's side. I was hoping she wouldn't venture down the same route with your upbringing. You never know. Miracles happen, she's still very young, and hopefully, she may be more level-headed by the time she's twenty-one." Mrs Montague said, "Thank you both for the refreshment. Other duties to perform."

"Thanks, Mrs Montague," Gerald expressed, "I hope she listens to you. She certainly doesn't to me," he sighed heavily. Cindy held Gerald's arm, watching Mrs Montague drive off.

Donald looked from his studio window to see Mrs Montague's limousine park, which brought a smile. He knew she'd be on the scene somewhere, suspecting she'd come from Strawberry Estate. She came upstairs, leaving her bodyguard by the car. Donald opened the door, greeting her with a hug. "Unhand me, Sir," Mrs Montague smiled. "Sophie, would you make Mrs Montague a cup of tea, please."

"Certainly."

Mrs Montague noticed straightaway Sophie's cleaning of the flat, the washing machine's running, and wasn't a dirty cup in the place; totally different from the way Christine behaved.

"I suspect you know where I've come from and why I am here with that wise head on your young shoulders, Donald."

"I suspect you kicked Christine's backside, and you're hoping to talk me into supporting Glencoe. I will, from afar. Sophie will not be returning; we will be married shortly. I'm quite happy for Justin to phone me for advice or any reason. I may venture for a holiday, that's all. I shan't be helping Gerald this year with his harvest. I will not work with Christine! She's had every chance I intend to give her."

Mrs Montague smiled, "Thank you, Donald, reliable and dependable, such a rare quality." Sophie grinned at the thought of marrying Donald, a dream come true; she'd only ever had one disastrous relationship wishing she'd met Donald before anyone else.

"I think it may be wise, although you are over eighteen, Sophie, to visit your parents as a courtesy, unlike you, Donald, to forget your manners."

Sophie sighed, "It wasn't Donald's fault Mrs Montague. I suggested I'm over eighteen; I do not need their permission. I suspect they've seen everything on the news, but I think you are right; please don't blame Donald for my mistake."

"You are like your mother, and I can see your father in your face," Mrs Montague said, understanding what she'd let slip.

"Sophie stared in shock, "You knew my real mother and father! I was adopted. How do you know them, Mrs Montague? Please explain."

Donald interrupted, "Mrs Montague can't say any more; she would be breaking the law. Except what she's told you, your parents are obviously watching you."

"Donald is correct, Sophie; they would lock me up and throw away the key if I revealed more than I have." Mrs Montague patted Donald on the cheek. Donald suspected a Royal person needed castrating; mistakes everywhere, he seemed to have a dab hand at finding.

"I must go; I have to press onto Glencoe and see what mess I'm left with before receiving a Royal phone call," she sighed heavily. "I suspect the news has already travelled by estate staff." Mrs Montague opened her handbag, removing a picture of her husband, "Donald, would you paint a portrait of my husband? He is suffering from cancer. I want to remember how he looks in the photo."

Donald took the photo, standing hugging Mrs Montague. She kissed him on both cheeks, "If only I were a single girl," she chuckled, walking downstairs. Donald watched from his elevated position Mrs Montague leave the yard. Donald immediately scanned the photograph of Mr Montague, transferring to his wall screen. Donald suspected Mr Montague must have been handsome in his younger days.

Sophie sat in the other room phoning the only parents she knew, apologising and explaining that she would visit with Donald shortly if they'd like to meet him. The reply was a resounding yes, which made Sophie feel more relaxed.

Donald soon had paint flying on the canvas, determined to give Mrs Montague the memory she desired. Donald texts Gerald, explaining he would not be helping with the harvest, and wanted nothing to do with Christine.

Gerald texts, "I understand."

Donald worked until the early hours, transferring the photo into oils. Mr Montague, looking at the rose garden with the vineyards in the distance with his walking cane. Donald sent a photo to Jack at seven in the morning. Not many minutes had passed before Mrs Montague phoned, "Donald, that looks beautiful. Can you arrange for transport to Jack please for framing? I'm preparing to visit Glencoe this morning; I rested at another estate overnight. Thank you once again, Donald, good day to you."

Donald carefully packed his artwork, arranging for a courier to transport the painting to Jack. Sophie's on the bed, asleep. Donald showered, changing into fresh clothes. He never seemed to tire when he had a paintbrush in his hand; he made two drinks and started breakfast.

***

Christine's out on The Rising Sun enjoying the early morning fresh air. Another glorious day wouldn't be long before the rape harvested. She cantered around the reserve along the track, watching Michael's girlfriend leaving with her mini for work. Monday already, Christine thought, to look across the road to Crabtree Farm; remembering the time she galloped to see Donald seemed a million years ago now.

She sighed heavily, stopping by the old strawberry shed tying her horse she entered, reliving her mistake. The thrill of the chase; bull-shit. In here, she'd lost everything valuable to her. She sat on a crate crying even her father knew she was naked with four men in France swimming. She returned to her horse mounting, wondering if she apologised to Donald and Sophie, may mend a few fences.

She galloped off towards Crabtree Farm, slowly trotting up the drive. Donald peered from his studio window as she entered the yard, suspecting trouble. He came running downstairs, leaving Sophie in the security of the studio. Christine didn't dismount; she surmised she wouldn't belong. "I thought I would apologise, Donald, for my behaviour at Glencoe; spiteful, angry and upset, I hadn't quite recovered from the loss of my mother."

"Find Christine." Sophie entered the yard; Christine tried not to glare at her. "Hi, Christine, what a lovely horse."

"Yes, lucky old me, nice to see you both," Christine turned her horse around, trotting off down the drive, feeling if she'd stayed any longer, she would have jumped off her horse and broke Sophie's neck. "She doesn't look happy, Donald; I don't think she's quite finished. If looks could kill, I'd be dead."

"I'm inclined to agree with you, Sophie; she'll have to get past me first."

Donald walked into the machinery shed, remembering the big Massey articulated tractor Christine and Gerald presented to him when he was poor.

***

Gerald and Cindy were taking a weekend break before harvest started. Christine's staying at home. She's conjuring a plan in her mind to find the best way to make Donald need her help, hoping she could build some bridges with him.

Christine waved goodbye to her father and Cindy. She phoned the Copthorne brothers explaining her father's away for the weekend and asking if they come around. She'd hated them for years and was about to use them to her advantage; she wondered what the cost would be?

She watched them arrive in their car; she nervously led them into the lounge. "Your phone call was rather mysterious, Christine?"

She spoke directly, "I would like the machinery store on Crabtree Farm in flames only the machinery store nothing else; otherwise, defeat the object. I will notify you when the coast is clear. No dogs, you have nothing to worry about."

"You must really hate him. We have friends, shall we say, who can handle those sorts of problems; they don't come cheap what are you willing to pay."

"What do you want," she asked calmly.

"Your mother was always obliging; we used to take photos of her like you when you were younger. We blurred out the face, so no one knew who they were; she would be very nice to us. We'd arrange things for her. I have a score to settle with Donald Selwyn after he broke my wrist and nose."

They hadn't noticed a drone scanned through the window seeing Christine standing. Mrs Montague watched in disbelief while the two Copthorne brothers slowly stripped Christine taking photos of her and placing her in different positions on furniture, each taking a turn to have sex with her. Mrs Montague presumed; Christine's lost her marbles anticipating trouble ahead for somebody. The Copthorne brothers were notorious for fixing accidents. Mrs Montague fearing the worst, immediately instructed other agents to monitor all conversations and notify her of anything significant involving Donald Selwyn, Sophie, or Crabtree Farm.

The Copthorne brothers left. Christine immediately ran upstairs, taking a shower, realizing She'd performed in a porn movie, especially when they licked her fanny and pushed a wine bottle inside her. She felt absolutely disgusted. Christine was determined to win whatever the cost. As her mother had advised use, anyone, to acquire what she wanted.

Christine rode to Crabtree Farm on The Rising Sun early the following day, noticing Donald's Bentley's gone. Sophie's mini parked in the corner, so they were together. Christine looked on her mobile; Donald had a tracker. She realised he was in Scotland, the other side of Glasgow. Christine rode out of the yard, dialling a number listening to it ring three times, and then disconnected that was the signal coast was clear.

She rode to Strawberry Estate, seeing a drone hovering over the field, suspecting she's watched. She stabled her horse by her father's horse. She instructed Stephen she was away for a few days. Christine packed a bag and locked the house, watching the drone observing her step into her Range Rover driving off; she left her tracker on so Mrs Montague would know where she was and couldn't be associated with what happened.

***

Donald and Sophie finally arrived on the other side of Tain by Bonar Bridge. They drove down the track, parking outside a Crofters house. Sophie introduced Donald to her mother and father, warmly embracing Donald. "We finally meet the famous artist Donald Selwyn," her mother said, displaying the newspaper cuttings she collected.

"I have something for you both," Donald smiled, running out to the Bentley, removing two portrait copies of him rescued by Sophie and the one he painted of Sophie in his studio on the farm. Sophie's mother, Mrs Mercantile, is in tears. "Would you like me to hang them for you, Mrs Mercantile," Donald offered, "Show me where you'd like them?"

Mr and Mrs Mercantile had a small extension to their Crofter's house, which they used as a living room; she pointed to where she'd like the two pictures. He fastened the pictures using Mr Mercantile's electric drill. "Sophie, you look so beautiful. Even as a baby, you were always a beautiful child," her foster mother proudly voiced.

Donald walked out with Mr Mercantile looking around the thirty acres. They had a couple of pigs and a large vegetable garden; an old Ferguson twenty that hadn't started for years appeared to be cemented to the ground. Both Sophie's foster parents were getting on in years. Donald lifted the bonnet on the Fergie twenty; this tractor could only be used for restoration. "We haven't the money son to invest. I have to manage our garden with hand tools now."

"Come with me, Mr Mercantile," Donald insisted. Mr Mercantile sat in Donald's plush Bentley, almost scared to move his feet if he marked the carpet. "Where is your nearest machinery dealer from here."

"A few miles up the road." Donald reversed his car, driving out onto the road. Sophie and her foster mother watched, somewhat puzzled, wondering where they were off. Within a short while, Donald pulled into an agricultural dealership. "Right, Mr Mercantile, I'll resolve your issues." The proprietor came over, recognising Mr Mercantile then Donald. "Mr Selwyn, I believe. How can I assist you?"

"The compact tractor over there with a loader, I want a reversible plough, power harrow, space drill, one that will fit the tractor, potato planter and potato lifter. We mustn't forget a suitable subsoiler, and we'll take one of those small muck spreaders over there; how much for cash? And can you sell a Ferguson twenty ideal for restoration?"

Mr Mercantile sat down on the wall; he'd never known anybody like Donald. The proprietor couldn't add up the figures quick enough. He'd never had an order that big in the years he'd been there on compact equipment. "Thirty-five-thousand pounds plus vat."

Donald ran to his glove box in the Bentley, removing a wad of cash; he counted out the money. "I'd like a receipt please and delivered to Mr Mercantile's Croft at your earliest convenience. Don't forget to sell the Ferguson twenty, please. I'm sure you could set Mr Mercantile up with a small diesel tank," Donald gave the proprietor another three hundred pounds.

Donald helped Mr Mercantile to his car; he was still in shock; he stayed quiet on the return journey to the Croft. Donald thought he'd upset Mr Mercantile, certainly not his intention trying to make life easier for him so he could enjoy the rest of his life. Sophie asked, "What have you done, Donald? father looks absolutely bewildered."

"Purchased equipment."

Mr Mercantile burst into tears holding his wife; she helped him inside. Donald's starting to feel as sick as a parrot; he'd obviously offended somebody. He stayed outside, leaning against the bonnet of his car, looking at the old sows uprooting the ground. Sophie said, "No one has ever helped my parents the way you have; he's shocked, he's not angry, Donald, neither is mum." Donald walked in, "I apologise if I caused you any upset. Only trying to help. I thought it only appropriate while I was here; I ask if you would consent to me marrying Sophie."

Mr and Mrs Mercantile look at Donald with tear-filled eyes, "Of course, we consent."

Donald ran to the boot of his Bentley, removing several bottles of malt whisky brought into the house. Mr Mercantile smiled. Donald and Sophie stayed at the local hotel in Bonar Bridge; there wasn't room in the Crofter's cottage.

At 3 o'clock in the morning, Donald received a phone call from the police. Crabtree Farm is on fire. Donald dressed quickly along with Sophie; they dashed to the Bentley. Sophie contacted her parents, explaining why they had to return to Donald's farm.

Donald travelled as quickly as possible and stayed within the legal speed limits. He's home by 10 o'clock in the morning, noticing the tractor shed destroyed. The barn, his fifth wheel and American truck had perished. Luckily the fire brigade had managed to save the cottage, and the flats weren't destroyed in the big house or his studio.

The police officer approached, advising, "no accident, Mr Selwyn. Do you have any enemies?"

"Not to my knowledge," Donald remarked, deep in thought.

Sophie commented, "What about Christine? She hasn't forgiven you, I can assure you, Donald."

Gerald came in his Range Rover with Cindy; they embraced one another. "You only have to ask Donald. I'm here to help, a disaster. Christine's in London staying in her mother's flat. Otherwise, I'd have blamed her straightaway," Gerald voiced suspiciously.

"Donald smiled, "I wanted a new barn."

Mary and Martin entered the drive they'd heard on the news and were also notified by the police. Mary and Donald stood, looking at the devastation. Donald placed his arm around his mother. "You realise, mum, dad, I can have a new barn, brand-new tractors," Donald chuckled.

The NFU representative talked to the fire brigade taking notes.

The people staying in the flats were evacuated to a hotel in Stratford for safety while everything was brought under control on the farm. The press photographed Donald and his parents, Sophie cuddling him. A reporter remarked, "Quite a mess, Donald, all indications arson. I can't imagine anyone disliking you."

Gerald thought for a moment, "Donald the Copthorne brothers, you beat the crap out of one of them."

The police officer noted the name, "What can you tell me about the Copthorne brothers?" Gerald explained everything he knew, which wasn't a great deal.

Everyone apprehensively entered the cottage. Mary made a drink. The smoke had penetrated the cottage. Donald ran upstairs into his studio. It had fared better slight smell of smoke. 11:30 a.m. Christine arrived in her white Range Rover, looking shocked, trying to control her facial expression, not wishing to give the game away. She came to the cottage. Mary glared at her passing her a coffee. Mary had learnt from past experiences with Christine that what you saw is not always the truth with her. Donald came into the cottage, "Harvest Donald, shortly, we can pop over here with our combines and store your oilseed rape for you. We have the capacity, don't we, father."

"I've already offered Christine, thanks," Gerald advised. Noticed a love bite on her neck, wondering who she'd been with this time. Christine finished her coffee and walked away, climbing into her Range Rover and heading down the drive, laughing at the top of her voice. She didn't think sufficient time to build another store, and his equipment was destroyed.

Donald and Sophie managed to sleep, although a heavy smell of smoke in the air. They dressed, walking around the devastation the following morning. Donald phoned the NFU. The claim is in the system and will be dealt with in due course. Donald explained he wasn't hanging about; he's authorising bulldozers. He wanted the site cleared and ready for the new construction. He would order new equipment harvest around the corner. The NFU reluctantly accepted his proposal. By midday, two excavators had arrived, separating the steel from the rubbish; the fire brigade had already ascertained the cause of the fire, and he wasn't destroying any evidence.

***

Christine on The Rising Sun surveyed what was taking place from her property. Lorries were coming and going. She knew from experience with Donald. If he wanted something, it would happen.

Donald had refunded the guests staying in the apartments suffering smoke damage; they certainly weren't fit for purpose. Michael and Angela arrived, parking by the studio. Angela and Sophie ran up into the studio to make coffee. Michael and Donald checked every apartment to see what was required to return to the standard that Donald expected. "I hear it's arson, Donald; who the bloody hell would want to upset you, one of the nicest guys I know," Michael expressed?

Donald shrugged his shoulders, "No idea Michael, only Christine and the Copthorne brothers, Robbie in Scotland, I've fallen out with."

"What will it cost Michael? I can't wait for the insurance company; dragging their feet, they don't care."

"If I said ten-thousand pounds to redecorate and power wash where I have to outside, that should cover the cost. I know you would want me to start half an hour ago. I can start in the morning," Michael smiled. "That reminds me, Gerald asked me to drive one of his combines. I refused. I don't want any contact with Christine; she's gone weird. She spent an hour on her horse, watching your driveway from her property."

Angela came down from the studio, hugging Sophie, "lovely to meet you, Sophie," Angela expressed warmly. Michael and Angela left. Mary and Martin came out from the cottage. They spent several hours washing the walls removing any signs of smoke from outside the cottage, surprised the thatched roof hadn't set fire.

Donald removed Mrs Montague's card from his wallet; he dialled the number. "Mrs Montague, Donald. I have a problem; we've had a fire. I suspect I need planning permission to erect new farm buildings; could you pull a few strings, speed the process."

Mrs Montague chuckled, "Yes, we heard about the disaster. We have our own suspicions; you proceed, and I will deal with the planning for you. I have received my husband's portrait; once again, Donald, you have excelled; thank you, good day."

Donald looked through the farmers' weekly with his father sitting at the kitchen table while Sophie and Mary continued to remove the grime left by the smoke. Donald sketched on a piece of paper what he'd like. Martin thought a brilliant idea a multi-purpose building plus a grain store purpose-built. "Shouldn't you wait for the insurance money, Donald," Martin suggested, concerned about the cost.

Donald removed his mobile and entered his bank account, showing his father. "What! Never."

"I don't think we need to worry about money, father," Donald smiled. Donald phoned a building company, explaining what he wanted. They would send someone to discuss matters further with him in the morning. Martin commented, "At least the wood processor wasn't damaged, Donald, but we lost everything else, including your lovely fifth wheel."

Donald smiled, "Two years ago, if this had happened, I'd be panicking; now, I'm not worried. I suggest you return to your holiday house in Devon and leave it to me. I don't want mum stressed or you for that matter."

Martin smiled, "Mary, pack your bags. We're going on holiday now, woman." Mary came dashing into the kitchen. "I can't! I have too much to do, Martin. Don't be bloody ridiculous."

Sophie cuddled Mary, "Donald and I can handle the situation. You go away and rest; sit on the beach, lick ice cream, don't forget to wear your sunblock," Sophie chuckled, "And a bloody face mask when you go shopping coronavirus is still prevalent."

Donald removed two thousand pounds from his wallet, kissing her on the cheek and placing in his mother's hand, "Go and enjoy yourself, mum."

Mary patted his cheek, "You always were a good boy, Donald."

Mary and Martin drove out of the yard within an hour, returning to their holiday accommodation in Devon.

At 9 o'clock the next day, the farm building representative came in, sitting at the kitchen table with Donald and Sophie showing what was on offer. Sorted within an hour and in stock; nothing odd about the building work Donald wanted. Promising to have constructed within a fortnight gave him a week before harvest. Donald wrote out a cheque for part of the work as a deposit. The representative commented, "We know who you are, Donald, the famous artist. We never considered money would be an issue with you." He smiled, finishing his coffee, leaving in his Range Rover.

The more Donald sat and thought about things, the more he concluded Christine's involved, although he thought he would never be able to prove the fact.

***

Christine, most days, rode her horse, The Rising Sun, to the same position in the field, carrying binoculars to check on the progress at Crabtree Farm. In some respects, she wished she hadn't bothered. Donald, with his money and contacts, she may have underestimated his ability to recover quickly from the disaster.

***

Donald's about to leave his mother's cottage with Sophie when the Case International representative comes into the yard, the same person he purchased the combine from last year. He jumped from his car, shaking Donald's hand, "You have quite a disaster here, Donald." Shaking Sophie's hand with a pleasing smile.

"You could say James; funny enough, I was thinking about you. As you can see, coming up the drive, we lost 99% of our equipment.

The only surviving thing was the wood processor and my grandfather's Ferguson twenty and trailer. They were in a different building which didn't catch fire."

They strolled into the cottage. Sophie made three coffees. "The way I see the future, James, I will be running this place on my own with Sophie before long; mother and father have had enough. They struggled most of their life to raise me and keep the farm running. Thanks to my art, I'm now in a fortunate position where I can be a weekend farmer."

"If I understand you right, Donald, you're looking for big horsepower and equipment to cope easily with three hundred acres a day? And in the shed for the rest of the year. I'm starting painting," James chuckled.

"You have it in one. I want a 620+ horsepower articulated tractor on rubber tracks, Case IH Quadtrac with hydraulics. I will have to buy a Lexion combine; you don't have one big enough," Donald suggested.

"We have one similar. I have one at the office you're welcome to view; it comes with a coffee maker and a forty-five-foot header on rubber tracks front and rear for those wet conditions. We'll match the Claas Lexion if not outperform, plus our patented thrashing system."

"I want two big grain trailers twenty-ton or bigger."

"I'll need another four hundred-plus horsepower tractor for those just-in-case moments. A ten-furrow plough and the largest set of power harrows you can lay your hands on, the tractors will drive. I almost forgot our JCB loader was destroyed. Do you have an equivalent?"

"Yes, no problem, Donald."

"How much have I spent," Donald asked curiously.

"Around 2 million, I think, you haven't included a drill, but we can discuss that later."

"That will do, James. I can purchase from you as I need. I won't be baling this year because we are all rape. I may grow wheat next year; we'll see."

" A definite order?" James asked.

"Why do you think I'm talking to you!" Donald asked, shrugging his shoulders.

"Thanks, Donald. We'll start moving the equipment here tomorrow morning. The combine can sit outside, waterproof. I will have to order the trailers, which should only take days. My boss will fall off his chair; neither he nor I expected such an order. If we can give you any more discount, Donald, we will; I'll check when I'm at the office."

Sophie looked at Donald, "You realise you've spent nearly two million, Donald. Doesn't that bother you?"

Donald shrugged his shoulders, "Must-have equipment. I want the cultivation and harvesting over quickly, then I can spend more time in bed with my future wife," he said, picking her up in his arms and carrying her upstairs to the studio.

***

Christine couldn't sleep; her guilty conscience was eating her alive. She dressed, out on The Rising Sun to her usual destination on Strawberry Estate. Horrified to see excavators arriving and lorry loads of building material, with police escorts because of the narrow lane. She couldn't believe she saw an enormous combine harvester coming along the road and an articulated rubber-tracked tractor following with a ten-furrow plough. As far as she could see, it appeared to be tractors and lorries approaching Crabtree Farm. Christine looked up to see a drone, Mrs Montague's watching her. Christine stayed for half an hour trying to calm The Rising Sun while the massive convoy passed, turning into Crabtree Farm and struggling up the narrow drive.

***

Michael was busy rectifying the apartments, ready to reopen. Donald looked at his purchases arriving. He wanted big, and he had big.

Luckily, they hadn't planted the two-acre paddock where Geraldine used to graze, the new equipment parked out of the way.

Gerald had heard the commotion from his farm, driving to Crabtree Farm. Observing his daughter over the hedge sitting on her horse. He continued up the drive watching the buildings erected, and concrete poured. Gerald saw the machinery in the paddock. He stared in disbelief, realising Donald wouldn't be beaten down by whoever was trying to destroy him. Gerald knew Donald had the money and the contacts to make it happen. He pitted anyone involved in destroying his farm; he doubted whether they would survive.

Camera crews had arrived to film the activity. Donald's a celebrity, whether he likes it or not. The public is interested to see him recover from the disaster. Christine sat in her bedroom watching the television, surveying the equipment Donald had purchased. She sighed; no matter what she did, she couldn't make him turn to her unless he wanted to, and while Sophie was with him, she stood no chance.

***

Mary and Martin were watching television, looking at their son's purchases. The paddock is full of brand-new equipment. Martin laughed, "Typical. I start retiring, and he has the best equipment to play with; I have to return home soon, Mary. I want to see this outfit for myself and what he's up to with the buildings."

***

Donald invited Gerald into the cottage for a cup of tea. "I would have never believed Donald. You could achieve so much in such a short time after the fire. I'm genuinely pleased for you both. You probably heard Michael is refusing to drive the combine. No one wants to work with Christine. The girl is changing somehow, Donald; she's turning out like her mother more's the pity."

"I don't think if I spoke to her, Gerald, it would help. I genuinely feel sorry for her; however, she betrayed me for no valid reason, which baffles me. Sophie and I will be marrying shortly, then perhaps she'll move on; find someone she can love."

"To be quite honest, Donald, I don't think she's fit to run Strawberry Estate or Glencoe. She will soon be twenty-one; I can't allow the shares of Strawberry Estate to be left in her care; unless she has her act together."

Gerald left a worried man with no idea how to help Christine. Donald and Sophie ran up into the studio. Donald started painting the horrific scene of his farm on fire while Sophie looked at horses on the Internet. For the past few days, Donald had noticed she kept returning to the one-horse called Cherokee, an Appaloosa five years old. From what Donald could sneakily survey the horse's all muscle. Donald saw the price fifteen thousand pounds; he nipped downstairs out of Sophie's earshot phoning his friend Derek, a horse trader. "Fancy hearing from you, Donald, a lovely surprise," Derek commented.

"I'm sure you've heard about Christine and myself and the fire," Donald asked.

"Yes, a sad affair. I can't believe Christine did the dirty on you after everything you gave her. Never mind, move on, Donald; learn from your mistakes. How can I help you?"

"A horse on the Internet, an Appaloosa, I think he's about five years old his name is Cherokee, could you purchase him for me. I think the price is fifteen thousand guineas and transport to Crabtree Farm for my future wife, Sophie, providing he has no defects."

Derek laughed, "You never read the advert properly, have you, Donald? He's one of my horses. I will deliver tomorrow morning. He's as sound as a bell, almost bombproof; you are a glutton for punishment; stay single. It's less trouble, lad," Derek rang off laughing.

Donald ran upstairs, trying not to grin, sitting back at his easel, finishing the disaster of Crabtree Farm. Sophie sat by him with her cup of coffee, watching how he applied the oils. Donald took a picture of the canvas and sent to Jack. Jack looked at the devastating photo. He phoned Donald, "Unfortunate Donald, what is the title."

"Burning Soul."

"I will fetch this one myself. I suppose your mother's not there; my stomach is burning for one of her cakes."

"I'll see what I can do for you, Jack."

"I'm coming now," Jack shouted.

"Sophie, you think you can make one of mum's cakes for Jack? He's on the way. You have about two hours. Tomorrow, your surprise will arrive."

"What, surprise? I'll have to phone Mary for the recipe. What surprise come on, tell me?"

"Go and make the cake, phone, mum."

Sophie rang Mary explaining the dilemma she was facing. Mary took her through a step-by-step process; luckily, Jack's delayed in traffic, so the cake's out of the oven long before he arrived. Sophie placed it in a tin out of the cupboard where Mary had advised.

Jack carefully placed the painting in the boot of his Bentley walking around the devastated farm. Sophie passed Jack the tin. "I've done my very best Jack followed Mary's instructions to the letter. If not to the standard you usually receive, I'm sorry."

Jack kissed Sophie, "You are an angel for trying; I will send you my full report. Now I must return and launch this magnificent artwork. I can see the money rolling in, Donald; your titles are so apt that the public loves you, Donald," Jack remarked, climbing in his Bentley and driving away.

After a week, Michael had finished repairing the damage to the apartments and power washing the grime off the exterior of the building. The letting agent inspected extremely pleased and announced that the flats were ready for holiday occupancy. Donald settled with Michael in cash. "Thanks, Donald, for the work. I appreciate I couldn't have handled the farm building replacements; that's way over my head."

Mrs Montague arrived in the yard. Donald greeted her, kissing her on both cheeks and giving her a hug. "That is inappropriate,

Donald," she smiled, "Because it's you I will permit," patting his cheek. "My husband is ecstatic with your artwork. The best news of all the doctors have managed to prevent his cancer from spreading. I believe seeing the portrait of himself boosted his morale considerably."

They entered the cottage, and Sophie made drinks. "What is the situation at Glencoe, Mrs Montague," Donald asked, concerned.

"Justin has appointed a new stable girl. I've managed to calm Jock. He wants to strangle Christine for offending you and dismissing Sophie. The remainder of the staff performs their duties adequately, although the establishment seems empty and has no life without you. I would ask you and Sophie to visit; you can use Christine's suite. She has no control over the property; I don't consider her fit to run the establishment after her last performance."

"I have a message for you both; it cannot be repeated. Elizabeth R wishes the pair of you every happiness; you should consider it an honour, Donald. She should even think about you or Sophie. Your artwork has affected many people, including myself and my husband. Once we have proof of who caused the fire, I can assure you they will be dealt with."

Mrs Montague gracefully rose to her feet. Donald kissed her on both cheeks giving her another hug; she grinned, shaking her head from side to side, leaving the cottage.

Donald said, "I will visit Glencoe in the next couple of days before I have to start harvest, Mrs Montague." She glanced back. He blew a kiss, and she grinned, climbing into her limousine, waving as she's driven away.

***

Christine steadily rode towards the reserve, watching the old sawmill from a distance noticing Colin Bradshaw from school entering the old strawberry shed. She dismounted, tying her horse, and she entered quietly. He's sat on a box with two of his friends and Pamela

Robinson, her best friend from school, smoking pot. "Well," Christine commented, "What have we here?"

Pamela smiled, "Sit by me, Christine; try a joint makes you feel relaxed and wonderful." Pamela giggled. Christine thought she had nothing to lose sitting by Pamela; she inhaled the joint, almost choking, and started to feel the effects. "You're right, quite nice, once you're used to it," she inhaled deeply. "Roll me another joint, please."

Christine tried to stand and went giddy, sitting down giggling. Colin rolled a joint, passing it to Pamela.

"Could I have another joint," Christine asked, "from somebody? I quite like the sensation," she giggled, feeling her troubles had vanished?

"Cost you ten pounds; grass doesn't come cheap, Christine," Colin advised inhaling his joint.

Christine giggled, realising she hadn't any money, "I will owe you, Colin; you know I'm good for the money."

"I'll pay you, Colin," Pamela giggled, standing, removing her clothes and laying on the hessian sack. Colin passed his joint to Christine, who watched Colin have sex with Pamela. Christine couldn't believe what she saw seemed okay in a strange way; her mind fuzzy; the more she inhaled the joint. Christine realised she was naked on the hessian sack, and everyone had gone. She suspected they'd had sex with her and left, including her best friend, without checking if she was okay. Christine quickly dressed, plastered in dust, headed home, stabling her horse, and ran for the shower. Her head screamed in agony. That's the last time she decided she would experiment with drugs.

***

Donald watched a horsebox come into the yard. Sophie looked, and they both ran downstairs, Donald not saying a word. The driver asked, "Sophie Mercantile here."

"Me," Sophie replied, taking the paperwork seeing she owned a horse she'd been looking at for days on the Internet, Cherokee.

She immediately kissed Donald, "You're a sneaky devil Donald; I love you."

The driver smiling, opened the side ramp backing Cherokee down slowly. Donald was surprised how big the horse towered must be seventeen hands, if not more. "That reminds me, Donald; Derek sent the saddle, bridle and blankets; he guessed you wouldn't have any."

Donald laughed, "He's right. Today, I must visit the wholesalers to collect sawdust and buy hay; mine went up in smoke." Donald wrote out a cheque passing to the driver. "Give my best to Derek, thank you."

The lorry turned around and left. Sophie placed her horse Cherokee in his stable, ensuring he had water, some hay in the net from when Christine was last here and sawdust. "I'll nip to the wholesalers and see a local farmer and purchase hay, want to stay or come to Sophie," Donald asked, suspecting no would be the answer.

"I'll come with you, Donald. I need to buy combs, brushes, buckets, and a few other essentials. No point in having a horse if you're not looking after it properly," she kissed him passionately. "You wait until I have you upstairs later," she grinned.

They jumped in his Bentley. He would have loved to have taken his American truck. Unfortunately, destroyed in the fire, soon in town at the wholesalers. Sophie knew exactly what she needed, ordering a ton of wood shavings and other supplements. Her horse would live better than they were, Donald thought. Donald decided the quickest solution to the hay problem was to see Gerald on Strawberry Estate; purchase a couple or three bales from him until he could sort out a proper supplier. Donald turned down the familiar drive; Gerald and Cindy came from the house and greeted Donald and Sophie, extremely curious as to why he'd come. "Need a favour, Gerald," Donald asked, stepping from his Bentley. "Sophie's horse has arrived; I haven't any hay. Could I buy a couple of bales from you?"

Christine's watching from the window, wondering why Donald would venture here, especially with his girlfriend. "I can see you're loaded down, Donald. I'll bring the hay over with my Range Rover. Cindy and I can have a cup of tea with you both. The atmosphere in our house is a little strained, as you can imagine."

Gerald jumped in his Range Rover, and Cindy drove around to the rear of the house, throwing three bales of hay on the tailgate, following Donald home. Sophie's using the next-door stable for storage and as a tack room. Donald promised to have Michael convert to hang things on the wall plus some storage bins for the horse food. They went up into Donald's private apartment away from the noise of the builders. Cindy had paused, stroking the head of Sophie's horse Cherokee, eventually running upstairs to join everyone else. "A beautiful horse, Sophie; he's like The Rising Sun, a good temperament."

Sophie smiled, "I suggest we go riding together, but that may upset Christine, and I don't want to cause any trouble."

"Sophie, I own Strawberry Estate, not Christine; you may ride on my estate whenever you want, and if she says anything, advise her to speak to me. It would be enjoyable if we could ride together when the weather and time allow. I'm afraid Christine has lost the plot as far as we are concerned. Honestly, I'm not convinced she wasn't involved in arranging the fire here."

"Thanks, Mr Gibbs," Sophie expressed, slightly concerned.

"Call me Gerald, Sophie, no formality amongst friends. You've done me no harm; only my stupid daughter messed up her future. That's not your fault or Donald's. Her mother is dead; those shares become mine. I own Strawberry Estate lock stock and barrel."

Donald exhaled, "You will have to leave them to someone, Gerald, before it's too late."

"I could leave for Cindy's son; he's like you, Donald, not frightened of work. His girlfriend is dependable. Christine can have Glencoe, then she's out of everybody's hair."

"I have to go to Glencoe myself in the next few days. I promised Mrs Montague; she helped me with planning consent for my new buildings; otherwise, I'd still be waiting. I think I start cutting here soon." Donald heard a vehicle; they looked out of the window. Mary and Martin had returned, Martin in his holiday sombrero-wearing a T-shirt with a pattern that drove your eyes crazy. Everyone came down from the studio, hugging each other in the yard. No one bothered anymore about the coronavirus. "I've come to prevent my son from spending money," Martin said, looking at the building work. "I must see what machines you purchased, Donald. I didn't realise we had a three-thousand-acre estate," Martin chuckled.

"No, dad, I purchased equipment big enough to complete each operation in a day. The rest of the time, I will only be a part-time farmer. The machinery can sit in the shed, costing me nothing."

Martin climbed aboard their new Quadtrac Case IH with over 620 hp with a ten-furrow plough on the back. "Donald, have you seen the computer stuff?"

"I haven't bothered to look too busy organising other things."

Martin climbed down, looking at the grain trailers, "Donald, they hold twenty-five tonnes each," he ran over to the combine, "Bigger than the one destroyed."

"Supposed to be as good as Claas Lexion, they think it can outperform in certain conditions. I don't know. They think it can cut three-hundred acres a day with no trouble. I only need someone here to empty the trailers in the grain store when they've finished building, which will have to be by the end of next week, or they won't be paid," Donald expressed firmly, "That's the agreement. You will also find father a five-thousand-gallon diesel tank by the new barn."

Mary was stunned by everything she saw climbing into a tractor; she sat in the comfortable seat with a plastic cover on, "What horsepower is this, Donald?"

"Only a baby mum four hundred plus hp four-wheel-drive, of course, you obviously notice that. I want something to pull the trailers to support the articulated tractor?"

"Dare I ask how much you spent, my son?"

"Two million, I think. I haven't calculated." Donald was not batting an eyelid. Martin and Mary stared at him in disbelief; Gerald exhaled, guessing expensive, but not that much.

"Some of the equipment is still at the supplier's were waiting for the sheds to be built. I have a new drill coming, can plant three hundred acres before I stop for lunch. You can see the new loader; you'll like that dad all-wheel steer, air conditioning, grain bucket, and bale grab still at the suppliers. I shan't purchase a baler until next harvest. I thought all wheat next year, we can either chop the straw or bale. I'll purchase for Sophie's horse and hay."

"What horse!" Mary asked, climbing down from the tractor.

"Sophie's! I purchased for her; she loves horses. I promised her I would buy one."

"Oh," Mary smiled, "Let's see the animal," they walked into the yard. Cherokee placed his head over the door, neighing. Mary patted him, "What a lovely animal; I'm sorry if I seemed shocked. The last time Donald purchased a horse for someone, he'd wasted his money."

"I'm marrying Donald, Mrs Selwyn," Sophie said abruptly. "I'm not a tart, I don't sleep around, and I only want Donald. I want to carry his child; I can't wait until we're married," she expressed firmly.

"Okay, I have the message," Mary said, surprised; Sophie would react that way, clearly showing her determination. Mary couldn't fault her.

Mary cuddled Sophie, "I didn't mean to be offensive. Only Donald's tolerated crap lately. I don't think it's over by a long chalk."

"Can you ride Mary," Sophie asked?

"As a teenager, yes."

"Good, change. I'll saddle Cherokee and see how you ride. I'm a qualified trainer," Sophie advised. "Mary, when I'm away with Donald in the next couple of days, you can feed him and ride," Sophie smiled cheekily.

"I'm too heavy," Mary suggested.

Martin commented, "You have a good arse woman," receiving a slap around the ear.

Donald's splitting himself laughing, watching Mary whisper in Sophie's ear what she weighed. "That will be fine and also help you lose weight."

Mary hurried and changed quickly into trousers and a jacket. Sophie made her wear a hard hat. Donald placed a hay bale close to the horse to help his mother mount. Mary carefully mounted, putting her feet in the stirrups has Sophie adjusted to make them more comfortable. Mary's smiling from ear to ear, "Great brings back memories."

Martin commented, "Doesn't it just my love, remember in the hay meadow."

Gerald and Cindy were watching.

Donald laughed, "The horse's eyes are popping out, mum! Lose some weight quick," he joked

Sophie slapped his leg with her crop.

"Ouch, that hurt."

Mary smiled, seeing Donald come off the worst for a change. Mary trotted out of the yard entering a field of rape with a set-aside headland. "Go around the field, Mary, steady, see how you cope," Sophie suggested. Everyone watched from the gateway, Mary riding around the twenty-acre field. She couldn't smile anymore by the time she returned to the gate. "I'd forgotten how lovely it is to ride a horse."

"Again, Mary," Sophie encouraged, "Keep riding around. He needs to exercise until you're tired, then come into the yard."

Martin kissed Sophie, "You made my wife a happy woman today. I never thought I'd see her on the back of a horse again, and I don't think she ever expected to ride."

Gerald and Cindy returned to Strawberry Estate. Christine watched Mary ride around the field from an elevated position with her binoculars, surprised she could even ride.

An hour later, Mary came into the yard. Sophie came down from the studio, helping Mary off Cherokee. "Oh, I'm stiff; my backside is numb." Mary waddled to the cottage returning with three large carrots. Cherokee rested his head against Mary while she slipped one carrot at a time into his mouth. Sophie remarked, "You have made a friend for life. Ride whenever you want to, Mary. I'm sure you know how to put a saddle and bridle on." Mary nodded, smiling, hugging and kissed Sophie on the cheek, "You are such a breath of fresh air, Sophie; I'm so pleased you're with Donald." Donald came down from the studio. "You'll never guess mum, Sophie, my latest artwork fetched fifteen million absolutely ridiculous. Some reports say it's heading for a Royal household, but not confirmed."

"I think Martin has the cheque from the insurance company. It doesn't cover a fraction of what we lost; thank god for you, son, we'd be on our knees."

"I haven't heard about the fifth wheel and my American truck either; the insurance company appears to be dragging their heels," Donald frowned. "Changing the subject, mum, I want to travel with Sophie to Scotland tomorrow. Would you mind looking after Cherokee? I've ordered some hay from a local haulier for him. Sophie has already ordered the bedding and plenty of food here for him. Of course, you can go riding around the estate," Donald grinned, "Perhaps you might bump into Christine, and you can kick her off her horse."

"That's not the attitude, son; you were never raised to be vindictive like that. Christine has her own problems, and we have ours; please concentrate on Sophie."

"Sorry, mum, you are correct; I won't lower myself to her level. As soon as the harvest ends, mum, I'm marrying Sophie."

Donald and Sophie set off for Scotland in his Bentley. A journey they haven't travelled for some time. First heading for Tain to visit Sophie's parents, Donald smiled, parking in the driveway and seeing Sophie's father on his new tractor ploughing. He'd extended his growing area by at least half an acre; he had the equipment to handle the work. Mr Mercantile noticed Donald's car stopping his tractor. He came over quickly, embracing his daughter and then Donald. Mrs Mercantile came out from the house, welcoming them both warmly. "We saw on the news Donald your farm the next thing new buildings and massive machinery delivered. The equipment you purchased me is wonderful. We are growing more vegetables now than ever, and I'm selling some to make a little income. Donald removed his wallet, placing a thousand pounds in Mrs Mercantile's hand, "That will help cover the cost of the cup of tea you're making me," Donald chuckled. "Unfortunately, we can't stay long. I'm here on business; Sophie and I plan to marry as soon as I've finished harvest. I will send a private helicopter for you both so you can attend the wedding; I'll cover the cost."

"I have to find someone to feed my pigs while I'm away," Mr Mercantile remarked, "And buy a new suit."

Donald removed another thousand pounds from his wallet, passing to Mr Mercantile, "That should cover the cost; you'll not have any excuse for not attending."

Donald moved away from the table with his camera taking several photos of Mr and Mrs Mercantile sitting at their oak table with a mug of tea with Ma and Pa engraved.

Sophie laughed, "You'll be in oils shortly, so don't be surprised if you see yourself on television," She kissed them both. "We must go, Donald, come on, we'll be in touch, love you both," she said, leaving.

Mr and Mrs Mercantile stood in the doorway waving while Donald and Sophie drove away. "You certainly made a big impression, Donald; Pa loves his tractor; I think they look younger since they met you. You made their life so much easier," she said, kissing him.

They finally arrived at Glencoe, warmly greeted. Sophie and Donald walk to the stables. The new stable girl glanced up and continued with her work; Justin joined them. "She's a bit fierce, Donald; she has a tongue like a razor blade that reminds me of Christine."

Sophie looked over the stable doors at the horses, "That one has a sore on his leg. That one has a scar on its neck, this one light on his front foot. Why?" Sophie went into the stable, lifting the hoof and finding a large stone trapped; she forced it out with her fingers patting the horse on the neck. Donald remarked, "I suggest you pack your bags and leave if this is the best you can perform. Call yourself a horse lover with horses in this state," he expressed with conviction.

Jock came down to the stables chuckling, "I heard you were here. The phones are red-hot, Donald. Are you sacking that bitch? She knows nothing about horses," Jock smiled, standing by Donald.

Donald turned to Justin, "Is this the best you can do, Justin? If you keep her on, she must be under Jock's supervision. He knows what's right and wrong with animals. If she doesn't like it, show her the door. Come along, Jock, you're smiling. You must need a drink." Jock patted Donald on the shoulder, "You're a sight for sore eyes, lad."

"A large malt whisky for my friend Jock, please," Donald ordered. "What's happening, Jock? Why has Justin employed that idiot to look after the horses?"

Jock shrugged his shoulders, "No idea, almost as if someone wants the operation to fail and will if it keeps on this way."

Justin came into the bar, "I have explained to her that Jock is in charge of the horses. She either carries out Jock's instructions to the letter or is down the road."

"Justin, what's going on? Your no fool is someone pulling your strings. You haven't phoned me lately, which I find rather suspicious."

"If you must know, Donald, everyone is disillusioned here since Christine sacked you and Sophie; everyone has lost the will to live for a better explanation. Glencoe knew nobody would get away with anything; they knew every penny they put into Glencoe would be for improvements."

"What's the state of accounts? Don't lie, Justin."

"Mrs Montague is permitting Christine one-thousand a month salary; she said it's a goodwill gesture. When she's twenty-one, she will take full control of the hotel. I will be gone by then, and so will the rest of the staff. No one wants anything to do with her, Donald. I know most of the staff are applying for employment, good reliable staff the hotel can't function without."

**

Mrs Montague's on a nearby estate in the security room listening to the conversation, now realising the severity of the situation. The hate for Christine is more intense than she anticipated. Her only hope is to keep Donald on her side; as long as he's associated with the hotel, the staff would remain loyal.

She's annoyed over the new stable girl. Donald had stepped in and stamped on everybody quickly as he always had. Mrs Montague ordered her driver to take her the short distance from her present location to Glencoe.

Donald glanced from the window, seeing Mrs Montague arrive with her bodyguard. She left him in the car entering the hotel in haste, locating Donald sitting at a table with Jock, Sophie, and Justin. Jock went to leave. Mrs Montague gestured with her hand, "Stay Jock, please, for a moment. Jock, take over the stables as Justin has suggested supervising the new girl. If she is no good, help her off the premises; unloved horses are not profitable."

"Donald, will you pay a monthly visit to Glencoe for the foreseeable future? Staff morale appears to be wavering; Justin needs your support on certain issues. I shan't insult you by offering to cover the fuel costs; you are already worth millions. The private suite is yours to use whenever you are here; you may stay for as long as you feel necessary to rectify any faults. I know you won't spare the rod; I've seen you in action myself," she smiled. "Sophie, if Jock needs any information regarding horse welfare. I'm sure he could phone you, and you advise him on what course of action to take."

Sophie smiled, "Certainly. I wonder if you would like to come to our wedding, Mrs Montague, hopefully after harvest."

"Send me an invitation," Mrs Montague standing, leaving the hotel less than happy because of Christine's behaviour.

Jock and Justin smiled, "You're back on the team."

"Apparently so, Jock; I'm tired. I'm off to bed," Donald said, standing.

"You hadn't better be," Sophie smiled, "I have plans for you."

Donald undressed, climbing into bed. Sophie joined him. The following morning, Donald strolled to the old sawmill, watching the water wheel majestically turn. Sophie had gone to the stables saddling a horse, taking a ride to the reservoir along the track to the conifer trees, taking in the early morning fresh air. She returned to the stables to find Jock with the stable girl. He's instructing her exactly how he wanted tasks carried out, leaving her in no doubt.

Sophie stabled her horse, returned to the hotel, and joined Donald for breakfast. Both decided to return home this morning. It was only intended to be a flying visit that appeared to serve its purpose. The staff were smiling apart from one. Justin came into the dining room with his cup of coffee, "I slept for the first time in ages, Donald; now we know you're on the team. Don't worry about the thousand pounds Christine receives a month. We can easily cover that. How long before your return, I suspect not until after harvest, must be close."

"Soon depends on the weather like everything else; hopefully, the new buildings are ready," he sighed heavily. "Are you ready to go, Sophie?"

"Yes, I've packed our bags before I went for a ride."

CHAPTER SEVENTEEN

UNEXPECTED PROBLEM

They set off on the long journey home. Sophie's feeling some discomfort, "I will have to see a doctor; I have a pain in my side," she complained.

They arrived home in the evening, heading for the studio. Mary noticed they'd arrived, not bothering to disturb, suspecting they needed to rest after the journey.

Around 2 o'clock in the morning, Sophie sat up in bed in agony, "I don't think it's food poisoning because I don't want to visit the toilet. Better take me to A&E Donald. I don't know what's wrong."

Donald quickly dressed. He carried her downstairs, placing her in the passenger seat of his Bentley driving out of the yard. Mary had heard the noise peering from the window and saw Donald's Bentley missing. She rang his mobile, "What's going on, Donald?"

"Sophie's in extreme pain, mum. I'm running her to A&E; I'll let you know when I know more."

Donald carried Sophie into accident and emergency; she was taken through within fifteen minutes for examination. Donald sat patiently, wondering what could possibly be wrong. The doctor advised Donald, "I'm afraid we have admitted Sophie. We need to test her liver; something isn't right, but we don't know what. She'll be in the ward in the next ten minutes. You can speak to her then."

"Private room, please. My name is Donald Selwyn. I will cover whatever she needs she must have, spare no expense doctor. Sophie is very precious to me."

"Yes, Mr Selwyn, now I recognise you; we have one spare private room if you could sign the paperwork at reception. I'll notify the specialist."

Within ten minutes, Donald's shown to a private room. Sophie was in bed. She hugged him, "This is private, Donald."

"It doesn't matter; I will pay whatever it takes to make you better; you're the best thing in my life, and nothing must happen to you," he kissed her forehead. Donald left as the doctors entered the room.

***

Mary sat drinking tea. Donald phoned, "Mum, there may be something wrong with Sophie's liver; they're running more tests. I'm on my way home."

"Stay strong, son; you may be worrying about nothing. We will have to face each challenge as it comes," Mary sighed, "I'll have breakfast ready for you."

"Thanks, mum. See you in a while."

Someone had informed the press, and the newspapers arrived at Crabtree Farm. A picture of Donald leaving his Bentley carrying Sophie into A&E. Donald shook his head in disbelief, convinced someone was stalking him. The caption read: "Mystery illness under investigation."

***

Christine sat at the breakfast table on Strawberry Estate, seeing the picture and the caption. Is this the break she's looking for, a way to walk into Donald's life? She'd have to monitor closely.

Gerald read the caption and immediately phoned Crabtree Farm. Mary explained the situation. "Give Sophie our best wishes for a speedy recovery, Mary."

***

Donald finished his breakfast with his mother and father. Mary advised she'd look after Cherokee and exercise. Donald and Martin walked through the newly completed buildings, including a new drying system. Simply drive over a grid, empty your trailer, the seed cleaned automatically, and moisture content tested if required; drying would automatically occur before storage. Donald had spared no expense. He didn't think there was any way he would want to reverse a twenty-five-tonne trailer into a grain store. Easier to drive over a grid empty and allow conveyors to do the work for you. "My God, son, you haven't spared any expense. We almost have a brand-new farm; in fact, you have better equipment than Gerald now; apart from my father's Ferguson twenty, the only thing left is the wood processor. I suppose we better set the combine, tractors and trailers ready to go, son."

Donald drove the articulated tractor into the new machinery store, detaching the plough. He glanced up to the roof, noticing the sprinklers were in place, costing an extra ten thousand pounds; he didn't care. No one would destroy his farm again. Donald gingerly attached the twenty-five-ton trailer. Martin's aboard the other tractor, an enormous 400 plus hp, he reversed to the other twenty-five-ton trailer hitching. Driving to the machinery store, parking inside. They walked back to the combine, the forty-five-foot header attached to the rear transport trailer. Donald ran, fetching the Ferguson twenty, detaching the new forty-five-foot header from the combine hitching to the back of the Ferguson twenty. He towed into the field, manoeuvring until the header was in the right place to attach to the combine in the field of oilseed rape.

Martin drove the combine around the rear of the buildings to the new diesel tank filling the combine to the brim with fuel. He returned to the header straddling the gateway. Donald watched him manoeuvre until he'd lined up properly, lifting the new header from its transport trailer. Donald moved the Ferguson twenty and trailer out of the way; they spent five minutes attaching an all-in-one hydraulic chest connection. They checked the combine is greased. Donald removed a moisture content tester from his pocket. While he tested the oilseed rape, Martin watched. "15% father, a dry night, no dew on the ground this morning, have you noticed?"

Martin nodded, "I think we'll have a cup of tea Donald; allow the sun to rise a little more, and we'll see what that beast is made of; can I drive, please," Martin grinned.

"You might as well, father; I've never seen you look so happy over harvest."

"I've never had new equipment before, son."

After a quick cup of tea, Martin climbed aboard the new combine and checked the setting on the computer and the recommendations. He started cutting, and Donald came into the field with both trailers. The combine's travelling that fast Donald had to run and jump on the ladder sitting in the cab with his father. Martin couldn't stop smiling; the machine absolutely charging across the field wasn't very long before one trailer filled. Donald transported to the new grain store system crossing his fingers everything would work properly. He pressed the start button on the grain storage system lifting the shoot on the rear of the trailer, watching the oilseed rape vanish. Donald lifted the trailer using the twin hydraulic rams until empty.

He returned to the field only to discover the next trailer completely full. He realised he would have to move, the combine, waiting for no one. By the end of the day, they only had twenty-five acres left on the farm to cut. Gerald came over, not believing the acreage the combine had covered. He looked at the new system Donald had built; an automated one-button cured all problems. Gerald sat in the cottage with Mary drinking a cup of tea, "I didn't think they'd cover that many acres considering they had to change fields, Mary."

"I have to confess I'm rather surprised. At least the seeds in the storage bins and not on the floor. From what Martin said, the combine keeps you well informed; if the thrashing system has a fault. I don't really understand it myself," she exhaled. "Remember Gerald, none of this would be possible without Donald and his money."

"Christine's in one of my combines and Stephen in the other. Too expensive to allow idiots to drive, I persuaded Michael to handle a grain trailer. Otherwise, I'd have to use outside labour, which I don't want to do."

"How is Christine, Gerald?"

"She appears to be settling down, I think. I know she sent a bouquet of flowers to Sophie this morning, which I thought was nice. Perhaps she's realised Donald, and she is really finished. More's the pity. He would have made a marvellous son-in-law, and I'm not talking about his money; he's genuinely a lovely person."

"Thank you for that comment, Gerald. We had not forgotten you helped us when we were in trouble." Gerald reached across with his hand squeezing Mary's; she stood, encouraging him to follow her. She turned quickly in the hallway, kissing him softly. They stayed there with Mary offering her breast to his lips for a moment. The minute his tongue touched her nipple, she lost self-control, suggesting, "Have to meet up soon somewhere we won't be disturbed, Gerald." She removed her nipple from his lips, slipping into her bra and encouraging him to go back to the kitchen before they were caught.

"If you like, I will talk to Martin tonight and Donald, perhaps to help you with the wheat. Martin could come over with our combine, Donald would come with a tractor and trailer, and you could complete ahead of time for a change."

"That would be marvellous."

Donald and Martin entered the cottage laughing, "Twenty-five acres, mum, we're finished."

"Good, you can help Gerald, and before you say anything, Donald, remember this farm wouldn't be here today if it weren't for Gerald and Christine when Martin broke his back. I offered on your behalf for Martin to take the new combine, and you with the trailer with the three combines running, two-thousand acres of wheat will vanish in a couple of days. Christine and Stephen will finish the rape tomorrow on Gerald's farm; you can all start the next day on the wheat."

Donald burst out laughing, and Martin, "You remember the last time your mother opened her mouth, giving orders."

"Yes, dad, cost me thousands."

"I will certainly come over with the combine, Gerald, and possibly Donald with the trailer; although he must see Sophie, you can't leave the girl alone. That reminds me, Donald, have you contacted her parents?"

"Blimey, no, dad, I'll do it now," Donald ran outside, dialling Mrs Mercantile's number. "Mr, Mercantile, I apologise for not contacting you sooner. I suppose you saw the newspapers?"

"Yes, lad, Sophie has phoned me. We understand Sophie explained you are paying privately. I couldn't wish for anything else; I'm sure she will receive the best care."

"If you'd like me to send a helicopter for you both, you can spend the day down here if you wish. Or a month, I will cover the cost. I don't want you worrying about expenses at a time like this."

"We understand why Sophie's so fond of you; thank you for your offer. We'll leave it a few more days to see how Sophie progresses. Let's find out what's wrong with her before we panic. Thank you for ringing Donald goodbye."

Donald entered the cottage, frowning, "I'm such a bloody idiot, mum. When it was in the papers, I should have realised that her parents would see; thankfully, Sophie phoned from the hospital."

"You can't think of everything, Donald," Gerald commented. "Thanks for offering to come and help me anything that secures the harvest, keeps the pennies in the bank," Gerald said, leaving.

Donald ran outside, detaching the one-grain trailer from the articulated tractor fitting the plough on the back. He apprehensively drove into the field, carefully starting to plough, becoming accustomed to the large outfit, flying across the field and continuing to plough until 6 30 p.m. He quickly showered, changed, drove to the hospital, and was allowed to see Sophie. "Have they discovered the problem?"

Sophie shrugged her shoulders, "My liver is failing, and I may need a transplant if they can find a liver. That's the last thing I expected to be wrong with me."

A consultant entered the room, looking at Sophie's notes and shaking Donald's hand. "We will try and flush Sophie's liver again. Not reacting the way it should. We don't know why. We've managed to control the pain; however, I wouldn't be surprised if she needs a transplant which leads us to our next problem, where do we find a liver from. There aren't that many donors; it has to be compatible."

"May I suggest, Sir, you email worldwide buy one? Money is no object," Donald assured, slightly panicking.

"Not quite as simple as that, Mr Selwyn, some real fraudsters out there; you pay up first and end up with a goat's liver if you're not careful. Although if we went through American hospitals, they are more credible. We must not start running around like headless chickens until we have all the facts," the consultant smiled, leaving.

Donald spent an hour with Sophie kissing her goodbye and leaving for the farm. He couldn't sleep and climbed aboard the tractor, continuing to plough, worried sick over Sophie and excited with his new purchase. Donald parked by the gateway and ran up to the studio, flopping on his bed, exhausted, only to be woken at 8 o'clock by his mother. "Breakfast, Donald."

Donald came down, walking across to the cottage. Mary took one look at him, "Have you had any sleep, Donald?"

"Not much. I ploughed 100 acres last night after I came from the hospital. Not good news, mum. They think she may need a liver transplant, so finding a suitable match can be difficult. I've offered to pay. That's not the problem."

"I think you had better go to bed, Donald. I'll help your father this morning. Only twenty-five acres to cut; besides, I haven't driven one of these new toys," she grinned. Walking out of the kitchen, following Martin to the tractor and trailer. She climbed in the cab, "I can't drive this. No gear levers."

Martin laughed, kissing Mary, "I can deal with love, only twenty-five acres you can play with the horse." She left the cab walking off, shaking her head in disbelief. Martin drove the tractor and trailer to where he was about to start cutting. He started the combine filling the trailer, moving to the store and emptying, returning to finish off what's left, with the tractor emptying the trailer again. Martin started his old Ferguson twenty; taking the header trailer over to the combine, he carefully detached the header, backing the combine away after releasing the hydraulic pipework. He felt pretty proud of himself; he's with the latest piece of equipment he hardly understood, having the privilege to drive thanks to his son. Martin parked the combine ready to move to Strawberry Estate in the morning, greasing to ensure the bearings wouldn't overheat, checking the engine oil and filling with diesel. Donald woke around 1 o'clock, coming downstairs and walking out into the yard to see his father had completed. He heard an engine. He looked across the fields, noticing his father ploughing with the ten-furrow plough and new 600+ horsepower case Quadtrac.

Donald noticed a white Range Rover coming up the drive. Christine, parking alongside him, lowered her electric window. "Father said you're helping us with the wheat; I'm to give you escort to our farm with your combine."

"Okay, we might as well take it, now, I suppose," Donald hitched the header trailer to the back of the combine and attached the electrics. Christine jumped in her Range Rover, placing an amber flashing beacon on her roof, leading the way. Donald followed her cautiously; they finally left the road, parking by the field to start in the morning.

Christine jumped out of her Range Rover, removing the flashing light from her roof and placing on the back seat. She approached Donald, "Sorry to hear about Sophie. I sent her flowers; I hope you don't mind?"

"No," he sighed, walking towards his own farm. "Donald, I'll give you a lift," Christine expressed, "Can't we be friends, Donald? Please, I can't undo the past."

Donald sighed, turning around and walking towards her. She quickly kissed him, "See, I'm not poisonous," she chuckled, climbing into her Range Rover. Donald popped around the other side; he sat quietly. Christine kept glancing at him, parking in front of Strawberry Estate house. "Come along, have a coffee with us, or I should say tea Cindy will never forgive me else." Donald followed her inside. Gerald's sat at the table drinking tea. Cindy had gone in his Range Rover shopping. Donald sat down. "You made the papers, Donald. Donald Selwyn spares no expense to save his future wife; the hospital is presently searching for a replacement liver."

Donald exhaled, "The press is always desperate for a story; last I heard, they were still trying to understand why her liver's failing. We discussed a replacement liver-only as a last resort, and I don't think we are yet at that stage."

Christine reached across, patting the back of Donald's hand, "I'm sure things will work out for the best," she left the table before she started grinning.

***

Mrs Montague had received information the Copthorne brothers instigated the attack on Crabtree Farm. She had received orders from Elizabeth R they could no longer be trusted, delving into highly embarrassing areas, such as drug trafficking. She arranged for the pair to be injected with a steroid their body couldn't handle. Keep fit fanatics enjoyed displaying themselves with men and women, considered distasteful in some circles. Within hours they were dead, and the television advised an accidental overdose of steroids and muscle enhancer, a new black-market product contaminated.

***

Christine's upstairs while Donald continued talking to her father. She switched on the television seeing the news flash concerning the Copthorne brothers and their demise. A cold shudder ran down her spine. She knew no accident and suspected Mrs Montague had worked out what happened at Crabtree Farm. Christine's only hope is if Mrs Montague accepts because Donald gave one of the brothers a good slapping, that's why the farm was torched. Christine quickly searched through her wardrobe, finding a short skirt and tight blouse, slipping on her favourite flat-soled shoes. She entered the kitchen, "I'll give you a ride home, Donald. I'm going into town if you're ready." Donald waved to Gerald, following Christine to her Range Rover. Christine jumped in eagerly, ensuring her skirt displayed as much leg as possible. She knew she caught Donald's attention, discreetly observing him glancing at her on the way home. She suspected still some attraction needed rekindling. Donald jumped out, "Thanks, Christine, see you tomorrow."

Donald watched Christine leave and climbed into his Bentley to drive into town to check on Sophie; her condition had worsened. The specialist entered, "I'm afraid we will have to operate; something is causing the problem, and we can't find it without an invasive examination. We have sedated her and should be in theatre later today." Donald nodded, leaving, having a horrible feeling he was losing Sophie.

***

Christine had dashed home, running upstairs, changing into her riding clothes saddling The Rising Sun and heading for Crabtree Farm. Mary riding Cherokee, enjoying every minute, Martin would have to wait for his lunch as far as she's concerned. "Hi, Mary," Christine voiced cheerfully, "Fancy venturing around our estate, ride together."

"Okay, I suppose it won't hurt; I can't belong."

They rode around Strawberry Estate, Christine making sure she said nothing inappropriate, hoping to get into Mary's good books. Donald would listen to her whatever happened. Mary looked at her watch, "Martin will kill me. It's 4 o'clock. I must go, Christine. We can do this again another day," Mary rode off quickly, returning to Crabtree Farm. Martin sat at the table with a pot of jam and a loaf of bread, not in the slightest impressed. Mary smiled, kissing him, "You forgive me, husband, having a good time." Mary observing Donald's Bentley had returned from the hospital.

Donald exhaled, sitting in front of a canvas. He started sketching Sophie on Cherokee; history repeating itself; he painted Christine on The Rising Sun. She betrayed him and Sophie on death's door if they couldn't find another liver.

Donald retired to bed at 4 o'clock and was woke at 8:30 by his mother for breakfast. After breakfast, Donald and Martin climbed aboard their new case tractor towing the twenty-five-ton grain trailer and made their way to Strawberry Estate. Attached the header to their combine noticing Christine coming down the lane with her Lexion combine, closely followed by Stephen with the other Lexion. She waved as she entered the field. Christine started cutting first, followed by Stephen, then Martin. Gerald had to join the grain carting with the three combines working at maximum capacity. They had cut over a thousand acres by 6 o'clock in the evening. Everyone stopped for a bite to eat, and within half an hour, the combines were rolling again. One-thousand-five-hundred acres were harvested by 10 o'clock in the evening, deciding to stop to control the moisture content.

Donald phoned the hospital for an update on Sophie's condition; all the nurses would say she was stable. Donald and Martin made their way home with the tractor and trailer and would return in the morning to wipe out the remaining five hundred acres. It shouldn't take many hours. Donald showered, sitting in front of his canvas, completing the painting he'd started. He betrayed Sophie in her wedding dress, hoping she would wear it one day. Donald finally retired to bed, exhausted. He realised it was pointless venturing to the hospital; she was so heavily drugged she probably wouldn't recognise him.

Mary woke Donald for breakfast; she could see that he was distraught by the expression on his face. Martin and Donald drove to Strawberry Estate on the tractor and trailer. The combines roared into life, with the trailers having difficulty keeping the combines empty; just after midday, the harvest finished. Martin loaded the combine header on the transport trailer, reversing and attaching. Donald led the way with the case tractor homeward bound for Crabtree Farm.

Christine showered and changed, driving over to Crabtree Farm. She knocked on Donald's studio door. "Come in," he said after looking out of the window, noticing her white Range Rover. She looked at the portrait Donald's painting of Sophie, " Beautiful, Donald," she commented. "How is Sophie? Any news?"

"Not really. I think desperately searching for a liver."

"Would you like me to make the coffee Donald or a cup of tea? I came over to thank you for helping us. You made preparing the ground so much easier we have more time."

"I wouldn't mind a coffee. We owe you anyway, Christine. You saved our skin when dad broke his back. You were very generous; you and your father, we wouldn't have survived without you two."

Christine returned with the coffees, "I wish I'd never interfered; I ruined your life and my own," she started to cry.

"Please don't cry, Christine, stay friends and leave it at that. Someone out there that will make you happy, I'm sure." Donald sighed, photographing his painting and sending it to Jack with the title. "Where My Angel Lives."

Jack phoned, "I will come to you, Donald. I can't imagine how you feel. A beautiful portrait. I think we should make a thousand copies. Hence, other members of the public have the chance to possess such beautiful artwork at a reasonable cost."

"Thanks, Jack; I don't want to be far away from Sophie now."

Donald's mobile rang. Mr Mercantile, "I've talked to the hospital. Sophie won't recover short of a miracle unless they find a liver in time. Could you possibly arrange for transport for myself and my wife, please? I asked the local farmer, and he said we could land a helicopter in his field. There are no electric cables or trees, just grass." His voice started to break under extreme stress.

"No problem, I'll give your phone number to the helicopter firm so you can explain where you want them to land. I will arrange accommodation for you, you can stay on my farm. I think we have a spare room, don't worry, all expenses will be covered by me," Donald assured.

"Thanks, Donald," Mr Mercantile rang off.

Donald phoned the helicopter company he used before providing Mr Mercantile's address and phone number; they were to fly direct to Crabtree Farm with Sophie's parents.

Donald stood. Christine, crying, held Donald, "A horrible life, Donald; everybody is suffering." Donald kissed her on the cheek and ran downstairs into the cottage. "Mum, do we have any spare accommodation?"

"Yes, apartment one for a week."

"Great send the bill to me for the week; I'm arranging for Sophie's parents to be flown from Scotland to land here. I suspect tomorrow morning, if not tonight. I'm waiting for confirmation."

"I see Christine's here," Mary asked curiously.

"She's behaving herself; she appears to be as upset as the rest of us."

"I wonder," Mary commented as Donald walked out the door.

He ran back in, "Jack's on the way, mum. Do you have a cake for him?"

"Don't I always," she smiles, watching Donald run out of the cottage. Christine came downstairs, meeting him in the doorway. She hugged Donald again, running for her Range Rover and jumping in driving off. The whole situation is tearing her apart; this would be hers if she weren't so stupid.

Donald left the yard looking across the fields seeing his father ploughing perhaps another day. The whole three-hundred acres were finished. Donald watched the drill coming up the drive with an escort. James wasn't joking when he said a minimum of three hundred acres daily. The machine is on enormous tyres, and you would definitely need satellite navigation. You would never see your last drill mark. Donald estimated the tank would hold eight tons of grain plus a separate compartment if you wanted to apply fertiliser simultaneously. James laughed, looking at the expression on Donald's face, "You ordered big, and I promised you big, the only one ever sold in the UK you can probably guess American."

Gerald had seen the flashing lights of the escort vehicle from his property. He couldn't wait to see what Donald had purchased this time. Gerald came up the drive. The tyres were at least six feet tall. Gerald stood laughing, "You won't wear the paint off the tines before you planted three-hundred acres, Donald."

"If you'd like one, Mr Gibbs," James smiled, "This machine is designed to plant over 1000 acres a day and requires a minimum of 400 hp to pull."

"The way I look at it, Gerald," Donald commented, "That should last me a lifetime unless I find an estate somewhere, either here or in Scotland."

Mary looked at the machine, "Oh Donald, you are ridiculous," she professed. "You have to buy everything bigger than anybody else," she laughed, "Thank god it's not my money," she said, walking to the house. "Tea Gerald if you move!"

"I'm coming," still laughing.

James remarked, "I'm sorry to hear about your girlfriend. That must be awful; I hope they find a liver. If we can be of service, Donald, give me a ring."

Donald smiled, walking off, attaching the folding power harrows to the Case IH 400 hp, hoping she'd have the power to drive. He entered the first field, setting the machine travelling fast and pleased the tractors on large tyres; otherwise, compaction could be a problem.

Gerald sipping his tea, suggested, "We're no better than the kids, Mary."

"We are more careful and a lot older. Martin in the bottom field," she grinned. Gerald couldn't believe what he saw. Mary slipped off her knickers, removing her large breasts from her bra, "If you're not interested, Gerald, fine. You have 15 minutes, I imagine." Mary walked along the narrow hallway. Gerald followed like a puppy dog discovering Mary on the bed waiting. He soon stepped out of his trousers. He'd never worked up, such a sweat, run the equivalent of 5 miles if not more and wasn't she demanding. He'd never know Mary to behave like this. The minute he touched her nipples, she would go wild. Gerald couldn't last any longer as much as he wanted to. Helping Mary to her feet, they both tidied quickly, returning to the kitchen and looking in the mirror. Mary straightened her pigtails and wiped her face on the towel to remove the perspiration. She was glowing like beetroot, and so was Gerald. He splashed cold water on his face, quickly wiping it off with the towel.

Gerald came out after having his cup of tea. He watched with Mary the speed Donald was travelling, thinking he didn't know everything about machinery. Donald's covering the acreage far quicker than his outfit. Realising the cost of the equipment Donald had purchased would take some recovering. He had almost three sets of power harrows in one line; you would need the 400 hp to drive the way the tractors barking under strain. The problem is Gerald thought, you'd only need a rubbishy driver could cost you thousands in repairs, he couldn't justify that.

After finishing ploughing, Martin travelled from the bottom field, watching Donald, then saw the new drill that belonged on an American farm. By the time you have one half in the field, the other half would be protruding out the other side.

Nevertheless, Donald had set out to make the farm easy to manage, and one man could easily cope with three-hundred acres with the size of equipment he purchased. Gerald driving off in his Range Rover, watching Donald travel across the field.

Martin stood in the gateway watching a helicopter hovering, landing in the paddock by the buildings making quite a noise with the echo it created.

Donald ran to the paddock helping Mr and Mrs Mercantile from the helicopter with their luggage. The helicopter immediately took off. "I have accommodation for you here in one of our apartments for a week."

Mr and Mrs Mercantile smiled in appreciation. They couldn't fault Donald; he bent over backwards to cater to their every need.

Donald showed them into apartment one. Mary greeted them, inviting to the cottage for refreshment, which they gladly accepted. Mr Mercantile commented, "Helicopters are not my favourite mode of transport. I know Sophie detests them; we used to have them on the estate where I worked. The Royals were forever flying in and out. We had the good fortune to adopt Sophie; she has been the light of our eyes. We managed to save enough money for the Croft; the rest is history. Although we were really struggling recently until Donald turned things around for Sophie and us. What is the latest on Sophie's condition? Do you know Donald?" Mr Mercantile asked.

"No change, as far as I know; I'm waiting for a phone call to say they have found a liver somewhere around the world," Donald expressed, tears on his cheeks. Mrs Mercantile cuddled him, "If it weren't for you, Donald, she'd probably be dead now; you have the contacts, the money to make things happen, we don't."

"I will take you to see her; I think she's still sedated. Nevertheless, we will go when you've had a chance to freshen. Sophie's in a private room."

Mary pointed to the screen on her computer, displaying a portrait of Sophie on Cherokee in her wedding dress, already reaching ten million. Mrs Mercantile looked at the screen. "You painted that Donald of Sophie on a horse in her wedding dress. When?"

Mary opened the door, pointing across the yard, "Sophie's horse Cherokee, Donald purchased before she was ill." Mrs Mercantile ventured out; Mary gave her a couple of carrots. The horse placed its head against her cheek, crunching on carrots. Mary pointed to the other side of the yard, "Sophie's car. My son is very much in love with Sophie, and there's nothing he won't do to make her well."

Mr and Mrs Mercantile had changed, climbing into Donald's Bentley. Mr Mercantile commented, "I used to have to polish the bloody Rolls-Royces, and you can guarantee they'd find every piece of shit on the road to drive through."

Donald laughed, "Only use a power washer on mine."

Donald drove to the hospital, entering Sophie's private room. The consultant sitting on a chair making notes. Sophie's barely awake. Donald introduced Sophie's parents to the consultant. He indicated to leave the room, and everyone stepped outside the door. "I'm afraid the situation is dire. We think we have a match in San Francisco; the price is a hundred thousand dollars; everything is money out there."

"Purchase!" Donald said without thinking twice.

"I already have on your behalf, Donald; I knew your answer. The liver is from a girl of a similar age; she was hit by a Lorry and pronounced brain dead at the hospital. They waited for her to die. Her liver is on the way. We have surgeons on standby to perform the transplant. That doesn't mean we're out of the woods; Sophie's body could reject the transplant; a hundred and one reasons it won't work. Although we can combat most situations with drugs, that's the only thing keeping her alive."

"Can you keep me up-to-date, please," Donald asked. The consultant nodded. They returned to Sophie, kissing her forehead, squeezing her arm, and leaving the room. Donald's struggling to hold his emotions together, glad to be in the fresh air. Donald steadily drove home to Crabtree Farm. Mr and Mrs Mercantile entered the apartment provided. Mary had made sure they had milk, sugar, and the basics, placing food in the freezer, unsure of what they liked.

Donald ran upstairs, sitting at his easel, realising the next few hours were critical for Sophie. He couldn't settle, ran downstairs, started the tractor and power harrows, continuing to cultivate the ploughing. Mary and Martin could hear the tractor in their bedroom; they couldn't imagine how Donald was feeling deciding to leave him; he would do no harm driving a tractor.

They realised Christine was eighteen, no one mentioned her birthday, and Mary had forgotten entirely. Remembering, Donald's eighteen in a week. So much going on dates slipped their minds. "He will be a man soon, Martin."

"A man a long time ago, Mary, we never noticed; you would think after all the good deeds he's performed for people he would have some luck. If there's a god, he's bloody cruel," Martin commented.

Christine couldn't sleep either; with her binoculars from her bedroom window, she could see a tractor working on Crabtree Farm. She dressed and drove to the field. Donald stopped opening the cab door. She climbed in, sitting beside him in her miniskirt. They smiled at each other. Donald said, "They found a liver, Christine; I hope it arrives in time."

"You have done everything you can, Donald like you always do, so whatever happens, you can't blame yourself," Christine said, patting his leg.

Christine stayed with him until 7 o'clock in the morning. She kissed him softly on the lips, "Bye, for now, my best friend," she said, patting his cheek.

Donald folded the power harrows on the back of his case tractor parking in the machinery store, ran upstairs to his studio, showered, flopping on the bed.

Christine lay on her bed. She realised she was clutching at straws. Although Donald's now more friendly towards her, she still has a mountain to climb and may stand a chance if Sophie doesn't survive. Even if she does, she has a long road to recovery and may not make it. Christine decided to keep chipping away at Donald's tough exterior, hoping he would finally forgive her sins. There had been a few since they parted, although that didn't count.

She saddled her horse in the morning, taking a steady ride across the harvested fields to Crabtree Farm. She entered the yard as Mary was mounting Cherokee. Mary commented, "You have radar or something, girl," laughing, "That reminds me, Christine, happy birthday, I forgot."

"Thanks, Mary, unimportant." They rode off together to Strawberry Estate; Cindy's on Gerald's hunter, called Pig as Gerald named him. They met up by the old sawmill, watching people turning up in their cars to watch demonstrations of how things worked many years ago.

***

Mrs Montague had now discovered the truth. Initially, Christine discussed the arson attack on Crabtree Farm with the Copthorne brothers. Mrs Montague had seen with her drone that Christine was engaged in sexual acts with the Cropthorne brothers. However, after the actual arsonist caught a lowlife who admitted the Copthorne brothers wanted revenge against Donald after one received a beating. She concluded that the lowlife in question has since fallen off London Bridge to a watery grave where the fish would enjoy their supper. Mrs Montague had decided Christine must be made aware her activities were known and would not be tolerated.

***

Christine, Mary and Cindy trotted along to Strawberry Estate house. Gerald carried a tray of tea to the garden table; everyone dismounted, tying their horse to a wooden bench, enjoying the sunshine and the warm air, and drinking a refreshing cup of tea. "Any news, Mary," Gerald asked, genuinely concerned.

"As far as I know, a liver is on the way from America. Donald paid, of course, the only way he could acquire one. I suspect some other poor soul will die, a terrible thing when money stands between you and life," Mary commented.

Gerald sighed heavily, "The old story of survival of the fittest, the world's gone to dog-eat-dog situation. Years ago, we all looked after one another; now, we would sooner shoot each other, ridiculous. If only I could turn the clock back on the years I've wasted," Gerald sighed, "Apart from meeting Cindy, she's the love of my life."

Christine rode to Crabtree Farm with Mary noticing her father never mentioned her as special in his conversation. Christine watched Mary cross the road, saying goodbye, and they went their separate ways. Christine returned, stabling The Rising Sun, dashing upstairs to her bedroom. She searched for a Sophie Mercantile. Much to her surprise, she saw a picture of Sophie in a silver tightfitting dress. She guessed about sixteen with an older man. Christine continued to read; Sophie used to sing, the only way she could fund her training to become proficient with horses. Christine noticed in one of the pictures she's convinced she could see Mrs Montague. Mrs Montague would only be involved if there were a Royal connection;

nothing's making sense to Christine. She searched the Internet, discovering Sophie's man, a horse trainer, married.

Further down displays the picture of a mangled car. "Girl survives driver doesn't." Christine printed the information off, wondering how she could show Donald without appearing to be trying to cause trouble. She looked from her bedroom window, seeing lights across the field. Donald out with the tractor. She placed what she'd printed off in her denim jacket, making a flask, and drove the short distance, parking her Range Rover on the side of the road. She walked across; Donald opened the door smiling. She climbed aboard, sitting in the buddy seat, "How is Sophie," Christine asked nervously.

"They have carried out the transplant, wait and see now," Donald sighed, noticing the folded papers inside Christine's denim jacket. "What's that?"

"Me being nosy." Donald grabbed it from the inside of her jacket. He stopped the tractor on the headland at the far end of the field, turning off the engine and the lights apart from the interior light. He sat there looking at the pictures, "I've seen this dress before. I gather from the article that her original boyfriend was killed in a road accident, and she survived."

"That's what I gathered. I feel sorry for her; she has you now to cuddle when she recovers," Christine sighed. "I remembered I have a flask of coffee in my Range Rover if you'd like a cup, Donald?" Donald smiled, leaving the tractor cab with Christine; they sat in the Range Rover discussing the article. "What she was involved in before I met her Christine is none of my business. I can understand your curiosity, wondering what she has you don't. The answer is nothing in the short time I've known her; she hasn't strayed with anyone else."

"Okay, rub it in, Donald. I'm such a tart friend," she said, removing her clothes and folding her seat back, "Make love to me one more time, friend."

Donald's surprised he's aroused and wasn't long before making love vigorously. Christine had never known him like this; she thought he was almost trying to punish her. Nevertheless, she's enjoying every minute. Finally, they tidied themselves. "Our secret, Donald," Christine professed. "I'm not out to cause trouble, would achieve nothing."

Donald felt more relaxed, although he's guilty as hell for what he'd performed, wondering how many secrets would come out of the woodwork concerning Sophie. He seemed to go from one traumatic adventure to the next. Christine jumped out of her Range Rover back door, kissing him passionately. "I shan't forget this moment for as long as I live." She jumped in the driver's seat of her Range Rover heading home crying, praying that she was pregnant. She hadn't taken contraceptives for months. Christine knew she couldn't be pregnant by anybody else. If she only achieved a child, she's desperate to have a part of Donald would be a start in the right direction, running upstairs and laying on her bed.

Donald returned to his studio, lying on the bed, feeling relaxed for the first time in weeks. The remainder of the week passed uneventfully. Sophie's sitting up in bed, looking more like her old self. Donald arranged for Mr and Mrs Mercantile to be flown home by helicopter, extremely appreciative of the accommodation and support for their daughter. Donald watched the helicopter take off from the paddock. Mary would often ride on Cherokee with Christine and Cindy around Strawberry Estate.

The season-changing planting of the winter wheat. Donald was thankful for the satellite navigation on his tractors, especially drilling. Donald planted the three-hundred acres in a day. He watched the equipment, and the tractor steered itself most of the time. Donald drove to Strawberry Estate with his new drill, helping Gerald plant his two-thousand-five-hundred acres. Gerald stood watching Donald fly across the field with the new drill. Gerald never planted so quickly before, as daft as the drill looked on Donald's three-hundred acres. Donald proved that you can shift and complete your workload on time if you have the right equipment.

***

Christine's riding with Mary and Cindy across the freshly planted fields of Strawberry Estate. Cindy commented, "You're not well, Christine. You should see a doctor; you look anaemic." She paused, having a horrible thought, "You're not pregnant?"

Mary stopped her horse, and Cindy waited for Christine's reply. "Yes, I'm pregnant, and before you ask, the father doesn't know, but he will, and I'm not disclosing his name, none of your business."

Cindy and Mary looked at each other, shrugging their shoulders, not knowing who the father could be. "Not Donald, Christine?"

Christine laughed, cantering off, leaving the others behind.

"That's a turn-up for the books," Cindy suggested, "That's the last thing I expected; who is the father?"

Cindy phoned Gerald, "Are you sat down, Gerald."

"Yes, why; I'm having a cup of tea reading the newspaper for once. I have nothing to do thanks to Donald and his new drill."

"Christine is pregnant." Cindy heard a cup smash on the floor.

Gerald shouted, "That's bloody hot. Are you serious, Cindy, because it's not funny?"

"Of course, I'm serious dopey! She knows the father; he doesn't know yet, and she will not tell us. She doesn't have to, Gerald; she's over eighteen."

Christine phoned Donald, "Donald, are you alone? Can you talk?"

"Yes, in the studio. Why?"

"Your mother and Cindy have discovered I'm pregnant, no one knows who the father is, and I shall keep it that way. You have nothing to worry about, Donald; something I want."

Donald exhaled, "I presume I'm the father?"

"Don't say anything, Donald, please. I'm not going to be accused of trapping you with a baby. I want you to marry Sophie. I like my own company, and I'll have a son or daughter to love."

"Are you definitely sure you're pregnant? We've been down this road together before," Donald asked calmly.

"According to the pregnancy test kit, yes, so if you're asked Donald, you have no idea what they're talking about. I want to prepare you if you have the inquisition treatment from your parents or mine. We're both over eighteen, so technically, it's none of their bloody business."

"Christine, if you want anything, phone me."

"I know that, Donald; bye for now."

Mary and Cindy said goodbye to each other. Cindy returned to the stables, and Mary rode home to Crabtree Farm. She stable Cherokee entering Donald's studio. He's sat at his easel painting. She looked at the picture for clues that Donald was guilty. "Hi mum, enjoy your ride," Donald asked brightly.

"You know Christine is pregnant, Donald? Anything to do with you," Mary asked, placing her hands on her hips, suspicious of him.

Donald shrugged, "I have better things to do with my life, mum."

Mary stormed out of the studio, not convinced he wasn't the father. Donald ran downstairs, jumping in his Bentley, dashing into town to the Range Rover dealership. He purchased the top of the Range Rover in black with a baby seat for Christine. Donald left strict instructions that the vehicle was to be registered in Christine Gibbs's name. They were not to disclose who'd purchased the vehicle; otherwise, they would see no further business from him. Donald left smiling. Although not quite the way he planned, the thought of having a child is quite exciting. He would have preferred the mother to be Sophie. He wondered how long the secret would stay a secret; he couldn't imagine the hell he would experience once everybody found out the truth.

Nevertheless, his lack of self-control placed him in that position. Donald returned to the studio, continuing with his picture of the three combines on Strawberry Estate harvesting the wheat. Donald painted a stalk flying across the field, carrying a parcel, which he thought quite amusing.

**

Gerald watched a new Range Rover arrive; Christine came downstairs wondering if her father had purchased a new vehicle. "Miss

Christine Gibbs, for you, we cannot disclose who from," passing Christine the keys. Christine smiled, rubbing her tummy. Gerald glaring.

"Daddies bought you a vehicle so we can travel safely together," She smirked.

Gerald walked into the house, determined to find out who the bloody father was. He realised he couldn't upset Christine in her condition. He's on the phone to Mary trying to work out who's the father, someone extremely wealthy, Gerald decided, after realising the new Range Rover cost over a hundred thousand pounds with the extras. What made Gerald more suspicious was black with smoked glass like her mother's Range Rover, which he thought odd.

Christine looked around her new vehicle. Sitting inside, smelled of new leather. She realised Donald still loved her, although they may have to accept a distant relationship; nevertheless, he's back in her life thanks to her condition.

***

Mrs Montague had monitored the mobile phone calls, excepting what had happened; she's beginning to realise Christine's genuine and not out to cause trouble. Although still hoped to have Donald in the future or as a lover. Under the circumstances, Mrs Montague thought it would be acceptable. She decided to stay out of the situation to see what developed. She's pleased Sophie is recovering, considering her Royal father died of the disease. And, of course, that's thanks to Donald's financing to ensure her recovery.

Donald sent a photo to Jack. Jack smiled, not saying anything putting two and two together, which he suspected everybody else would too. Jack texts Donald, "Transport to London, please."

Donald smiled, placing the portrait in the boot of his Bentley. He'd clocked up some miles, although the old beast purred along like a sewing machine.

***

Christine's clearing an adjacent room to hers to convert into a nursery. She had seen the doctor who confirmed she was definitely pregnant, deciding not to know the sex; she likes surprises, which would be the best one of her whole life.

Donald parked in Jack's compound. Jack grins from ear to ear. Donald looked somewhat puzzled at him, "What's the matter, Jack!"

"Stalk in the picture carrying a parcel. A blind man would know what you were referring to."

"I thought you knew Christine's pregnant, nothing to do with me. I have my girlfriend, Sophie; hopefully, she will be out of hospital in the next couple of weeks to convalesce."

Jack looked at him, "I'll believe you. Thousands wouldn't," placing Donald's latest artwork on the easel, fixing a temporary frame. Jack took several photos, pressing the send button. Donald left the gallery driving off to Harrods, selecting everything a baby would need from cot to toys spending ten thousand plus a further five hundred for delivery. Donald paid in cash, no trace to him, giving the address for delivery. Donald walked out of the store grinning, steadily driving home.

Gerald's on the phone at 10 o'clock the following day with Mary. "I've had a bloody lorry delivering from Harrods, full of baby things from a cot to God knows what you could think of, for a baby."

"Gerald, this sounds more like Donald every minute; he was in London yesterday taking his artwork to Jack. I can't accuse him without real proof; he seems totally disinterested, and Christine stays tight-lipped. We will have to wait until somebody slips up, then we'll find out."

Christine stood in the hallway listening to her father on the phone with Mary; she found it highly amusing. She made her annual visit to the doctor for a check-up only to be told there were two heartbeats, and she's definitely carrying twins. Christine sat for a moment in shock, leaving the doctors sitting in her Range Rover, texting Donald, "Twins! That will hurt!"

Donald texts back: "Can't blame me. I'm not the father!'"

Donald jumped in his Bentley tearing off and returning to Harrods, selecting almost similar things as the first time around, paying in cash and giving the same delivery address as before. He drove to the hospital to see Sophie, discovering she was back in the theatre. Something had come detached, bleeding internally.

Donald thought judgement on him for being such a bastard. He sat for an hour; the surgeon came out of the theatre. "We have solved the problem, Mr Selwyn. She should heal rapidly now; hopefully, you can have her home in three weeks."

"Thank you, doctor." Donald left the hospital; seeing Christine parked by his Bentley, she stepped from her new Range Rover. "Fathers going mad, Donald trying to find out who the father is," she laughed.

"Another delivery for you in the morning," he grinned.

"I'll need a bigger nursery, quite happy with the thought of one baby, now two. I think that's unfair; although the way you attacked me in my Range Rover, I thought the worlds coming to an end, we must do that again sometime," she grinned. "Can a fat girl have a cuddle and a kiss? I bought flowers for Sophie."

Donald gave her a hug and a kiss. "Sophie's come out of theatre, complications; I think she will make a speedy recovery now, I hope," he said, disheartened. He walked into the hospital with Christine. She passed the flowers to the reception for Sophie.

They returned to the street only to see Gerald driving by slowly in his Range Rover, staring at them both suspiciously. They walked across the road, entering a coffee shop. "Strange, Donald, we appear to get on better now, not boyfriend and girlfriend, if you know what I mean," Christine remarked, sipping her coffee.

"This may sound insulting, Christine; the children are definitely mine?"

"I'll take a DNA test; I have nothing to hide," she chuckled. "That's strange coming from me."

Donald laughed, "No, I believe you. You have no reason to lie; I suspect when we were in the Range Rover, that's the only time we've been together in months."

"You are correct; I hadn't seen anyone for some time. I must learn the hard way I always do, Donald. However, I may have something I want for once," she said, rubbing her tummy, "And from the person I love, sorry, it's the truth."

"You are a crazy bitch, Christine, fancy wrecking our relationship. We had everything. I could kick your arse," Donald frowned.

"You already have; I'm suffering for nine months and pay for the next eighteen years."

Donald choked on his coffee, wiping his mouth with a napkin. "I think we might as well admit. We both love each other."

"Leave everything as it is, Donald; you have Sophie to look after. I have what I want here; that's all that matters, for now, okay, friend," she smiled, leaving the coffee shop. Donald followed, passing her one thousand pounds from his wallet, "Nip around to the Range Rover dealership. They will fit another baby seat."

Christine kissed him, "You'll be a wonderful father, even if you don't have a child to hold now."

Donald watched Christine drive off in the direction of the Range Rover dealership. He climbed into his Bentley, receiving a text message from Jack that his latest artwork had reached eight million, and the bidding wasn't finished. Jack sent another text: "Gerald's asking questions and Mary."

Donald drove steadily home, suspecting that the phones would be red-hot tomorrow morning when another Harrods vehicle arrived carrying baby products. Donald didn't care if he were responsible for producing children. He would stand by them regardless of the consequences. If anybody didn't approve, tough. He would maintain his silence for as long as Christine insisted on the best way forward; he didn't want to hurt Sophie.

Donald sat at his computer, selecting a company to tarmac the drive he's sick and tired of hitting ruts every time he used his vehicle, which would undoubtedly prevent anyone from suing the farm. Donald phoned a company, and their representatives said he'd be there within a couple of hours. Taking Donald by surprise, they weren't lying. Tarmac International came in the yard. Donald walked down the drive with the representative. He concluded around hundred-thousand-pounds to do a decent job that would carry the weight of lorries, tractors etc. The best news was they were working for the council four miles away, ideal for them to start on Crabtree Farm drive simultaneously, so in theory, they could start in the morning.

Donald shook his hand, "Excellent, go ahead." Donald signed the paperwork, returned to the yard with the Tarmac International representative, and waved, watching him leave.

Martin came out of the cottage chuckling, "What's that about Donald? Your mother is on the warpath; she thinks you're a naughty boy. You strayed somewhere," Martin chuckled, "Lucky little devil."

"I've authorised the tarmacking of our drive only a hundred thousand pounds. I thought quite cheap. Starting tomorrow with any luck. If you see excavators working around here, you know why. You can explain to mum you didn't manage to squeeze any information out of me," Donald grinned.

"You spent a hundred thousand pounds on the bloody old drive, still serviceable," Martin complained.

"I don't know what damage it's done to my Bentley or your Range Rover. The average family car the drive will knacker, and we could be sued. That's my reason behind having the work carried out. It won't affect the appearance of the farm."

"You have a valid point, son. You might also put some people off visiting, and you make hundred-thousand-pounds while drinking a cup of tea, so you won't notice money missing from your account."

Mary stood in the doorway with her hands on her hips, fuming, "I've looked at Jack's website and realise your last painting has a stalk carrying a parcel. Are you owning up finally, Donald," Mary shouted.

Martin intervened, "What business is it of yours, Mary. The lad is over 18 and one of the most responsible people I know. I should shut up if I were you. He's paid out a hundred thousand pounds to have the bloody drive tarmacked, so were not prosecuted by visitors for trashing their cars on the ruts."

Donald shook his head, walking to his studio, realising the noose was tightening whether he liked it or not. Donald started painting, depicting Christine on a swing with a boy and a girl on either side of her. He guessed he was walking on hot coals by painting something suggestive. Nevertheless, brought pleasure to his mind; he'd nearly completed by morning, hearing a commotion outside. He could see excavators had arrived. Tarmac International was as good as their word. They first repaired all the ruts in the road, placing small kerbs on either side of the drive. Far more than he'd expected, he suspected a quick coat of tarmac would be all he received for his money. They stopped short of entering the yard. Martin and Mary looked at the devastation down the drive, which appeared to be a mess; guessing when the tarmac was laid and the concrete had dried would look different.

The following day the tarmacking machine arrived along with lorry loads of tarmac, carrying base tarmac. They didn't bother with the topping an industrial road and needed the strength not to look fancy. Within hours finished. Tarmac International had vanished apart from their representative coming up the drive and finding Donald looking at the finish. Donald wrote a cheque; the drive came with a five-year warranty subject to the tarmac not being disturbed by farm implements scratching the surface. They shook hands, and the representative left. Donald drove up and down in his car to ensure his backside wasn't being punished as it usually had. Donald placed his latest portrait in the back of his car, heading for London, phoning Jack arriving sometime later. Jack looked at the portrait, "You are trying to convince me, Donald, you're not the father of the forthcoming children?"

"I'm saying nothing; I know Christine is carrying twins. She told me common knowledge. I thought would be a beautiful picture."

"Donald, you wrapped the swing with heart-shaped flowers. You dressed the children and the mother in white outside Strawberry Estate house on the front lawn. I know the place inside out, Donald; you painted her engagement ring on her finger. Gerald will have his shotgun ready and blow your brains out, Donald."

"Nobody has any proof, all circumstantial evidence. I'm painting a friend on my canvas; it means nothing; I might make a few pounds," Donald smiled.

"Bear in mind, Donald, you are a long time dead. Your artwork will treble in price, and I must admit, I made a fortune when you became an artist; as a friend, I don't want to see anything happen to you."

Donald slowly drove home, deciding to call in at the hospital; he wanted to see Sophie and entered her room. She's sat up in bed looking quite herself; he kissed her on the lips, exhaling, "You look absolutely gorgeous, Sophie. Anything you need?"

"I have six months of convalescence, and I want to ravish you," she chuckled.

The consultant said, "Miss Mercantile, I'm pleased to say, Friday you can leave here; do nothing strenuous. I suggest you take a holiday somewhere; walking is good, no vigorous exercising."

"How do you fancy a month at Glencoe Estate? We can visit your parents and have a good time together."

"That sounds great, Donald; I should be able to travel comfortably in your Bentley."

Donald returned home to Crabtree Farm. "Mum, Sophie's coming out of hospital Friday. I'm taking her directly to Glencoe Estate for a month. Would you mind looking after Cherokee?"

"I don't mind looking after Cherokee since Sophie made me ride; I haven't enjoyed myself so much. I would like to know the father of the twins Christine's carrying. We've had twins in our family history, Donald. You know the truth will come out eventually."

Donald started laughing, "You don't quit, mother; when the truth comes out, it does; until then, we will all have to wait and see," he smiled, patting his mother's cheek.

Donald text Christine with his plans. Christine text: "Have a good time." Christine's starting to feel the discomfort of pregnancy, the sex part OK; for the rest, she wasn't so impressed. Gerald, determined to find out who the father is, suspecting whoever's involved is supporting Christine, gave her 100%. However, he appeared invisible and dared not face him.

***

Friday morning, Donald had packed his and Sophie's suitcase loading in the Bentley; he arrived at the hospital at ten, carefully assisting Sophie into the passenger seat. He drove off steadily, phoning ahead, notifying Justin to prepare the suite for him and Sophie. Sophie phoned her parents, explaining she was on the way to Glencoe Estate for convalescence with Donald. She would call around in the next couple of days. They arrived at 10 o'clock in the evening. Sophie's tired; other than that, okay; she had a course of pills with her must take to stem any rejection of the new organ. The chef had stayed behind, asking Donald if he required a meal. Donald passed him fifty pounds, "No, thank you, we'll be fine tonight. I appreciate you waiting for us to arrive."

They settled down for the night. Donald was struggling to sleep; he didn't know whether he was suffering from a guilty conscience or what was wrong with him. He glanced from his balcony seeing the waterwheel turning, illuminated. He quietly dressed, trying not to disturb Sophie. He hadn't long started walking before Sophie realised he wasn't in the room. She switched on the bedside table light. Noticed Donald's mobile by his bedside light. She reached over, suspecting he'd used his date of birth as his code; she wasn't wrong; she searched the messages, curious to see what had gone on while she was ill. She came across the messages from Christine concerning her pregnancy. Sophie realised Donald was the father. Christine's not chasing him, noticing the last message; enjoy yourself at Glencoe with Sophie.

Sophie wondered whether she should confront him. She suspected it would end their relationship; she wouldn't be alive now if it wasn't for him. The doctors had explained Donald had paid a hundred thousand pounds plus her medical bills to ensure she lived, so he must love her. Sophie couldn't understand why Christine was so desperate to have Donald's children if she didn't want the man himself?

Sophie remembered being besotted with a married man, a horse trainer; she barely escaped with her life after the accident, discovering she was one of a string of women her so-called boyfriend's seeing. She exhaled, excepting she's no angel. She turned Donald's mobile off, placing it exactly where she found and pretending she knew nothing.

Donald watched the waterwheel turn, reliving the moment he'd spent with Christine rectifying the estate. Donald slowly returned to the hotel, quietly climbing into bed, feeling Sophie cuddle close to him.

They rose at 7 o'clock dressing; you could hardly see the scar from Sophie's operation. They went down for breakfast. The staff applauded as they walked into the dining room. After breakfast, they strolled along the track by the stream past the sawmill continuing to the reservoir, seeing Jock approaching in his truck. Jock shouted, "We sacked that silly bitch, have a new girl now. She's good," he waved, continuing down the track. Donald and Sophie both laughed; Jock's a character.

Sophie's trying to strengthen her muscles after lying in bed for over a month. They sat on the sluice gate on the reservoir, watching horses approaching from the stables with the new girl leading the way with paying customers following. Jock at the rear, everything seemed to be working as originally designed. The new girl said politely, "Good morning, Mr Selwyn, Miss Mercantile."

Sophie and Donald waved, descending to the hotel to find Mrs Montague sitting outside at a table drinking tea and her chauffeur standing by the car. Donald smiled, "Hello, stranger."

Mrs Montague shook her head, chuckling, "You don't change, Donald. I've ordered tea; I saw you coming; please sit with me. How are you, Sophie? I know Donald was frantic. I can assure you that he wouldn't spare any expense to save you, Sophie, and he would do anything for anyone in trouble."

"I'm fine, thank you, Mrs Montague or I will be in a month when I can ride my horse; I miss riding terribly."

"Don't rush things, Sophie. You're not quite nineteen, your whole life ahead of you, the pair of you," she smiled, enjoying the sun on her face. "I've seen some of your recent artwork, Donald; very suggestive, if you know what I mean?"

"Mrs Montague, you must have a first name," Donald asked.

"Why do you ask? I'm content with you addressing me as Mrs Montague, my title."

"How is Mr Montague's health these days?"

"Very satisfactory, thank you for asking. Sophie, you are aware Christine is pregnant?"

Donald went into a cold sweat.

"Yes, she came in to see me. I believe Christine's having twins and may soon be regretting her condition; she's already starting to feel discomfort."

Donald's not aware Christine had seen Sophie without him knowing; Sophie certainly hasn't mentioned a visit.

"I thought I'd mention I don't want you putting two and two together ending up with forty-six. Donald helped with the harvest," Mrs Montague smiled, looking at Donald, knowing he's guilty; she's covering for him.

"Never crossed my mind, Mrs Montague. That relationship is dead and buried as far as Donald is concerned. What Christine wants will never happen; we are marrying as soon as I recover from my present predicament. I hope to conceive, and we can start our family."

Mrs Montague's trying not to grin, looking at the death wish expression on Donald's face. Donald nervously smiled, standing, easing the chair away for Mrs Montague. He kissed her on both cheeks giving her a slight hug and patting her backside. She glared at him, "Sir, you take liberties," she walked off to her car; Donald could hear her trying not to laugh with her hand to her mouth.

Donald suspected more was going on than he realised. Christine visited Sophie, and neither of them had informed him. They climbed into Donald's Bentley, heading for Bonar Bridge, a couple of hours away if traffics cooperating. They parked outside her parents Croft warmly greeted them. Mrs Mercantile commented, "I never thought I'd see you alive again, my love, a miracle. Your father and I have prayed every night, hoping you would recover." Donald walked outside, looking at the thirty acres asking, "Mr Mercantile, you actually own this, Sir?"

"Not quite, I think another five years, then I can tell the bank to take a running jump."

Donald lent on the bonnet of the compact tractor writing a cheque out for Mr Mercantile for the sum of fifty thousand pounds, "Here, Sir, hopefully, this should cover what you owe the bank?"

Mr Mercantile shook his head in disbelief, "Why do you give your money away so freely, Donald?"

"I could drop dead in the next ten minutes or live another forty years. I don't know how long I have on this planet; I want to make sure the people I like have an easier life than before I met them. I love your daughter immensely, although I barely qualify to be in her presence."

Mr Mercantile patted Donald on the shoulder, "There are far worse sinners out there, Donald, than you."

Mr Mercantile showed his wife the cheque; she placed her hand to her mouth, "You realise we are free of a mortgage now, love," she smiled.

"I know everything we make from now on is our own, not the banks first."

Mr Mercantile passed Donald a small whisky. "You can't have any lass, not after your operation. To good friends and a future son-in-law."

Sophie grinned, looking forward to her future with some optimism, wondering if she should become good friends with Christine when they return to Crabtree Farm. At least she'd be able to monitor the situation more closely. The other option would be to make Donald purchase an estate in Scotland.

Sophie and Donald enjoyed a pleasant afternoon with Sophie's parents, finally saying goodbye and returning to Glencoe Estate. They retired early, Sophie's determined to enjoy Donald, which he found somewhat surprising in her delicate condition. After breakfast, Donald decided to risk driving the Bentley around the estate, surprised by how mobile the vehicle was off-road. Sophie's laughing, enjoying the adventure.

Finally returned to the hotel, his Bentley resembled a vehicle that had gone through a hedge backwards. They decided to drive into town, driving his Bentley through a car wash, returning the vehicle to its former glory, and visiting Maggie's shop. She greeted him with a kiss and carefully embraced Sophie. "At long last, Donald, you realise what I was informing you is the truth about Christine. I have a new man in my life, thanks to you, my shop has never been so busy. The Donald Selwyn tartan I sell worldwide on the Internet."

Donald and Sophie walked out of the shop, quickly getting into the Bentley. He could see tourists approaching and driving off. "You realise that woman fancies you, Donald?"

"I know it's my charm," he laughed. Sophie slapped his leg smiling. The rest of the month passed uneventfully. Now the beginning of November, quite a chill is in the air. Donald and Sophie packed their bags; she's feeling a different woman and looking forward to trying to ride Cherokee when she returns to Crabtree Farm.

They steadily drove home, took several breaks, and finally arrived at Crabtree Farm at ten in the evening. Donald carried the bags to the studio; they had a quick cup of tea and retired to bed. Mary suspected Donald returned last night; she heard the vehicle looking out of the window this morning, confirming seeing a frost glisten on the car roof. She made breakfast phoning across to the studio. Donald and Sophie went to the cottage to have a light breakfast. Sophie is careful about what she's consuming for a while, not wishing to stress her new liver. Mary commented, "You should see the size of Christine now carrying twins; she was only a stick, to begin with," Mary chuckled. Donald didn't comment either, Sophie. Donald asked his father, "Have you checked the antifreeze in the tractors, dad? They should be okay; I want to ensure it hasn't been forgotten."

"Already checked, son. I'm not having one million worth of equipment trashed by frost," he smiled. "I'm riding this morning," Sophie announced.

"Over my dead body," Donald said, staring at her, "You'll damage your liver, and you're finished. Be sensible, Sophie, plenty of time to ride horses."

Sophie frowned, "Will you be like this when we're married, bossy?"

Mary laughed, " Frosty out there this morning, Sophie; if Cherokee slips could do untold damage, you'll never find out how bossy Donald is if you don't marry him."

"Marry him; I stand more chance of catching a cold than him getting off his backside."

Donald glared in disbelief, blamed for the delay, "Just say the word Mrs, we'll be married; you could have a cheap and cheerful registry office. I don't think your parents will be impressed. You can have a Christmas wedding," Donald paused. "I'm not having a Christmas wedding. That's tempting fate," remembering what happened with Christine. "It's either now or postpone until spring; the choice is yours, Sophie."

Mary watched Sophie counting on her fingers. "You're pregnant, aren't you, Sophie?"

"I think so. I hadn't planned, and of course, while in the hospital, I wasn't taking any precautions. I suddenly had the urge to attack Donald; it wasn't quite his fault; I'm three weeks late."

"Oh, wonderful, Sophie, you've had a liver transplant. Are you really trying to kill yourself? I suggest you see the doctor today without fail and discuss the options and the risks involved before continuing with the pregnancy," Mary insisted. "In fact, I will come with you; Donald hasn't the brains to work it out," Mary said, glaring at Donald. "Come along in my Range Rover, Sophie; I thought you were smarter than that."

Donald exhaled, "Mum's right Sophie. I don't want you to die, I don't want you to have an abortion, but it's the lesser of the two evils."

Sophie grabbed her coat, travelling with Mary to the local surgery. Mary's doctor agreed to see Sophie and take her on as one of his patients. They waited an hour and finally were allowed in. Sophie explained the position. The doctor looked at Sophie's records from the hospital on his computer, " I think you can continue with the pregnancy very early days. I will have to monitor you regularly. I shall want to see you every week. Make an appointment at reception."

"Thanks," Sophie said, somewhat relieved. "One last thing, doctor, can I ride my horse if I'm careful?"

The doctor smiled, "You are a glutton for punishment, Sophie, yes if you're very careful. Remember, there is not another liver available."

Sophie immediately cuddled Mary as they walked out of the doctor's office. Mary shook her head slowly from side to side, smiling. They drove steadily to the farm at 11 o'clock in the morning; the sun had risen, melting any frost on the ground. Mary helped Sophie saddle Cherokee; she climbed aboard gingerly, wearing her hardhat and thick coat. The smile on her face could have lit the sky. Donald noticed from his studio, suspecting the doctor must have okayed or mother wouldn't have allowed her on the horse. Sophie shouted, "Donald, I'm still pregnant and can continue carrying."

Sophie set off down the drive avoiding the shady patches on the tarmac so the horse wouldn't slip, crossing the road onto Strawberry Estate. Christine, with binoculars, recognised the horse Cherokee and Sophie. She jumped into her father's Range Rover, driving down the track to intercept. Sophie stopped alongside Christine, slowly dismounting. They hugged each other as best they could. Christine, with her bulge, looked the size of a battleship. "I'm pregnant too, Christine; wonderful the doctors are slightly concerned about my new liver. I'm glad I haven't twins, I hope. You look very uncomfortable."

"You're not joking, Sophie; once I have these children, we can go riding together. I can't climb on The Rising Sun in this condition; I think I'd break his back."

Gerald came walking down the track looking annoyed, "Thank you for asking, stealing my Range Rover, Christine. Hi, Sophie, you look well."

"I should; I'm pregnant." Gerald stopped in his tracks, re-evaluating who could be the father of Christine's children. Sophie carefully mounted Cherokee riding off. Christine slid into the passenger seat of her father's Range Rover; he gave her a lift to the house. "Are you still not saying who the father is? I'm convinced it's Donald. I don't know why he's the only one daft enough to have you."

"Thanks, father, I love you too," Christine remarked, easing herself out of the Range Rover and walking inside the house.

Sophie carefully dismounted in the yard at Crabtree Farm. Mary came out to assist, "You okay, Sophie?"

"Yes, I saw Christine; I hope I don't have twins."

"Ran in my family for years; I was lucky I only had Donald, don't be surprised if you have twins Sophie."

"Don't say that, Mary, please; you're frightening the life out of me."

Donald came downstairs from the studio, hugging Sophie. "Donald, you planning we live in the studio with a child or children. Your mothers informed me twins run in her family! Will there be sufficient room? We have to plan ahead, Donald," Sophie remarked seriously.

"Don't worry, Sophie, I'll build you a new house. Wait, let's make sure you're definitely pregnant."

Mary thumped Donald on his shoulder, annoyed, "Are you really my son? The doctors confirmed she is pregnant; her condition won't change unless she does something silly."

Donald kissed his mother and Sophie on the cheek, walked off, and jumped in his Bentley, heading down the drive only to be blocked at the end of the drive by Robert Morgans Range Rover.

Donald stepped out of his Bentley, somewhat puzzled, "Hi, Mr Morgan."

"Morning, Donald. I don't know whether you are aware, Donald; I'm selling Mill Farm 1500 acres and taking early retirement. I wondered if you'd be interested in purchasing. I'd rather make a private sale; I make more money than an auction. I have considered Gibb's offer from Strawberry Estate; he will only penny-pinch and want to argue for six months. I have good land, you should know, adjacent to yours."

"I wouldn't want the machinery, Mr Morgan. Only the grain storage, outbuildings and house. What sort of money are you looking for?"

"Fifteen million."

"I'll give you ten million. I don't need to see your land; I know what it's like. I've walked it many times on shoots. You can sell the farm machinery; it will provide extra money."

"Come on, Donald, play fair thirteen million five hundred thousand, don't forget the farm is planted with wheat. We have a deal. You know the land is worth every penny."

"Okay." Donald held out his hand. Mr Morgan and Donald shook hands, "Have your solicitor prepare the transfer of ownership, and my solicitor will check its kosher."

Mr Morgan smiled, "Pleasure to do business with you, Donald. That's a load off my mind; at least I know the farm will be looked after and not become a number. You will have to dodge the bullets. Gibbs won't be happy he missed the sale."

Donald shrugged his shoulders, "Too bad, business is business."

Donald phoned the farm solicitors, making them aware of the pending transaction. Donald's solicitor knew the other solicitors involved, so he would keep Donald posted on events that shouldn't be a problem.

Donald drove to the Case IH dealership, finding James. They shook hands warmly, "James, I need a self-propelled sprayer. I have purchased another farm of about one and a half thousand acres to spray, which isn't a lot. I don't want to spend hours sitting in a sprayer if I don't have to."

"This one over here, Donald, is a brand-new self-steer fully computerised. It works out everything for you the amount of chemical, water the lot, and it matches the new drill I sold you."

"Okay, deliver when you're ready. Thanks, James; while I think about it, I'll have another twenty-five-ton grain trailer, another case 400 hp tractor like I have now. I quite enjoy driving. The power harrows on the back made her bark; she soon covered the ground."

***

Gerald received a phone call from his solicitors informing him Mill Farm's no longer available for purchase, sold to Mr Donald Selwyn. Christine's eavesdropping on the conversation on the phone was somewhat heated, to say the least. She knew Donald's planning investments for his children. She didn't want any more acres, could make a substantial living off their estate. Why go looking for more trouble? Plus, she had Glencoe in profit for the first time in forty years, not a tax loss anymore.

Donald returned home. Mary looked at the expression on her son's face as she stepped from the cottage, closely followed by Sophie. "What have you done, son?" Mary asked suspiciously.

"Purchased a house for Sophie and our forthcoming child, that's all."

Mary looked shocked. "Where?"

"Mill Farm. I own Mill Farm," Donald said, casually walking towards the studio.

"You own what!" Mary emphasised, trying to grasp what her son had said. Martin came dashing outside, standing with Mary and Sophie.

"You said to me this morning about accommodation for Sophie and child or children if she's turning into a battery hen. Robert Morgan spoke to me at the bottom of the drive offering me Mill Farm, so I purchased. We have another thousand plus acres; I have all the equipment I need to deal with. I have purchased another tractor and trailer and self-propelled sprayer."

"And how much did that cost?" Mary asked, placing her hands on her hips. Martin's holding his forehead. "I suppose with the new equipment, around fourteen million," Donald shrugged his shoulders, continuing to the studio as if nothing had happened.

Sophie looked at Mary, speechless. Donald said, "You can have horses, Sophie, if you wish, plenty of room," he continued upstairs.

Gerald came into the yard in his Range Rover, jumping out and shouting, "You realise Mary, what your son has done, stolen Mill Farm from under my nose. I'd work for months trying to achieve a decent deal." Donald came running down from the studio. No one would shout at his mother. He grabbed Gerald round the throat, "The reason you didn't acquire the farm, Gerald, you're a tight old bastard, and Mr Morgan couldn't be bothered with you anymore. Off my property." Gerald jumped in his Range Rover, leaving immediately. Mary, Martin, and Sophie were silent. Not expecting Donald to react that way; nevertheless, Gerald was shouting at his mother.

Gerald returned to Strawberry Estate, entering the house and slamming the door. Christine jumped in her black Range Rover, never remembering her father to be that angry. She came over to Crabtree Farm, easing herself out of her Range Rover. Mary greeted her. Sophie and Donald came down from the studio. Christine's helped into the kitchen, "What happened? My father's at home slamming doors over that bloody farm I didn't want, just more work and headaches. I have enough problems at Strawberry Estate."

Donald sighed, "Probably my fault Christine, he was shouting at my mother. I grabbed him around the throat and told him he's a mean old bastard, that's why he didn't have the farm. Mr Morgan said he couldn't be bothered to argue with your father anymore, so he sold it to me."

Mary made Christine a cup of tea. "I'm glad you purchased Donald; you are investing for the children's future." Nobody spoke while drinking tea.

Donald helped her to her Range Rover, "Sorry, Christine," Donald expressed.

"Doesn't matter, Donald. When he calms down, he will realise his mistake, not yours," she kissed Donald on the cheek, glancing at Sophie to see her expression of concern. Christine drove off grinning, returning to Strawberry Estate house, seeing her father sitting with Cindy at the kitchen table. "You shouldn't have shouted at Mary father. She had no idea what Donald had done; besides, we don't need any more problems. Donald needs more acres if he wishes to survive in farming."

"I wish I hadn't shouted at Mary. I suppose you're right, Christine. We don't need any more headaches."

"This farm and Glencoe will suit my twins; they can each have a property or share the two and split the income," Christine smiled, walking out of the kitchen.

Cindy remarked, "She's fully committed, Gerald; I've never known Christine to be so positive. Have you seen everything that came from Harrods in the children's nursery must have cost thousands? The only person that fits that criteria is Donald. I find it strange, neither owning up. I know one thing for sure if Christine were in trouble, you'd see Donald move; he wouldn't risk the unborn children hurt."

"I thought I would lose my teeth this morning because he grabbed me around the throat," Gerald frowned.

"My son would have reacted exactly the same if you shouted at me; a natural reaction protects one's loved ones, Gerald. You should have discussed the situation calmly with Donald."

"I suppose you're right; let's look at the children's nursery. I haven't bothered much. Christine's organising the room; she has more motherly instinct than her real mother had. Josephine demanded a nanny."

They entered the room to find Christine still opening some of the boxes, each cot of a neutral colour, until you pressed a button. Then the whole cot changed colour displaying pretty patterns, you pressed another button, and nursery rhymes would play. Gerald suspected the bloody thing would take off if she pressed another button. The nursery was fantastic. With so many toys and gadgets, the babies would be spoiled from the minute they left the womb. The father had to be a millionaire. Donald fitted the bill perfectly. The more Gerald thought it over, had to be the logical choice. He's the only one sensitive enough to purchase such a variety of things.

"Christine," she glanced at her father. "Donald's the father; I don't care what you say; no other person I know would lavish you with so many gifts and your unborn children. You might as well come clean and own up. I don't care; I'm not causing trouble, and neither will Cindy; we know Donald will provide for you."

Christine smiled, "You really do want to lose your teeth, father; I wouldn't accuse Donald of being the father," she grinned, turning back to what she's engaged in.

Gerald frowned, leaving the nursery with Cindy. "It has to be him, Cindy," he whispered.

CHAPTER EIGHTEEN

REORGANISING

Mrs Montague received a phone call in her limousine. "Your Majesty."

"Mrs Montague, I'm informed by one of my estate managers a further twenty-five thousand acres are available for purchase between Glencoe Estate and mine. I think it would be very appropriate if you could persuade Donald to purchase from a security point of view most beneficial. I can't purchase it myself. Otherwise, the public will think their Queen has disposable money in this fragile economic climate. I don't want to annoy too many in government. They're trying to control the coronavirus."

"I understand completely, your Majesty; I will report shortly."

Mrs Montague drove to Crabtree Farm. Donald looked from his studio window, surprised to see the limousine suspecting trouble for a personal visit. Mary had already hijacked Mrs Montague, insisting she had tea and a slice of cake in the kitchen.

Donald came into the kitchen, kissing Mrs Montague on both cheeks. "Donald, we have a minor problem. land has become available on the border of one of her Majesties estates and Glencoe. To be quite honest, the land is worthless from an agricultural standpoint; hills, rocks, and moorland ideal for pony tracking and wildlife. We were reliably informed travellers are in the process of purchasing the land. Obviously, neither you nor her Majesty finds this acceptable. I understand ten million will purchase the property after consulting the owner who is moving abroad for tax reasons."

Mary butted in, "Why can't her Majesty purchase herself?"

"Her Majesty could easily afford the land; public opinion would dictate she doesn't flaunt her wealth while the country is in recession from the coronavirus. Not only that, she concluded, Donald would also enjoy extending the boundaries of Glencoe to incorporate more tracking, generating more income."

"Something very wrong with this deal. My son spends his money extending the boundaries of Glencoe. What does he receive in reward?"

"Nothing, his children, will," Mrs Montague glared.

Mary went quiet, realising confirmation Donald's the father of the twins Christine's carrying, the only logical explanation.

"Okay, I will travel to Glencoe and look over the property myself, Mrs Montague; I'm sure you'll be there to guide me through the purchase."

Mrs Montague left the kitchen, kissing Donald on both cheeks; she stepped into her limousine. Sophie came down from the studio, "What's going on, Donald?"

"Nothing. I have to return to Glencoe; would you like to come or stay here?"

"I'll come. We can find time to see my parents, can't we, future husband, " she chuckled.

They quickly packed their bags heading for Glencoe, arriving in the early hours. The journey was never any easier, especially now the weather changing and snow on the hills. Donald had explained that he had to inspect land bordering Glencoe Estate. Donald summoned Jock, who arrived after breakfast with his truck. Donald climbed aboard, leaving Sophie in the warm hotel. Jock drove steadily across the hills.

Mrs Montague's description of the land is correct; streams, rocks and hills lovely from a viewing standpoint, probably very suitable for the odd mounting goat or deer other than that bloody useless. Jock drove on until they reached quite a large property nestled amongst trees, very run-down. Donald steps from the truck, meeting Mr Clooney, the present owner in the process of packing, ready to leave the country. Donald introduced himself, offering, "Five million? I can pay you immediately; you're obviously in a hurry. I will only need deeds of ownership transferred from your solicitors to mine."

"Seven million, we have a deal, Mr Selwyn."

"Okay," Donald replied, wondering if he'd spent too much money.

Mr Clooney phoned his solicitors explaining the deal. They were to proceed with the transfer of ownership once the seven million was transferred into their account.

Donald realised he actually owned the land and the house, not Glencoe, ideal. He now had his own home in Scotland plus land; admittedly, it wasn't much use, but he could join forces with Glencoe to increase their incomes.

Donald travelled to Glencoe in Jock's truck, advising his solicitors on the pending deal. Mrs Montague waiting in the hotel for his return sitting at a table drinking coffee. Sophie and Donald joined her. "I purchased Mrs Montague in my name, a house with the property I can have once renovated. I'm not prepared to transfer ownership to Glencoe, an investment for any children I have." Mrs Montague grinned, realising the estate was safe in Donald's hands. When he passed on, his children would continue the legacy. She wondered if he realised both Christine and Sophie were of Royal connection. Mrs Montague surmised what would be the odds of that happening.

Sophie commented, "You'll have to start painting Donald; you will be broke at the rate you spend money."

"You underestimate Donald, Sophie," Mrs Montague remarked. "If you knew what Donald's worth in this country and abroad, you'd be shocked."

Mrs Montague kissed them both on the cheek, leaving satisfied the lands now secure, phoning her Majesty to confirm the situation is now resolved.

Justin joined them at the table. "Justin, I own twenty-five-thousand acres bordering Glencoe; work out a deal where we can share the income from the tracking, bird spotting, etc."

"Certainly, Donald, and congratulations. If I were you, I'd turn the property into a hotel like this one; they are virtually identical in size? I think you'll find there are forty bedrooms. The place needs renovation. Once completed would be a fabulous location, and with your reputation, the place would be packed. I know a good manager," Justin smiled.

Donald and Sophie smiled, finished their coffee, and headed for Bonar Bridge to see Sophie's parents. Spending half a day there before returning to Glencoe. Donald had a phone call from his solicitors confirming he's now the proud owner of Mill Farm and could move onto the property as soon as he wished, the house currently vacant. "A little job for you, Sophie, will you have a look at Mill Farm and decide on the furniture which room you wish to use as a nursery. I believe stables you may wish to utilise. The same will apply to Dorking Moor Estate I just purchased. We have to decide whether we wish to have a hotel as an income or for ourselves?"

"I think Dorking Moor Estate would warrant a hotel. We could have a suite for ourselves, much like Glencoe. People are desperate for work Donald, and the holiday business is booming," Sophie suggested.

Reasonably early the following day, they headed for home Crabtree Farm after breakfast. Mary had already seen the newspapers. "The artist Donald Selwyn purchased Dorking Moor Estate twenty-five- thousand acres of unspoiled beauty."

"I'll kill him; he's trying to buy the country, Martin?"

Martin sipped his tea, reading the newspaper. "You obviously missed what was said; the artist Donald Selwyn purchased Dorking Moor Estate twenty-five thousand acres. There is no mention of Glencoe Estate. Donald isn't that stupid, Mary."

Mary exhaled, ringing Donald. He answered, "Yes, my lovely mother, how can I help you?"

"Less of the flannel Donald," listening to Sophie screaming with laughter. "Who handled the deal for Dorking Moor Estate twenty-five thousand acres?"

"Your loving son, mother, nothing to do with Glencoe."

"Donald, you drinking and driving? I can hear your car, don't forget you have Sophie in the car with you and your unborn child, be responsible."

Sophie had the giggling fits, "Stop teasing Donald. You're hurting my stomach."

"Mother, I'm perfectly sober. I'm having fun with you. Relax, mother, you will have a bloody heart attack. " Dad, take mother to bed," Mary immediately disconnected the call. Martin rose from the kitchen table; Mary stared at him, running out of the kitchen door, laughing. "I'm coming, woman. I'll give you a run for your money."

3:30 in the afternoon, Donald and Sophie came into the yard entering the cottage. Mary had already poured the tea. Donald explained the events. Mary was delighted; he owned the property, although she thought he was spending too much money. "Mother, why don't you and Sophie visit Mill Farm and decide what to do with the house? I'm sure you'd enjoy that trip."

Mary immediately grabbed Sophie's hand, "If you're not too tired, Sophie."

"Definitely not," she ran out of the door with Mary, climbing into Mary's Range Rover and heading for Mill Farm. Mary suspected a preservation order on the property's timber work and the exterior superb. She estimated it must be at least fifteen bedrooms plus. Mary looked under a brick at the side of the front door, the keys. She laughed, "Nothing has changed." The furniture was gone. The bare shell of the house, sinks, toilets and the usual fittings remained, discovering a large cellar. When on the upper floors, they could see Crabtree Farm plainly. They could have walked quicker than driven, only a field separating the properties. Sophie looked around, somewhat bewildered, "What shall I do, Mary? What's Donald expecting me to work out?"

"The first thing we do is phone Michael," Mary said, removing her mobile. "Michael, you know Donald's purchased Mill Farm. We're there now. Any chance you can come, look at things if you're not too busy?"

"Give me five minutes; I'll be with you, Mary."

Michael arrived in his works transit provided by Gerald. They joined Michael outside. He's removing a ladder, inspecting, checking the external beams and plaster. He said, "You need work carried out. I suspect a preservation order is on the property, so I'll have to check what I'm allowed to do, if straightforward," he said. "I suppose six thousand pounds with general repairs." Michael went inside, "I need to know your colour schemes; obviously, painting is cheaper than wallpaper. Give me a list of what you want, and I can give you a fair price, Sophie."

"Thank you, Michael," Mary smiled, "We'll be in touch, and want completing, pretty ASAP."

Michael nodded, driving away. Sophie looked lost, shrugging her shoulders. Mary placed her arm around her shoulder, "Don't worry, love, I'll help you. Explain what you'd like, don't worry about the cost; Donald can easily afford it, and I'll advise you if practical."

Mary grabbed a colour scheme brochure from her back seat. They sat inside each room on a large windowsill seat, deciding and writing a list. Sophie selected the best room for a nursery. "Tomorrow, Sophie, we'll go into town together and select appliances for your kitchen and scullery."

Sophie started to cry, "I'm scared, Mary, for the first time. I'm scared of being a failure. I don't want Donald to be disappointed with me."

"Not a cat in hells chance Donald will ever be disappointed with you, Sophie. Donald's learning about life. A big step for him as well, so you're not alone. I'm just over there. You can see Crabtree Farm from here. If Donald is a pain, you come and see me; I'll straighten him out," Mary reassured.

They locked the house, keeping the keys while driving to Strawberry Estate and finding Michael working on a building down the yard. Mary passed him a colour scheme chart for each room. "I suppose you are looking about twenty-thousand pounds for the whole job. A lot of areas to cover, Mary and two of the rooms you're wallpapering. I can start next week; I should be free. Hopefully, I will complete it before Christmas, depending on how well the paint dries in these conditions. It would help immensely if the heating is on, perhaps, light the fires. I can't touch the external work until spring next year; nothing would dry outside in this weather. A couple of good frosts would destroy whatever I do."

"Go ahead, Michael, thank you. I'll have a key cut so you can come and go as you please. I'll arrange for Donald to have the fires lit; you're right, have some heat in the property, make your job no end easier, thank you, Michael," Mary said, driving off.

"We haven't discussed with Donald, Mary; he'll have a fit."

"You have to learn, Sophie; women are in charge. Donald's only the breadwinner," she chuckled. Mary explained to Donald, "All done."

Donald shrugged his shoulders, "Fine by me; don't forget to purchase the furniture," he remarked, returning to his studio.

"You're right, Mary," Sophie expressed, "He doesn't care."

Donald stared at his blank canvas, wondering what he wanted to paint. Glanced from the window observing his new sprayer arrive, new tractor and trailer. Martin shouted up the stairs, "Donald, avoid your mother; you'd better come and look at your purchases," Martin laughed.

"Why have you bought a bloody sprayer and another tractor and trailer," Mary shouted.

"I have to spray the crops, mother. I purchased this particular model because it works out quantity's for you, so both father and I can use it without having a degree," he grinned. "The new tractor is an addition for the other farm. I will have to employ someone to assist. Otherwise, you two will never use your holiday cottage in Devon."

"You're not employing staff; your father and I are not crippled. I could have driven that one if you hadn't stolen the gear levers from the tractor. I'm not incompetent, Donald."

Donald grabbed his mother's hand. Martin and Sophie laughed as he made her sit in the new tractor seat. "Start the engine, mother," she turned the key; the engine started after putting her foot on the clutch. "Now move that, push that, there you are, drive the tractor, don't need gear levers. Reverse it in the shed, and don't hit the other equipment; use your mirrors." Donald watched his mother reverse the new tractor and trailer into the shed. She didn't hit anything, to his surprise. She climbed out of the cab grinning, "Martin could have shown me; he's just a male chauvinist pig," Mary protested.

Martin shrugged his shoulders, watching Gerald park in the yard. The first time since he'd shouted at Mary, he'd ventured to Crabtree Farm.

He removed a bouquet of flowers from the passenger seat, passing to Mary, "Please accept my apologies, Mary, for my rude behaviour."

"Apology accepted, Gerald. I wasn't offended. I've had worse said to me, although Donald wasn't in earshot." Donald held his hand out. Gerald shook it gladly.

"I think Christine will be in hospital shortly; I'm not convinced everything is okay with her. She doesn't say much she exercises with Cindy, which is good for the babies apparently," Gerald sighed. "I hear you purchased more property in Scotland, Donald. What are your plans?"

"Turn the property into a hotel, beautiful walks and scenery, the public should enjoy along with Glencoe. We may join forces; Justin's looking at the figures now. I'm sure he will consult Christine in due course."

"She still won't tell me who the father is," Gerald said, looking at Mary, "You know, don't you, Mary," he watched her smile.

Mary grabbed Gerald's arm, walking off. Donald, Martin, and Sophie watched, intrigued.

"Gerald, Mrs Montague visited us the other day concerning the property for sale in Scotland. I questioned why Donald should buy the property for Glencoe. She replied it's not for Donald, for his children. Say nothing, Gerald; we could open a can of worms that neither of us can control, play stupid for the moment. Once the children are born, a giveaway, I'm pretty sure. I have a sneaking suspicion Sophie already knows the truth but is not letting on."

"When and how did this happen?" Gerald frowned.

"We both know how Gerald, when is a good question. When Sophie was in the hospital. Donald spent some nights on the new tractor power harrowing perhaps; they liaised then?"

"I can't understand Christine's insistence that the children are not Donald's and Donald's supporting her decision. That brings us to the question, what about Sophie? She's pregnant; is he starting a bloody harem?" Gerald frowned. "You should see what's arrived from Harrods, every convenience for a child. We had two lorry loads. You must come down and see Mary." Mary walked over to Gerald's Range Rover, he jumped in the driver's seat, and they left the yard, not saying a word to anyone.

CHAPTER NINETEEN

WHO KNOWS WHAT?

Gerald and Mary ascended the plush carpeted stairs. Christine was resting on her bed; they entered the nursery. Mary stood in amazement. She had never seen anything like it, a children's paradise, their own personal grotto. Christine was very uncomfortable, holding her stomach, entering the nursery and not looking well sitting down on a chair. "Lovely Mary, don't you think?" Christine suggested.

***

Donald's busy painting a portrait of his new property. Sophie ran in, "My mother's not well, Donald; I'm off home to help." She quickly packed a bag.

Donald asked, "You want me to come; the roads could be treacherous, Sophie?"

"No, I'll be okay. The road to Tain is usually quite clear, and Bonner Bridge, just beyond, I will drive carefully, I promise," she kissed him on the cheek and lips driving out of the yard.

Donald looked at the weather report. The weather appeared to be okay on the route she was taking. He'd given her a thousand pounds cash in case of emergencies. Her car was virtually brand-new, so it should be reliable.

***

Christine tried to stand and collapsed. Gerald immediately phoned for an ambulance. The paramedic suspected the children were trying to leave the womb early. Mary phoned Donald asking if he would collect her. "Christine's in hospital, and Cindy's over at her son's farm for the day." Donald didn't hesitate, grabbed the keys for his Bentley, and drove over to Strawberry Estate. Mary jumped in his car; she could see the worried expression on his face. "What's wrong, mum?" He asked, trying to stay calm.

"The paramedic thinks the twins are trying to leave the womb; let's hope they don't; she hasn't been pregnant long enough."

Donald said nothing driving home steadily, explaining Sophie had gone home, her mother unwell.

"I would have thought you'd have taken her son in these conditions," Mary expressed concern.

"I offered mother," she said, "she could manage."

"You're starting to disappoint me, son, letting her drive on her own in these conditions."

Donald removed his mobile. Sophie had already pulled off at a service station with her car backfiring on the M6, phoning the RAC, who had arrived looking at her car. "Hi Donald, everything okay? I'm parked at a service station?" she advised.

"I'm coming to collect you. Stay at the service station."

"How do you know I'm broken down?"

"I didn't; what's wrong?" Donald asked, worried.

"According to the RAC patrol-man, something's wrong with the engine; he said it's been apart before, probably suffering from the same complaint."

"Ask the RAC to transport the car directly to the garage we purchased from. My solicitors will take over from there; I will come and collect you. Stay in the warm."

"Okay, I love you, Donald."

"I love you too, Sophie. Stay in the warm, give me half an hour or an hour. I should be with you, depending on the traffic."

Donald hugged his mother, "Sometimes, mother, I wonder where my brains are. You are right; I should never have let her go in this weather alone."

Donald quickly packed a bag and jumped in his Bentley, phoning the garage where they'd purchased the mini, explaining he would fry them alive in the courts. They immediately offered him a full refund. Donald pressed on as quickly as he could, arriving in two hours. He walked into the service station cafeteria area, seeing Sophie with her bag drinking coffee. She ran over and hugged him. "Sorry, Donald."

"No worries, love had a full refund. The garage didn't argue; I threatened to tear their arms off in court. I hate dodgy dealers; we'll buy you something brand-new that is bombproof," he smiled, "we'll Carry on to your mothers before the weather changes."

They climbed into Donald's warm Bentley, heading up the motorway calling in at Glencoe to stay for a few hours until morning, not wishing to disturb her parents in the early hours. They set off again in the morning, arriving to see the doctor leaving. Sophie looked at the expression on his face realising something seriously wrong. Sophie ran inside, finding her father making tea and her mother resting on the settee by the fire. Sophie and her mother hugged each other. "What's wrong, mum?"

"I have cancer. The doctor said maybe six months," Mrs Mercantile burst into tears. "I have to go into hospital."

Sophie looked at Donald for a solution. "Can they operate? Mrs Mercantile."

"No, Donald, short of a miracle, you and your money can't resolve this."

"Mother, Donald can pay for the best surgeons, can't you, Donald," Sophie expressed reassuringly, trying to be strong.

The ambulance arrived. Mrs Mercantile carefully loaded into the ambulance, heading for Edinburgh. Donald made a few phone calls explaining he was happy to pay for Mrs Mercantile's treatment. He expected every effort to be made to resolve the cancer issue when she arrived.

Donald realised if it wasn't for his money, he wondered how many people would genuinely be interested in him. Mrs Mercantile suggested it doesn't matter how much money you throw at a problem; it sometimes won't change the outcome. Donald wondered if Sophie was in love with him or his money. The same applied to Christine had she purposely become pregnant for financial reasons. If it weren't for his talent, he'd be plain old Donald, perhaps a rugby player, a good rugby player.

***

Christine is now comfortable in the hospital; she would have to stay there for at least two weeks to rest completely. Otherwise, the babies would abort. She discovered she's carrying a boy and a girl, a completely ready-made family, which made her smile.

Cindy collected Gerald from the hospital, relieved a disaster averted. Gerald phoned Mary explaining the situation and Christine's carrying a boy and a girl. Mary smiled, "That was lucky, Gerald, we were there. God knows what would have happened if no one were in the house."

***

The snow had started to fall. Donald walked across the paddock stroking the pigs; he suddenly felt alone, wondering where his life was heading, concluding that he's only a meal ticket for many people.

Donald received a phone call from his solicitors informing him he now owned Dorking Moor Estate. Donald drove to Edinburgh, transporting Mr Mercantile and Sophie. Sophie's mother is already in surgery to investigate, if possible, to remove cancer from her liver. Since Donald had intervened, there appeared to be more urgency. It's the old saying, Donald thought, money talks. They waited six hours, and the surgeon came to see Mr Mercantile. "A very successful operation. We think early days may have removed the tumour in time before it spread. Only time will tell."

Mr Mercantile collapsed onto a chair, suspecting if Donald hadn't intervened less of an urgency to deal with his wife's cancer. Sophie sat with her father while Donald purchased plastic cups of tea that could be better described as engine oil by the taste.

Sophie and her father stayed in a small hotel. Donald returned to Bonar Bridge, asking the neighbouring farmer if he would feed the pigs for a few days while Mr Mercantile was with his wife in the hospital.

Donald returned to Glencoe, then drove to Dorking Moor Estate, finding the caretaker employed by the previous owner, an elderly man earning a dismal amount of money to supplement his pension. Going by the name Eric McTavish, which Donald thought was odd. Eric opened the house showing Donald around the forty rooms, some suffering from water damage. The roof is obviously in a bad way. Donald asked, "Eric, you know of a builder locally?"

Eric passed him a card, "This company had already costed repairs, Mr Selwyn. I'm sure they'd be interested if you gave them a ring, especially when they know they will be paid. The previous owner is a little devious with his money."

Donald phoned the number on the card, surprised Maggie answered the phone. "Maggie," Donald asked, "You own a building company?"

"No, Donald, my future husband does; he carried out the original quote for repairing the roof. The interior comes to a hundred-seventy-thousand. Donald, I have the quote in front of me."

"Maggie, you know of an architect we're turning this place into a hotel. Forty bedrooms, the same as Glencoe. I want a suite for my personal use."

"My future husband can do that; I'll have him draw plans for you, Donald. Preventing further water damage is essential, or the cost would escalate."

"Brilliant. I know I have little to worry about if you're involved. Eric will be here holding the keys to gain access once you have the drawings, Maggie, ring me."

"Okay, Donald, bye for now."

"How are you paid, Eric, by the previous owner?" Donald asked, concerned.

"He gives me a few pounds in cash occasionally, very occasionally," Eric lifted his eyebrows.

Donald passed Eric a card and two thousand in cash. "Ring me if you need to, Eric, look after the place for me."

Eric shook his hand eagerly; Donald liked the look of the house with stone pillars supporting the entrance, the property allowed to decay. Donald looked around the other buildings, mainly agricultural, coming across two old cottages, one Eric obviously lived in. "Eric, your place looks a little worse for wear. Do you have any building issues?"

"She's a little damp in places, but it's home somewhere to live."

Donald rang Maggie. "Maggie, please look at Eric's cottage fairly urgently. He appears to have damp patches; rectify."

"We'll be out tomorrow, Donald."

Donald patted Eric on the back, "Thank you, you have my phone number, just ring me." Donald climbed into his Bentley, heading for Edinburgh. The weather is very unsettled, cold, sometimes snowing and rain, soon be Christmas again. Donald pulled into a Land Rover dealership purchasing a bright orange Range Rover for Sophie. Donald thought; it almost made your mouth water like bitter orange, looking at the colour. They promised to have the vehicle ready for the road in two days and delivered to the hotel the garage only two miles from where Sophie's staying. Donald knew she didn't like big vehicles. Nevertheless, if you have a prang in this weather, you need some steel between you and the other vehicle. Plus, he wanted protection for his child when born.

Donald parked outside the hotel carrying suitcases for him and Sophie. Donald explained he'd found her a vehicle and purchased. She kissed him, saying, "I won't argue; I don't like big vehicles, although I know why you purchased to protect my sorry arse from injury."

Donald phoned his mother, explaining the events. She likewise concerned explaining Christine and her condition. Donald sighed heavily. Sophie had listened to the conversation placing his free hand on her covered stomach, "Remember Donald, I'm carrying your child too."

Donald had a distinct feeling; she knew more than she was letting on. He always thought, in a few months, the balloon would explode in his face. He'd either end up with no girlfriend or in a lawsuit for financial support, or she would shoot him.

The following two days passed uneventfully. Donald had a chance to walk around Edinburgh, looking at the spectacular architecture. Sophie's new Range Rover arrived, and her father burst out laughing, "You will not be lost in that girl. I should imagine they can see you on Mars."

Sophie climbed inside, "lovely Donald, plenty of room and a baby seat."

"I'm heading home, Sophie. If you need anything, ring and come once your mother and father are safely home, and there are no issues."

Mr Mercantile smiled, patting Donald on his shoulder, "She'll be there, lad, don't worry, you've done us proud. You saved my daughter's life and now, my wife. We will never be able to pay you back."

Sophie kissed him on the lips, "Drive careful, Donald, please," she said, waving goodbye to him.

Donald joined the M6; his Bentley had spent most of its life racing up and down the motorway. To be quite honest, he couldn't wait to be home. Jack phoned, "I haven't had any artwork recently, Donald, is everything okay?"

Donald explained the situation to Jack. Jack responded, "I'm afraid you will have to become accustomed to the leeches sticking to you. They will suck you dry because you have what they haven't, money. Tread carefully; if you were broke tomorrow, they wouldn't look at you twice. They move on to the next meal ticket. However, what I can inform you. Thanks to your endorsements and art, you're worth a hundred million in your Swiss bank account; I won't give you access yet," Jack chuckled.

"I owe you, Jack, for looking after me."

Donald arrived home in the early hours. The weather is appalling. Rain and frost are a great combination if you have a death wish to travel in. He ran up to his studio, flopping on his bed, exhausted; that's where he stayed until morning, receiving a phone call from his mother at 8:30 a.m. " Donald, breakfast."

Donald sat down to a lovely breakfast with his father. "I had Gerald slaughter the rest of the pigs, Donald; we don't need the headache. Your mother and I are supposed to be semi-retired, and all she ends up looking after is Sophie's bloody horse. We appreciate she's helping to look after her mother at the moment, and she has had health issues."

Donald lowered his knife and fork to the plate, "Solution, father, sell me the farm and move out. You have property down in Devon I purchased. I can employ people," Donald rose from the table, walking out of the door; Donald glanced back, "I will move to Mill Farm as soon as Michael's finished. Then I'll permanently be out of your hair and Sophie's horse."

Mary shook her head from side to side, "Martin, you are as tactful as a bulldozer. I said I don't mind looking after the horse; I have great pleasure riding."

Donald jumped in his Bentley driving to Mill Farm, finding Michael working inside. "How much longer, Michael?"

"The decorating is almost finished; we still have appliances to fit which weren't chosen before Sophie left for Scotland. I'm in limbo waiting for someone to purchase, then I can plumb in."

"Leave it with me, Michael; the appliances will be here later today or first thing in the morning."

Donald drove straight into town, calling in at a store. He purchased a washing machine, dryer, dishwasher, and everything he could think of to fit out the kitchen. He moved on to a superstore selecting furniture for the whole house to be delivered in the morning.

He drove to Crabtree Farm, sitting at his easel painting away with no idea where the picture was heading. He threw the paintbrush at the canvas, swearing and going to bed, fed up with life.

Sophie phoned at midnight, disturbing him. Donald explained that he'd purchased appliances and furniture for Mill Farm in no uncertain terms, turning off his phone. Sophie's quite shocked by his abruptness.

The following day, she drove her parents home, worrying about Donald, he seemed to be under pressure, and she didn't know why. She left in the evening heading for Crabtree Farm. The gritters were out, still snowing and raining. What a combination. At 6 o'clock in the morning, Donald peered from the studio window to see Sophie's bright orange Range Rover. She could not hide in that car; he chuckled, coming downstairs. They went into the cottage for breakfast. Sophie explained the situation with her parents, especially her mother. Sophie turned to Donald, "Have I upset you, Donald? You were rather nasty to me on the phone. I can't be here and there. I'm afraid my parents will come first. They're the only friends I've had in this world; if you don't want me to stay, say so now, and I'll leave."

Mary and Martin stared in disbelief. Donald sat, shocked by her comment. "Whatever gave you that silly bloody idea," Donald retaliated? "You phoned at midnight. I had to purchase appliances and furniture for the house because you didn't organise it with mother; so, you'll have to like it or lump it. Don't start on me, Sophie. I have businesses to run."

Mary intervened, "The pair of you calm down before the situation explodes in your face, and you'll say something you really regret. We understand your position over your parents Sophie that couldn't be helped. You must also understand Donald has to make money to keep everything running; you must be tolerant, the pair of you."

Sophie stood, "I will go to Mill Farm; I'm knackered. I've driven all night to be with you," Sophie burst into tears.

Donald immediately cuddled her, "I'm sorry, Sophie, it's me. I'm so stressed, and I don't know why. I can't even paint a portrait; perhaps that part of my life is now over, who knows. Come on, have you upstairs in bed to sleep," he emphasised.

Sophie retired to bed. Donald stared at his easel, looking at the canvas for a miracle to happen to show him the direction he needed to go. He's producing his first abstract painting. Donald looked at the pure mess on his canvas, like his mind sending a photo to Jack, waiting for the insults. Donald entitled the artwork "Frustration." He thought an apt description; he had blended colour into colour for no particular reason or order.

Jack phoned, "What's happened to you, Donald? It will sell because you painted, certainly not your usual standard. Transport to my studio in the morning, watch the roads, quite treacherous," Jack rang off.

Donald left at 6 o'clock the following morning for London. The roads were treacherous; gritting lorries ensured the motorways were clear, not paying much attention to the side roads. Donald left his artwork with Jack after watching the price start at five pounds on the computer wouldn't even cover the cost of his fuel, let alone the oils. Donald suddenly found himself in a fog bank, trapped between two lorries. His Bentley caught fire, and he struggled to escape, grabbing his thick coat, and making his way to the barrier off the motorway, along with the other dozen or so involved in the accident. Donald watched his Bentley burn, so many memories vanished into thin air. Once the accident was on the news. "Donald Selwyn's Bentley is on fire." The rubbishy artwork Donald had presented to Jack had reached fifteen million pounds. Everyone suspecting Donald's either injured or dead would increase the value of his art many times over.

Sophie phoned his mobile crying, relieved he was okay. Christine watched the news from her hospital bed, panicking her children's father had died.

Donald's finally released from the hospital; making his way to a train station, he headed home, arranging for Sophie to collect him from Birmingham station.

Donald sat quietly in the passenger seat, listening to Sophie explain how worried she was and the rest of the family. Donald wondered if he'd died, what difference would it have made? He's just a meal ticket. He visualised the family like a ravenous dog chewing at his bank account, deciding who had what.

The following day Donald went into his solicitors, making out a Will ensuring his unborn children were catered for along with their mothers if he should die prematurely.

Donald left the solicitors and caught a taxi to the hospital, finding Christine sitting in bed, bored stupid. They greeted each other warmly with a kiss. "I've come from the solicitors. I've made sure you and the children are well provided for Christine, and the same applies for Sophie in the event of my death, which nearly happened yesterday."

"You are silly, Donald. You won't die."

"I've purchased Dorking Moor Estate and turning into a hotel. I must go now; I have to purchase myself another vehicle. I'm rather sad my Bentley burnt; I become very attached to her."

He kissed Christine goodbye. Donald walked out of the hospital; Angela pulled up alongside, "Can I give you a lift, Donald? I'm heading home," she smiled encouragingly.

Donald climbed into her mini, sitting comfortably in his camel hair coat. Donald asked with curiosity, "How come you're finishing work early, Angela?"

"My half-day if we have to work extra hours, we are not paid for them. We have to take them off in lieu."

They pulled into the yard at Crabtree Farm. "Would you like a coffee before you go, Angela," Donald offered.

"Why not," she said, following Donald upstairs. Donald realised Sophie was missing. He looked out of the window seeing her Range Rover gone, suspecting she was paying a visit to the doctor for a check-up. Donald made two coffees. Angela's studying herself in the full-length mirror in the studio. Donald watched through the doorway as she paraded herself in front of the mirror. Much to his astonishment, she unbuttoned her blouse, removed her bra, looked at herself in the mirror, and then removed the rest of her clothes; Donald exhaled. Gorgeous is an understatement. She had a fabulous pair of tits. Although he suspected Angela saw him watching, he stepped back into the kitchen.

Donald prayed Sophie would not return home; how could he explain the situation had no idea. Donald called out, "Coffee."

Angela came into the kitchen, suggesting, "Michael wondered if you would paint me nude on a portrait to hang on our bedroom wall. You think that's too kinky?" She smiled, accepting her mug. Totally unconcerned, Donald could see everything.

Donald shrugged his shoulders, "I don't quite see the point; he has the real you. What more does he need? I certainly wouldn't. I don't find it necessary to paint a portrait of Sophie naked; besides, as you age, you would hate the portrait without imperfections."

"That's a very valid point," Angela frowned, "Never crossed my mind. Thanks, Donald," she said, finishing her drink. "I must go. I have to cook Michael lunch," she kissed Donald, dressed and ran off downstairs. Donald sighed, watching Sophie's orange Range Rover come into the yard. She entered the studio frowning, "The doctors complaining my blood pressure is too high," she said, flopping down on the bed. "I have to rest; this is your fault, Donald. You're so scrumptious and irresistible."

"That's not the reason you drink too much coffee." They embraced for a moment.

"Go away. We can't do that."

Donald returned to his canvas, receiving a phone call from Maggie, "Hi Donald, we found the damage on the roof at Dorking Moor Estate. We also had a look at the caretaker's cottage and sealed the leak. Before doing anything else, we must see what alterations need to be made to turn it into a forty-bedroom hotel. The village is quite excited about having more employment, so I don't think you'll be short of applicants."

"Sorry, Maggie, I'll have to ring off; I have another incoming call; I'm trying to sort another vehicle."

The Bentley dealership from Cheltenham phoned Donald. "Mr Selwyn, we are deeply sorry you were involved in an accident. Your Bentley was destroyed, but at least you escaped unhurt. Will you be replacing your Bentley, Sir, with an identical model or something else?"

Donald thought, very fond of his old Bentley, "What have you in stock that would interest a poor artist," he chuckled.

"We have an identical vehicle to yours; the only difference is the car is gold in colour. Obviously, we can order anything you wish, such as the artwork on your previous vehicle."

"One presumes I would blind half the country driving around in such a bright colour. I like it; please deliver at your earliest convenience. I'm without a vehicle."

"Thank you for your order, Mr Selwyn. We estimate two days should suffice to have the vehicle to your standard and requirements. I presume you require a small cash safe fireproof fitted?"

"Yes, very handy not only for cash but documents."

Donald walked across the fields to Mill Farm, unlocking the front door and discovering the place was immaculate. Michael had completed his work, the furniture arranged, which could be moved later, if not exactly where he wanted it or Sophie. Donald's extremely impressed with the seventy-two-inch plasma television on the wall.

To his surprise, Sophie had arrived in her bright orange Range Rover, which always made him smile. He couldn't have picked a worse colour no wonder they were so keen to sell; no way you could have an affair in that vehicle, wouldn't be a lay-by you could hide in. Sophie walked in and had a look around, "Beautiful, Donald." Sophie's mobile rang. "Calm down, father. Okay, I will come; give me a chance to pack a bag. According to my father, my mother's relapse. Cancer has spread not just her liver but everywhere. He wants me to come and say goodbye to my mother," Sophie said, wiping her eyes with a handkerchief.

"The roads are treacherous, Sophie; I haven't my new Bentley. You want me to drive your Range Rover. I don't want you having an accident in your condition; the last thing we need so close to Christmas."

"The motorways are clear, Donald. I have my lovely new Range Rover; she will look after me," Sophie smiled, patting Donald's cheek-kissing him on the lips, "See you soon, bye." Sophie left packing a bag and headed for Bonar Bridge, driving steadily.

Donald locked the front door on Mill Farm, walking across the field to his studio on Crabtree Farm. He sat quietly at his easel and threw the paintbrush across the room in frustration; his mind wouldn't settle. He made a coffee sitting down to watch the television. Donald jumped to his feet, staring at the screen in horror. He saw an orange Range Rover down an embankment as if driven off the road, not appearing to be damaged. Donald, panicking, fumbled with his mobile frantically, phoning the police. Donald explained who he was and the woman Sophie Mercantile his fiancée. Donald swallowed hard, no other vehicle involved. Sophie had gone off the road and was pronounced dead at the scene; an autopsy would hopefully reveal why.

Two days later, the coroner discovered Sophie had a massive heart attack while driving and dead before the vehicle stopped. Donald was inconsolable. The minute his new Bentley arrived, he drove off for Scotland to visit Mr and Mrs Mercantile. Donald parked on the side of the motorway, placing a bouquet of flowers where Sophie had died and continued to Mr and Mrs Mercantile. Warmly greeted by Mr Mercantile informing Donald Mrs Mercantile had died at the same time as Sophie. Sophie and her mother were cremated, along with her unborn son. Donald called in at Glencoe Estate after the funeral, which some staff members had attended. Christmas Eve, Donald had not purchased any presents for anyone. He didn't think he would ever celebrate Christmas again, and he certainly wasn't becoming involved with anyone else. He's not 20, and he'd suffered two failed relationships.

Donald drove home on Christmas day, the motorway almost clear of traffic. Donald's mobile rang Christine, she was crying. "I don't know what to say, Donald; I can't make things better for you. I don't even know why I'm phoning you. You must hate me," Christine rang off. Donald continued to drive; he was in no rush to go anywhere.

Donald finally parked in the yard at Crabtree Farm. His mother opened the cottage door. "I don't want to talk, mother. Please leave me alone," Donald ran up into the studio. Donald made a coffee using powdered milk and opened a bottle of whisky sitting in front of his blank canvas, opening the gates of hell in vibrant oils, trying to express the pain he's feeling over the loss of Sophie and his unborn son. Donald glanced down at the whisky glass, realising no matter how much he consumed, the pain would return in the morning.

***

Mrs Montague was in France with her husband monitoring events; she couldn't believe anyone could have such bad luck as Donald. He'd never harmed anyone, and this is his payment, more pain. Although Mrs Montague realised this opened the door for Christine, suspecting Christine would never behave herself, Donald would be acutely aware. Mrs Montague suspected the only thing to do was sit back and see what happened next. Mrs Montague suddenly smiled, conjuring a plan in her mind and deciding to phone Mary.

Boxing Day, Donald sent Jack a photo of his latest creation. Jack studied the photo; he could see the pain and torment of Donald's suffering. He texts Donald, "Transport when you're ready."

Donald took a stroll, sitting on the bench where he'd buried Biscuit and where his grandfather's ashes were scattered. In contemplation, he walked across the field to Mill Farm, turning up the heating to prevent the water pipes from freezing.

***

Christine's sitting at the breakfast table with Cindy and her father, drinking a cup of tea. "Donald is the father of my children; you might as well know now Sophie's dead. I was determined if the last thing I ever did. I wouldn't destroy Donald's chance of happiness by exposing the fact I'm carrying his children. I seduced him, not the other way around."

"That confirms everybody's suspicions," Gerald commented, pleased Donald is the father and disgusted with his daughter at the same time. "You mind if I inform Mary?"

"Yes, I will explain to her. About time; I answered for my actions. Determined at the outset not to be like my mother and failed miserably for some time; since I conceived, I see things differently. You wouldn't understand, father," Christine sighed, slipping on her coat.

Christine slid into her black Range Rover Donald had purchased for her a while ago, driving to Crabtree Farm. She stepped from her Range Rover, warmly greeted at the door by Mary, "Would you like a cup of tea, Christine?"

"After what I say, I don't think I'll be welcome here. You might as well know now Sophie's dead. I carry Donald's children, don't blame Donald; I seduced him. I was determined not to ruin his and Sophie's relationship. I made Donald promised not to reveal the truth to anyone. I'm the bitch around here, no one else. I'm ashamed of many things I've done apart from having Donald make me pregnant, which I'd planned because I love him desperately. Yet, I'm still a miserable human being."

Christine turned to walk away. Mary grabbed her, "Sit down. Christine took some guts standing there. You are definitely your mother's daughter; nothing frightened her either. You're carrying a boy and a girl, a complete family in one package," Mary chuckled.

"Definitely not planned; I would have been thrilled with one of either sex. A complete family is extremely uncomfortable; I thought I lost them a couple of weeks ago. The doctors have managed to control things. Although they suspect they will be born prematurely, they want them to stay there for as long as possible."

Gerald and Cindy came into the yard at Crabtree Farm. "Don't worry, Mary, I have explained to them shouldn't be any blazing arguments; I hope it won't alter anything. I know Donald has already made a Will splitting some of his wealth between the three children, which he will now have to adjust since Sophie's deceased with her son."

"Your well-informed Christine," Mary commented, "You know more than me."

"Donald and I talk a lot; he's preparing for any eventuality other than the one that just took place, which is a shock to us all. Who would have suspected Sophie would have passed away like that? It makes it worse that she was pregnant," Christine sighed.

Gerald said, "I suspect my daughter has explained her devious behaviour," Gerald frowned.

"Devious or not, Gerald, Christine had the guts to face me with the truth. Give her some credit. Donald will provide for the children, that's for sure," Mary expressed.

Martin had said nothing sitting at the far end of the table, listening. Donald came in, observing everyone. "I've confessed, Donald, you're the father of the children I'm carrying; we have no need to stay quiet anymore."

Donald didn't care who knew what; it wouldn't change the outcome. "I'm taking a portrait to London. You want to come for a ride, Christine unless you think it would be too uncomfortable for you to travel that far?"

Christine grinned, "I'm definitely coming, Donald; I'm sick to death of four walls."

"Mother, Cherokees yours if you want him. If not, I'll phone Derek; he can be disposed of," Donald suggested with determination in his voice.

"Yes, thanks, son. I'll have to find stables close to our house in Devon; he can spend the summer with me," she grinned.

Everyone watched Christine leave with Donald. He placed his portrait in the boot of his new gold-coloured Bentley and set off for London.

Cindy, Gerald, Martin, and Mary sat around the table drinking tea, trying to work out what had just happened. "They won't be back together, will they, Mary," Gerald asked.

"I wouldn't have thought so, although knowing Christine, she has a way of getting whatever she wants sometimes. Although I know Donald has a long memory, like an elephant. He doesn't forget, very rarely forgives," Mary sighed, "At least we have another generation to take over the farms. Christine explained Donald has prepared his Will, leaving everything to the children."

Cindy gasped, "Already, don't you find that suspicious any of you? He's not 20. Although Donald is that way inclined, he likes to be organised."

They all looked at each other, wondering what was going on in Donald's mind for him to make a Will so early in life.

***

Christine commented, "Your son and daughter are playing rugby in my stomach." She placed his hand on her stomach; he could feel them moving. Christine moved his hand onto her covered breast, "I'm the size of Geraldine." Donald burst out laughing, the first time he'd laughed in ages.

They finally arrived at Jack's studio late afternoon. Jack looked at the portrait, saying a few pleasantries to Christine. He blamed her for most of what went wrong in Donald's young life. He placed the portrait on his easel, fitting a temporary frame and taking a few photos; within seconds after pressing the send button on the computer, the bidding had reached seven million. Donald held his forehead in shock; Christine placed her hand over her mouth. "That's ridiculous, Donald; although the pain you suffered is easily recognised in the portrait, how can you price someone's pain?"- Jack stood open-mouthed; he'd never expected a figure like that in all the years he's been an art dealer, never seen a price jump so spontaneously.

Donald and Christine set out heading for home. Now Donald had a new car without the artwork; nobody paid much attention to him. Occasionally, Christine noticed a female would come alongside in the middle lane looking at Donald and then accelerate off, making Christine grin with satisfaction. They finally arrived at Crabtree Farm. Christine kissed Donald, climbed into her Range Rover and headed home. Mary watched from the cottage window, realising still a considerable affection between those two. Donald retired to bed.

***

Early the following day, Maggie texts a message to Donald. "The drawings were now ready for Dorking Moor Estate conversion. Could you possibly come up to discuss the alteration?"

Donald texts, "On my way in half an hour, meet me at Glencoe Estate." Donald quickly packed a bag dashing downstairs and heading for Glencoe, arriving in the afternoon. Maggie's waiting for him having a drink at the bar. Donald asked, "Where's your future husband, Maggie?"

"Called out on an emergency, burst pipe somewhere. I understand the drawings, so I can show you." They went up into the private suite laying the plans on an oak table. Maggie never mentioned Sophie once; she didn't think necessary. Maggie explained anything Donald didn't understand on the drawing. The cost would be around one million, they estimated. Donald sat in thought for a moment.

Maggie went to the loo. Donald continued looking at the plan; Maggie returned; removed her clothes, sliding into bed. Donald glanced back, realising she was naked after she folded the blanket. "I've waited a long time, Donald." Not many minutes before Donald's making love to Maggie, he'd had an affection for her for some time, determined to control himself at the outset and now didn't give a bugger. Everybody's screwing everybody, he decided. They spent a couple of hours in bed together, finally showered and dressed, running downstairs. "Go ahead, Maggie, with the alterations, please."

Maggie whispered in his ear, "There's nothing wrong with you in the slightest," kissing him on the cheek and grinning as she left Glencoe.

Donald had an evening meal and retired to bed. He spent the next day walking around Dorking Moor Estate. Eric, the caretaker, was grateful Donald had repaired the cottage. The place is now warmer and drier. Donald walked to the rear of the old estate buildings, discovering an old petrol paraffin Ferguson twenty. Donald checked the engine oil. Eric joined him, "She's a good old tractor used here for odd jobs; she hasn't run for a while."

Donald slid the starting handle into its location, cranking the engine over; she spluttered into life on petrol. Eric pointed to a large tank in the corner where the TVOs stored, filling her tank; after she'd warmed for a few minutes, they switched the fuel over to TVO. She spluttered and coughed for a while. Donald climbed aboard, and memories flooded back of his grandfather's tractor, although she's a diesel. Donald set off across the estate, dodging the boulders and trying not to get stuck in the wet patches; suddenly, the weather changed as a blizzard approached. He quickly returned the tractor to the shed. Eric, laughing, "I could have told you, lad, before you set out a bad idea."

"I have a present for you, Eric, in my boot," Donald smiled, dashing out, returning with a crate of whisky, opening his wallet, and handing Eric another thousand pounds. Eric couldn't stop smiling; he'd never been treated so generously before by the owner of Dorking Moor Estate. Donald explained to Eric alterations taking place shortly as soon as the weather permitted. He's not to worry; he would always have a home here. Eric smiled in appreciation. Donald asked before leaving, "I presume you have a gun licence, Eric? Help yourself to any game, providing for your own consumption and not for sale. I don't think the estate will go bankrupt if it loses a deer occasionally."

"Donald, would you put two new batteries on the tractor? I know my way around the twenty-five-thousand acres; I won't get stuck," Eric chuckled, "I can use the little trailer to bring a deer home."

Donald smiled, phoning the Massey Ferguson dealership on the other side of Inverness. "Certainly, Donald, I'll have a mechanic out there in the next couple of hours with two batteries, and we'll give her a good service."

"There you are, Eric; your problem is solved. We'll fall out if I find out you have banquets at my expense," Donald laughed.

Eric smiled, "You don't stab a man in the back who looks after you," Eric winked.

Donald jumped in his Bentley and returned to Glencoe, finding Jock. Jock commented, "A bad affair Donald over Sophie, you have my sympathies. I can't imagine how you must feel, and I know I speak for everyone else here."

"I have to move on, Jock. I can't dwell on the past too much; it rips me apart. I've come to speak to you about Eric. I've permitted him to shoot deer for his consumption on Dorking Moor Estate. If you could monitor the situation, it would be appreciated. I don't know him like I know you."

"Needn't worry about Eric; he's as honest as the days long; he'll only take what is necessary to sustain himself. He's not a thief or a liar, a well-respected man in the community treated like dirt by the last owner of Dorking Moor Estate. We already know how generous you've been with him; he'll not betray your trust, Donald, have no fear."

"Thank you, Jock; I appreciate your insight," Donald remarked, entering the hotel upstairs to Christine's private suite. He rested for the remainder of the evening, setting out early the following day for Crabtree Farm. The roads were reasonable to travel on once he's passed Glasgow, travelling on the motorways far easier. He glanced across to where he'd left the bouquet of flowers for Sophie, still there, feeling tears on his cheeks, swallowing hard, trying to control his emotions. Nothing made sense to him at this precise second.

He parked outside the house on Mill Farm, walking inside to check nothing was frozen. Heard a Range Rover park behind his Bentley. Donald looked out the window, surprised to see Christine. She knocked and entered, "You mind if I come in, Donald?"

She carefully sat down on the plush settee gazing around the room, noticing the television resembling a cinema screen. Donald searched the cupboards finding powdered milk, making them both a coffee. Christine removed a piece of paper from her denim jacket. Donald sat beside her.

"I want you to read this," she said calmly.

Donald carefully unfolded the piece of paper, revealing a DNA test confirming he's definitely the father of the twins. "What's the point in that? I took your word for it," Donald asked, puzzled.

"I think it's time, Donald, for me, if you never speak to me again afterwards, I will have cleared my conscience; that's important to me. You're not like what you hear, but it's the truth. I had sex with Oliver once and Tim, four French boys plus both Copthorne brothers, and one or two others, not forgetting what my mother tried to arrange before she died; you can punch me in the face. I don't care. Although, in my own defence, I've owned up some of the affairs were not while we were together, so technically, none of your business."

Donald sat drinking his coffee, "What you expect me to say, Christine, you're a naughty girl, everything is forgiven? Since we weren't together, I've had my fair share, so why discuss the matter further?"

"Donald, I love you, don't ask me to explain my mistakes; because I can't other than I thought I could get away with it, like my mother, all I've achieved is wrecking what I want."

"Hypothetically, Christine, we start seeing each other again; you have the two children. You see a man you fancy, and I can go to hell while you have your pleasure. I'm expected to accept your story when you come running back. No, thank you. I'm quite happy to provide for the children. Sue me if you wish. I don't care. With your track record, I could bury you in court."

"I don't blame you for responding that way, Donald. I have no intentions of cheating on you if we ever rekindled our relationship; there again, I didn't the first time around and look what happened. Things would be different this time with far more at stake; my children would anchor me to my husband, I'm sure."

"Much like your mother, she spent most of her life naked with other men than she ever had with Gerald. You had a great role model, Christine. You are very strong-willed and will do exactly what you want to do at the time and bugger the consequences or anybody else's feelings."

Christine took a deep breath placing her cup on the table; she rose to her feet, heading for the door. Donald would not relent now. She suspected he would; the minute the children were born, only a matter of months, she would win, convinced. She climbed into her Range Rover. Donald was watching from the window. She knew his feelings for her still existed. Christine had proven the children were his, no escaping the fact, and no doubt in his mind now. Donald shut down the house on Mill Farm, heading home to the studio.

Donald awoke to a change in the weather at the beginning of February, the chill in the air receding. Donald knew the seasons were changing, according to the experts, global warming. Definitely, is something going on in his short existence. Things you could rely on, like the weather during the six-week school holiday, no longer existed; instead of brilliant sunshine, the weather could be anything it wanted.

Donald realised he now had three properties, two of them quite large. He would have to find a hotel manager when Dorking Moor Estate house was converted into a luxury hotel. More than a thousand acres at Mill Farm, the three hundred acres at Crabtree Farm, he thought, he'd combine together. Crabtree Farm has fifty acres of oilseed rape and two hundred and fifty acres of wheat this year. Mill Farm milling wheat already had its own drying and storage system, so there's no urgency to sell until the price is high to maximise profits for both properties.

Donald glimpsed at his canvas, sketching out Dorking Moor Estate house. What he envisaged the place would look like when the alterations were finished and repairs to the external of the property. The pillars were impressive; they almost looked like marble. Maggie had estimated six months to complete the work, most internal, so the weather wouldn't affect the progress.

Donald sat peaceably drinking his coffee, finally enjoying the solitude. He glanced from his window, seeing a limousine come into the yard. Only one person could possibly be, Mrs Montague, who hadn't seen her for some time. Her bodyguard knocked on the studio door, entering, standing aside, allowing access for Mrs Montague, accompanied by another young lady. Donald wiped his hands quickly on a cloth. "Donald, I would like to introduce you to my daughter Isabella; she has the Queen's ear on some matters."

"Pleased to meet you," Donald offered his hand. Isabella looked at him shaking his hand and quickly releasing it with a pleasing smile. "Mrs Montague, I thought you and I had a private relationship; now you're coming with other women," he joked.

Isabella looked away, not wishing her mother to see her smiling at the comment. "Behave yourself, Donald; I shan't threaten you with my bodyguard. I saw what happened to the last one most regrettable."

"Come through to my apartment; I will make you refreshments," Donald offered, leading the way. Isabella scanned the apartment with eyes like her mother's, missing nothing of importance to her. Donald made the coffees in cups and saucers and placing on the table. Isabella had dressed like an ordinary teenager apart from the clothes were far more expensive than you'd buy at the local shop. She'd ensured every part of her figure was emphasised by her clothes.

"Why have you come to see me, Mrs Montague? You don't do anything without reason?" Donald asked curiously.

Mrs Montague took a deep breath, "Sophie's death was totally unexpected. We can't imagine the pain you have suffered. Certain people are aware of what you spent to save Sophie's life. For her to die of a heart attack after everything you provided was unbelievable. I have arranged for the engagement ring you purchased to be sold. Isabella arranged for Sophie's Range Rover to be disposed of, and the monies recovered were transferred to your account." Isabella listened intently. You can ascertain she's a recording machine; nothing missed and stored for future reference.

"Thanks, Mrs Montague. I tried so hard; I should have realised when the doctor had mentioned her blood pressure and, on top of that, her mother's illness. I suspect the stress was all too much for her. My car out of action after an accident, although I should have driven up there with her, as usual, it's my fault," Donald swallowed hard, holding back the tears.

"I have seen the autopsy report, Donald, unlike yourself. Sophie was dead two minutes before the car went off the road. Even with resuscitation, the damage was irreversible."

"Thanks, Mrs Montague, for the information; I still feel a failure."

"I believe everyone is aware you are the father of Christine's twins since she decided to enlighten everyone after the death of Sophie. I have no doubt in my mind you will support the children with whatever they need to succeed in life, including leaving your estate to them."

"Yes, I have already made a Will. Hopefully, I will provide them a secure future after my death."

"I believe Christine has confessed her indiscretions in the hope of encouraging you to consider rekindling your relationship, using the children as a form of bribery, which I find distasteful. I know your behaviour has been exemplary. Your affairs were after the relationship was finished, not during. Apart from when Christine made herself pregnant using an enticement in the coffee, she brought it especially to encourage you to make love to her. Once she's pregnant, she's working on the principle; that you would never leave your children uncared for."

Donald sat shocked. Isabella made three more coffees returning to the table, "I can see from your expression, Donald, the information a revelation," Isabella remarked.

"Well, yes, Christine had planned. Mrs Montague, I didn't think you had any children," Donald asked.

"Why should I reveal to you, Donald, my daughter, at finishing school, and her life is private? Isabella has never mixed with the riffraff of life."

"You still haven't explained why you're here, Mrs Montague. I'm certainly not marrying Christine; you can forget that idea."

"Your opinion, Isabella am I correct in my assessment," she asked her daughter.

"I would say so, mummy; he is of a pleasant disposition and could be moulded with a little effort into something great, although his reputation as an artist excels in the highest places. Elizabeth R finds him very amusing."

"Then we agree, daughter," Mrs Montague said, smiling broadly.

Donald asked, "You two agree on what? May I ask if it concerns me."

Isabella enlightened, "I am renting one of your apartments for a month. We have spoken to your mother, and she agrees." She advised, " No good asking you with your mind in its present state, suffering from so many traumas. Let's see what transpires; you will have the privilege of taking me out and entertaining me for the month. I can assist you with business decisions." Isabella glanced from the window, "Oh good, my car has arrived." Donald glanced from the window seeing a black Wrangler Jeep driven into the yard and a car collecting the driver speeding off.

Mrs Montague stood, turning to face Donald, "I'm placing my daughter in your care. Don't disappoint me, Donald."

"Just a minute, Mrs Montague, who the bloody hell do you think you are! How dare you dump your daughter on me." Mrs Montague's bodyguard made the mistake of approaching Donald. Donald lashed out with his enormous fist. Mrs Montague's bodyguard flew down the stairs without touching a step. Mrs Montague held her head, "Donald, I wish you would control your temper. I am not dumping my daughter on you. Isabella is here to help you. Now I have to see what's left of my bodyguard. By his groaning, not much." Isabella's laughing.

Martin came from the house, assisting Mrs Montague's bodyguard to his feet, taking him into the cottage. Mary wiped the blood from his face where he'd collided with the bottom of the stairs. Isabella walked across the yard, stroking Cherokee's head. "Can I have permission to ride him, Donald, while I'm here?"

"Mother's horse, ask her, Isabella. Which apartment are you in?" Donald opened the limousine boot. "Apartment four on the ground."

Donald carried her two large suitcases into the apartment, passing Isabella the key left in the door. He continued upstairs to his studio, not speaking to anyone returning to his artwork. Sorry in some respects, he had struck Mrs Montague's bodyguard. Nevertheless, he'll not be hit first. Mary came upstairs, "Isabella is here to help

Donald. You may think your Mr wonderful, but you're not. You have all this money; two businesses of your own plus Crabtree Farm; when I sign over to you, I'm not dead yet," Mary emphasised, "You only have shares."

"Keep it, mother. I don't need Crabtree Farm for me to survive. I wonder why Mrs Montague sent her daughter here when I'm not a Royal. I've nothing to do with Christine. Sophie is dead; my only chance of happiness has gone. I shall stay on my own; I don't need anyone thank you."

Donald pushed past his mother before she responded; running downstairs, he jumped in his gold Bentley driving to Mill Farm. Searching the cupboards, they were bare. Donald jumped in his Bentley dashing into town, purchasing a new wardrobe and a small box of groceries. He returned to Mill Farm switching on the computer setting up an account with Morrisons to have his groceries delivered in the future, and phoned Susan. "Hi, Donald, you're the last person I thought would phone me," she chuckled.

"I'm wondering, Susan; how would you like to keep house for me, say two or three times a week at Mill Farm."

"I'll pop over, and we can talk," she lowered the receiver. Weren't many minutes before Susan parked outside Mill Farm. She entered, seeing everything brand-new. She already knew what had happened to Sophie tragically not to be. Donald made them both a coffee they sat at the kitchen table. "Your life's like mine, Donald, a bloody disaster. I have one or two cleaning jobs to keep the wolf away from the door, and of course, I still have the car Gerald kindly purchased for me," she sighed heavily.

"I guess things might be tight for you after the episode with Gerald. Anyway, that's water under the bridge. You've done me no harm and dared to come to Crabtree Farm and explain things to my parents and me. I would prefer you not to read my mobile messages," he chuckled. "Nothing here worth stealing if you need anything you ask. I ask no more of you than that. Once my hotel is finished in Scotland, I can arrange for you to visit with your daughter or your boyfriend."

Susan laughed, "Boyfriend, you must be joking. Mr right hasn't come along yet for me," she smiled.

"I believe Gerald used to pay you three-hundred pounds a week, is that correct, Susan?"

"Yes, but almost full-time, and of course, nothing went through the books. Otherwise, I'd lose my benefits," Susan grinned nervously.

"How long have you lived where you are at the moment?" Donald asked.

"About seventeen years, I moved in just before my daughter was born. Why?"

"Apply to the Housing Association to purchase the property; you should get a good discount on the property's true value. I will purchase for you, no strings attached. It won't be more than one-hundred-fifty-thousand pounds, I shouldn't think with your discount."

Susan held Donald's forehead, "Do you have a fever, Donald? Are you unwell? You realise what you've just said?" She asked, completely shocked.

"I was poor once, Susan and know what it feels like, wondering where the next pounds coming from. Our farm never used to be financially successful. We hadn't the acreage to make a serious profit supporting three people, not forgetting grandfather some of the time."

"Christine's such a fool. I'm so sorry things didn't work out for you and Sophie; with all your grief, you still have time to think about me, not even a real friend or relation," Susan burst into tears.

Donald smiled, "Inform me as soon as the place is valued. If they question you about affording, explain to them the property will be purchased on your behalf. Any arguing, let me know; in the meantime, I will pay you two hundred a week," he said, passing her a key, "Pop down here and keep me straight. Do whatever you think needs doing, as regards purchases. I have a Morrison's account; we can go online together, you say what you want, and I'll order it for you."

"We better start now, Donald," she switched on the computer, typing out a list of things she needed for the house, from a new vacuum cleaner to a mop and bucket for the scullery. "There you are, everything I should need for a while." she turned away while Donald placed the order; she kissed him on the cheek, "Has anyone ever told you your Mr wonderful, Donald," Susan smiled.

Donald chuckled, "Go home. Hopefully, I will see you soon. Your products will be delivered this afternoon, start whenever you like," passing her a hundred pounds from his wallet. She was about to leave when a black Jeep arrived. Susan and Isabella studied each other as they passed in the doorway, smiling politely.

Isabella made her way to the sink, removing a cup from the cupboard; she made herself a coffee as if she owned the place. Donald stood, arms folded, preparing for a few choice words; he wasn't taking any crap from anybody. "After the older woman Donald," Isabella commented, trying not to grin, looking at her long black hair in the window's reflection.

"I may well do, actually, my cleaner. I've taken her on to look after Mill Farm. I take it you have no bloody objections."

"You don't like me, Donald," Isabella asked directly.

"I don't know you, to be quite honest. I suspect you're like Christine and her mother, for that matter."

Isabella, so incensed, threw her empty cup, striking Donald on the forehead. Donald grabbed her arm, throwing her over the kitchen table. He spanked her backside until she screamed, throwing her on the floor. "You spoiled bitch, clear off." The cup had gashed the top of his eyebrow; he walked to the bathroom and cleaned the wound. Placed a plaster across the cut venturing downstairs to find Isabella had made two coffees. "Now we have cleared the air, perhaps you can be civilised. You always beat women?"

Donald didn't answer, trying to calm down, drinking his coffee. "We are taking your latest artwork to Jack in the morning. If we leave fairly early, we should miss the London congestion."

Donald grunted. "Your mother is right! You do sulk; she blames herself you were spoiled," Isabella grinned.

Donald turned to face Isabella with a face like thunder, then burst out laughing; he didn't see the point in arguing.

"I think you should have one or two things straight in your mind, Donald. Firstly, I am not a tart; I am nothing like Christine or her mother. I am slightly older than you and obviously a lot wiser from what I can see of your performance."

Donald chose not to respond, watching Isabella log into his computer, appearing to know his account passwords, horrifying. She saw the expression on his face, "Don't be alarmed, Donald. I know where you hide your money; it doesn't interest me in the slightest other than to ensure you are receiving the highest interest possible."

Donald shouldn't be shocked. Mrs Montague had contacts; he hadn't had any money stolen. Therefore, he had little to worry about, certainly no flies on Isabella. He left her sitting at the computer, walking around the buildings checking the grain storage facility on the farm, quite an expanse. The sparrows were perched on the rafters, searching for any morsel they missed when the grain store was cleaned. When Donald returned to the house, Isabella left a note on his computer. "Do not touch security software downloading."

Morrisons van arrived; he helped the man unload everything he purchased, placing it in the scullery for Susan to sort out when she came. Donald sat eating a packet of crisps and watching television, noticing from his sitting-room window Cherokee with Isabella on his back; he watched her jump the hedge approaching the house. Crazy girl, he thought. Donald opened the front door. "You need to order fertiliser, Donald. Come on, wake up, should be in stock by now," she ordered, riding off and calling back, "I'll check the crops around here. Guess you obviously haven't."

He thought Isabella was trying to get under his skin, succeeding much to his annoyance. Donald checked the horrendous fertiliser prices, wondering whether he should go organic next year. He could arrange for Seven Trent to apply sewerage to the thousand-plus acres. They would undoubtedly be pleased with the acreage and make that last for the year.

Donald ordered several tons of fertiliser to be delivered to Crabtree Farm. At least it wouldn't be nicked from there. Thieving from farms is now a regular occurrence, not only here but also in Scotland.

Within half an hour, Isabella came riding to the house. Donald opened the front door with his arms folded. "The crops are faring quite well; I presume you've ordered the fertiliser. Your new sprayers arrived at Crabtree Farm; you managed to do something right. Do you have the brains to operate it, Donald?"

Not bothering to reply, Donald walked back into the house and shut the door, watching her ride off towards Crabtree Farm, preparing to jump the ditch. Cherokee applied the brakes, and she flew over his head, landing in the ditch full of water. Donald nearly wet himself laughing as she stood plastered from head to toe in mud. Donald walked across, opening the gate as she mounted Cherokee. "There you are, Isabella, that'll teach you to show off, silly bitch." She didn't respond, galloping through the gateway around the perimeter of the field to Crabtree Farm. If she's trying to impress Donald, she certainly went a long way to achieving that today. Donald locked the house returning to the studio; he paused to speak to his father in the yard, "Dad, I've ordered fertiliser. If I'm not here, can you unload it in the shed? Please, for both farms."

Martin burst out laughing, "No problem, son. Cherokee taught Isabella a valuable lesson. Don't mess with the Selwyn's; a wonder butter melts in her mouth. Her being here is nothing to do with me, son. You can blame your mother for that one, but I'm sure you'll knock her into shape."

"Why is she here, dad?"

"Your mother is worried Christine may influence you, and you will lose all your hard-earned wealth. Mrs Montague and your mother have come to some agreement."

"What puzzles me, dad? I'm not Royalty or anything to do with them, so why the interest. It may be because my son and daughter aren't born and are slightly royal. Christine has already been into hospital once."

"Speak of the devil," watching Christine's black Range Rover come into the yard. "This should be interesting, son," Martin chuckled. "I'm glad I'm not in your shoes."

Christine approached, kissing Donald, "You have a cuppa for a friend? And your rugby team."

Donald helped Christine upstairs into the studio. She looked at the portrait of his new estate adjacent to her own. "Spectacular, Donald, when finished, how long before you open?"

Isabella walked into the studio. If looks could kill, Isabella would be dead. Christine observed how she was dressed. Although not indecent, in a pink V-neck jumper revealing a modest cleavage, she was obviously wearing a bra underneath and a white skirt with authentic leather shoes. Christine remembered she used to have a waistline like that; it seemed a lifetime ago. "Christine, we finally meet; I'm Isabella Donald's financial adviser. Mrs Montague, my mother, insisted I help Donald organise his finances, so he isn't ripped off by gold diggers."

Christine grabbed Donald's arm and placed his hand on her stomach, "There are two financial packages here; you will have no control over, I promise you. Donald will care for his son and daughter, whether you like it or not," Christine smirked.

"Providing they are Donald's, of course, don't bore me with the DNA reports. You can purchase of any street corner for the right money."

"Donald." Christine protested, "You let her speak to me like that?"

"I've seen the DNA report; Isabella looks genuine to me. I think you're cruel."

"I suppose possible they're yours. There again have been a few men, haven't there, Christine, even when you were with Donald and certainly plenty afterwards," Isabella smirked.

Donald could see they were provoking each other. He stood between them. "Not in your condition, Christine. I've lost so many things precious to me. I don't want to see the children harmed. Isabella, pack it in; obvious you're trying to provoke her. I'd let her rip your eyes out if she weren't pregnant. I've seen this girl in action."

"Oh, you mean like this, Donald." Isabella switched the plasma screen on and typed a code on his computer. Donald stood, staring along with Christine. Christine is naked on the floor with the Copthorne brothers taking turns to have sex with her and using sex toys. Christine turned away. Isabella discontinued the transmission, calmly leaving the studio and returning to her apartment, grinning. No way Christine could beat her.

Christine sat on a chair for a moment sobbing, then rose to her feet. Donald helped her down the stairs into her Range Rover, and she drove off. Donald returned to his studio, checking the paintings ready to take to Jack in the morning. He realised Mrs Montague and her daughter had access to everything. He understood Christine would do whatever it took to win. She professed she hated the two brothers and was on her back with them both in the next breath, enjoying the experience immensely from the sound.

At 5 o'clock in the morning, Donald heard someone knocking on the studio door. In his pyjamas, he answered, finding Isabella dressed and ready to go. "Come on, London, this morning; I don't want to be trapped in rush-hour traffic."

Donald quickly showered while Isabella made him coffee. He promptly carried the painting downstairs, placing in the boot of his new gold-coloured Bentley. Isabella climbed into the passenger seat wearing her jeans, blouse, and denim jacket. When they arrived on the outskirts of London, she started giving Donald directions to improve their progress through London. Isabella seemed to know every street like the back of her hand. Donald thought she probably spent most of her life in London or some city.

Jack greeted Isabella as if he'd known her his whole life. Donald thought strange; most things in life he found weird these days. Jack looked at the portrait, "So this is your latest acquisition, Donald. I will have to visit when finished it looks very posh. Although you never know, I'm not sure it will fetch a reasonable price. What title will you give this portrait."

"Sanctuary."

Isabella watched intently. Jack framed the picture and took photos, placing on his website and pressing the send button. Two and a half million appeared instantly. Jack held his forehead, "There must be somebody waiting for your next portrait. I wonder if a secret hoarder is trying to purchase all your portraits, presuming the price will only rise as time progresses. I've known it happened before but very rarely."

Isabella commented, "Jack, I've checked on Donald's Swiss investments; he is now worth over one hundred million. A shrewd move on your part hiding some of his wealth, stop the little sticky-fingered devils bleeding him to death, which I will now prevent," she assured with her mother's pale blue eyes.

Donald flopped down on the chair, realising Jack was looking after his interests, and Isabella appeared to be. What is her motive? They left Jack's gallery not quite 10 o'clock in the morning; Donald parked outside a coffee shop. Isabella looked puzzled as he left the car, opening the passenger door, holding her hand helping her out. "Come on, I'll buy you coffee and a sticky bun. If you're socialising with ordinary people, you will have to become used to their ways," he grinned, suspecting she'd never entered such a place in her life.

Donald sat at the table; Isabella joined him. He passed her the menu. The waitress came to the table, holding her notepad. Donald smiled pleasantly, "I'll have the full English breakfast, please, and two extra slices of toast and a pot of tea for two. What would you like, Isabella?"

"I'll have the same, please."

Donald was surprised; he suspected Isabella would look at the cups with a magnifying glass before drinking from them, let alone eat here.

She tucked into her breakfast as if she hadn't eaten for a week, much like himself. Donald hadn't had breakfast before they set out; not eaten recently. His appetite had gone after facing problem after problem.

"Isabella, why are you hanging around with me. What are you and your mother up to, and mine? All I have is money. I don't mix in high society circles. The only person I've met close to Royalty is your mother, and she won't run away with me, I asked."

Isabella spilt her tea, laughing, the first time Donald had really seen the ice break in her expression. She wiped her mouth with her napkin composing herself. "Thank you for trying to choke me. Mother said, if she weren't married, she would have run away with you for sure; that's one hell of a compliment from my mother. She's extremely fussy about everything, including her men. My father spent three years begging before my mother relented."

The waitress approached, placing the bill on the table. Donald opened his wallet, and the bill came to thirty-four pounds. He gave her fifty pounds, "Keep the change."

She smiled, "Your Donald Selwyn, the famous artist, aren't you?" She asked timidly.

"Yes, I am he," Donald grinned.

"Mr Selwyn, I have a magazine with one of your portraits. Would you sign for me, please?"

"Of course." She scurried off, returning with the magazine. "What's your name?"

"Simone."

Donald wrote, to my true love, Simone, from Donald Selwyn. "Do you know Jack Potter's art gallery two streets down? If you go in there, pass him this card from me; he will give you a print that you can keep for yourself." Donald scribbled a message on the back of the card. Jack would know it's from him. Isabella watched in amazement the way Donald performed with people. He may not be high society, but he's generous and kind to everyone unless you upset him, which she had achieved on two occasions. She's now seeing the real him in action, realising what her mother's saying is correct; you just want to cuddle him. Simone kissed him on the cheek, "Thank you so much, Mr Selwyn. Please come here again."

Donald smiled, "Thank you for a lovely breakfast. I will certainly eat here again," he said, holding the door for Isabella to leave.

They set off for home. Donald watched Simone run down the street in his rearview mirror, holding his card. Isabella glanced back, "You made that woman's day, Donald; you give away so much. Mother explained how many thousands of pounds you spent on

Christine. You saved Sophie's life. You give to charity, and I witnessed first-hand how you made a woman's heart jump for joy in an otherwise miserable existence."

"Don't you go soft on me, Isabella; I'm not falling in love, I'm not marrying, and I'm staying happy single old me."

Isabella didn't answer. They joined the M40. She watched girls in Ferraris waving at Donald, children from coaches and the back seats of cars. A varied selection of people wanted to know Donald, spanning the classes. She guessed Christine would continue to fight for Donald, although she suspects things may change once the children are born, especially if they're not his. She suspects this is the case. Donald's unaware of Christine's exploits with young men at school when she'd sample the fruits of lovemaking with Donald.

They arrived at Crabtree Farm just after lunch. Donald parked his Bentley. Isabella suggested, "You can pay for lunch. I can drive my new Jeep; daddy purchased something I'd wanted for a long time."

Donald climbed into the passenger seat; she started the engine reversing out of the yard and heading into town, parking in sheep Street. Donald grabbed her hand, which surprised her, taking her into the Rose and Crown, one of Michael's favourite pubs, sitting at a table, "What would you like to drink, Isabella?" Donald asked.

"I fancy a non-alcoholic wine; I'm driving. Remember, mother would hang me if I were caught breaking the law." Donald purchased a bottle of non-alcoholic wine, returning to the table with the bottle and two glasses. Isabella ordered a salad and Donald steak, chips, and peas. Isabella burst out laughing as the oval dishes were placed in front of them. Much to Donald's surprise, Michael and Angela came in. Donald invited them to join him and introduced everyone, although Angela already knew Isabella. "I'll cover the meals," Donald advised. Michael had the same as Donald. Unlike the men in their lives, Angela had salad, not wishing to pile on the pounds. Michael commented, "You've had it rough; lately, Donald, I wish you every happiness in whatever you do mate. If it wasn't for you, I don't know where I'd be today."

"Angela," Isabella remarked, "We'll have to rewrite Donald's Will, you know why in case. Don't look at me like that, Donald. I know a little more than you, and so does Angela. She's not permitted by law to expose what she knows; otherwise, her career would be over."

Angela reiterated, "listen to Isabella, Donald, you're too nice a chap to be taken for a ride."

"You two certainly know how to cheer someone up." Donald sighed heavily, walking to the bar. "Drink, Michael?"

"Okay, my afternoon off," Donald ordered two treble whiskies and two pints of beer, returning to the table. When everyone had finished eating, neither Michael nor Donald steady on their feet. Angela remarked, "Donald's had it rough, Isabella. I know Christine too well, both her mother and her; I wouldn't trust any further than I could throw them."

"I agree with your assessment as long as those children belong to Donald; she will have his undivided attention and her claws firmly in his wallet; that's all she's after."

"I agree with you. Unfortunate, Sophie died; the guy doesn't have a break; of course, you could always win his affections. I see the way he looks at you," Angela grinned.

"I'm not his type, I don't think; he thinks everyone from my sort of background is a tramp and has the morals of a dog," she exhaled.

Angela glanced at the bar. "We'd better help these two home before they drop on the floor, and we can't move them." Isabella removed Donald's wallet paying the barman. Angela struggled with Michael, pushing him into the car. Isabella assisted Donald to her Jeep, finally persuading him to climb in and fit his seatbelt. He grabbed her head, kissing her passionately on the lips, which surprised her. She didn't say anything suspecting he wouldn't have done anything like that if he weren't intoxicated. She drove home to Crabtree Farm, realising she could not help him up the stairs. Instead, she helped him into her apartment, laying him on the bed. He immediately started snoring, and Isabella burst out laughing. Donald is a character, nothing like the people she's used to mixing with, all trying to brag, better than the next person, much like herself when she first met Donald. All she achieved was falling into a ditch full of water and mud.

Isabella's phone rang. She answered, "Mummy, everything okay with you and daddy?"

"Yes, Isabella, report daughter, why can I hear someone snoring? You and Donald have not! I hope?"

"No, we have not! I finally have his finances in order; I may have to stay for another month. I have met Christine and embarrassed her by making Donald aware of the truth about the Copthorne brothers. I have spoken to Angela, who works for Donald and Christine's solicitors, arranging to reorganise Donald's Will. If she has the idea of disposing of Donald to gain access to the money, she will be shocked. We all suspect she would if the opportunity presented itself; unless he relents and marries her, she would bleed him dry slowly."

"Could you imagine the damage that would cause to Elizabeth R. If Christine's permitted to venture down that path, Isabella? I will book your apartment for another month. Hopefully, you will have resolved all issues by then; if not, I will have to take other steps..."

"Okay, mummy give my love to daddy and thanks for my new Jeep; it's wonderful to drive."

Isabella made strong coffee sitting Donald up on the bed. He held his head gently, sipping his coffee, looking around the room, realising where he was. He stood immediately, almost spilling his coffee, "What the bloody hell am I doing in here," hearing an articulated lorry park outside the yard, realising a lorry load of fertiliser. Donald struggled out through the door. Isabella said immediately, "You are not driving any machinery in that state, Donald; I'll unload the lorry."

Donald fell over laughing, "You couldn't start the bloody loader, let alone unload it, girl," he said, struggling to his feet, leaning against the gate post.

Isabella ran into the machinery shed. He heard the loader start, much to his surprise. Martin came running out from the cottage, looking somewhat bewildered. "Who's driving the loader, Donald? You're certainly not in a fit state, son."

Martin supported Donald watching Isabella working the all-steer loader, removing one-ton bags from the lorry and placing them in storage. In Donald's wildest dreams, he never considered Isabella knew anything about farming equipment. However, he thought her parents had a vineyard and would undoubtedly have access to machinery.

He couldn't imagine Mrs Montague allowing her daughter to touch a tractor or her father, let alone be proficient in operating. She signed for the fertiliser. The articulated lorry left. She placed the loader in the machinery store, put the signed ticket in Martin's hand, and returned to her apartment, closing the door, grinning. Isabella had never seen Donald look so surprised in the time she'd known him; he obviously thought she couldn't operate anything. Is he in for a shock? She persuaded her mother to extend her stay to show him how much of a real woman she could be when provoked.

Martin helped Donald upstairs to his apartment, leaving him on the bed to sleep off the alcohol. Around 10 o'clock in the evening, Donald finally sat on the corner of the bed with a stinking headache. Making a strong coffee, he placed a blank canvas on his easel, sketching the loader and Isabella removing the ton bags of fertiliser from the articulated lorry. Donald painted her exactly the way he saw her; by 6 o'clock in the morning, he'd finished.

He carefully carried the portrait to the boot of his Bentley, tearing off for London determined to shock Mrs Montague, suspecting she had never seen her daughter operating a loader. He never thought he could surprise Mrs Montague; she probably knew everything. Nevertheless, he loved the painting, the vibrant colours of the machine and Isabella's lovely long black hair in her jeans and blouse, nothing inappropriate at all. He incorporated a glancing smile he thought would melt even the most hardened soul.

Donald parked at the rear of Jack's shop; Jack was amazed to see him, especially when he unloaded the canvas after only visiting yesterday. "Make sure Mrs Montague has a photo, Jack, please; perhaps you could print off a couple of copies, no, make it a dozen."

"What's the title Donald," Jack asked, seeing absolutely nothing exciting about the portrait other than the beauty of Isabella.

"Confidence."

Jack frowned, "Okay, don't expect this to reach more than twenty pounds, Donald, nothing in the picture. That reminds me, I gave a woman you sent me a copy of the painting in the magazine of Jerusalem."

"Thanks, Jack, mate."

Donald drove down a couple of streets, parking outside the café. Simone greeted him, "Mr Selwyn, I have a copy of Jerusalem. What can I get you for breakfast."

"The same as I had last time, please, Simone."

"No young lady this time, Mr Selwyn?"

Donald shook his head, smiling, "No, just me."

Donald finished his breakfast. Simone placed the bill on the table, placing a finger to her lips. "I paid for that one, Mr Selwyn; you're so generous."

Donald opened his wallet, "Don't be silly," passing her a hundred pounds to cover breakfast. "See you again soon, Simone." Such a small amount brought so much happiness to a woman's expression. Donald wondered how hard she had to work to make ends meet. Donald drove to Mill Farm, finding Susan cleaning; she greeted him. "The Housing Association said a hundred and seventy-five thousand pounds, Donald." She showed him the letter as proof she wasn't lying. The thought of not paying rent, only utility bills a dream come true for Susan if he decided to go ahead and purchase the house for her. "Come on in my Bentley; we'll drive to the Housing Association." They entered the offices speaking to someone concerning the purchase.

Donald explained he was supplying the money and the property solely in Susan's name. Donald rang his solicitors, explaining what he'd done. They were to represent Susan during the transfer of ownership to ensure completed correctly. Donald left a cheque with the Housing Association. Donald slowly drives to Mill Farm. Susan, in tears, never imagined she would own her house in her wildest dreams. They parked outside Mill Farm. Isabella's Jeep was parked by Susan's car. When they entered, Isabella was busy on the computer. She glanced to see the state of Susan with her makeup running down her cheeks, crying. Isabella asked, "Are you okay, Susan," deeply concerned while Donald made the coffee. Susan explained to Isabella what Donald had done.

They sat at the kitchen table. Isabella removed her mobile, searching through photos, "You wouldn't happen to know anything about this portrait Donald? My mother has been on the phone, asking me several questions."

Donald grinned, "I thought a lovely portrait. I don't think it will sell," he chuckled, "Jack doesn't think it will."

"Oh no," she showed him the price, "Hundred thousand pounds, Donald already; you are so lucky you had some prints made, so my mother could have one; my father thinks, absolutely wonderful."

Isabella showed Susan, "He's so talented; Donald sees the beauty where others only see ugliness."

Susan dried her eyes, applying more makeup, "When you reach my age, you need every assistance you can find to improve your looks," she chuckled.

"Donald, you haven't a fertiliser spreader, you realise?" Isabella announced.

"I've purchased as I go along, and Gerald's covered most of the fertilising and spraying on Crabtree Farm."

"I think you should purchase one, Donald. You shouldn't rely on others, should be self-sufficient and capable of handling all the operations yourself."

"I have to agree with Isabella, Donald," Susan voiced. "I know it's none of my business; Christine can twist her father around her little finger. And if you want the honest truth, there is talk around the village; that she's responsible for the fire. Copthorne brothers were working for her."

Donald looked surprised at Susan's comment, dialling Jason at Case IH. "Hi, Jason, Donald Selwyn. Do you have such a thing as a self-propelled fertiliser spreader; all our tractors are on big tyres, and I don't want the job of changing."

"I have everything," Jason chuckled, "Must be big and capable of applying fertiliser to all your properties within a day; that's your usual criteria."

Donald laughed, "You're learning, I could do with the machine yesterday, so my business manager tells me."

"The earliest two days, Donald, and the cost is hundred-ninety-thousand plus VAT."

"See you in two days, or my business manager will bite you," Donald laughed.

"Donald," Isabella cautioned, "I hope you haven't purchased anything ridiculous!"

Donald punched in the name of the machine on the computer. Isabella gasped, "Must be carrying ten-ton at a time, massive," she read down the specifications. "All computerised that should be easy to program. I presume this farm was mapped along with your own. Save a fortune on fertiliser wastage."

Donald walked to the cupboard, placing a folder on Isabella's lap, "Knock yourself out, woman," he smiled.

Weren't many seconds before Isabella had the information she required and a bag of memory sticks that could program the computer automatically on the fertiliser spreader. Donald sat disappointed. He thought he'd beat her at her own game, sadly mistaken. She laughed at his expression, "Donald, I have a degree in many subjects. I spent most of my education in a girl's convent. The most exciting thing was a magazine if we could sneak one in without mother superior finding out. We were there to learn and nothing else to distract us."

"So, you haven't been running wild with all the high society men?"

Isabella laughed, "You have a weird imagination, Donald, don't judge everybody by Christine's standards. Far more to life than sex; my mother and father have been together for many years and are perfectly happy. Allow me to show you an example of my father's respect for my mother."

Isabella punched in a code on the computer keyboard, displaying Christine's bedroom in France. Donald watched along with Susan. They saw Mr Montague assisting the inebriated Christine to her bed, sitting her on the edge. He went to walk away; she stood, removing her knickers and laying on the bed, offering herself to him. He walked out of the door. Isabella pressed the delete button, and the programme vanished. "Cameras all around my mother's castle in France; they were fitted because of thieving by the staff and visitors but have since served their purpose of eliminating suspicious instances, should someone choose to cause trouble. My mother said she's awfully tempted by you, Donald. Even at her age, you would have to be someone special to interest, my mother."

"To be quite honest," Susan remarked, "I always thought your mothers a right old battle-axe."

"You can have whatever opinion you wish, Susan. You will not beat my mother. If it weren't for the fact you had a daughter, you would be locked away and the key flushed down the toilet. I can promise you that's the only reason mother showed compassion. You were stealing from Mr and Mrs Gibbs. I would advise you not to try it with Donald."

Donald intervened; he could see nails at ten paces. "That's enough, the pair of you. That's history we can do nothing about. I don't think Susan would steal from me. I have given her more than anyone else ever has," Donald confidently professed.

"I didn't steal! Josephine asked me to conceal certain items; so she could take them to London to be pawned to help support her gambling addiction." Susan glared. "Your surveillance and spies aren't that good. Josephine could run circles around the lot of you, and so will Christine. You mark my words; she will have whatever she wants, including Donald."

Isabella realised the information her mother had accumulated was wrong about Susan. They naturally presume the servant stole the silver. "Please accept my apologies, Susan, if wrongly accused; why have you not said anything before now?"

"Part of my contract, have you ever read it, Isabella. I'm not permitted to expose what happened in the house or any orders Josephine or anyone else gave me. The only thing I confessed is to Donald over Christine and her lies."

"I've seen your contract and understand your reluctance to speak out."

Donald cuddled Susan, remarking, "That stinks, so the accusations of theft were lies, Susan. You were acting on Josephine's instructions."

Susan nodded, "Josephine knew my husband had a criminal background and why I'd applied for the position to keep my daughter safe. She knew if anything went missing, the first person they would look at would be a servant, not her. I imagine about twenty-thousand pounds of silver has ended up in pawn shops in London over the years. Josephine wasn't bad if she won on the roulette tables; she would often give me an extra hundred pounds for helping her," Susan sighed. "Of course, I ruined everything for myself. I lost my temper with Christine; I knew she was screwing other boys and for her to object to me wearing her mother's jewellery, which Josephine had given me permission, on other occasions, was mean. I lashed out, nearly costing me my life if not for your mother's bodyguard, Isabella."

Isabella made three coffees inviting Susan to sit at the table. She exhaled, "My mother will be livid. She hates being wrong."

Isabella hadn't realised she was wearing a pair of earrings with a micro receiver. Her mother's listening and absolutely livid. She'd made some grave errors in her assessment of the situation, which could have put Susan behind bars for something that wasn't her fault; she was only working on instructions from Josephine.

Donald sat astounded by the revelations feeling extremely sorry for Susan. He was pleased he now employed her and provided her own house and a secure position. Donald opened his wallet, "After what I've heard here today, I'm disgusted," he handed Susan a thousand pounds, "Call that a belated bonus," he said, kissing her on the cheek, "And I thought I had problems."

"Donald, your silly, too generous. You've spent a fortune on buying me a house. I have a lovely job working with you. Thanks to you, I have more security now than I've had for years," she cuddled him.

"Put the money in your pocket and go home. Use the money for redecoration or something," Donald smiled, watching her walk out.

Isabella returned to the computer, typing a coded letter to her mother, not realising she'd already listened to the conversation.

"Donald, would you take me to Scotland, please. I'd like to see the other property you recently acquired; I can make a full assessment. The fertiliser spreader won't arrive for two days we can be there and back in that time. I'll drive some of the way," she smiled reassuringly.

They returned to Crabtree Farm. Donald explained to his mother and father he had purchased a new spreader; he would apply the fertiliser in a couple of days when the machine arrived. They had nothing to worry about. He's taking Isabella to Scotland; she wished to see his other property to make a full assessment.

Mary grinned, "Okay, son, we'll hold the fort here when you return; your father and I are off to the Devon property to have a holiday." Mary asked Isabella if she would look after Cherokee while gone for a month.

"Yes, Mrs Selwyn, I'll gladly look after Cherokee; I'm booked here for the next two months?"

"I think you'll find your mother has decided you will stay until the end of summer. We've chatted on the phone," Mary grinned, knowing that would annoy Donald immensely.

Isabella looked surprised, "No peace for the wicked," she winked at Mary.

Martin came up from the cellar with a jug of cider, "Fancy a drop, son, you Isabella?"

"Rather, Mr Selwyn," Isabella smiled, taking a glass filled to the brim, knocking it back as if a glass of water, "not bad."

Donald emptied his glass without any trouble. Isabella commented, "When you've lived in France, Donald, you become virtually immune to alcohol, especially if you live on a vineyard. All you drink is wine and spirits. I mustn't have any more driving tomorrow some of the way to Scotland," she grinned with satisfaction.

Mary could see Donald's puzzled by Isabella; he couldn't quite understand where she was coming from. She could operate a loader like a professional. She could drink cider-like water without effect. "You know, next time we have cider Mr Selwyn, a nice piece of cheese adding flavour to the palate."

Mary couldn't resist; she stood embracing Isabella, "You are a breath of fresh air, Isabella. I hope you enjoy the trip tomorrow with my confused son," Mary chuckled.

Donald and Isabella said goodnight to each other. Donald ran up to his studio, picturing Isabella sitting at a wooden table with a flagon of cider, a large piece of cheese on a cutting board and a crusty loaf. He painted away until six in the morning; he'd finally finished. He parcelled the portrait, addressing to Jack. Donald sent a photo ahead with the title: "Mysterious Woman."

Isabella's banging on his door at 7 o'clock. She looked at Donald's expression, "Have you had any sleep, Donald?"

"I'm okay, you could drive first, and I'll deal with the complicated bits around Scotland," he smiled.

Donald texts the courier service he usually uses and makes his mother aware the portrait to be collected was marked extremely fragile. The courier service understood the penalty for damaging one of Donald's portraits. Cost Donald a thousand pounds to transport to London on the same day.

Isabella drove Donald's Bentley cautiously, becoming used to the horsepower and the vehicle's speed. Donald was asleep until they reached Glasgow. Isabella pulled over into a service station. "Time to wake up, Donald, your turn to drive," She patted his cheek softly.

Donald woke, rubbing his eyes, realising close to Glasgow. "Have I been asleep all the way?" He asked, puzzled, stepping out of the car with Isabella and heading into the coffee shop. "Yes, you snore

Donald terribly; even the stereo couldn't drown out your noise," she chuckled.

Donald had two cups of coffee and a hearty breakfast; Isabella settled for a croissant. Donald looked at his wristwatch; made good time unless Isabella ignored the speed limit. Donald took over driving; he could see Isabella occasionally glancing at him, "What's the matter," he grinned.

"I'm thinking of all the people you've helped since you were wealthy, even some that have betrayed you. You never complain."

Donald shrugged his shoulders, "I can do nothing about the situation. Christine's the first person to really hurt me. Sophie the second, which wasn't her fault, God bless her soul." Donald swallowed hard, trying to hold back his emotions. Isabella could see he was upset; she refrained from asking any more questions. They parked outside Glencoe Hotel. Donald carried two overnight bags. Justin greeted him with a hug glancing at Isabella, "Your new lady Donald?"

"No, Justin," Donald laughed, "She's my financial adviser; she looks after my affairs," Donald glanced at Isabella with her blushing expression.

"I suppose you don't happen to have two rooms, Justin?"

"We do, Christine suite; you normally use; one other vacant for two nights."

"Isabella can have Christine's suite more suited for her. I'll take the other room," Donald smiled.

"The spare room is opposite Christine's suite," Justin advised.

Donald carried the luggage showing Isabella into Christine's suite; he walked across the hallway into the other room to freshen. He texts Isabella, "Meet you in the bar in ten minutes," he attached a smiley face.

Isabella smiled, showering and changing, finding Donald downstairs in the lounge sitting at a table, "What would you like to drink, Isabella?"

"A glass of wine, please." Donald walked to the bar returning with a bottle of wine with a glass and a malt whisky for himself.

Isabella inhaled the fragrance of the wine, pouring some into a glass; she looked and tasted, taking the bottle back to the bar. Justin stood intrigued. "The wines off. You can't serve this almost vinegar."

Justin tasted and emptied the remainder of the bottle down the sink; selecting another bottle of wine, he opened it, poured a little into a glass, passing to Isabella. "That's better; needs to breathe for a minute other than that, thank you."

Mrs Montague walked in. Donald stood, pulling out a chair for her; he kissed her on both cheeks giving her a little squeeze. "Donald, I have mentioned before. Mind your manners and don't take liberties."

Isabella grinned; her mother glared at her. Mrs Montague removed her mobile. "Would you care to explain this portrait, Donald Selwyn? Are you taking liberties with my daughter?" Isabella immediately stood, moving behind her mother to see what was on her mobile. She placed her hand to her mouth, observing how beautiful Donald had betrayed her.

"That's why I had to drive to Scotland, Donald. You worked all night. Mummy, I had a glass of cider with Mrs Selwyn. I commented cheese would have been appropriate to enhance the flavour. Donald was listening; that's where the painting came from and his imagination to create such a lovely setting."

"Sit down, Isabella," Mrs Montague ordered, "You realise, Donald, the portrait has reached a ridiculous sum. The tabloids are humming, asking the question! Donald Selwyn's future bride."

Donald shrugged his shoulders, "I can't help what people think, Mrs Montague. I can assure you nothing inappropriate has taken place."

Mrs Montague looked at both their expressions. "Isabella, am I to believe you are now enjoying your stay at the Selwyn's. You endeavour to organise his finances and advise him on the correct course of action?"

"Yes, mummy."

"Isabella, I have received information; I made a grave error of judgement concerning Susan and the part she played with Josephine."

"Yes, mummy, Donald rectified the situation; he purchased Susan's council house for her and has given Susan suitable employment. I apologised on your behalf."

Mrs Montague frowned, "Extravagant as always, Donald."

"You didn't say that when I produced a portrait of you, Mrs Montague." She rose from her chair. Donald kissed her on the lips. She hit him with her cane, "Behave, Donald," turning away, grinning, leaving rapidly, sliding into the back of her limousine, and driven away quickly.

"How dare you kiss my mother on the lips, very inappropriate, Donald," Isabella scolded.

"I'm taking a walk to the sawmill. You want to come or stay here?"

"Fresh air would be good before a meal." Isabella ran upstairs, returning with her sheepskin coat. They walked along by the stream; Donald had so many times in the past with Christine and Sophie. Neither of them spoke, pausing by the waterwheel that had never stopped turning since the day he brought it back to life with his finances. Jock approached on horseback; he dismounted, hugging Donald, "A sight for sore eyes, everything is running perfectly, and who is this young lady?" Jock asked, grinning.

"My name is Isabella," she held out her hand. Jock shook gently.

"The builders are making good progress on Dorking Moor Estate. Eric shot him a stag a fortnight ago. He's living like a king."

Donald passed Jock a fifty pounds, "Keep your eye on things, Jock."

"That I will, boss. Isabella, grab him before somebody else does," Jock chuckled, riding off.

Isabella's laughing, "Is there no one on this estate that doesn't adore you, Donald? No matter where we go, everybody wants to know you."

"Must be my aftershave! I'm me, take it or leave it," he said, closely followed by Isabella, walking back to the hotel. They had a pleasant evening meal and all the other guests.

After breakfast in the morning, they set out for Dorking Moor Estate. They arrived at ten o'clock. Donald's surprised to see Maggie wearing a hard hat with a clipboard walking around the exterior of the building. She caught sight of him running over, immediately kissing him on the lips, which took Isabella by surprise; she would greet Donald in such a fashion. "I would like you to meet Isabella; she appears to be in charge of me," Donald grinned.

Maggie scoffed, "Woman in charge of you, Donald, never, I've seen some try and fail," she laughed, kissing him again.

Maggie passed Donald and Isabella hard hats before entering the building, which resembled a bomb site. Maggie explained where everything would be, from the kitchen to the refurbished lounge and dining area. Isabella asked, "I believe the budget is one million. Can you advise me on expenditure to date, and will you come in on target?"

Maggie showed Isabella the figures. Isabella smiled, "Women in charge, Donald, her calculations are excellent," Isabella grinned, satisfied.

"Who's looking after the shop, Maggie, and where is your future husband?"

"I have a young school leaver looking after the shop; we're never busy this time of year unless Donald Selwyn pays me a visit. Then you can't get through the door. Unfortunately, John is in hospital with two broken legs, he fell off scaffolding on another job. I told him before that he can't walk on air."

Isabella burst out laughing at Maggie's comment. "Come along, Maggie. I haven't paid a visit to your shop for ages," he said, placing his arm around her waist. Maggie jumped in her car, the one Donald had purchased some time ago, and Donald followed in his gold-coloured Bentley parking outside the shop. Almost as if people were hiding around every corner waiting for Donald to arrive, suddenly the shop is swamped. Isabella was astounded; people love Donald, and he's only an artist. He had never appeared on television or promoted himself other than through his art. Twenty minutes later, Maggie came out of the shop, kissing Donald, leaning against his Bentley. "I don't know how you do it, Donald. We're sold out of Selwyn tartan's, a hundred gone in the last half hour."

"Maggie," Donald asked earnestly, "How would you like to manage my new hotel when finished. I want someone at the top I can trust."

Maggie whispered, "Only if you have sex with me every month," Donald turned bright red. Maggie moved away, laughing, looking at his expression. "I'll have to see what commitments I have before saying yes, Donald. I don't want to stretch myself too thin on the ground and be inefficient," she grinned.

Donald smiled, jumping in his Bentley; Isabella climbed into the passenger side, and they returned to Glencoe. Isabella commented, "That woman is all over you like a rash, Donald, and she's about to marry someone. Don't you think that's rather naughty you tease her?"

Donald patted Isabella's leg, "Maggie and I go back a long way; she's always teased me, not the other way around. Justin, her father, runs Glencoe; that's why I offered her the position to run my hotel, extremely clever like you."

"Thank you for the compliment, Donald," Isabella smiled. After the evening meal, they retired to their rooms to prepare for the next day's journey home. A faint knock at the door. Donald looked at his watch, 11 o'clock. "Come in."

Much to Donald's surprise, in walked Maggie; she closed the door quietly behind her, locking and removing the key placed on the sideboard. Donald watched her remove her clothes, sliding in beside him. It wasn't many minutes before they made love. Isabella heard the door open and shut; she opened her door quietly, peering through Donald's keyhole. She definitely could see Maggie with Donald. She scurried back to her own room, closing the door quietly. Donald's a single man; he didn't force Maggie to come to his room. Maggie had decided to cheat on her future husband. Isabella couldn't imagine Donald cheating on anyone after what her mother said about him.

Donald and Isabella sat having an early breakfast. She asked cautiously, "You sleep well, Donald?"

"Actually, yes, I slept very comfortably last night. I don't usually settle in strange beds," he confessed.

"I suppose it helps if you have someone relieving your stress and keeping you warm," she grinned.

"I suppose it does; I must remember that," Donald remarked, realising she knew. He wasn't giving her the satisfaction of confessing. He'd done nothing wrong, single, and so is Maggie technically.

Isabella didn't push the subject anymore. Donald loaded their suitcases into the boot of the Bentley. He paid his bill at reception, driving the first part of the journey home. Isabella drove the last part of the journey arriving at Crabtree Farm around 4 o'clock in the afternoon. Donald carried Isabella's bag to her apartment number four and his own into the studio. He made a coffee sitting down to relax, watched television for a moment, falling asleep on the settee.

Isabella rose bright and early, walking over to the machinery store and seeing the massive new fertiliser spreader had arrived. She filled it with diesel parking by the fertiliser store; using the loader, she filled the spreader. Jumping from the loader cab and sitting inside the luxurious cab of the spreader. Programmed the computer slipping in the memory stick which transferred the information about the fields she's to spread fertiliser on. Within two hours, she had spread fertiliser on nearly three hundred acres.

Donald and Martin came out to see what was happening. Isabella backed the fertiliser spreader, ready to load again. They looked at each other in total shock. Not what they were expecting to see. They watched Isabella reload the fertiliser spreader, taking off down the drive and heading for Mill Farm.

Gerald came up the drive in his Range Rover, lowering the window, "Who the bloody hell is that! She nearly pushed me off the road."

"We're not quite sure! Isabella's mother is Mrs Montague, and the girl operates machinery like Christine; she knows everything we are discovering."

Gerald stepped from his Range Rover, "Christine never told me about Isabella; I didn't know Mrs Montague had children. I always thought she's an old baron cow," Gerald grinned, following Martin and Donald to the cottage. Mary's pouring tea, smiling, listening to them discussing Isabella and Mrs Montague. Gerald left after half an hour more puzzled than when he first arrived, wondering what Mrs Montague was planning. She always had a purpose in everything she was involved in.

By 12 o'clock, Isabella came into the yard driving the new fertiliser spreader backing over the drain. She removed the pressure washer from the store. She switched on, cleaned the spreader and removed the acid from the machine to prevent corrosion. Donald came out, removing the lance from her hand. He kissed her on the cheek, "Have a coffee Isabella, mums waiting for you in the kitchen; I'll wash this down."

Isabella walked into the kitchen, exhaling, "Some fields are rough on Mill Farm and wet. The new machine Donald purchased is wonderful to drive and rapid, excellent choice."

"I think you shocked one or two people today, Isabella," Mary grinned, "They've never seen a woman like you before. How are you progressing with Donald?"

"Okay, thanks. Donald's very generous and kind; some women seem to take advantage of him, like Maggie, although he's single. I shouldn't want to be Maggie's husband; I wouldn't trust her."

"Elaborate, Isabella," Mary asked curiously.

"Well, I heard someone enter Donald's room late in the evening. After looking through the keyhole, I discovered it turned out to be Maggie," she grinned. "I don't think I need to explain anything else."

Mary laughed, "Maggie's been after Donald for ages. That will never happen. I doubt whether anyone will conquer his heart; unless they're exceptional and can drive a tractor properly," Mary grinned.

Isabella smiled, leaving the kitchen looking over the fertiliser spreader, checking Donald had washed thoroughly. "Donald, the chassis on the inside looks coated in dust," she said, taking the lance from him, spraying him with water making him run to escape a drenching. Donald watched from a concealed location. Isabella finished washing the new machine. He sneaked behind her, grabbing the lance soaking Isabella from head to foot. She screamed, running for her apartment, giggling, the water extremely cold. Donald turned off the pressure washer packing away, running to his studio to change; he was soaked. Mary had watched from the window suspecting the first step to something special for her son. He really needed someone like Isabella to control him. Unfortunate the way things had turned out with Christine, she thought, sighing heavily.

Isabella dried her hair and changed. Venturing outside, she parked the fertiliser spreader inside the machinery store, leaving on a slope so the water would drain off the machine more easily.

***

Gerald's sitting at the kitchen table on Strawberry Estate. Christine's making tea. Cindy had gone shopping. "Why didn't you mention Christine, Isabella, apparently Mrs Montague's daughter."

"Didn't think you were interested, father, nothing you can do about the situation. Neither can I. I'll have my children to look forward to shortly," she said, rubbing her tummy.

Gerald sighed, left the house, jumped in his Range Rover and drove away without saying another word. Christine finished her cup of tea strolling to the stables to talk to The Rising Sun; she hadn't ridden him for months and would dearly love to. She sighed heavily, returning to the house, wondering how she could win Donald's affection. She knew the children would help, enough to secure his love and money she's unsure.

***

Isabella saddled Cherokee riding around both properties, trying to decide in her own mind what she wanted in her future; someone wealthy is essential. Although she had a small fortune, her parents had set aside for her.

Donald drove around to Mill Farm, finding Susan dusting. She noticed Donald come in; she made coffee for them both. Susan smiled excitedly, "The house is mine Donald, all mine; no more worrying about paying the rent. You can't imagine what a load off my mind." Donald removed his wallet, handing over three hundred pounds. She kissed him, "You sure you don't want to marry an older woman, Donald." He burst out laughing.

Isabella returned Cherokee to his stable, watching Mr and Mrs Selwyn leaving for Devon to their holiday retreat. Isabella jumped in her Jeep, heading for Mill Farm, suspecting Donald would be there if not in his studio. She parked outside the Elizabethan farmhouse, carefully wiping her shoes on the coconut mat before entering. Susan made her a coffee she sat at the table. "Excellent, Isabella, you are full of surprises. I didn't think for one moment you could operate the fertiliser spreader, let alone the loader. You appear to be a genius at whatever you touch," Donald smiled.

"Thanks. Nice to know I'm appreciated. Your mother and father have set off for Devon; I watched them leave while stabling Cherokee."

"Your lumbered for the next month," Donald smiled, "You're in charge of Cherokee."

Susan suggested, "Would you like me to look after the studio for you, Donald, while your mother is away? No trouble. If I can't help you, a poor job, after all, you've done for me."

"Thanks, Susan, yes, please, if you could keep the studio tidy for me; my apartment mainly I'm a slob, I'm afraid," he grinned.

"I've finished here, Donald; I'll visit the studio and check before going home."

"Just as you wish, Susan," Donald smiled, watching her leave.

Isabella moved to the computer to check statements. Donald glanced over her shoulder. She discovered the password to his personal account, which he thought rather naughty. She knew he was worth over thirty million in one of his accounts. Donald had always spread things around a little just in case. "May I ask why you're in my personal account, Isabella? Business, I understand; my personal life is taboo. I know you are aware of what is in my Swiss account, which I must confess when I thought it over, rather disturbed you had access."

Isabella turned to face him, "If you must know, I'm not interested in how much money you have, Donald. I am checking your money to ensure no hackers are bleeding your account. You'll find Christine will be at the top of the list if there's a way to bleed you dry; she will find it, I promise you." Isabella rose to her feet, sidestepping Donald out of the front door; he heard her drive away.

Donald exhaled, not knowing who to trust or who to believe. He locked the house and climbed in his Bentley returning to Crabtree Farm. Susan had already gone; he ran upstairs, seeing a note on his easel. "See you next week, sexy."

Isabella came up into the studio seeing the note pinned to his easel. She shook her head, "I suppose you'll be in bed with her next; you're chasing my mother, so why not have her? She should be a pushover like Maggie," Isabella stood with her arms folded.

Donald's fuming and deeply concerned, she knew about Maggie and him. He took a deep breath and walked past her downstairs, jumping in his Bentley; he drove off headed into Coventry. He needed a substantial pickup truck. He found his way to where he purchased the RV. He noticed a selection of new pickup trucks, one with a diesel engine, the exhaust pipes running up the back of the crew cab, and oversized tyres. Hoping he could float on water with them if conditions on the farm became sticky. He paid for the truck, asking to be delivered to Crabtree Farm.

He drove steadily home, wondering if the information he'd received concerning Christine was accurate. Although what he'd seen of her with the two brothers would certainly confirm his suspicions, she couldn't be trusted. He drove to Mill Farm to avoid confrontation with Isabella and exhaled, making a coffee while watching television.

***

Mrs Montague entered the yard at Crabtree Farm in her limousine and parked. Her chauffeur bodyguard opened the door for her to step out. Isabella greeted her mother with a kiss on either cheek; they walked into the apartment sitting at a small table. Isabella made them both a drink. "What are your plans concerning Donald?" Mrs Montague asked, "From what I've seen of your behaviour, Christine stands more chance of succeeding than you."

"Whatever makes you say that, mother?" Isabella asked, confused.

Mrs Montague pointed to her earrings, "I'm listening in, Isabella; why make Donald aware of his liaison with Maggie. You don't own him. You haven't said boyfriend, fiancé! What is your game? No, you prefer to rub it in his face; women are attracted to him. I would say this, Isabella, if I were not married to your perfect father and a few years younger, I would have Donald eating out of my hand. Don't be obvious; make him want you for what you are, an attractive, clever girl like your mother, although I think you have your father's brains."

Isabella sighed, "I am interested, mummy. I'm trying very hard not to be obvious like all the other women surrounding him, trying to prove I'm a worthy person. I think I've impressed him with my machinery skills. Of course, if we were to become a couple, that would be essential to our future success. I don't know what to do about Christine; she worries me, mummy."

"You have approximately two months to impress Donald if you're seriously interested, Isabella. I'm trying to find the perfect husband for you; few high society males are available with integrity. Most are scum; I wouldn't wipe my boots on. I want my daughter to have the best chance of a happy marriage with a man who will love her like my husband loves me unconditionally. The decision is yours, Isabella, at the end of the day. I have opened doors for you to walk through and take what's on offer if that's what you want out of life. Or you can risk someone like a Copthorne, who'd be with a prostitute drinking and gambling every weekend and spend all your savings."

Isabella exhaled, "We will have to see what transpires, mummy; sometimes I think Donald would be so easy to love, and other times, is he really my type," she shrugged.

Mrs Montague shook her head in disbelief. She had pulled so many strings to arrange for her daughter to be here, including talking to Mary, who she knew she could trust. Mary wanted her son to be settled after the disaster with Sophie. She feared Christine would creep back into his life and destroy him.

Mrs Montague left in her limousine. Isabella ran up into the studio switching on Donald's computer. She selected the chemicals required for spraying the crops to prevent bug infestation and give the best chance of a bumper harvest. Donald entered the yard, parked his Bentley, and ran into the studio, finding Isabella on his computer. She printed off the chemicals required and the cost. Passed the sheet of paper to Donald with a brief smile. He realised she wasn't snooping, only thinking ahead, everything for the farm's success. He looked at the price and exhaled, "By the time we finished paying for fertiliser and chemicals, not much left for profit, especially if we have an iffy harvest."

Isabella, on a blank piece of paper, started calculating. Donald watched in amazement at the speed her brain was working. He knew his mathematics wasn't that good; hers were excellent from what he could see; within one minute, she calculated the estimated tonnage, the cost of production in equipment and diesel, plus the estimated profit. Donald stood open-mouthed even if she wasn't right; the speed she calculated was outstanding. "I think I should take you out for dinner, Isabella, don't you," he smiled.

"Yes, I'd enjoy that. Allow me to change; I've seen to Cherokee he settled for the night." She scurried off, excited Donald would take her out. She could assess what he thought of her by where they dined. Donald dressed in a suit he'd used for Christine's birthday party, which failed miserably. He phoned the Hilton in Birmingham, securing a table. He suspected Mrs Montague would beat him with a big stick if he didn't treat her daughter to every luxury.

Donald ran to apartment number four and knocked on the door; Isabella opened. Donald almost fell over. Isabella in a full-length sparkling evening gown with a matching purse. "You look stunning, Isabella," he escorted her to his car, opening the door for her. Mrs Montague's listening through Isabella's earrings, excited about the situation. She knew where Donald was taking Isabella, which she considered very appropriate, no fish and chips around the backstreet. Isabella chuckled, "Keep your eyes on the road, Donald, less on my cleavage. Otherwise, we'll be in hospital; I'm not that attractive."

"Sorry, I don't mean to stare. I feel like I'm taking out a Princess tonight," Donald smiled, feeling an absolute prat for his last comment.

They arrived at the Hilton and were escorted to a table in a secluded part of the restaurant. Donald passed the wine list to Isabella, "You're far more qualified than I am; you know what's good or not."

The waiter approached with a bottle of non-alcoholic champagne on ice, "Mr Selwyn, a pleasure to serve you again." Donald passed him twenty pounds. The waiter had remembered him from last time as an excellent tipper. He would make sure Donald's evening's memorable with the young lady. Another waiter approached, carrying a bouquet of flowers, offering Isabella. She's absolutely stunned. She had not expected this sort of treatment from Donald; even his suit of high-quality material would be permitted into most circles without question. Mrs Montague had tapped into security cameras at the Hilton, watching Donald and her daughter drinking a glass of wine, Mr Montague smiling, both holding hands, praying for success for their daughter and a fantastic future to follow like they had themselves.

Isabella ordered wine for herself, appreciating Donald couldn't drink and drive, although the non-alcoholic champagne was okay for him. They started the three-course meal. Mrs Montague could see from the body language that both were extremely comfortable.

She could almost feel the magnetism from where she was sitting. Donald paid, leaving a hundred-pound tip for the waiter.

They finally left the restaurant, slowly driving home to Crabtree Farm. Donald opened the car door escorting Isabella to her apartment door. "Thank you for coming this evening, Isabella, delightful. We must do it again sometime," he smiled, kissing her lips. She swallowed hard, looking into his eyes, feeling his hands gripping her waist. She placed her arms around his shoulders, kissed him softly and walked into her apartment, shutting the door and throwing her purse across the room with excitement. Donald ran upstairs, hung his suit in the wardrobe, jumped into bed, and quickly fell asleep.

Donald awoke the following day to someone screaming, glancing from his elevated position and seeing Isabella looking in Cherokee stable. He quickly threw on his work clothes running downstairs. Isabella's in tears, Cherokee's dead on the stable floor, his throat cut. Donald phoned the police immediately, no accident, police Range Rover arriving in a short while. Donald explained events leading them to find Cherokee. Donald finally escorted the shocked Isabella into his mother's cottage, making a drink. Isabella's trembling; she'd never seen anything like that before. Within hours the press desperate for a story. Mary had seen the news on television from her holiday retreat. Martin and Mary, alarmed, drove home, arriving in the afternoon. After forensics had finished, the police allowed Cherokee taken to the knacker's yard to be turned into dog meat.

Donald's livid; he had such a lovely evening and a disaster that he could have done without by morning. Mary cuddled Isabella, "Don't worry, Isabella, you are not to blame. I know who I think could be responsible."

Donald, with the power washer washing away the blood, seemed to take forever for the stains to disappear.

***

Christine watched the news grinning. No one would suspect her in her present condition to be involved, especially Mrs Montague.

Christine suspected Mrs Montague wouldn't want her daughter any-where near if there were a chance of her being injured. Gerald and Cindy had gone away for a few days leaving Stephen in charge of spraying and fertilising. Christine would provide him with memory sticks and rates of application for each crop.

***

Mrs Montague came into the yard at Crabtree Farm; she's already been briefed by the police on events. She was satisfied that Donald would prevent anything from happening to her daughter. Mrs Montague had seen him in action twice. Both times her bodyguards lost the battle. She entered the cottage warmly greeted Mary and everyone else sitting around the oak table. "I suppose we all know who's responsible, directly or indirectly," she commented, sitting down to a cup of tea.

Donald had enough; he stormed out of the cottage jumping in his Bentley and driving to Strawberry Estate, parking outside the house. Christine had seen him approach. She looked at herself in the mirror, looking as attractive as possible. She opened the front door, "Hi Donald, lovely to see you, please come in," she offered. Donald walked in. "Go through into the lounge."

Donald stood by the fireplace controlling his temper, "You know anything about Cherokee's demise, Christine? Is this one of your spiteful jokes?" he asked seriously.

"How could you possibly accuse me, Donald? I'm about to be the mother of your children. I love you with all my heart. Why would I inflict pain on you?" She pretended to lose her balance. Donald quickly grabbed her, easing her down onto the settee. She kissed him passionately, sliding his hand onto her large breast, "I love you, Donald," she hugged him. Donald held her feeling emotions; he hadn't for so long. Realising it would never work, he eased away from her. Kissed her on the forehead walking out, driving away, really wanting to stay, knowing the consequences if he did. A life of misery and torment wondering whether his girlfriend would be in bed with somebody else.

He returned to Crabtree Farm. Mrs Montague was still there; she wouldn't be surprised if Donald came into the cottage with blood over his hands after strangling Christine. She knew he was competent if he chose to take that path. "I challenged her; she denies having anything to do with Cherokee's death. She wouldn't confess anyway. We don't have the proof to accuse her; although suspicion would dictate, she's as guilty as hell," Donald said, sitting down.

"Why would she want to kill Cherokee?" Mary asked, deep in thought. "Sophie stood between her and Donald; Sophie is no longer with us, so why kill the horse now? Just to intimidate us, what is she trying to achieve. Perhaps frighten Mrs Montague into removing her daughter from here as a safety precaution," Mary suggested, "At least if Isabella isn't here; Christine wouldn't consider Isabella a threat preventing her from rekindling her relationship with Donald."

"Excellent deduction Mary; I have no need to remove my daughter. Undoubtedly, Donald would break anybody in half who approached her as a threat. My bodyguard suffered a fractured jaw after one punch from Donald."

Martin laughed, "Sherlock Holmes is at work again." Everyone glared at him disapprovingly.

Mrs Montague rose to her feet, kissing her daughter on both cheeks, "Stay close to Donald Isabella; he will safeguard you. Although I don't think Christine will push her luck too far, she knows what happened to her mother." Mrs Montague left the cottage, climbed into her limousine, and quickly drove off. She removed her mobile. "Yes, it's me, monitor Strawberry Estate, and especially Christine Gibbs, thank you."

CHAPTER TWENTY

NO SECOND CHANCES

Donald sighed heavily, "I wish Biscuit were here; he'd have taken on anybody who's causing trouble. Such a lovely dog, my best friend."

Isabella is about to return to her apartment. Donald grabbed her hand, "You are staying with me. I'll sleep on the couch. You have my bed; you'll be safe if you're in the same room as me."

"Donald's right, Isabella," Mary expressed, "play safe for a few days and see what happens."

Isabella left, returning to her apartment, grabbing her night bag nervously, and following Donald into his apartment. She went into the bathroom, changed into her pyjamas, sat, and drank coffee. Donald placed a canvas on the easel, sketching Isabella in a lovely evening gown. She came into the studio, placing her hand on Donald's shoulder, realising who he was painting.

***

Mrs Montague's watching the monitors for any signs of activity around Strawberry Estate. She's almost falling asleep, glancing at the clock 1:30 in the morning. A car parked outside Strawberry Estate house. She sat up quickly, paying attention. Extremely difficult to make out who the person was. The drones struggled in the darkness to give a clear image. She watched Christine open the door and greet the young man with a hug taking him into the lounge. Now the drone could see clearly Christine had not bothered to draw the drapes. Mrs Montague realised one of the boys Christine had sex with and was sent to America by his parents to avoid the scandal. He was allowed to return home now the dust had settled. Mrs Montague couldn't hear any conversations, although she noticed Christine pass him a package which Mrs Montague suspected drugs. Perhaps a secret hiding place on Strawberry Estate where Josephine hid drugs for Dixon, and Christine discovered the location.

Much to Mrs Montague's dismay, she observed Christine removing her clothes; she looked away. What might be transpiring made her feel sick, especially with Christine in her present condition? She switched off the monitor. Mrs Montague made a quick phone call relaying the car's registration to the police, advising, "He may be in possession of drugs and responsible for the death of Cherokee, the horse on Crabtree Farm." She didn't mention Christine; she's of Royal blood and must not be brought to the public's attention and linked to Donald Selwyn or her daughter, for that matter. Mrs Montague thought she would have eliminated her if Donald had not known about the twins and the possibility he could be the father.

The following morning Mrs Montague parked outside Strawberry Estate house; her bodyguard opened the door for her to step out. Christine watched from the landing, frowning; coming downstairs, she opened the front door. Mrs Montague's bodyguard grabbed Christine's arm, escorting her into the lounge. Christine said nothing suspecting Mrs Montague had cottoned on to something.

"Where are the drugs hidden, Christine? Or shall I call the police in and have the place demolished? You can explain why to your father," Mrs Montague threatened, glaring. Christine exhaled, not saying a word, and followed her into the cellar to a dark corner. She removed a brick. Mrs Montague's bodyguard found a package. "I presume where your mother concealed drugs for Dixon, Christine. Answer me!"

"Yes, Mrs Montague, I've known for some time; I've never taken drugs."

"No, you trade them for favours, don't you. Is Tim responsible for Cherokee's demise? Christine, answer me! My patience is wearing thin with you if you'd like to end up in the channel like your mother; keep behaving as you are, and I will arrange for you. I can't make it any plainer than that girl! If anything happens to my daughter, you will die the second I find out. I will open the gates of hell on you, spoilt little bitch," Mrs Montague shouted, losing her usual composure for a moment.

"I'm not responsible for the death of Cherokee. I don't know who is, and I certainly wouldn't go after your daughter; I'm not that stupid. Donald, once he's seen his children, will naturally return to me their mother."

Mrs Montague laughed, "You must live in cuckoo land Christine." Mrs Montague removed her mobile, showing her performing with Tim. "When Donald sees that you will be lucky if he ever speaks to you; don't worry, he will provide for the children if they are his, a job to know with you. You are outperforming your mother as a prostitute." Mrs Montague turned, heading up the cellar stairs out of the front door. Her bodyguard carried the packet of drugs, which he placed in the limousine boot. Mrs Montague phoned the police, "Have you charged the boy Tim Jenkins? I reported last night for transporting drugs. Release him, keep the drugs and make sure his parents know those are your instructions."

Mrs Montague, in her limousine, pouring herself a glass of sherry, pleased with the outcome. Didn't matter if Christine had organised the slaughter of Cherokee using Tim Jenkins. Christine now understood she was facing a watery grave if she made one more mistake.

**

Donald's busy placing chemicals in the lock-up where they are stored for security, preventing anyone from meddling with such dangerous products. Isabella returned to her apartment; enjoyed sleeping in Donald's bed. She showered and changed, looking on the computer for a weather report. Two clear days, and nearly at the end of March, she wanted to spray the oilseed rape. Donald heard the new sprayer start, watching Isabella drive into the yard, parking by the storage shed. She climbed down from the cab, grinning. Donald shook his head, laughing, "Is there nothing you can't do, Isabella?"

She patted his cheek, checking the sprayer drain plug was secure; she placed the hosepipe in the tank, removing a notebook from her pocket. She determined the amount of chemical she would require and water to spray the fifty acres of oilseed rape. She placed the liquid concentrate in the hopper, which transferred to the main tank and agitated thoroughly, mixing the contents. Mary came out with a mug of coffee and passed it to Isabella. "Where's mine," Donald protested.

Mary advised, "In the kitchen, fetch," she remarked, watching Donald frown and head for the kitchen.

Mary quickly asked, "Isabella, your night out? I haven't had a chance to talk to you alone."

"A wonderful night, Mary; you don't mind me calling you Mary?"

"Of course not, don't be silly."

"I enjoyed every moment; Donald is a real pleasure to be with. Everything ruined the next morning when I discovered Cherokee."

Mary patted Isabella on the shoulder, "You'll get there. Just be patient; I can sense he really likes you, and so do I," Mary kissed Isabella on the cheek heading for the cottage.

Donald watched Isabella drive out of the yard into the first field of rape; she unfolded the booms automatically from the cab. Donald couldn't grasp how proficient she was. Isabella could outperform him on every level. She must have a brain like a computer, he decided, suspecting she learnt her skills with the sprayer in the vineyard. By lunchtime, she had sprayed the fifty acres and, in the yard, washed out the sprayer, checking the jets were clean before parking the machine away until the wheat needed spraying.

Donald walked across the yard; Isabella ran over to join him. "Donald, there are slugs on fields four and five. Appears to be some damage I think you should treat."

Donald laughed, "You mean I can do something, Isabella?"

"Only if you go in a straight line, I'll set the rate for you to save wastage," she grinned. Isabella ran off laughing, suspecting that annoyed him. She ran into the machinery shed with Donald close on her heels. He grabbed her around the waist, kissing her on the lips. She looked at him with a pleasing smile, "Work to be done," she kissed him quickly on the lips, checking the setting on the slug pellet dispenser attached to the quad bike. Donald placed two sacks of pellets on the front rack of the quad bike, strapping down. He filled the hopper on the rear, driving out of the machinery shed treating fields four and five. Isabella's correct; the slugs were having their last meal at his expense and noticed a patch in field seven and treated. Donald placed the quad bike in the machinery shed, entering the cottage and seeing Isabella enjoying a meal Mary had prepared for her. Donald sat down, "You were right about the slugs, Isabella, and some were in field seven, so I hit them."

Donald noticed the courier van come into the yard. "Excuse me," he smiled, running up into the studio, carrying a portrait parcelled for Jack. Donald returned to finish his meal. "What have you sent to Jack this time, Donald?" Mary asked.

"Nothing really, mum, Isabella asleep on my bed in her pyjamas," he remarked, watching Isabella's eyes enlarge. "You hadn't better, Donald."

Donald spent the night on the couch, and Isabella had his bed. Donald walked down to his grandfather's ashes and Biscuit's grave. He sat on the bench, wondering what the future held, would he always be able to paint. He didn't think he could ever give up farming in his blood. The smell of the soil turning as the plough cut through the ground, watching seeds grow. The usual panic to harvest, wondering if the weather would destroy everything. Donald's thoughts were interrupted. His mobiles ringing, he answered. "I'm on my way into the hospital, Donald; your children are about to be born. Are you coming to hold my hand, please? I'm frightened," Christine asked.

"Yes, I'm coming." Donald switched his phone off and ran into the yard, jumping in his Bentley, saying nothing to no one charging out of the yard. Mary phoned, "Whatever is the matter, Donald?"

"Christine's in labour; she's asked me to hold her hand. I can't refuse mum; she's all alone," Donald rang off.

Mary frowned, sitting down at the table, "Christine's gone into labour; she's a month early by my calculation there again if the children are Donald's."

Isabella sighed, "Just when I thought I was in with a chance."

"Don't be silly, Isabella. Donald would support the devil if he were in trouble; sometimes, I wonder where his brains are. Nevertheless, if they are his children, you can't blame him. That doesn't mean he will run off with her; she has a track record. Two years back, I'd have said you stood no chance."

Donald arrived at the hospital and was allowed to see Christine after she explained he was the father. Within five hours, Christine gave birth to a boy and a girl, slightly premature but healthy. Donald waited for Christine to be moved into the maternity ward and allowed to see her. "I'm naming my daughter Josephine after my mother and my son Eric. I like the name," she smiled. Donald noticed Cindy and Gerald coming into the ward; he kissed Christine on the forehead, "Well done, two lovely children. If you need me, ring."

Gerald remarked, passing Donald, "Thanks."

Donald drove home slowly, deciding whether he should try again with Christine for the children's sake if nothing else. Donald parked in the yard at Crabtree Farm. Mrs Montague's limousine parked. Mary opened the cottage door indicating with her finger to come in. Donald sat down at the table by Mrs Montague, kissing her on the cheek, making her grin. "Donald, you have been with Christine at the hospital? I take it there were no issues with the births?"

"None, straightforward, not as I'm an expert, although I played midwife to five hundred ewes if that counts," he commented.

Mrs Montague chuckled, "On a more serious note, Donald. The Cherokee incident, I have carried out some investigating. What I'm about to disclose to you must never be repeated, you understand, Donald?"

Donald nodded. Mrs Montague explained she had a drone monitoring Christine. She removed the tablet showing Donald; Christine naked with Tim on the carpet. She disclosed the conversation of Christine supplying drugs to Tim Jenkins, sent to America by his parents. Mrs Montague studied Donald's expression for a reaction. He shrugged his shoulders, sighing heavily, "I will support the children; I'm not having Christine back; my life would be nothing but hell."

Mrs Montague scrolled through pages on her tablet, "Would you care to explain this, Donald," she asked, trying not to smile, displaying a picture of Isabella in her evening dress holding a bouquet of flowers with the title, "Perfection."

"To be quite honest, Mrs Montague, I don't know whether your daughter is a computer or a robot. Nothing she can't do. I have to confess she's far better than me on many tasks."

Isabella grinned, "Perhaps you should reward me with another evening meal or purchase me a horse. I must have earned one by now. Mary and I can share."

Mrs Montague started to laugh, standing to her feet. Donald gave her a hug. She tapped him with her cane, "Behave yourself, young man. I have a husband; I must go to him. You are a bad influence, Donald Selwyn," she chuckled, walking out the door.

Isabella and Mary were already sitting at the computer together, looking down horses for sale. Donald walked out of the cottage, running into his studio, still wondering about the children. He couldn't believe how Christine had turned out, remembering the first time he made love to her on his bed. He surmised he should have waited longer, sending her on a journey of discovery, ruining everything. Or was she always like her mother anyway, and whatever he did would not have altered the course of her life?

Isabella came upstairs into the studio carrying a printed piece of paper with a picture of a horse and sitting beside Donald. She kissed him affectionately, which surprised him, "I'm apparently your girlfriend if you're buying me a horse," she smiled.

"Is that what you want Isabella to become involved with some-one who already apparently has two children, two failed relation-ships. That isn't an outstanding portfolio; sure you want to become involved with me?"

"Let's not rush anything. I am extremely fond of you, and I think you like me; one step at a time, no rush. Although you can pay for the apartment, I don't see why I should," she grinned.

Donald laughed, "And you still expect me to buy you a horse?"

"Not just me, your mother. We will share when I'm not busy on the farms. To be quite honest, I find this whole situation quite exciting. I'm venturing into territory I don't know about other than farming."

"Isabella, you must realise I will have to contact Christine; the children are mine. I won't ignore them. I want to ensure they have a secure future."

"I would expect no less of you, Donald. That doesn't mean to say you have to sleep with her again; otherwise, forget any relationship with me," Isabella assured.

"Agreed," Donald said, making coffee and looking at the horse. His mother and Isabella had selected a seventeen hands palomino named Spartacus. Donald phoned Derek. "Hi Donald, bad do about Cherokee, they catch the little bastard, a lovely horse."

"Unfortunately, not. I would strangle him myself. Anyway, since my mother had taken such a shine to Cherokee. My new girlfriend decided they would like to share a horse. I have selected a palomino named Spartacus. You know anything about him?"

"Course I do, Donald. He's from my stables," Derek chuckled, "Excellent temperament providing you don't upset him. He can be a little difficult then; unless you're an experienced rider. He bites and kicks." Derek started laughing, "Sorry Donald, sometimes I have a terrible sense of humour; all in all, a brilliant horse, he's seven years old. You can have him for twelve-thousand including his saddle and bridle, and I'll make sure he's re-shoed before delivered."

"Okay, when he's ready, deliver. I'll send a cheque with the driver providing he has four legs," Donald started laughing along with Derek.

Isabella ran downstairs into the cottage, explaining that Donald had purchased the horse to Mary. They hugged each other. Isabella climbed into her Jeep and drove to Mill Farm, checking the wheat for any signs of mildew and other unsavoury diseases. She noticed Susan cleaning the house she went in. "Hi Susan, you okay?" Isabella smiled.

"Yes, thanks, Isabella; please advise Donald, if he's not living here, not to buy fresh food; I've had to throw it in the bin."

"Take home if still in date," Isabella suggested. "You're not stealing, so don't worry, I've given you permission. I detest wastage; I will have to knock Donald into shape," she grinned, scribbling on paper. "I give Susan permission to take food home if not used in time." She signed Isabella.

Susan smiled, "Thanks," she pinned the piece of paper on the noticeboard so everyone could see and wouldn't question if she was caught carrying something out of the house. "I take it you and Donald are an item now. I understand Christine has given birth to twins?"

"Yes, to both questions," Isabella remarked, making Susan a coffee. They sat at the kitchen table.

"You're not like your mother, Isabella."

Isabella choked on her coffee, "My mother is old school; she takes no prisoners. You must remember she has Elizabeth R ear, and I can assure you the Queen keeps my mother on her toes, always a crisis somewhere for her to deal with."

"I'm pleased you and Donald are together. Your mother will kill you if you behave like Christine or Josephine. I think the reason Christine's that way inclined is because of the way her mother treated her. Josephine had this obsession with trying to find suitors for her in the hope of securing Christine's future ridiculous at her age. I remember one incident as plain as day. I came in with refreshments. Christine's standing by the sofa. I think about thirteen. Josephine sat on the arm of the chair, watching. I place the drinks on the table and about to leave. Josephine ordered me to stay voicing, "You will say nothing, Susan." Christine glanced at me. I thought she was almost saying, help me with her eyes. The man on the sofa lifted little Christine's skirt, pulling down her knickers. Christine stepped back. Of course, her mother grabbed her shoulders, shaking Christine to standstill. The man opened Christine's blouse. She barely had formed any breasts. Christine was crying; she broke away, running out of the room. Josephine dropped her knickers, standing in place of Christine. I think you can imagine where Josephine ended up on the carpet. I walked out of the room shocked and disgusted. Although she suggested I should entertain some of the men on various occasions, I'm a single woman and might enjoy the experience."

Isabella finished her drink, not saying anything washing the cup in the sink. Susan was surprised, realising first impressions were not always correct about a person. Isabella jumped in her Jeep, returning to Crabtree Farm; she barely jumped out of her Jeep when Donald scooped her up in his arms and kissed her on the cheek, "Where have you been?"

"Checking the wheat on Mill Farm for bugs and mildew."

Donald's new American truck came into the yard; Mary stared from the window, with Martin following. The driver passed Donald the paperwork and keys and jumped in another vehicle leaving the property. Donald walked around the vehicle, noticing a significant eagle transfer on the bonnet. Isabella started laughing; Mary and Martin joined in. Donald stood looking puzzled.

"What's so funny?"

"Only you, Donald, could buy something so impractical. What possible use could this thing be apart from posing? The only advantage I can see is you can look over the hedge as you drive along the road; you're that high off the ground," Isabella laughed.

"One moment, ladies and gentlemen, when my beloved mother and father want to transport Spartacus to Devon so mum can ride there. They will need something to pull the horsebox," he said, thinking of a good reason to have the truck.

Mary's still laughing, "What's that over there, Donald, my Range Rover that will pull the horsebox."

"I'm not talking about one of those cramped old horseboxes; we are talking about a horsebox," Donald quickly went on his mobile phone, displaying an enormous horsebox, similar to a fifth wheel caravan assembly, showing everyone.

"Donald, be practical." Martin walked over, patting Donald on the shoulder, "You won't win, lad; those two will win hands down. Quit while you're ahead."

Donald threw his arms up, climbing into his new pickup. Isabella slid onto the other side. Donald struggled to turn around in the yard heading down the drive. Isabella commented, "I like the bench seat. I can sit close to you."

Donald parked outside a fish and chip shop on the outskirts of the village just before the Case IH dealership. "Fancy some! Or does one not eat this sort of food!" he said, mimicking a posh voice.

"One does! I'll have a large piece of fish, a small portion of chips with curry sauce and mushy peas."

"Are you really Mrs Montague's daughter? I wouldn't have thought you'd have ever eaten this type of cuisine, Isabella."

"When you have spent as many years as I have in a convent inhaling the fragrance of fish and chips cooking down the road, you learn ways of acquiring. The paperboy used to have a crush on one of my friends, if she gave him a kiss, he would nip down and purchase, and we'd share," she grinned cheekily.

Donald burst out laughing, placing his arm around her waist. They entered the chip shop. Donald ordered two of the same. They stood outside with their chips on the bonnet of Donald's new truck enjoying their meal. They finished eating, disposing of the newspaper, throwing in the litter bin, and wiping their hands on napkins. Climbing in the truck, continuing along the road to the Case IH dealership. Jason laughed, "I know where you've been, Donald, the chip shop. You have tomato sauce on your bottom lip." Donald quickly wiped.

"Isabella, is there anything you can't drive on my farm?" Donald asked, "Have you ever ploughed?"

"Yes, I have, and you don't have anything I can't operate, Donald. I spent six months in America. I operated some of the biggest tractors made and used a large plough on my auntie's farm. Why do you ask?"

"Start that beast over there, Isabella." She shrugged her shoulders, climbing aboard the 600+ horsepower articulated Quadtrac on rubber tracks, within; seconds, she's operating the machine. "That's the same as I've already purchased, Jason; I'll have another ten-furrow plough. We should be able to plough thousand-five-hundred acres in a couple of days. I better have another one of those power harrows behind the 400 HP Case IH. I like the one you sold me last year, we can have his and hers! Save the arguing," Donald grinned.

"Donald, will you stop spending; we could manage with the one you have. I can drive during the day, and you can drive through the night."

Jason looked to Donald, "Yes, or no? You want me to order another ten-furrow plough? That's a brand-new tractor Isabella sat in, not sold, unless your purchasing, of course," Jason laughed.

"I'll take it, Jason, because I may expand even more when another farm becomes available locally." Isabella exhaled. Donald grinned, "Jason, can you have Isabella's name sign written on the door? No chance she can blame me if she damages her tractor," he laughed.

"Donald, you are the craziest customer I have, but the best," Jason remarked, returning to his office and placing the order for the new plough.

Isabella and Donald climbed into his new American truck; she slid close to him on the bench seat, kissing his cheek. "I can see the method in your madness, Donald. If the weather is foul, at least with two 600 hp plus tractors and two ten-furrow ploughs, we should be able to tear across the land fairly quickly. Not forgetting the two power harrows, we should be able to prepare the fields quicker and efficiently. My only suggestion for the moment is to leave the new equipment at Crabtree Farm. If we leave at Mill Farm, it will make it easy for someone to vandalise unless you intend to move there permanently."

"You have a valid point, Isabella." Donald drove home steadily and parked in the yard at Crabtree Farm. Ran upstairs to the studio. Donald made several phone calls to security firms acquiring quotes to have both farms installed with surveillance cameras and monitored twenty-four hours a day.

Isabella took the phone from his hand, disconnecting the call. Donald looked rather annoyed at her. "Mummy, how would you like to bug Crabtree Farm and Mill Farm for your loving daughter and monitor twenty-four hours a day?" Donald playfully slapped Isabella's backside. She grinned, "I thought you'd like to know Donald and I are dating, taking things very slowly, mummy, and see what transpires, bye."

Mrs Montague grinned. She already knew most of her daughter's jewellery was bugged and her mobile. Finally, she thought her prayers were answered. Dispatching a crew to conceal cameras and microphones around the two properties made her feel more secure having her daughter there. Christine can try to bypass the security, and she'll definitely be caught or her accomplices.

***

Christine's finally collected from the hospital by her father. She immediately went to bed, having the two cots Donald had purchased on either side of her bed. She's determined to breastfeed her children. She would make Donald pay to have her breasts repaired if they sagged after working out at the gym and failed to rectify any faults with her figure. She's determined to show Donald what's on offer should he return.

***

At 10 o'clock the following day, the horsebox arrived in the yard. Mary came out of the cottage quickly; Isabella ran from the studio. They stood there like excited schoolchildren waiting for their present. Donald watched from the studio as Spartacus was removed from the horsebox. Donald walked down after writing out a cheque to give to the driver. "Thank Derek for me." Donald carried the saddle, bridle, and everything else that came with Spartacus into the neighbouring stable converted into a tack room by Michael some time ago.

***

Cindy had become quite broody, helping Christine change and bathing the children. A month had passed, and Christine finally had a routine with the children, receiving full support from Cindy and her father, who now doted on the children. Christine's relieved instead of her father rejecting her, Gerald and Cindy doted on her every wish, sometimes smothering, she thought, but nevertheless, better than not caring.

***

Donald realised some time had elapsed since Christine left the hospital with the children. He hadn't made any attempt to contact her or vice versa. Donald sent a text message asking if convenient for him to come and see the children?

Christine replied with a text immediately. "You are welcome to see your son and daughter." Donald kissed Isabella on the cheek. "I'm nipping over to Strawberry Estate to see the children. I won't be long, don't worry, Isabella, I don't cheat, and I definitely don't lie."

She tried to produce a reassuring smile, although deep down inside, she was petrified; Christine would destroy the fragile relationship she had achieved with Donald so far. Isabella watched him jump in his American truck nipping down the drive.

Donald parked outside Strawberry Estate house; he knocked on the door. Gerald greeted him, less than pleased to see him. He reluctantly showed Donald upstairs with a clear warning, "Behave yourself, Donald, on my property. Do not upset my daughter or her children." Donald's shocked by his remark.

Nevertheless, Christine's in the nursery she had created with everything Donald had sent her from Harrods. Gerald quietly opened the nursery door. Donald entered Gerald close behind him. Christine sat in her nursing chair; she smiled, tapping the seat next to her for him to sit down. Eric's breastfeeding, and Christine sitting topless, which Donald thought was unnecessary to display herself. He didn't say anything and wasn't looking for an argument. She passed Eric to him, taking Josephine from her cot and attaching to her nipple. Christine was drinking lots of water and eating fruit in the hope of producing sufficient milk for the first few months of their life.

Christine whispered, "I didn't think you would come. I suspected you wouldn't want to know your children," she sighed.

"To be quite honest, Christine, unsure of what to do. I didn't want to interfere, although I wanted to see the children. I had a glimpse in the hospital when they were born; they've grown."

"Eric's like his father, he has big hands, and he's just been sick over his father quite normal for him," she said, "he's a pig; he loves his breast," she smiled, passing Donald a cloth.

Christine stood passing Donald, Josephine, removing Eric and placing him in his cot. "The only things these two are proficient at are breastfeeding and dirty nappies. I'll be glad when they're older." Christine re-fastened her top covering her breasts, joking, "They never used to be that big, Donald."

"Is there anything you want, Christine, money or any product or equipment that would make your life easier?"

She removed Josephine from Donald's arms, placing her in her cot, returning sitting on Donald's lap, which he didn't object to; not wanting to cause any trouble, which could become a volatile situation if he wasn't careful by the tone of Gerald's voice, things had changed. Christine started kissing Donald. "Please, Christine."

"The only thing I need is you in my life with the children. I know I've made mistakes, and I won't again. I promise, give me one more chance, Donald, please, to prove myself."

Christine stood, holding Donald's hand, leading him out of the nursery, quietly closing the door. She's carrying a baby monitor with her so she would know the minute one of them cried. They went downstairs into the kitchen, finding Gerald sitting with Cindy; both looked at Donald like dirt. Gerald commented, "You needn't come too often, Donald. We can manage, and we certainly don't need your money."

"Father, that's unfair; Donald is the father. He didn't do anything wrong; he's unaware I wasn't taking contraception. I purposely made myself pregnant. I wanted his children, and I want him."

"I'm quite happy to support you, Christine and the children; you have the farm and Glencoe Estate."

"You forget father whose money made Glencoe work wouldn't be a success if it weren't for Donald. My fault I'm in this mess; I fooled around, not Donald."

Mrs Montague suddenly arrived, unexpected, she let herself in accompanied by her bodyguard. She's expecting trouble and about to dish it out if provoked. "What do you want, Mrs Montague?" Gerald asked, less than enthusiastic to see her.

"I've come to make one or two things straight. Donald and Christine will not be rekindling their relationship. I have sufficient evidence if you wish Gerald to put Christine behind bars for life. She is indirectly responsible for the fire at Crabtree Farm. She's also responsible for organising the death of Cherokee, the deceased Sophie's horse. Donald will support his children, and I'm sure if Christine asked him for anything, he would provide for her, but he is not ruining his life wondering which bed she's in next. She's simply a tart like her mother, you should know from your own experiences, Gerald, yet you wear blinkers! Donald, go!" Mrs Montague ordered. Donald looked at Christine in tears. She knew every word Mrs Montague had spoken was the truth.

Donald climbed into his American truck, slowly leaving the property, suspecting he would never enter the drive again. Mrs Montague's on the warpath and shocked Christine may be responsible for organising the fire on his farm and the death of Cherokee; the one remaining memory he had of Sophie. Donald returns to Crab-tree farm.

Isabella's waiting in the yard stroking Spartacus after Mary had returned from a ride. She helped Mary put him in the stable. Donald said, "Your mother's there, Isabella laying the law down. She doesn't take any prisoners on a good day. I don't think I will be welcome there again; more's the pity; I would love to stay in touch with my children," he sighed, walking away and making his way upstairs into the studio sitting in front of a blank canvas.

Isabella's now sleeping in her apartment; everyone felt no danger after Mrs Montague had laid the law down at Strawberry Estate, making them aware of the consequences of crossing her.

Time's marching on, moving to near the end of April. The new 620 hp Case IH Quadtrac arrived with the new plough attached with Isabella's name sign written on the driver's door, which made everyone laugh. Isabella sprayed the wheat on Mill Farm, not taking long with the unit she used. Donald received a phone call from Maggie; the work progressed far better than anticipated. Would he come to Dorking Moor Estate and carry out an inspection. Donald booked two rooms at Glencoe Estate, feeling inappropriate to use Christine's suite considering the situation. Isabella accompanied him, arriving at Glencoe early on Friday night. Justin explained things were changing. Christine's making more decisions regarding the running of her estate. After today, he's no longer welcome; no cooperation between the estates as initially planned. Donald placed his suitcases back in the boot of his Bentley. "Isabella, we'll find another establishment; we're only here for two days."

"Donald," Justin asked, "Could I apply for the manager position when your hotel is ready. I know you've offered the position to Maggie; she feels she's too busy with other projects. I think you'll find most of the staff will leave here and apply to work for you once you're operational; no loyalty here anymore; Christine has ruined everything. Let her sink in her own stupidity."

"I'm inclined to agree with you. My patience is wearing thin with her," Donald frowned, "Is Mrs Montague aware of the situation?"

Justin shrugged, "I don't know whether she'd improve the situation or make it worse."

Donald drove away, finding a bed-and-breakfast in the village. They were more than welcome; the residents knew what Donald had achieved for Glencoe and the village through his presence.

Early the following day, Donald and Isabella made their way to Dorking Moor Estate. Eric, the caretaker, came out to greet them, unlocking the main front door. Donald and Isabella inspected every room spotless. Donald asked, "How many people were working here, Eric? I didn't expect the project to be finished until nearly Christmas."

"Nearly fifty people here at times, Maggie's cracking the whip something fierce. She's determined to finish the project on time, if not before. The landscapers in tomorrow plant new shrubbery preparing the lawns. Maggie found some old pictures of the estate before in disrepair. She'd use them to reproduce the splendour of the estate. Thousands of people queueing to come here, Donald, by the time she's finished. She also has a crew starting on the three cottages. She said would cost you extra, but they would have to be brought up to standard for staff to live in."

"How are you keeping Eric? Do you have any problems?" Donald asked, opening his wallet and passing him one thousand pounds.

"Not with a generous boss like you. No, I shot me a stag and brought him down on the tractor and trailer, some lovely beasts there. Donald, you need a stable block here. We have better riding country than Glencoe."

Donald glanced at Isabella; she lifted her eyebrows, nodding slightly. "He makes sense, Donald; why should Glencoe reap the benefits when you have more to offer here. Their accommodation is not as good as you're offering."

"I offered to join forces. It would have made more sense than in competition, still their choice. Eric, do you think you could take us around the estate? You drive the Ferguson twenty, and we'll sit in the trailer so I can assess the scenery and ensure it warrants stables and horses. What's that building up there?"

"An unfinished project, water turbine they laid the cable and water pipe twenty years ago to the house, fitted the turbine and run out of money. The project never finished, would have supplied the house and surplus to go into the grid."

Donald and Isabella looked at each other, grinning. Eric removed his tractor and trailer from the barn. "Take me to the turbine first; I want to see what's left to do."

Eric slowly made his way up the hillside; standing in the trailer was more manageable than sitting down. The ride was rough, but the scenery was spectacular the higher they travelled. Donald opened the old wooden shed door, realising the turbine wasn't there. Only a stopcock controlled the amount of water flowing to the turbine, which must be somewhere by the house. Donald and Isabella continued walking up the steep gradient seeing the pipework taking the water from the lake. "Take us back to the house, Eric," Donald asked, realising Eric didn't quite understand how the setup worked. Donald ran into the basement of Dorking house, seeing a similar control panel to the one at Glencoe. He ran outside to the rear of the house, discovering another building some distance away, following a slight crease in the ground, suspecting that's where the electric cable and water pipe ran. Inside the building, a brand-new water turbine never used connected.

Maggie came on site. Donald grabbed her and explained what he had discovered. She was not to damage the pipework supplying the water or the electric cable to the house. Donald ensured the valve was closed on the turbine returning to the shed on the hill. He opened the valve using a crowbar driving back to the house, slowly watching the turbine rotate. Isabella had gone into the cellar disconnecting the mains power and switching over to the turbine; everything worked, much to their surprise. The discharged water entered the stream flowing from Glencoe, continuing its journey to God knows where. Eric scratched his head, "I wonder why never used. I remember the work carried out. I don't remember completed."

Donald kissed Maggie on the cheek, "Excellent job, Maggie. I understand your landscaping tomorrow."

"No, today."

"And you're spending more of my money on the cottages; how much more?" Donald chuckled.

"About two-hundred-fifty-thousand-pounds, all you need to bring them up to spec Donald. You can't expect people to live like animals. Within fourteen days, we'll be finished. Everything will be completed."

"No, you won't; I want the stables refurbished at the rear, I know they are dilapidated, but I'm sure you can rectify."

"You're probably looking at another hundred thousand, Donald; are you sure? Father phoned me this morning. The little bitch is taking charge. Although she won't have any staff, I warned you, they all want to move here by the sounds of things," Maggie laughed, "I don't have any time for her, stuck-up bitch."

"Go ahead with the work, Maggie, ASAP, please. Opening for business in fourteen days."

"I love it when you're all manly with me, Donald!" Maggie laughed, "Perhaps later," she grinned.

Isabella interrupted, "I don't think so, Maggie; he's mine; any hanky-panky it will be with me."

Maggie laughed, walking off to organise the crew who had arrived with lorry loads of material.

Donald made a phone call to the local press within minutes, swamped by reporters. A story from Donald Selwyn would be a headliner; he rarely gave interviews, and any usually incorporated a disaster somewhere. Donald leaning against his gold-coloured Bentley with Isabella beside him. "Good morning, ladies and gentlemen of the press. I thought you'd like to know Dorking Moor Estate will be opening its doors on May fifteenth for business. If you care to view what's on offer, there are two bars, a fitness room and forty bedrooms, and horse riding around the beautiful estate."

"We understood you were part of Glencoe Estate, Donald. What has changed?" A member of the press asked.

"I'm advised yesterday by the manager I'm no longer welcome on the estate; obviously, he's working under orders from the owner, one presumes."

"We understand you are the father of Christine Gibbs's children, is that correct, Donald, and will you play a part in their lives?"

"I don't really have any comment other than to wish Ms Gibbs every happiness in whatever venture she decides to pursue."

"Isabella Montague, are you in a relationship with Donald?"

"We are close friends," she smiled. "I'm his financial adviser."

"You were seen eating at the Hilton with Mr Selwyn, kissing him and eating fish and chips. You still deny there is anything between you?"

Donald laughed, kissing Isabella on the lips. The cameras went wild. "Does that answer your question?" Isabella grinned. The press went inside the hotel, photographing rooms and facilities. Donald and Isabella jumped in his Bentley, returning to their bed-and-breakfast accommodation, collecting their things, and going home with no reason to stay here a moment longer. They arrived at Crabtree Farm at three, both shattered from the journey.

The following day the papers were full of Donald's new enterprise Dorking Moor Estate, a new hotel opening in May. Donald phoned Justin, giving him the position of manager. Any other staff that wishes to follow him would be given a position at the hotel.

***

Christine's devastated; she had advised Justin to inform Donald he wasn't welcome at Glencoe. She hadn't realised its effect on all her staff. They had resigned, and the hotel bookings were cancelled. Glencoe Estate was derelict, and the horses were released by the stable girl to roam freely. The only thing left operational are the farms and the staff, only three of now.

Mrs Montague arrived, parking outside Strawberry Estate house, coming in with her bodyguard. Gerald and Cindy could see that she was livid with Christine by the look on her face. "Explain yourself,

Christine. Your big mouth is working without your brains in gear. You now have a derelict hotel, no staff, no customers; don't you dare blame Donald. I've spoken to Justin; Donald was paying for two rooms, he wasn't using your suite, he's a paying guest, informed he wasn't welcome. You are crazy like your mother, and I think you should join her. I have Elizabeth R breathing down my neck; you have placed the whole estate at a security risk." Mrs Montague threw a document on the table. "Sign!"

Christine, Gerald, and Cindy studied the document. "You expect me to give Glencoe Estate to Donald Selwyn to control and look after until his children are of age, to take control? I will not," Christine shouted.

"You prefer prison," Mrs Montague removed her mobile, "Can you give me the chief of police, please. Mrs Montague speaking."

Christine quickly scribbled her signature on the document, realising she would lose her children, freedom, and Strawberry Estate. Mrs Montague switched her phone off. "You may not visit Glencoe Estate. Donald may take his children, but you are banned. Those are Elizabeth R's instructions. I dare you to cross her. Now I must persuade Donald to pick up the pieces; otherwise, my head will be on the chopping block with yours, girl. Consider yourself fortunate you have Donald Selwyn's children; otherwise, you wouldn't be here. I promise you!"

Mrs Montague stormed out of the house heading for Crabtree Farm. She found her daughter sitting on Spartacus after returning from a ride around the fields. Isabella dismounted and placed her horse in the stable, hugging her mother. "You smell of horse, Isabella. Where is Donald? I may need your assistance, daughter persuading Donald."

"He's painting mummy upstairs."

Isabella and her mother walked upstairs, finding Donald painting a portrait of his new hotel set in the hills. Donald stood, wiping his hands, kissing Mrs Montague on both cheeks and once on the lips. She hit him with her cane, "Stop doing that, Donald! Manners, you are taking liberties, young man." Isabella's laughing, "And you can be quiet, Isabella, not funny."

Donald rubbed his leg where Mrs Montague had hit him with her cane; she showed him the document signed by Christine. He read very carefully, passing to Isabella. "No, I'm not interested; it makes me look like the village idiot. One minute I'm there, the next I'm not."

"Donald, you realise Christine will not benefit in the slightest, all for the children, your children and possibly ours eventually."

Mrs Montague stared at her daughter, "You had better not, Isabella. You're not married. I think you'd better come home with me if you're behaving like that; I had enough of Christine trying to become pregnant and driving Donald mad."

"Mummy, don't be silly. Donald and I have not; we are taking things slowly. I'm saving myself for the right man," she grinned, looking at Donald.

Donald frowned, "Why do I suddenly feel my life is organised again. Okay, pack bags and return to Glencoe pronto, Isabella. See if I can straighten the mess out without looking an idiot at the same time."

Mrs Montague smiled, kissing Donald on the cheek; he kissed her on the lips; she hit him with her cane, shaking her head, chuckling walking downstairs. Donald rubbed his leg, realising he'd end up with bruises if he kept kissing her that way, although all in good fun.

Donald and Isabella arrived in the early hours at Glencoe Estate. Justin's still in his cottage. He came out to greet Donald and Isabella, the hotel staff notified, Donald's in charge permanently, and Christine Gibbs finished. Justin, in his wisdom, had phoned the guests that had cancelled, explaining the press were misinformed. Donald hadn't left Glencoe, joining forces with his new establishment Dorking Moor Estate. Most guests rebooked, and the travel agencies knew the new situation. Dorking Moor Estate is booked already before opening for the next twelve months.

Jock came to the hotel early the following day, "Everything explained to us, Donald, about time they disposed of that silly bitch."

"How well do you know my new estate, Jock?"

"I know most of it, Donald; why do you ask?"

"Meet up with Eric, work out the best routes for horses and your truck. We combine the two hotels on the tourist trail, on horseback and by vehicle."

Jock smiled. Donald commented, "Don't smile, Jock. You worry me."

"With fifty thousand acres, Donald, you will need more horses. Eric's already informed me you're repairing the stables at your new establishment. We can ride over the mountains, call in at Dorking Moor for refreshments and change horses and trackback. Otherwise, too much for the horses to complete the whole journey, especially if they have inexperienced riders."

"Well thought out, Jock. Regarding the wildlife on both properties, I will need you to personally cull; we can use the meat in the hotels."

"I understand, Donald, a few animals need to be culled, as much as I detest shooting. We have too many Stags."

Donald patted Jock on his back, "You're a good man Jock. I'll leave everything in your capable hands as soon as the stables are ready; I'll purchase more horses."

Donald walked into the hotel, finding Justin. "Justin, do you think you could manage two hotels?"

"Shouldn't be a problem, Donald, if I can have an assistant manager at Dorking Moor to keep on top of things."

"The next problem, Justin, we have a thousand sheep on Glencoe Estate. We need to increase the area we use for making hay, with extra horses to feed. I don't have any suitable land for making hay on Dorking Moor. I will have to purchase my hay from here or another source."

"I think we could make another hundred acres suitable for hay-making. We need to drain, and the man for that job, Robbie. Unfortunate, he's not here."

"You have any idea where he is, Justin?"

"Last I heard, he's in a bedsit odd jobing," Justin exhaled, "What a waste."

"You can employ him again, Justin; if you think it's a good idea, make him aware of where he stands. We want no trouble with him chasing women."

Justin nodded in agreement, "I'll give him a chance; Maggie's settled with her new man, and she doesn't come here very often now; you have her too busy," Justin smiled.

Donald walked outside, seeing Isabella on a horse returning from her ride. She dismounted, suggesting, "The countryside is outstanding, Donald, on both properties. I've spent three hours riding around. Jock's with Eric working out the tracks to use safe for the public to travel on." Donald went back inside, leaving Isabella to stable her horse. Justin smiled, "Robbie's starting in the morning and staying in the cottage where he and his mother used to live. I've ordered roles of plastic draining pipe. Robbie can use the JCB you acquired and lay the piping to drain the land."

"Justin, can I give you another headache? Would you interview the staff for Dorking Moor? You know what we need; I'm opening on the fifteenth of May, which isn't far away. Can you manage?"

Justin opened his drawer, dropping a folder on his desk. "You look in there, Donald, fifty applicants who want to work for you, from stable girls to chefs. I've already interviewed the ones I thought would be suitable." Justin laughed, looking at the expression on Donald's face of pure shock.

"Okay, Mr manager. I will leave everything in your capable hands; thank you so much, Justin; you've taken a load off my mind. We'll soon be harvesting at home. I have one thousand five hundred acres. Although I should have Isabella with me this time, she's a godsend."

"Perhaps you should show her your intentions, Donald. If you know what I mean, a good woman is hard to come by, one you can trust."

"I think you're right, Justin. Could you possibly lay on a special meal and a table for two tonight, say 8 o'clock?"

Justin nodded, seeing Isabella come into the office. "Come with me," Donald insisted. Isabella looked intrigued and smiled following. She climbed into his Bentley, and he sped off, heading for Inverness. "Where are we going, Donald?" She asked curiously. Isabella noticed the sign for Inverness; Donald parked outside a jewellers shop. He jumped out of his car, opening the passenger door for Isabella and the jewellery shop door. Her eyes enlarged, wondering what he was planning. "Isabella, select a ring of your choice." She placed her hand to her mouth in shock. Isabella was definitely not expecting that. "You mean engagement ring, Donald, so soon, are you sure?"

Donald nodded, "I'm sure, surer than before."

Mrs Montague's listening, eating her lunch, almost choking on her food. She's more surprised than Isabella. She didn't think Donald would make such a gesture so early on, after the loss of Sophie. Mrs Montague thought Isabella would struggle to secure Donald after his catalogue of disastrous relationships.

Isabella spent an hour; Donald thought she had tried on every engagement ring in the shop, finally settling for a cluster of diamonds for fifteen thousand pounds. Isabella looked at him, "Are you really sure, Donald? Don't you break my heart?"

"As sure as anyone can be, Isabella," he said, kissing her.

They left the shop, Isabella's beaming from ear to ear, suspecting her mother's listening. They stopped at a fish and chip shop, laughing, sitting in the Bentley with chips, fish, curry sauce and mushy peas. Isabella commented, "I never thought life could be this wonderful, Donald. You make me very happy."

"That works both ways, Isabella. I wanted to strangle you when I first saw you. You're exceptional; besides, your cheap labour for driving the tractors on the farm," he laughed. She threw a chip at him, poking out her tongue.

CHAPTER TWENTY-ONE

REVENGE

Christine's livid about losing Glencoe Estate to Donald. She would have to be extremely clever to outwit Mrs Montague. Whatever happened, she mustn't be involved; otherwise, her days may be numbered. Providing she had the children, they may safeguard her to some degree. Christine saddled The Rising Sun leaving her children with Cindy and her father. Somehow, she would have to persuade someone to help her. She rode along the track approaching the sawmill seeing visitors watching timber processed the old-fashioned way. Her father, in his wisdom, had taken on two young offenders recently released from prison on work experience; of course, her father paid handsomely for having them on the farm.

Christine tied The Rising Sun to a tree some distance from the mill so he wouldn't be spooked. She leant against the wall, deciding who would be her victim and who's most likely to cooperate out of the two men. She noticed one had taken a particular interest. He smiled at her, slowly working his way towards Christine. She moved out of view of everyone, searching the sky for any signs of a drone, suspecting Mrs Montague would know she was riding and wouldn't suspect anything. She made her way to the old strawberry shed a few yards away, standing in the doorway, seeing the young man had noticed her. He smiled, and within a few minutes, he followed her after checking no one was watching. Christine sat on an old box he sat close by. "Hi there, I haven't seen you before," he grinned.

"No, I haven't been out for a while thanks to my boyfriend dumping me, leaving me with two children to look after on my own. You're not from around here, are you?" She asked curiously.

"No, I'm from the other side of Leeds on work experience; we stay in a hostel on the other side of town. What a dump, better than prison. Caught stealing from a farm. They tried to accuse me of poisoning the animals, but they couldn't prove it. I was jailed for another crime," he grinned. "The farmer short-changed my old man, cheated him out of a couple of thousand pounds, so I thought it was payback."

"I'm trying to think of a way of having my own back. He only lives at Crabtree Farm; he cheated on me, stole some money, left me with the babies."

"That sort of lowlife is dealt with severely in prison; he'd end up in a body bag. You know how to put him out of business without him discovering it's you? A friend told me when I was in prison, he'd done the same to a neighbour. You acquire a large syringe filled full of roundup or something that kills everything and inject it into the containers of concentrated herbicide. They won't notice for two or three weeks, and the crops will suddenly die, no chance of recovery," he laughed, "The farmer went bust, and the kid only got six months, mind you, only thirteen."

"That's a brilliant idea; they haven't sprayed their wheat. The chemical store is not visible from the house. Although it's locked, it has a sign on the door advising you what's inside," she sighed.

"Easy! Pick the lock I can anyway," he smiled.

"What would you charge me to deal with the problem so I can have my own back?"

"You'd have to supply roundup or something and a large syringe. I mean a massive one and a very fine needle; otherwise, see the puncture marks and give the game away. You be nice to me; I'll look after you. You're on benefits, I suspect. I'm not taking any money, that's for sure."

"Okay," Christine watched him unbutton her blouse; she released her bra. He started kissing her. She stood and removed her jeans, laying on the old hessian sack. She's already on the pill; she wasn't taking any chances of becoming pregnant again; once is enough to experience the pain. They finally dressed. "No names," he smiled, "For the moment, maybe afterwards, we will see. See you here at the same time tomorrow. You supply the stuff and leave the rest to me." He kissed her passionately, which she rather enjoyed; he certainly knew how to make love to a girl. He ran out of the shed returning to the sawmill. Christine ensured she was tidy, looking to see if a drone was there before returning to The Rising Sun, mounted, and riding to the stables. Jumped in her Range Rover, heading into Birmingham where she wouldn't be known. She purchased a syringe and a gallon of roundup concentrate from one shop. She hid in the boot of her Range Rover returning home.

***

At 8 o'clock in the evening, Donald knocked on Isabella's bedroom door. She opened, and he held her hand, "Come with me." Donald led her downstairs into the secluded part of the dining room, seating her at a table and passing her a bouquet of flowers. He'd paid the staff extra to stay on and serve his meal. The chef had prepared venison as the main course starting off with soup. Donald remembered the name of the wines she'd ordered at the Hilton having a glass himself this time. He wasn't driving anywhere tonight. Isabella realised how serious Donald was about her. First, the engagement ring and now an exceptional meal for them to enjoy together. Isabella hadn't noticed when they were in the jewellery shop Donald had secretly purchased diamond earrings and a necklace for her. He slid the boxes across the table. She stared in disbelief, undoing the ribbons and looking at the expensive earrings and necklace. "Donald, you shouldn't have. The ring cost a fortune which I love immensely, beautiful."

***

Mrs Montague's watching on her surveillance camera couldn't smile anymore if she tried. Even her husband tuned in a little concerned Donald's a commoner. Mrs Montague remarked to her husband, "The earrings and necklace were over twenty thousand pounds; Donald is definitely serious about our daughter. I hope to God she doesn't make a mistake. Isabella has one of the most generous men I've ever met, apart from you," she said, kissing Mr Montague.

Isabella and Donald finished their meal, slipping on their coats, walking along to the waterwheel and back, meeting Robbie in the doorway, who looked a little worse for wear. "Thanks, Donald, for giving me another chance; I'll not forget," he said, scurrying off, almost afraid to be near Isabella.

"I presume that's Robbie; you recently gave permission to be reinstated?"

"Yes, be careful around him. He'll have you in bed."

Isabella glared at Donald, "Don't you dare compare me to your other relationships. They are not in my league." Isabella stormed into the hotel, running upstairs. Donald thought, big mouth; he'd managed to ruin a perfect evening.

***

The next day Christine concealed what she'd purchased in a shopping bag, walking around to the stables, saddling The Rising Sun. She left him where she had before and made sure the young man saw her, making her way to the old strawberry shed. She sat in there patiently after checking no drones in the sky. He joined her a few minutes later, looking in the bag, "That will do. I checked Crabtree Farm out last night. I found the store, no dogs, one horse and his parents didn't come out in the evening, even when I knocked a bucket."

***

Mrs Montague notified someone's snooping around the farm; they suspected a common criminal. He hadn't broken into anywhere and had left. Security not related anything to Christine at this stage.

***

Christine removed her clothes and lay on the hessian sack allowing the young man to take his pleasure. She couldn't stop smiling at the thought of all Donald's crops destroyed; he wouldn't realise for weeks. They finished and tidied themselves. "Don't come here again; I won't be here. I'm off home for a month, maybe longer. I have to appear in court on other charges," he smiled, running out of the door, taking the carrier bag with him.

***

Donald retired to bed, a faint knock on the door. "Come in." Isabella entered wearing her dressing gown and sitting beside him on the bed; she kissed him affectionately. "I'm sorry for what I said; I don't like compared to other women. I'm me, and I'm yours if you want me, but not tonight. I don't want to rush, Donald. I want to make sure you really want me," she kissed him again, patting his cheek and returning to her room.

***

The security officer had fallen asleep and surveillance cameras surveying Crabtree Farm not recording. The lock picked on the chemical store, and the young man injected roundup into every plastic container after removing the caps carefully. Injecting close to the side of the top seal so barely a pinprick could be seen through the silver foil unless you were looking hard. He dispensed a gallon of roundup amongst the other containers. He locked the store, leaving the farm, placing everything in a large bin outside his temporary accommodation, burying it with other rubbish. He flushed the rubber gloves he was wearing down the loo so no trace of his DNA. He awoke the following day to see the bins emptied, grinning, preparing to leave for Leeds.

***

Isabella and Donald left early the following day heading for Crabtree Farm, taking most of the day to travel. Donald ran up into his studio, realising Susan had paid a visit. He couldn't find anything when she tidied the woman went to town. He fell into bed too knackered to care about anything. Donald awoke to the sound of the sprayer parked in the yard; he looked out of his window seeing Isabella. The woman had more energy than he ever had, he thought, dressed quickly, running downstairs holding a cup of coffee in one hand, trying to wake up. She removed two plastic containers of chemicals from the store. Isabella held up to the light. "Donald, something strange with the colour," she pulled the plastic cap phoning her mother. "Mummy is surveillance working correctly; something's happened to the chemicals; they're the wrong colour unless they adjusted the consistencies. What have they added, although the container doesn't state they have?"

Mrs Montague checked surveillance noticing the security guard was asleep on the internal camera. she had no idea what had happened at Crabtree Farm without the surveillance officer pressing the record, which he obviously hadn't. "Isabella, do nothing, touch, nothing! I have someone on the way to test the chemicals; you have no idea what's in there." Mrs Montague shouted down the phone, "Dismiss that man on duty last night." She drove as quickly as possible to Crabtree Farm, arriving as the chemicals were tested in the containers. The police had come trying to lift fingerprints. Unfortunately, Donald's and Isabella's were everywhere, as you would expect from moving the containers. Mary and Martin had made coffee for everyone, alarmed at the thought that someone had managed to bypass security and possibly contaminate the chemicals used to spray the crops. The police officer approached Mrs Montague, "We had a case once before; someone injected roundup into other spray containers, put the farmer out of business, and killed everything he had. The lad's still in prison, so it can't be him."

The results were verified. "Every one of your containers is contaminated with roundup. If you'd have sprayed, sufficient to destroy the plants." Donald dashed upstairs, reordering replacement chemicals for the contaminated ones.

Mrs Montague looked at her daughter's ring and grinned, kissing her on the cheek, "A lucky girl and well spotted. Thank god for your education Isabella and working on the vineyard. You learnt an awful lot; very proud of you."

Donald kissed Isabella on the cheek, "So am I. We would have lost everything; Isabella is a genius. Pretty apparent, Mrs Montague, someone really has it in for me, determined to put me out of business, one way or another."

"From what I can ascertain from surveillance on Strawberry Estate. The most Christine has performed is riding The Rising Sun most days, and she went shopping once. Unfortunately, the security guard watching your premises fell asleep. However, the night before, he detected what we considered a common criminal looking around. Now obvious more than that."

Isabella washed out the sprayer, ensuring no residue remained in the tank. Mary and Martin looked at each other and then at Donald, "Who the hell have you upset, Donald, other than Christine?"

"Can't be Robbie. He's reinstated at Glencoe and not before time; he's nearly on his knees, a skeleton of his former self. Gerald's upset over me buying Mill Farm; as you know, I can't imagine him that vindictive."

A white van arrived in the yard carrying replacement chemicals. Isabella filled the sprayer with water adding the chemicals after checking for any puncher marks, although the chemical suppliers had taken extra precautions with the shipment and actually marked the plastic tops, which would indicate if they were moved after sealing. By 5 o'clock in the afternoon, Isabella had sprayed the acres of wheat, praying none of the chemicals was contaminated; otherwise, they would be lost. Donald wouldn't go bankrupt, but that wasn't the point. It would indicate someone had outwitted her, which would be more devastating than losing the crop.

Donald sent Isabella into the cottage for a drink. He started washing out the sprayer system, ensuring no residue was left in the tank; otherwise, it would contaminate the following application. No chemicals left on site. Everything used; he'd only purchased enough for the one application.

***

Mrs Montague convinced Christine had something to do with what had occurred; she had no proof. She couldn't fly a drone all day. Christine's clever enough to notice a drone in the air she had spotted in the past. Mrs Montague certainly couldn't warrant someone on surveillance; the disaster had been averted by her daughter. She decided the next surveillance security guard who fell asleep would be in a body bag.

***

Donald reversed the sprayer in the machinery shed while Isabella went to shower. Isabella excelled at whatever she performed, and Donald realised that the worst the situation could become longer he stayed single. Donald knocked on the door of apartment four. Isabella answered; with a towel wrapped around her, she stepped aside for Donald to come in, still drying her hair. "Will you marry me, Isabella?" He asked straight out.

Mrs Montague listening to the conversation, dropped her cup of tea in the surveillance room. That's the second time Donald had taken her by surprise, and if her daughter didn't say yes, she's driving over to Crabtree Farm to kick her backside.

"Of course, not yet. We can formally announce our engagement. I want to be married at Dorking Moor Estate next summer after harvest. I want to make sure you are a worthy husband and deserve this wonderful girl," she grinned, running into her bedroom, locking the door to dress. Isabella knew she was driving Donald crazy and enjoyed every moment.

"Do we have to wait that long, Isabella? Tomorrow afternoon would suit me better!"

Isabella's laughing as she opened the door, kissing him, "You will wait if you want me. If you look at another woman, I'll be gone."

***

Mrs Montague grinning her daughters in charge; admittedly, she wouldn't have waited so long. Nevertheless, it would prove Donald's loyalty to Isabella. Mrs Montague immediately phoned the news desk, informing them of the official engagement of Isabella Montague to Donald Selwyn. The television was on in Isabella's room. Donald sat down after making coffee for them both, hearing the announcement on television along with Isabella. She placed her hand to her mouth, realising her mother's listening and had arranged the announcement.

***

Christine's feeding her children, watching the television hearing the announcement. She realised something had gone wrong after surveying police cars and vans visiting Crabtree Farm. She would have to stay silent; she couldn't afford to be connected to what took place. She's pretty sure the boy she'd seen would say nothing. Christine sighed heavily, deciding the chances of her and Donald again remote.

She had lovely children and knew Donald would ensure they were well provided for. She suspected she would be making serious money when Donald had finished with Glencoe. The only way she could win was if Isabella were to disappear, which she would have to ponder on for the future before they were married. Christine knew her father was against Donald having anything to do with her children. Although they would be the key once they could walk, they would pull on Donald's heartstrings.

"You better dress. We're out this evening to celebrate," Donald remarked, grabbing her around the waist and kissing her lovingly. Isabella grinned, "Of course, I would expect nothing less of you. I only want fish and chips tonight. That's what I fancy; I'm not dressing up."

Donald shook his head, laughing, "Make you fat."

"I'd rather be fat from fish and chips than something else," she remarked, lifting her eyebrows.

Martin and Mary came out of the cottage, "We saw on the news Mrs Montague making an official announcement, brilliant son, you couldn't have picked a better girl." Everyone hugged each other.

"We're nipping out to celebrate on fish and chips; that's what Isabella wants," Donald laughed. "I may have finally found a cheap wife to keep."

"How do you know I'm not having cravings, Donald," Isabella stared at him. Mary glared. Martin looked. Isabella laughed at Donald's bewildered expression, "Don't be silly, Donald, I'm only teasing!" She ran across the yard laughing, jumping into the Bentley, locking the door. Donald waved to his mother and father, climbing in the driver's seat and heading toward town. They entered a fish and chip restaurant and decided to have their favourite fish and chips, mushy peas, and curry sauce served on plates rather than newspapers. Cameras flashed through the window; Donald waved. He didn't care. Isabella grinned; she finally achieved what she wanted to find someone she felt she could trust with her heart. "Donald, you already have two children. When we're married, I don't think there's any need for me to be pregnant straightaway. We can wait a few years; they will have my mother's estate in France plus whatever else we decide to leave them."

"Blimey, you are planning things; what happens if you have two children or four, perhaps six."

"That will not happen. I may give you two children. We will have to see; the rest is fantasy in your mind. I'm not providing you with a rugby team."

"You never know; you might enjoy the process and ravish my body," Donald laughed.

Isabella grinned, enjoying the remainder of her meal. They finally made their way back to Crabtree Farm. Isabella went into her apartment. Donald ran upstairs to the studio, phoning Mark at home from Seven Trent. "Hi, Mark, Donald Selwyn. Would you be interested in applying sewerage to fifty acres of oilseed rape stubble this year with the possibility of a further one thousand plus acres once I've removed the wheat? The only thing is you have to be quick because of ploughing and planting again."

"Fabulous Donald, we were struggling to find farmers interested; thanks. As soon as you've removed the rape, I'll have the equipment there; the same goes for the wheat. We will have three lorries feeding the umbilical cord, so we won't be waiting like last year."

"Thanks, Mark," Donald rang off.

Maggie phoned, "Everything is ready, Donald. The landscaping was finished, my father showed the new assistant manager around, and the new staff ready to open on the fifteenth. The water turbine is working wonderfully; I'm sending your final bill in the next few days. By the way, the stables weren't as bad as they looked. You're engaged. I hope it all works out for you this time, Donald. As long as you realise you're becoming involved with one of the most dangerous women in Britain, Mrs Montague," Maggie chuckled, ringing off.

Donald looked at the calendar next Wednesday, the fifteenth of May, making him exhale. Time certainly creeps up on you. Donald glanced out of his window, noticing a brand-new horsebox in the far corner of the yard wasn't there when he left with Isabella. Donald came down shining his torch, looking around the new horsebox. Mary and Martin came out of the cottage seeing the torchlight. Martin's carrying a shotgun, Mary shone her torch in Donald's face, laughing, "Don't shoot him, Martin! He hasn't paid for the horsebox."

"When you order, mother?"

"A few days ago, on the farm's account. Jason from Case IH arranged for me, and you pay, so we won't worry about it too much, will we, Martin?" Martin shrugged his shoulders.

"You'll notice I've had a towing hitch fitted to my Range Rover; you're paying for that, son," she grinned. Isabella came out hearing the disturbance. "My mother's raiding the piggy bank, Isabella. Do you know any think about this?"

They entered the cottage. Donald stared at Isabella suspiciously, "You know anything about this, Isabella?"

"You would accuse your future wife; honestly, Donald! How could you?" Mary burst out laughing along with Martin. "Because my future husband sometimes forgets to twist the agent's arm when you spend so much money, you are entitled to a discount. The horsebox and the towing hitch were with the compliments of Jason after you spent two million pounds with him last year and some this year."

Donald's silent. Isabella's correct. Sometimes, he didn't push hard enough for a discount. Isabella patted his cheeks, "Never mind, future husband, I will teach you how to purchase products at the right price." Mary and Martin sat at the table, almost in tears watching Isabella embarrass Donald. Everything she said was the truth, and he couldn't deny it.

Mary finally spoke, "We're leaving tomorrow, taking Spartacus with us to Devon. He needs a holiday." Mary couldn't prevent giggling. The tears ran down her cheeks; seeing the expression on Donald's face was priceless, "You better paint something else, son. I might need to purchase something next week," she laughed even more.

Donald walked out of the cottage returning to his studio, laughing. He'd never known his mother and father to be so happy and himself for a change.

Isabella helped Mary in the morning persuade Spartacus in the horsebox, which he didn't seem very impressed with. Although once Mary gave him a few cubes of sugar, he would have sat in the back of the Range Rover. Mary and Martin set off for Devon; she'd arranged for a nearby stable for Spartacus to stay while there.

Donald had painted a portrait of Spartacus with Isabella on his back using Dorking Moor Estate as the background. He'd sent it to Jack two days ago with the title, "Spartacus." Donald went online, finding that bidding was not permitted to start until the fifteenth of May. Donald smiled. Jack's a shrewd old devil; he knew how to maximise profits. Isabella came up into the studio, "My mother's been on the phone expressing how wonderful her daughter looks on Spartacus. My father said he wants to purchase."

Donald placed a blank canvas on the easel, grinning, "Say nothing, Isabella. I will paint the same picture with your mother on Spartacus. It should excite your father and mother."

Isabella kissed him, "Wonderful, Donald, she'll be so surprised."

Donald started straight away; paint flowed like a river replicating the portrait of Isabella and Spartacus on Dorking Moor Estate. He worked for the next two days finalising the picture placing Mrs Montague on Spartacus. Incorporating a side-saddle as ladies used many years ago in her riding clothes. Donald placed it in the boot of his Bentley. Isabella slid in beside him, grinning, "Mother will be so surprised." 9 o'clock in the morning outside Jack's art gallery. Jack released the security gates giving them access, surprised he wasn't contacted before delivery. Both Donald and Isabella knew the farms were monitored. "Jack, can you please frame it and send it to Mr Montague? Send with our compliments."

Jack had barely placed the portrait on the easel after fitting a frame when Mrs Montague walked in. She tapped Donald on the shoulder with her cane, looking at him, then at the portrait. "My husband will be overjoyed to receive such a beautiful portrait of his wife," Mrs Montague paused, seeing the title. "My True Love."

Donald shrugged his shoulders, "Seems appropriate, Mrs Montague. I thought we'd run away together."

Mrs Montague grinned, "In another lifetime, maybe Donald, you have the closest thing to me, my daughter; what more could you ask for."

"Absolutely nothing Mrs Montague."

Isabella's shocked to see her father walk into Jack's art gallery. He never usually left France. He placed his arm around his wife, admiring the portrait Donald had produced. Shaking Donald's hand, "You are talented, Donald. What a beautiful likeness of my wife in an exquisite setting."

Mr and Mrs Montague left, leaving Jack to parcel and send it to France. Jack remarked, "I've had offers of over ten million for the portrait of Isabella on Spartacus. I suggest you allow me to run a thousand prints, sell at five hundred a copy with your signature, Donald."

"I'll leave it entirely in your hands, Jack; you know what you're doing. I only paint."

"You are so wrong, Donald. Any idiot could paint a woman on a horse, the way you apply the oils, the brush strokes, the feeling in the picture, the whole composition. When people buy your artwork, they feel they have a part of you."

"Don't you go all soppy on me, Jack?" Donald laughed.

Isabella and Donald made their way home to Crabtree Farm, preparing for their scheduled opening of Dorking Moor Estate Hotel. They decided to spend a couple of days in the hotel before it officially opened to ensure it functions as it should. The following day, travelling to Scotland, arriving at Dorking Moor Estate in the afternoon. The place had never looked so spectacular as it did at this precise moment. Donald took several photographs, greeted by the assistant manager, Mr Jenkins, a man in his fifties who had spent some time in hotels. Donald had provided uniforms for all members of staff supplied by Maggie's shop. Isabella and Donald were shown to their private suite; the furnishings were excellent, nothing out of place.

Donald and Isabella walked around the hotel, checking every room, determined; that it would not be a failure. Both Glencoe Estate and Dorking Moor Estate were booked solid; people were queueing to acquire rooms in the new hotel. Donald went down into the kitchen, looking at the brand-new appliances. The chef and staff busily stacked shelves, cupboards, and fridges where the meat would be stored. Justin arrived to carry out his final inspection.

Donald walked around to inspect the refurbished stable block discovering a young girl in the tack room, her long red hair draping over her shoulders. She's writing down a list of things she needs, noticing Donald. "You would think the bloody owner would have the horses here by now; what am I supposed to do?" Isabella followed in behind Donald. "No good; I'm sorry I can't take you riding. I don't have any horses." Donald burst out laughing along with Isabella. The young girl suddenly realised who she was speaking to, placing her hands over her mouth, "Oh my god, it's you, I mean Mr Selwyn, sorry Sir," she spluttered. Isabella's in stitches.

"You are?" Donald asked.

"Emily Perkins, Mr Selwyn."

Justin came to the stables. "I see you've met Emily; she's a little young. She has good qualifications, Donald, similar to Sophie."

"Excellent, now, where are the bloody horses; otherwise, she'll strangle me," Donald laughed, watching Emily smile with relief; he saw the funny side of the situation.

"I sent the horsebox ahead from Glencoe. I've struggled to find good horses; I managed to find nine. Perhaps Isabella and Emily can inspect the horses, and you can purchase Donald. They are on the other side of Inverness. We need them today ready for the opening. I've ensured each horse comes with saddle, bridle and blankets as part of the deal," Justin assured.

"Emily in my Bentley." Isabella sat in the front, Emily and Justin in the back. Emily sat quiet, feeling embarrassed she'd shouted at her employer, which was not a good start. Donald glanced in his rear-view mirror at Emily. "I've had a lot worse said to me, Emily, don't worry, you were correct, but you can blame Justin, not me. I left him in charge," Donald laughed. "What he knows about horses you could write on a postage stamp, including me," Donald remarked, watching Emily chuckle.

They finally arrived at a large livery. The horsebox was already parked; Sandra had driven from Glencoe Estate in charge of the horses there.

Donald was introduced to the establishment owner and taken immediately to the holding paddock, where the horses were held before purchase. Sandra, Isabella, and Emily walked amongst the horses inspecting for any defects. A veterinary report had taken place the day before stating the horses were in good health at inspection.

Sandra and Isabella returned to Donald, leaning on the gate. Emily's spending some time with one horse. Donald called out, "What's the matter, Emily?"

"Unfortunately, this poor horse is only good for dog meat. I can see the start of arthritic joints." Emily looked at the horse's teeth, "Too old for what we want."

The owner looked embarrassed, realising Emily had noticed the one horse they were desperate to dispose of. "I have another," not bothering to argue with Emily's assessment. Donald smelt a rat. They were obviously trying to stitch him on one horse. Thanks to Emily, they failed miserably. Another horse brought into the paddock Emily inspected carefully, "This one is okay, Mr Selwyn; don't pay a lot for this bunch; the saddles are probably worth more than the horses." Donald loved Emily; she took no prisoners and said what she meant, his kind of employee. Donald studied the veterinary report; most horses were over eight years old. He didn't want skittish young horses with the public. These had obviously been used for general riding. "What's your price?"

"Twenty thousand pounds."

Donald glanced at Emily, moving her head slowly from side to side. "Twelve thousand, including the saddles etc. My final offer, Sandra, return the horsebox to Glencoe."

"Okay, Mr Selwyn, we have a deal," the owner reluctantly accepted, realising they wouldn't achieve a better price.

"Sandra, Emily, will you transport the horses to Dorking Moor Estate, please, the saddles etc." Donald opened his wallet, removing fifty pounds and placing in Emily's hand, kissing her on the cheek,

"Clever, you're an asset." Emily turned bright red, not expecting a fifty pounds or a kiss on the cheek from Donald Selwyn with praise after she insulted him on their first meeting. Donald returned to his Bentley, removing twelve thousand pounds in cash and acquiring a receipt from the owner stating what he'd purchased. Isabella and Justin sat in the Bentley; Donald joined them, returning to Dorking Moor Estate. Isabella commented, "Emily is a clever girl, Donald. I hadn't noticed the joint problem on the horse, and I've been around horses all my life. I have to protest; will you reframe from kissing other women if you want to marry me." Justin laughing, sitting in the back of the Bentley. Isabella turned and glared at him, "Not funny, Justin," watching Donald grin as Isabella chastised Justin.

Justin remarked, "She has a tongue on her just like our Maggie," Donald laughed, stepping out of the Bentley. "Return to Glencoe before Isabella strangles you, Justin; thanks for your help, mate. Catch you later."

Jock came down the hill blasting his klaxons, making sure half the world could hear him coming. Donald smiled, watching him park his truck. "I thought you might like to come for a ride, Donald and Isabella if you're so inclined. I'll show you the routes we picked for the truck and horses across your new estate."

"Brilliant, Jock. Reminds me I haven't seen Eric this morning."

"Gone to the doctor to acquire pills for his chest; he's lived in that damp old cottage for years until you had it fixed. He often has a chest infection, although that may change once the damp dissipates from the cottage."

"Come on, then let's go," Donald sighed, climbing into Jock's truck with Isabella sitting on the middle seat. Jock set off not concerned about the gradients his truck's tackling or how the lorry leaned, giving the impression that it would roll over any minute. Both Donald and Isabella were gripping the seat, worried the vehicle would roll over. Jock chuckled, seeing their horrified expression at times. "Jock, the scenery's spectacular; I suppose you're used to seeing every day," Isabella remarked.

"No, something's always different; no two seasons are the same." Jock pointed, "There's the rogue stag." Jock stopped the truck, grabbing his rifle from behind the seat; he shot the stag driving over with his truck, gutting the animal. Isabella turned away. Donald helped Jock throw the carcass on the back of the truck returning to the hotel. Jock skilled skinned the beast within minutes, cutting it up into manageable joints to be hung. Donald helped him carry into the kitchen for the chef to hang and use when ready. Isabella had gone to the stables seeing the first four horses had arrived.

***

Christine had received a visit from the police regarding the slaughtering of Cherokee and the attempt to ruin the crops on Crabtree Farm. Gerald's so incensed that he contacted the family solicitors to protect Christine, convinced his daughter's innocent. Mrs Montague had monitored and had instructed the police to question Christine; to make her realise she was under suspicion and may curb any other attempt to ruin Donald Selwyn's life and her daughter's.

***

Gerald suggested Christine spend a few days shopping in her mother's old London flat. He and Cindy would look after the twins. Christine packed her suitcase heading for London. She entered her mother's apartment, opening all the windows to allow fresh air to circulate, removing the stale smell. Since her mother's death, no one had been in the flat. She searched through her mother's clothes finding a dress she would wear to the roulette tables. Christine tried on looking in the mirror; nothing she couldn't see of her figure. Christine laughed, changing, placing the dress in the closet. Christine searched through the draws coming across a wad of cash totalling ten thousand pounds, which she suspected was from her mother's winnings. Today's turning out to be good so far, she thought.

Christine ventured to the club her mother would often visit, watching everybody gambling. Millions of pounds were changing hands every night, mostly ending up in the club owners' hands. The chances of winning are slim. Christine played one or two slot machines placing her last coin in a machine. She pulled the handle watching the cylinders rotate; she'd won fifty thousand pounds jackpot. She took the ticket to the cashier, who gave her the option of having the money paid directly into her bank account, which Christine thought more sensible than carrying that amount of money on the streets of London. Christine's given a receipt confirming the cash in the process of transfer.

Christine left the casino thrilled. Finally, her luck changing, she thought, returning to her mother's flat. Christine continued to search her mother's apartment, stumbling across more drugs she suspected were here for Dixon; she guessed they had some street value, so she left them concealed for the moment. Suddenly a light turned on in her head. If the drugs were found on Crabtree Farm or in one of Donald's vehicles, his reputation would be shattered? Isabella would unquestionably believe, leaving the door open for her to recover what's hers.

***

The fifteenth of May had arrived. The press had come along with a camera crew filming people arriving, approximately a hundred in total, the first bookings for the hotel. Justin's there along with the assistant manager, Mr Jenkins. Emily had saddled three horses making sure the guests could see what was offered. Jock came along with his truck.

***

Christine's at home watching television, absolutely fuming it wasn't her in the film, observing Isabella kissing Donald and holding his arm as if they were a married couple. The first hundred guests were treated to champagne as they entered the premises. A press member asked, "Donald, we have followed your story since you first placed a paintbrush on canvas. You are now a multimillionaire with properties in Scotland and the UK; how do you feel?"

"A very fortunate individual, hopefully, I have created a few jobs along the way using my wealth. I'm blessed after so many disasters to have Isabella, the greatest gift, far more valuable than money."

Christine watching television, threw orange peel at the screen, "What a load of bull shit," she shouted.

Within three hours, Emily's on her first track around the estate with four customers desperate to see the countryside. Mr Jenkins approached Donald, "Mr Selwyn, I think you can safely say we have a successful start; may it continue." Donald nodded in agreement, watching Mr Jenkins move away talking to Justin. Donald found Jock, taking his arm and leading Jock to the open kitchen window. "Do you have a meal for Jock, a nice piece of venison? Give him all the trimmings. He's the man who supplies your larder; treat him nice," Donald laughed, walking away, remembering as a child, if he went around the back of the school to the kitchen, sometimes the cook would give him a little treat.

Finally, the day ended; Isabella and Donald retired to their suite. Donald took the small room with a bed where children would generally stay, and Isabella had the large bed in the main bedroom. She's determined he would not be sampling the fruits of her body, although she's desperate to let him, not until she's convinced he only had eyes for her. Her mother told her many years ago men always look that's okay, as long as they don't touch other women. Isabella's mother had made her take contraceptives early on in life if she had the miss fortune to be attacked. However, she's saving herself for Mr right. At twenty years old, she thought, time for her to settle down with her perfect man when she found him. Most of her friends were already married; some had children others were in the middle of a divorce after their husbands were caught cheating. She wanted none of that. Just the perfect man and marriage, which may be hard to achieve, as her mother suggested. Donald's the best chance to achieve her goal and be happy like her mother.

After breakfast, Donald left the hotel with Isabella, leaving it in Justin's hands. He's highly impressed with the way things have gone. The building refurbishment cost him over one million with the furnishings on top, so he hoped money well spent almost two million. Isabella commented, "I've been thinking, Donald, have harvest out the way and married this year. We've usually planted everything by the eleventh of October."

"I'm not having a Christmas wedding," remembering the past disasters.

"Third time, lucky Donald," she grinned, "I wouldn't mind a Christmas wedding at Dorking Moor Hotel."

***

Christine carefully placed the drugs in her suitcase, preparing to return to Strawberry Estate. She couldn't be seen anywhere near Crabtree Farm; she would have to find herself another idiot to perform the task of placing the drugs somewhere on the farm. She would notify the police anonymously, which should put pay to his relationship with Isabella. Her mother certainly wouldn't want her daughter with someone like that.

Christine hadn't realised her mother's apartment was bugged. Mrs Montague was notified of Christine's discovery and transporting of the drugs in her suitcase. Mrs Montague's intrigued. She guessed Christine's up to no good, but this time, she had surveillance.

***

Donald and Isabella returned to Crabtree Farm late in the afternoon. Donald carried Isabella's bags to her apartment. Donald's about to leave, Isabella kissed him passionately, holding his hand, taking him into the bedroom. She lay on the bed. Donald lay beside her, and immediately they started kissing and caressing each other. Finally, Isabella relented, a moment she'd longed to experience. Isabella's body quivered, watching Donald slowly removing her clothes, finally penetrating. She closed her eyes holding Donald close, feeling him gently thrusting and the enormity of what she was receiving. After what seemed to be an eternity, both showered in the morning together. "If my mother finds out, she will probably want to kill you, Donald, and me. She wanted me to wait until we were married."

"Okay, marry today, your everything I want, so why wait?"

Isabella kissed him, "I don't know why I feel I can trust you. I feel safe with you, Donald."

They both dressed, having a light breakfast.

***

Christine returned home and enjoyed a few hours with her children. Gerald advised, "Careful around the sawmill one or two unsavoury characters from prison on work experience. You don't know what they're like, Christine, but it's good money to allow them to work other than thieving." Christine decided to take a ride on The Rising Sun.

June had arrived, harvest was approaching, and the barley ears slowly turned golden. She rode down to the old sawmill leaving The Rising Sun where she had before, just what she needed, unsavoury characters with the brains of a dog and easily manipulated. She approached the sawmill watching the public; at least forty people appeared to be watching.

The boy had returned from Leeds. She smiled, watching him approach, making their way into the old strawberry shed. He commented, "That was close; I didn't think they'd realise the chemicals were contaminated; somebody must be clever."

"I have an idea," Christine smiled, unbuttoning her blouse and releasing her bra. "I've managed to acquire drugs if you would hide them on the farm, somewhere easy to find and notify me of the location. I could anonymously notify the police. His reputation would be ruined, his girlfriend would run for the hills," she smirked, watching him release her jeans; he made love to her on the old hessian sack. They tidied themselves. He remarked, "Give me the drugs tomorrow and leave the rest to me."

Christine grinned, "I've saved a little something for you," she gave him twenty pounds.

"I can't take that. Spend it on your kids, and give them a better start in life than I've had. I'll deal with that bastard for you, be here tomorrow," he rushed out of the strawberry shed, returning to the sawmill before he's missed.

***

Mrs Montague was notified by surveillance. Christine had left her horse tied to a branch, entering the old strawberry shed with one young man on work experience. Mrs Montague grinned; she now realised how Christine had arranged for the chemicals to be contaminated at Crabtree Farm. The subsequent day surveillance noticed Christine returning to the same place, carrying a shopping bag. She spent some time in the old strawberry shed with the young man and returned home. Mrs Montague contacted her agents. Christine must not end up in the papers; one scandal from this young lady is enough. Two would be outrageous, and Elizabeth R would want Mrs Montague's head on a block.

Mrs Montague standing in the surveillance room watching the cameras on Crabtree Farm. She was surprised to see her daughter sliding into bed with Donald before marriage. However, she's twenty years old; Isabella could please herself but had rather hoped she would wait. She tapped the surveillance operative's shoulder, "Turn the bedroom camera off now."

Around midnight they saw someone approaching the buildings carrying a small package. Mrs Montague noticed Donald come into focus on one of the cameras. She instructed her agent to stay hidden for the moment; otherwise, Donald may consider him a target. Donald grabbed the young man, hit him once, and he's knocked out for the count, switching on the machinery shed lights. Mrs Montague's agent quickly announced himself and explained who he was.

Mrs Montague rang Donald's mobile, confirming the man in black, her agent, would take care of the lad Donald had knocked out. Mrs Montague's agent walked over to one of Donald's tractors, removing the package of cannabis, "You were set up, Donald." Isabella came running into the machinery store holding Donald's arm. Her mobile rang, "Isabella! I thought you were waiting until you were married."

"I was mummy. You know what it's like to be held in Donald's arms; you go all mushy."

Mrs Montague chuckled, "Marry him, stop delaying Isabella."

"I brought forward the wedding, mummy, to Christmas, not long."

"Good." her mother rang off.

***

Around 9 o'clock the following day, Mrs Montague arrived at Strawberry Estate. Gerald opened the door, allowing her in. Mrs Montague strutted straight into the kitchen, sitting at the table. "Where's Christine?"

"Out on her horse; is there a problem, Mrs Montague?" Gerald asked, watching Cindy place a cup of tea on the table for Mrs Montague.

Mrs Montague exhaled, "Christine has not taken my advice. She has convinced, on two occasions, one of the boys from prison to assist her in a revenge attack on Donald Selwyn and his farm. On the first occasion, she arranged to have the chemicals used to spray the crops contaminated. My daughter, Isabella, thankfully realised the chemicals were contaminated. She has a degree in science and obviously used chemicals in the vineyards at home. Christine travelled to her mother's apartment, discovering drugs, which we presume hidden for Dixon by Josephine. Still full of spite for her mistakes, Christine convinced the young man to plant the drugs on Crabtree Farm so Donald would be convicted of meddling in narcotics. I don't think Christine realises how much trouble she's in, Gerald."

Cindy and Gerald looked at each other. Gerald remarked, "I had no idea, Mrs Montague. The whole situation is Christine's stupidity;

she's the one cheating on Donald, not the other way around. What happens now? Her children, I know she loves them dearly."

"Personally, we should lock her up and throw away the key. I think Elizabeth R would have her beheaded if the practice was still legal."

"Is there anything we can do? I think the girl's mind is twisted," Cindy expressed, extremely concerned for the children.

"All I can offer is an ankle bracelet restricting her movements, although that would not have prevented her from arranging the last two attacks on Donald. I think she will have to have psychiatric treatment. I will have her driving licence suspended until the psychiatrist satisfied Christine is no further threat. If you agree to monitor her, Gerald and Cindy, I will implement what we've discussed. If not, I'm afraid she will have to be locked away until we feel she can be released. The children will be taken into care or left with you. I suspect Donald would jump in with both feet to rescue the children and arrange for them to be cared for at Crabtree Farm."

"We agree with your suggestion," Gerald said quickly, not wanting to see Christine incarcerated and possibly lose his grandchildren.

"I think it would be wise to allow Donald to see the children; he's a good person, and the children need to know their father. You realise Donald has the money and the power to have Christine considered an unfit mother; he could take the children if he wanted through legal means. I can assure you that he would have the full support of the courts. Therefore, I suggest you treat him with utter respect, which he deserves."

Gerald exhaled, "I'm inclined to agree with you, Mrs Montague, we blamed Donald for a lot, and it's not his fault in the slightest."

Christine came into the kitchen, bluffing her way out, "Lovely to see you, Mrs Montague. I presume more trouble somewhere. What am I accused of now?" Christine smiled.

"We now have the proof concerning the contamination of chemicals and planting drugs on Donald's farm. Of course, we caught your accomplice; he will be facing more charges."

Christine nervously laughed, "Yes, I'm a mastermind; I'm off to rob the crown jewels next week."

"If you wish to stay out of prison, Christine, you will listen carefully. Gerald and Cindy have agreed to monitor you. You will have an ankle bracelet fitted, your driving licence will be suspended, and you will see a psychiatrist until he is satisfied you are well enough to be left without supervision. You will permit Donald Selwyn, the father of your children, to see them regularly. Or the alternative is to throw you in jail and stay there, not seeing your children until I remember to release you, which would be very unlikely considering your track record, Christine," Mrs Montague threatened.

"Listen! Christine to what Mrs Montague is offering; otherwise, you will lose, especially your children. Donald never harmed you. You created this situation yourself; it's over, Christine, accept the fact and move on," Cindy suggested.

Christine took a deep breath, "Okay, perhaps I need to see a psychiatrist. I may be going mad; Donald is eating me alive."

Mrs Montague commented, "Your guilty conscience eating you alive, Christine, not Donald. You can't accept that he's guilty of nothing, you've planned every sordid episode in your life, and now you will pay the price one way or another."

Mrs Montague rose from her chair, walking out of the house with her bodyguard. "Crabtree Farm, please," she ordered.

Donald came out of his mother's cottage, followed by Isabella greeting Mrs Montague with a kiss on either cheek, once on the lips. Mrs Montague hit Donald with her cane, "You don't learn, boy, do you," she grinned.

Isabella embraced her mother, "lovely to see you. Please come and have a cup of tea, mummy and explain what's happening. I'm intrigued."

Mrs Montague explained events. Donald sat shocked at how severely Mrs Montague had dealt with Christine, knowing she's of Royal blood.

"Now to the interesting part of my visit, you will be married on Christmas Eve at my castle in France; Mr Montague covers expenses.

I am quite happy to forward Elizabeth R's comment; she's over-joyed with the outcome. I'm disappointed with you, Isabella, for not waiting until you were married. I can understand Donald is out of control." Donald placed his arm around Mrs Montague's shoulder, kissing her cheek, "Hello, mummy," he laughed. Mrs Montague lashed out with her cane catching him on the knuckles. "Ouch," Donald laughed.

"You will address me Sir as Mrs Montague at all times; show some respect, Donald." Mrs Montague glanced at Isabella, "You can refrain from grinning, maintain standards, and yours are slipping by the day, Isabella."

"I apologise, Mrs Montague," Donald expressed.

"Good, I'm glad we have that settled. I will keep you appraised of arrangements. A helicopter will collect you and Donald, including your parents, flying you directly to my property in France. Good day to you both," Mrs Montague left abruptly.

Isabella frowned, "I'm twenty, not three. I wish mummy would stop treating me like a child. I suspect everything will be a formal dress, how boring. I was looking forward to marrying at Dorking Moor Estate, sorry, Donald."

"Doesn't matter where to me, providing I have you in the end, give your mother what she wants to shut her up. Give her half a dozen grandchildren to look after; she wouldn't come around so often," Donald laughed.

Mrs Montague's heading for London, listening to the conversation between Isabella and Donald, making her smile.

Isabella and Donald jumped into his American pickup truck driving to Mill Farm, finding Susan removing cobwebs from the windows as they drove past. They waved to one another and continued to the fields of wheat. Isabella jumped out, inspecting the ears of grain, "Swelling nicely, Donald, I don't think we need to apply any more fertiliser, no disease to worry about at the moment."

They return to Crabtree Farm, walking into a field of rape. "This will be early, Donald," Isabella advised, "if we're not spraying Roundup, we'll have to cut high; otherwise, too much green residue going through the combine. Perhaps we should buy a topper, a gullwing or something along those lines to cut the stubble after combining and speed up the process. Would cost next to nothing in diesel to cut the stubble shorter ready for cultivation."

"I was thinking, Isabella, we could bale the remains of the rape, and the wheat straw, perhaps sell for biofuel. I haven't costed; I thought my genius future wife would. I appreciate extra work; I don't know what it's worth."

"Like anything else, Donald depends on the quality and extra work. We have the equipment apart from the baler, but it is a horrendous price. If you're lucky, your average is about two tons to the acre, so you are looking at two thousand tons of wheat straw, providing you can bale dry enough and store. Don't forget nobody wants wet straw apart from the mushroom growers," she chuckled. "I would sooner sell the straw in the field, no layout by us."

"I see your point; a lot of hard work for minimal gain and certainly not over the first two years, I shouldn't think. I'll have to sulk!" Donald remarked, running up into his studio. Ordering two lorry loads of timber from the Forestry Commission so he could process leaving a pile to dry during the summer, ready for the approaching winter. One load would stay at Crabtree Farm, and the other goes to Mill Farm; he could easily transport the wood processor to the other farm. Donald noticed a message from Christine in his mailbox on the computer with two photos, one of Josephine and the other of Eric. Donald smiled, wishing in some respects things could have been different.

Donald sat at his easel, sketching his daughter and son onto the canvas with Christine holding one in each arm. He didn't have any bitterness towards Christine, just sad. He spent several hours painting. Isabella's in her flat working on her laptop, catching up with Donald's expenditure, which is excessive at times, on ridiculous items like an American pick-up costing over fifty thousand pounds. She couldn't help loving him for all his faults and guessed she wasn't perfect either. Isabella stayed in her own flat for the night. Donald continued painting into the early hours until he was completely satisfied.

At 6 o'clock in the morning, Donald placed his portrait of Christine and their children in the boot of his Bentley and took a deep breath, heading for London. When Isabella awoke, discovering he was gone, she rang his mobile, "Where are you, Donald?"

"Nearly in London, I'm off to see Jack. I need a painting framed."

"Why didn't you take me?"

"I couldn't sleep, so I left early; I thought you might need a rest and a break from me."

"Whatever gave you that idea, Donald, because I disagreed with you wasting more money. I'm afraid you'll have to become accustomed to that. It will happen very often. You spend money like water," she cautioned.

"Look at it this way, Isabella, it's my bloody money; I'll spend how I want to, thank you," he switched off the phone, becoming angry; she would not rule his life.

Isabella gritted her teeth, returning to her laptop and accounting. Mrs Montague had heard the conversation, concerned about Isabella applying too much pressure on Donald. She couldn't suddenly expect to jump in and rule his life. The only thing Donald had purchased which could be considered extravagant or wasteful was his American pickup truck. Everything else had a monetary value, her engagement ring, earrings, and necklace. The boy is worth millions. Why is Isabella penny-pinching?

***

Donald showed Jack his painting. "That's exquisite, Donald. Shall I send a print to Christine? What's the title, Donald?"

"My Children."

"Nothing else fitting to say," Jack patted Donald on the shoulder, "Stay strong, Donald. Life is not perfect; at least you can do what you like with yours; remember many poor people who have no choice in what they do."

Donald smiled, leaving Jack's gallery and heading home; it wasn't many minutes before the portraits on the web and bidding went straight to six million. Jack phoned Donald as he drove home, "Donald, my website has gone wild, straight to seven, no eleven million; I've never seen a portrait make so much money in such a short time."

"Thanks, Jack," Donald turned into Strawberry Estate drive, sitting in his Bentley. Donald wrote out a cheque for one million pounds from his personal account. Gerald greeted him, "Hi Donald, long time no see," he smiled.

Donald passed Gerald the cheque. Gerald stared in disbelief, "Why, after what she's done to you?"

"I can easily afford Gerald; I don't want Christine to be short of money. Hopefully, she will spend on the children."

Christine noticed from the landing Donald parked outside. She ran downstairs like the wind coming out to greet him. Gerald passed the cheque. Christine placed her hand to her mouth, bewildered, "The children are asleep now, Donald. I'm sorry, you want me to wake them?"

"No Christine, thanks, be other days," he said, driving off quickly with tears streaming down his cheeks. He couldn't bear the pain parking at the bottom of his drive, trying to regain composure before driving the last few yards.

***

"Christine, you realise you've destroyed Donald, and he still gives you money. If I had my gun, I'd bloody shoot you for what you've done to him and others."

"Believe it or not, father, I am ashamed of myself. I can't undo what happened, although I am learning to live with the pain myself."

***

Donald made his way up the drive, parking in the yard and running straight into his studio. Isabella's sat working on her computer. She turned to face him, realising he was upset for some reason; she could see where tears had run down his cheeks. She didn't say anything turning back to her computer, expecting he would explain eventually. Isabella looked on Jack's website finding the portrait Donald had taken, a painting of Christine and his two children.

She looked at the price of twelve million; Isabella shook her head in disbelief. The sums of money people would pay for art is ridiculous. Nevertheless, they would never be short of money. She checked Donald's bank account, forty-seven million. She wondered how someone with so much wealth could be so unhappy. She switched off the computer, slowly entering Donald's apartment; he was lying on his bed. Isabella made two coffees resting beside him; he sat up, "Have you looked at Jack's website?" Donald asked calmly.

She nodded. "That's why I went alone; I didn't want to upset you. I couldn't stop painting the picture, although it destroyed me inside. This will probably annoy you even more. I gave Christine one million towards the upkeep of my children."

"You just made twelve million, Donald. I don't think one million will be missed; no one will ever accuse you of not providing for your children. One of the reasons I love you so much," she said, kissing him tenderly.

Donald finished his coffee looking at his wristwatch, 5 o'clock, "Come on, Isabella, we'll have fish and chips tonight. I quite fancy, not good for the figure but great for the soul," he smiled.

Isabella grabbed her coat, holding Donald's hand; they walked to the Bentley, heading into town, casually entering their favourite chip shop, ordering their usual. Both Donald and Isabella looked in disbelief seeing Mrs Montague walk into the chip shop sitting beside Isabella, removing her glove and stealing chips with curry sauce from Isabella's plate. "Would you like a portion Mrs Montague; I will purchase gladly?" Donald offered.

She grinned, "No, thank you, Donald, young once too, you know Isabella's father and I used to nip across the field stealing the neighbour's plums," she smiled, remembering the good old times. "Occasionally, he would set his dog loose, but we never were caught. I was passing and saw your Bentley. I commend you, Donald, and your generosity. A million pounds is a considerable amount of money to give someone who's tried to ruin your life; you're very gracious. I know it's for your children; nevertheless, well done, you will never be accused of failing to provide for your loved ones. This brings me to another point, Isabella, do not criticise Donald. Most of the time, he spends wisely. We are frivolous occasionally, including you, young lady; need I remind you about the expensive bicycle you purchased? You only ever rode twice," Mrs Montague smiled.

"You have listened to private conversations, mummy."

"Yes, Isabella and I will continue to do so whether you like it or not, young lady. Someone must step in and prevent you from making a fool of yourself."

Donald ventured to the counter, ordering the same meal he had, walking out to the limousine and passing to Mrs Montague's chauffeur. "Mrs Montague sends them with her compliments." Donald smiled, watching him open the newspaper on the bonnet and start consuming. Donald returned inside laughing. Mrs Montague glared at him, "What have you said to my chauffeur- bodyguard?"

"I said you sent them out with your compliments."

Donald returned to the counter, returning with a plate for Mrs Montague. She took a deep breath removing another glove. Donald fetched four coffees and took one out to the chauffeur in a plastic cup. "Donald, you must understand that standards have to be maintained. Discipline is essential amongst the staff."

"Kindness can go a long way, Mrs Montague. I learned that many years ago. I always found if you treat people fairly, they usually return the compliment. I owed him fish and chips anyway for punching him."

"I have to say, Isabella, this fish is lovely, as good as my chef serves."

Mrs Montague had sufficient, not clearing her plate, but you could ascertain she enjoyed every mouthful. The shop owner had never seen a limousine and a Bentley parked outside his shop before; he took a photo in the doorway.

Mrs Montague wiped her mouth on a napkin, watching her chauffeur throw the empty carton and newspaper in a bin. "Thank you for the meal Donald," Mrs Montague kissed both on the cheek and left the premises. The chip shop owner came over rather excited, "You are Donald Selwyn, the artist?" he asked with an Italian accent, "And your wife?"

"Very soon," Donald smiled, standing. "We will see you again. You make lovely fish and chips," Donald expressed, leaving. They steadily drove home to find his mother and father had returned from Devon with the horsebox and Spartacus, frantically nodding his head over the stable door. Mary came from the cottage, passing them each a stick of rock. Donald laughed, "I finally have a present from my mother. I suppose you want to hear all the gossip!"

"No need, Donald. Mrs Montague has kept me appraised of events, some I found extremely shocking. We are flying to France for the wedding. That should be an experience I've never been abroad."

Isabella remarked, "You will really enjoy yourself, Mary. The wine will be flowing, that's for sure, and you probably, gain a stone in weight; we all will. Banquet after banquet, if I know my father and two hundred guests, nobody knows only him and mother."

"Put your foot down," Mary suggested, "You're twenty years old, Isabella, not a baby; you choose where you want the venue and who you want at your wedding. If they don't like it, tough luck. I know Donald would tell them for sure."

"I can't do that to my father, Mary; he's recently recovered from cancer. I don't want to stress him anymore; a small sacrifice to give happiness to my father."

"I'd forgotten," Donald expressed, "I would do the same; a few months to go, things may change, you don't know."

"The only change is we are married, nothing else," Isabella assured.

"Why are you back early, mother? I thought you were on holiday, a retreat with Spartacus and my father," Donald inquired.

Mary grinned, "We wanted to check the crops are looked after; this is still our farm Donald. You don't own everything, son, until we are six-foot underground."

"Oh, I think I need to move to my own residence." Donald stormed out of the cottage; Isabella shrugged her shoulders, following him. "Once again, my true love," Martin remarked, "That big gob of yours has made a smashing job of wrecking a good working relationship. You allow him to run the farm one minute; you jump on him the next. I think you need to see a psychiatrist, woman."

Isabella followed Donald upstairs into the studio, "Take no notice Donald, parents are all the same. One-minute father allows me to plan the planting of vines, and the next, he jumps all over my plans," Isabella exhaled.

"No, this is a good opportunity to move to Mill Farm; leave them to cope."

"What about the equipment?"

"They've had the insurance money from the fire. They can buy their own bloody equipment; I'm moving what I purchased to Mill Farm."

The following day the first lorry load of timber arrived from the Forestry Commission. Donald had the driver unload around the rear of the buildings. Donald phoned Susan, explaining a lorry load of wood from the Forestry Commission arriving. Could she ask him to unload by the woodshed? Donald removed the wood processor on the back of one of his new tractors processing the lorry load of timber in half an hour. Donald folded the wood processor into transport mode to travel down the road. Isabella followed him with the loader; they processed the timber delivered into a massive pile of blocks by the woodshed on Mill Farm. Donald returned the processor to Crabtree Farm. Isabella left the loader in one of the buildings; she travelled back with Donald, "Are you sure, a little drastic, Donald."

"Yes," he said abruptly, backing up to a grain trailer. Isabella started the other tractor, attached to a grain trailer; everything transported Donald had purchased to Mill Farm within three hours. The storage facility on Mill Farm for large equipment was more spacious, and he could easily park all his new toys. Donald checked the diesel tank by the building; he was given a key for the tap to prevent people from stealing. He checked the tank almost empty. The previous owner had informed him would hold at least eight thousand gallons. Donald ordered five thousand gallons to play safe. Donald and Isabella walked across the fields to collect their vehicles and clothes.

Donald decided to convert one of the bedrooms into an art studio in Mill House. Neither Mary nor Martin came out to challenge or ask Donald what was happening. Martin walked around the buildings seeing everything's gone apart from the wood processor and his Ferguson twenty. Martin sighed heavily. Mary came to join him, "Oh well, better buy yourself an old tractor and combine; our son has flown the nest or fallen out on his head. Silly boy, you could never say anything to him without having a reaction."

"No, I'm not buying bloody equipment. I'll ask Gerald if we can work out a deal; I quite like being lazy. I've done my time on tractors unless you want to go and buy something Mary, you want to drive; because I won't," Martin stormed off towards the cottage.

Isabella at Mill farm selected her own bedroom with a lock on the door. "I thought we would sleep together, Isabella."

"Not until we're married." Donald started setting up a room as an art studio, collecting all his art equipment from his old studio. Neither Mary nor Martin tried to talk to him, he'd made his decision, and they were leaving him to it. Donald had arranged for Susan to clean; his mother could let the room gain more income as a penthouse suite affair.

***

Christine's taken once a week to a private psychiatrist. Cindy would shop for an hour while Christine received her treatment. The psychiatrist in his fifties was a well-respected man in his field. Christine's determined to regain her driving licence and freedom; she's far from finished on her quest to recover what she believed belonged to her, Donald.

She remembered her mother had advised her to use anyone to achieve what she wanted. She visited the psychiatrist for several weeks, dressing a little more revealing each time. Christine made sure she looked as attractive as possible, giving an innocent appearance. She visited the loo before her session, removed her bra, made sure her cleavage was visible and removed her knickers. She entered the psychiatrist's office after called. She smiled pleasantly, crossing her legs, making sure her thigh was visible to him. As far as she's concerned, a man is a man like her mother had said. They could all be manipulated one way or another, especially if you were attractive.

The psychiatrist asked her how she felt about Donald and her situation. Christine explained she was no longer interested in Donald. She needed to move on with her children to find someone, settle down and start a new life. Christine could see how he looked at her figure; she guessed it wouldn't be long before she had her own way.

***

Isabella would visit Crabtree Farm and ride Spartacus. Donald refused to step foot in the place. He still believed they were wrong whether they owned the property or not; he's running the show, providing them with an income. He thought it was unfair of them to rub in his face that he didn't actually own Crabtree Farm entirely. Isabella returned from riding Spartacus. "Ridiculous, Donald, you can't keep feuding with your parents."

"I'm not feuding with anyone; my property that is theirs. Are you happy to continue sharing Spartacus? Or do you want me to buy you a horse?"

Isabella said nothing. She was fuming with his attitude; she strutted into the lounge watching television. Time's moving on nearly the end of June. The harvest wasn't far away; somehow, she would have to get people talking again; although his parents weren't much help, they were as stubborn as he is.

***

Christine prepared herself to visit the psychiatrist; Cindy drove her into town. Christine entered the private facility and was finally allowed in to see him. Christine lay on the couch. She'd already removed her knickers and bra. Decided to gamble by the way he was looking at her. She slowly unbuttoned her blouse, parting. She parted her legs, raised her skirt, felt his hand between her legs, closed her eyes, and the rest is history. He's like a raging bull, never treated like this before. After a while, they both tidied their selves. Christine kissed him passionately on the lips for an old man she thought that's some experience, "See you next week," she smiled, leaving.

***

Donald looked at his blank canvas, desperate to paint, but nothing came to mind. He came downstairs sitting in the lounge beside Isabella, watching a soap, bored stupid. Isabella cuddled up to him. He placed his arm around her, drifting off to sleep on the settee. They awoke in the early hours when the fire had burnt down. Donald threw more logs on the fire, trying to rekindle the dying embers. He exhaled, "I suppose I will have to give in; I'm not moving to Crabtree Farm. I like it here."

"That's a sensible decision, Donald; now you can have your reward," she grinned, lying on the carpet, receiving half an hour of vigorous sex, almost sending her crazy with exhilaration. Isabella drove to Crabtree Farm the following day, feeding Spartacus with Mary, "Don't worry about the harvest, Mary. I've taken care of it."

Mary grinned, "I guessed you would. Men are all the same pig-headed and stupid." Mary walked off into the house, grinning. Isabella assessed at the beginning of August that the rapeseed would be ready for harvesting. Donald prepared the combine attaching two trailers to the 400 hp tractors and the third trailer to his Quadtrac 600 hp.

***

Christine continued her visits to the psychiatrist, which now became a routine; she would walk in, remove her clothes and lay on the couch. She had to admit that she enjoyed how he made love to her, although she preferred Donald. They dressed, kissing passionately for a moment. "I think you can now visit Christine once a month; otherwise, people may become suspicious. You can have your driving license reactivated and your ankle bracelet removed. I don't consider you dangerous any longer," he smiled.

Christine kissed him again, "You won't regret it, doctor, thank you," she kissed lovingly on the lips enjoying her last few weeks immensely. She'd never been made love to that way before, although she preferred Donald.

***

Donald started to combine the oilseed rape on Crabtree Farm. Isabella operated the trailers transporting the seed to storage. By the end of the day, fifty acres were cut. Donald returned the combine to Mill Farm, notifying Seven Trent to begin spreading sewerage on Crabtree Farm's fields.

The following day, Donald saw the umbilical cord running across the field and sewerage injected into the ground. They had changed the system from the previous year. Instead of spraying, now inject, trying to curb some of the smell after receiving complaints from a nearby town if the winds were blowing the wrong way. Donald thought they had little to complain about, considering they created most of the manure. Donald's surprised neither his mother nor father ventured into the field while he was harvesting.

Donald attached his ten-furrow reversible plough to his Quadtrac articulated tractor and the other ten furrow reversible plough to Isabella's tractor. The following day, he and Isabella started ploughing, following one another up and down the same furrow with their reversible ploughs. Acres vanished in minutes.

Gerald sat on the side of the road in his Range Rover, watching these two enormous tractors performing, admiring Donald's decisions regarding equipment. Donald and Isabella had to wait for a day, allowing sewerage to be injected into the ground on the rest of the field before they ploughed. Although three tankers were on the road transporting, there were traffic issues at certain times of the day. Nevertheless, within a week, everything had been injected with sewerage. Isabella and Donald had ploughed fifty acres; they parked their tractors in the shed, hugging each other, dashing into the shower together, enjoying their intimate moments.

***

Mrs Montague had received the psychiatrist's report stating Christine's obsession with Donald was under control. He recommended her driving licence be returned and her ankle bracelet removed, which showed they trusted her. This would speed the healing process from her traumatic experiences. Mrs Montague sanctioned Christine could now drive, and the horrible ankle bracelet was removed. Although Christine still paid monthly visits to the psychiatrist, which would continue for a year as a safeguard, Christine didn't mind. They enjoyed sex together every time.

***

Donald greased the combine, starting to cut the wheat on Crabtree Farm. Two hundred and fifty acres vanished in the day, and he moved on to Mill Farm. Isabella transported the grain to the storage facility, checking the moisture content. Donald's combine performed excellently, managing over two hundred acres a day. Not cutting too low to the ground so he could travel faster, the monitors kept him informed of his progress. Within seven days, the harvest finished the grain store heaving; Donald had never seen so much grain in one place other than on Gerald's estate. Donald and Isabella were heading towards town, noticing Christine driving one of her Lexions combines; she waved, and they waved to be polite. Donald notified Seven Trent they could now apply sewerage.

Isabella and Donald sat in their favourite chip shop, watching Isabella's mother park outside. She allowed her chauffeur inside; he purchased fish and chips and sat at a secluded table. Mrs Montague ordered herself a portion of fish and chips, sitting with Donald and Isabella. "Apart from the noise around the buildings from machinery, what's happening? I thought I would advise you; that Christine is considered well enough to return her driving licence and remove her ankle bracelet. The psychiatrist feels he only needs to see her once a month for another year."

"That's good news," Donald expressed, "I hope she finds what she's looking for out of life. I wish her every success."

"I've spoken to your father concerning your wedding; you're not happy, Isabella? You think all pomp and ceremony, and your father will invite his old cronies you wouldn't recognise."

"Yes, mummy, I don't want to be horrible to daddy; he's recovering from cancer."

"You finished harvest; I know you have to prepare the ground and plant, with your equipment won't take long. I suggest you and Donald meet with your father, Isabella and me to discuss what you'd like. I think you should hold the venue in France, your place of birth."

Donald laughed, "I didn't realise I'm marrying a French bird; you speak perfect English."

Even Mrs Montague had to laugh. "Donald, you are crazy. You agree with my suggestion, the pair of you?"

"I think it would be advisable, Isabella, if we travel to France now. Leave Seven Trent to spread the sewerage; we can't plough until they are ahead of us."

"Excellent, Donald," Mrs Montague voiced cheerfully.

"We can drive over tonight, Isabella," Donald remarked, excited about the trip.

"I suppose we can share the driving; it won't take too long on the shuttle," everyone finished eating, including the chauffeur, who smiled at Donald. Donald kissed Mrs Montague on the lips. She hit him with her cane shaking her head in annoyance.

Donald called in at the local garage and filled his Bentley to the brim heading to Mill Farm; they packed a few clothes and headed for the shuttle. Texting Mary and Martin of their destination along with Susan. By 10 o'clock the following day, they arrived at Mrs Montague's castle. Isabella's driving, and Donald's asleep in the passenger seat. She parked the Bentley on the gravel outside the front of the stately home. Waking Donald as her father came out, Rupert escorted them to their separate rooms, making Isabella grin. They both freshened; Isabella knocked and entered Donald's room, kissing him softly, "Don't worry, Donald, once we are married, just you and me, none of this pomp and ceremony."

Mrs Montague's listening to the conversation, realising they would have to tread carefully even with their daughter. Otherwise, the wedding could explode in their face, and they wouldn't achieve what they had set out for Isabella. They sat around a large table, having lunch. Donald wondered where to start, such a variety of choices. Isabella's father spoke calmly, "I understand from your mother, Isabella, you would prefer a quiet wedding and, according to your expression, none of my pompous arses, attending the ceremony?"

"Daddy, this is my day and Donald's, not your friends. I'm quite happy to have the wedding here. However, I had planned for Dorking Moor Estate, the reason for that location making it easier for Donald's family and friends to attend. I'm not Royalty father, and I don't need a lavish wedding. I have no need to prove anything to anyone; I'm my own person."

"Well said, Isabella," her mother remarked. "Nevertheless, certain standards have to be maintained. Otherwise, Elizabeth R will be breathing down our necks. She's rather fond of Donald; although she has never met him, she admires his artwork and how he conducts himself. The wedding will be broadcast and videoed for posterity; the only daughter of Rupert Montague marrying Donald Selwyn, the artist."

Isabella looked at Donald with everyone watching him crush nuts in his bare hands without using a nutcracker. "Your opinion, Donald, do you have any preferences?"

Rupert Montague interrupted abruptly, "Doesn't matter what Donald thinks; he will have to do as he's told on this occasion!"

Mrs Montague closed her eyes, realising that if Donald hit her husband, he would die. Isabella glared at her father, "How dare you speak to him like dirt. He's not one of your servants' father, and neither am I."

Donald quietly rose from the table; Isabella ran after him, walking out of the room. "Take me home, Donald. We'll arrange our own marriage," upset with her father's comment.

Rupert Montague rose from the table, "ill-mannered commoner, couldn't she find someone better. He has no breeding."

"Isabella will now marry Donald not here, in England without either of us attending. This situation might have been avoided if you'd used your brains instead of your mouth."

Within ten minutes, Donald and Isabella were heading for the channel tunnel. "That was interesting; perhaps you should find somebody else, Isabella, more suited to your standing in life," Donald suggested.

Isabella glared at him, "What are you saying, Donald? You don't want me? If that's the case, I will collect my belongings from your farm and drive home to France."

"I think you're a fish out of water, Isabella; you're used to mixing with snobby people. I'm not; they don't interest me. I'm not kissing anybody's arse, including your mother and father; I've tolerated their crap because of you. That stops right now! You're either with me or bugger off back to France."

"We are staying together, Donald; I don't think it's necessary to insult my parents unduly. They are old school, used to that way of life. They don't live in the same world as ordinary people, and you must accept that fact."

"I'm not here to be insulted, Isabella; I will not accept orders from your father. I'm definitely not his servant and never will be."

"I don't expect you to be his servant or anybody else's. Let's work out our own marriage plans. We have time. I will send an invitation to my mother and father. They can either come or not," Isabella commented resolutely.

Donald and Isabella took turns, finally arriving home at Mill Farm. Susan was surprised to see them both. Donald explained why. "You can't expect anything else, Donald," Susan advised, "You're not even on their radar; you are scum unless you have a title with those sorts of people." Donald immediately kissed Susan, taking her by surprise. "I have a title, I'm a laird, I own an estate in Scotland. I'm not common rubbish!" Isabella's standing in the doorway into the lounge listening to him and Susan talking. "See, Donald, you have a title."

Donald watched the tankers drive through the yard carrying sewage to the umbilical cord spreading on the harvested wheat fields. Isabella immediately designed and ordered a thousand cards with Donald's title and status to be printed and sent to Mill Farm. "I've notified mummy and daddy of your status Donald, and advised, we are marrying at Dorking Moor Estate, your property and mine shortly as your wife."

***

Mrs Montague read the email along with Rupert Montague; fuming, especially Rupert, he realised Donald had a title and would have handled the situation differently. However, they would have to make the best of a bad situation no good crying over spilt milk. "Stay out of it, Rupert; I will see if I can mend fences in a couple of days. If not you will have to travel to Scotland for the wedding at Christmas when they're marrying. It's a pity it's not in August, then the midges would remind you to keep your mouth shut," Mrs Montague stormed off.

***

Early the following day, Donald started ploughing the two hundred and fifty acres of wheat stubble at Crabtree Farm, moving on to the thousand acres of wheat stubble treated with sewage. Isabella joined him later with her tractor and plough. Mary's watching from Donald's abandoned studio with binoculars seeing the two ploughing. She wondered why they had returned from France so early, suspecting something had gone wrong. Curiosity is killing her; she jumped in her Range Rover driving to Mill Farm into the field where Donald and Isabella were ploughing. They parked on the headland, leaving their tractor cabs after stopping the engines. Mary stepped out of her Range Rover, hugging Isabella first and then Donald pinching his cheek. "Come on, you two spill the beans. Who upset who?" Isabella explained.

Mary laughed, "I wish I were there to see your face, Donald. Lucky Mr Montague is an old man you'd have sat him on his arse, like Martin. So, what are your plans now?"

Isabella explained, "Donald actually has a title. He's a laird because he owns an estate. We are having the wedding at Dorking Moor Estate where I wanted originally. I've invited both my parents and rubbed it in their faces. Donald has a title; that's all I can say, Mary. We still haven't decided everything."

"For curiosity Donald, what are you planting at Crabtree Farm this year?"

"Wheat, you should have a good wheat crop once replanted, which will occur before October. We will plough my thousand-plus acres here and plant with rape. That will give these fields a break from constant wheat-growing; do you agree, Isabella?" Donald asked.

"Yes, we can use some of Crabtree Farm's rapeseed to plant a thousand acres here and some wheat seed from here to plant Crabtree Farm. We need to have treated, which I'll arrange for tomorrow. Please don't sell any of your oilseed rape, Mary."

"Wasn't intending to, or Martin, we're making you two earn your money for a change," Mary grinned, climbing into her Range Rover, "When you two feel we are good enough to visit, please come for tea," she smiled driving off.

Donald's relieved he's now on speaking terms with his mother. He gave Isabella a kiss and a hug. They climbed aboard their machines, continuing to plough until 5:30 p.m., parking the equipment in the shed. They drove to Crabtree Farm. Mary had anticipated they would come making one of her lovely cakes. Martin's smiling: he'd had a few glasses of cider. Donald's passed a large slice of cake which he devoured eagerly; Isabella had a smaller portion; nevertheless, the plate cleared. "I've had a phone call from your mother, Isabella; she wants me to persuade you two to have a wedding in France. I explained I couldn't. You can have your wedding wherever makes you happy. Hopefully, the only wedding you have. So why should you change your plans for anyone else? It's your day."

"I suspect that went down like a mouthful of mustard, Mary."

Mary shrugged, "Can't be helped, the truth."

The following day Donald and Isabella continued ploughing until they finished by the end of the week. Donald attached the two large power harrows to the 400 hp Case IH tractors. Isabella, ahead of him, destination Crabtree Farm, wasn't long before they had prepared three hundred acres for drilling. Isabella had a company treat sufficient oilseed rape and wheat seed ready for planting. Donald attached the enormous drill to the tractor. Isabella drilled the three hundred acres quickly within a day on Crabtree Farm.

Donald had already started preparing a thousand acres on Mill Farm for planting with oilseed rape. Isabella began planting the next day until she caught up with Donald, joining him with the other power harrows until they had finished preparing for drilling. Isabella continued drilling until the work was completed. The last week was hectic, barely had a moment's peace having to refill the diesel storage tank.

Isabella's mother arrived at Mill Farm. Donald and Isabella had finished their lunch prepared by Susan, who had gone home. Mrs Montague entered, looking at them both, suggesting, "You appear to have me over a barrel. What must I do for the wedding to take place in France?" she asked calmly, "Your father is beside himself, regretting what he said to you, Donald."

"Nothing you can say or do, mummy. I've decided the wedding will be held at Dorking Moor Estate Hotel where all our friends can easily travel. Not your day, mother; it's mine and Donald's."

"Your father and I will not attend the wedding in Scotland, Isabella. A wretched place, the midges eat you alive how Elizabeth R tolerates the place, I don't know."

"You will not bribe me, mummy; I'm sure someone will give me away. I have a closer relationship with Mrs Selwyn than ever with you mummy! If that's what you call a good upbringing, I'm bewildered you couldn't wait to place me in a convent school."

Mrs Montague walked out the door and climbed into her limousine, disappearing down the road. "That went down like a ton of bricks," Donald remarked.

"I don't care, Donald, I have what I want, and that's all that matters. I think we are good together; we complement each other in work and love," she grinned, "That reminds me, your business cards arrived." Isabella opened the box, placing six in Donald's wallet. He looked at one, "Donald Selwyn Laird of Dorking Moor Estate Hotel and Artist." He grinned. Donald started kissing Isabella's neck. She smiled, "I know what you're after," holding his hand and leading him upstairs.

Donald hadn't bothered to celebrate his birthday; he was too busy and didn't want to know he was a year older. Isabella hadn't realised they were so preoccupied deciding what to do about the wedding. "Pack your bags; we'll go to Dorking Moor for a week. I need time to unwind," Donald suggested. "I'm fed up with people trying to organise my life and yours." The following day, they set off for Dorking Moor Estate sharing the driving, making the trip much more manageable.

***

Christine drove to London to stay in her mother's old flat. She now realised the place bugged after the drugs episode, the only way Mrs Montague could have found out. Christine visited the casino where she'd won fifty thousand pounds on a slot machine. She realised gambling's a waste of time unless you were extremely fortunate to pick the suitable game to play or a device which paid out occasionally to keep the punters interested.

She had only taken fifty pounds in cash with her, playing one or two slot machines and noticing a young man watching her. Anyone in here she anticipated was up to no good; she didn't think he's a bouncer wasn't big enough, more like security. She started grinning at his persistence; he wasn't bad looking, not much older than her. He Finally approached, " Christine Gibbs, I believe?"

Christine looked somewhat puzzled, "Yes, how would you know me?"

"We have a mutual friend; he worked on your father's estate. My younger brother on work experience; you wouldn't know his name because he wouldn't have given you. Although he tried to assist you in certain matters, shall we say."

"You don't look much older than him; he's very kind. We didn't exchange any details, he said, better that way. What happened to him?"

"Nothing, we can't figure out why? He was charged, sent to prison for about three weeks, released on good behaviour and told not to be a naughty boy again, not permitted to return to your farm to continue his work experience."

"That's odd." Christine knew immediately Mrs Montague had something to do with the decision to cover up.

"Where are you staying? My nickname is Titch."

"In my apartment, however, I think it's bugged; that's how they found out about your brother, I suspect. How old are you?" Christine asked curiously.

"Twenty-five on my last count," he smirked, "We'll go somewhere, no cameras, let me leave first, and you follow five minutes later; I'll meet you on the street. If you'd like me to complete my brother's offer to help, I will. Your apartment isn't bugged. You're not important enough anybody would think your Royalty."

Christine watched Titch leave, realising this may be a golden opportunity, but at what cost to acquire what she wanted.

Christine left the casino casually, walking down the street. A taxi pulled alongside, the door opened Titch, and she climbed in. The cab took them into the back streets of London. Titch paid the taxi driver escorting a nervous Christine into an old bedsit where Titch lived. "No bugs in here. You can say what you like. I don't like my brother set up, I know it wasn't you, and you didn't say anything to anybody else; otherwise, I'd have found out I have a lot of connections. From what my brother told me, Donald Selwyn, who just happens to be a famous bloody artist, stitched you up, got you pregnant and ran for the hills, leaving you with nothing but two kids. However, you're not penniless by any means. It's still a dirty trick. You want him dead, crippled or what?" Titch asked seriously.

"I don't think Donald's the problem, a girl he's with, Isabella Montague. If she was to disappear, he might reconsider."

"My friends have heard of her; there are certain people you don't touch. Otherwise, opens the gates of hell and would ruin businesses thriving around London unnoticed. You better have Donald's hands chopped off; he'd be buggered."

Christine stood, "I might as well go," she sighed heavily, "Nothing anyone can do about the situation. I don't want Donald injured; I'm very much in love with him. Isabella, I wouldn't give a damn what happened to her; I'd shoot her myself, only I haven't a rifle. We only have shotguns at the farm."

"You are not thinking straight, Christine. You want an untraceable rifle and lightweight. A two-two will do the job from quite some distance if you hit her in the head."

"Where do I acquire one of those from, and what will it cost me?" Christine asked, disillusioned.

"Acquiring, you leave to me; my brother mentioned the old strawberry shed can be left there for you to collect along with ammunition. Remember to wear gloves. You can't have your fingerprints found, including on the bullets. Throw in an old pond, a deep one when you've finished. Some on the farm don't disturb the embankment and leave any footprints. The police will have dogs everywhere, but they can't sense stuff underwater. I shouldn't think they would drain ponds, especially if you have more than one and don't look disturbed."

"How much?" Christine asked nervously.

"Thousand-five hundred will cover the rifle and half a dozen bullets because if you can't hit her with the first one in the head, five more won't matter unless you hit her in the heart."

Titch started removing Christine's clothes, not resisting staying for the night, allowing him to take his pleasure several times. Her mother's right: part your legs, and young men will do anything, even if they bore you unless they were Donald.

***

Isabella and Donald arrived at Dorking Moor Hotel, entering their private suite and changing for dinner. Jenkins fussing trying to impress Donald and Isabella. Donald called him over, "Jenkins, calm down. You're starting to look an idiot."

Mr Jenkins glared at him, leaving the dining room. "I don't think you'll see him again tonight, Donald," Isabella commented.

They finished their meal, had a few drinks at the bar and retired to bed.

The following day Isabella decides to ride with Emily and several of the guests around the estate, enjoying the fresh air, and trying to avoid the midges. The deer roaming free, grouse taking off gliding across the heather and open moorland. Donald drove to Glencoe Estate, finding Justin in the office. "How are things Justin," Donald asked brightly.

"They were fine until you upset Jenkins; you realise he used to work for the Hilton group; he's paid to fuss," Justin advised.

"I don't like someone hovering over me like a praying mantis when I'm trying to eat. Straighten Jenkins out or replace him," Donald ordered, annoyed, walking out of the office. Donald continued walking towards the waterwheel, something he loved to watch.

Donald glanced across, seeing the JCB digging a trench across a stretch of ground, suspecting Robbie, draining more land to supply hay for the animals. Jock came down in his truck. Donald climbed in, "How are you this morning, Jock?"

"The Assistant manager at Dorking, he's stuck-up. Donald doesn't represent the Scottish traditions. I'd shoot him by mistake as a peacock." Donald laughing. "It's all right for you, Donald. We have to work with the bugger. Emily is a wonderful girl; she treats the horses excellently. Jenkins keeps trying to skimp to maximise profits, which is okay, but not for the animals or staff."

"Drive to the office, Jock." Jock parked his truck outside the hotel. Justin came out. "Repeat to Justin what you've told me this morning Jock," Jock explained.

Justin's horrified, "I didn't realise you're the first to speak out, Jock. I will deal with the situation immediately." Justin jumped in his Land Rover, heading for Dorking Moor Estate Hotel.

Donald looked at his watch, "11 o'clock, Jock, I think a little dram is in order, and you keep speaking your mind, Jock. You're the only one I can rely on around here. Otherwise, the place would be in rack and ruin if we had cowboys working for us." Jock smiled. "Don't smile, Jock; it worries me when you're happy." They both went inside to have a small whisky.

Donald returned to Dorking Moor Estate Hotel to find Maggie's car parked outside and Mr Jenkins driving away. Isabella stood in the hallway, talking to Maggie and Justin. "Look out, Donald," Maggie advised, "I'm the manager while my father finds a replacement for that idiot. I promised to tuck you in bed every night," she winked, watching the expression of thunder appear on Isabella's face. "If there's any tucking in Maggie, I'll do it with Donald," she emphasised. Justin left laughing, returning to Glencoe Estate.

CHAPTER TWENTY-TWO

FINALISING THE DEAL

Christine made her way to a mother's apartment in the early hours, wondering if she was going too far killing someone, which seemed drastic. Although if she wanted Donald, maybe the only option left, providing she could escape prosecution. Christine visited a cashpoint in the evening, heading for the casino. Titch is there. She passed him the money discreetly and left, returning to her mother's apartment. She set off home early the following day to Strawberry Estate, convinced she's followed. Ensured she didn't break the speed limit or do anything silly on the road to attract unwanted attention.

***

Maggie changed into her manager's uniform, matching everyone else in the hotel beside the nametag displaying her title. Donald thought the staff seemed to be more relaxed, definitely less tension in the air, except when Maggie passed him pinching his bum, which Isabella saw. Donald displayed an embarrassed expression, watching Maggie laugh as she walked behind the bar talking to the staff. "Donald, you dare go near Maggie, and we are finished," Isabella whispered.

Donald glanced at her pinching her backside. She jumped, realising Donald's to blame, "Not in public, Donald; if you want my body, take me to bed, don't tease." Donald threw Isabella over his shoulder; Isabella was speechless, watching everyone laugh in the bar as he carried her upstairs. He opened the suite door, throwing her on the bed. She giggled, never experiencing anything like this, although embarrassed at the outset. They stayed there together for some time, enjoying each other's company.

After the evening meal, Isabella and Donald sat with Maggie to organise the wedding. Once he knew how many of his friends wanted to come, Donald would book seats on an aeroplane for Inverness. The guests could be collected from and brought to the hotel. Party all night and return home the next day, he would cover the expense of the flights and hire a minibus to collect and return to the airport. Donald and Isabella decided on a buffet-style wedding; it made everything simpler. People could help themselves and not be forced to eat what they didn't like, which Donald considered waste and Isabella.

The wedding would be held at noon, giving everybody a chance to arrive from the airport. The flight home would leave at 10 pm the next day, returning everyone home. "Maggie," Donald asked, "Make sure all the hotel staff are permitted to share in the celebration. I appreciate you can't leave Glencoe unattended; perhaps staff could spend an hour here and then swap and let the other half come. Under no circumstances are they to spend their money on a present for Isabella and me. They need their hard-earned money for themselves."

"We need to know numbers, Donald, so the chef prepares sufficient food." Maggie telephoned the vicar, "Would like to book you for the first of December, 12 o'clock at Dorking Moor Estate to conduct the ceremony between Donald Selwyn and Isabella Montague. I presume you will be free?"

"I suppose I'd better; Donald destroyed the last ceremony I was conducting. Will he definitely be marrying this girl, or will he throw another tantrum?"

"Choose your words carefully, vicar," Maggie advised, "The only one likely to afford the church repairs is Donald Selwyn. Otherwise, you'll probably find the church is sold for private dwellings, and you'll be shipped off to some island where there's no heating."

"Point taken, my child, god's cheque book does not receive many donations these days." .

Donald took the receiver from Maggie. "Donald Selwyn here, Sir, price your roof repairs and inform Maggie; I'll see if I can arrange for repairs. I'd hate my favourite vicar to go damp."

"Thank you, Mr Selwyn. I look forward to seeing you at twelve noon on the first of December, good day, Sir."

Maggie laughed, "I don't know why you're bothering to marry, only a piece of paper. The vicars are corrupt like anybody else; he knows when his bread is buttered. He comes here for a few drams knowing the visitors will buy him several drinks."

"Send the vicar a crate of whisky with my compliments. Put it on my tab that should cheer him up," Donald chuckled. "When are you marrying Maggie?" Donald asked curiously.

"You haven't asked me, Donald; I've waited for a long time," she joked.

"Be serious, Maggie," Donald laughed, watching Isabella fuming.

"I've decided not to marry were living together; neither of us wants children and happy with our arrangement. Don't fix what isn't broken."

Donald and Isabella return to their suite. Isabella using her laptop, emailed her mother with the date and time of the wedding. "She probably won't come just to spite me. I don't care; I have my life ahead of me with a wonderful man if I can keep Maggie out of your bed."

Donald was puzzled at her remark. "Yes, Donald, I know Maggie would be in your bed in seconds. I remember the first visit to Scotland together. I heard her creep into your room before we went out; otherwise, I wouldn't be here now."

Donald sat quiet nothing he could say the truth. They stayed one more night and slowly drove home to Mill Farm. Isabella wasn't surprised she hadn't heard anything from her mother or father, suspecting they wouldn't come. When they arrived at Mill Farm, Susan was in the kitchen. Donald carried the suitcases upstairs. Isabella stood by Susan talking. The next minute a sound of breaking glass. A bullet had come through the window into the kitchen.

Donald came running downstairs after hearing Isabella scream, finding Susan lying on the kitchen floor. He immediately pulled Isabella down out of sight of the window. Donald checked Susan for vital signs; she was breathing. The bullet had grazed her head, nothing else. He phoned the police. Within minutes an armed response team were on the farm. Donald explained nervously, using his mobile. They are on the kitchen floor, the door's unlocked, they could enter no one other than him, Isabella, and Susan, in the house.

CHAPTER TWENTY-THREE

THE HUNT

Police had soon secured the farm, and a police helicopter airborne, arm response team burst into the house, searching every room. An ambulance crew finally attended, taking Susan away underarm guard. Donald thought something from a movie seen. A police officer noticed the bullet had lodged in the door jamb after striking Susan on the side of her head.

The police immediately tracked Christine Gibbs, discovering she was on a monthly visit with her psychiatrist. They burst into his consulting room, finding him and Christine naked and having sex on the couch. Christine quickly dressed, explaining she had been here for the last hour with Dr Roberts, her boyfriend. Dr Roberts played along with her story, realising it would look better from his point of view regarding his position as a psychiatrist. The police were somewhat surprised Christine was not involved in the assassination attempt. Now left with no suspect.

Donald phoned the glaziers insisting bullet-proof glass fitted to the downstairs windows. Donald and Isabella were informed that Susan had regained consciousness in the hospital, a near miss. The police returned to Donald, asking him to list enemies or people he may have upset. Donald couldn't think of anyone other than Christine. Donald remarked, "Has the hallmarks of Christine's marksmanship. She couldn't hit the backside of a bus when we were on her shoot. If she's aiming for Isabella, that would explain why she hit Susan instead."

They noticed from the window a helicopter landing. Mrs Montague and her bodyguard came towards the house. They looked to the window, observing her daughter having a whisky at the kitchen table. They walked in, "You can't stay here, Isabella, too dangerous," Mrs Montague ordered.

"I'm not going anywhere without Donald. We have no idea who they were after; I don't have any enemies, only Christine, same as Donald."

Mrs Montague made a cup of coffee for everybody, realising she may persuade her daughter and Donald to hold the wedding in France, a more secure location. After making everyone a drink, Mrs Montague talked to the chief of police on-site. He explained where Christine was, which ruled her out; no way she could travel the distance in time. That didn't mean to say she had not organised something. However, after checking her bank records, the most she spent recently was one thousand five hundred pounds which she took to the casino according to the cameras.

Forensic removed a bullet from the wooden door jamb and reported to the chief of police and Mrs Montague. A 2.2 bullet not usually an assassin's choice of weapon. Nothing's adding up; Mrs Montague returned to the kitchen. "Perhaps you should reconsider your location for the wedding? France would be far more secure with the number of staff we have," she suggested crossing her fingers.

Isabella's making toast for herself and Donald, "I will not be bullied; how do you know the bullet was for me, mother? It may have been for Susan considering her husband is a criminal. Has anyone thought of that possibility?"

Mary and Martin were finally permitted onto the farm, joining everyone else in the kitchen, slightly panicking, observing armed police. Donald explained the chain of events. Mary exhaled, "A professional would not have missed; I shouldn't imagine. They weren't after Donald. He's upstairs, so it's one of the two girls," Mary surmised. "How close together were you two?" Mary asked, looking at Isabella for an answer.

Isabella moved from her stool, standing on a flagstone tile, "I was here, Susan slightly to my right and two tiles forward by the sink. We were virtually in line depending on where the gun's fired." The police officer noted what Isabella had said, looking at the hole in the glass on the small window pane. He walked out of the door crossing a ten-acre field. Within a few minutes, forensics stood by the hedge. A policeman had obviously discovered where the bullet was fired from.

The television stations were alive with the event. A news helicopter took aerial views of Donald's property, which Donald thought wouldn't help matters if another attempt. Donald laughed nervously, "At least Susan's okay; she will probably make a few pounds out of this selling her story to the press."

***

Dr Roberts cancelled his appointments for the day, whispering in Christine's ear, "follow me in my black BMW." Christine left sitting in her black Range Rover, watching Dr Roberts leave the practice. She followed him for several miles, parking outside a large house. He opened the door inviting Christine in. Christine surmised he obviously wasn't short of money, noticing an indoor swimming pool through the glass. "Thank you, Christine, you save my career; suggesting we were in a relationship means I can't be dismissed. I may be disciplined, but that's all."

Christine smiled, "To be quite honest, I enjoy my time with you. You're gentle and fulfilling," she said, taking her clothes off and jumping in the pool, "What are you waiting for, boyfriend? I never had my full hour of treatment," she chuckled.

Dr Roberts removed his clothes, joining her in the pool, enjoying their time together immensely. Christine thought he may be old, but he knew what to do, which made her feel fantastic, and that's all that mattered to her.

***

The glaziers arrived, repairing the window while waiting for the bullet-resistant glass. Most of the police officers had gone, including the helicopter. Whoever is the assassin had covered their tracks. Susan would be released in the morning from the hospital, suffering no irreversible effects from the incident.

Mary and Martin went home. Mrs Montague finally left feeling uneasy about leaving her daughter in a potential death threat situation. She had ordered surveillance to alert her of any intruders at Mill Farm.

***

Strawberry Estate house was thoroughly searched by the police for any signs of a 2.2 rifle. Christine came home, and her father noticed her hair was wet. He asked, somewhat surprised, "Why is your hair wet, Christine, not raining?"

"Swimming with Dr Roberts in his private pool, the police interviewed us both concerning something to do with a shooting at Mill Farm," she mentioned unconcerned.

"The police searched the house from top to bottom; Cindy's gone with the twins in their pushchair, so they weren't upset by the commotion. I'm surprised you're not worried about Donald, Christine?"

"Why should I," she shrugged her shoulders, "I have to move on with my life, father. Who's shot anyway for curiosity's sake?"

"Susan, we think they were aiming for Isabella; it certainly wasn't Donald. He was upstairs, apparently. Mrs Montague is on the warpath; someone taking a pot-shot at her daughter has already signed their own death warrant," Gerald advised. Observing Christine's expression, not convinced she's not involved somehow. Christine shrugged her shoulders, running upstairs to her bedroom, finding turmoil after the police searched; she grinned and had the perfect alibi, changing her clothes.

***

Donald and Isabella retired to bed; locking the bedroom door in case of an intruder would give him time to prepare to deal with any situation he hoped. Surveillance reported to Mrs Montague at 9 o'clock in the morning. The only thing seen on the cameras around Mill Farm is a deer, a fox and the usual barn owl taking great pleasure crapping on one camera.

***

Christine finished her breakfast, leaving Eric and Josephine with Cindy. "I'm off for a ride this morning. You okay to have the children?" Christine asked.

Cindy nodded, noticing Christine's becoming less interested in the children.

Christine saddled The Rising Sun, slowly riding along the track, scanning the sky for a drone, and looking at her wristwatch. Suspecting Mrs Montague would be monitoring her, she would have to change her plans if that were the case. She tied her horse and walked into the old strawberry shed, surprised to find no one there. She's about to leave. Titch entered the building, "I hit the wrong bloody woman; I'm glad I didn't kill her. They won't be able to trace anything, Christine. Don't worry; the gun is long gone. I'm afraid we'll have to think of something else," he frowned. He removed Christine's clothes, which she didn't object to. She knew a price to pay and wasn't punished, although he's nowhere near as good as Dr Roberts. Titch stood, tidying himself, "leave everything with me. We won't have contact again for a while; I'll arrange something; you will know when I'm successful."

Christine was about to speak she heard a dull thud; Titch dropped to the ground, blood pouring from his head. Christine stared in disbelief. Mrs Montague's bodyguard stepped forward, pointing his handgun fitted with a silencer at Christine. "A message from Mrs Montague, go home, Christine; the next bullet in my gun is for you. You will join your mother if you go anywhere near her daughter or Donald. Now go and say nothing if you value your life."

Christine ran out of the strawberry shed like the wind, mounting The Rising Sun, hyperventilating. Couldn't believe what she had experienced. She glanced back, watching a black Range Rover with smoked glassed windows drive away, suspecting Titch's body in the back to be discreetly dumped.

Mrs Montague smiled after hearing her bodyguard laying down the law. Christine, seeing a dead body in front of her, Mrs Montague presumed would frighten the life out of Christine. Instructed her bodyguard to dump Titch's body in the back streets of London; he couldn't be connected to Strawberry Estate.

Christine ran into the house. Cindy looked at her expression, Christine's complexion pure white as if she'd seen a ghost. Christine picked up her children, cuddling them both, realising how close to death she had come with her crazy obsession with Donald. She had to re-evaluate her life. She couldn't continue down this road unless she had a foolproof plan or if god were on her side. Something happened to Isabella and Donald's relationship, opening the door for her and the children. Much to everyone's surprise, Donald parked outside Strawberry Estate house knocking at the door, let in by Cindy. He looked at Christine and the two children, "May I hold, Christine, please?"

She smiled, "Of course."

Donald sat at the kitchen table, holding Eric and Josephine in each arm. Grown so much over the past few months, smiling at Donald as if they knew he was their father, not frightened. The first time he'd held his children properly since they were born. Cindy inquired, "How are you and Isabella? It must have been a horrifying experience?"

Donald nodded, "For Isabella, Susan especially. I had a phone call fifteen minutes ago from Mrs Montague; she advised me the other person had been dealt with and to move around freely." Donald suggested, "She said a bullet in her gun with somebody's name on should they step out of line."

Christine nervously smiled, suspecting that message was for her. "When slightly older, Donald, perhaps you'd like to have the children stop at your place for a night or two. I know they would come to no harm with you?"

Cindy and Donald were both taken back by her remark. "Really!" Donald expressed, "Wonderful, Christine, would give you a break. I'm sure Isabella would love to have the children. If you prefer, I will employ a nanny. She could travel between both properties with the children. What's your view, Cindy, Christine?"

Cindy remarked, "Give us time to think it over, Donald. We'll have to discuss it with Gerald; I love having the children," Cindy glancing at Christine.

"I suppose a nanny would free everyone, especially during harvest, a busy period. I'm quite happy for Isabella to look after our children, Donald, providing you are, of course?" Christine remarked cautiously.

"Anything you require, Christine, for the children?" Donald asked sincerely.

"No, I'm fine for money, Donald; I wouldn't mind having their father with me," she smiled.

Donald carefully passed the twins to Christine and Cindy, "I must go; I have work to do," he kissed Christine on her cheek, walking out of the door. Donald drove away quickly, returning to Mill Farm and finding Isabella carrying out housework duties, which he thought odd; he didn't expect her to do those chores. She poured him a coffee, "Well, do tell, you smell of babies," she exhaled.

Donald chuckled, "Don't say you're becoming broody, Isabella. We could always nip upstairs."

She scoffed, "You must be joking. Look like a football for six months, then have to change nappies, have sick all down your top, and screaming kids in your ears, no thank you, not until I have to," Isabella said firmly.

Donald was surprised by her remark; nevertheless, he had two children to take over his small empire. He may expand if the right property comes his way and at the right price. After Isabella's remark, Donald left the kitchen, taking a shower, smelt of babies. He considered the possibility she felt threatened by Christine and dismissed the idea as silly. He entered his studio, looking out the window, only to see a taxi coming along the drive. He ran downstairs realising he hadn't seen Susan, never visited her in hospital, shameful he thought.

Susan stepped from the taxi with her head bandaged. Donald paid for the cab. "I'm sorry, Susan, I haven't come to see you. How are you feeling?" Donald asked, extremely concerned, guiding her into the house.

"I'm okay, thanks, Donald; I guess you're all over the place, quite a shock, fortunate to escape with a scratch," she smiled, sitting at the table. Isabella made Susan a coffee.

"The police still don't know who they were aiming for, whether you or Isabella, more likely to be Isabella than you, Susan, I'd have thought?"

"The only things I have of value are the house and my daughter, one of which you purchased for me."

"I suppose you need a few weeks off, Susan, or will you quit altogether? Quite understandable," Donald remarked.

"Neither! I should be at work tomorrow morning. I will draw the curtains in whichever room I'm in," Susan chuckled.

"No need, Susan, to draw the curtains; I have bullet-resistant glass fitted to all the lower windows. This is where we spend most of our time. I'm not having you shot at or anyone else. I'd love to know who's behind the attempt; although Mrs Montague assured us it won't happen again, she must know something and not let on?"

"That's mummy," Isabella voiced, "You really don't want to upset her. She can open the gates of hell better than anyone I know."

Susan finished her coffee, took her car keys, she headed home. Donald was extremely pleased she wasn't quitting; he likes Susan; she knew what needed attending and got on with it more than most people would. Donald returned to his studio in Mill House, sitting there staring at a blank canvas, the state of his mind blank. Isabella went into town to select her wedding dress, grinning and seeing her mother walking toward her. "You still have trackers, and listening devices fitted to me, mother," Isabella chuckled.

"Of course, the only time they're turned off, when you make those silly noises in bed, nobodies that good, you're faking," Mrs Montague grinned.

"Considering Donald is the only man I've been with mother, I can't make a comparison. However, you shouldn't be listening to my private life; every sound I make is genuine. He's an animal, those great hands of his; he can do wonders with your senses."

Mrs Montague smiled, "I never thought you and I would have a conversation like this, Isabella. Is there no way I can persuade you to hold the wedding in France far more secure, my dear?"

"Not since daddy insulted Donald. I wanted the wedding at Dorking Moor Estate, originally my choice, not Donald's; he affords me every luxury I wish. You couldn't want a better man. He's loving, caring, almost too good to be true," Isabella smiled.

"That's why I selected him for you, daughter," Mrs Montague grinned, "I knew he'd be good, and he makes money in seconds when painting; the world seems to love his art, including your father."

They walked into a bridal shop, spending an hour selecting a dress. Isabella wanted not white but more of a cream with lots of laceworks. "How much?" Isabella asked. "Donald wouldn't care if I were in wellington boots; I don't know why we're bothering with the expense, mummy."

The sales assistant remarked, "Eight thousand pounds, Madam, for that dress."

Isabella exhaled, "I'm not paying that!"

Mrs Montague intervened, "My daughter will take the dress, thank you. Looks beautiful on you, Isabella. I will arrange for transport to Dorking Moor Estate and your unhappy father. Next shoes."

They walked along the street together, "You realise, Isabella, the first time we have ever shopped together; we usually have the servants to do. What a strange sensation. I quite enjoy shopping," she suggested, walking into a shoe shop.

They spent another half-hour selecting shoes. Mrs Montague paid the five-hundred-pound bill, taking the shoes to join the wedding dress she would transport to Dorking Moor Estate.

***

Donald had painted a kitchen scene where the bullet had entered the window, betraying a woman on the floor wounded and Isabella standing shocked. Although you couldn't ascertain from the face, actually Isabella. He photographed the portrait sent to Jack. Jack had heard about the incident and was pleased to learn everyone was okay. Jack studied the photo Donald had sent him, an interesting composition, although not exactly worth millions like his usual work. Jack realised he couldn't be on form every time he placed a paintbrush on canvas.

Donald jumped in his Bentley, heading for London with his portrait, not impressed himself. He turned into Jack's Fort Knox establishment around teatime. Jack placed the portrait in its usual place with a frame temporarily secured. Jack considered a dismal figure; the bidding started slowly at five hundred pounds. Jack asked, "What's the title, Donald?"

"Revenge!"

Jack typed in the title that made things move, one million. Everyone knew what had happened to Donald at Mill Farm, a one-off immortalising the memory in oils.

Donald slowly drove home, thinking next week, he's heading for Dorking Moor Estate to marry Isabella, wondering if he's making the right decision. With Sophie, it was simple; she's like him and had no ulterior motive other than to love him. Isabella's the daughter of Mrs Montague, a frightening combination. Her comments about babies didn't impress him, almost like she would have to tolerate another chore. He couldn't imagine marrying his first love Christine; although she had his children, he would not be able to trust her any further than the front door.

Donald sighed heavily. A lorry in the opposite carriageway lost its load, burying Donald's Bentley in steel piping. Donald regained consciousness; blood on his face from where the roof had collapsed, hitting him, and the glass shattered, cutting his cheek. He could move his hands and feet, hearing someone shout. "You okay?"

Donald said, "Yes, although I can smell diesel," he replied, concerned. Donald sat patiently while the steel tubes were carefully craned away one at a time until they could cut out the driver's door. Donald released his seatbelt and was helped out by a fireman. He hadn't walked away many yards before the car burst into flames. Donald glanced back, breathing a sigh of relief, as close as he wanted to come to death. He was helped into an ambulance.

Donald was taken to a hospital in Oxford, the closest to the accident. He's thoroughly checked over and released an hour later with minor abrasions on his cheek from broken glass. Isabella, in her Jeep, came to collect him, upset; she wouldn't allow him to drive to London anymore. The M40 had turned out to be a menace. The second time he'd had an accident on the motorway, he'd driven to Scotland many times and treble the mileage without a scratch.

She hastily parked her Jeep and ran into the hospital. She found him talking to a pretty nurse at reception, drinking coffee. Isabella placed her hands on her hips, "Future husband, you are in the doghouse," she suggested.

Donald smiled, "Could happen to anyone Isabella, not the road, just circumstance. The lorry driver didn't purposely lose his load; I didn't drive underneath for fun. When my numbers up, it's up; neither you nor I will prevent the outcome."

Isabella kissed him, "Now you are a philosopher; that's all we need," leading him out of the hospital. Donald gave a brief statement to the awaiting press, allowing them to take a few photos sitting in the passenger seat of Isabella's Jeep. She drove off like the wind. Donald commented quickly, "One accident today is enough, thank you." She grinned, looking at his terrified expression. She'd learn to drive in France, "Donald, you should learn to drive in France the only rule out there is the winner takes all," she laughed.

Cutting across the country through Banbury and home to Mill Farm. Isabella chuckled, "Since you've had the accident, Donald, your last portrait reached seven million. Everybody's waiting for you to die; the minute Jack said he heard you had an accident, the price when off the scale. When I'm a married woman, you'll be able to look after me properly. I met mummy in town today, we purchased my wedding dress and shoes. Another thing, she's transporting to Dorking Moor Estate for the wedding. She's still trying to persuade me to hold the venue in France. I'm not; I want to be married at Dorking Moor Hotel."

**

Christine's watching television, seeing the news report of Donald Selwyn buried in steel tubing on the M40 escaping with minor injuries. Christine breathed a sigh of relief; she didn't want anything happening to her future husband, although he may not realise it now. Mrs Montague initially had put the fear of god into her. She's surprised Mrs Montague's bodyguard hadn't dispatched her along with Titch when they had the chance. Christine couldn't understand why.

**

Donald ordered another Bentley, black, this time four-wheel-drive SUV, excepting the vehicle's robust construction, saved his life which he's grateful for, admittedly, his old car a right off; nevertheless, he wasn't. The suppliers said they would have one with him tomorrow morning delivered to Mill Farm. Donald turned his phone off, thinking third time lucky, he hoped. Walking around the farm looking at his new toys in the machinery shed, remembering not so long back when he would spend hours repairing equipment because they couldn't afford to purchase new ones. Donald received a phone call from his mother after seeing the news. Donald advised nothing to worry about. He's home and safe; they should prepare for the wedding not long now.

Donald returned to the house, running upstairs, looking in the other bedrooms, deciding which he would convert into a nursery for his twins when they stayed. He wondered whether he should prepare two rooms, one for when Isabella decided to have a child; because of the age differences, he couldn't have three together, which could be dangerous. Isabella joined him, "What are you doing, Donald?"

"Preparing two nurseries, one for when the twins stay and the other when you decide to have a child. I didn't think we could have the three together because of the age differences; you couldn't have a tiny baby with two older children."

"So, you intend to have Christine's children stay here sometimes, and I'm producing babies the minute we're married," she frowned.

"Christine said she wouldn't mind if we had Eric and Josephine stay over, perhaps for a weekend. I presume you would prefer to have children while you were young?"

"Who's going to look after Eric and Josephine. I presume I'm lumbered, thanks, Donald!"

"Oh, I've obviously made a mistake; thank god I found out before we were married."

Isabella stared in shock at his comment, watching him walk down the stairs. Donald jumped in his American pickup truck and drove away. Isabella panicked, phoning Donald, who refused to answer his phone. Isabella phoned her mother, explaining what she'd said to Donald. "Where are your brains, Isabella? You've shot yourself in the foot; pack your bags and come home. The relationship is finished. Isabella, placing yourself between Donald's twins and him is a suicide mission."

Donald drove to London to Harrods purchasing toys for the twin's room at Mill Farm. He didn't see the point in setting up another nursery. The chances of his and Isabella's relationship lasting were slim; he certainly wasn't marrying someone with that attitude. Donald slowly returned home, receiving a phone call from Christine, "Hi Donald, I have discussed what you suggested of employing a nanny who could travel between our properties. The children would always have someone with them they were familiar with. I have to say a brilliant idea, Donald; I must insist I choose the nanny."

"That's okay in principle, Christine; I'm paying for her, so I want to meet her before any decisions are finally made. I don't want my children mixed up with Count Dracula's sister." He heard Christine burst out laughing. "Okay, Donald, I'll place an advert and ensure they are fully qualified. I can imagine you being a nightmare father," she disconnected the call.

The more Donald thought about having children at his place, the more he smiled, wondering if one of them would be an artist like him. Donald finally parked outside Mill Farmhouse, walking inside and finding Isabella in tears at the kitchen table. He made them both a coffee, passing her a mug. "No good crying that won't resolve any issues," Donald said coldly. "Christine's phoned me; I'm employing a nanny for Eric and Josephine. The nanny will travel between Christine and me, so they always have someone they know. Look on the bright side Isabella; you needn't have anything to do with them. I appreciate they're not your children, so why should you be interested."

"That's unfair, Donald," she sniffled. "I don't want any children now. I want to live my life first and have fun with my husband. I don't give a damn if you have Eric and Josephine over here. You're right. I don't want to be tied down with children. If you employ a nanny, that doesn't mean I would ignore them; I will spend some time with Eric and Josephine. You forget I have to keep accounts and monitor your money. I have a hundred and one jobs to do."

"Point taken," he sighed heavily, wondering whether he should delay any wedding; he didn't want to tie himself down with a less than perfect relationship.

At 10 o'clock the following day, Donald's new Bentley arrived gleaming; Donald thought that won't last long. The places he travelled, at least, weren't gold. He rather hated the colour after a while too much in your face. Mrs Montague arrived in her limousine, walking into the house, looking at the expression on Isabella's face and Donald's. "You are marrying in less than seven days. Are you sure you two are making the right decision after what I've heard; it's easier to walk away now than wait until you're married and discover it's not what you want."

"Mrs Montague," Donald smiled, placing his arm around her waist, "Have you finally realised you're in love with me and want to elope."

She hit the back of his leg with her cane. "Behave, Donald, serious. I'm not having my daughter unhappy."

"Mummy, I'm twenty years old, not three. I can resolve my own issues. Donald and I have discussed matters; as far as I'm concerned, they are resolved, you agree, Donald," Isabella glanced at him.

"It's up to you, Isabella; I will have Eric and Josephine over here to stay for weekends or a week. I don't know; I haven't discussed it with Christine. We employ a nanny, so that will not involve you unless you wish. You stated you don't want children straightaway. You want to wait until you're old and decrepit when the chances of a successful birth are slim. Perhaps, you shouldn't have any children, Isabella, if they don't interest you. I already have two, so it doesn't matter."

Mrs Montague glared at Isabella, "Don't you want a child Isabella of your own who will take over my property in France? I would expect one child from you, Isabella, if not two. Are you really my daughter," Mrs Montague shook her head, walking out of the house, extremely disappointed with Isabella's attitude, understanding why Donald's cross.

"Thank you, Donald," she said, passing him a knife from the kitchen drawer, "Would you like to stab me in the back now or later," she stormed off. Donald exhaled; he could do without the crap and wasn't marrying a barren old cow only interested in his money. Donald phoned Angela, "Angela, could you do me a favour, pop over to Mill Farm and help me put a prenup together?"

Angela laughed, "You are joking, Donald, surely?"

"No, I'm not! I want to protect what I have; some may consider I haven't worked very hard to achieve my wealth. Maybe. I don't intend to lose in the law courts to a scheming bitch."

"Are you sure you should be marrying Donald? Certainly sounds like dangerous ground you're walking on," Angela advised.

"Maybe nerves on both parts; nevertheless, I must have a business head on my shoulders sometimes."

"Give me ten minutes; I'm saying goodbye to Michael; he's off to Strawberry Estate house to prepare a room for the nanny," she chuckled.

Isabella's listening to the conversation, exhaling, trying to decide whether she wanted to stay with Donald or return to France as her mother suggested. She would not be bullied into having children until she was good and ready. If Donald wanted a prenup, she didn't care; she had her own money besides her mother's properties worth, far more than Donald's likely to earn. She would have a prenup to make sure he couldn't have anything of hers.

Isabella came downstairs. "I want a prenup," she advised abruptly, "You're not having your sticky fingers on my mother's property, worth far more than you're ever likely to earn. I suggest we both agree, I keep what is mine, and you keep what is yours. Neither party can be accused of marrying the other to increase their wealth. And just to set the record straight, I will have children when I'm ready, not when you want them or my mother if you don't like it, tough. I suggest you call the marriage off if you can't accept those terms."

Angela arrived, coming into the house carrying her notepad. Isabella made coffee, "Angela, very simple whatever Donald has, he keeps including his money, and whatever I own I keep. That way, no one can be accused of marrying the other for their wealth."

"What a shame I didn't bring my duelling pistols; an exciting arrangement." Angela wrote down the necessary details, slowly drinking her coffee, looking at Donald and Isabella glaring, neither backing down. "I could save you both heartaches, don't marry, start over. The way you two look at each other, you could scratch each other's eyes out; what will it be like when you're married?"

"You have a point, Angela," Donald remarked, "Still, I have nothing to lose with the prenup in place, and neither does Isabella."

Angela shrugged her shoulders, shaking her head in disbelief, "Okay, I have all the details I need. I'll instruct your solicitor Donald to contact Miss Montague's counterpart with the instructions."

"Thank you very much, Angela. At least now no robbing bitch will have my money and property." Isabella was so incensed by his remark she threw her mug, striking Donald on the forehead and running off upstairs. Donald shook his head, bending down to pick up the broken pieces, put them in the bin, walk to the cupboard, and remove a mop to dry the floor. Angela exhaled, kissing Donald on the cheek, leaving. Isabella came downstairs, "Sorry, Donald, I shouldn't have thrown the mug. You're such a bastard. I don't know why; perhaps you should have, Christine."

"No, you drive a tractor far better than her; besides, if Christine had thrown the mug, she'd have missed she couldn't hit the backside of a bus."

Isabella started laughing, "What a ridiculous argument," she said, kissing him passionately on the lips. "Damn, I forgot to include you could only have my body twice a week in my prenup," Donald chuckled.

Isabella grabbed his hand, "I need some attention," guiding him upstairs.

Mrs Montague's listening convinced the relationship was doomed, although, like the prenup idea, alleviating any concerns either party had. They could now concentrate on loving each other. Hopefully, Isabella would relent, providing a son or daughter to take over the estate in France before she passed on, which she hoped wasn't for many years. Of course, Elizabeth R may request Isabella to fill her shoes in the distant future when she has matured and understands her requirements.

The Montagues were the equivalent of the secret police in Tudor times. The Royals and the Montagues went back many centuries. Hence, the property in France was given to Montague's ingratitude for their services to the Royals centuries ago.

Donald heard the front door open. Susan said, "It's only me," making Donald laugh. Isabella ran to her room; Donald dressed, grinning. What seemed insurmountable problems had drifted into history. Donald concluded the stress of preparing for the wedding. They ran downstairs, finding Susan had already made three coffees. "I presume you're coming to the wedding, Susan?" Donald asked.

"I don't remember being invited, Donald. I certainly never received an invitation."

"I'm inviting you now. Drive to Birmingham Airport. You'll be flown to Inverness with everyone else, transported to my estate in Scotland, party all night fly home the next day. Plenty of men in kilts," he whispered in her ear. "Some don't wear anything underneath; you're all right there."

Susan punched Donald on the arm, "You're terrible. I'm coming. Thank you for the invitation; where do I acquire the ticket?"

"Waiting for you at the airport; you leave at seven a.m. take off on the first of December, so I think you'll be at the hotel at twelve noon for the wedding. I can't remember half of what's arranged anymore. A ten-minute ceremony where I stick my head in a noose." Isabella punched him on the other arm, grinning.

Susan remarked, "Thank you both it should be an adventure. Long time since I've had a day away from home. "I see an advert for a nanny to look after Christine's children."

"I know we are sharing the nanny, so the children have someone with them they know when they travel between properties."

Susan nodded, carrying on with her work looking forward to the trip to Scotland, hoping she would meet someone interesting. She didn't want to stay single for the rest of her life if possible.

***

Christine was inundated with applicants. She made the applicants apply in writing rather than talk to them over the phone, supplying their qualifications and work experience. Christine knew Donald wouldn't pay for rubbish or anyone he didn't trust. The postman delivered a sack full of mail within three days of the ad. She spent the morning sifting through, selecting what she thought would be suitable and phoned Donald. "I could do with your help; I've had that many applicants, I've slimmed the candidates down. Would you interview with me, Donald, please? After all, you're paying their salary."

"When?"

"Tomorrow morning, I know it's only a day before you travel to Scotland, but the sooner we resolve this issue, the better."

Donald exhaled, "Okay, I'll see you at 9 o'clock in the morning; I presume we are interviewing at your place?"

"Yes, of course; bye for now."

Isabella was listening to the conversation, not impressed Donald would be spending time with Christine, Isabella trying to convince herself Donald wouldn't go back to her under any circumstances.

***

Donald arrived at 9 o'clock in the morning at Strawberry Estate, invited into the house by Christine. Cindy had agreed to sit in on the interviews as an independent who would look at things from a different perspective. Christine had whittled down to five candidates allowing an hour per candidate. Showing them their room, introducing them to the children and the facilities examining their qualifications and experience. By 1 o'clock in the afternoon, Donald, Cindy and Christine all liked one candidate. She came with Royal references, propelling her above the other candidates. Her qualifications are to look after a child impeccable and her education. Her name's Miss Caroline Crombie: she's thirty-five years old. Donald left everything to Christine to arrange with Cindy. Donald knew if Cindy's involved, wouldn't be any mistakes; Donald wrote a cheque for five hundred thousand pounds passing it to Christine. "Towards her salary and anything else you need to purchase."

Christine showed Donald two bank books. She'd split the million pounds he gave her before between Eric and Josephine. Donald smiled, pleased with what she'd decided. Whatever happened, the children would have cash when they were older. Donald said goodbye returning to Mill Farm, finding Isabella packing suitcases, appearing worried. "What's the matter, Isabella."

"Worries me when you're with Christine. I don't want to suddenly find out she's pregnant again and you're the father. You two have history."

Donald sat on the side of the bed. "If you're that unsure, Isabella, let's not marry if you feel you can't trust me. We are wasting our time; I will not neglect my children. I certainly wouldn't cheat on you or anybody else, not in my nature," Donald assured.

"Probably nerve's Donald, ignore me; I'm silly and irrational," she exhaled.

The night seemed to last forever neither could sleep nor wanted to make love. Morning arrived too soon, barely having a couple of hours' sleep. They made breakfast together. Donald loaded the suitcases heading for Dorking Moor Estate. They stopped a couple of times on the way, having a cup of coffee in a motorway service station, both trying to keep their eyes open. Donald wondered what Isabella was thinking and vice versa. They finally arrived carrying the suitcases to their suite. One day to recover from the journey before the wedding. Mr and Mrs Montague had flown in by helicopter, landing before dusk shown to their room to freshen before the evening meal about to be served.

Maggie had set the table aside so Donald, Isabella, and her parents could sit together; Maggie chuckled, thinking of the last supper. She watched Donald and Isabella come to the table, joined by Mr and Mrs Montague shortly after. She felt if looks could kill, everyone would be dead. Mr Montague had ordered steak and a bottle of wine; he suspected the hotel wouldn't have. Maggie's one step ahead of him. She'd done her research and knew exactly what he would ask for, guessing he's a miserable old bastard trying to cause trouble. She looked at the expression on his face when the bottle appeared. Mrs Montague grinned, enjoying her salmon; Mr Montague couldn't find fault with his meal and stayed silent. Mrs Montague, after the evening meal, disappeared upstairs with Isabella to check the wedding dress and everything else was in order.

Mr Montague moved to the lounge; Donald walked outside for a breath of fresh air, the tension thick. You could have cut the atmosphere with a knife, remembering his last disastrous attempt at a wedding in Scotland. Donald received a text from Christine, "good luck and keep smiling. Eric and Josephine send their love to their father."

Donald strolled around to the stables stroking the horses, Emily's sitting in the tack room, cleaning the saddles. Donald walked in, taking Emily by surprise. "Why are you still here?" Donald asked suspiciously.

Emily smiled pleasantly, "I have nowhere else to be. I don't have a boyfriend, and if I had, I'd probably shoot him; none are reliable. I can sit here, clean my saddles, talk to myself or the horses, and everything is perfect in the world," she smiled.

Donald sat beside her, phoning the hotel, "Could a member of staff please bring a meal out to the tack room and a pot of tea for Emily, a double malt whisky, and one for myself, charge to me, Donald Selwyn."

"Donald, you realise a sackable offence if I drink on duty without Justin's consent or Maggie's," she grinned.

"I can do what I like, Emily; I'm the boss. I own everything, and the rest can take a running jump. Does the hotel provide you with meals during the day?"

"No, we have to pay like a customer."

Maggie came out to the tack room, carrying a tray and another waiter with a meal. "Maggie, I don't know who's responsible for making the rules here. All staff members can eat here, including Emily; I'm not running a concentration camp."

"I thought it odd when Justin made the rules the same applies at Glencoe. I guess you will burn his ears. Father is trying to keep expenditure under control, Donald, to make money," she sighed heavily.

"You sort your father out, Maggie because if I do, he won't like what he hears. Advise him that staff are entitled to a meal. I don't mean caviar; I mean a sensible dinner. That's the keyword if they start abusing the situation, I'll sack them; I will not be made a fool of by anyone. The waiter left the plate and tray with Emily's meal, and Maggie left a pot of tea and two whiskies.

Emily tucked into her food as if she was starving, enjoying her cup of tea and sipping her whisky, which she thought a little naughty. Nevertheless, the boss said, okay, so it didn't matter. Donald sat drinking. Isabella came into the light seeing Donald sitting and talking to Emily while she enjoyed her meal. "I see, fraternising with the staff," Isabella laughed, "Don't worry, Emily, Maggie warned me Donald is on the warpath, obviously not with you."

"He is not like other bosses, Isabella; he is kind and considerate and appreciates what people do; he is not a stuck-up slob."

"I guess you and my father separated as soon as the meal was finished, Donald. You have nothing to say to him, do you?"

Donald shook his head, "No, he's not my cup of tea; I like ordinary people who speak their mind. I'm not an arse kisser." Emily almost choked on her cup of tea, laughing.

"You could be civilised, Donald. No need to be downright rude. He made an effort to come here; it wouldn't hurt you to show respect if you understand the word." Donald pushed Isabella out of the way. "I suggest you and your parents climb aboard her helicopter and piss off back to France. I'm not marrying you," Donald jumped in his Bentley driving off. Isabella stood, shocked, unable to grasp what had happened. Emily remarked, "That serves you bloody right. You didn't expect him to stand there and be insulted, Isabella. You must be bloody crazy."

Isabella went to slap Emily's face, not realising Emily's trained in martial arts. Emily launched a blow smacking Isabella in the eye; she fell to the floor like a stone, struggling to her feet, walking to the hotel. Isabella explained to Maggie what had happened privately, so her parents wouldn't find out. "If you went to hit Emily, you can't blame her for defending herself, your own fault Isabella, and if you've insulted Donald, you might as well jump on a plane and go home. I think I know where he'll be. I'll see if I can calm the situation for you; I wouldn't hold your breath. The last woman who pissed him off ended up left at the altar."

"I know I was trying to mend a few fences and ended up crashing through with my choice of words. See what you can do for me, please, Maggie. I do love Donald; he frightens me. I don't think I have the necessary talents to keep him happy in marriage."

"You don't need any talents with Donald. He's the easiest man you'll ever come across as long as you're loyal; that's all that bothers him, and he wouldn't betray you either, definitely not with Christine. I'd marry him tomorrow," Maggie confessed, leaving Isabella in the office, jumping in her car and driving to Glencoe along to the illuminated waterwheel. Donald's sat on timbers trying to calm down.

Maggie started laughing, and Donald grinned. "You fancy a quick one in the workshop, Donald," she smiled, lifting her eyebrows.

"You don't change Maggie," giving her a cuddle.

"I'm on a mission of mercy. Isabella is distraught; she'll have a black eye, thanks to Emily. She went to slap Emily, not realising Emily's trained in martial arts, so you can imagine the outcome," Maggie laughed.

"That will go down a bundle with her parents. Is Emily all right, Maggie?"

"Emily is fine. I can't discipline her for self-defence; no one has the right to hit somebody else. I think you had better return to Dorking Moor Estate to mend a few fences; all the ammunition Mr Montague requires to cause trouble."

Donald kissed Maggie. "I told you, Donald, you should have married me," she chuckled, climbing into her car and followed to Dorking Moor Estate by Donald in his Bentley. Donald entered the office. Isabella sat with a bag of ice against her eye to prevent the swelling. "I'm sorry for what I said, Donald; I want to marry you. I'm scared; I don't know why a big step has many variables. I suppose it's because I can't control the situation," she sighed heavily.

"I'm as worried as you. Let's look at your eye Isabella," she removed the bag of ice. Donald dried with a towel, "I think, ok,

Isabella, you could always wear a patch and pretend to be a pirate," he laughed.

"I'll have to apply extra makeup; hopefully, no one will notice." Donald and Isabella held each other for several minutes, Isabella heading for the bedroom, making sure she avoided her mother and father. Donald noticed the tack room light on. He walked around to the stables, Emily still working, at 10 o'clock in the evening. "Haven't you a home to go to, Emily?"

"Sorry about Isabella. She came at me, Donald; I only defended myself," she expressed sincerely.

"Isabella explained, no worries, you haven't answered my question."

"I have accommodation in the village, a bedsit. I prefer to be here than sit bored stupid, watching television the same programmes I watched when I was five years old. I'm paying fifty pounds weekly for a shit hole to live in. That's half my salary gone more or less."

Donald opened his wallet, passing Emily two hundred pounds. "Here, I'll sort out your accommodation problem. I remember someone else in the same predicament when I first met her," he sighed heavily, remembering the accommodation Sophie lived in.

"You're talking about Sophie; we were good friends; you were to marry her." Emily packed her things away, walked towards her small car, heading home.

Donald found Maggie grabbing her torch, holding her hand, walking out, and looking at the buildings. "Maggie, a priority some of our staff are suffering not only are their wages crap. I appreciate we can't pay out more than the going rate; otherwise, we'll go bust. Perhaps find some buildings around the back here suitable to convert into one-bedroom accommodation. At least we could give the staff a perk, minimal or no rent. The electricity we have is free anyway, thanks to the turbine."

"When tomorrow is out the way, Donald, I'll be straight on it. You have a heart of gold," Maggie smiled. "An old brick barn along the lane belongs to the property. I think you could convert into six flats; you need Mrs Montague to speed up the planning permission."

Neither realised Mrs Montague was standing behind them. "And what is Mrs Montague to approve?" she asked suspiciously.

Donald placed his arm around Mrs Montague's waist. She looked at him suspiciously in the floodlights. "My lovely mother-in-law, we want to convert a barn into approximately six self-contained flats for staff. Could you arrange for planning permission?" he asked, kissing her cheek.

Mrs Montague removed his arm, "That's enough flirting; I've seen Isabella; she may have a black eye in the morning. However, from her accounts of what happened, her own fault. Yes, you may convert, keeping the shell of the building in keeping with the area. I can't understand why you and my husband can't be civilised to one another. I suppose he's losing his daughter, and you don't like him because of the insults regarding your standing in society."

"That's not why, Mrs Montague," Donald kissed her on the lips, "I want to run away with you." Maggie's screaming with laughter, looking at Mrs Montague's face. She lashed out with her cane catching Donald on the back of the leg, making him jump in agony. "You animal!" Mrs Montague walked off, shaking her head, smiling, wishing in some respects she was Isabella; she surmised Donald's a pushover.

Everyone up early the following day. Donald was kicked out of his own suite and given a small room to dress, while Isabella was made ready by her mother. Maggie's preparing the hotel for the event. The local vicar phoned, checking Donald hadn't cancelled the wedding. The aircraft landed in Inverness in good time, and the guests were transported directly to the hotel. It was the first time Mary and Martin had seen the estate since Donald had acquired it. Mary determined to go horse riding if she could slot in before heading home. She noticed someone in the tack room. Mary made her way over, "I'm Mrs Selwyn, Donald's mother; any chance sometime in the morning before I have to fly home, I could have a ride around the estate. I appreciate its cold."

Emily held out her hand, "Pleased to meet you. Yes, if we meet here, say 8 o'clock in the morning about daylight, I'll take you into the hills; wrap up warm it will be freezing, nothing like where you come from, I mean really cold," Emily warned.

"Thank you, Emily. Are you coming to the wedding?"

Emily shrugged her shoulders, "I didn't know I was invited. Besides, I won't be Isabella's favourite person. I gave her a black eye yesterday."

Mary chuckled, "Whatever for."

Emily explained. Mary laughed, "Her own fault shouldn't treat people like dirt."

The vicar arrived having a couple of malt whiskies. They entered the large lounge filled with the fragrance of flowers, a white archway for Mr Montague and Isabella to walk through, where Donald was waiting patiently for the ceremony. Isabella looked stunning in her wedding dress. Donald trussed up like a chicken in his suit, which he detested wearing, a tie he avoided wearing as a rule.

Jack flew from London for the ceremony joining everyone else. Isabella's eye was slightly swollen. Her mother used makeup to disguise as best she could. Finally, Donald kissed the bride; they were now officially man and wife. Emily had stood at the back, virtually out of sight. Isabella caught sight of her throwing her bouquet directly at her. Emily looked very embarrassed catching. Isabella gave Emily a hug as they walked into the buffet-style service. Donald was rather pleased with Emily, and Isabella had no animosity. Donald whispered in Emily's ear, "You will have new accommodation shortly; it won't cost you anything."

Emily kissed Donald on the cheek, "Thanks."

The rest of the day went off without a hitch. Even Mr Montague appeared to be more friendly towards Donald. In the evening dancing. Jock came across from Glencoe Estate in his best tartan. Susan's dancing with every spare man available. She's having one heck of a time. Isabella and Donald watched, bemused by her behaviour; she's really letting her hair down. Donald whispered in Isabella's ear, "I said the men wore nothing under their kilts. It's gone to her head," Isabella screamed with laughter, with her parents looking at her very peculiarly. Mary and Martin had fallen asleep on the sofa.

Mary woke early, looking at the time, realising she planned to meet Emily at 8 o'clock, wondering what she was to wear. Maggie came to the rescue finding suitable riding clothes for Mary and a thick warm coat and gloves. Maggie couldn't believe Mary would want to venture into the hills in this weather.

Mary joined Emily, who'd already saddled two horses; they greeted each other with a hug and rode off. Mary couldn't believe the wildlife; although the tracks were well worn and easy to follow in winter, the grouse could be seen and the deer. They spent two hours up in the hills before returning to the stables absolutely froze, warming themselves on the small fire in the tack room. Emily put the horses in stables. Mary grabbed her hand, "Come along, Emily; you can have breakfast with me."

"You sure, Mrs Selwyn, I shouldn't be dressed in my riding clothes in the hotel."

"I'm dressed no differently to you; come along, you worry too much," sitting at a table. Mary ordered breakfast for them, glancing to the window and seeing snow starting to fall. Mary noticed most guests only having coffee holding their heads and catching sight of a helicopter landing from the window. Mr and Mrs Montague climbed aboard, flying off before the weather stopped them altogether.

Donald and Isabella came downstairs, joining Mary and Emily for breakfast. Martin's still snoring away in another room on a settee. "You haven't ridden this morning, mother?" Donald asked, looking at the way she was dressed.

"Yes, Emily took me up into the hills, spectacular views Donald and lots of wildlife. We had a great time apart from freezing."

Maggie came over. "The plans are available now, Donald, for the alterations to the old barn. We estimate it would take about a month to convert," she whispered the cost in his ear.

"Go ahead, make sure Emily has the first choice of rooms and a strictly no smoking policy in any of the rooms."

"Your mother and father left early, Isabella," Mary remarked.

"Not my father's idea of a good time; he prefers France and his own estate. I'm surprised he turned up for the wedding, to be quite honest," Isabella sighed.

Everyone who came to the wedding made their way to the awaiting minibuses later in the day and were taken to Inverness Airport to return home. Donald and Isabella looked at each other. "We are married, Donald. I'm now Isabella Selwyn."

"Strange, I don't feel any different," Donald remarked, "The advantages, of course, I now have a hot water bottle to cuddle in bed," he smirked, watching Isabella grin. They sat on the window seat, watching the snow gently falling. The hills were no longer visible; the clouds were now so low, almost as if the sky had reached the earth.

Donald received a phone call. Isabella watched the expression of joy drain away from his facial expression seeing the tears form in his eyes. Donald listened to the information. Mr Mercantile has passed away and will be buried with his wife and daughter tomorrow. The solicitors informed him Mr Mercantile had left his estate to Donald Selwyn in gratitude for trying to save his daughter's life and his wife. Donald burst into tears as he explained to Isabella.

Isabella thought what a great start to their married life. Nevertheless, she would have to help Donald through this traumatic time bringing memories to the surface he had buried. Maggie advised where they could buy a black dress and suit. She's convinced Donald would go to the funeral if he had to walk there. They drove into town to purchase new clothes and footwear, returning to Dorking Moor Estate, trying to enjoy the rest of their honeymoon.

Mrs Montague had heard the news; she suspected Isabella would hold Donald together and help him, not believing what had happened.

Donald and Isabella attended Mr Mercantile's funeral, and very few people attended. They drove to the solicitor's office, collecting the keys to the property and deeds of ownership. everything was left to him. Donald drove to the Croft, noticing the old pigs released to survive on the vegetation until the problem was resolved. They had destroyed Mr Mercantile's garden. Donald entered the Croft, seeing the copies of the paintings still on the wall. Donald collapsed on the settee, heartbroken.

Donald had pulled himself together within a few minutes, venturing outside to see the equipment he'd purchased Mr Mercantile in a shed. Donald phoned Glencoe to arrange for Jock to collect the pigs today and to be slaughtered and the meat split between the two hotels. Donald went inside, finding Isabella had made two coffees. "What do you intend to do with the property, Donald?" Isabella asked nervously.

"Nothing for the moment; I need to think things through when my brain is working properly and not so full of emotion." Donald and Isabella emptied the cupboards containing food and opened the fridge, turning it off; otherwise, the place would be full of vermin, especially at this time. They placed the discarded food in the wheelie bin for the refuge collectors to deal with at the end of the road.

Donald knew there were thirty acres of land which could be cultivated. Mr Mercantile had struggled for years, scratching a mere living for his family. Donald wondered if he could turn the thirty acres into growing vegetables for the two hotels or at least one of them, which would be his own. The equipment is already here. Isabella asked, "What's going on in that mind of yours, Donald? You're up to something. I've seen that look on your face before. Talk it over first and make sure it's feasible, please; I'm your partner in crime now, remember," she chuckled.

Donald explained his idea to Isabella. She thought for a moment about the pros and cons. "You couldn't pay them a salary Donald not a good salary anyway; the cost of production would outweigh what you could purchase from a wholesaler. However, if they live in the Croft rent-free on the conditions, they grow the vegetables for the hotels. They would be paid for their time in planting and harvesting. They could perhaps work at either hotel carrying out odd jobs to supplement their income."

"I knew I had married you for a reason," he said, kissing her on the lips and giving her a cuddle.

Donald and Isabella made their way to Dorking Moor Hotel, changing out of their present attire, and talking to Maggie about their plans for the Croft Donald had inherited. "I may know of a suitable couple. They rent a house, he works on a farm, and his wife grows vegetables in their large garden to supplement their income. When they're not busy on the Croft, they could attend the gardens at both hotels. We could share the cost."

Isabella and Donald smiled, looking at each other. "We have a plan," Donald remarked, "shall I leave it to you to talk to them, Maggie?"

"Okay, I'll phone Veronica in a minute, she's at home, and her husband's name is Rory Davies."

Maggie returned an hour later from the office. "Mr and Mrs Davies want to know when they can move in," she smiled. "Donald, you must provide transport like a transit van to transport the vegetables from the Croft to the hotels."

"What does Rory actually do on the farm where he works?" Donald asked. "I want to meet them both while I'm here with Isabella; she knows the right questions to ask, don't you, my wonderful wife," making her smile.

"Rory's a tractor driver, mechanic. Veronica attended agricultural college."

"Okay, invite them over for dinner. We can discuss matters further, Maggie."

Maggie went off to make a phone call arranging for Rory and Veronica to join Donald and Isabella for an evening meal at the hotel. At 7:30, Rory and Veronica arrived looking nervous, entering the plush hotel. Maggie greeted them warmly, guiding through to where Donald and Isabella were sitting.

The discussion mainly about Rory's skills with machinery and Veronica's knowledge of growing vegetables soon became abundantly clear to Donald. These were the right couple, aged thirty, an excellent age. Donald explained a vehicle would be provided to transport the goods from the Croft. Everything would be provided. They would only need to make a list after talking to Justin, who would explain what they mostly consumed in vegetables. The property would be rent-free in return, looking after and producing the two hotels' products. Start with Dorking Moor Hotel; any surplus can go to Glencoe Estate. When they weren't busy on the Croft, they could work on the gardens at the hotels; the two hotels would share the cost, so they would always have a salary.

Rory and Veronica shook Donald's and Isabella's hand, eager to start. Rory would hand his notice in tomorrow, have to work a week's notice and move to the Croft. To which Donald agreed, Rory asked if he could use the new van to transport their belongings. Donald passed him one of his cards, "Any issues that can't be resolved by either hotel manager, you phone me directly."

Both excited about the new venture, Rory and Veronica made their way home. Donald and Isabella retired upstairs. "They seem a nice couple," Donald commented.

Isabella smiled in agreement, "Yes, Maggie certainly knows the best people for the position; she could be a valuable asset Donald, although I suspect she will want to help her partner shortly."

Once Donald and Isabella had finished breakfast, they drove off to Inverness, striking a good deal on a Ford transit van, arranging for delivery to Dorking Moor Estate. They spent the rest of the day walking around Inverness and Nairn, only a short distance away.

They returned to Mill Farm Saturday morning, in some respects, glad to be home. Susan had made a smashing job of tidying the house; you couldn't fault her housekeeping. Christmas is in a few days, and the start of a new season is approaching. Mary, dressed resembling a range rider, rode across the field through the gate Donald had fitted to join the two farms on Spartacus. Mary tied Spartacus to the wing mirror on Donald's American truck. She came into the house wearing her new Driza-bone coat and cowboy hat. Donald and Isabella burst out laughing. "All the fashion," Mary voiced cheerfully, "I've come to ask when you are selling the oilseed rape and wheat? We've had one or two enquiries."

Isabella wrote down the names of the two companies wishing to purchase and what they'd offered. "That's not enough, Mary, if we're to keep you in the standard of living you want," Isabella grinned.

Donald noticed an unfamiliar vehicle coming up the drive; he opened the front door seeing Caroline Crombie step from the vehicle. "Good morning Mr Selwyn," she voiced, pushing past him wiping her feet on the coconut mat, looking around the house, running upstairs, checking on her bedroom and the nursery; she came down, making herself a coffee sitting at the table. "I hope your tarmac the drive soon, Mr Selwyn, jolt Josephine and Eric's spine when travelling here."

Mary laughed, "I don't know which planet you're from, woman. Donald rode on my knee from two months old; he loved the jolts."

"I will remind you, Miss Crombie, who is paying your salary," Donald advised firmly. "If you wish to continue working for me, I suggest you shut up, don't dictate to me. There's the door use it; come back when you have some manners." Caroline Crombie frowned and left immediately.

Donald phoned Christine, "Don't send that bitch down here with an attitude. I will sack her. I will not be dictated to by a bloody nanny," Donald turned his mobile off before Christine could reply. Donald hadn't realised Caroline Crombie was making Christine's life a misery. Christine immediately phoned Donald, "Please dismiss her. We picked a nightmare; she's driving me crazy," Christine expressed, frustrated.

"Oh, sorry, Christine, I thought you sent her down here to annoy me, so you're suffering. I gave her a bollocking if she didn't take the hint inform me. We'll have her replaced. Bye for now."

Isabella and Mary were laughing. "You certainly know how to pick them, Donald," Mary advised, placing her leather cowboy hat on looking in the mirror, grinning. "Talk about a poser mother," Donald smiled, opening the door for her. Isabella and Donald stood in the doorway, watching her release Spartacus from Donald's wing mirror, riding across the field towards home.

Donald kissed Isabella on the lips. She watched him race upstairs, guessing he was painting, not a bad thing. They had spent money lately. Admittedly, he's worth millions. She thought a few more wouldn't go amiss, clearing away the dirty cups and checking the fridge, realising very little in the house. She moved to the computer, ordering groceries from Morrisons, which would be delivered later today.

Donald couldn't reframe from smiling the way his mother was posing; she was on canvas whether she approved or not. He pictured the horse by an old wooden gate with his mother holding the reins standing by Spartacus. By midnight Donald had finished standing back and looking at the portrait. Everyone would know his mother; he hadn't missed a detail, and to be quite honest, he thought she looked quite attractive in her Driza-bone coat and leather cowboy hat. At two in the morning, he sent a picture to Jack as Isabella came into the room with a mug of coffee. She stood with her hand to her mouth, realising immediately who he painted, passing the mug to Donald. She sat in his chair, studying the detail. "Donald, beautiful."

"And so are you," Donald remarked, kissing her on the cheek and smiling at Isabella's expression.

Donald received a text message from Jack, "My gallery, 9 o'clock in the morning, don't be late!! PS bring cake!" Donald and Isabella both laughed. Donald texts his mother, looking at the clock on the wall. Now 3 o'clock in the morning. She texts, "Here at six, I have one in the cupboard; I guess you're off to London."

Donald and Isabella grabbed a couple of hours' sleep before collecting the cake and heading for London. The sleety rain is quite heavy. Nevertheless, his Bentley ploughed on through regardless of the weather. Isabella caught some extra sleep while Donald drove to London; they parked at the rear of Jack's gallery, quickly carrying the portrait inside to avoid becoming wet. Jack placed it on the easel, fixing a temporary frame he always had, taking shots transferring to the web. After nine in the morning. Donald phoned his mother, "Check Jack's website, bye."

Mary immediately switched on the computer, scanning and seeing herself and Spartacus. Martin peered over her shoulder, "Our lad is talented, Mary. You look scrumptious," he said, kissing her neck and sliding his hands onto her large breasts.

"A piece of cake in the cupboard Martin. That's all you have this morning," she grinned.

Isabella's watching the bidding within twenty minutes, the portrait had reached one million five hundred thousand pounds. She shook her head in disbelief; people absolutely love Donald. At the bottom of the portrait, she noticed the title, "My Mother," she thought it a sweet touch. Donald asked, "Would you make two hundred prints for me, Jack, and send one down to mother, please."

Jack smiled, nodding, cutting himself a slice of cake, not offering anyone else. Donald and Isabella left, calling in at the café along the road. Donald wrote on the back of his cards, "Give Simone a copy of my latest Jack."

Simone came over he passed her the card. "Thanks, Mr Selwyn; you're usual. I read in the paper that you finally married; congratulations to you both," Simone said joyfully.

"Thanks, Simone, two breakfasts, please."

Donald glanced through the window as Simone walked away with their order; he saw someone lean out of a car window brandishing a shotgun. He launched over the table, covering Isabella with his body as both barrels from the gun were discharged, shattering the window. Donald heard the tyres screaming from the car as they sped off to escape. The police were there in seconds as Donald helped Isabella to her feet, checking she was unhurt. Isabella noticed blood on Donald's neck. She made him remove his coat quickly, seeing pellet holes through the leather material from the shotgun cartridges. Donald was taken to hospital, and Isabella followed in the Bentley. The newspapers wild Donald wondered if his life would ever be normal, who would want him dead. He couldn't believe Christine. They appear to have a good, friendly relationship now; besides, he would have thought she would go after Isabella, not him, or perhaps they were after Isabella?

Donald was on his belly in casualty as they removed the pellets from his neck and back one at a time. Isabella sat beside him, holding his hand, trying to hold back tears of love she had for him. He'd risked his own life to save her; she could have easily been injured.

Mrs Montague arrived at the hospital. She had a face like thunder; she'd heard the reports of how Donald had protected her daughter, which she suspected he would do in any situation. He's better than any bodyguard she'd employed. However, she wanted answers. Whoever's behind the shooting would have to leave the planet to avoid her wrath. Isabella stepped out of the cubicle and talked to her mother in the corridor, explaining events. Mrs Montague stepped in. Donald stood kissing Mrs Montague, "I know why you came to see me without my shirt on," she couldn't hit him. "Be nice, mother-in-law," he joked, trying to make light of the situation, although he's worried.

Mrs Montague grinned, patting his cheek, "You saved Isabella; I will find who is responsible, Donald, I promise you," she kissed him, leaving.

Donald was released; the pellets only caused surface damage besides his coat and shirt. The pain of glass in the shop window had taken the force out of the shot. Donald's back was sore, so Isabella drove home in the afternoon. Mary had heard the news phoning Donald's car; Isabella explained as she drove home what had happened.

Donald retired to bed when they reached Mill Farm, laying on his belly; within a couple of days, he's back to his usual old self, a relief to everyone.

***

Mrs Montague left no stone unturned, immediately suspecting the brother of Titch, who she had her bodyguard dispose of. Mrs Montague understood how the underworld worked, especially around London; the last thing they needed was heat from the police. Mrs Montague put the word out, "She wanted the culprits or else!"

The underworld knew when Mrs Montague said: "Or else!" She would unleash the gates of hell on their organisations, costing millions. A message is relayed to Mrs Montague on a postcard, "The persons involved are floating in the Thames; it will not happen again." Mrs Montague smiled, satisfied with the information she'd received; even criminal organisations respected Elizabeth R and would not cross the line.

Mrs Montague drove to Mill Farm, finding Donald and Isabella drinking coffee; Donald stood. Mrs Montague pointed her cane, "Sit. You're taking too many liberties; I will not tolerate."

Donald exhaled; sitting, Isabella grinned. Mrs Montague smiled, "I have some news for you both. The culprits dealt with very severely, shall we say."

"You wouldn't happen to know how to deal with a nanny? Miss Caroline Crombie."

"Why, Donald, is she threatening your manhood? She's excellent; she will look after your two children perfectly in their early years. Unlike their mother, they won't turn out to be tramps. I suggest you listen to her carefully. I think she advised you to have the driveway tarmacked, an excellent idea, like riding across a playing field to visit you two. I might send you the bill for the damage to my limousine, or Elizabeth R will."

"Mummy, don't bully Donald. You realise the cost would be over a hundred thousand pounds to tarmac to the house?"

"He can afford it, the painting of his mother has reached five million, and it's about time you were pregnant. I want to be young enough to enjoy my grandchildren. Yes, I said, Children or do you need a manual Isabella on the procedure."

"How dare you, mummy, I will have children when I'm ready and not before."

Mrs Montague passed a box of pills to Donald, "Swap her contraception; she won't know whether it's the right one or not," Mrs Montague grinned, "I always win, Isabella."

Donald's laughing: he never believed Mrs Montague would be so devious, especially with her daughter.

Isabella sat quiet, frowning, determined not to give in to her mother snatching the box of pills from Donald's hand. Mrs Montague smiled, "How do you know the ones you're taking are the real ones, Isabella? I may have arranged for them to be changed already," Mrs Montague chuckled, walking out of the house.

"You haven't changed my pills, have you, Donald?" Isabella asked, searching his expression.

"Don't be silly, Isabella. Why would I do that," he sighed heavily, leaving the house.

CHAPTER TWENTY-FOUR

TRYING TO PLEASE

Donald contacted Tarmac International, the company he used to rectify the driveway at Crabtree Farm. They prepared and laid tarmac at Mill Farm, costing Donald hundred and fifty thousand pounds.

***

Michael Pearce preparing to marry Angela seemed inseparable, almost like soulmates. As an added bonus, Michael had won custody of Charlie, his son, now extremely boisterous, attending preschool most days.

***

Miss Caroline Crombie, the nanny, pleased the driveways tarmacked on Mill Farm. Christine had purchased a small people carrier for the children with Donald's approval.

Christine is visiting her psychiatrist at his home, receiving more than professional help on her visit.

Isabella had sprayed the crops on the two farms. They decided to visit Glencoe and Dorking Moor Estate, not forgetting the Croft at Bonar Bridge, to see how things were progressing there.

Isabella packed two suitcases; Donald placed them in the boot of the Bentley, heading for Dorking Moor Estate with Isabella driving. They swapped before Glasgow; Donald drove the last section arriving at Dorking Moor Estate Hotel in the late afternoon. Greeted by the new female manager, Maggie and Justin had appointed. A Miss Rosemary Chuckle, a tall slim woman, smartly dressed as you would expect of a hotel manager. She greeted Donald and Isabella at reception. "You're my new manager," Donald expressed warmly.

"Yes, Mr Selwyn, pleased to meet you for the first time, and you must be Isabella Selwyn; I've heard a lot about you," she smiled politely.

Rosemary asked a staff member to carry Donald's luggage to his room. Donald smiled, "I can manage, thanks," walking to his private apartment, Donald looked out the window, noticing Emily grooming one of the horses. Donald kissed Isabella on the cheek running downstairs out to the stables. He placed his arm around her shoulder. She glanced at him and smiled, "Hello, boss," making him laugh.

"You're still here; almost 5 o'clock, Emily. How do you like your new accommodation?"

"Brilliant, Donald; I couldn't wish for anything better. I'd buy you a coffee, but I'm not allowed in the hotel in my riding clothes because they smell of horses," she frowned.

Donald frowned, "We are in the heart of Scotland, cow muck everywhere, wild animals roaming free. The new manager informed you that you can't enter the hotel in your riding clothes?" Donald held Emily's hand, "Come along with me."

She looked somewhat puzzled giggling, "You're married. You can't run away with me, Donald."

Donald entered the hotel with the unwilling Emily suspecting she'd receive a roasting from the new manager. Isabella came downstairs to join him, looking somewhat puzzled. The new manager approached, "You know the rules, Emily. Why are you in here?"

"Don't answer that question, Emily. I will! Emily works here, she may be in her riding clothes, and she may smell of horses. This is the countryside, not the Hilton. If I hear one report from Emily, you have chastised her unfairly. You see that door, Rosemary; you will use it before she does. Now get your act together, manager and concentrate on what's important. Excuse me, ladies and gentlemen,"

Donald voiced. Watching everyone in the bar turn to face him, "Do you have any objections to my stable manager in her riding attire coming into the bar?"

A resounding "No." Rosemary walked off, daring not to say anything else to Donald or Emily. Isabella grabbed his arm, "You sure know how to make friends, Donald."

"I know a natural talent I have." Emily looked embarrassed, especially when paying guests started talking to her and purchasing her a drink.

Justin came into the bar shaking his head, smiling, "Every time you come to Scotland, my phone's red-hot, Donald. We have to have standards. Rosemary's only enforcing what she thought correct; now it looks like I'm to lose another good manager," Justin sighed.

"Good, I prefer Maggie; where is she?"

"On her honeymoon, they finally found the time to marry since you stop pestering her for building repairs."

"I never had an invitation," Donald said, feeling quite insulted.

"You were purposely not invited. They wanted a quiet registry office wedding, not half of Scotland queueing for your autograph. Haven't you noticed, Donald? Both bars are full here, and at Glencoe, just in case you come in, now they know you're here. You are great for business but a bloody nightmare; otherwise," Justin grinned, walking away.

Isabella said, "He's right; you are a bloody nightmare, and that's why I love you so much, Donald."

The following day, Isabella, Emily, and five others set off track into the hills. Rosemary's sitting at a table having a morning coffee; Donald joined her. She glanced up. "You don't mind if I join you, Rosemary," Donald asked politely.

"No, please do, Mr Selwyn." A member of staff supplied Donald with a coffee.

"You ride horses, Rosemary?" Donald asked, trying to make conversation.

"No, doesn't interest me," she answered, disinterested in holding a conversation with Donald. Donald picked up his cup and saucer, moving away. He decided she wouldn't be here long with an attitude like that. Jock came into the hotel, giving Donald a hug. Rosemary looked over her newspaper, watching disapprovingly. "I have a stag on the truck, Donald."

Donald stepped outside with Jock, "Blimey, he's a big one. How the hell you lift that on the truck on your own?"

"I didn't Emily help me, and Isabella," he grinned, "Gutted the animal after shooting, and they came along with tourists."

Donald helped Jock carry the animal to the kitchen. Jock hung on two hooks, quickly skinning. Rosemary appeared, standing with her arms folded, advising, "Have you ever considered hygiene? People have to eat the food that comes out of here."

"Let's tie her up and skin her, Jock. She can go in the next pot."

"Ha-ha, very funny; ensure you sterilise everything when you two have finished making a mess. I'll have to inform the chef he can check you've performed your duties adequately."

"You can see why she has not married Jock; no one would have her." Jock almost fell over himself, laughing.

Rosemary turned and walked out of the kitchen, absolutely fuming, phoning Justin to complain. Justin explained, "Jock is skilled; certainly wouldn't leave anything contaminated in the kitchen. I suspect he would normally skin the animal outside but didn't want to stress any of the guests. That's why he's in the kitchen. Be tolerant, Rosemary; otherwise, you won't last long here. Donald won't tolerate you; he doesn't think twice about sacking anybody. I can promise you, just do your job, and you'll be fine; this isn't London or France. In Scotland, we do things differently here."

Rosemary exhaled, "I understand, Justin, thank you for the advice."

Donald thought he'd been rather mean to Rosemary. He knocked, walking into her office, "Come along, I will buy you a coffee," he smiled pleasantly. "I apologise for my remarks, which were rather rude and unnecessary."

"Thank you, Mr Selwyn."

"Donald, please," they made their way into the lounge. The waitress brought two coffees over. "Right, start again and see if we can be civilised to one another," Donald expressed. Rosemary and Donald spent the next hour conversing instead of rubbing each other up the wrong way, which would only achieve her dismissal.

Donald noticed Emily and Isabella returning to the stables and the other riding guests. Isabella helped Emily unsaddle the horses; both came in having a coffee sitting with Rosemary and Donald. Emily remarked, "Three of the horses need re-shoeing. It may be advisable to alter the tracks we've chosen, which are extremely hard on the horses and will considerably shorten their working life. Some of the stones on the hills are quite sharp."

"You better look, Rosemary," Donald suggested, "You are supposed to be general manager of the estate under Justin's supervision."

"I would be quite happy to take Emily's advice; she is the stable manager and knows what is best for the animals. If we're seen to be not taking care of them, a backlash from the public, make suitable changes, Emily ask Jock for assistance and his opinion, affects both hotels."

"I think you should learn to ride, Rosemary; Emily can teach you. I was rescued once from the mountains, so I think it's essential the manager experiences what the public is seeing. You can honestly voice an opinion once you understand," Donald grinned, knowing Rosemary had never ridden.

"No time like the present," Emily voiced. "I'll saddle horses while you change Rosemary," she expressed, trying not to grin.

Rosemary exhaled, "I think the owner should accompany me," she smiled pleasantly; she was already informed Donald didn't like riding horses, so she thought tough.

Isabella was in stitches; she knew Donald was not fond of horses. Emily grinned as she left to saddle the horses. Picking the largest they possessed to cater for Donald's weight. Rosemary changed into her jeans and warm coat, placing a net over her head to avoid midges, sometimes a nuisance. Isabella stood in the hotel doorway watching Donald and Rosemary riding off together, with Emily trying not to grin at their expressions of horror sitting on the back of a horse. They travelled for nearly an hour, steadily climbing. Emily started to point out the problems. Donald dismounted, and Rosemary walked along, looking at the narrow track worn away by wild animals and sheep down to the jagged bare rock. "I've seen enough," Donald voiced, "What do you suggest, Emily?"

"I suggest considering the track only a metre wide coating with gravel. The problem is transporting the gravel here. We would damage too much of the surrounding area. We can start a new track a couple of metres to one side, so the horses were walking on a softer surface. The trouble is once it becomes wet, the ground will be destroyed by the horses," Emily shrugged her shoulders.

Donald called Glencoe Estate, "Could I have a meeting in an hour, please, Justin, with Rory, Veronica, Robbie, Jock, Emily and Rosemary with me." Donald mounted his horse, Rosemary, likewise making their way down, returning to the stables. Isabella could see the expression on Donald's face; he wasn't a happy bunny. He explained to her he was holding a meeting at Glencoe. They travelled in Donald's Bentley heading for Glencoe, greeted by a worried Justin at the entrance. He had set aside a private conference room, wondering what was happening. The other staff members had arrived, sitting nervously, coffees brought in for everyone. Donald explained the problem.

"I noticed the problem, Donald, and hope to present you with a solution. I can't think of one now," Jock voiced, "Other than as Emily has suggested moving the horses to one side of the track."

"I would use a small dumper," Rory voiced, "Such as a roughneck; they're about the same width as the track at the narrowest point. Thanks to Emily the other week, she took Veronica and me on a track, a beautiful ride and extremely scenic. Anyone who didn't enjoy the ride would be mad or blind."

"I. I could come with the JCB if you hired two roughneck dumpers; I could keep them loaded. We wouldn't have to cover the whole track only where the stone is jagged, don't you agree, Emily?" Robbie asked.

Emily nodded, "Yes, that would be excellent. I think the track this side of Glencoe is fine; the problem is with Dorking Moor Estate."

Isabella had already worked out the quantities, "You will need approximately three thousand tons, Donald, applied at 15.4 centimetres."

"We appear to have a plan," Donald remarked, smiling. "I will leave it to you, Rosemary and Justin, to arrange. I would use the company where I purchased the farm machinery; they have a hire business. Acquire two roughnecks from him. Ensure no disruption for the guests; find somewhere secluded to tip the gravel. We don't want to ruin any of the landscape. Rosemary, I know everyone wears a tracker after Justin's insistence. I think we should now include two-way radios for everyone who works at the hotel outside. Emily can contact the two roughneck drivers so the horses aren't spooked. The last thing we need is a dead guest or injuries."

"Don't sit on your hands, Justin. I want the work completed within the next seven days and without excuses. Thank you, everyone," Donald said, standing. "Come along, Rosemary, Emily, I'll give you a lift to Dorking Moor, and of course, I mustn't forget my special wife," he smiled, tapping her backside. "Rory," Donald asked, "How are things at the Croft? have any issues? I'd like to pay you a visit."

"We have the thirty acres planted, Donald. The small tractor you purchased for Mr Mercantile originally is excellent. Justin is wonderful to work with, and Rosemary, we have no issues. I wished you had come ten years ago," Rory smiled, "I've never enjoyed myself so much, and I think I speak for Veronica," she smiled. "Donald, for next year, could I possibly have a cabbage planter? It would speed up the process, and a sprayer to go on the back of my compact tractor for this year?"

Justin voiced, "Give me the figures, Rory, although I suspect Donald will purchase anyway in the next couple of days if he's paying you a visit," Justin smiled. Everyone went their separate ways.

Donald lay in bed. He noticed during the meeting how Rosemary and Robbie kept glancing at one another; he had a sneaking suspicion something was going on. However, Robbie's now single and could please himself, providing he didn't disrupt the running of the hotels. Donald suspected Rosemary would be fully aware of Robbie's track record with the female sex and avoid him like the plague. Again, she might not be looking for anything serious or a permanent relationship.

Donald finally fell asleep. The following day after breakfast, Donald noticed forty-ton lorries arriving carrying gravel tipping in a neat pile behind the barn out of sight. Within half an hour, a low loader had arrived, transporting two roughneck dumpers which were unloaded placing behind the barn out of sight. Robbie arrived an hour later with the JCB excavator and Rory and Veronica in their white van. Donald watched from his window loads of gravel heading up the track on the narrow-wheeled base dumpers, causing no damage to the track. Every hour two more lorries returned with another load of gravel. Donald walked through the trees at the back of the hotel, standing behind a large pine tree. He noticed Rosemary kissing Robbie standing by his JCB, waiting for a roughneck dumper to return.

Donald retreated. Now he knew what was going on between those two. Donald's determined not to interfere; none of his business. Only if it affected the hotels would he take steps. Donald phoned Justin making him aware of the situation. Justin's to say nothing providing had no effect on the hotels.

Donald drove to Glencoe Estate, entering Justin's cottage, to the room set aside for him to paint. He pictured in his mind the meeting with everyone sitting around the table. Justin brought him a coffee around 11 o'clock in the evening. Isabella had already phoned complaining that he should be in bed with her. Donald finally finished using an old hairdryer to speed up the drying process of his oils. Although they were quick-drying, nothing was quick enough for Donald. He entitled the painting. "The War, room." He sent a text message to Jack, asking for ten prints to be made, naming everyone in the meeting to receive one.

Jack responded, "Boring! paint something more exciting."

Donald exhaled, leaving the painting with reception to be collected by a courier. Donald drove to Dorking Moor Hotel, finding Isabella asleep in bed; he showered and joined her.

After breakfast, they ventured to the Croft. Donald's stomach's churning, reliving the times he visited here with Sophie; taking a deep breath, they were greeted at the door and invited in to find the place redecorated. Although they'd left the prints of Donald's artwork on the wall. Donald's shown around the thirty acres, five of which were potatoes and the remaining vegetables. Donald took Rory to the machinery supplier, where he originally purchased the equipment for Mr Mercantile. Ordered a new sprayer and a single-row cabbage planter to go behind the compact tractor. Donald agreed with Rory that a couple of pigs wouldn't go amiss, dispose of unwanted vegetables and create manure. Donald purchased two pig huts to be delivered to the Croft. Half an acre of less fertile ground was set aside for the pigs. Rory would erect the fencing after Donald supplied the posts and wire.

Rory had spent some time with pigs on the farm he'd left. Donald suggested Rory should purchase the two sows; they wouldn't bother with a boar easier to have artificial insemination. Rory would go to the market next week and buy the animals, taking Justin with him and the horsebox to transport.

Isabella and Veronica enjoyed discussing what they could grow here and what would be the most suitable for the hotels the surplus can go to market.

Donald and Rory returned to the Croft to have a cup of tea. Everyone was pleased with the outcome. Donald and Isabella returned to Dorking Moor Hotel, satisfied with what they'd seen and achieved.

Emily greeted Donald with a broad smile. "The track is so much better now, Donald. The horses really enjoy the trip. You can see by their behaviour that there shouldn't be any hoof problems; a more comfortable ride for the visitors."

"Saddle three horses. We'll have a look," Donald said, watching the surprised expression on Isabella's face and Emily not believing what he'd said.

Within half an hour, riding together. Robbie had returned with the JCB to Glencoe. The roughneck mini dumpers were taken away; they had served their purpose. Everyone had worked extremely hard to make the track serviceable for the horses. They reached the affected areas where the most jagged stones were no longer visible. They met Jock coming the other way with three guests from Glencoe Estate; Jock smiled as they passed each other, heading for the stables on Dorking Moor to change horses to continue the round-trip.

Donald dismounted, digging down with his hand, checking the gravel to ensure the correct depth was laid. He mounted his horse, and they continued riding for another hour, enjoying the breath-taking scenery. Donald's immensely enjoying riding a horse, which he finds surprising. Both Emily and Isabella could see the relaxed expression on his face. They turned around, heading down the hill to Dorking Moor Hotel, helping Emily unsaddle the horses. Donald hadn't seen Rosemary today, which he thought rather intriguing; she reminded him of a ferret sniffing around.

Mrs Montague arrived, a surprise. Donald thought no dramas as far as he knew. That's her usual reason for an appearance. He greeted her as usual with a kiss on the cheek and one on the lips feeling the cane strike the back of his leg. "You don't learn, Donald, do you. You enjoy me hitting you. Are you weird!" Mrs Montague voiced, trying to be annoyed watching him place his arm around her waist, giving her a hug. "Be nice, mother-in-law or else," he grinned.

"Donald, your behaviour is outrageous," Mrs Montague suggested.

"Why don't you change from your granny suit into riding clothes, allow Emily to take you up into the hills and relax."

Isabella's virtually on her knees, laughing at her mother's expression and how Donald's treating her. "Mummy, enjoy yourself, go for a ride into the hills, take your bodyguard if you want."

Mrs Montague pushed Donald away. "I wasn't aware your mother wore bullet-proof clothes, Isabella," Donald joked.

Isabella screamed with laughter; everyone looking at her. She whispered in Donald's ear, "That's mummy's girdle." Mrs Montague's bodyguard could see the playful attitude of everyone and didn't intervene, besides; not wanting to take on Donald particularly, the last time he lost heading downstairs without touching the steps until he hit bottom.

Mrs Montague strutted through into the lounge, leaving Donald and Isabella smiling. Donald looked to Mrs Montague's bodyguard, "Have a coffee on me. I'll look after the old dragon." Mrs Montague's bodyguard grinned, heading to the bar to drink his coffee and smiling at Donald.

Donald and Isabella entered the lounge. "Have you finished making fun of me, Donald? Extremely embarrassing. I will go riding but not today, thank you, I have never ridden here in all the time I visited Glencoe or Dorking Moor. I've only ever viewed from a helicopter or by drone."

Donald ordered coffee for everyone. "What is the purpose of your visit, Mrs Montague?" Donald asked curiously.

"Pleasure, no issues you need to concern yourselves with. I can observe from both expressions that you are happy together; that is the most satisfying part of today."

"How would you like some juicy gossip Mrs Montague, although I suspect you already know the situation," he asked, watching her beautiful pale blue eyes light up and Isabella's. "You realise this cannot be repeated," Donald expressed, "Technically, it's none of our business, although I want to see the outcome?"

"Come along, Donald," Mrs Montague encouraged. Isabella sat all ears listening.

"Rosemary and Robbie are having a little hanky-panky; I caught them kissing around the rear of the barn. They didn't see me; I was hiding behind a tree," he grinned with satisfaction.

"You jest, Donald," Mrs Montague voiced.

"You can't be serious, Donald," Isabella expressed, "He's not her type, surely?"

"Perhaps she likes a little rough," Donald laughed, "Who knows what's under his kilt."

"Don't be vulgar, Donald," Mrs Montague chastised. "We will have to watch, a younger man and an older woman, especially with Robbie's background."

"They can't be meeting here or at Glencoe; she can come and go as she pleases, unlike Robbie in theory. Mind you, he could sneak off whenever he liked. He would have to leave his tracker on-site. Otherwise, we would know where he is. He would have to make sure he's in an area you can't receive a signal so no one could contact him," Donald surmised.

Donald received a phone call from Justin, "Donald, Rosemary's with Robbie in his cottage. I've driven past, seeing her car parked outside. Not a problem, providing it doesn't affect her work and judgement."

"Thanks for the update, Justin."

Donald explained to the others. Mrs Montague commented, "Everybody knows now, so we have to watch and keep our eye on things," she smiled. "I must go things to do and places to be."

Rosemary came into the lounge, much to everyone's surprise. "Could I speak to you privately, please, in my office?" Rosemary walked towards the office, opened the door went inside; standing behind her desk? "I should imagine the gossips have enlightened you; I see Robbie, a casual relationship, nothing serious. I am aware this may cause issues in some quarters. Do you have any objections, and if so, what are they?"

Donald spoke, "Personally, no one here really cares what you do in your private life, providing it doesn't affect the hotels or their reputation. However, Robbie has a stigma, providing you are aware of those facts and wish to see him, your choice. The minute it affects the hotel or your judgement, you will be dismissed. I can't make it any plainer than that," Donald said, leaving the office followed by the others, who thought he'd made his position very plain, leaving Rosemary in no doubt where she stood.

Isabella ran to catch Donald, holding his arm, kissing him on the cheek, "Nicely said, Donald, I think you, impressed mummy." Mrs Montague drove away in her car. Donald and Isabella stayed one more night before heading home early the next day. They arrived at Mill Farm around lunchtime, discovering Caroline Crombie with the twins to their amusement. Susan had a face like thunder. She immediately approached Donald, "Do I have to take orders from Caroline Crombie? The woman's a bloody nightmare, Donald." Donald and Isabella both laughed, watching Caroline Crombie come downstairs. "Could you possibly be quiet? I have Josephine and Eric asleep it's their rest period," she turned on her heels, heading upstairs.

Susan, Isabella, and Donald sat around the kitchen table having a coffee, "I suppose she will be useful, Donald, when I have my child in nine months," Isabella said without batting an eyelid. Mrs Montague in France choked on her dessert. Mr Montague patted her on the back frantically; she gasped for air, "I will kill Isabella," she spluttered, "The girls trying to kill me with surprises."

Donald stared at Isabella along with Susan, "Can you repeat what you've said, Isabella, in case my hearing is failing?"

"According to the test kit, I'm pregnant, considering I've only been to bed with you. You are the father of whatever I'm having. Early days," she smiled, "I will be approximately two months pregnant after harvest. I have comfortable machinery to ride in so I can continue working. Once I've disposed of the lump, Caroline Crombie can take over, and I can continue working."

"When you suddenly decide you wanted children, Isabella?"

"I worked out you were paying for a nanny, so why not utilise her to her full potential? With her available, it won't inconvenience my work program. You complained you wanted to ruin my figure for some months," she grinned. "I assure you will have the bill for repairing my figure."

Caroline Crombie came downstairs quietly, making herself a coffee. Donald invited with a gesture of his hand for her to join at the table. "You are pregnant, Isabella," Caroline remarked, "I will write you a suitable diet; we must look after the unborn infant. The earlier we start, the better. No more fish and chips, I don't think." Donald was astonished at the comment, looking at the expression on Isabella's face. Isabella glanced at Susan, "You needn't smile either, Susan. You will be looking after the baby sometime," Isabella chuckled, "While I work on the farm with my husband."

What happens next is another story

by Isabella Montague

Printed in Great Britain
by Amazon

82821909R10464